Performance Measurement, Management, and Appraisal Sourcebook

Edited by

Douglas G. Shaw,
Craig Eric Schneier, Ph.D.,
Richard W. Beatty, Ph.D.
and
Lloyd S. Baird, Ph.D.

Human Resource Development Press
Amherst, Massachusetts

Published by Human Resource Development Press, Inc.
22 Amherst Road
Amherst, Massachusetts 01002
1-800-822-2801

Printed in the United States of America

ISBN 0-87425-265-2

Production services provided by Susan Kotzin

Cover design by Old Mill Graphics

Editing services by Robie Grant

Table of Contents

PART II

Introduction

Performance measurement and management has become a critical management process to many leading U.S. companies over the past several years. As more companies have seen both competition and their customers' expectations increase, they have realized the importance of strategy *execution* over strategy *definition* in attaining sustainable competitive advantage. Hence, to remain competitive they must select the right measures, define stretch goals, track and measure both results and the process for attaining the results, and attach meaningful consequences to performance.

In the eight years since the publication of *The Performance Management Sourcebook,* companies have increasingly linked their performance management processes to their key business goals. Performance appraisal was typically an annual event aimed at measuring and improving individual performance, often conducted independent of a company's or a unit's business plans. We now see more and more integration of business plans and performance measurement and management systems, with the overall goal of improving business, team, *and* individual performance. Performance management processes have moved out of the sole domain of personnel and human resource functions and into the management mainstream at many leading companies. Where they are successful, they are business tools, operated by line managers.

Through our work in performance measurement and management, which spans many years, several consulting firms, and numerous organizations in a variety of industries, we have uncovered no collection of materials that reflects the new realities of performance measurement, management, and appraisal. Managers and students told us of their need for a business-relevant collection of articles on performance measurement, management, and appraisal.

Our *Sourcebook's* intended audience therefore includes business leaders, managers, human resource professionals, and students. We have attempted to include material we believe is useful for each of these audiences.

Organization of the *Sourcebook*

Section I, "Toward a New Perspective on Performance Measurement, Management, and Appraisal," expands on the notion that performance management must be viewed as central to the planning and management processes of companies. It also provides data that show how many companies are falling far short when it comes to effectively communicating expectations, managing performance, and rewarding results.

Section II, "Performance Measurement: A Key to Successful Strategy Execution," includes several articles on selecting what types of performance to measure for different parts of the company, and also reviews the establishment of performance standards.

Section III, "Developing a Performance Measurement and Management Approach," reviews goal-based and competency-based approaches, key legal implications, and perspectives on the effectiveness of performance management systems.

Section IV, "Managing, Appraising, and Developing Performance," provides several readings on key components of a performance management process, including establishing expectations, coaching, collecting and documenting performance data, conducting performance reviews and appraisals, developing performance, and linking performance assessment to rewards.

Section V, "Successful Implementation of the Performance Measurement, Management, and Appraisal Process," provides several leading companies' experiences with these processes. We believe that an understanding of how specific companies have used performance management processes is very helpful to business leaders, managers, and human resource professionals as they consider their current processes and what improvements they may make.

We have greatly expanded and updated the second part of the *Sourcebook* to provide more questionnaires, cases, role plays, and practical suggestions our clients, students, and readers have found useful.

We would like to thank the numerous clients, colleagues, and students we have worked with over the years that have helped us further our knowledge and understanding in this field. We also appreciate the work of those individuals and publications that have graciously permitted us to draw upon or include their work in this *Sourcebook*. Finally, we would like to acknowledge the first two editors' assistant, Theresa Scheese, for her skill, speed, and patience.

Craig Eric Schneier
Pennington, NJ

Richard W. Beatty
Princeton, NJ

Douglas G. Shaw
Newton, PA

Lloyd S. Baird
Belmont, MA

August 1995

I.
Toward a New Perspective on Performance Measurement, Management, and Appraisal

Performance Measurement and Management: A Tool for Strategy Execution

by Craig Eric Schneier, Douglas G. Shaw, and Richard W. Beatty

In many organizations performance measurement and management (PMM) systems are little more than human resource bureaucracies with forms, rules, and review layers. These paper-driven systems are burdens to managers and hence are completed marginally, if at all. They are typically seen by raters as extra work and by ratees as at best irrelevant, at worst demotivating. Most PMM improvement efforts center on the most visible aspect of PMM—the form. But these quick fixes attempt to treat symptoms (e.g., leniency), while diseases (e.g., lack of managerial accountability for performance improvement or development) go unchecked. Rather than periodic revisions to the rating scales, PMM can be made relevant by linking it to strategy execution. PMM can be a vital tool for strategy execution by signaling what is really important, providing ways to measure what is important, fixing accountability for behavior and results, and helping to improve performance. In this article a PMM process is described which begins with identification of Critical Success Factors (CSFs) derived directly from business strategy. These are the basis for a PMM process that is a welcome managerial tool. The successful use of PMM as a device for strategy execution is illustrated via a case study.

As business strategies become increasingly generic (e.g., customer service; penetration of global markets), the execution of strategy distinguishes high-performing from average companies. Leaders of America's best-known companies are increasingly aware of the need for execution:

> *"At best the plan is 20 percent of the game. Execution is 80 percent of it."* (John Trani, head of GE's medical systems business [reported in Huey, 1991].)

> *"It is my absolute conviction that you can outmanage your competition by having brilliant strategies, but those brilliant strategies have to be executed brilliantly."* (Leo Gerstner, CEO of RJR Nabisco [reported in Irvin and Michaels, 1989].)

Strategy execution has been operationalized as reduced cycle time (e.g., Stalk & Haut, 1989), better customer service (e.g., Zeithaml et al., 1990; Schlesinger & Heskett, 1991), superior quality (e.g., Crosby, 1979; Juran, 1989), flexible manufacturing (e.g., Hayes et al., 1988), and empowered workforce (e.g., Block, 1987), effective management of change (e.g., Beer et al., 1991), or responsive organization structures (e.g., Bartlett & Shoshal, 1989; Charan, 1991), among other concepts. Each view of better execution advocates a strong measurement emphasis, from 3M's "Project '95," aimed at reducing all manufacturing cycle times by 50%, to Motorola's "six sigma," aimed at improving all products' quality to 99.9997% defect-free.

Yet, as organizations struggle to reduce their cycle times or improve their products' reliability, their performance measurement and management (PMM) systems offer little help. At the macro (organization) level they have been maligned for concentration on short-term, period-to-period financial performance measures to the exclusion of qualitative data and comparisons to competitors (Eccles, 1991). At the micro (individual) level, they have been maligned for a concentration on psychometric nuance, such as the number or title of rating scale categories which lead to no real improvement in rating accuracy (Landy & Farr, 1980; Austin et al., 1991). They are either ignored by senior executives or so lenient as to be useless as a basis for reward allocation (e.g., Longenecker & Gioia, 1991). IBM's experience is indicative:

> *Under the new guidelines, IBM will more strictly enforce a system under which it ranks employees on a numerical scale. Few employees now carry a rank below three (on a four-point scale), but the guidelines will force managers to rank people as fours. Anyone with a rank that low will face pressure to resign, and quickly. (Wall Street Journal,* October 1, 1991, parentheses added.)

IBM's PMM system was obviously not facilitating strategy execution.

It is argued here that PMM is critical to strategy execution and an approach is described that has elevated PMM beyond a personnel *form* to a strategic *tool* in several companies.

PMM: What Exists Is Not What Is Needed

The Wrong Measures

Many have detailed the inadequacies of PMM systems (Schneier, 1992; Carroll & Schneier, 1982; Bernardin & Beatty, 1984; Mohrman et al., 1989). As a tool to help execute strategy, most PMM systems are woefully deficient (See Figure 1). Companies need a process to help identify and measure "what counts"—those few activities that lead to success of individuals, teams, units, and the organization. Most PMM systems measure performance only at the individual level and measure a set of un-

defined, generic personal characteristics (e.g., "initiative") or a set of specific, yet narrow technical skills (e.g., "financial analysis") derived from job descriptions. These sets of criteria rarely track with the company's strategy or even with what is truly important for success in any given position.

Consider the recent experience of the procurement function of a division of a Fortune 50 company. An analysis of slipping market share pointed to poor product quality. Quality breakdowns were traced to raw materials. The division attempted to implement a sourcing strategy that included developing partnerships with a select few suppliers in order to focus on product quality and reliability in use. Despite its rhetoric, the number of suppliers and their materials' quality remained constant. The single largest impediment to this major, cross-functional effort was that the procurement people interacting with the suppliers on a daily basis were still being measured on the discounts they were able to obtain from suppliers. In other words, their success was assured if they dealt with numerous, competing suppliers and pressured them for discounts, with little regard to material quality. Subsequent costs related to downtime from the failure of the product were not on the procurement unit's measurement "screen."

The Wrong Judgements

In addition to measuring the wrong aspects of performance, PMM systems typically require numerous, finite evaluations that too many managers are unwilling and/or unable to make on a performance scale. Leniency, as in the IBM example described above, becomes the norm. Research (e.g., Landy & Farr, 1980) has shown that changes in scale definitions, labels, "anchors," or examples, or even the number of scale points lead to little that is definitive regarding rating accuracy. Further, it has been argued, as well as empirically demonstrated, that a performance rating is more reflective of the *rater's* personality or judgment style than the *ratee's* actual performance (e.g., Borman, 1983). Hence, the emphasis is on *rating* performance, not improving it.

The Wrong Owners

The PMM system is too often viewed as the province of the human resources unit, not the manager's

4

Figure 1. Performance Measurement and Management (PMM): What exists is not what is needed

What Most Companies Have...	What Most Companies Need...
1. A staff-driven rating *scale* and *forms*	1. A management *tool* and *process*
2. Supervisor-driven *ratings*	2. Subordinate, supervisor, team member, customer-driven *assessment*
3. A focus on evaluation performance *after* the fact	3. A focus on setting expectations *up front, coaching, developing* and *improving* performance *continually*
4. Measuring *generic* aspects of people or jobs	4. Measuring those *"Critical Success Factors"* that assure goal attainment, strategy execution
5. Consequences of performance centered around *base compensation*	5. *Positive* and *negative, financial* and *non-financial* consequences of performance utilized effectively
6. *Human resources accountability* for *"fixing"* the system	6. *Managerial accountability* for *designing, operating,* and *improving* the *process,* with human resources technical assistance
7. *Ambiguity* and *inconsistency* around "what it takes to make it" in different units, at different levels, for different managers; uneven expectations	7. *Clarity* about success for individuals, teams, units, across the Company
8. Performance *hurdles set too low,* or *not set at all,* given what is required for the organization to compete successfully	8. Performance *hurdles set to stretch* people, *ever-increasing,* reflecting customers' ever-increasing demands and competitors' ever-increasing skills

accountability. It is likely that human resources designed and implemented the system. PMM is hence seen as extra work by managers, who resent completing forms merely to process a salary increase and are not skilled at providing constructive performance feedback. Lack of managerial accountability for PMM leads to perhaps the system's most telling deficiency: PMM is routinely ignored. In one recent study, almost half of the executives interviewed indicated they did not receive perform-ance reviews, and those that did described them as rushed and vague (Longenecker & Gioia, 1988).

The Wrong Impact

Most researchers and practitioners agree that the impact PMM systems should have is on perform-ance—to develop it and to improve it. The typical PMM policy statement or CEO's exhortation in the front of the managers' PMM Guide usually contains a direct reference to improved performance as the key objective of PMM. While the evaluative and developmental impacts of PMM are different and hence difficult to reconcile in practice, the facts are that individual-level, hierarchically-based performance appraisal has been a failure: it has not improved performance (see e.g., research cited in Mohrman et al., 1991), and it is not a viable force for development in most organizations, according to survey after survey (see e.g., *Training*, 1988).

What has the PMM system impacted, if not performance? The impact of individual-level PMM has been most notable on the merit pay system, where a rating is used to derive and justify (albeit weakly due, for example, to extreme leniency) a base salary increase.

PMM Strategy Execution: A Framework

Both discussions of strategy execution (e.g., Schneier, 1991; Hrebineak & Joyce, 1984; Ulrich & Lake, 1991), and executives' own experiences (e.g., Rodgers, 1990; Tichy & Charan, 1990) suggest the importance of PMM. T.J. Rodgers is founder and CEO of Cypress Semiconductor, whose 1991 return on equity is over twice its industry's average. He discusses PMM as follows:

> *All of Cypress' 1,400 employees have goals, which, in theory, make them no different from employees at most other companies. What does make our people different is that every week they set their own goals, commit to achieving them by a specific date, enter them into a data base, and report whether or not they completed prior goals. In any given week, some 6,000 goals in the data base come due. Our ability to meet those goals ultimately determines our success or failure.* (Rogers, 1990, p. 87)

At Cypress, PMM is not merely a paperwork exercise for managers based on a rating scale, it is a key to business performance. At Federal Express a Service Quality Index (SQI) measures 10 key aspects of overall company performance and is flashed daily via closed-circuit television to all employees. At Johnson and Johnson adherence to its famed "Credo" is measured via employee surveys and used to help determine executive compensation. For these companies, PMM is central to business operations and critical to success, both individually and organizationally.

PMM facilitates execution of business strategies by:

1. signaling what to measure;
2. determining appropriate ways to measure; and
3. fixing accountability for performance on the measures.

Unless all three of these activities occur, strategy execution is in jeopardy. People will focus on the wrong measures, fail to know when or agree if targets are reached, aim too low and achieve too little, and/or see no consequences for missing the targets (or perhaps for hitting them). (See Figure 2.)

Each aspect of a PMM strategy execution model is described below, as is the importance of aligning key organizational capabilities—structure, skills, style, and systems—with strategy to assure execution.

Identifying Critical Success Factors (CSFs): The First Step Toward Strategy Execution

Regardless of how formally a business strategy is documented, the essence of the strategy can be distilled into the few factors that must be executed

Figure 2. Performance measurement and management and strategy execution

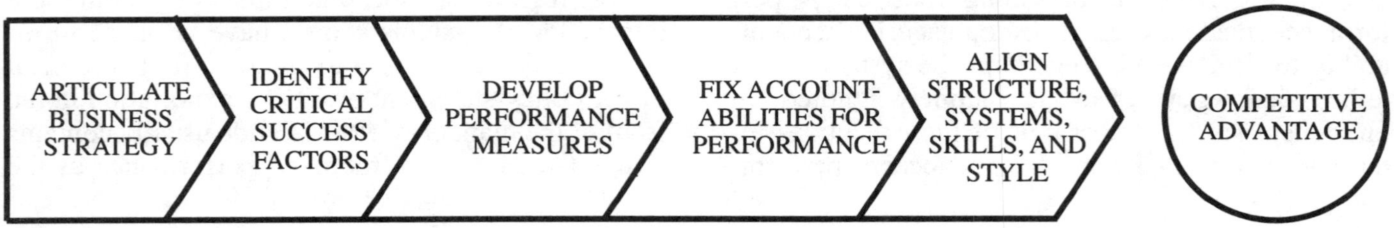

ARTICULATE BUSINESS STRATEGY → IDENTIFY CRITICAL SUCCESS FACTORS → DEVELOP PERFORMANCE MEASURES → FIX ACCOUNT-ABILITIES FOR PERFORMANCE → ALIGN STRUCTURE, SYSTEMS, SKILLS, AND STYLE → COMPETITIVE ADVANTAGE

with excellence to gain and sustain competitive advantage. For example, many companies' strategies speak to cost-competitiveness: Wal-Mart competes on "everyday low prices." But a key to success for Wal-Mart is its superior capability in purchasing and logistics, enabling low prices everyday (Stalk et al., 1992). While many companies have a customer service strategy, a CSF for Domino's Pizza is custom order processing and, of course, delivery, given its 30-minute delivery time guarantee. These CSFs are strategy-driven, and they are specific, operational embodiments of what it takes to win. They are neither always obvious nor generic.

Two frameworks are useful to assist in identifying critical success factors (CSFs), Rockhart's (1979) MIT study, and Tregoe et al.'s (1989) "driving forces."

Rockhart (1979) advocates the following as sources of CSF's:

1. **The characteristics of an industry.** There are specific factors that must be addressed in a given industry to survive and prosper. For example, hotels and airlines must ensure that their fixed assets are well-utilized (i.e., high occupancy rates), or they will face severe cash crunches, to say the least.

2. **An organization's competitive strategy and industry positioning.** Within an industry, competitors may have different business strategies and typically will not enjoy the same position. In its early years, for example, Compaq Computer could not rely on customer service to gain a fast hold in the marketplace; they chose to fill a niche—"portable" computers—as an entry strategy. Hence, in the early 1980s, innovation was a CSF for Compaq, whereas for IBM, market dominance was critical.

3. **Environmental factors (i.e., economic and political).** Prior to the mid-1970s, few companies worried about the availability of energy supplies. With the oil embargo, securing oil became a CSF for companies in several industries. In another industry, setting up and operating efficient overseas (i.e., US) manufacturing plants became a CSF for Japanese automobile companies as they encountered more and more resistance from the public and governments in the US and Europe.

4. **Temporal factors.** Specific circumstances may give rise to temporary critical success factors that may become less critical once a crisis is averted. Companies that have just completed a leveraged buy-out may see the ability to generate cash as a CSF. Cash flow may not take on this heightened importance once the debt is paid down.

Just as two companies in the same industry may not have the same CSFs, two divisions or businesses in the same corporation may have different CSFs. For example, the private banking, commercial banking and investment banking units in a large money-center bank have some overlap, but some unique CSFs. In one of the nation's largest bank corporations, the private bank uses personal service, leading to the cashé that attracts moneyed clientele. For the investment bank, a network of investors able to commit huge sums on a telephone call is critical. For the commercial bank division, success has followed strong analytical capability and a conservative lending policy (see Bullen & Rockart, 1981, for a review of CSF generation).

Tregoe & Associates (1989) have developed the notion of "driving force," used to generate a strategic vision. There are eight key variables that serve as the source of strategic vision, but each has also helped companies see the CSFs which fall from their strategy (see Figure 3). The sources of the driving force provide a lens through which a company can view and assess its ability to execute a strategy.

Core Skills, Core Competencies, Capabilities, and CSFs

Like the driving force, notions of core skills (Irvin & Michaels, 1989), core competencies (Prahalad & Hamel, 1990), and capabilities (Stalk et al., 1992) help a company point to what it must do exceptionally well to execute strategy and sustain competitive advantage. Each concept is somewhat different, but each is essential for successful strategy execution.

For Irvin and Michaels (1989) core skills:

Link strategy (thinking) and execution (doing). If you want brilliant execution, strengthen the right core skills, the ones that provide the most economic leverage. If you do a good enough job, the core skills

Figure 3. Sources of strategy and Critical Success Factors (CSFs)

After Tregoe et al. (1989); driving forces are not mutually exclusive in that companies address several simultaneously to develop strategy and CSFs.

1. Products/Services Offered
   Common characteristics of products/services described, but subject to expansion.
   Objective is to rapidly develop/acquire new products/services that fit the profile, seeking broader markets to exploit.
   Product/service value/differentiation sought.
   Product development and marketing emphasized.
   Example: J.M. Smucker

2. Markets Served
   Strong, well-defined relationships with customers.
   Objective to identify and fill customer needs.
   Marketing and marketing research, along with R&D, are emphasized.
   Example: Consumers Packaging

3. Return/Profit
   Ability to meet return and profit goals determines business portfolio; asset divestiture/acquisition.
   Example: Variety Corporation

4. Technology
   Body of knowledge or technological capability leads to success.
   Objective is to leverage technological expertise, applying it to products/services.
   Example: 3M

5. Low-Cost Production
   Production of products/services is lower than competitors.
   Cost-efficient operations, from economies of scale, superior manufacturing processes, and/or ability to match utilization of productive facilities to their capacity.
   Customers buy on price; typically commodity businesses.
   Example: International Paper

6. Operations Capability
   Flexible use of productive capacity as in "job shop" manufacturing and/or unique products/services, is critical to success.
   Specialized target markets must be identified and penetrated.
   Scheduling, expediting, coordinating human and material resources, and budgeting are emphasized.
   Example: Bechtel Group

7. Method of Distribution/Sale
   Distribution channels and/or sales capability allow for large market share and competitively advantaged pricing.
   Additional products/services may be added to exploit the channel.
   Example: Book-of-the-Month Club

8. National Resource
   Ownership/control over a natural resource leads to success, as well as the ability to process the resource into more and more marketable products/services.
   The quality, quantity, or location of the resource may lead to an advantage.
   Example: Shell Oil

themselves, even more than the strategy, will become the basis for your continued success (p. 5).

Irvin and Michaels (1989) discuss Marriott's ability actually to provide high quality service to business travelers (i.e., execution) as a core skill leading to its success, as opposed to merely a stated strategy of providing excellent service to the business traveler. Other companies in Marriott's industry fail to execute as well. Like CSFs, core skills are strategy-driven and specific; they must be operationalized for key positions and reinforced by those at the top.

Core competencies, as defined by Prahalad and Hamel 1990, have three acid tests:

1. Provide access to a wide variety of markets.

   Example: Casio's expertise at display systems lead to calculator, miniature TV, dashboards, etc., markets.

2. Contribute significantly to customers' perception of products' benefits.

   Example: Honda's engine expertise helps assure that its engines are a core product, viewed favorably by customers, hence contributing heavily to its end-products' (e.g., lawn mowers) success.

3. Not easily copied.

   Example: 3 M's expertise in "sticky tape," leveraged via a culture that reinforces innovation and risk-taking, leads to numerous successful products.

Stalk et al.'s (1992) notion of capabilities is very similar (some would say the differences are semantic) to the concepts described above. Capabilities are critical to strategy execution, and strategy execution, as argued above, is the key to competitive advantage:

> ...the essence of strategy is *not* the structure of a company's products and markets, but the dynamics of its behavior. And the goal is to identify and develop the hard-to-imitate organizational capabilities that distinguish a company from its competitors in the eyes of its customers. (p. 62)

Processes, particularly those that cross business units and/or functions and are linked to customers, provide strategic capability. Wal-Mart's capability in warehousing—the continuous delivery of goods to warehouses and the continuous dispatching of these goods to stores—almost eliminates inventory. Transportation, buying, information systems, financial analysis (regarding investment decisions), logistics, and asset (e.g., warehouse) management are a few of the functions that come together to make the warehousing process a competitive advantage for Wal-Mart. They are able to replenish store shelves twice a week, versus once every two weeks for their competitors (Stalk et al., 1992).

The Power of CSFs: Fast Food

A striking illustration of the power gained by identifying and utilizing CSFs to execute strategy can be seen in a comparison of McDonalds and Burger King. Experts have pieced together a set of CSFs for these "fast food" retail stores (see Figure 4). In the late 1960's both Burger King and McDonalds had approximately 100 stores, essentially no rivals, and a similar strategy, but over the next two decades McDonalds was relentless on its adherence to the CSFs, arguably executing its strategy much better than Burger King, and growing and profiting handsomely. The size and profitability of the two chains are very different today.

Developing Performance Measures That Drive Strategy Execution

Once CSFs (or driving forces or core competencies) have been identified, the second key step in the development of a PMM process to enhance strategy execution is to develop performance measures for the CSFs. CSFs tell *what* must be done to win; performance measures are needed to determine *how well* we must perform and how we will know if we succeeded. Strategies are rarely executed if a general mandate or vision (e.g., "compete globally") is not operationalized via CSFs (e.g., speeding the right financial and sales data to offices all over the world simultaneously). But measures to determine the necessary speed and right data are also needed. These, of course, determine and communicate performance targets and bring the CSF to bear on specific positions, both prerequisites for effective strategy execution. Figure 5 provides illustrative performance measures for a set of CSFs. Some are obvious, some less so, but if the CSFs do not have predetermined, specific measures, and/or

Figure 4. The power of Critical Success Factors (CSFs)

McDonalds was relentless in adhering to CSFs, Burger King less so . . . *

Fast Food CSFs	McDonalds	Burger King
Site Selection	"Penchant for finding the plum"	"Generally good locations"
High Quality Service	"Unparalleled consistency"	"Suffers from operational sloppiness"
Product Innovation	"A knack for product development"	"Spotty record with new products"
Communications	"Surrogate mom"	"Comes off as aggressive, masculine and distant"

And McDonalds' resultant financial performance reflects the difference†

Performance	McDonalds	Burger King
Royalties Paid by Franchisee	3.5%	3.5%
Number of Employees‡	60	60
Average Cost of Hamburger	$.63	$.63
Average Start-up Cost*	$435k	$1MM
Average Annual Revenue*	$1.5MM	$1MM
Average Annual Profit*	$234k	$140k

*Irvin & Michaels, 1989, p. 7.
†Heskett et al., 1990, p. 207.
‡Per restaurant.

Figure 5. Developing performance measures for Critical Success Factors (CSFs)

Based on company documents, reports in business press.

Company	Illustrative CSF	Illustrative Measure/Goal
Rubbermaid	New Products	Reduce new product development cycle
Alcoa	Safety	Improvement in safety rewards (?)
Federal Express	Customer Service	12-factor Service Quality Index (SQI) covering measures such as late deliveries, lost and damaged packages, missed pick-ups
Hewlett-Packard	Innovation	Percent of revenues from products that are two years old or newer
Xerox	Customer Service	Service call measures: frequency, responsiveness, length, copy quality
Domino's Pizza	Home Delivery Time	Percent deliveries within 30 minutes
3M	Manufacturing Cycle Time	Reduce cycle time by 50% within five years
Nissan Motor (Infiniti)	Customer Service	Increases in customer satisfaction survey scores and $100,000 bonus to dealers
Bell Atlantic	Develop, install network allowing advanced services	Percent of phone lines equipped with "Signalling System 7"
Coca Cola	Penetrating and operating in foreign markets	Number of days to set up operating/bottling in a country
GM	Operating efficiency	Reduce number of direct labor hours to produce a car
Motorola	Quality	Six sigma quality (99.9997% defect-free) products by 1992

if the measures derived from CSFs are not in the PMM system, PMM becomes an administrative exercise, not managers' "real work." Measuring procurement managers on raw material cost, but not on quality in the case of the manufacturing company cited earlier, is an example of a PMM system incompatible with company CSFs.

Another common PMM problem is the system's reliance on duties derived from a job description. One financial service company's PMM system tracks and evaluates analysts on how well they productively prepare reports, because the job description contains a duty called "report writing." However, internal customers, when asked said that the reports provide only redundant data and should not

be written by financial analysts, but by the accounting unit. As long as the analysts' PMM measures report writing, the analysts write reports. A worldwide consumer goods manufacturer has shifted to a CSF of product line extensions. Its PMM system rates, but does not define, initiative, motivation, and task knowledge, among other generic criteria, for every position. These characteristics may be admirable, but their relation to executing strategy (more line extensions) for each position is unclear. That is, what does the staff accountant do differently to take initiative and what task knowledge is now important, given the line extension CSF? That many managers fail to complete appraisal forms in this consumer goods manufacturer, and that most who do complete them do so in a "perfunctory" (to quote one executive) manner, is not surprising. Yet the company measures numerous aspects of its operation in detail. The PMM process is not related to strategy and hence is not used in its execution. It is seen as an HR system, not a managerial tool.

A Company's Use (or Misuse) of PMM Is Determined by Its Culture, Not Its Appraisal Forms or Rating Scales

Leniency, leading to inaccurate assessments, is a longstanding problem in PMM systems, particularly at the individual level (see e.g., Austin et al., 1991). This problem has been researched as a psychometric one, but the causes perhaps stem more from a company's culture than the psychometric properties of its appraisal forms.

PMM systems are a reflection of the values a company has around performance and the performance culture is illustrated not by value statements, but by action (see Figure 6). Key questions that are used to assess a performance culture are:

- How hard do people actually work?
- Are performance expectations explicit?
- How high are the expectations for performance?
- Is failure to meet expectations noticed and tolerated?
- What is the relative importance of effort expended and of outcomes (results) attained?
- What happens to those who exceed expectations versus those who merely meet them?
- Do people receive candid performance feedback?
- Are developmental needs identified, discussed, and acted upon?

As Figure 6 describes, companies with an "Up or Out" culture around performance communicate high expectations and do not tolerate failure to meet them. Poor performers are routinely dismissed. In these cultures, leniency on appraisal forms is not a serious problem and measures are plentiful and visible. In contrast, companies with an "Entitlement" ("Hire Adequate, Retain, Redeploy") performance culture typically have inflated ratings. Managers who are brutally frank about performance would violate the performance culture norms. Dismissing

people for failure to perform is also taboo. Those who meet and those who exceed performance expectations are treated essentially the same regarding rewards.

The PMM System Must Fit the Performance Culture—Or Help Change It

Different performance cultures can be described and can lead to success, given certain competitive, economic environments (see Figure 6). As Figure 6 indicates, competitive environments facilitate or deter survival in each performance culture. Many heretofore successful companies are finding it difficult to remain in the "Competence" culture due to increased competitive pressures, higher cost structures, and higher customer expectations. They are moving to "Selectivity" cultures by necessity as an assurance against an eroding competitive position. Companies in transition from a Competence to a Selectivity culture have problematic PMM systems. Old performance expectations were too low, measures too ambiguous, ratings too lenient, feedback too sugar-coated, and rewards too homogeneously administered to reflect today's competitive realities. IBM, noted earlier, is a case in point, as it has mandated a less lenient performance rating distribution and a "get tough" policy with regard to poor performers. The recent popularity of downsizing, particularly at the white-collar level, is evidence of companies' attempts to shift to more rigorous performance cultures. PMM systems can assist in this shift and hence can be a powerful lever for change.

Fixing Accountabilities for Performance: Assuring Execution

As Figure 2 notes, the final key step in developing a PMM process to drive strategy execution is to hold performers accountable. CSFs and measures must be operationalized at the unit, team, and individual levels. Specific outcomes and behaviors can be specified and then linked to consequences. Most PMM systems fail as tools for strategy execution because managers have not determined what people and teams must actually *do* and *achieve,* given the company's set of CSFs. Johnson and Johnson specifies what people must do via its Credo survey and fixes accountability via compensation. GE's chairman has publicly described negative consequences

Figure 6. Performance cultures and Performance Measurement and Management (PMM) implications

Performance Culture	COMPETITIVE: UP-OR-OUT	SELECTIVITY: HIRE THE BEST, PUSH THEM, DEVELOP THEM	COMPETENCE: HIRE WELL, KEEP AS LONG AS CONTRIBUTING	ENTITLEMENT: HIRE ADEQUATE, RETAIN, REDEPLOY
Illustrative Key Practices Related to Managing People, Performance	• Hire only those with high potential • Cultivate an individual "star system" • Tell people early if they'll make it; remove ones who won't • Turnover encouraged • Set extremely high expectations	• Retain people as long as contribution is increasing • Provide first-rate development, not just training • Cultivate teams, synergies • Set high expectations, clear accountabilities • Provide performance feedback regularly • Set high standards	• Hire good people, potential unsure • Provide opportunity to improve, develop • Cultivate a "family," avoid confrontations, dismissals • Turnover avoided • Performance standards vary in degree of rigor • Provide "benefit-of-the-doubt" in ratings	• Move people to a job of best fit, given capability • Promote cooperation, loyalty, security, "family" • "Sugar-coat" or do not offer performance feedback • Provide continual training opportunities • Routes to the top well-known and inflexible • Time in grade, not high performance, brings rewards
Competitive Environment that Enables Companies with Philosophy to Win	• Image and name of key people bring sales • Highly competitive industry • Dominating companies prevail • Aggressiveness well rewarded financially	• Synergies, innovations lead to sales • Highly competitive, dynamic industry • Leading companies have superior core competencies visible to customers	• Leading companies have market dominance, slack resources • Industry not highly volatile • Slow growth, yet returns available over time	• "Regulated" and/or "protected" industry • Leading companies have a "franchise" (e.g., size, location) that funnels sales to them • Core technology is not quickly obsolete

13

(i.e., termination) for those who not only do not achieve business results but also fail to show behavior consistent with GE's values. Those who exhibit the desired behaviors and attain the results are rewarded differentially. Recent actions make the system real.

PMM as Strategy Execution: A Pharmaceutical Case Study

A Fortune 100 East Coast pharmaceutical company (here called Global Health) had a typical PMM system. Their system for managers, technical experts, and professionals contained a series of five-point scales measuring various types of knowledge, several skills, and about a dozen personal characteristics. In addition, each manager had a set of goals to attain. But the results of all of these measurements and appraisals were boiled down to a single score on a five-point scale. Over 70 percent of all those rated received the rating (one below the highest) called Excellent. The score was forwarded to the Compensation Department to determine merit increases. Over two-thirds of Global Health's employees received a 5 percent base salary increase, interestingly enough, the exact amount of the merit budget. A survey indicated considerable dissatisfaction with the PMM system: almost no performance feedback was provided to those rated; top performers were discouraged as they received the same salary increases as those rated lower or who had done little; and managers complained bitterly about completing the long, complex forms and the trite, meaningless narrative they were forced to produce for each subordinate. After offering several voluntary training courses (run with only a handful of attendees), making numerous attempts at increasing or decreasing the number of scale points, deciding on a "forced" distribution, and selecting new titles for the scale values, it was decided that a new PMM approach was needed.

A line management Global Health task force revised the process along the lines of Figure 2. Once the company's CSFs were identified, performance measures were developed. Finally, accountabilities for individuals and teams—those behaviors, outcomes, and consequences for performance required to assure the CSFs were met—were developed (see Figure 7).

Test Top Management Support by Deriving Concrete Implications of Principles

How did the task force operate? They provided the basic PMM framework and assisted managers and their subordinates in developing measures and accountabilities. The company's top executive group identified the CSFs. The task force ran into one problem however. Top management at Global Health had readily agreed to support line management, as opposed to human resources, accountability for PMM. The task force decided to test this support by developing a set of PMM principles and related implications (see Figure 8).

Once the top executive group approved the implications, the PMM process could be designed and implemented. For example, the executive group supported the notion that collaboration is important. But heretofore, those who were not collaborative team leaders were still highly compensated and promoted. Hence top managers' support was nominal, and the principle of accountability had no credibility. Once the executives agreed to the principle, however, they were also now agreeing with the task force's implication for that principle: assessments of team leaders in writing would be obtained from team members and would be used as input for promotion and compensation decisions (see Figure 8). Such agreements pave the way for managerial accountability for PMM and hence for effective PMM implementation at Global Health.

A CSF for Global Health was shortened cycle time for approval of its products. The PMM process helped identify specific performance measures, mechanisms for measuring performance, and accountability targets for this CSF (see Figure 8). Direct ties to Global Health's CSFs moved PMM out of the category of extra work for managers. Operational performance measures for key jobs helped assure that PMM focused behaviors and outcomes on what counts. The implications for the PMM principles further operationalized PMM and gave it "teeth."

The Global Health task force needed very little debate concerning whether and how to deliver PMM training: managers whose incentive pay is based on their subordinates' assessments of their PMM practices *want* PMM training. The task force trained a cadre of interested managers and HR professionals to deliver practical assistance to "natural"

Figure 7. How Performance Measurement and Management (PMM) facilitates strategy execution: Global Health Corporation (not the company's actual name)

Business Strategy	Critical Success Factors	Performance Measures	Mechanisms for Measuring Performance	Team/Individual Manager Accountability
Penetrate, then dominate North American market for dermatoloty compounds	Shortened cycle for discovery to FDA approval	Number of compound submissions	Team member surveys of leaders	Annual incentive (partially) based on:
	R&D talent attraction/ retention	Number of compound approvals	FDA decisions	Reduction in (unwanted) turnover of senior staff
	Successful worldwide (chemical) compound teams	Project/team leadership	Team member feedback	FDA submission of three compounds
		Turnover of senior scientists	Turnover rates	FDA approval of of three compounds
		Collaboration	Superior's observations	Job rotation, promotion (partially) based on:
			Self-assessment	Team member, sub-ordinate, leadership assessment
				Verbal praise, spot bonus awarded for:
				Team leadership effectiveness
				Hiring new senior technical talent

Figure 8. Global Health Corporation's* Performance Measurement and Management (PMM) principles and implications lead to effective PMM process design and implementation

(*not the company's actual name)

Sample PMM Process Principles	Illustrative Operational and Design Implications
Managers have accountability for performance measurement, management, and development	Each manager's success is (partially) based on his/her performance management effectiveness No manager receives a higher overall performance evaluation, used for incentive pay allocation, than the evaluation received for performance management skills/duties Subordinates will provide input into their managers' evaluation
Not only results obtained, but behavior exhibited, is evidence of successful performance and is manageable via the performance management process	Poor performance of subordinates reflect adversely on their managers' performance Both behavior and results will be measured Each manager specifies and communicates behavioral performance expectations for subordinates Relative weighting of results and behaviors can vary across positions and/or over time
Teamwork and collaboration is a key to success in the business	Self-assessments will be used as input into an overall evaluation "Skip level" discussions (managers talking to their subordinates' subordinates) and customer and supplier input will be used to assess performance. Team leadership and performance will be tracked and will be used in conjunction with individual performance to determine compensation
Performance measures and the measurement process are driven by business strategy and goals	Results and behaviors, based on critical success factors, will be developed initially for each key position by managers and incumbents The top executive team will prepare their performance measures and accountabilities with the CEO

teams. They were credible and did not need canned classroom training. The task force also spent very little time deciding on rating categories. They saw no need for such categories except to send an overall message about performance. They quickly settled on three performance levels: exceeds expectations, meets expectations, does not meet expectation. Most people are doing well and meeting expectations, but could use some development. A minority are truly stellar or very poor performers. Why have more rating categories than the three groups to further separate people? Specific, candid feedback, not rating, is what was needed at Global to improve performance. Since the PMM measures drive the business results, they, not ratings, were the focus of the PMM process.

Making Change Last: Structure, Systems, Skills, and Style

Global Health was able to overcome some tough PMM hurdles—measurement relevance, managerial accountability, top executive participation—because its process was driven by and seen as a mechanism to execute business strategy. However, in order for the PMM process to facilitate strategy execution on an ongoing basis, important aspects of Global Health had to change: structure, systems, skills, and style. For example, effective world-wide chemical compound teams were a Global Health CSF. These teams, composed of people from sales, marketing, research, manufacturing, finance, and government relations were given the awesome responsibility of marshalling Global's resources around the world to turn a chemical compound into a drug, refine it, test it, obtain FDA approval for it, manufacture it, market it, and sell it. The teams became a reality only when the traditional functional, hierarchical structure in Global Health was altered (DeVanna & Tichy, 1990). In some cases, team leaders were taken out of the hierarchy and in others they had network reporting relationships.

Many of Global's senior scientists, appropriate candidates for worldwide compound team leaders, had marginal leadership and management *skills*. Some were coached and improved. Their team leadership skills were enhanced and their managerial style (e.g., verbal communication, listening, participative decision making, tolerance for other cultures) was altered to fit a collaborative model. Other obvious candidates, due to their experience, visibility, level, and expertise, were passed over as team leaders because they could not function well in a collaborative setting.

Finally, Global's *systems*—such as budgeting, planning, compensating, staffing—were called into question by the emerging PMM system. In order for worldwide compound teams to succeed, a PMM process identified appropriate performance measures linked to CSFs and built accountability in key jobs for high performance. But appropriate rewards for performance were necessary. Under the old performance appraisal system, most of Global's employees received the same rating and hence the same compensation increase. A revised reward system was proposed. Based on the collaboration PMM principle (see Figure 8), the entire compound team's performance was measured, not merely individual member's performance. The PMM system facilitated the relevant quantifiable (e.g., speed of FDA approval) and qualitative (e.g., effective collaboration) measures based on the CSFs (see Figure 7). All members of teams that succeeded were given bonuses. Individual performance was rewarded with job assignments, promotions, and recognition, important to the highly skilled, marketable Global scientists.

Design PMM Processes to Execute Strategy, Not Merely to Appraise Performance

Global Health was not dissimilar from many of today's companies. It had reorganized and downsized. Its overseas markets offered growth potential, but it faced unrelentless competitive pressure both abroad and at home. Its internal functional boundaries were loosening, and it was attempting to push decision making down. But Global knew the keys to its sustainable competitive advantage: deep scientific talent that could fill its pipeline with new drugs and teams of specialists working together who could quickly get the drugs approved and to market.

Like many companies, Global had a PMM system that was not part of the essence of its business. PMM was a paperwork exercise, perceived to be the province of human resources, containing forms with numerous ratings on overly-general aspects of jobs, and used primarily to assure essentially a cost-of-living merit increase. Global's task force did not attempt to fix the PMM system by substituting new scales for old, by shrinking the space for comments on the forms so they could be completed quicker, by mandating forced rating distributions because managers were not rigorous enough or candid enough, or by requiring managers to attend training classes. None of these treatments will cure the PMM disease of irrelevance. Simply put, what Global did was to consider how its business strategy could be better executed. It found that identifying what counts, measuring it, holding people accountable for it, coaching them to get better at it, and rewarding it were the simple, yet powerful solutions.

17

Craig Eric Schneier is President of Craig Eric Schneier Associates, a Princeton, New Jersey management consulting firm; he teaches in the Graduate School of Business, Columbia University. From 1987 to 1991, he was Managing Principal of Sibson & Company (Princeton, NJ). Dr. Schneier consults with numerous companies helping executives to improve work effectiveness and productivity, to implement culture change, and to develop and use performance management systems. He is the author and co-author of numerous articles and several books, including Personnel Administration, *3rd ed. (Addison-Wesley) and* The Training and Development Sourcebook, *2nd ed. (HRD Press).*

Douglas G. Shaw is a Principal of Sibson & Company and directs work with clients in several areas, including work effectiveness, performance management, and rewards systems. Prior to joining Sibson in 1985, he was a consultant at Towers, Perrin, and Cresap. He has written several articles and chapters on different management and human resource topics.

Richard W. Beatty is a Professor in the Institute of Management and Labor Relations, Rutgers University. He has also held faculty positions at Washington University and University of Colorado. Dr. Beatty is a consultant to organizations in human resource management systems, performance management and reward systems, improving work effectiveness, and implementing change. His many articles and books include Performance Appraisal *(Kent) and* Personnel Administration, *3rd. ed. (Addison-Wesley).*

References

AMA (1991). *Blueprints for service quality: The Federal Express approach.* New York: American Management Association.

Austin, J.T., Villanova, P., Kane, J.S., & Bernardin, H.J. (1991). Construct validation of performance measures: Issues, development, and evaluation of indicators. In G.R. Ferris and K.M. Rowland (Eds.), *Research in personnel and human resource management* (Vol. 9, pp. 159–234). Greenwich, CT: JAI Press.

Barlett, C.A., & Ghoshal, S. (1989). *Managing across borders.* Boston: Harvard Business School Press.

Beer, M., Eisentate, R.A., & Spector, B. (1990). *The critical path to corporate renewal.* Boston: Harvard Business School Press.

Bernarden, H.J., & Beatty, R.W. (1984). *Performance appraisal.* Boston: Kent.

Block, P. (1987). *The empowered manager.* San Francisco: Jossey-Bass.

Borman, W.C. (1983). Implications of personality theory and research for the rating of work performance in organizations. In F. Landy et al. (Eds.), *Performance measurement and theory,* (pp. 128–165). Hillsdale, NJ: Erlbaum.

Bullen, C.V., & Rockart, J.F. (1981, June). *A primer on critical success factors.* Boston: Center for Information System Research (MIT).

Buzzell, R.D., & Gale, B.T. (1988). *The PIMS principles.* New York: Free Press.

Carroll, S.J., & Schneier, C.E. (1982). *Performance appraisal and review systems.* Glenview, IL: Scott Foresman.

Charan, R. (1991). How networks reshape organizations—for results. *Harvard Business Review, 69*(5), 104–115.

Conference Board (1989). *Current practices in measuring quality.* Research Bulletin No. 234, NY.

Crosby, P.B. (1979). *Quality is free.* New York: McGraw-Hill.

Deming, W.E. (1986). *Out of the crisis.* Cambridge, MA: Massachusetts Institute of Technology Press.

DeVanna, M., & Tichy, N. (1990). Creating the competitive organization of the 21st century: The boundaryless corporation. *Human Resource Management, 29*(4), 455–472.

Drucker, P. (1991). Japan: New strategies for a new reality. *Wall Street Journal,* October 2.

Eccles, R.G. (1991). The Performance Measurement Manifesto. *Harvard Business Review, 69*(1), 131–139.

Hayes, R.H., Wheelwright, S.C., & Clark, K.B. (1988). *Dynamic manufacturing.* New York: Free Press.

Heskett, J.L., Sasser, W.E., & Hart, C.W.L. (1990). *Service breakthroughs.* New York: Free Press.

Hrebiniak, L.G., & Joyce, W.F. (1984). *Implementing strategy.* New York: Macmillan.

Irvin, R.A., & Michaels, E.G. (1989, Summer). Core skills: Doing the right things right. *The McKinsey Quarterly,* 4–19.

Juran, J.M. (1989). *Juran on leadership for quality.* New York: Free Press.

Landy, F.J., & Farr, J.L. (1980). Performance rating. *Psychological Bulletin, 87,* 72–107.

Longenecker, C.O., & Gioia, D.A. (1988, Winter). Neglected at the top—Executives talk about executive appraisal. *Sloan Management Review,* 41–47.

Longenecker, C.O., & Gioia, D.A. (1991, Fall). SMR Forum: Ten myths of managing managers. *Sloan Management Review,* 81–90.

Lovelock, C.H. (1991). *Federal Express quality improvement program.* Lausanne, Switzerland: International Institute for Management Development (IMD).

Maskell, B. (1991). *Performance measurement.* Cambridge, MA: Productivity Press.

Mohrman, A.M., Resnick-West, S.M., & Lawler, E.E. (1989). *Designing performance appraisal systems.* San Francisco: Jossey-Bass.

Mohrman, S.A., Mohrman, A.M., & Cohen, S.G. (1991). *Human resource strategies for lateral integration in high technology settings.* Los Angeles: Center for Effective Organizations, University of Southern California, CEO Publication 691–11 (196).

Prahalad, C.K., & Hamel G. (1990). The core competencies of the corporation. *Harvard Business Review, 68*(3), 79–91.

Rockhart, J.F. (1979). Chief executives define their own data needs. *Harvard Business Review, 57*(2), 81–93.

Rodgers, T.J. (1990). No excuses management. *Harvard Business Review, 68*(4), 84–98.

Schlesinger, L.A., & Heskett, J.L. (1991). The service-driven company. *Harvard Business Review, 69*(5), 71–81.

Schneier, C.E., Beatty, R.W., & Shaw, D.G. (1992). Why measure the CEO's performance. In R.J. Niehaus & K.F. Price (Eds.), *Bottom line results from human resource planning* (pp. 247–260). New York: Plenum.

Schneier, C.E. (1991). Executing strategy: The new battleground in business competition. In C.E. Schneier (Ed.), *Human resource strategies for the '90's: A basis for competitive advantage* (pp. 3–11). New York: AMACOM.

Schneier, C.E. (1991). Measuring and assessing top executive performance. In M.L. Rock & L.A. Berger (Eds.), *The compensation handbook* (pp. 520–532). New York: McGraw-Hill.

Schneier, C.E. (1989). Implementing recognition and rewards at the strategic level. *Human Resource Planning, 12*(3), 205–220.

Stalk, G., & Hout, T.M. (1990). *Competing against time.* New York: Free Press.

Stalk, F., Evans, P., & Shulman, L.E. (1992). Competing on capabilities: The new rules of corporate strategy. *Harvard Business Review, 69*(2), 57–69.

Stanich, P.J. (Ed.) (1982). *Implementing strategy: Making strategy happen.* Cambridge, MA: Ballinger.

Tichy, N., & Charan, R. (1989). Speed, simplicity, and self-confidence: An interview with Jack Welch. *Harvard Business Review, 66*(5), 112–120.

Tichy, N., & Charan, R. (1990; Nov.–Dec.). Citicorp faces the world: An interview with John Reed. *Harvard Business Review,* 135–144.

Training (1988, June). Appraising performance appraisals, 16–17.

Tregoe, B.B. et al. (1989). *Vision in action.* New York: Simon & Schuster.

Ulrich, D., & Lake, D. (1990). *Organization capability.* New York: Wiley.

Zeithaml, V.A., Parasuraman, A., & Berry, L.L. (1990). *Delivering quality service.* New York: Free Press.

The State of Performance Management: Selected Statistics

by Douglas G. Shaw and Craig Eric Schneier

---

1. **We're not providing clear direction to employees...**

   - 70% say managers don't provide clear goals and directions *(Personnel)*

   - 64% not confident senior managers know the right direction for their business *(Conference Board)*

   - 75% believe that their company's strategy implementation is worse than their strategy development *(Journal of Business Strategy)*

   - 55% say their managers are poor or average in providing direction *(Industry Week)*

   - 50% believe middle managers do not understand corporate objectives; 66% believe that supervisors do not sufficiently understand corporate objectives *(Journal of Business Strategy)*

2. **We're not managing performance well...**

   - 70% say performance expectations are not clearly defined *(Conference Board)*

   - 70% have never had meaningful performance discussion with their manager *(Wall Street Journal)*

   - Clear performance standards are not established for upper middle management (39%), for middle management (47%), nor for first level management (49%) *(Industry Week)*

   - 65% say the most important information needed concerns ways to improve performance *(Wall Street Journal)*

   - 80% say their boss does not follow up on their reviews *(Across the Board)*

   - 71% of professionals believe their company's system for evaluating performance is not fair *(Personnel Journal)*

   - 47% of middle managers do not have a clear understanding of how their performance is judged *(Personnel Journal)*

   - 75% of managers are dissatisfied with their review *(Academy of Management Review)*

   - 73% of managers are dissatisfied with the amount of feedback they receive *(Academy of Management Review)*

   - 66% of managers believe the quality of the feedback they receive is inadequate *(Academy of Management Review)*

3. **People want more challenge in their work...**

   - 66% would rather accept a more challenging job than keep high-paying job *(USA Today)*

   - 90% say they are willing to work harder to help their organization succeed *(Wall Street Journal)*

   - 75% believe they could be significantly more effective in their jobs *(Leaders;* Harper and Row)

   - 88% say it's important to them to work hard and do their best *(Gallup Poll)*

- 52% say challenging work is one of the top two reasons they are loyal to their company *(Industry Week)*

4. We're not making good performance count. . .

- 52% say poor performance is tolerated too long *(Wyatt Company)*
- 80% don't see a relationship between good work and rewards *(Bureau of National Affairs)*
- Whereas 98% believe pay should reflect performance, only 48% believe their company's pay system does *(Wall Street Journal)*
- 80% say recognition for a job well done is one of the top two reasons for their loyalty to their company *(Industry Week)*
- 70% want more recognition of their efforts *(Yankelovich, Skelly and White)*
- 70% of professionals believe their pay is not tied to performance *(Personnel Journal)*

5. We're not holding managers accountable for performance management. . .

- Only 40% of managers are rewarded for effective people management *(Wall Street Journal)*
- Only 14% of CEOs have formal appraisal systems or documents *(Sibson & Company, Inc.)*

6. We're not making executive/management development a priority. . .

- 70% say they should be allowed to participate in a formal review of their supervisors' performance *(Robert Half International)*
- 56% of top executives do not have clear development goals *(Industry Week)*
- 64% of middle managers do not have clear development goals *(Industry Week)*

Demand Better Results— And Get Them

by Robert H. Schaffer

One of the most dramatic, large-scale productivity improvements I am familiar with occurred in a regulated public utility—an industry not noted for such performance breakthroughs. In the early 1960s, this company's productivity was about average among 20 similar companies in North America, as both work load and work force were rapidly rising. In 1966, the trend shifted: the work load continued to rise, but the number of employees began to drop. By 1968, the company's productivity ranked among the best in its industry. The difference between average and best performance was worth savings of more than $40 million a year— well over one-third of its net income at that time.

What produced this gain? Neither new technology nor labor-saving machinery was a significant factor. No significant change in management took place. The company was not reorganized. Nor were programs incorporating management by objectives, organizational development, mathematical modeling, or management information systems responsible for the shift. The key to the turnaround was a decision by the principal operating officer (with backing from the chief executive) that the company must and could make substantial productivity gains. Naturally, many supportive programs and activities were necessary to translate this determination into results. These activities, however, would have produced little if a clear demand for improved performance had not been placed on the company's management team.

Most organizations have the potential for as great—or greater—gains. Very few, however, ever realize them. Few managers possess the capacity— or feel compelled—to establish high performance-improvement expectations in ways that elicit results. Indeed, the capacity for such demand making could be the most universally underdeveloped management skill.

Why Demands Aren't Made

Pushing for major gains can appear very risky to managers, and these perceived risks exert tremendous inhibition on performance expectations. If the newly installed manager asserts that significant gains are possible, he may threaten his predecessor and current boss—and thus arouse their antagonism—by implying that they had settled for less. Even if he has been in the job for a while, he subjects himself to the same estrangement.

Great demands increase the risk of resistance from subordinates and of the embarrassment of failing to reach ambitious goals. Managers who set unusually high demands may be challenged by others. They must therefore be sure of their facts and clear about directions. The struggle to upgrade performance may expose their uncertainties, weaknesses, and inadequate knowledge. More modest expectations reduce all these risks.

In addition, establishing well-defined and unequivocal expectations for superior performance creates the worry that the failure of subordinates to produce will require drastic action. Musing out loud about a long-needed productivity improvement effort, the vice president of a manufacturing operation asked, "What would happen if we set specific targets and my people didn't meet them? I'd have to do something—maybe let some of them go. Then I'd have to bring in people I trusted even less." Before even determining whether he could create an effective strategy, this man was paralyzed by the anticipated consequences of failure.

The fear of rejection is also a powerful motivator. Asking subordinates to do much more than they assert they can do runs the risk, at least in a manager's mind, of earning their resentment, if not their dislike. Many managers have been only too eager to adopt the model of the manager portrayed by the human relations movements of the 1950s and 1960s—the loving, understanding, and supportive father figure. The model of the stern, demanding manager was portrayed as a villain.

Although many exponents of human relations did emphasize the importance of high expectations and tough goals, managers frequently overlooked those parts of the message. They saw that high expectations for performance could lead to psychological rejection by subordinates. The prevailing opinion was that by adopting the right techniques, managers could avoid confronting subordinates on performance expectations and asking them to produce much more than the managers estimated they were likely to give anyhow.

Are managers conscious of the discrepancy between the performance they are requiring and what might be possible? To an extent, they are. Most sense that their organization could achieve more, but their vision is obstructed. To avoid the uneasiness and guilt brought on by too clear a vision of performance gaps, managers unconsciously employ a variety of psychological mechanisms for obstructing the truth.

Evasion through rationalization. Managers may escape having to demand better performance by convincing themselves that they have done all they can to establish expectations. For instance, they may claim that everyone already knows what must be accomplished. When asked whether they have made the goals clear to their people, these managers respond with a variation of "If they don't know what the goals of this outfit are by now, they don't belong in their jobs."

Sincere in their belief that their subordinates are doing their best, managers frequently look for sub-standard performance elsewhere. Do the following statements sound familiar?

"We can reduce back orders, but you're going to have to pay for plenty of overtime."

"If you want us to cut inventories any further, be prepared for delayed shipments."

"Ever since they trimmed our maintenance budget, we haven't been able to keep this plant operating properly."

Performance improvements always seem to call for an expansion of resources or an increase in authority. Overlooking the possibility of obtaining greater yields from available resources, managers often fail to impose greater demands and expectations on their employees. And when managers do try to demand more, their subordinates are quick to point out that they are doing all that can be done. Thus all levels of management may share the illusion of operating at the outer limit when, in fact, they are far from it.

To avoid having to impose new requirements on subordinates, a manager may decide to take on the job herself. She reassures herself that her people are already overloaded or that they lack some qualification that she possesses. At the other extreme is the manager who covers up his reluctance to make demands with toughness, gruffness, or arbitrariness. He may threaten or needle subordinates without actually specifying requirements and deadlines for results. In the folklore of management, such toughness of manner is equated with a preoccupation with achievement.

Reliance on procedures. Managers can avoid the necessity of demand making by putting their chips on a variety of management programs, procedures, and innovations that they hope will produce better results. But while such mechanisms may help an organization respond to demands, they are no substitute for good management.

For example, a manager may try an incentive system aimed at seducing subordinates into better performance through the promise of "goodies." Many top officers are perpetually preoccupied with new kinds of salary, profit-sharing, and stock-option plans and with promotions, titles, and other so-called incentives. Management assumes that if the right carrots are held out, managers and employees will run like rabbits.

Infusions of new managerial technology also may appear to be the key to performance improvements. Management will install information systems, mathematical planning models, industrial engineering studies, training programs, or any of dozens of other programs offered by technical staff or outside consultants. Top management may even reorganize the company—or parts of it. Perhaps convinced of the magic in their medicines, even the best-trained staff technicians and management consultants become the unwitting coconspirators of managers who fail to establish higher performance requirements for subordinates. In one well-known international company, an internal consulting group put together a mathematical planning model to maximize corporate profits in interdivisional negotiations. But the president used a flimsy excuse to escape from the struggle of requiring his division heads to operate within the framework of the models.

Attacks that skirt the target. A manager may set tough goals and insist they be achieved—and yet fail to produce a sense of accountability in subordinates. For example, managers often define even significant goals in vague or general terms that make accountability impossible. The R&D director is told that she "must get more new products out this year"; the personnel director hears that "turnover must be reduced"; management at a transportation company insists that "safety is our number one objective." When reporting time comes, who can say whether these objectives have been met?

Similarly, a manager may establish goals but insist that subordinates can't be held accountable because they lack the authority to get the job done. The case of a petrochemical plant whose product quality was well below par illustrates this point. Quality depended on how well a number of interdependent departments processed components. Top management charged department heads to improve operations and monitored these activities, but it failed to hold any individuals responsible for the quality of the end product on the grounds that none of them was in sufficient control of all the factors. The quality improvements failed to meet expectations.

Sometimes, when pressed by superiors, a manager will establish expectations in a way that tells subordinates that he is merely following instructions from above. In fact, he unconsciously hopes that his subordinates' performance will fall short, "proving," as he has asserted all along, that the new stretch goals cannot be attained.

Ironically, management-by-objectives programs often create heavy paper snowstorms in which managers can escape from demand making. In many MBO programs, as lists of goals get longer and documents get thicker, the focus becomes diffused, bulk is confused with quality, and energy is spent on the mechanics rather than on results. A manager challenged on the performance of her group can safely point to the packet of papers and assert, "My managers have spent many hours developing their goals for the year."

Strategy for Action

The avoidance mechanisms just described act as powerful deterrents to dramatic performance improvement—but they do not have to. There are ways to accelerate progress.

If management is willing to invest time and energy, there is a way it can expect more and get more. I have seen the process work in a variety of organizations: in a refinery that expanded its output while reducing its force by half; in a large, urban teaching hospital that shifted its mission and direction radically; in a poorly maintained detergent and foodstuffs plant that became more competitive without more investment; and in school systems where determined leaders generated innovation despite the inertia of tradition.

The essence of the five-step strategy outlined here is to make a successful initial attempt at upgrading expectations and obtaining a response and then to use this achievement as the foundation for increasingly ambitious steps. A series of demands, initially limited, then more ambitious—each supported by careful plans, controls, and persistence—makes success more likely than does a big plunge involving demands for sweeping changes.

Select the goal. Start with an urgent problem. Are the costs of one department too high? Is a budget being seriously overrun? Is a quality specification being consistently missed? Is there a shortfall in meeting a sales quota? Beginning with problems like these is essential to generating the feeling that achievement of the goal is imperative, not merely desirable.

Retrospective Commentary

In company after company, I have asked managers to estimate how much more their organizations would produce if overlapping functions were eliminated, if units began to work more in sync with each other, if people worked more closely to their real potential, and if they dissipated less energy in political hassles, self-aggrandizing behavior, useless meetings, and projects that go nowhere. Not surprisingly, almost everyone has selected the "25 to 50%" and the "over 50%" categories.

With all this latent potential evident, why hasn't there been more progress toward meeting the global competitive challenge? I am as convinced as I was 17 years ago that the principal reason is that "few managers possess the capacity—or feel compelled— to establish high performance-improvement expectations in ways that elicit results." This capacity continues to be the most universally underdeveloped managerial skill.

There is no doubt that companies today are more impressed with the need for performance improvement than they were in 1974. They are making vast investments in new tools, new plants, and new technology. They have cranked up massive programs in continuous improvement, customer service, total quality, and culture change that dwarf the efforts of the 1960s and 1970s. Senior executives, corporate staff groups, university professors, and consulting firms have thrown themselves into the battle. The Malcolm Baldrige National Quality Award furnishes a national rallying point.

If these programs were put under the spotlight, however, they would be discovered to serve frequently as convenient escape mechanisms for managers avoiding the struggle of radically upgrading their organizations' performance.

Ironically, the "thinkers" who have invented the latest organizational effectiveness strategies unwittingly provide new busywork escapes. By putting so much emphasis on processes and techniques, they have slighted the importance of results. Thousands of employees are trained in seven-step problem solving and statistical quality control; thousands of managers are "empowered"; and thousands of creative reward and communications systems are in place. In the absence of compelling requirements for measurable improvement, however, little improvement occurs.

For example, teams of consultants and social scientists set up more than 40 different programs in a large international corporation in an effort to make it a "total quality company." In publicizing this undertaking, the company proudly asserted that it did not expect significant results until the *fourth* year.

Companies will never achieve competitive performance levels as long as their executives believe that the right training and development activities, applied with enough diligence, will eventually be rewarded with the right bottom-line results. That is a siren song for all those managers who don't have the stomach for the necessary personal struggle. No combination of programs and training can inject the required experience, skill, and confidence.

Contrary to the mythology, setting high-performance imperatives does not conflict with empowering people. Empowerment comes as people rise to the challenge of tough demands and, through effort, meet them. Listen to two Motorola employees describe their experience on a project to turn out a product for Nippon Telephone and Telegraph:

- "The customer came and told us that nothing except absolute excellence would be accepted. The team was really turned on by the challenge of doing something that was considered impossible."

- "People were challenged every day. There was a strong drive to succeed in this program. It was the most exciting time of my life."

Those are empowered people.

To create this kind of environment, managers have to personally experiment with demand making on some urgently needed improvement, like accelerating the development of new products, making far-reaching gains in quality, or improving customer relationships. Demand making can enliven organizations with the challenge of tough goals and the gratification that comes with success. Without an ever-sharpening demand framework, improvement programs and activities are merely diversions from the real work of making our corporations more competitive worldwide.

As you select the goal, assemble the information needed to frame the performance demand. You need this information not only to define the need and specify the target but also to convince people why performance improvement is essential.

It is also a good idea to sound out your subordinates on the opportunities for improvement; their responses will give you a sense of their readiness. To illustrate, the management at a newspaper publishing plant tried to launch a comprehensive improvement effort. The needs were so great and resistance by managers at lower levels so strong that very little was accomplished. Interviews with the composing room supervisors, however, revealed that they shared upper management's distress over the number of typographical errors in news and advertising matter. This information made it possible to design an initial project mobilizing supporters of change.

The more participation by subordinates in determining goals, the better. Managers should not, however, permit their dedication to the participatory process to mean abdication of their own responsibilities.

Specify the minimum expectation of results. Broad, far-reaching, or amorphous goals should be narrowed to one or two specific, measurable ones. A manager may protest with "I have too many things that have to get done to concentrate on only one or two of them." But the fragmentation of a manager's attention in trying to push them all ahead can keep her perpetually trapped in the same defense mechanisms from which she is trying to escape. Whether the first-step goal is a modest advance or a bold one, it must focus the energy of the organization on one or two sharply defined targets.

For example, one company, in treading a path between mass production and tailored engineering, was losing money because it could not clarify its proper place in the market and develop the appropriate products. Top management spent hundreds of hours conferring and making studies to define the business, the product line, and the pricing strategy. This produced more frustration than progress.

The undertaking was transformed, however, when the president asked the executives to select from a dozen new products the one they agreed would most likely be profitable and conform to their vision of the business. He directed them to sketch out a market plan and pricing policy for this product. They were to draw from this effort some generalizations that could be applied to policy determination. The president was convinced that the group could produce the result in a short time. And he was confident that the initial step would provide insights into the next steps to clarify the company's direction.

Communicate your expectations clearly. Share with the persons responsible, both orally and in writing, the determination of the goal, the locus of responsibility, the timetable, and the constraints. Make clear that you are not asking for permission to set the goal, not securing their advice on whether the goal is attainable, and not implying that if they do not meet the target, you will nevertheless appreciate their efforts. Make sure they understand that this is not a goal that *should* be achieved; it is one that *must* be achieved.

Monitor the project, but delegate responsibility. Work-planning disciplines are essential to preventing these projects from fading into the ether. Trying to keep the goals, commitments, and plans only in your mind is sure to undermine the project; rather, have the manager responsible for each goal or subgoal provide you with a written work plan of steps to be taken to reach the goal. This plan should also specify how progress will be measured and how it will be reported to you.

Moreover, assign responsibility for achieving each goal to one person, even though the contributions of many may be essential for success. Consider the case of a company whose technically complex new product was failing to perform as promised. The president talked about the problem with her marketing, engineering, and manufacturing vice presidents; each claimed that his function was doing its job and that the problems originated elsewhere. After spending much more time than usual with her subordinates, the president was still able to effect only a slight improvement.

The turnaround came when she told her departments heads that it was unwise for her to get involved in trying to solve the problem. That was *their* job. She gave them full responsibility for reducing the frequency of unacceptable products to a target level within three months. She assigned to one executive the responsibility for shaping an integrated plan and for making certain it was adequate

26

to achieve the result. In addition, the president requested that each of the other managers produce a plan specifying his or her own functions, contributions, and timetable. After many months of struggling for a solution, the company for the first time pinpointed a goal to be achieved, established responsibilities for achievement, and introduced work-planning disciplines to manage the process in an orderly way.

When responsibility for results is not explicitly assigned, subordinates tend to "delegate" it upward, especially if the boss tries to play a helpful role in the project. Top management must ensure that project members clearly understand their responsibility and must not permit them to turn offers of help and support into opportunities to pass the buck.

Expand and extend the process. Once some success has been achieved on a first set of demands, it should be possible to repeat the process on new goals or on an extension of the first. This will lead to further expansion.

Consider the efforts of a large railway express terminal that handled tens of thousands of shipments daily. It was performing very poorly on many counts: costs were high, productivity was low, and delivery deadlines were often missed. Studies had identified the potential for saving hundreds of thousands of dollars, but those savings were illusive. Then the head of the terminal and his boss ceased talking about what was going wrong and all the improvements that were needed. Instead, they identified the most crucial short-term goals.

From these few they selected one: getting *all* of one category of shipments out on time each day. It was not an easy goal, but it was clear and understandable; it could be sharply defined and measured, and action steps could be quickly identified. Meeting that target was the all-important first success that launched the terminal on an ambitious improvement program. Once the first traffic category was under control, top management planned a series of slightly more ambitious improvement programs. Gradually, the terminal's managers gained confidence in asking for more, and their staffs gained confidence that they could respond. Eventually, many of the sizable savings promised in the earlier studies were realized.

Psychodynamics of Action

While moving ahead through successive sets of demands, top management has some essential work to do on the psychological front as well. The methods and procedures for negotiating goals with subordinates are well known; almost overlooked but more significant are the often unconscious negotiations that managers carry on with themselves. They frequently bargain themselves down to comfortable expectation levels long before they confront subordinates. They must learn to share the risk taking that they want their subordinates to assume. They may have to live with the "testing" subordinates subject them to, and they may need to engage in consciousness-raising to make sure they do not slip into rationalizations for failing to see that their directives are carried out.

Managers often unintentionally ensure that they will share in the glory of their subordinates' successes but that lower levels will take the blame for failures. For example, a plant manager had been pressuring the head of maintenance to realign the responsibilities of supervisors and workers as a way to increase efficiency. The step would make a number of persons redundant. Low-level managers and supervisors resisted the move, warning of various disasters that would befall the plant.

The deadlock was broken only when the plant manager—through transfers, early retirements, and a very modest layoff—reduced the maintenance force to the level needed after the proposed reorganization. Once the most painful step had been taken, maintenance management quickly installed the new structure. Instead of insisting self-righteously that the key to action was overcoming the resistance of maintenance management, the plant manager assumed the risk and reduced the staff.

When managers expect better results, subordinates may express their own lack of self-confidence in the form of tests. For example, they may continue to do exactly what they have been doing, suggesting that they heard the boss's words but disbelieve the message. Or they may imply that "it can't be done." Some subordinates may advise managers that for their own good—considering the high risks involved—they should lower their sights. They may even withdraw their affection and approval from their managers.

Such testing is usually an expression of subordinates' anxiety over whether they can actually achieve the goal; it is a way to seek reassurance from the boss. If the boss is as anxious as they are, he will be upset by the testing and may react against what he perceives as defiance. If he has self-confidence, he will accept the testing for what it is and try to help his subordinates deal with the problem—without lowering his expectations.

In breaking out of productiveness-limiting traps, consciousness-raising may be needed to help managers assess more objectively their approach to establishing demands. Consultants—inside or outside—can help managers gain the necessary perspective. Or several managers who are working through the same process may join forces, since each can be more detached about the others' behavior than about his or her own. They may meet periodically to probe such questions as: Have you adequately assessed the potential for progress? Have you made the performance requirements clear to your associates? Are these goals ambitious enough? Are you providing your subordinates with enough help? Are you sharing the risks with them? How well are you standing up to testing? Have you defined goals that at least some of your subordinates can see as exciting and achievable?

Perhaps the most important function of consciousness-raising has to do with getting started. It is very difficult to alter the pattern of relationships between superiors and subordinates, especially if they have been working together for a long time. You cannot take the first step without worrying that your people may say (or think), "Oh, come off it. We know who you are!"

The Rewards Are There

The strategy for demanding better performance—and getting it—begins with a focus on one or two vital goals. Management assesses readiness and then defines the goal. The organization receives clearly stated demands and unequivocally stated expectations. Management assigns the responsibility for results to individuals, and work-planning discipline provides the means for self-control and assessment of progress. Management keeps wired in, tenaciously pushing the project forward. Early successes provide the reinforcement to shoot for more ambitious targets, which may be extensions of the first goal or additional goals.

There is no limit to the pace or scope of expansion. As this process expands, a shift in management style and organizational dynamics gradually takes place: sophisticated planning techniques, job redesign, closer line and staff collaboration, and other advances will come about naturally.

With clearly conveyed, "nonnegotiable" expectations and a step-by-step expansion strategy, you may find that the anticipated difficulties and dangers never materialize. If your subordinates are like most, they will respond to the higher demands. They will be able to accomplish what is expected—or most of it. And despite a bit of testing or hazing, most of them will enjoy working in a more results-oriented environment. Thus you will be creating greater job satisfaction and mutual respect, better relationships among levels, and a multiplied return on the organization's human and material resources.

Since 1960, Robert H. Schaffer has headed a Stamford, Connecticut, management consulting firm that bears his name. Through the Association of Management Consultants, he also trains consultants. In 1988, Harper Business Books published his book The Breakthrough Strategy: Using Short-Term Successes to Build the High-Performance Organization. *For the reissuance of this article, which originally appeared in HBR November-December 1974, he has written a retrospective commentary.*

II.
Performance Measurement: A Key to Successful Strategy Execution

A. Determining What to Measure

Core Skills: Doing the Right Things Right
    by Robert A. Irvin and Edward G. Michaels, III
Make Performance Gages Perform
    by Bob Malchione
A Need to Crunch the Right Numbers
    by Joseph M. Sieger
Successfully Integrating Total Quality and Performance Appraisal
    by Mark R. Edwards, Ph.D.
Performance Appraisals and Deming: A Misunderstanding?
    by Jim M. Graber, Roger E. Breisch, and Walter E. Breisch
If Earnings Aren't the Dial to Read
    by Robert A. Kaplan and David P. Norton

B. Measuring Performance for Different Parts of the Organization

Emerson Electric: Consistent Profits, Consistently
    by Charles F. Knight
Why Measure the CEO's Performance
    by C.E. Schneier, R.W. Beatty, and D.G. Shaw
The Executive Appraisal Paradox
    by Clinton O. Longenecker and Dennis A. Gioia
How the Right Measures Help Teams Execel
    by Christopher Meyer

C. Setting Performance Standards

Why to Go for Stretch Targets
    by Shawn Tully

Core Skills:
Doing the Right Things Right

by Robert A. Irvin and Edward G. Michaels III

For years, the primary focus of management was on strategic issues. This was a natural consequence of the external forces—the energy crisis, double digit interest and inflation rates, rapid technology advances, and deregulation—that triggered fundamental changes in industry structure and led many companies to rethink both their market positions and their sources of competitive advantage. Today, however, we believe that a new management focus is emerging which, in many industries, is already playing a greater role than the creativity of strategies in driving corporate performance—the superior execution of the core skills of the business.

In many businesses, opportunities to develop novel, and sustainable, sources of competitive advantage are few and becoming fewer. Skill-based competitive advantages, however, generally have significant impact on economic performance and are extremely difficult for competitors to replicate. Developing superb execution of core skills, though not mysterious, requires an enormous, integrated effort driven from the top and sustained over time.

We have recently completed research in the insurance industry, which focused on identifying property and casualty "winners" (i.e., those companies that have consistently outperformed the industry). Our research suggests that "winners"' have been helped by a sharp product/market focus and by structural distribution-based advantages. But they have succeeded largely by superior execution of the core skills of pricing/underwriting, claims, investment management, and marketing.

In the following article, Bob Irvin and Ed Michaels summarize the forces that have led to the emergence of core skills as a focal point for management. They then describe the five "secrets" of skill building and the nature of the systematic effort it requires.

Peter Walker
McKinsey & Company

RJR Nabisco's Lou Gerstner, probably America's most famous new CEO since Lee Iacocca, was quoted recently as saying:"It is my absolute conviction that you can outmanage your competition by having brilliant strategies but those brilliant strategies have to be executed brilliantly."

It's a sign of the times that he added the point about brilliant execution. More and more, CEOs today are concluding that a good strategy by itself is not enough. So they are also focusing on strategy's partner, core institutional skills, as an essential key to achieving sustainable competitive advantage. These skills are, after all, what enable you to get your strategy executed. They are the critical capabilities that an organization as a whole has—as distinct from the capabilities of individuals in the organization.

The difference matters. The question an insurance company needs to ask, for example, is not, "Do we hire smart people from good schools and give them effective underwriting training?" Rather, it is, "Do we, as an institution, have the core skill of making wise underwriting decisions?" Such a skill would, no doubt, require us to hire smart people from good schools and give them effective underwriting training. But it would require us to provide continuous coaching, information systems that support the making of fact-based underwriting decisions, an ability to analyze the effectiveness of those decisions over time, incentives and development programs to reward effective underwriting, and performance guidelines that are clear and constantly reinforced.

Core skills, as we think about them, link strategy (thinking) and execution (doing). If you want brilliant execution, strengthen the right core skills, the ones that provide the most economic leverage. If you do a good enough job, the core skills themselves, even more than the strategy, will become the basis for your continued success.

A Foundation for Success

The lesson takes some getting used to: you *can* build sustainable competitive advantage on a base of first-rate core skills. Take Marriott Hotels for example. The company's strategy is straightforward and certainly no secret: go after business travelers with consistently excellent service. Almost any lodging chain could adopt that strategy; in fact, a lot of others have. What makes Marriott special— what gives it its edge—is its ability to execute the strategy brilliantly.

Marriott is excellent at selecting good sites, designing and building appropriately sized hotels, opening them smoothly, and marketing them well. But what travelers see and remember is Marriott's core skills of providing consistent high-quality service. How do they do it? By institutionalizing a "fanatical eye for detail" across the company, now some 200,000 employees strong.

This attention to detail begins with the hiring process. As Ron Zemke reported in *The Service Edge,* the company interviewed 40,000 applicants for 1,200 positions when it opened the Marriott Marquis Hotel in New York a few years ago. It is led tirelessly from the top. On a recent tour of a company hotel with a *Fortune* magazine writer, Bill Marriott is said to have "grimaced at the lack of glaze on the pastries" until the hotel manager reassured him that they would get a glaze before leaving the kitchen. And it continues through every ho-

tel operation. Maids, for example, follow a 66-point guide to making up bedrooms.

Paying such close attention to detail creates a set of boundaries within which employees are personally empowered to take initiative in providing excellent customer service in every area from sophisticated meeting planning to returning lost galoshes. Consequently, Marriott consistently comes out on top in customer surveys conducted by *Business Travel News* and has an occupancy rate that is 10 points higher than the industry average.

Or take Wal-Mart. Yes, their strategy of focusing on smaller towns was crucial to their success. And, yet, their "everyday low price" strategy got them well established. But now as they move into larger cities with a format not so different from that of K-mart and other discount retailers, Wal-Mart continues to rack up impressive gains. (Their sales are up 29 percent for the most recent quarter; K-mart's, 4 percent.) Why? Simple: their core skills in purchasing, logistics and customer service are better than those of the competition.

The marketing vice president of a major vendor says of Wal-Mart's purchasing capability, "They are very, very focused people, and they use their buying power more forcefully than anybody else in America. They talk softly but have piranha hearts, and if you aren't totally prepared when you go in there, you'll have your behind handed to you." Wal-Mart's logistics strength is based on a sophisticated distribution system, with 14 computerized facilities and a fleet of 6,500 trucks. Says the CEO, "Our distribution facilities are one of the keys to our success. If we do anything better than other folks, that's it."*

There it is again: a clear strategy executed brilliantly because of better core institutional skills. These companies have an ability to get extraordinary results from ordinary people by being clear about what *they* need to be good at and then gearing hiring, training, coaching, information systems, rewards, management style, and culture to building and nurturing those core skills.

Once you get used to looking at the world this way, the reasons for a lot of successes and failures come into focus. Did you know, for example, that in 1968 McDonald's, Burger King and Burger Chef

---

* "Wal-Mart—Will It Take Over the World?" *Fortune,* February 30, 1989.

all had under 1,000 outlets and were in a tight race for control of the fast food market? Or that Burger King and Burger Chef were backed by parents with deep pockets (Pillsbury and General Foods, respectively)? Why does McDonald's now have over 10,000 outlets with sales growing at 13 percent per year, Burger King about 5,500 outlets with sputtering sales, and Burger Chef a mere 21 outlets? Core skills is why—an institutional knack for finding excellent sites, offering consistent products and service and developing new products. Customers and industry observers recognize these core skills and the superior performance with which they are associated. (See, for example, Exhibit I, which summarizes how these observers contrast McDonald's execution of these skills with that of Burger King.)

Marriott, Wal-Mart and McDonald's provide visible examples of the power of core skills in service industries. But core skills are equally important in manufacturing industries. Consider VF Corporation, the maker of Lee and Wrangler jeans, Jantzen swimsuits and Vanity Fair lingerie. VF has been the leader among the *Fortune* 500 during the past 10 years in return to shareholders with a whopping 35.4 percent average annual return. Why? VF has achieved this impressive record in large measure because of strong core skills in manufacturing, operations planning and disciplined product line development. They make high-quality apparel at competitive (or lower) costs and thereby offer consumers superior value. Second, they forecast demand and both plan and run operations with less inventory, fewer plants, and fewer closeouts than can most of their competitors. Finally, they are able to manage the risk inherent in the apparel business by institutionalizing a focused and disciplined approach to the line development process. These three core skills have helped them achieve an average 22 percent ROE during the last 10 years while integrating and adding enormous value to several apparel company acquisitions.

The bottom line

So, you might ask, what's new about all this? There have always been companies that are just "better at it" than others. Unless you were going head-to-head with them, however, that did not really matter. Besides, it is—and always will be—tough for any manager to make a company much "better at it." So why all this talk about core skills? Well, two reasons:

First, we believe that, in the future, strength in the right core skills will be *the* key to sustainable competitive advantage.

And second, we have identified five "secrets" to building core skills and have designed a logical, strategy-driven process that can give top managers a firm grip on this critically important but slippery challenge.

Exhibit I. Contrasting Execution of Core Skills

Core Skills	McDonald's	Burger King
Site selection	"Penchant for finding the plum"	"Generally good locations"
High-quality service	"Unparalleled consistency"	"Suffers from operational sloppiness"
Product innovation	"A knack for product development"	"Spotty record with new products"
Communications	"Surrogate mom"	"Comes off as aggressive, masculine and distant"

Source: *USA Today; Business Week; Wall Street Journal.*

The Key to Advantage

Core skills have always been important, but we believe they will be increasingly central to success in the future. Three converging trends are responsible:

1. *The structural barriers are breaking down* that used to protect industries like automobiles, aircraft engines, steel, banking, energy and retailing. Today, these barriers—geographic, regulatory, scale and technology—are either eroding or already gone; and as they break down, the basis for competition shifts back to "who's better at it." Often that's all there is left.

Automobiles are a classic example of the breakdown of geographic barriers. Consumers can now choose from a broad selection of cars from around the world, and costs and quality levels are beginning to converge. Hence, what determines a given producer's success is not the robustness of its domestic market, but rather the strength of its core skills of tailoring cars to customer niches, improving quality/reliability, and getting products quickly to market.

Much the same is true of *regulatory barriers* (which have long provided protection to companies in industries like transportation, health care and telecommunications) and *scale barriers* (which have protected such operations as steel making, electricity generation and metropolitan newspaper publishing). Health care companies and hospitals, for example, are having to learn how to control costs, segment customers, keep up with expensive, rapidly advancing technology, and forge better relationships with doctors and clinics. By eating away at the dominance of major metropolitan dailies, suburban newspapers are forcing them to be better at the core skills of local reporting, circulation and customer service. Even *technology barriers* are eroding. Ever-more-rapid advances in electronics, for instance, produce ever-weaker barriers for the current state of the art. As in Wonderland, you have to run hard just to stand still.

2. *Strategies have become similar and transparent* in many industries. Which regional bank isn't focusing on affluent and wealthy customers and small businesses? Which airline isn't going after the business traveler? Which consumer goods company isn't trying to grow its major brands internationally, develop innovative new products for emerging niches, and wring more out of marketing expenditures? These strategies make sense. No wonder so many of them look alike. The real battle lies elsewhere.

Today, it's not figuring out where to compete or even how to compete that's tough. It's competing that's tough! Focus and execution are the name of the game. Driven, in part, by a newly efficient market for corporate control, many companies have now clarified their product lines, spun off divisions that didn't fit, and downsized headquarters' staff in order to focus better on their true core businesses. The winners will be the companies that execute the best—that is, the companies that possess superior core skills.

As we've said, having clear strategies is essential. Having brilliant strategies is terrific. But only if those strategies are brilliantly executed will they lead to lasting competitive advantage.

3. *The era of "human capital" is upon us.* As markets and technology become more global and more dynamic, the old scientific management approach of "command and control" is increasingly outmoded. Because the world had become too complex for management to be able to prescribe all-purpose solutions from the top, organizations have to become more adaptive. That means broader job classifications, more extensive use of teams, and more frequent job rotation will all become common. In such an environment, people—human capital—will be the scarce resource.

To realize the full potential of their human capital, companies must be willing to invest in assets like information systems and training programs that are less tangible than plant and equipment. Only then will they be able to build the necessary competence at all organizational levels to respond with the speed and creativity required by today's competitive pressures. Nurturing this competence means finding ways to unleash the "brain power" of people. And focusing this brain power in support of the superior execution of strategy is what core skills are all about.

"Secrets" of Skill Building

If core skills are so important, you may ask, why haven't I heard of them before? Actually, you have. You may have called them "what we need to be good at around here to win." Consultants often call them "key factors for success." Employees call them "what I am trying to do every day."

"We need to be more innovative, like 3M"; or "We need to be better at customer service, like Nordstroms"; or "We need to get to market quicker, like the Japanese"—when you hear statements like these, people are really talking about core skills. Most senior executives intuitively accept their importance and the need to pay attention to them. The problem is that they don't really know *how*.

This is no indictment. Building core skills is extremely difficult. Organizations and individuals easily get "grooved" in certain ways of doing things, and instilling a core skill like "first-time quality in manufacturing" may require changing the behavior of thousands of people in dozens of plants. This isn't easy. But it is possible! And it is increasingly necessary for competitive success. The good news is that our experience suggests people are actually quite willing and able to change as long as they have a clear understanding of what's expected of them and why it's important, as well as some latitude to exercise judgment and solve problems creatively.

During the past three or four years, our firm has worked with approximately 200 companies to help them improve their core skills. Along the way, we've identified five key elements that companies frequently overlook. We call them the five "secrets" of building core skills.

Secret #1: Forge a clear link between strategy and skills

A company's strategy, which should embody the value it proposes to deliver to its customers, determines the skills it needs. Many companies, however, are not sufficiently clear or rigorous about this linkage.

Because Frank Perdue promises to deliver more tender chickens, his organization has to excel at the breeding and logistics skills necessary to deliver them. Because Volvo promises to deliver more reliable, tougher and safer station wagons, it must be skilled at designing and manufacturing them. Be-cause Domino's Pizza says it will get a fresh pizza delivered hot to your door within 30 minutes, each of its 5,000 outlets needs to be skilled at making a good pizza quickly and at customer order processing and delivery. Strategy drives skills. Simple stuff, to be sure, but if you miss this linkage, your company may end up doing some things right, but not doing the *right* things right.

Secret #2: Be specific—and selective—about core skills

Managers often describe the core skills their companies need to build in terms that are too general. Saying that you need to be first-rate at customer service or marketing is not good enough. Let us illustrate. The employees of a department store committed to being better at customer service won't know what to do differently because "customer service" doesn't paint a specific enough picture of the behavior desired of them. In fact, a department store needs to be good in at least three different types of customer service: with hard goods like refrigerators or furniture, customer service must have a high component of product and technical knowledge; with fine apparel, what counts is expertise in fashion counseling; with basics and sundries, the need is for friendly, efficient self-service. Each of these service goals translates into a different set of day-to-day behaviors expected of employees. Unless you specify precisely which you want, even willing employees won't change their behavior very much because they won't know how.

We sometimes help companies think about how to leverage the strong core skills they have in order to grow into related business areas. In such cases, being specific about the skills you want to leverage is especially important. Otherwise, you can easily be fooled about how extendable your skills really are.

A while ago, for example, we were asked to help a utility think about possible diversification. We jointly came to the conclusion that they were excellent at operationally- and technologically-intensive, quasi-regulated service businesses. This realization led us to conclude they should pursue cable TV, waste and energy management, and home security companies, but not the health care, real estate, or financial institutions that had initially appeared attractive based on the demographics of their service areas.

The trick is to focus on a few (say, two to five) genuinely "core" skills—those with the most economic leverage, those most central to your ability to execute your strategy. They will not, of course, include everything you need to do right. (The department store noted above also needs to handle credit decisions well.) They will simply be the most important things to do right. And that's plenty to focus on. Trying to build three core skills at once is tough enough: trying to build twenty is impossible.

Secret #3: Clarify the implications for pivotal jobs

Think back to the department store again. You can see that the definition of different types of customer service drives through to the identification of several specific jobs whose performance will determine whether customers think the store is good at customer service: the product salesman for refrigerators, the fashion counselor for fine apparel, and the cashier for sundries. Pushing the skill definition to these specific jobs, which we call "pivotal" jobs, allows you to describe in specific terms what you want the holders of these jobs to do or not to do, which kind of people to hire, which kind of training and coaching to give them, which rewards will motivate them, and which kind of information they need.

For example, at Nordstrom, the excellent Seattle-based fashion specialty retailer, the pivotal job is the front-line sales associate. Because Nordstrom is clear about the type of person they want for this job—someone interested in a career, not just a summer position—they look more for a service orientation than prior experience. They pay better than the industry average and offer an incentive for sales that allows top sales associates to make over $80,000 a year. Nordstrom stresses customer service above all else. The company philosophy is to offer the customers, in order, "the best service, selection, quality and value."

This clarity about priorities helps sales associates determine appropriate service behavior. So does the excellent product and service training they receive. And so does the customer information system that provides them with up-to-date sales and service records on their customers. Nordstrom recognizes that their business success depends on the success of pivotal jobholders in delivering value to custom-ers, and they have geared their entire organization to support these front-line associates.

Whatever your business, pivotal jobholders hold the key to brilliant execution of your strategy. If you are clear about the skills required by your strategy, the nature of the pivotal jobs, the behavior required of them, and the policies, culture and systems needed to support them, you are well on your way to success. All too often, however, companies stop short. They think too generally about what their organizations need to be good at, and they fail to take the time to drive those conclusions through to their implications for pivotal jobs.

Secret #4: Provide leadership from the top

Whether they call them core skills, key factors for success, or "what we need to be good at," most executives we've met know at least intuitively which core institutional skills their companies need. And they know, as well, that these skills are about people—hiring the right people, training them, providing the right coaching, offering appropriate incentives and rewards, and so on. Since this "looks like, flies like, and quacks like" a people problem, these managers often do not lead the process but delegate the task of building core skills to their human resources (HR) departments. True, they may exhort the troops, launch a task force, and encourage the HR folks to develop slogans, offer training and propose an incentive plan. A year later, however, these managers are inevitably asking what happened to their programs to improve customer service. The lament is familiar: "I don't sense we are doing any better."

What you must do to provide leadership, of course, varies with the situation. But here are some key ingredients that we've seen work time and again:

- Appeal to the pride of your organization. Most people want to do a superior job, especially for a company that expresses its mission with an idea bigger than just making money. Providing them with a single noble purpose—be it "quality, service, cleanliness, value" at McDonald's or "innovation" at 3M—will unleash energy, but keep it focused.

- Clarify the importance and value of building core skills. Provide your organization with a good economic understanding of their value, as well as a clear picture of the consequences of *not* paying attention to them.

- Be willing to do the tough things that break bottlenecks and establish credibility for the belief that "this change is for real." Usually the toughest things involve replacing the people who are change blockers, committing key managers to the skill-building effort, and spending money on it.

- Treat the program to build skills as something special, not business as usual. Reflect this in your own time allocation, in the questions you ask your subordinates, in the special assignments you give people, in your choice of the special measurements (which we call "closely watched numbers") you look at, and so on.

- Overcommunicate to your superiors, your subordinates, your customers, and especially your pivotal jobholders. Talk and write incessantly about your skill-building program—about the skills you're trying to build, about why they're critical, about early wins, heroes, lessons learned from failures, milestones achieved. One client repeated his core institutional skill goals so often that they almost became a litany: "We will operate a transit system that is safe, clean, comfortable, reliable, attractive, and economical." He could explain and measure each one. It got so his employees could repeat them in their sleep. That's the kind of communication you want.

We recently conducted a survey of McKinsey teams whose clients had begun programs to build core skills some time ago. One-third said their clients had built superior skills. One-third said they were making good progress; and one-third said the effort was sputtering or never got off the ground. The single most powerful discriminating factor between success and failure was the commitment of top leadership to the effort. Whether the challenge is building claims management skills in an insurance company, relationship management skills in a bank, or "making it right the first time" skills on a factory floor, the effort has got to be a sustained top priority of senior management.

Secret #5: Empower the organization to learn

Organizations, like individuals, learn best by doing. Building new core skills is pre-eminently a learning process. As we've said, you should sketch out for employees the boundaries of their playing field by defining your strategy, the skills you're trying to build, the pivotal job behaviors you want, and the convictions you want them to hold about what's right. But within these boundaries, you should give them a lot of room to run—to try things, succeed, fail—and so learn for themselves exactly what works and what doesn't. They will figure out for themselves details you could never prescribe from above. As our former McKinsey colleague Bob Waterman used to say, "Good things will mysteriously begin to happen." Stories will spread about successes, people will learn from each other, and gradually your employees will gain confidence that they *can* do what is required.

Take, for example, the 10,000 route sales people of Frito-Lay. Michael Jordan, the company's president, says that these people with their "store to door service" control the destiny of Frito-Lay. Wayne Calloway, PepsiCo president and past CEO of Frito-Lay, describes this pivotal job as follows: "Our sales people are entrepreneurs of the first order. Over 100,000 times a day they encounter customers who are making buying decisions on the spot. How in the world could an old-fashioned sort of management deal with those kinds of conditions? Our approach is to find good people and to give them as much responsibility as possible because they're closest to the customer, they know what's going on."*

And listen to what Jan Carlzon, the CEO who turned around SAS by improving his organization's skills of customer service and on-time departure, recently said when asked if he was worried his people will make mistakes: "To the contrary, I *want* them to make mistakes. But you must provide a framework in which people can act. For example, we have said that our first priority is safety, second is punctuality, and third is other services. So, if you risk flight safety by leaving on time, you have acted outside the framework of your authority. The same is true if you don't leave on time because you are

---

* Ron Zemke and Dick Schaaf. *The Service Edge.* New American Library, 1989, p. 342.

is true if you don't leave on time because you are missing two catering boxes of meat. That's what I mean by a framework. You give people a framework, and within the framework you let people act...the dangerous thing is to not make decisions."[†] Just so.

A Systematic Approach

Well, if core skills will be increasingly important and if there are some "secrets" to building them, how can a management team address this need? Through both observing and working with companies trying to build core skills, we've developed a strategy-driven, fact-based approach that incorporates these "secrets." This process, which we call Building Institutional Skills, is laid out conceptually in Exhibit II. It starts high in the organization, with strategy, goes deeper and deeper to pivotal jobs, then comes back up with designing and implementing programs to "make it happen." (See "Some Success Stories.")

Our approach starts with clarifying the company's or division's strategy and value proposition—that is, a statement of what benefits an identified target group of customers will receive, at what relative price. The key to doing this effectively is to see yourself as your customers see you. Remember the Domino's example: a fresh, hot pizza delivered to your door within 30 minutes (at an implied price of 15 to 20 percent more than pizzas bought in a mom and pop restaurant). *That's* how the customer sees Domino's.

Next, be explicit about the few core institutional skills the organization as a whole must possess to deliver this value proposition. It's crucial to get them right, and to not select too many. That means first assessing how strong each of these skills is relative to what's needed and to how good competitors are, as well as estimating the value of strengthening them. Doing this helps you know which skills to build first. It also helps you explain why they're important. Insurance companies, for example, have been able to build support for—and a great sense of urgency about—strengthening their skills at settling claims by demonstrating that doing so would lower their loss ratio three to four points or more.

Third, for each deficient core skill, identify the one, two, or three pivotal jobs that must be per-

Exhibit II. Building Institutional Skills: Process for Diagnosis and Design

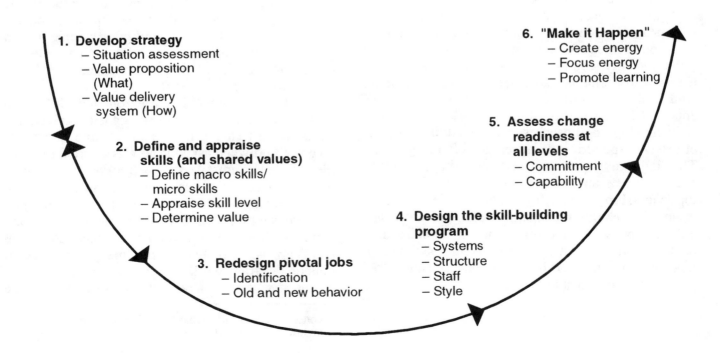

1. **Develop strategy**
   – Situation assessment
   – Value proposition (What)
   – Value delivery system (How)

2. **Define and appraise skills (and shared values)**
   – Define macro skills/ micro skills
   – Appraise skill level
   – Determine value

3. **Redesign pivotal jobs**
   – Identification
   – Old and new behavior

4. **Design the skill-building program**
   – Systems
   – Structure
   – Staff
   – Style

5. **Assess change readiness at all levels**
   – Commitment
   – Capability

6. **"Make it Happen"**
   – Create energy
   – Focus energy
   – Promote learning

formed brilliantly. Because pivotal jobs are positions that directly affect the delivery of value to customers they are usually close to the front line and involve people who design, make, or sell the product or service. Identifying these jobs requires close analysis of the company as your customers see you. What's the value you provide from their point of view and who controls it? Then describe the pivotal jobs in detail: job objectives, use of time, and criteria for success. Clarify the desired behavior by contrasting it with the current behavior in these jobs.

Fourth, design the systems, structure, staff and management style needed to influence, support and empower the pivotal jobholders to move toward the desired behavior. You can't expect superior execution of your strategy unless all this infrastructure is properly aligned to help build and sustain your core skills. Top management's job—indeed the job of the whole organization—is to make sure that the pivotal jobs get performed right. As Jan Carlson has said to his people, "If you're not serving the customer, your job is to be serving someone who is."

Some Success Stories

We all still have much to learn about the important process of building core skills. However, we have observed promising results in companies using the six-step approach outlined in this article or, at least, major aspects of it. Here are a few examples:

- An American insurance company dramatically improved its skill at claims management and consequently reduced its loss ratio by 7 points, improving profits $150 million. In this case, the pivotal job design was the key lever.

- A Canadian railroad has improved its on-time delivery percentage from 45 percent to nearly 90 percent over the last two and a half years by following this approach. Improved systems and pilot projects to determine how to empower dispatchers and other pivotal jobs were the key levers.

- A transit system widely recognized as one of the poorest run in the United States within three years received an award as the best managed system in North America. To get there, they focused on the core skills of safety, reliability and efficiency. The key levers were hands-on top management leadership of mechanics and drivers and a system of a dozen or so closely watched numbers to track weekly (by vehicle and overall) how the system was doing against its targets.

- An apparel company improved its core skill at production planning and inventory management and took $100 million out of inventory. Here the key lever was a series of computer systems jointly designed by front-line operations planners and systems people.

- A European computer manufacturer was able to improve its after-sales service quality and move from the bottom rank of performers to competitive parity by focusing on the systems changes (call dispatch/assignment, escalation, spare part availability, performance indicators, etc.) required for the field engineers to be both effective and efficient.

- A large automotive manufacturer in North America was able to move the performance of one of its large plants from near the bottom of the list to being the best plant in its system by focusing on the skill of "making it right the first time." Here the key levers were job redesign and clarification, worker empowerment, and a series of "debottlenecking" actions.

The good news, then, is that core skills *can* be built. CEOs should feel about embarking on a program to build core skills the way George Bernard Shaw said he felt about turning 90: "Fine, considering the alternative." The alternative is to try to compete without adequate core skills. In the future, that will mean losing.

Next, assess the organization's receptiveness to change. This step requires managers to evaluate the commitment to and capability of making the necessary changes at each level in the organization. This assessment lays the groundwork for planning the actual steps necessary to "make it (the skill-building program) happen." Understanding where you have support, where you have opposition, and where you have potential support but suffer from lack of understanding allows you to tailor your program much more effectively.

The last step on our chart, "make it happen," requires the most time. Building one core skill, much less several, is typically a two- to three-year undertaking. It must be thought through carefully and led by senior management. And it must call upon a variety of mechanisms to create energy (for example, simple and meaningful change themes, debottlenecking actions), focus energy (for example, specific targets for measuring progress), and promote learning (for example, pilots).

Done well, a program to build core skills can help make a company a real winner. Even more, these skills can truly become the essence of your company. They not only enable you to execute your current strategy; their strength will provide the basis for your next strategy when the current one reaches its limit. You can then choose to build a new strategy based on your core skills, or let them lead you to appropriate acquisitions and diversifications, as Con Agra has done with more than 50 successful acquisitions in the last 10 years.

Core skills, then, are what we believe to be the next key to competitive success for most companies. Even if you don't have barriers to protect you, even if you don't have a unique strategy, even if most of your employees are neither superman nor superwoman, you can still be a big winner if you've developed the right core skills. You can be like the Green Bay Packers football team in their heyday, about whom an opposing coach once said, "We know exactly what they're going to do; all we have to do is stop them." Of course, hardly anybody did.

Bob Irvin is a Principal and Ed Michaels a Director in the Atlanta office. They are both leaders of McKinsey's Building Institutional Skill Center of Competence. Peter Walker, a director in the New York office, leads the Firm's Insurance practice.

Make Performance Gages Perform

by Bob Malchione

If you wanted to know the temperature outside, you would use a thermometer. If you wanted to weigh a block of cheese, you would use a scale. Unfortunately, no simple instrument exists to measure a company's performance.

There's another problem as well. Performance measurements at most companies are out-of-step with the business environment. Too many corporations still use traditional measurements that focus more on internal goals of cost and efficiency when what matters today is meeting rising customer expectations by emphasizing time and quality.

For example, Company A's customers almost always receive their orders when the shipping department promises. Yet the company has been losing customers to higher-priced competitors. Why? Its internal measurement of "ship-to-promise" fails to detect the external reality that its customers want the product even sooner and will pay a premium to get it.

In another case, Company B's distribution outlets are measured on how many orders they can fill off the shelf. When the product isn't in stock, however, some customers go elsewhere, and the number of orders lost goes undetected.

Traditional measurements also too often focus on particular departments at the expense of overall business goals. Company C's distribution center is measured on product turns, so it takes only the number of parts it has ordered from the factory, regardless of the quantity the factory has made. Yet when the distribution center runs out of inventory, orders remain unfilled even though the organization has already committed time and money to producing the product.

Clearly, each business is different, and needs it own set of performance measurements. But there are some common rules to follow when developing performance measurements so that you focus the company in the right direction and don't spend a significant effort on performance measurements that won't help your company attain its goals.

First, start on the outside of your business.

Ask yourself, "What do customers really want and when? What do our best competitors give customers that we do not?"

Second, don't let control measures get in the way of customer responsiveness.

Backlog is a time-honored measurement of a company's strength and companies are comfortable when the backlog is high. But high backlog also means slow response to customers. So if you are serious about responsiveness, don't reward backlog. Reward throughput.

Third, think of process and product as equals.

The performance measurements you use should make product and process equally visible to your people. Too many employees think in terms of fixing the product as it moves through the production process when their focus should be to make the process as flawless as possible. So reward people who fix the process.

Fourth, don't let operating measures obscure overall business goals.

When you measure more processes and more variables, it's easy to lose sight of the overall goal. Watch customer retention, customer gains, and customer losses. Share this information with your people so they can look beyond to the larger picture. And train your people to think of the company as one integrated delivery system for the customer's benefit.

Fifth, establish new measurements.

Externally focused, process-oriented, and system-wide performance measurements are essential to gain a competitive advantage today. But they won't happen without strong management support.

That process starts with communication. Convincing an organization to rethink measurements that have been part of its mindset for years is not easy. Rules give people security and a sense of purpose.

Management has to explain the rationale behind the new measurements if it wants employees to understand that customer satisfaction, time, and quality really matter. Give your people a chance to design the new measurement, figuring out which options make sense and which will just get in the way.

Management also must show its commitment to the new measurements by sticking to them even if results are slow to materialize. They must also monitor measurements to make sure they keep pace with the rapidly changing competitive environment.

If performance measurements aren't aligned with the business' goals, the organization will not achieve advantage. Changing a business' goals without changing the measurements is to not change at all.

Mr. Malchione is a consultant with the Chicago office of the Boston Consulting Group Inc.

A Need to Crunch the *Right* Numbers

by Joseph M. Sieger

Many companies are managing with the wrong numbers.

Look at Philip Morris, for example. In its 1991 annual report, it maintains that a key strategic goal is to assure the consistency and quality of its brand names. But one national brand manager recently told Price Waterhouse: "Top management only gets quarterly sales results, operating profit and market share. We do not use—and they do not see—numbers that tell them what's happening to brand quality." The result? "They are destroying brands," the manager said—and brands are critical to the long-term performance of consumer products companies.

Unlike Philip Morris, other companies are beginning to realize they need better ways to measure their performance. Companies like 3M, Analog Devices, Du Pont, First Chicago, Ford, General Motors, Hewlett-Packard, and International Business Machines are developing new measures geared to strategic performance.

3M's goal is to develop a steady stream of innovative products as quickly as possible. So it now measures product development speed and the number of new products, not just line extensions, that a team creates. And this works: New products now account for one-third of sales. One team came up with a digital color match print system in less then three years—after companies like Xerox failed to do it in five.

There are other examples: First Chicago knows that a money transfer costs less than $10 if done correctly, but a mistake can raise the cost to almost $500. So it measures frequency of mistakes. Ford now measures the number of parts that go into a product; it knows how important that number is to assembly costs.

Good performance measurement systems enable lower-level managers to know what they need to do to support corporate strategy. The systems also help senior managers gauge how well the strategy is working and what needs more attention. The new measures are prescriptive and predictive and often concern nonfinancial phenomena. Although financial measures continue to be important in managing a company—and reporting its results to the outside world—nonfinancial measures can move companies closer to the goals they have laid out for themselves.

43

Successfully Integrating Total Quality and Performance Appraisal

by Kathleen A. Guinn

Many leaders of the Total Quality Management movement contend that the American tradition of performance appraisal is completely inconsistent with a "total quality" culture. But despite long-standing, widespread discomfort with performance appraisal, most companies have not rushed to toss it out: Performance appraisal appears to be as American as apple pie and the Fourth of July.

In fact, companies need not sacrifice performance appraisal on the altar of total quality. They can address the concerns that total quality leaders raise by building a stronger performance appraisal, one that is equally effective for individuals or work teams. Accomplishing this means shifting the performance appraisal focus from an annual event to a longer-term process called "performance management" that incorporates performance appraisal as one phase.

Performance management is not just a new name for performance appraisal, just as "Total Quality Management" means more than just quality control. Performance management is a comprehensive process of planning, managing, and reviewing performance. Each phase of this process is equally critical to the success of the whole, requiring special tools for both managers and employees and providing unique benefits. Overall performance management requires that managers and employees look at performance from an entirely different perspective, and use those new tools to carry out the assessment tasks.

Performance Management in Relation to TQM

The process of performance management actually reinforces total quality management (TQM). Because it gives managers the skills and tools to carry out the "management" part of TQM, performance management can enable managers to sustain TQM as a vital part of the organization's culture. To be most effective, managers should (1) model performance management from the top of the organization down; (2) give line management "ownership"; (3) make sure performance management is integral to "the way we do business."

A performance management process that reinforces TQM differs significantly from traditional performance appraisal in five critical ways:

- Customer expectations, not the job description, generate the individual's performance expectations.

- Results expectations meet different criteria than management-by-objectives statements.

- Performance expectations include behavioral skills that make the real difference in achieving quality performance and total customer satisfaction.

- The rating scale reflects actual performance, not a "grading curve."

- Employees are active participants in the process, not merely "drawn in" to management's actions.

The Principles of Performance Management

Managers should examine these principles individually to understand how each contributes to the process as a whole.

Customer expectations, not the job description, generate the individual's performance expectations. Traditionally, managers develop performance expectations by using a job description defining how the job should be performed. The underlying assumption is that there is a "standard of achievable perfection" which is static over time and across individual performance. But this approach often generates a "tyranny" of the performance standard, reflected in the common response, "Sorry, that is not in my job description."

Using customer expectations as the source of performance expectations means looking at how others use the outcomes of the job. Employees and managers can then set performance expectations to meet or exceed the customer's expectations. This applies whether the customer is external or internal to the organization.

Customer expectations are not the only performance expectations for the employee. They are the root from which managers and employees can generate specific results objectives for discussion. In addition, arriving at the end stage—with fully developed performance expectations—calls for integrating results expectations with the requirements of the organization's business plan.

The critical change managers must implement to support total quality is redirecting the focus to customer expectations. This is the first step in developing performance expectations. To redirect the focus, every employee in the organization—from the CEO to the front-line employee—identifies his or her customers' expectations, using the following three-part process:

Part 1: Listing the product or service the job provides.

Part 2: Identifying the internal or external customer who receives each product or service.

Part 3: Listing the customer's expectation for each product or service.

Each employee should talk directly to the customer in order to identify the customer's expectations. While the employee may be able to assume or anticipate the customer's requirements, direct communication ensures the accuracy and completeness of the employee's understanding. Companies can establish procedural guidelines to prevent this step from becoming an unwieldy free-for-all. It is important to carry out this step effectively—it reinforces the importance of the customer's expectations as the definitive measuring stick for quality work.

With the customer's expectations identified, the employee can begin assessing which expectations he or she is currently meeting and what areas need changes and improvements in performance. Once this foundation is set, the employee and manager can develop specific performance expectations.

Working through this step reinforces employees' awareness of customer expectations and directs their efforts to make continuous improvements in line with these expectations. In the end, both managers and employees are more confident that any subsequent performance expectations will meet or exceed customer expectations. (See Table 1.)

Results expectations meet different criteria than management-by-objectives statements. Once the employee has defined the customer expectations, the next step is identifying actions to meet or exceed those expectations. (See Table 2.) The employee and the supervisor together consider these customer expectations in conjunction with the business plan and begin to establish priorities for improvement opportunities. Using any of the analytical tools provided through a TQM process, the employee sets "continuous improvement targets." Although these continuous improvement targets (CITs) are measurable results of performance, they are not management-by-objectives (MBO) statements.

CITs are stated differently than traditional MBOs. Because they are process-oriented, they avoid imposing the traditional "performance standard." A clearly communicated CIT:

- is measurable or observable;
- is within the employee's control or influence;
- has resources allotted to enable the employee to achieve it; and
- has significant impact on the work process required to achieve the customer's expectation.

Table 1. Customer Expectations List

Position	Products/ Services Provided	Customer	Customer Expectations
Plant Manager	Cost Control	Vice President	Effectively achieved cost control; legitimate explanations provided for variances; corrective action plans identified as needed
Operating Supervisor	Effective Crew Management	Dept. Manager	Yield; housekeeping; products meet specifications; safety; attendance; cost of overtime; cross-training; direction; problem resolution
		Employees	Safety; housekeeping; cross-training; problem resolution; accurate and timely direction; respect
Customer Service Representative	Resolve Order Discrepancies	External Customers	Order meets specifications and is received when needed
		Expediter	Discrepancies negotiated to meet production needs
		Sales Team Leader	Provide complete information on discrepancies and their effects on customer and company
Programmer Analyst	Analytical Work on New Systems	User Dept.	Objectives of request met; understands what is being requested and what is needed
		Project Supervisor	Established deadlines met; work completed on priority basis
		Programmer	Specifications clear and appropriately detailed; available to respond to questions; provides clear responses

Note: All the examples in Tables 1, 2, & 3 are taken from actual expectations established for jobs at Republic Engineered Steels, Inc., headquartered in Massillon, Ohio.

When goal statements are phrased in terms of continuous improvement, employees clearly understand that they cannot "rest" at some "standard level." Furthermore, they are more apt to attempt action in areas requiring more difficult solutions— they know management will not penalize them for failing to attain some arbitrary level, but will acknowledge them for any improvement, no matter how small.

Table 2. Identifying Continuous Improvement Targets

Position	Continuous Improvement Targets	Tracking Source
Plant Manager	Effectively allocate funds within budgetary constraints	Accounting reports
Operating Supervisor	Reduce amount of extra processing needed to meet product specifications for straightness	Product specifications; production report
Customer Service Representative	Improve completeness of order-taking	Sales error claims; order entry error
Programmer Analyst	Reduce post-installation changes	Installation follow-up report

Using employees' existing baselines of achievement as the starting point makes them compete against their "personal best," rather than striving toward an arbitrary standard that seems unattainable or uncontrollable. When employees meet or exceed the customer's expectation in one area of performance, they can turn their attention toward another area for continuous improvement. Because employees benchmark their own performance against customer expectations that rarely remain static, they will not exhaust their continuous improvement opportunities.

Table 3. Defining Continuous Improvement Skills

Position	Skills	Job-related Example of Continuous Improvement Skills	Tracking Source
Plant Manager	Analytical Thinking	Analyzes expenditures to identify savings opportunities; anticipates consequences of spending or saving dollars; rapidly identifies key issues in complex situations; identifies several possible explanations for a situation	Direct observation; self reports
Operating Supervisor	Coaching	Provides help to crew as required to reduce extra processing; resolves other problems; maintains morale and attendance	Direct observation; self reports; third-party reports
Customer Service Representative	Negotiating	Convinces customer to accept order early or to not cancel or reschedule delivery; "sells" an order discrepancy to customer to retain sale	Third-party reports; self reports
Programmer Analyst	Listening	Asks questions to clarify user's message; checks understanding by repeating back; shows close attention to what speaker is saying	Direct observation; third-party

47

CITs are effective performance expectations for either individuals or teams. If the structure of the production process or work environment is built on teams, the teams carry out the same CIT identification process.

Performance expectations include behavioral skills that make the real difference in achieving quality performance and total customer satisfaction. A total quality culture demands that employees pay attention to "how" they make their continuous improvements, that is, to the behavioral skills they use to achieve their improvements. Quality is, after all, the "attention to detail" or the "analytical thinking" (both behavioral skills) an employee uses to accomplish a task or carry out a procedure. For example, effective customer service includes the "initiative" or the "listening skills" employees use while meeting a customer's need. These Continuous Improvement Skills (CISs) are as important to TQM as the more results-oriented CITs.

When managers focus performance expectations on both the process improvements (CITs) and the behavioral skills (CISs) used in providing a product or service, total quality and excellent customer service become "the way we do business." While employees cannot ever expect to have complete control over the external forces that influence results, they can control their behavior in accommodating the factors that are outside their control. Including behavioral skills among the performance expectations provides an opportunity for acknowledging the overall efforts employees devote to accomplishing desired improvements, and helps employees focus on the process without losing sight of the results.

Since CISs address the more subjective aspects of performance, employees and managers should define them in a way that minimizes potential negative effects. (See Table 3.) There are two new conceptual tools for both managers and employees: guidelines that clearly communicate behavioral performance expectations, and criteria for objectively observing behavioral performance on the job.

A clearly communicated CIS is:

- observable;
- related to a CIT; and
- accomplishable, as evidenced by specific job-related examples.

Managers and employees can refer to the *Continuous Improvement Skills Dictionary* for help in following these guidelines. (See Table 4.) The dictionary clarifies a given expectation by providing behavioral indicators for each skill, which managers and employees can easily rephrase to relate specifically to one or more CITs. Following the guidelines for a clearly communicated CIS not only ensures legal defensibility for this more subjective aspect of performance, but, more important, also establishes the fairness and relevance of the behavioral expectation in the eyes of the employee. The organization's ultimate benefit is the performance improvement that results when employees effectively use the right skills.

The second tool managers and employees need is criteria for objectively observing behavioral performance on the job. There are four means to observe or track behavioral performance on the job:

- direct observation, when the supervisor sees the employee in action
- written materials, in documentation such as reports, memos, or letters written or prepared by the employee
- third-party reports, such as compliments, complaints, or comments, whether verbal or written, from customers, coworkers, superiors, and subordinates
- self-report, or communication directly from the employee about what he or she actually did

Objectivity in observation requires gathering complete information about the behavior. "Complete" information includes data about the:

- context—details about the employee's situation
- action—what the employee actually did or said
- outcome—what happened as a result of the employee's action

With complete information, both the manager and employee will feel considerably more confident that they are analyzing and appraising the behavior objectively. During the "managing phase" of performance management, the supervisor and employee share information about the work-related behavior as completely as possible. In this way, the

48

Table 4. Sample Dictionary Page

Attention to Detail: Thoroughness in accomplishing a task through concern for the areas involved, no matter how small.

Behavioral Indicators:

- Provides accurate, consistent numbers on all paperwork.
- Provides information on a timely basis to others who need to act on it.
- Provides information in a useable form to others who need to act on it.
- Maintains a checklist, schedule, or calendar to ensure that small details are not overlooked.
- Double-checks the accuracy of information and work products.
- Carefully monitors the details and quality of others' work.
- Expresses concern that things be done right, thoroughly, or precisely.

Continuous Improvement: Constantly looks for incremental improvements in work processes and results.

Behavioral Indicators:

- Pays attention to the processes or elements leading to the accomplishment of results, looking for ways to improve quality and efficiency.
- Seeks to constantly improve level of results.
- Seeks to constantly improve efficiency.
- Looks for small improvement, not just "major blockbuster."
- Questions established procedures, suggesting ways to improve efficiency.

Creativity/Innovation: Demonstrates the ability to generate novel and valuable ideas and to use the ideas in developing new or improved processes, methods, or systems.

Behavioral Indicators:

- Tries new methods for completing required tasks, refining the methods until a "better way" has been determined.
- Works to develop new approaches when problem-solving; seeking ideas or suggestions from others as appropriate.
- Identifies novel approaches for completing work assignments more effectively or efficiently, and works within the "established" system to push for "a better way."

Customer Service Orientation: Demonstrates concern for meeting internal and external customers' needs in a manner that provides satisfaction for the customer with the resources which can be made available.

Behavioral Indicators:

- Asks questions to identify customer's needs or expectations.
- Checks understanding by stating what he or she understands are the customer's needs or expectations and asking the speaker to verify or clarify.
- Demonstrates close concentration on the message being verbalized.
- Stays calm in the face of a customer's anger or lack of control.
- Keeps own emotions from interfering with responding effectively to customer's needs.
- Takes a variety of actions to meet customer needs, as required, until need is met.
- Responds quickly when problem occurs.
- Questions customers to assess satisfaction with service being provided.

manager reinforces or coaches performance to help the employee achieve the agreed-upon performance expectations. The emphasis in this phase is on the trend in behavior, not just isolated incidents.

The rating scale reflects actual performance, not a "grading curve." TQM advocates often claim that the performance rating scales most companies use create potentially destructive competition, particularly when they apply "forced distribution." Forcing a manager to apply a normal distribution curve to performance ratings may control the manager's action, but does little to improve the manager's judgment.

However, a manager can improve that judgment with a legitimate reference point for comparing the employee's performance. Clearly established performance expectations provide that reference point. Comparing an employee's actual performance against expected performance also avoids detrimental intra-team competition, because managers assess employees against their individual benchmarks, not against the performance of others.

Actual performance, even that of superstars, is a combination of strengths and weaknesses. (See Figure 1.) A manager's judgment will be less reliable the narrower the band of acceptable performance is. TQM leaders appropriately criticize rating scales, since they usually require a manager to make fine distinctions—distinctions that often are unreliable and unnecessary—among performers. In contrast, a rating scale that reinforces a total quality culture accommodates the fact that actual performance is not a straight line.

In fact, when actual performance is compared against expected performance, rating scales are unnecessary except to link into the organization's traditional merit-based compensation structure. As companies increasingly adopt more nontraditional pay designs, they may dispose of rating scales or redesign them to more accurately reflect actual performance, allowing for those peaks and valleys.

A three-point rating scale requires fewer distinctions within the wide range of acceptable performance, thus avoiding unnecessary negative effects on the employee. (See Table 5.) And because goal-setting is directed toward continuous improvement, the overall planning process itself encourages employees to work toward their "personal best," not for a "grade" they will get on a rating scale.

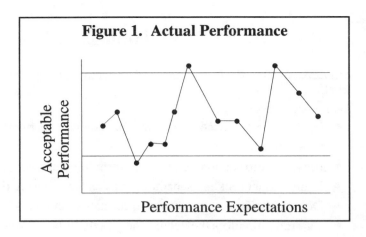

Figure 1. Actual Performance

Acceptable Performance (vertical axis)

Performance Expectations (horizontal axis)

Employees are active participants in the process, not merely "drawn in" to management's actions. In order to actually achieve total quality—and exceptional customer service—managers must empower employees to take responsibility for their own performance. It is not enough that they be "involved" with their managers; they must be actual partners. The employees are the players on the field; managers are their coaches, providing strategic direction, feedback, pointers on improving the plays, and pats on the back for good performance. Employees must feel that they can take the ball and run (*i.e.*, they are responsible for identifying their CITs and the skills that will help them improve). They also need to be willing to assess their actual performance against

---

Table 5. Sample Rating Scale

- *Achieved Improvement Targets*—Actual improvements were accomplished in areas of opportunity.

- *Showed Little or No Improvement*—Little or no improvements were accomplished despite areas of opportunity.

- *Accomplished Significant Improvements*— Actual improvements were accomplished significantly beyond what was thought possible, and the manner in which they were achieved was highly effective.

Note: In pioneering the integration of its TQM and performance management processes, Republic Engineered Steels, Inc. is using this rating scale.

their own expectations and take the initiative to ask for feedback.

In short, managers should expect employees to be self-managing—identifying and monitoring their customers' expectations (without making or implying agreements for which resources are not available), defining their own CITs and CISs, and reviewing these with their managers to ensure they align with the organization's business plan.

Most important, employees must understand their role in the performance management process. Being partners means that the employee can and should carry out planning, managing, and appraising activities without waiting for a supervisor to initiate them. If employees do not receive feedback or coaching, or participate in a progress review during the year, they need to ask for it. Employees should initiate the performance appraisal (or a self-appraisal) by assessing their own actual performance against expectations, using the same form—and the same content—the manager uses. If the content of the performance appraisal is a surprise at the end of the year, the employee is as much at fault as the supervisor.

This means that employees need to learn the same skills that managers use. In fact, employees need the same training that supervisors do to plan, track, and appraise performance. When employees and managers become true partners in managing performance, employees are legitimately accountable for what they do. At that point, at every level, the focus will be on improving the work process in order to attain quality performance.

Conclusion

The benchmarks for quality and customer service never remain static. The approach to performance management is one of constantly defining, achieving, and redefining performance, in a way that keeps every job challenging and propels the company to grow competitively. Thus, performance appraisal need not be inconsistent with total quality management. It does have an effective role when it becomes one step in a process of managing performance, providing the opportunity for strategic analysis and planning on an individual level. As part of the performance management process, with its broader perspective and unique tools, performance appraisal and total quality initiatives can combine to strengthen the employee skills that create—and support—a quality-oriented organizational culture.

Kathleen A. Guinn is a Consultant with the Hay Group, Pittsburgh, PA.

Implementation Strategies for Multiple Rater Systems

by Mark R. Edwards, Ph.D.

Almost every textbook and major author on performance appraisals has recommended multiple rater evaluation systems.[1] A multiple rater performance appraisal (MRPA) system replaces the traditional evaluation by the supervisor only.

Such a system, however, poses certain procedural and cultural obstacles to implementation. If these barriers can be overcome, the use of multiple raters can become an effective reality.

MRPA systems work best when: (1) Ratings are scored using a systematic process that moderates predictable sources of bias and; (2) results provide input only for the purpose of improving supervisory appraisal judgments.

When used according to these constraints, multiple raters offer many advantages, including:

- Employees select members of a personal evaluation team (which includes the supervisor)

- Performance information is highly reliable—consistent with research showing that co-workers are the best source available for merit ratings[2]

- Data about promotability and career development obtained from colleagues is the most valid source for predicting organizational advancement[3]

- Performance information is trustworthy and credible because each performer can believe in the systematically combined judgments of various colleagues (of his or her choice) and the supervisor

- Evaluation results are keyed more to overall performance (as seen by multiple raters), than to the relative rating rigor of immediate supervisors

- Different perspectives may significantly augment information known to the immediate supervisor

- Employees receive recognition from colleagues for teamwork and contribution to work group effectiveness

- Each participant receives feedback indicating his or her behavioral strengths and weaknesses as a rater, thus exposing unfair rating strategies[4]

- MRPA systems provide multiple procedural and statistical safeguards that aren't available in single rater plans[5]

Substantial advantages from multiple rater systems are realized only by organizations that have overcome the initial obstacles to implementation.

Many people who are considering MRPA systems have fears that turn out to be red herrings and are solved easily. Although each organization has a unique situation, there are eight concerns common to firms using MRPA systems.

The process will take too long. This concern often is paired with the statement, "Supervisors don't have enough time to do single rater appraisals, so how can we expect them to do multiple rater evaluations?" This legitimate worry reflects the reality that if a new evaluation system adds a substantial time cost, already overtaxed supervisors won't support its use.

Surveys of plan users, however, indicate that the process requires no more time than single rater systems. In addition, many supervisors report a decrease in evaluation time (resulting in increased time available for the more constructive tasks of providing results feedback and performance coaching).

A rating team member typically can evaluate the work behaviors of a ratee in fewer than eight minutes. Because most people rate six or fewer colleagues, the total time required of each participant is less than an hour.

After the time issue has been addressed, critics argue that the process must be inaccurate if so little effort is required. The fact that there is substantial inner-rater agreement in more than 90% of MRPA evaluations shows that raters don't need a lot of time to accurately assess people with whom they regularly work.[6]

MRPA will require too much administrative time. This is a primary concern. Administrative staff anticipate facing a complex and time consuming process.

In actual operation, however, only one administrative assistant is needed to oversee the project during the evaluation period (approximately two months), so long as coordinators are selected from each participating area to help with the process.

Every area coordinator has the responsibility of ensuring that each participant has selected an evaluation team and that each team member has returned an evaluation form. Little time is required for this process, because usually the coordinator only needs to follow up with 5–10% of the participants. These individuals are either delinquent in selecting an evaluation team or slow in returning their evaluation forms.

The objection that the MRPA process must be too complex to administer efficiently can be overcome by piloting an MRPA procedure to demonstrate the simplicity of each administrative activity. Taken together, all of the administrative activities associated with the project require a modest investment of time and resources. Each activity has been flowcharted, and examples of memoranda and training materials have been developed for most practical applications.[7]

Our employees won't accept the system. This problem is twofold. First, there is the issue of whether nonsupervisory employees will find MRPA an acceptable evaluation tool. The assumption that nonsupervisory employees won't want to participate is sometimes expressed as the fear that they will say, "We don't get paid to make evaluation decisions." Solving this concern hinges on how employees originally are approached about participating in the plan.

Before implementing the appraisal process, ask employees whether they would prefer to have supervisor-only performance evaluations or the supervisor's performance judgment supplemented with MRPA input from colleagues. Usually, more than 90% indicate that they would prefer an MRPA.

If employees are asked to participate in multi-rater colleague reviews to provide co-workers with information in addition to supervisor-only judgments, nearly everyone says yes. If asked to make evaluation judgments similar to supervisors, most people say no.

Traditional norms assume that employees believe supervisors should be solely responsible for evaluation decisions. MRPA experience has disproved that assumption, as field tests in many different organizations have established that more than 90% of employees prefer that their colleagues' input be added to supervisor-only performance information.

Most users find consensus evaluation information more credible than supervisor-only assessment data. Not surprisingly, after participating in the MRPA evaluation process, many nonsupervisory employees no longer feel comfortable with supervisor-only evaluations and request continued participation in the alternate process.

The second part of the concern about organizational tradition is whether supervisors will accept this plan. A few die-hard, autocratic supervisors may resist the concept, saying that their management prerogatives are threatened.

In practice, most supervisors prefer the MRPA validation by credible work associates in making performance-based evaluations. The input typically supports or improves the supervisor's understanding of employee performance. As importantly, the MRPA reduces the supervisor's need to "play God" in making evaluation judgments.

The best way to solve legitimate management concerns about supervisory acceptance is to pilot the project. In the pilot, every rated employee receives a performance profile consisting of a bar graph that represents results of the MRPA for each evaluation criterion and a composite of all criteria.

The supervisor also receives a companion profile that shows his or her rating as well as the team's consensus. Usually managers see their judgments validated by the combined similar opinions of other team members, thus increasing the supervisors' faith in the consensus evaluation process.

One of the best endorsements of the system's value came from a manager who noted that the consensus evaluation was 90% "correct." He could, therefore, focus attention on the employees (represented by the 10% "incorrect" team evaluations) whose work contacts with colleagues demonstrated behaviors that were different from what he observed.

Safeguards Allay Fears About the System

We won't be able to find enough good raters. Although most organizations have sufficient internal contacts for an evaluation team of five, some performers simply don't give colleagues an adequate opportunity to examine their performance. In those cases, the process can work with four (or even three) raters who have observed work behaviors.

To keep distress about rater quality in check, some projects have captured information about the degree of contact between rater and ratee. Analyses of this safeguard indicate that work contact occurring twice a month, on average, provides sufficient behavioral observation for reliable ratings.

In addition, when individuals have less contact, they tend to use the *no opportunity to observe option* on the rating form far more often than raters who have regular contact. Ratings from individuals who have minimal observation opportunities lack consistency when compared with other raters who have more contact.

As a process safeguard in rater selection, the immediate supervisor can use knowledge about working relationships to sign off approval for evaluation teams. This allows supervisors to veto raters who

lack the opportunity to observe representative performance of particular ratees.

As an additional net, the supervisor's companion profile reports the number of team respondents (on each evaluated criterion for a ratee) and the degree of consensus among them.

Supervisors will use the process to renege on their important management responsibility of evaluation. A major strength of the system is that it provides a complete picture and the necessary information to support decisions about people. Its flip side, however (and a potential risk), is that some weak supervisors may try to abdicate responsibility with a don't-ask-me-the-team-said-it approach. This represents the most serious problem associated with consensus evaluation.

The solution to abdication is simply to build subordinate development and supervisory responsibility into the model through special behavior criteria for managers. A supervisor then can be evaluated by the rating team on the management evaluation criteria.

By integrating criteria related to responsible supervision into the assessment of managers, individuals who don't abdicate but actually provide structured work objectives and ongoing performance feedback to their subordinates will be identified and rewarded.

Another option is to have two teams evaluate every supervisor's management system criteria (behaviors and skills). The first evaluation team consists of colleague input, while the second team collects subordinate input.

The subordinate-only input provides an excellent picture of which supervisors truly support the management system and develop the people under their direction. This team provides a view of supervisory behaviors and skills that can be used along with the MRPA profile to target necessary development.

Users will tend to focus unduly on the length of the bars in the evaluation consensus profile. This issue arises because the MRPA bar graph profile tends to be viewed as an absolute performance measure. Therefore, users tend to envision the ideal bar length as being toward the maximum end of the rating scale and may find dissatisfaction in the discrepancy between their expectations and the reality of the graph.

To address this concern, supervisors should emphasize the shape of the graph instead of the length of the bars. The shape of the profile provides important information about the performer's relative strengths and weaknesses. Relative bar lengths indicate performance areas that should be targeted for training and development, as well as areas that are strong.

A closely related problem is the management and employee emphasis on the composite score derived from the MRPA on separate evaluation criteria. The composite score provides a weighted criteria summary for each performer and represents a summary statistic.

Participants want narrative feedback as well as consensus rating information. Although an MRPA gives substantial, efficiently gathered performance information, the process doesn't provide specific narrative data about the behaviors associated with various ratings. Written or verbal narrative feedback provided by the supervisor through the management system may solve this problem.

Some organizations allow MRPA participants to add a typed narrative statement about the ratee for any evaluation criteria they choose. This information is given to the supervisor, who passes it along to the subordinate during the review.

Some people may try to game the system. Any performance evaluation model, whether single or multiple rater, is a human system susceptible to distortion.

Multiple rater appraisals merely offer different opportunities than supervisor-only ratings for distorting the measurement of performance. Although studies specify that friendship, favoritism and competition bias have negligible impact on multiple rating systems, many users don't trust this research.[8]

To best address the question of distortion in the rating process, an intelligent scoring system can be designed to anticipate game players. The scoring system then moderates the distortion from predictable games (or at least identifies when people try to fix the system).

One scoring system, TEAMS Intelligent Consensus technology, does both. This software removes extremely high and low ratings before scoring, thereby removing distortion introduced by raters who are extremely lenient or harsh on each evaluation team.[9]

In addition, rater feedback systematically identifies extremely high or low rating patterns compared to the consensus of other raters.[10] Rater feedback flags individuals who are using inappropriate procedures and targets needed rater training.

Rater feedback also flags collusion of raters who have combined to try to beat the system. Such provisions ensure the highest quality performance information (with the least distortion).

The performance management system is a cornerstone of human resources management and, therefore, is highly resistant to substantial changes. Experience, however, indicates that most of the claimed obstacles to appraisal system change are rhetoric.

The obstacles to MRPA are surprisingly easy to overcome. Organizations using MRPA evaluation, such as Westighouse, Fidelity Bank, Current Inc. and Arizona State University, have found that implementation problems are solvable.

When organizations overcome initial barriers and adopt an MRPA, the appraisal system becomes fairer and more accurate. Organizations then can enjoy substantial benefits from appraisals, including the knowledge that the most deserving performers will be identified accurately and rewarded appropriately. Such employee knowledge contributes directly to productivity.

Footnotes

1. Bernadin, H.J., and Klatt, L.A., "Managerial Appraisal Systems: Has Practice Caught Up with the State of the Art?" *Personnel Administrator.* November 1985, pp. 79-85.

2. Latham, G.P., and Wexley, K.W., *Increasing Productivity Through Performance Appraisal.* Reading, Massachusetts: Addison Wesley, 1981, pp. 84-85.

3. Korman, A.K., "The Prediction of Managerial Performance: A Review, " *Personnel Psychology.* 1968, pp. 295-322.

4. Edwards, M.R., and Sproull, J.R., "Rating the Raters Improves Performance Appraisals," *Personnel Administrator.* August 1983, pp. 77-83.

5. Sproull, J.R., and Edwards, M.R., "Safeguards Can Improve Performance Appraisal," *Business.* April-May-June 1985, pp. 17-27.

6. Edwards, M.R., "Wolf-hunting: Are There Wolves in Your Organizations?" *Review of Public Personnel Administration.* Summer 1983, pp. 117-127.

7. Edwards, M.R., and Verdini, W.A., "Engineering and Technical Management: Accurate Human Performance Measures = Productivity," *Journal of the Society of Research Administrators*. Autumn 1986, pp. 33-48.

8. Latham, G.P., and Wexley, K.W., *Op.cit.*, pp. 84-87.

9. Edwards, M.R., and Sproull, J.R., "Team Talent Assessment: Optimizing Assessee Visibility and Assessment Accuracy," *Human Resources Planning*. Autumn 1985, pp. 157-181.

10. Edwards, M.R., and Sproull, J.R., "Solving the Double Bind in Performance Appraisal: A Sage of Wolves, Sloths and Eagles," *Business Horizons*. May/June 1985, pp. 59-68.

Mark R. Edwards, Ph.D., is a professor and the director of the Laboratory for Innovation and Decision Research at Arizona State University. His most recent article for PERSONNEL JOURNAL, *"A Joint Effort Leads to Accurate Appraisals," appeared in June 1990.*

Performance Appraisals and Deming: A Misunderstanding?

by Jim M. Graber, Roger E. Breisch, and Walter E. Breisch

W. Edwards Deming, a tireless apostle of quality, blames performance appraisals for poor quality. In his typically animated fashion, he has denounced them as one of the seven deadly diseases afflicting Western management.[1]

However, organizations will not abandon performance appraisals without a fight, because they have the potential to improve performance, strengthen communication, help reward employees fairly, and provide legal defensibility. There are some appraisal approaches that do not suffer from the afflictions Deming has identified. Some might even support quality efforts.

Deming's lack of enthusiasm is understandable. Why would anyone support a process that typically:

- Doesn't improve performance?

- Angers and alienates many employees?

- Sometimes makes organizations more prone to legal difficulties, rather than validating their approaches and actions?

- Takes a considerable amount of time and requires a lot of paperwork without providing a return on this investment?

Indeed, it is accurate to think of performance appraisals as the pariah of human resource management. Effective methods for compensation, testing and selection, and labor relations have been developed and are widespread in other related disciplines. But when it comes to appraisals, failure is widespread and social scientists and consultants are helpless.

And yet, Deming is shooting at a moving target. The intractability of performance appraisals has spawned a wide variety of approaches. Deming's negative comments about appraisals might apply to some and be invalid about others.

Deming's Charges

Deming identifies many problems with performance appraisals:[2]

- They nourish short-term performance and annihilate long-term planning.

- They are destructive to the individual being reviewed. They leave employees bitter, crushed, battered, desolate, feeling inferior, and unfit for work because they are afraid to present a divergent point of view or ask the boss a question that might appear to bring his or her wisdom into doubt.

- They are detrimental to teamwork because they foster rivalry, politics, and fear. Employees are rewarded for promoting themselves for their own good; the organization is the loser. After all, if employees take time out to help another department, others might receive all the credit, while the helper loses time that could have been spent working on personal goals. Making someone else look good is a dual liability because it takes time away from one's own concerns while strengthening someone else's case for scarce promotions.

- They focus on the end product, not leadership to help people.

- They do not reward attempts to improve the system or take a risk. They reward people who do well under the old system. Taking a risk can result in a lost promotion and finding oneself permanently behind in the race for upper management.

- The measures used to evaluate performances are not meaningful because supervisors and subordinates are pressured to use numbers and count something. Promotions must be defended with numbers.

- The measures discourage quality. People will concentrate on meeting numbers; they won't take time to improve a design if their goals involve quantity or deadlines. An arbitrator who is evaluated on the number of meetings he conducts will take three meetings to accomplish what could have been done in one. A purchasing agent who is evaluated on the number of contracts accomplished will not take time to learn about the losses his purchases caused.

- Despite apparent variation in performance, factors outside an employee's control—an action of the system or expected statistical variance, for example—account for the differences in performance. Even large differences can generally be ascribed to chance.

Analysis of the Charges

If they are true, Deming's charges are a serious indictment of performance appraisals. These charges apply to a number of performance appraisal systems, most notably those derived from the precepts of management by objectives (MBO). In fact, it is possible to specifically identify which aspects of MBO lead to each of the problems mentioned by Deming.

There are four critical design flaws of MBO. Each has significant effects:

1. MBO focuses exclusively on results.

   - Employees are often graded on things that are influenced by factors out of their control, such as co-workers, managers, the steps taken by the competition, and the health of the economy. The result can be an unfair process, cynicism, and employee discontent.

   - Coaching employees is not facilitated. An evaluation only indicates whether the goal was met, but it doesn't help determine why. It does not help people improve.

   - Short-term results are valued over long-term results. MBO preaches loudly against evaluating activities. Presumably, it would be an intrusion to indicate to any executive how to reach a result. Additionally, it is argued, one can do all the right things and still be unsuccessful, or vice versa.

   What happens when a result cannot be accomplished in less than one year? Any result that requires more than one year can be measured only by the activities taken to get there. A refusal to measure and give credit for activities means that short-term goals will predominate.

   Finally, a preoccupation with results, without any consideration of methods, often leads to negative side effects. This philosophy is aptly described as the ends justifying the means. The damage caused by this philosophy is legend.

2. MBO is typically quantitative.

   - The goals that are set for performance appraisals are often arbitrary and contrived. For example, how does one know whether a 5% or 10% improvement is justified? Many people end up being unfairly rewarded or penalized.

   - Quality goals have often been overlooked because it often takes more effort to attach a number to quality and is more difficult to gain universal acceptance of the importance of quality. In addition, quality might conflict with quantity and come out the loser.

   - Only a small percentage of employees' performance is evaluated. Since so much of the job is not touched upon, the evaluation is, by definition, unfairly skewed and affects employee morale. An important consequence is that the system is much less defensible should a legal challenge be made.

3. MBO is concerned with a few aspects of the job and special projects for the year to the exclusion of ongoing responsibilities.

- Little or no attention is given to many important ongoing activities and significant behaviors. MBO focuses employees' attention on results; they tend to ignore everything else. Far more is lost than just attention to teamwork and quality. There are dozens of other significant employee activities that receive no attention: administrative duties such as budget preparation, annual and long-range planning, and equipment and facility management and procurement; human resource management such as staffing, labor relations, training and development, counseling, and performance appraisals; work flow management such as division of labor, communication within the work unit and to higher management, work monitoring and quality control, coordination with other departments, managing and developing subordinates, and change and conflict management; and issues of professionalism such as staying current in one's field, supporting the organization, and professional and equal treatment of others in the organization.

4. MBO discourages setting difficult objectives that involve more work and more risk.

- Taking risks might be applauded in others, but the savvy players will set goals they are sure they can accomplish.

In sum, all of the ills described by Deming can be explained by these four main design characteristics of MBO.

And yet, among the ruins of performance appraisal failure lie the seeds of success. That is, it is logical to assume that, if performance appraisal systems could be developed without the problematic design flaws, they might circumvent Deming's criticisms.

Successful Performance and Planning Review

Let's look at a different set of performance appraisal design characteristics:

- Division, department, and individual goals must be determined by customer's needs. Performance planning for individuals begins with setting clear goals and metrics for the entire organization based on customers' needs. These must then be translated into goals and metrics for all subgroups and processes within the organization. Each individual should identify his or her internal and external customers and document their needs in relation to organizational goals. Only then can individuals set priorities, goals, and metrics that fully support the organization and its customers. Performance planning done in isolation, while it might be compatible with work group goals, nearly guarantees that the performance of the organization will fall short.

  Successfully accomplishing many organizational objectives involves the effort of more than one work group. Group objective setting and problem solving, occasionally using task forces, will help define the roles of subgroups and individuals within the context of organization goals.

- Performance appraisals should be devoid of arbitrary or excessive numbers and percentages. Rather than using percentages and numbers in performance appraisals, it is preferable to require that tasks be completed thoroughly and efficiently. Clearly, there is more subjectivity involved in determining whether a task has been done efficiently than in determining, for example, whether 10 cars have been sold. However, frequent coaching and discussions between employees and supervisors, self-reviews, and monitoring the fairness of the review process serve to clearly define subjective standards.

  Getting away from numbers opens up the performance appraisal process to setting expectations in many new and significant job areas. It is also a more credible approach from the employees' standpoint because supervisors lack the time and resources to track quantitative performance measures accurately.

  When numbers are an appropriate means for measuring performance (successful salespeople will tell you their success is directly connected to the quantity of calls they make), statistical methods can help set baselines. Groups and individuals can determine realistic expectations by looking at historical data. They can then set goals that are realistic and meaningful.

- Performance appraisals should be comprehensive. Expectations should be developed for every important aspect of a job. How can someone begin to manage his or her performance when expectations haven't been developed and subsequently evaluated? The philosophy should be "If it's important, we will develop expectations and make evaluations no matter how challenging."

  A distinction should be made between ongoing responsibilities and new or special priorities. Attention should be given to both. Once expectations have been defined for regular parts of the job, however, more time can be spent on emerging priorities.

  Expectations should be developed for teamwork, communication, employee development, job enrichment, employee participation, and other areas that build the organization.

- Performance appraisals should be based on activities and results. Activities are the steps taken to achieve results. People knowledgeable about any given job can identify the activities that tend to lead to success. For example, no matter how tedious the process, it is essential that a chemist thoroughly review previous research findings and current products on the market before trying to develop a new antibiotic. Using activities and results means that employees are being evaluated on elements they truly control. Furthermore, the appraisal form becomes a useful diagnostic and coaching tool that can help determine where an employee might have gone wrong. Finally, the steps required to reach long-term results, from organizational focus to cultural change, can be addressed by measuring significant activities.

- Performance appraisals should be criterion-based. People should be evaluated against standards and expectations, not against each other. Forced distributions of ratings are competitive and terribly destructive to morale. All employees should have the opportunity to receive an outstanding rating. It is healthy to adopt the philosophy that the job of every supervisor is to develop and motivate employees so that a high percentage of them will, in fact, be legitimately outstanding.

- Performance appraisals should be participative. Employees should play an active role in developing performance expectations for their jobs. Similarly, they should evaluate themselves on these expectations periodically. Formal performance evaluations should be structured so that the employee leads off the evaluation process, with the supervisor patiently listening and noting remarks and then indicating where he or she agrees or disagrees. A participative approach will improve the quality and relevancy of the whole process while increasing fairness and reducing the devastation that Deming speaks of.

- Performance appraisals should define outstanding performance. Much of the game playing in appraisals stems from a looseness in the way expectations are defined. It is not adequate to evaluate an employee on the trait "teamwork." The meaning of this term within the context of a particular job or even a single responsibility must be defined. Furthermore, an effort must be made to define an outstanding level of teamwork. Misunderstandings occur when an average level is defined and employees are told that they must exceed that standard to achieve an outstanding rating. Too frequently, an employee will guess wrong and define what it means to exceed the standard differently than the supervisor will.

- The development of performance expectations should be facilitated. Developing clear, comprehensive performance standards for most jobs is a difficult and often labor-intensive task. It seems to be most effectively accomplished by a small group of people knowledgeable about the job (typically job incumbents and supervisors) with the help of a third-party facilitator. The facilitator leads the meeting, walks the participants through the process of developing job expectations, and records the responses of the participants. Shortly after the meeting, a rough draft developed by the facilitator is presented to the meeting participants. Using a trained facilitator ensures that the kinds of performance appraisal design criteria identified are met. It results in more positive reactions to the performance appraisal process.

- Supervisors must receive thorough performance management training. Every important aspect of a supervisor's job begins with training; performance management is no exception. The best performance management system can be made ineffective by a few supervisors bent on finding fault rather than leading their employees to improved performance.

Performance planning and review processes based on these design characteristics will provide many benefits:

- Employees will learn about organizational plans and goals. Further, they will feel more positive about their contributions; they will gain a better understanding of the value they bring to the organization.

- Employees will get an opportunity to participate in setting personal, department, and division goals. Participation in this process leads to greater commitment and accomplishment.

- Employees will gain greater insight into what is acceptable performance and what is outstanding performance.

- Employees can help evaluate the variety of activities they perform relative to the organization's needs. Priorities can be set to ensure that critical activities get the attention they require.

Organizational vs. Individual Goals

Suppose your organization wants to reduce the time it takes to process an order from three weeks to two days. Optimizing the performance of individuals will not be enough. Quantum performance gains are achieved through system changes. For example, significantly reducing new product development time will require that the product design, process engineering, and tool development phases occur concurrently, not sequentially as they have in the past.

System changes require organization performance planning. Goals, methods to reach them, milestones, and final measures of success must be worked out with all concerned participants. When group goals are achieved, appropriate recognition for all involved parties should follow. Similarly, accountability is shared, not assigned to one individual. While it is sometimes possible to split a systems change into individual responsibilities with attendant rewards or penalties, it would be ill-advised. There is a risk of creating inappropriate (i.e., competitive) interpersonal dynamics and of treating people unfairly since individuals seldom have the knowledge, authority, and control to carry out a systems change by themselves.

In short, every individual's goal should be linked to the organization's mission, but not every organizational goal can be or should be translated into individual goals.

Customer Evaluations

The importance of customer evaluations in the performance review process cannot be overstated. Individuals will devote the majority of their time and effort to satisfying those in the organization who have the most control over their reward systems; in most situations, this means satisfying the supervisor. This is acceptable when the supervisor's goals are 100% in line with those of the work group's internal customers. Usually, however, supervisors' goals are more in line with those of their own supervisors. And so it goes. Employees continually focus upward in the organization rather than peripherally toward their customers. The boss is satisfied first, and if the customer happens to be satisfied, that's nice too.

The solution? Allow customer satisfaction surveys to play a role in performance evaluations. Internal customers can and should be asked whether others in the company support their efforts to meet department and organization goals.

Infusing Quality into Performance Appraisals

Solid, quality-related goals should make up a high percentage of the written performance expectations that direct and evaluate employees. The process for ensuring they do is straightforward. A group knowledgeable about the job should be asked:

- What is the difference between average and outstanding quality for this responsibility?
- What do you have to do to make the quality of your work outstanding?
- If you were training someone to perform this responsibility, what would you emphasize?
- What are the tricks of the trade?
- What are some quality-related events or activities you have witnessed that impressed you?
- Think of a person who is extremely dedicated to quality. What examples can you give to support your argument that he or she is exceptional?

Answers to these and similar questions result in a clear definition of quality. The result is clear targets to shoot at and fair and useful criteria for performance evaluations.

Don't Forgo Performance Planning and Review

Despite Deming's criticisms of performance appraisals, they do perform a number of valuable services when implemented properly. There should be little doubt in anyone's mind that the goal-setting process is powerful. Research during the last 30 years has repeatedly shown that goal setting enhances performance. These findings have been confirmed by experiences in thousands of organizations, although it has also been demonstrated that setting the wrong goals can lead to undesirable effects.

Regardless of whether an organization conducts formal performance appraisals, we have yet to discover one that does not give promotions. Promoting one individual over another is, like it or not, an evaluation. Even worse, it is a ranking. It is better to have formal criteria for promotions rather than an informal, subjective system.

Employees want to know how they are doing. Annual performance appraisals might cause consternation once a year, but a lack of clear goals causes confusion and aimlessness every day. Moreover, performance appraisals are the basis for legal defensibility for any personnel action taken, from promotion to termination.

Deming has strong opinions. His criticism of performance evaluations certainly has merit. There are, however, considerations and design characteristics that can make performance planning and review a valuable practice.

References

1. W. Edwards Deming. *Out of the Crisis* (Cambridge, MA: Massachusetts Institute of Technology. Center for Advanced Engineering Study, 1982), pp. 101-120.
2. Ibid.

Jim M. Graber is an organizational psychologist at Graber Management Consultants in Evanston, IL, and a member of the faculty in the department of management at the University of Illinois in Chicago. He has a doctorate in psychology from Claremont Graduate School in CA.

Roger E. Breisch is a senior consultant at The Webber Group, Inc. in Wheaton, IL. He has a master's degree in business administration from the Massachusetts Institute of Technology in Cambridge. Breish is a member of ASQC.

Walter E. Breisch is a senior consultant at The Webber Group, Inc. in Wheaton, IL. He has a bachelor's degree in chemical engineering from the Illinois Institute of Technology in Chicago. Breisch is a senior member of ASQC.

If Earnings Aren't the Dial to Read

by Peter F. Drucker

The pressure for short-term earnings on the part of security analysts and asset managers is unlikely to abate in the foreseeable future. Businesses, thus, have to accommodate themselves to it. But most chief executive officers have learned by now that short-term earnings are quite unreliable, indeed often grossly misleading, as measurements of a company's actual performance.

Most experienced executives have also learned that there is no magic formula for measuring business performance. Just as an automobile needs a number of dials on the dashboard and also needs to have its tire pressures checked once in a while, a business needs a number of "dials" to have control. But the number is small; five such "gauges" will tell how a business is doing and whether it is moving in the right direction.

The first true measurement of a company is its standing in its markets. Is market standing going up or going down? And is the improvement in the right markets? A pharmaceutical company, for instance, may need to know how its products are doing overall, but also how they are doing in both the human-health and the animal-health markets; how human-health products are doing with younger doctors, that is, with tomorrow's main customers; how they are doing in hospitals as well as with physicians and with specific groups, e.g., urologists. It also might need to know its market standing in specific competitive arenas such as anti-inflammatory drugs.

But a company also needs to know how its products or services are doing in respect to market share compared with alternatives of customer satisfaction. How does the structural steel our company produces stack up against pre-stressed concrete and on-site stressed concrete, the alternative materials in commercial and office construction?

Early Warning

The second "dial" on a company's "instrument board" measures innovative performance. Is the company's achievement as a successful innovator in its markets equal to its market standing? Or does it lag behind it? There is altogether no more reliable early warning of a company's imminent decline than a sharp and persistent drop in its standing as a successful innovator. And equally dangerous is a deterioration in innovative lead-time, that is, in the time between the inception of an innovation and its introduction as a successful product or service in the market.

And does the ratio of successful innovations to false starts improve or deteriorate? Again the dial should show innovative action by major segments, and especially in the segments where future growth is likely to occur. Digital Equipment Corp. has done so much better these past few years than most other computer companies (including IBM), not primarily because it produced more successful innovations, but because it concentrated its innovations on the growth markets in data processing.

The third set of measurements on the executive control panel measures productivity. It relates the input of all major factors of production—money, materials, people—to the "value added" they produce, that is, to the (inflation-adjusted) valve of total output of goods or services minus whatever is spent on buying supplies, parts or services from the outside. Each factor has to be measured separately.

Indeed in the large organization—whether a business, a hospital or a university—the productivity of different segments within each factor needs to be measured, e.g., blue-collar labor, clerical labor, managers and service staffs.

Ideally, the productivity of each factor should increase steadily. At the very least, however, increased productivity of one factor, e.g., people, should not be achieved at the expense of the productivity of another factor, e.g., capital—something that American industry has been guilty of far too often. Such a "trade-off" usually damages the company's break-even point of operations. Increased productivity in good times is then paid for by decreased productivity when a company needs productivity the most—in poor or depressed times.

No one needs to be told that productivity is in trouble in the U.S. But it also is in trouble worldwide. Since 1973, the rate of productivity increase has been falling steadily in all industrially developed countries, including Japan and West Germany. Whatever the causes—and no single one has yet been convincingly identified—this represents a tremendous opportunity for the individual business. The company that systematically concentrates on its productivity is almost bound to gain competitive advantage, and pretty fast.

The fourth "dial" shows liquidity and cash flows. It is old wisdom that a business can run without profits for long years provided it has adequate cash flow. The opposite is not true, however. There are far too many businesses around—and by no means only small ones—that have to abandon the most profitable developments because they run out of cash. And increased profits, e.g., through rapid expansion of sales volume, which weakens rather than strengthens liquidity and cash position, is always a danger signal. It commonly means the company "buys" rather than "earns" its additional sales—through overly generous financing of its customers, for instance. And "bought" markets don't last. But also an expected need for additional cash usually can be filled, and at a reasonable cost.

If a company waits till it needs the cash—for instance to finance the development of an unusually promising new product line—it may, in the end, have to sell the new product line to a competitor at a fire-sale price. Indeed, a liquidity crunch is usually more damaging than a profit crunch. In a profit crunch a company typically sells off or cuts out its least profitable and most nearly obsolete businesses or products. In a liquidity crunch it typically sells its most profitable or most promising units, since these bring in the most cash soonest.

Yet liquidity is easy to measure and projection is usually all that is needed to identify future cash flows and cash needs.

The final "dial" should measure a business's profitability—which is both more and less than conventional profit. Profitability measures show the capacity of a company's resources to produce a profit. They thus exclude profits or losses from nonrecurring transactions such as the sale or abandonment of a division, a plant, a product line. They also do not include overhead-cost allocations. But they also do not try to measure the profit in any given time period, focusing instead on the profitability of the going concern.

The easiest way to do this is probably to show operating profits on a 36 months' rolling basis—adjusted, if needed, for inflation or for fluctuations in foreign-exchange rates. When December 1986 is added, December 1983 is dropped, and so on. And the profitability trend is then projected three ways to test its adequacy: (a) cost of capital; (b) new ventures, new products and new services (is profitability going up at these margins, or is it declining?); and (c) the need for profitability to be tested in respect to its composition.

No Precise Readings

Total profit is profit margin multiplied by turnover of capital. And usually profitability can be raised far more easily by increasing the turnover of capital—either by reducing the capital needed to produce, market and service a given unit of output, or by making the same capital serve a broader volume of output or a wider range of markets—than by increasing profit margins. But ideally both should improve simultaneously. And if one of the two profitability factors improves at the expense of a deterioration in the other one—e.g., if higher profit margins are being obtained by more liberal financing of the company's customers and distributors—the quality of profitability is deteriorating even though absolute profit may remain the same and may even be going up.

What exactly the best measurement is in each of these areas is hotly debated by economists, accountants and management scientists. For the practitioner, however, it makes little, perhaps even no difference which of the measurements he adopts. None of them is perfect; and practically all are adequate. And no matter which specific measurement a company chooses, it will not give precise readings; all of them have built in a substantial margin of error, if only because accurate information does not exist in any of the areas.

But again this is not crucially important for the practitioner. What matters to him is not the absolute magnitude in any area but the trend—what mathematicians call the "slope of the curve"—that the measurements will give him no matter how crude and approximate the individual readings are by themselves. Without such information a business does not really know how it performs and whether it is headed in the right direction; it may not wake up early enough to the need to take corrective action. These measurements of performance give control. They should be on the desk of every CEO or on the walls of his chart room the second Monday of every third month.

Mr. Drucker is Clarke professor of social sciences at the Claremont Graduate School.

Putting the Balanced Scorecard to Work

by Robert S. Kaplan and David P. Norton

Today's managers recognize the impact that measures have on performance. But they rarely think of measurement as an essential part of their strategy. For example, executives may introduce new strategies and innovative operating processes intended to achieve breakthrough performance, then continue to use the same short-term financial indicators they have used for decades, measures like return-on-investment, sales growth, and operating income. These managers fail not only to introduce new measures to monitor new goals and processes but also to question whether or not their old measures are relevant to the new initiatives.

Effective measurement, however, must be an integral part of the management process. The balanced scorecard, first proposed in the January-February 1992 issue of HBR ("The Balanced Scorecard—Measures that Drive Performance"), provides executives with a comprehensive framework that translates a company's strategic objectives into a coherent set of performance measures. Much more than a measurement exercise, the balanced scorecard is a management system that can motivate breakthrough improvements in such critical areas as product, process, customer, and market development.

The scorecard presents managers with four different perspectives from which to choose measures. It complements traditional financial indicators with measures of performance for customers, internal processes, and innovation and improvement activi-

ties. These measures differ from those traditionally used by companies in a few important ways.

Clearly, many companies already have myriad operational and physical measures for local activities. But these local measures are bottom-up and derived from ad hoc processes. The scorecard's measures, on the other hand, are grounded in an organization's strategic objectives and competitive demands. And, by requiring managers to select a limited number of critical indicators within each of the four perspectives, the scorecard helps focus this strategic vision.

In addition, while traditional financial measures report on what happened last period without indicating how managers can improve performance in the next, the scorecard functions as the cornerstone of a company's current *and* future success.

Moreover, unlike conventional metrics, the information from the four perspectives provides balance between external measures like operating income and internal measures like new product development. This balanced set of measures both reveals the trade-offs that managers have already made among performance measures and encourages them to achieve their goals in the future without making trade-offs among key success factors.

Finally, many companies that are now attempting to implement local improvement programs such as process reengineering, total quality, and employee empowerment lack a sense of integration. The balanced scorecard can serve as the focal point for the organization's efforts, defining and communicating priorities to managers, employees, investors, even customers. As a senior executive at one major company said, "Previously, the one-year budget was our primary management planning device. The balanced scorecard is now used as the language, the benchmark against which all new projects and businesses are evaluated."

The balanced scorecard is not a template that can be applied to businesses in general or even industry-wide. Different market situations, product strategies, and competitive environments require different scorecards. Business units devise customized scorecards to fit their mission, strategy, technology, and culture. In fact, a critical test of a scorecard's success is its transparency: from the 15 to 20 scorecard measures, an observer should be able to see through to the business unit's competitive strategy. A few examples will illustrate how the scorecard uniquely combines management and measurement in different companies.

Rockwater: Responding to a Changing Industry

Rockwater, a wholly owned subsidiary of Brown & Root/Halliburton, a global engineering and construction company, is a worldwide leader in under-water engineering and construction. Norman Chambers, hired as CEO in late 1989, knew that the industry's competitive world had changed dramatically. "In the 1970s, we were a bunch of guys in wet suits diving off barges into the North Sea with burning torches," Chambers said. But competition in the subsea contracting business had become keener in the 1980s, and many smaller companies left the industry. In addition, the focus of competition had shifted. Several leading oil companies wanted to develop long-term partnerships with their suppliers rather than choose suppliers based on low-price competition.

With his senior management team, Chambers developed a vision: "As our customer's preferred provider, we shall be the industry leader in providing the highest standards of safety and quality to our clients." He also developed a strategy to implement the vision. The five elements of that strategy were: services that surpass customers' expectations and needs; high levels of customer satisfaction;

Rockwater's Strategic Objectives

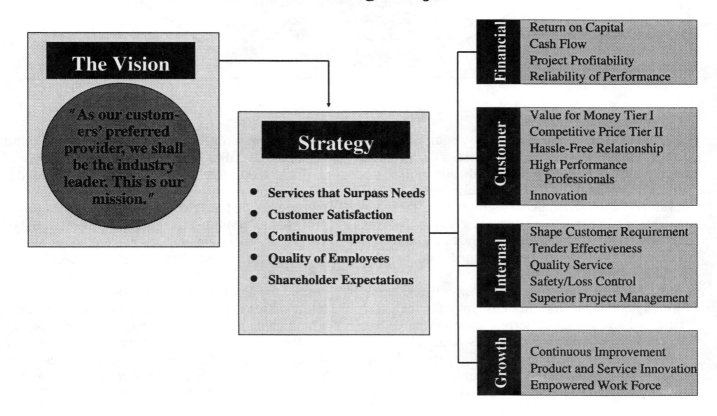

67

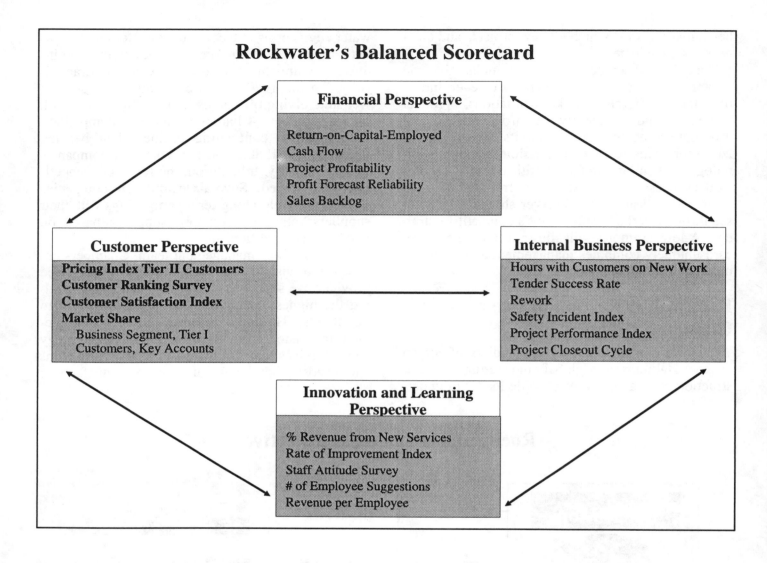

Rockwater's Balanced Scorecard

Financial Perspective

Return-on-Capital-Employed
Cash Flow
Project Profitability
Profit Forecast Reliability
Sales Backlog

Customer Perspective

Pricing Index Tier II Customers
Customer Ranking Survey
Customer Satisfaction Index
Market Share
    Business Segment, Tier I
    Customers, Key Accounts

Internal Business Perspective

Hours with Customers on New Work
Tender Success Rate
Rework
Safety Incident Index
Project Performance Index
Project Closeout Cycle

Innovation and Learning Perspective

% Revenue from New Services
Rate of Improvement Index
Staff Attitude Survey
# of Employee Suggestions
Revenue per Employee

continuous improvement of safety, equipment reliability, responsiveness, and cost effectiveness; high-quality employees; and realization of shareholder expectations. Those elements were in turn developed into strategic objectives (see the chart "Rockwater's Strategic Objectives"). If, however, the strategic objectives were to create value for the company, they had to be translated into tangible goals and actions.

Rockwater's senior management team transformed its vision and strategy into the balanced scorecard's four sets of performance measures (see the chart "Rockwater's Balanced Scorecard"):

Financial Measures: The financial perspective included three measures of importance to the shareholder. Return-on-capital-employed and cash flow reflected preferences for short-term results, while forecast reliability signaled the corporate parent's desire to reduce the historical uncertainty caused by unexpected variations in performance. Rockwater management added two financial measures. Project profitability provided focus on the project as the basic unit for planning and control, and sales backlog helped reduce uncertainty of performance.

Customer Satisfaction: Rockwater wanted to recognize the distinction between its two types of customers: Tier I customers, oil companies that wanted a high value-added relationship, and Tier II customers, those that chose suppliers solely on the basis of price. A price index, incorporating the best available intelligence on competitive position, was included to ensure that Rockwater could still retain

Tier II customers' business when required by competitive conditions.

The company's strategy, however, was to emphasize value-based business. An independent organization conducted an annual survey to rank customers' perceptions of Rockwater's services compared to those of its competitors. In addition, Tier I customers were asked to supply monthly satisfaction and performance ratings. Rockwater executives felt that implementing these ratings gave them a direct tie to their customers and a level of market feedback unsurpassed in most industries. Finally, market share by key accounts provided objective evidence that improvements in customer satisfaction were being translated into tangible benefits.

Internal Processes: To develop measures of internal processes, Rockwater executives defined the life cycle of a project from launch (when a customer need was recognized) to completion (when the customer need had been satisfied). Measures were formulated for each of the five business-process phases in this project cycle (see the chart "How Rockwater Fulfills Customer Needs"):

- *Identify:* number of hours spent with prospects discussing new work;

- *Win:* tender success rate;

- *Prepare and Deliver:* project performance effectiveness index, safety/loss control, rework;

- *Closeout:* length of project closeout cycle.

The internal business measures emphasized a major shift in Rockwater's thinking. Formerly, the company stressed performance for each functional department. The new focus emphasized measures that integrated key business processes. The development of a comprehensive and timely index of project performance effectiveness was viewed as a

key core competency for the company. Rockwater felt that safety was also a major competitive factor. Internal studies had revealed that the indirect costs from an accident could be 5 to 50 times the direct costs. The scorecard included a safety index, derived from a comprehensive safety measurement system, that could identify and classify all undesired events with the potential for harm to people, property, or process.

The Rockwater team deliberated about the choice of metric for the identification stage. It recognized that hours spent with key prospects discussing new work was an input or process measure rather than an output measure. The management team wanted a metric that would clearly communicate to all members of the organization the importance of building relationships with and satisfying customers. The team believed that spending quality time with key customers was a prerequisite for influencing results. This input measure was deliberately chosen to educate employees about the importance of working closely to identify and satisfy customer needs.

Innovation and Improvement: The innovation and learning objectives are intended to drive improvement in financial, customer, and internal process performance. At Rockwater, such improvements came from product and service innovation that would create new sources of revenue and market expansion, as well as from continuous improvement in internal work processes. The first objective was measured by percent revenue from new services and the second objective by a continuous improvement index that represented the rate of improvement of several key operational measures, such as safety and rework. But in order to drive both product/service innovation and operational improvements, a supportive climate of empowered,

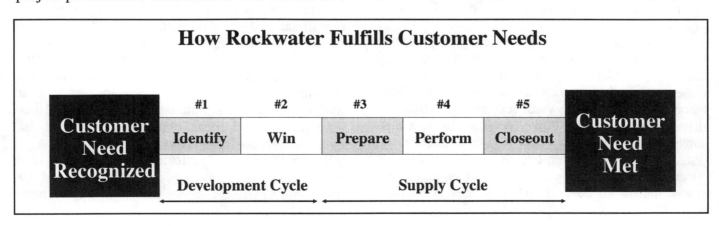

How Rockwater Fulfills Customer Needs

Customer Need Recognized	#1 Identify	#2 Win	#3 Prepare	#4 Perform	#5 Closeout	Customer Need Met
	Development Cycle		Supply Cycle			

motivated employees was believed necessary. A staff attitude survey and a metric for the number of employee suggestions measured whether or not such a climate was being created. Finally, revenue per employee measured the outcomes of employee commitment and training programs.

The balanced scorecard has helped Rockwater's management emphasize a process view of operations, motivate its employees, and incorporate client feedback into its operations. It developed a consensus on the necessity of creating partnerships with key customers, the importance of order-of-magnitude reductions in safety-related incidents, and the need for improved management at every phase of multiyear projects. Chambers sees the scorecard as an invaluable tool to help his company ultimately achieve its mission: to be number one in the industry.

Apple Computer: Adjusting Long-Term Performance

Apple Computer developed a balanced scorecard to focus senior management on a strategy that would expand discussions beyond gross margin, return on equity, and market share. A small steering committee, intimately familiar with the deliberations and strategic thinking of Apple's Executive Management Team, chose to concentrate on measurement categories within each of the four perspectives and to select multiple measurements within each category. For the financial perspective, Apple emphasized shareholder value; for the customer perspective, market share and customer satisfaction; for the internal process perspective, core competencies; and, finally, for the innovation and improvement perspective, employee attitudes. Apple's management stressed these categories in the following order:

Customer Satisfaction: Historically, Apple had been a technology- and product-focused company that competed by designing better computers. Customer satisfaction metrics are just being introduced to orient employees toward becoming a customer-driven company. J.D. Power & Associates, a customer-survey company, now works for the computer industry. However, because it recognized that its customer base was not homogeneous, Apple felt that it had to go beyond J.D. Power & Associates

and develop its own independent surveys in order to track its key market segments around the world.

Core Competencies: Company executives wanted employees to be highly focused on a few key competencies: for example, user-friendly interfaces, powerful software architectures, and effective distribution systems. However, senior executives recognized that measuring performance along these competency dimensions could be difficult. As a result, the company is currently experimenting with obtaining quantitative measures of these hard-to-measure competencies.

Employee Commitment and Alignment: Apple conducts a comprehensive employee survey in each of its organizations every two years; surveys of randomly selected employees are performed more frequently. The survey questions are concerned with how well employees understand the company's strategy as well as whether or not they are asked to delivery results that are consistent with that strategy. The results of the survey are displayed in terms of both the actual level of employee responses and the overall trend of responses.

Market Share: Achieving a critical threshold of market share was important to senior management not only for the obvious sales growth benefits but also to attract and retain software developers to Apple platforms.

Shareholder Value: Shareholder value is included as a performance indicator, even though this measure is a result—not a drive—of performance. The measure is included to offset the previous emphasis on gross margin and sales growth, measures that ignored the investments required today to generate growth for tomorrow. In contrast, the shareholder value metric quantifies the impact of proposed investments for business creation and development. The majority of Apple's business is organized on a functional basis—sales, product design, and worldwide manufacturing and operations—so shareholder value can be calculated only for the entire company instead of at a decentralized level. The measure, however, helps senior managers in each major organizational unit assess the impact of their activities on the entire company's valuation and evaluate new business ventures.

While these five performance indicators have only recently been developed, they have helped Apple's senior managers focus their strategy in a num-

Building a Balanced Scorecard

Each organization is unique and so follows its own path for building a balanced scorecard. At Apple and AMD, for instance, a senior finance or business development executive, intimately familiar with the strategic thinking of the top management group, constructed the initial scorecard without extensive deliberations. At Rockwater, however, senior management had yet to define sharply the organization's strategy, much less the key performance levers that drive and measure the strategy's success.

Companies like Rockwater can follow a systematic development plan to create the balanced scorecard and encourage commitment to the scorecard among senior and mid-level managers. What follows is a typical project profile:

1. *Preparation*

The organization must first define the business unit for which a top-level scorecard is appropriate. In general, a scorecard is appropriate for a business unit that has its own customers, distribution channels, production facilities, and financial performance measures.

2. *Interviews: First Round*

Each senior manager in the business unit—typically between 6 and 12 executives—receives background material on the balanced scorecard as well as internal documents that describe the company's vision, mission, and strategy.

The balanced scorecard facilitator (either an outside consultant or the company executive who organizes the effort) conducts interviews of approximately 90 minutes each with the senior managers to obtain their input on the company's strategic objectives and tentative proposals for balanced scorecard measures. The facilitator may also interview some principal shareholders to learn about their expectations for the business unit's financial performance, as well as some key customers to learn about their performance expectations for top-ranked suppliers.

3. *Executive Workshop: First Round*

The top management team is brought together with the facilitator to undergo the process of developing the scorecard (see the chart "Begin by Linking Measurements to Strategy"). During the workshop, the group debates the proposed mission and strategy statements until a consensus is reached. The group then moves from the mission and strategy statement to answer the question, "If I succeed with my vision and strategy, how will my performance differ for shareholders; for customers; for internal business processes; for my ability to innovate, grow and improve?"

Videotapes of interviews with shareholder and customer representatives can be shown to provide an external perspective to the deliberations. After defining the key success factors, the group formulates a preliminary balanced scorecard containing operational measures for the strategic objectives. Frequently, the group proposes far more than four or five measures for each perspective. At this time, narrowing the choices is not critical, though straw votes can be taken to see whether or not some of the proposed measures are viewed as low priority by the group.

4. *Interviews: Second Round*

The facilitator reviews, consolidates, and documents the output from the executive workshop and interviews each senior executive about the tentative balanced scorecard. The facilitator also seeks opinions about issues involved in implementing the scorecard.

5. *Executive Workshop: Second Round*

A second workshop, involving the senior management team, their direct subordinates, and a larger number of middle managers, debates the organization's vision, strategy statements, and the tentative scorecard. The participants, working in groups, comment on the proposed measures, link the various change programs under way to the measures, and start to develop an implementation plan. At the end of the workshop, participants are asked to formulate stretch objectives for each of the proposed measures, including targeted rates of improvement.

6. *Executive Workshop: Third Round*

The senior executive team meets to come to a final consensus on the vision, objectives, and measurements developed in the first two workshops; to develop stretch targets for each measure on the scorecard; and to identify preliminary action programs to achieve the targets. The team must agree on an implementation program, including communicating the scorecard to employees, integrating the scorecard into a management philosophy, and developing an information system to support the scorecard.

7. *Implementation*

A newly formed team develops an implementation plan for the scorecard, including linking the measures to databases and information systems, communicating the balanced scorecard throughout the organization, and encouraging and facilitating the development of second-level metrics for decentralized units. As a result of this process, for instance, an entirely new executive information system that links top-level business unit metrics down through shop floor and site-specific operational measures could be developed.

8. *Periodic Reviews*

Each quarter or month, a blue book of information on the balanced scorecard measures is prepared for both top management review and discussion with managers of decentralized divisions and departments. The balanced scorecard metrics are revisited annually as part of the strategic planning, goal setting, and resource allocation processes.

Begin by Linking Measurements to Strategy

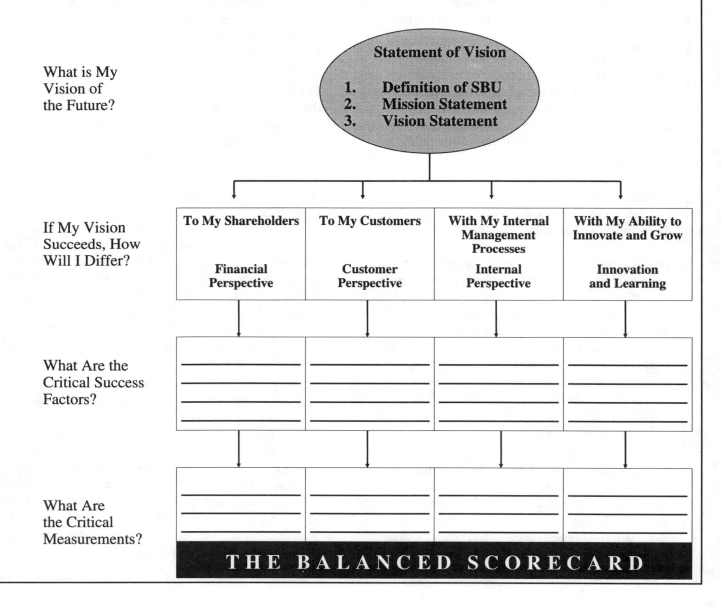

ber of ways. First of all, the balanced score card at Apple serves primarily as a planning device, instead of a control device. To put it another way, Apple uses the measures to adjust the "long wave" of corporate performance, not to drive operating changes. Moreover, the metrics at Apple, with the exception of shareholder value, can be driven both horizontally and vertically into each functional organization. Considered vertically, each individual measure can be broken down into its component parts in order to evaluate how each part contributes to the functioning of the whole. Thought of horizontally, the measures can identify how, for example, design and manufacturing contribute to an area such as customer satisfaction. In addition, Apple has found that its balanced scorecard has helped develop a language of measurable outputs for how to launch and leverage programs.

The five performance indicators at Apple are benchmarked against best-in-class organizations. Today they are used to build business plans and are incorporated into senior executives' compensation plans.

Advanced Micro Devices: Consolidating Strategic Information

Advanced Micro Devices (AMD), a semiconductor company, executed a quick and easy transition to a balanced scorecard. It already had a clearly defined mission, strategy statement, and shared understanding among senior executives about its competitive niche. It also had many performance measures from many different sources and information systems. The balanced scorecard consolidated and focused these diverse measures into a quarterly briefing book that contained seven sections: financial measures; customer-based measures, such as on-time delivery, lead time, and performance-to-schedule; measures of critical business processes in wafer fabrication, assembly and test, new product development, process technology development (e.g., submicron etching precision), and, finally, measures for corporate quality. In addition, organizational learning was measured by imposing targeted rates of improvements for key operating parameters, such as cycle time and yields by process.

At present, AMD sees its scorecard as a systematic repository for strategic information that facilitates long-term trend analysis for planning and performance evaluation.

Driving the Process of Change

The experiences of these companies and others reveal that the balanced scorecard is most successful when it is used to drive the process of change. Rockwater, for instance, came into existence after the merger of two different organizations. Employees came from different cultures, spoke different languages, and had different operating experiences and backgrounds. The balanced scorecard helped the company focus on what it had to do well in order to become the industry leader.

Similarly, Joseph De Feo, chief executive of Service Businesses, one of the three operating divisions of Barclays Bank, had to transform what had been a captive, internal supplier of services into a global competitor. The scorecard highlighted areas where, despite apparent consensus on strategy, there still was considerable disagreement about how to make the strategy operational. With the help of the scorecard, the division eventually achieved consensus concerning the highest priority areas for achievement and improvement and identified additional areas that needed attention, such as quality and productivity. De Feo assessed the impact of the scorecard, saying, "It helped us to drive major change, to become more market oriented, throughout our organization. It provided a shared understanding of our goals and what it took to achieve them."

Analog Devices, a semiconductor company, served as the prototype for the balanced scorecard and now uses it each year to update the targets and goals for division managers. Jerry Fishman, president of Analog, said, "At the beginning, the scorecard drove significant and considerable change. I still does when we focus attention on particular areas, such as the gross margins on new products. But its main impact today is to help sustain programs that our people have been working on for years." Recently, the company has been attempting to integrate the scorecard metrics with *hoshin* planning, a procedure that concentrates an entire company on achieving one or two key objectives each year. Analog's hoshin objectives have included customer service and new product development, for which measures already exist on the company's scorecard.

But the scorecard isn't always the impetus for such dramatic change. For example, AMD's scorecard has yet to have a significant impact because company management didn't use it to drive the change process. Before turning to the scorecard, senior managers had already formulated and gained consensus for the company's mission, strategy, and key performance measures. AMD competes in a single industry segment. The top 12 managers are intimately familiar with the markets, engineering, technology, and other key levers in this segment. The summary and aggregate information in the scorecard were neither new nor surprising to them. And managers of decentralized production units also already had a significant amount of information about their own operations. The scorecard did enable them to see the breadth and totality of company operations, enhancing their ability to become better managers for the entire company. But, on balance, the scorecard could only encapsulate knowledge that managers in general had already learned.

AMD's limited success with the balanced scorecard demonstrates that the scorecard has its greatest impact when used to drive a change process. Some companies link compensation of senior executives to achieving stretch targets for the scorecard measures. Most are attempting to translate the scorecard into operational measures that become the focus for improvement activities in local units. The scorecard is not just a measurement system; it is a management system to motivate breakthrough competitive performance.

The Scorecard's Impact on External Reporting

Several managers have asked whether or not the balanced scorecard is applicable to external reporting. If the scorecard is indeed a driver of long-term performance, shouldn't this information be relevant to the investment community?

In fact, the scorecard does not translate easily to the investment community. A scorecard makes sense primarily for business units and divisions with a well-defined strategy. Most companies have several divisions, each with its own mission and strategy, whose scorecards cannot be aggregated into an overall corporate scorecard. And if the scorecard does indeed provide a transparent vision into a unit's strategy, then the information, even the measures being used, might be highly sensitive data that could reveal much of value to competitors. But most important, as a relatively recent innovation, the scorecard would benefit from several years of experimentation within companies before it becomes a systematic part of reporting to external constituencies.

Even if the scorecard itself were better suited to external reporting, at present the financial community itself shows little interest in making the change from financial to strategic reporting. One company president has found the outside financial community leery of the principles that ground the scorecard: "We use the scorecard more with our customers than with our investors. The financial community is skeptical about long-term indicators and occasionally tells us about some empirical evidence of a negative correlation between stock prices and attention to total quality and internal processes."

However, the investment community has begun to focus on some key metrics of new product performance. Could this be an early sign of a shift to strategic thinking?

Implementing the Balanced Scorecard at FMC Corporation: An Interview with Larry D. Brady

FMC Corporation is one of the most diversified companies in the United States, producing more than 300 product lines in 21 divisions organized into 5 business segments: industrial chemicals, performance chemicals, precious metals, defense systems, and machinery and equipment. Based in Chicago, FMC has worldwide revenues in excess of $4 billion.

Since 1984, the company has realized annual returns-on-investment of greater than 15%. Coupled with a major recapitalization in 1986, these returns resulted in an increasing shareholder value that significantly exceeded industrial averages. In 1992, the company completed a strategic review to determine the best future course to maximize shareholder value. As a result of that review, FMC adopted a growth strategy to complement its strong operating performance. This strategy required a greater external focus and appreciation of operating trade-offs.

To help make the shift, the company decided to use the balanced scorecard. In this interview conducted by Robert S. Kaplan, Larry D. Brady, executive vice president of FMC, talks about the company's experience implementing the scorecard.

Robert S. Kaplan: *What's the status of the balanced scorecard at FMC?*

Larry D. Brady: Although we are just completing the pilot phase of implementation, I think that the balanced scorecard is likely to become the cornerstone of the management system at FMC. It enables us to translate business unit strategies into a measurement system that meshes with our entire system of management.

For instance, one manager reported that while his division had measured many operating variables in the past, now, because of the scorecard, it had chosen 12 parameters as the key to its strategy implementation. Seven of these strategic variables were entirely new measurements for the division. The manager interpreted this finding as verifying what many other managers were reporting: the scorecard improved the understanding and consistency of strategy implementation. Another manager reported that, unlike monthly financial statements or even his strategic plan, if a rival were to see his scorecard, he would lose his competitive edge.

It's rare to get that much enthusiasm among divisional managers for a corporate initiative. What led you and them to the balanced scorecard?

FMC had a clearly defined mission: to become our customers' most valued supplier. We had initiated many of the popular improvement programs: total quality, managing by objectives, organizational effectiveness, building a high-performance organization. But these efforts had not been effective. Every time we promoted a new program, people in each division would sit back and ask, "How is that supposed to fit in with the six other things we're supposed to be doing?"

Corporate staff groups were perceived by operating managers as pushing their pet programs on divisions. The diversity of initiatives, each with its own slogan, created confusion and mixed signals about where to concentrate and how the various programs interrelated. At the end of the day, with all these new initiatives, we were still asking division managers to deliver consistent short-term financial performance.

What kinds of measures were you using?

The FMC corporate executive team, like most corporate offices, reviews the financial performance of each operating division monthly. As a highly diversified company that redeploys assets from mature cash generators to divisions with significant growth opportunities, the return-on-capital-employed (ROCE) measure was especially important for us. We were one of the few companies to inflation-adjust our internal financial measures so that we could get a more accurate picture of a division's economic profitability.

At year-end, we rewarded division managers who delivered predictable financial performance. We had run the company tightly for the past 20 years and had been successful. But it was becoming less clear where future growth would come from and where the company should look for breakthroughs into new areas. We had become a high return-on-investment company but had less potential for further growth. It was also not at all clear from our financial reports what progress we were making in implementing long-term initiatives. Questions from the corporate office about spending versus budget also reinforced a focus on the short-term and on internal operations.

But the problem went even deeper than that. Think about it. What is the value added of a corporate office that concentrates on making division managers accountable for financial results that can be added up across divisions? We combine a business that's doing well with a business that's doing poorly and have a total business that performs at an average level. Why not split the company up into independent companies and let the market reallocate capital? If we were going to create value by managing a group of diversified companies, we had to understand and provide strategic focus to their operations. We had to be sure that each division had a strategy that would give it sustainable competitive advantage. In addition, we had to be able to assess, through measurement of their operations, whether or not the divisions were meeting their strategic objectives.

If you're going to ask a division or the corporation to change its strategy, you had better change the system of measurement to be consistent with the new strategy.

How did the balanced scorecard emerge as the remedy to the limitations of measuring only short-term financial results?

In early 1992, we assembled a task force to integrate our various corporate initiatives. We wanted to understand what had to be done differently to achieve dramatic improvements in overall organizational effectiveness. We acknowledged that the company may have become too short-term and too internally focused in its business measures. Defining what should replace the financial focus was more difficult. We wanted managers to sustain their search for continuous improvement, but we also wanted them to identify the opportunities for breakthrough performance.

When divisions missed financial targets, the reasons were generally not internal. Typically, division management had inaccurately estimated market demands or had failed to forecast competitive reactions. A new measurement system was needed to lead operating managers beyond achieving internal goals to searching for competitive breakthroughs in the global marketplace. The system would have to focus on measures of customer service, market position, and new products that could generate long-term value for the business. We used the scorecard as the focal point for the discussion. It forced division managers to answer these questions: How do we become our customers' most valued supplier? How do we become more externally focused? What is my division's competitive advantage? What is its competitive vulnerability?

How did you launch the scorecard effort at FMC?

We decided to try a pilot program. We selected six division managers to develop prototype scorecards for their operations. Each division had to perform a strategic analysis to identify its sources of competitive advantage. The 15 to 20 measures in the balanced scorecard had to be organization-specific and had to communicate clearly what short-term measures of operating performance were consistent with a long-term trajectory of strategic success.

Were the six division managers free to develop their own scorecard?

We definitely wanted the division managers to perform their own strategic analysis and to develop their own measures. That was an essential part of creating a consensus between senior and divisional management on operating objectives. Senior management did, however, place some conditions on the outcomes.

First of all, we wanted the measures to be objective and quantifiable. Division managers were to be just as accountable for improving scorecard measures as they had been for using monthly financial reviews. Second, we wanted output measures, not process-oriented measures. Many of the improvement programs under way were emphasizing time, quality, and cost measurements. Focusing on T-Q-C measurements, however, encourages managers to seek narrow process improvements instead of breakthrough output targets. Focusing on achieving outputs forces division managers to understand their industry and strategy and help them to quantify strategic success through specific output targets.

Could you illustrate the distinction between process measures and output measures?

You have to understand your industry well to develop the connection between process improvements and outputs achieved. Take three divisional examples of cycle-time measurement, a common process measure.

For much of our defense business, no premium is earned for early delivery. And the contracts allow for reimbursement of inventory holding costs. Therefore, attempts to reduce inventory or cycle times in this business produce no benefit for which the customer is willing to pay. The only benefits from cycle time or inventory reduction occur when reduction in factory-floor complexity leads to real reductions in product cost. The output performance targets must be real cash savings, not reduced inventory levels or cycle times.

In contrast, significant lead-time reductions could be achieved for our packaging machinery business. This improvement led to lower inventory and an option to access an additional 35% of the market. In this case, the cycle-time improvements could be tied to specific targets for increased sales and market share. It wasn't linear, but output seemed to improve each time we improved throughput times.

And in one of our agricultural machinery businesses, orders come within a narrow time window each year. The current build cycle is longer than the ordering window, so all units must be built to the sales forecast. This process of building to forecast leads to high inventory—more than twice the levels of our other businesses—and frequent overstocking and obsolescence of equipment. Incremental reductions in lead time do little to change the economics of this operation. But if the build cycle time could be reduced to less than the six-week ordering time window for part or all of the build schedule, then a

breakthrough occurs. The division can shift to a build-to-order schedule and eliminate the excess inventory caused by building to forecasts. In this case, the benefit from cycle-time reductions is a step-function that comes only when the cycle time drops below a critical level.

So here we have three businesses, three different processes, all of which could have elaborate systems for measuring quality, cost, and time but would feel the impact of improvements in radically different ways. With all the diversity in our business units, senior management really can't have a detailed understanding of the relative impact of time and quality improvements on each unit. All of our senior managers, however, understand output targets, particularly when they are displayed with historical trends and future targets.

Benchmarking has become popular with a lot of companies. Does it tie in to the balanced scorecard measurements?

Unfortunately, benchmarking is one of those initially good ideas that has turned into a fad. About 95% of those companies that have tried benchmarking have spent a lot of money and have gotten very little in return. And the difference between benchmarking and the scorecard helps reinforce the difference between process measures and output measures. It's a lot easier to benchmark a process than to benchmark an output. With the scorecard, we ask each division manager to go outside their organization and determine the approaches that will allow achievement of their long-term output targets. Each of our output measures has an associated long-term target. We have been deliberately vague on specifying when the target is to be accomplished. We want to stimulate a thought process about how to do things differently to achieve the target rather than how to do existing things better. The activity of searching externally for how others have accomplished these breakthrough achievements is called target verification not benchmarking.

Were the division managers able to develop such output-oriented measures?

Well, the division managers did encounter some obstacles. Because of the emphasis on output measures and the previous focus on operations and financial measures, the customer and innovation perspectives proved the most difficult. These were also the two areas where the balanced scorecard process was most helpful in refining and understanding our existing strategies.

But the initial problem was that the management teams ran afoul of both conditions: the measures they proposed tended to be nonquantifiable and input- rather than output-oriented. Several divisions wanted to conduct customer surveys and provide an index of the results. We judged a single index to be of little value and opted instead for harder measures such as price premiums over competitors.

We did conclude, however, that the full customer survey was an excellent vehicle for promoting external focus and, therefore, decided to use survey results to kick off discussion at our annual operating reviews.

Did you encounter any problems as you launched the six pilot projects?

At first, several divisional managers were less than enthusiastic about the additional freedom they were being given from headquarters. They knew that the heightened visibility and transparency of the scorecard took away the internal trade-offs they had gained experience in making. They initially interpreted the increase in visibility of divisional performance as just the latest attempt by corporate staff to meddle in their internal business processes.

To offset this concern, we designed targets around long-term objectives. We still closely examine the monthly and quarterly statistics, but these statistics now relate to progress in achieving long-term objectives and justify the proper balance between short-term and long-term performance.

We also wanted to transfer quickly the focus from a measurement system to achieving performance results. A measurement orientation reinforces concerns about control and a short-term focus. By emphasizing targets rather than measurements, we could demonstrate our purpose to achieve breakthrough performance.

But the process was not easy. One division manager described his own three-stage implementation process after receiving our directive to build a balanced scorecard: denial—hope it goes away; medicinal—it won't go away, so let's do it quickly and get it over with; ownership—let's do it for ourselves.

In the end, we were successful. We now have six converts who are helping us to spread the message throughout the organization.

I understand that you have started to apply the scorecard not just to operating units but to staff groups as well.

Applying the scorecard approach to staff groups has been even more eye-opening than our initial work with the six operating divisions. We have done very little to define our strategy for corporate staff utilization. I doubt that many companies can respond crisply to the question, "How does staff provide competitive advantage?" Yet we ask that question every day about our line operations. We have just started to ask our staff departments to explain to us whether they are offering low cost or differentiated services. If they are offering neither, we should probably outsource the function. This area is loaded with real potential for organizational development and improved strategic capability.

My conversations with financial people in organizations reveal some concern about the expanded responsibilities implied by developing and maintaining a balanced scorecard. How does the role of the controller change as a company shifts its primary measurement system from a purely financial one to the balanced scorecard?

Historically, we have had two corporate departments involved in overseeing business unit performance. Corporate development was in charge of strategy, and the controller's office kept the historical records and budgeted and measured short-term performance. Strategists came up with five- and ten-year plans, controllers one-year budgets and near-term forecasts. Little interplay occurred between the two groups. But the scorecard now bridges the two. The financial perspective builds on the traditional function performed by controllers. The other three perspectives make the division's long-term strategic objectives measurable.

In our old environment, division managers tried to balance short-term profits with long-term growth, while they were receiving different signals depending on whether or not they were reviewing strategic plans or budgets. This structure did not make the balancing of short-term profits and long-term growth an easy trade-off, and, frankly, it let senior management off the hook when it came to sharing responsibility for making the trade-offs.

Perhaps the corporate controller should take responsibility for all measurement and goal setting, including the systems required to implement these processes. The new corporate controller could be an outstanding system administrator, knowledgeable about the various trade-offs and balances, and skillful in reporting and presenting them. This role does not eliminate the need for strategic planning. It just makes the two systems more compatible. The scorecard can serve to motivate and evaluate performance. But I see its primary value as its ability to join together what had been strong but separated capabilities in strategy development and financial control. It's the operating performance bridge that corporations have never had.

How often do you envision reviewing a division's balanced scorecard?

I think we will ask group managers to review a monthly submission from each of their divisions, but the senior corporate team will probably review scorecards quarterly on a rotating basis so that we can review up to seven or eight division scorecards each month.

Isn't is inconsistent to assess a division's strategy on a monthly or quarterly basis? Doesn't such a review emphasize short-term performance?

I see the scorecard as a strategic measurement system, not a measure of our strategy. And I think that's an important distinction. The monthly or quarterly scorecard measures operations that have been configured to be consistent with our long-term strategy.

Here's an example of the interaction between the short and the long term. We have pushed division managers to choose measures that will require them to create change, for example, penetration of key markets in which we are not currently represented. We can measure that penetration monthly and get valuable short-term information about the ultimate success of our long-term strategy. Of course, some measures, such as annual market share and innovation metrics, don't lend themselves to monthly updates. For the most part, however, the measures are calculated monthly.

Any final thoughts on the scorecard?

I think that it's important for companies not to approach the scorecard as the latest fad. I sense that a number of companies are turning to scorecards in the same way they turned to total quality management, high-performance organization, and so on. You hear about a good idea, several people on corporate staff work on it, probably with some expensive outside consultants, and you put in a system that's a bit different from what existed before. Such systems are only incremental, and you don't gain much additional value from them.

It gets worse if you think of the scorecard as a new measurement system that eventually requires hundreds and thousands of measurements and a big, expensive executive information system. These companies lose sight of the essence of the scorecard: its focus, its simplicity, and its vision. The real benefit comes from making the scorecard the cornerstone of the way you run the business. It should be the core of the management system, not the measurement system. Senior managers alone will determine whether the scorecard becomes a mere record-keeping exercise or the lever to streamline and focus strategy that can lead to breakthrough performance.

Robert S. Kaplan is the Arthur Lowes Dickinson Professor of Accounting at the Harvard Business School.

David P. Norton is founder and president of Renaissance Strategy Group, a consulting firm located in Lincoln, Massachusetts.

Emerson Electric: Consistent Profits, Consistently

by Charles F. Knight

When I meet with people outside Emerson, I'm often asked: What makes Emerson tick? That question typically reflects an interest in the company's consistent financial performance over the past three-and-a-half decades—but my answer deals with issues that go far beyond financial statements.

Simply put, what makes us "tick" at Emerson is an effective management process. We believe we can shape our future through careful planning and strong follow-up. Our managers plan for improved results and execute to get them. Driving this process is a set of shared values, including involvement, intensity, discipline, and persistence. We adhere to few policies or techniques that could be called unique or even unusual. But we do act on our policies, and that may indeed make us unusual.

Several assumptions underlie our management process. We believe, for example, that profitability is a state of mind. Experience tells us that if management concentrates on the fundamentals and constantly follows up, there is no reason why we can't achieve profits year after year—even in manufacturing businesses that many observers consider mature and unglamorous. We also believe that companies fail primarily for nonanalytical reasons: management knows what to do but, for some reason, doesn't do it. That is why Emerson has a strong action orientation; we see to it that our strategies get implemented properly.

A third belief is that the "long term" consists of a sequence of "short terms." Poor performance in the short term makes it more difficult to achieve strong performance in the long term. The basis of management is management from minute to minute, day to day, week to week. Finally, it is crucial to "keep it simple." While effective management is simple in theory, it's difficult in practice. As Peter Drucker has noted, managers seem naturally inclined to get caught up in complicated ideas and concepts—ideas that look great on paper but just don't work. A corporation has to work hard to have a simple plan, simple communications, simple programs, and simple organizations. It takes real discipline to keep things simple.

My answer, therefore, to those who ask what makes us tick is far-reaching in its implications but uncomplicated in its substance: what we do at Emerson to achieve consistent performance at high levels is just solid management, rigorously executed. Interestingly enough, given our consistent performance, the dynamic impact of Emerson's approach to management is sometimes overlooked. Wall Street analysts, for example, tend to portray our stock as a good investment, but they also consider us a conservative and unchanging company. Yet a close look at what Emerson has accomplished in recent years reveals that we have changed a great deal.

For example, through our Best Cost Producer Strategy, we have spent more than a quarter of a billion dollars on restructuring and now have best cost positions in all of our major product lines. We've moved from an export-led to an investment-led international strategy, resulting in a rise of international sales from about 25% to about 40% in the past five years. As a result of a $1.6 billion investment in technology during the 1980s, new products—those introduced in the past five years—as a percent of sales have increased from 9% to 20%. All the while, we've adhered to the discipline of

---

Emerson's Record

During the past several decades, St. Louis, Missouri-based Emerson Electric Co. has posted an enviable record for a U.S. manufacturing company. In 1991, Emerson marked its thirty-fourth consecutive year of improved earnings and earnings per share and its thirty-fifth consecutive year of increased dividends per share—a performance matched by only a handful of manufacturing companies in the world and unmatched by any U.S. company that makes comparable products or serves similar markets.

Since 1956, Emerson's persistence has rewarded investors, yielding an annual total return that has averaged 19.1%. According to a recent study by A.T. Kearney, Emerson is one of only 11 U.S. corporations that outearned its cost of capital during each of the past 20 years and one of only 22 industrial companies whose ratio of market price to book value ranked in the top 20% of U.S. corporations during each of the past 10 years.

Although it is one of America's leading manufacturing corporations, Emerson is hardly a household name. Many products bearing its brand names are better known commercially than Emerson itself. Among them are Skil, Dremel, and Craftsman power tools, Ridgid professional plumbers' tools, In-Sink-Erator waste disposals, Copeland compressors, Rosemount instruments, and Browning, Morse, Sealmaster, and U.S. Electric Motors in the power transmission market.

Emerson's 40 divisions make a wide range of electric, electromechanical, and electronic products for industry and consumers. The divisions are collected into eight businesses: fractional horsepower electric motors; industrial motors and drives; tools; industrial machinery and components; controls and components for heating, ventilating, and air conditioning equipment markets; process control equipment and systems; appliance components; and electronics and computer support products and systems.

— The Editors

---

constantly increasing earnings, earnings per share, and dividends per share (see Emerson's earnings and return on equity charts).

The driving force behind all that change is a simple management process that emphasizes setting targets, planning carefully, and following up closely. The process is supported by a long-standing history of continuous cost reduction and open communication and is fueled by annual dynamic planning and control cycles. Finally, it is nourished by strongly reinforced cultural values and an approach to organizational planning that is as rigorous as our approach to business planning. It is an environment in which people at all levels can and do make a difference.

The Basics of Our Approach

In my view, the job of management is *to identify and successfully implement business investment opportunities that permit us to achieve the financial targets we set.* That definition is carefully phrased, and it constitutes the foundation of our approach to management.

The first step is to "set financial targets," since almost everything we do is geared toward reaching our financial objectives. When I came to Emerson in 1973, the company was already a strong performer whose stock traded at a premium relative to other industrial companies. We wanted to maintain this performance. We analyzed Emerson's historical record and the records of a set of "peer companies" that the stock market valued highly over the long term for growth and consistency. We concluded that, to maintain a premium stock price over long periods of time, we needed to achieve growth and strong financial results on a consistent basis—no swings of the pendulum, just constant improvement starting from a high level.

Consistent high performance requires ambitious and dynamic targets. Every year we reexamine our growth targets to see whether they remain valid, and we have recalibrated our growth objectives several times because the business environment has changed, or Emerson has changed, or we've learned something that causes us to see the world a little differently. In the early 1970s, for example, the general level of economic activity, plus the energy shocks and the inflationary aftermath, forced us to rethink our nominal and real growth rates. In recent years, we've targeted growth rates relative to economic growth as a whole, based on revenue targets above and beyond economy-driven expectations.

We have not modified our other financial goals, despite pressure to do so. During the 1980s, for example, we were criticized because we refused to increase our debt position. Given the then-prevailing attitudes toward leverage, our financial position appeared unduly conservative. But we regard our finances strategically: maintaining a conservative balance sheet is a powerful competitive weapon. When we see an opportunity that we can finance only by borrowing, we have the capacity. By the same token, we're not encumbered by interest payments, which are especially burdensome during economic downturns—as the experience of the 1990s bears out so far.

Once we fix our goals, we do not consider it acceptable to miss them. These targets drive our strategy and determine what we have to do: the kinds of businesses we're in, how we organize and manage them, and how we pay management. At Emerson, this means planning. In the process of planning, we focus on specific opportunities that will meet our criteria for growth and returns and create value for our stockholders. In other words, we "identify business investment opportunities."

From a management standpoint, the most important decision a company makes is the level at which it plans and controls profits. For a corporation of our size, approaching $8 billion in sales, we are relatively decentralized. Our division presidents are responsible for identifying business investment opportunities and planning and controlling profits by product line. We do not have groups or sectors or other combinations commonly found in large, diversified companies. Although we recently adopted a new structure that gathers similar divisions into businesses to exploit common distribution channels, organizational capabilities, and technologies, we never aggregate financial reports for purposes of planning or controlling profits at levels between the division and the corporation as a whole.

Once we identify business investment opportunities, the next step is to "successfully implement" them. This is where many companies fail. Often implementation goes astray because the people who plan are separated from the people who have the re-

---

Emerson's Best Cost Producer Strategy

In recent years, the Best Cost Producer Strategy has been fundamental to Emerson's profitability and its success in global markets. Developed in the early 1980s, the strategy consists of six elements:

- Commitment to total quality and customer satisfaction.
- Knowledge of the competition and the basis on which they compete.
- Focused manufacturing strategy, competing on process as well as product design.
- Effective employee communications and involvement.
- Formalized cost-reduction programs, in good times and bad.
- Commitment to support the strategy through capital expenditures.

---

sponsibility to make the plans work. The plans go to the bottom of an operations manager's drawer, and that's the end of them. At Emerson, the people who plan are the people who execute. They have ownership and involvement; it's their plan, not a corporate plan. That ownership makes all the difference.

Sometimes companies fail to execute because people are not permitted to complete the implementation. Systems in other companies may require putting good people on a fast track, giving them more responsibility, and promoting them. As a result, people are not permitted to stay involved long enough to complete what they start. In contrast, we try to focus on jobs and projects rather than status; we compensate people based on the importance of their jobs, not on the number of people reporting to them or the arbitrary need for a promotion.

The structure and everyday operation of Emerson embodies this basic approach: set tough targets, plan rigorously to meet them, and follow through on the plans.

Two Underlying Principles

The first pieces of our management process were put in place during the 1950s, when my predecessor, W.R. "Buck" Persons, established two fundamental principles—continuous cost reduction and open communication—as central to everyday management.

The first of the two has correctly been described as a "religion" and "a way of life" at Emerson. Every year for the past three-and-a-half decades (in good times and bad), the company has set cost-reduction goals at every level and required plant personnel to identify the specific measures necessary to achieve those objectives. Over that period, Emer-

son's cost-reduction programs have targeted improvements of 6% to 7% a year, in terms of cost of sales. During the 1980s, when fierce global competition challenged many of our businesses, we redoubled our efforts, aiming for still higher levels of annual improvement. Our present cost-reduction goals, developed by each division, average about 7% of the cost of goods sold.

We identify the programs that will give us 70% to 80% of our cost-reduction targets before the year starts. We know exactly what we're going to do:

More Than 30 Years of Increased Earnings at Emerson

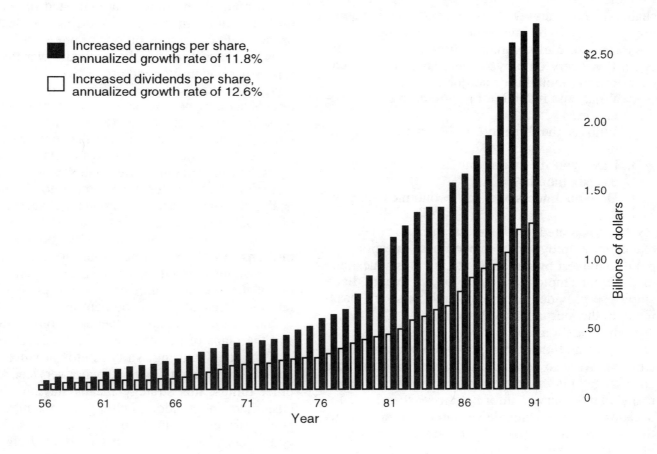

■ Increased earnings per share, annualized growth rate of 11.8%

□ Increased dividends per share, annualized growth rate of 12.6%

we'll install this machine tool to streamline that process, saving two-and-a-half man-years; we'll change this design on that part, saving five ounces of aluminum per unit at 75 cents a pound; and so on. Division and plant management report every quarter on progress against these detailed targets. Although this entire saving does not reach the bottom line, without this program combined with price changes, we would not be able to stay ahead of the inflation that affects our costs, and our margins would drop.

The second principle—open communication—is also fundamental to the management process. For decades, Emerson division presidents and plant managers have met regularly with all employees to discuss the specifics of our business and our competition. We continue this practice today because we believe people are more likely to be receptive to change if they know why, when, and how it's coming; they need to be involved in the process.

As a measure of communication at Emerson, we claim that every employee can answer four essential questions about his or her job:

1. What cost reduction are you currently working on?
2. Who is the "enemy" (who is the competition)?
3. Have you met with your management in the past six months?
4. Do you understand the economics of your job?

When I repeated to a business journalist the claim that every employee can answer these questions, he put it to the test by randomly asking those questions of different employees at one of our plants. Each employee provided clear and direct answers, passing both the journalist's test and ours.

Communication is a two-way street. We listen to employees and make changes when we hear a better idea. We also conduct, and spend a lot of time analyzing, opinion surveys of every employee. At many plants, survey information reaches back for decades and is a valuable resource that enables us to track trends. I personally review a summary of every opinion survey from every plant. When I spot a downward trend, I immediately ask the managers in charge for an explanation. It has to be a good one.

Best Cost Producer

Continuous cost reduction and effective communication became two central elements of Emerson's Best Cost Producer Strategy, which we developed during the early 1980s to meet global competition. The four other elements of this strategy are: an emphasis on total quality, a thorough knowledge of the competition, a focused manufacturing strategy, and a commitment to capital expenditures.

The Best Cost Producer Strategy begins with a recognition that our customers' expectations for quality, broadly defined, are getting higher every day. To remain competitive, we have to meet or exceed the highest standards in the world for product performance, on-time delivery, and service after the sale. In this context, for example, the ideal of "zero defects" is not some high-tech dream: we've gotten to the point where defects are counted in parts per million—and I'm not just referring to electronic products. For example, on one of our electric motor lines, we have consistently reached fewer than 100 rejects per one million motors.

We also stress the importance of analyzing and understanding the competition. Simply comparing ourselves with ourselves teaches us nothing of value. We use the products and the cost structure of our competitors as the measures against which we assess our performance. We do this in detail, legally and ethically, by taking apart competitors' products, analyzing the cost of components, knowing regional labor rates and freight costs, and more. If we want to make intelligent decisions about investing millions of dollars in a new plant to make circular saws, we must assemble as clear a picture as possible of the cost structures and overall plans of both our domestic and global competitors.

Once we understand the needs of our customers and the plans of our competitors, we develop a focused manufacturing strategy to produce more competitively and to provide better service. Among other things, this strategy means staying close to customers and vendors, helping them achieve their goals as well as our own. It also means that we compete on process, not just product design; that we focus strictly on manufacturing and aren't afraid to say so; that we address the issue of our installed manufacturing base and are willing to relocate

Return on Equity: Emerson vs. Standard & Poor's 500

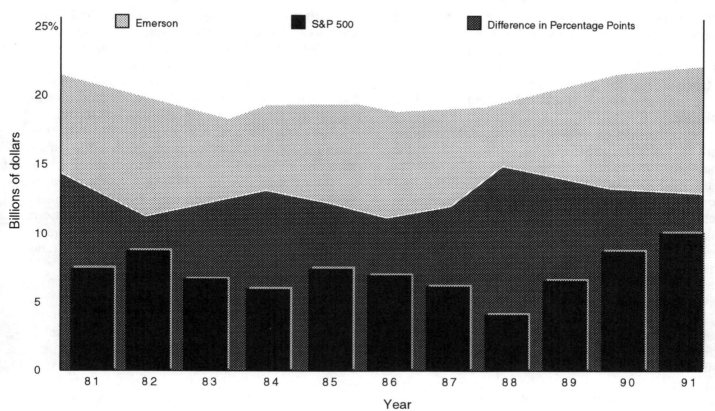

plants, invest in technology, and make other tough decisions when necessary.

Finally, we support the elements of our Best Cost Producer Strategy through an ongoing program of capital investments. This commitment to capital expenditures is crucial: it's the only way to improve process technology, increase productivity, gain product leadership, and achieve critical mass regularly. This investment program is made possible by our strong cash flow and balance sheet, which we view as a major competitive asset; effective asset management plays a major role in freeing up the needed cash.

These elements of strategy are not especially new or original. We think the key to success is closely tracking performance along these dimensions and attacking deviations immediately. Ten years ago, Emerson was not globally competitive in all its major product lines. Today we are, thanks to the intensity of our manufacturing approach and to the management process through which we make it work.

Making the Future Happen—Planning and Control

At Emerson, rigorous planning has been essential to the company's success since the 1950s; it's no coincidence that our long record of improved annual earnings dates from the same period. As CEO, more than half of my time each year is blocked out strictly for planning. Emerson President and Chief Operating Officer Al Suter and other senior managers spend even more time in planning sessions. We devote so much time to planning because that is when we identify business investment opportunities in detail—and because good planning takes time.

Each fiscal year, from November through June, selected corporate officers, Al Suter, and I meet with the management of every division for a one- or two-day planning conference, usually held off-site. These division conferences are the culmination of our planning cycle. The mood is confrontational—by design. Though we're not trying to put anyone on the spot, we do want to challenge as-

85

sumptions and conventional thinking and give ample time to every significant issue. We want proof that a division is stretching to reach its goals, and we want to see the details of the actions division management believes will yield improved results. Our expectations are high, and the discussions are intense. A division president who comes to a planning conference poorly prepared has made a serious mistake.

Corporate management sets the stage. We require only a few standard exhibits, including a "value measurement chart," a "sales gap chart," and a "5-back-by-5-forward" P&L statement. (See the four corresponding exhibits, which are reproductions of actual Emerson charts.) While the list is short, it takes substantial planning and backup data to develop these exhibits. To prepare properly requires that division presidents really understand their business. Every piece of data we ask for is something division management needs to know itself.

The value measurement chart captures on a single page such vital data as long-term sales and profit growth, capital investment, and expected return. The chart displays the amount and type of investment and return on capital over the preceding five years, allowing us to see quickly the return on incremental capital. Add to this a forecast of capital investments and returns over the next five years, and we can see whether the division is earning, or expects to earn, a return on total capital greater than our cost of capital. In other words, we can tell in a glance whether the division is creating stockholder value.

The sales gap chart and sales gap line chart display current sales and make projections for the next five years based on an analysis of the sources of growth: the market's natural growth rate, the division's change in market penetration, price changes, new products, product line extensions, and international growth. Should the projected growth not meet or exceed our target, the division faces a gap. Then it is management's job to tell us the specific steps it will take to close the gap.

The 5-back-by-5-forward P&L chart arrays current-year results in the context of 5 years of historical information and 5 years of projections. This exhibit shows not only sales growth but also gross profit margin, SG&A expense, operating profit margin, capital turnover, and returns on sales and capi-

tal. We look at 11 years' worth of data to spot trends. If they're down, then we want to see why we can't make the margins we used to make and what actions will bring them back. If they're up, we ask, "How much further can we drive them?"

Together, those four charts tell us basic information about the business, alert us to any problems, and provide clues to the steps divisions must take to outperform the competition and produce results for stockholders. Beyond the required exhibits, the planning conference belongs to the division presidents. We're there to help them improve their plans and their results. We want to hear division management's views of customers and markets; its plans for new products; its analysis of the competition; and the status of such manufacturing issues as quality, capacity, productivity, inventory levels, and compensation.

We also believe in the logic of illogic. Often, a manager will give a logical presentation on why we should approve a plan. We may challenge that logic by questioning underlying assumptions illogically. The people who know their strategies in detail are the ones who, after going through that, are able to stand up for the merits of their proposal. In the end, the test of a good planning conference is whether it results in managers taking actions that will have a significant impact on the business.

Since operating managers carry out the planning, we effectively establish ownership and eliminate the artificial distinction between strategic and operating decisions. Managers on the line do not—and must never—delegate the understanding of the business. To develop a plan, operating managers work together for months. They often tell me that the greatest value of the planning cycle lies in the teamwork and discipline that the preparation phase requires.

The Measure of Managers

The measure of Emerson managers is whether they achieve what they say they will in a planning conference. We track the implementation of our plans through a tight control system. That system starts at the top, with a corporate board of directors that meets regularly and plays an active role in overseeing our business. Management of the company is directed by the office of the chief executive (OCE), which presently consists of me, Al Suter,

The Value Measurement Chart Assesses Value Creation at a Glance*

	Line No.	5th Prior Year Actual FY 1986		Current Year Forecast FY 1991		5th Year Forecast FY 1996		5 Year Increment Historical CY vs 5th PY		5 Year Increment Forecast 5th Yr vs CY		10 Year Increment 5th Yr vs 5th PY	
		Amt.	% Sales	Amt.	% Sales	Amt.	% Sales	Amt.	% Sales	Amt.	% Sales	Amt.	% Sales
		A	B	C	D	E	F	G	H	I	J	K	L
Growth Rate and Capital Requirements													
Working capital operating - Y/E	1127	117.1	29.8%	120.2	21.8%	153.3	18.5%	3.1	1.9%	33.1	12.0%	36.2	8.3%
Net noncurrent assets - Y/E	1128	92.9	23.6%	150.0	27.2%	221.6	26.8%	60.2	35.9%	71.6	26.0%	128.7	29.6%
Total operating capital - Y/E	1129	210.0	53.4%	270.2	48.9%	374.9	45.3%		37.9%	104.7	38.0%	164.9	37.9%
Average operating capital	1130	201.1	51.1%	267.1	48.4%	370.4	44.7%	66.0					
Incremental Investment	1584							16.1		103.3		169.3	
Net. oper. prof. aft. tax (NOPAT)	1119	33.4		49.5		79.0		24.4%		16.1		45.6	
Return on incremental investment								8.2%		24.4%		26.9%	
NOPAT growth rate								5.8%		8.2%		9.0%	
Capital growth rate										5.8%		6.3%	
Rate of Return													
Return on Total Capital NOPAT / Avg. Oper. Cap.		16.6%		18.5%		21.3%		159.0					
Net sales	0001	393.2		552.2		827.9		7.0%		159.0		434.7	
Sales growth rate								10.1%		7.0%		7.7%	
NOPAT margin		8.5%		9.0%		9.5%		2.41		10.1%		10.5%	
Operating capital turnover		1.96		2.07		2.24				2.41		2.57	
Cost of capital		12.0%		12.0%		12.0%		8.0					
Capital charge (L1130 x L3000)	3000	24.1		32.1		44.4		8.1		8.0		20.3	
Economic profit (L1119 – L3000)	3001	9.3		17.4		34.6				8.1		25.3	

✳ In millions of dollars

Vice Chairman Bob Staley, Vice Chairman Jan Ver-Hagen, and seven other business leaders, and three additional corporate officers. The OCE meets from 10 to 12 times each year to review and discuss issues facing the divisions individually as well as the corporation as a whole.

Input from the divisions arrives in the form of their presidents' operating reports (PORs), monthly submissions that summarize the divisions' results and immediate prospects (see the president's operating report chart). We view the budget process used by many companies as static. In contrast, the

The Sales Gap Chart Forecasts Five-Year Plans*...

	Line No.	Prior Year Actual FY 90	Current Year Expected FY 91	FY 92	Forecast FY 93	FY 94	FY 95	FY 96	5 Year Source of Growth %	5 Year Company of Growth %
		A	B	C	D	E	F	G	H	I
Current year domestic sales base @ 10/1 prices	1		305.7	305.7	305.7	305.7	305.7	305.7		
Domestic Excluding Exports — Served Industry – growth/(decline)	2			3.0	24.6	39.0	49.6	58.3	21.1%	3.6%
Penetration – increase (decrease) (including – new line extensions/buyouts)	3			6.3	14.1	21.0	29.8	37.6	13.6	2.0
Price increases – current year through 5th year	4		3.3	7.6	14.7	21.6	29.5	38.0	12.6	1.7
Incremental new products — Prior 5 year introductions	5		16.1	16.4	17.7	17.4	17.5	19.0	1.1	
Incremental new products — Current year through 5th year	6		1.4	5.6	11.6	18.5	25.9	34.2	11.9	
Other	7		3.1	1.4	1.6	2.3	2.5	2.8	-0.1	
Total Domestic	8	363.7	329.6	346.0	390.0	425.5	460.5	495.6		8.5
Current year international sales base @ 10/1 prices	9		202.9	202.9	202.9	202.9	202.9	202.9		
International Excluding Sales to US — Served industry – growth/(decline)	10			(0.1)	8.8	17.0	24.8	35.4	12.9	3.3
Penetration – Increase/(decrease) (Including – new line extensions/buyouts)	11			(0.5)	18.8	27.2	36.2	45.1	16.4	3.6
Price increases – current year through 5th year	12		2.0	4.9	8.5	12.5	16.9	21.7	7.1	1.4
Incremental new products — Prior 5 year introduction	13		6.9	7.1	6.7	7.1	8.0	9.2	0.8	
Incremental new products — Current year through 5th year	14		1.1	4.5	6.3	10.1	14.3	16.9	5.7	
Currency	15		9.3						-3.4	
Other	16		0.4	0.8	0.7	0.9	1.0	1.1	0.3	
Total International	17	204.3	222.6	219.6	252.7	277.7	304.1	332.3	100.0	8.3
Total Consolidated	18	568.0	552.2	565.6	642.7	703.2	764.6	827.9		8.4
Annual Growth %			-2.8%	2.4%	13.6%	9.4%	8.7%	8.3%		
Gap — 15% Target – nominal				635.0	730.2	839.8	965.7	1,110.6		15.0
Sales gap – over/(under)				(69.4)	(87.5)	(136.6)	(201.1)	(282.7)		
US Exports (excluding to foreign subsidiaries)		35.3	31.3	33.7	35.9	39.9	43.9	47.6		8.7
Foreign subsidiaries (excluding sales to US)		169.1	191.4	185.8	216.8	237.8	260.3	284.7		8.3

＊In millions of dollars

POR is a dynamic tool: we update expected annual results each month and make rolling comparisons against historical and projected performance.

The divisions themselves are governed by their own boards of directors, with a member of the OCE serving as chairman. Other members of the board include the division president and the president's direct reports. The division boards are partly a legacy of Emerson's growth through acquisition, but more important, they are a reflection of the level at which we plan and control profits. The boards meet monthly to review and monitor performance. In ad-

...While the Sales Gap Line Chart Projects Sales Growth Against Other Targets

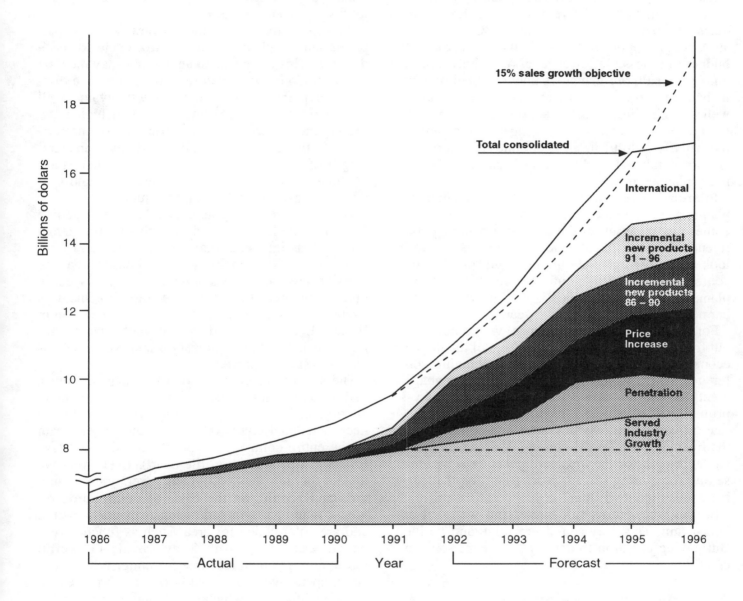

dition, the president and chief financial officer of each division meet quarterly with corporate operating and financial management to discuss short-term operating results and lock in on the current quarter; we call these sessions "president's councils."

Each division president, along with appropriate staff, meets once a year with senior corporate officers for separate financial reviews. These reviews occur late in the fiscal year and are a review of performance against financial plan, with a detailed financial plan of the coming year.

At the financial review, we push the divisions to think through different scenarios and to plan and advance actions that different contingencies will require. We use a technique called ABC budgeting: an A budget applies to the most likely scenario, a B budget to a possible lower level of activity, and so on. As a result, our managers know well ahead that, if their business environment changes, they have a well-thought-through set of actions they can take to protect profitability. This contingency planning is particularly helpful in an economic downturn; we are not paralyzed by bad news because we've already planned for it.

Information generated for and during the division planning conferences and financial reviews becomes raw material for the corporate planning conference. We consolidate the data and take a fresh look at the aggregate at our corporate "preplanning conference" about a month before the corporate planning conference, which is held in late September near the start of each fiscal year.

For the preplanning conference, we combine input from the divisions and an analysis of the macroeconomic environment. The annual planning conference itself, which includes corporate management and the top officers of each division, serves primarily as a vehicle for communication. Corporate officers share overall results and communicate the financial plan for the coming year as well as the strategic plan for the next five years. It is an ideal setting for sharing success stories and for challenging conventional wisdom.

So the wheel turns full circle, and we do it all over again. This may sound repetitive and boring. But paying attention to detail makes Emerson successful.

Management Development

We manage organizational needs with the same intensity as we manage our businesses. Emerson's approach to the development of people is founded on two principles: first, the corporation has the obligation to create opportunities for talented individuals; and second, these individuals have the obligation to create their own careers. We provide the opportunities; it's up to our people to take advantage of them.

Our organization planning reflects the critical importance we attribute to human resource issues and our dissatisfaction with standard, off-the-shelf appraisal and compensation packages. We rely primarily on two techniques.

The first is the organization review, which is part of the annual planning and control cycle for each division. This review is an annual half-day meeting centering on basic human resource issues in a division. In preparation, a division will evaluate all managers who are department heads or higher, assessing them according to specific performance criteria. At the meeting, we talk about key managers' length of service in a particular assignment, their potential to move to a more difficult job, and specific responsibilities they might assume.

We try to identify young people who look like "high potentials" and develop plans to offer them a series of assignments that will enhance and augment their skills. Finally, we try to ensure that the division has—or knows how to get—the specific human resource skills it will need to implement its strategy. If a business plans to open an operation in Eastern Europe, for example, we want a demonstration that it has the organization and personnel capacity to succeed there.

The second technique is one we adapted from a major engineering construction firm. We maintain an organization room at headquarters, where we keep personnel charts on every management team in the entire company, corporate and division (see Emerson's personnel profile chart). Every year we update this information, which covers more than a thousand people, on the basis of organization reviews. The charts include each manager's picture and are color-coded for areas such as function, experience, and career path. They provide a powerful visual aid to human resource planning. When a position opens, we know quickly which candidates are most qualified and which people might succeed the candidates we move up.

Both of these organization planning techniques support our focus on follow-through and implementation by letting us know when people should not be moved. For the benefit of implementation, we avoid moving people who are in the middle of important assignments.

Emerson's management personnel come from four sources. The first—and by far the largest

The 5-Back-By-5-Forward Chart Provides 11 Years of P&L Measures*

	Line No.	Actual/Restated					Current Year Expected	Forecast				
		5th PY FY 86	4th PY FY 87	3rd PY FY 87	2nd PY FY 88	Prior Year FY 90	FY 91	Next Yr FY 92	2nd Yr FY 92	3rd Yr FY 94	4th Yr FY 95	5th Yr FY 96
		A	B	C	D	E	F	G	H	I	J	K
Order entries	1142	71,363	77,057	92,716	100,164	126,591	128,247	142,612	157,972	173,743	189,896	207,133
Sales backlog (year end)	1144	13,310	14,051	17,098	16,534	29,334	29,842	31,509	33,082	34,805	36,591	38,363
Net sales	0001	71,163	76,316	89,669	100,728	113,791	127,739	140,945	156,399	172,020	188,070	205,361
Annual growth % – nominal			7.2%	17.5%	12.3%	13.0%	12.3%	10.3%	11.0%	10.0%	9.3%	9.2%
– real							11.3%	7.8%	8.4%	6.7%	6.8%	6.1%
Cost of sales	0009	36,02	39,382	46,478	51,593	60,003	67,651	74,432	82,109	89,966	98,173	106,997
% to sales		51.7%	51.6%	51.8%	51.2%	52.7%	53.0%	52.8%	52.5%	52.3%	52.2%	52.1%
Gross profit	0010	34,361	36,934	43,182	49,135	53,788	60,088	66,513	74,290	82,054	89,897	98,364
% to sales		4.3%	48.4%	48.2%	48.8%	47.3%	47.0%	47.2%	47.5%	47.7%	47.8%	47.9%
SG&A expenses	0011	21,773	22,558	26,246	29,941	32,163	36,150	40,169	44,887	49,714	54,366	59,555
% to sales		30.6%	29.6%	29.3%	29.7%	28.3%	28.3%	28.5%	28.7%	28.9%	28.9%	29.0%
Operating profit	0012	12,5	14,376	16,936	19,194	21,625	23,398	26,344	29,403	32,340	35,531	38,809
% to sales		17.7%	18.8%	18.9%	19.1%	19.0%	18.7%	18.7%	18.8%	18.8%	18.9%	18.9%
Other (inc) / ded.(exl. int.)	0235	423	1,090	1,395	1,232	1,488	1,764	1,766	1,794	1,530	1,438	1,423
Earnings before interst & taxes	0240	12,165	13,286	15,541	17,962	20,137	22,174	24,578	27,609	30,810	34,093	37,386
% to sales		17.1%	17.4%	17.3%	17.8%	17.7%	17.4%	17.4%	17.7%	17.9%	18.1%	18.2%
Interest (income) / expense, net.	0230	(771)	(1,041)	(1,127)	(1,326)	(1,781)	(2,224)	(2,330)	(2,576)	(2,734)	(2,903)	(3,070)
Pretax earnings	0015	12,936	14,327	16,668	19,288	21,918	24,398	26,908	30,185	33,545	36,996	40,456
% to sales		18.2%	18.8%	18.6%	19.1%	19.3%	19.1%	19.1%	19.3%	19.5%	19.7%	19.7%
Income taxes	0016	5,445	6,789	7,788	8,447	9,668	10,551	11,753	13,101	14,497	15,948	17,387
Effective tax rate		42.1%	47.4%	46.7%	43.8%	44.1%	43.2%	43.7%	43.4%	42.2%	43.1%	43.0%
Net earnings	0017	7,491	7,542	8,880	10,841	12,250	13,847	15,155	17,084	19,047	21,048	23,069
% to sales		10.5%	9.9%	9.9%	10.8%	10.8%	10.8%	10.8%	10.9%	11.1%	11.2%	11.2%
Return on total capital	1324	20.4%	19.7%	20.3%	23.6%	23.8%	25.1%	26.1%	28.0%	30.1%	32.0%	33.9%
ROTC excluding goodwill	1323	27.3%	28.0%	27.2%	31.5%	31.5%	32.5%	32.9%	34.7%	36.6%	38.3%	40.2%

✳ In thousands of dollars

group—consists of long-term employees. We believe that operating the company successfully requires management continuity. The typical Emerson division or corporate officer is in his or her late forties and has about 15 years of service. About 85% of promotions come from within Emerson; we believe that this approach to management development contributes to good morale and helps our culture remain cohesive. A second major source of personnel is acquisitions. Many of our division presidents and business leaders joined the company this way; if they stick around—and, in most cases, they do—they tend to thrive in the Emerson system.

Third, every year we recruit 10 to 20 high-potential young people and put them in jobs for which they are not yet qualified. The best make it; the others don't. It's that simple. We carefully track these people, and we retain a majority of them; some have become division presidents and corporate officers. Finally, we hire experienced people for certain jobs because we believe that occasionally bringing in new thinking is very important. We also hire from the outside when we need specialized experience that we do not have internally.

To keep people motivated and involved, we've tried to avoid problems that can paralyze corporations—things like organization charts and large headquarters staffs. We don't have a published corporate organization chart at Emerson. No such piece of paper exists because we want people communicating around plans, projects, and problems, not along organization lines.

I am a believer in small, talented, functionally oriented corporate staffs. But we work hard at not loading up on staff because a large staff creates work. For every person we hire at corporate, we have to hire others in the divisions. A number of years ago, one of the best staff people I've ever known came to me with a list of programs Emerson's operating management wanted to implement and the seven people he would need to hire to help carry out these initiatives. I sat down with him and said, "Let's cut the number of programs in half. How many people do we need to hire now?" He said, "Three." Then I said, "Let's cut the number of programs in half again. Now how many people do we need to hire?" He said, "None." As it turned out, we were able to complete all the programs the businesses wanted with no additions to corporate staff.

There are two lessons to be learned from this story. The first is, don't underestimate the capacity of well-managed organizations to get important things done—less important things probably will not get done, but important things will. And the second is, don't burden very talented staff people with a lot of administrative responsibility; the loss of their productivity is rarely worth the extra capacity the additional people provide.

So, whenever someone considers hiring additional personnel, the presumption is that the answer will be no. In 1991, Emerson has about the same number of people at headquarters—approximately 300—as it did in 1980, when the company was one-fifth its current size.

Emerson's compensation policies help involve and motivate our people. Simply, we pay for results. Each executive in a division earns a base salary and is eligible for a year-end "extra salary," which is based on the performance of the division according to measurable objectives. This extra compensation is calculated as a multiple of an extra salary "centerpoint," which we establish as part of the total compensation target at the beginning of each year. Depending on how well the division performs, the multiplier applied to the centerpoint ranges from 0.35 to 2.0. If the division hits its forecasted target for performance—numbers based on commitments that were mutually agreed on during the annual financial review—the multiplier is 1, and members of the management team will receive their centerpoint extra salary. Doing better increases the multiplier, and doing worse lowers it.

The formula for computer compensation targets changes over time, depending on the needs of the business. At present, sales and margin have a 50% weighting, with inventory turnover, international sales, new product introductions, DSOs (a measure of accounts receivable), and individual management objectives accounting for most of the rest. Other factors that may be included in the formula are geared to the economics of a particular division. In addition, stock options and a five-year performance share plan make up an important part of the total compensation package.

Systematic Process—and Benefits

Emerson's annual planning and control cycles provide important advantages in addition to good

Each Month the President's Operating Report Updates Expected Annual Results*

Line No.		Current Year						Prior Year		% Act/Exp Over/(Under) Prior Year
		Actual or Expected	% Sales	Prior Expected	% Sales	Forecast	% Sales	Actual	% Sales	
	1st Quarter Ending December 31									
1	Intercompany sales	36		36		34		37		-2.7%
2	Net sales	29,613		29,613		29,463		25,932		14.2
3	Gross profit	14,065	47.5%	14,065	47.5%	3,790	46.8%	12,384	47.8%	13.6
4	SG&A expenses	8,312	28.1	8,312	28.1	8,281	28.1	7,650	29.5	8.7
5	Operating profit	5,753	19.4	5,753	19.4	5,509	18.7	4,734	18.3	21.5
6	Earnings before interest & tax	5,280	17.8	5,280	17.8	5,048	17.1	4,343	16.7	21.6
	2nd Quarter Ending March 31									
7	Intercompany sales	5		5		9		56		-91.1%
8	Net sales	33,324		33,324		31,765	46.6%	26,661		25.0
9	Gross profit	15,283	45.9%	15,283	45.9%	14,812	28.1	12,518	47.0%	22.1
10	SG&A expenses	9,301	27.9	9,301	27.9	8,937	18.5	7,395	27.8	25.8
11	Operating profit	5,982	18.0	5,982	18.0	5,875	17.7	5,123	19.5	16.8
12	Earnings before interest & tax	5,785	17.4	5,785	17.4	5,612		4,918	18.4	17.6
	3rd Quarter Ending June 30									
13	Intercompany sales	25		25		39		146		-82.9%
14	Net sales	32,845		32,845		33,424	46.9%	30,678		7.1
15	Gross profit	15,353	46.7%	15,353	46.7%	15,664	28.2	14,310	46.6%	7.3
16	SG&A expenses	8,916	27.1	8,916	27.1	9,399	18.7	8,424	28.5	5.8
17	Operating profit	6,437	19.6	6,437	19.6	6,265	16.9	5,886	19.3	9.4
18	Earnings before interest & tax	6,126	18.7	6,126	18.7	5,645		5,378	18.0	13.9
	4th Quarter Ending September 30									
19	Intercompany sale	94		94		94		25		276.0%
20	Net sales	36,611		36,611		35,722	47.1%	30,521		20.0
21	Gross profit	17,109	46.7%	17,109	46.7%	16,832	28.1	14,576	47.3%	17.4
22	SG&A expenses	10,537	28.7	10,537	28.7	10,029	19.0	8,695	28.5	21.2
23	Operating profit	6,572	18.0	6,572	18.0	6,803	22.8	5,881	19.3	11.7
24	Earnings before interest & tax	6,122	16.7	6,122	16.7	8,146		5,498	18.0	11.3
	Fiscal Year Ending September 30									
25	Intercompany sales	160		160		176		264		-39.4%
26	Net sales	132,393		132,393		130,374		113,792		16.3
27	Gross profit	61,810	46.7%	61,810	46.7%	61,098	46.9%	53,788	47.3%	14.9
28	SG&A expenses	37,066	28.0	37,066	28.0	36,646	28.1	32,164	28.3	15.2
29	Operating profit	24,744	18.7	24,744	18.7	24,452	18.8	21,624	19.0	14.4
30	Earnings before interest & tax	23,313	17.6	23,313	17.6	24,451	18.8	20,137	17.7	15.8
31	Pretax earnings	25,154	19.0	25,154	19.0	24,771	19.0	21,918	19.3	14.8
32	Net Earnings	14,361	10.8	14,361	10.8	14,024	10.8	12,250	10.8	17.2
	Expected 1st Quarter Next Fiscal Year									
33	Intercompany sales	67		65				36		86.1%
34	Net sales	32,830		32,311				29,613		10.9
35	Gross profit	15,142	46.1%	15,143	46.9%			14,065	47.5%	7.7
36	SG&A expenses	9,179	27.9	9,217	28.6			8,312	28.1	10.4
37	Operating profit	5,963	18.2	5,925	18.3			5,753	19.4	3.7
38	Earnings before interest & tax	5,628	17.1	5,619	17.4			5,280	17.8	6.6

✳ **In thousands of dollars**

Emerson's Personnel Profile

Legend

(1) Position Title
(2) Incumbent Manager
(3) Incumbent's Years of Service
(4) Incumbent's Base Salary (in $M)
(5) Incumbent's Performance (see Coding)
(6) Incumbent's Readiness for Promotion
(7) Incumbent's Potential (see Coding)
(8) Replacement's Years of Service
(9) Replacement's Name
(10) Replacement's Degree of Readiness for Promotion
(11) Replacemnt's Base Salary (in $M)

1	Department Head			
2	Jane H. Doe			
3	10		4	75
5		6	2	7

8	7	9	John T. Smith	10	②	11	50
8		9		10	○	11	
8		9		10	○	11	

Performance Coding (Number 5)

(Orange/Gold) — **(1) Outstanding:**
Awarded only to those managers who have made significant, easily recognizable contribution; performance so clearly outstanding as to be obvious to all. Results obtained for in excess of the requirements and indicate early promotion potential. Rating must be supported with specifics.
Note: A "good" manager may have an outstanding year and be rated "outstanding." However, the manager whose performance exceeds requirements but does not make a "significant" contribution should be rated "commendable."

(Green) — **(2) Commendable:**
Performance exceeds expectations. Employee's day-to-day performance "excellent," but no special contribution can be cited.

(Blue) — **(3) Competent:**
Performance completely satisfactory and sufficient in every respect. Meets all end results expected of a seasoned and well-qualified employee.

(Yellow) — **(4) Adequate:**
Results not yet completely meeting requirements of all objectives. Result fall somewhat below expected levels of accomplishment. Need for futher development recognizable, but progress clearly evident.

(Red) — **(5) Needs Improvement:**
Unacceptable performance. Results noticably below the expected level; may have to be replaced if no major improvement.

(White) — **(6) New in Position:**
No evaluation.

Potential Appraisal (Number 7)

(Orange/Gold) — **(1) Outstanding:**
Qualifications for advancing to high-level (executive) position – "high performance"

(Green) — **(2) Exceeds Expectations:**
Clear potential for advancing to high-level position or for substantially increased responsiblities of present level.

(Blue) — **(3) Some Potential:**
Potential to handle expanded responsiblities of present level and perhaps one level highter.

(Yellow) — **(4) Limited Potential:**
At or near capacity in present position or limited due to personal factors.

(Red) — **(5) Not Promotable:**
Below average potential.

(White) — **(6) New in Position:**
Not evaluated

Degree of Readiness Coding (Number 10)

(1) Ready Replacement
Within 30 days (nominal orientation)

(2) Pending Replacement
Within 1 year (after specific experience in select areas)

(3) Future Replacement
Within 3 years (after specific experience or development)

(4) No Movement
No upward movement or increased responsiblities foreseen

plans and tight controls: the process fosters teamwork, communication, understanding of the business and the marketplace, improved management skills, and focus on the fundamentals; it serves as an ongoing mechanism to identify and assess management talent; and it helps assimilate new acquisitions into the company.

The most important benefit, of course, is the bottom line. The proof lies in constantly improving results and long-term, high levels of total return to stockholders. We are opportunists, constantly on the lookout for new management techniques. When a new idea surfaces—such as a method of measuring value creation or focusing, factories or a statistical process control technique—we take a hard look. If we think the idea has merit, we'll adapt it into our management process and operations.

Occasionally, I'm asked whether the Emerson management process is exportable to other companies. The quick answer is yes—it happens every time we make an acquisition—but it is never easy. As has happened here, building a smooth-running operation will entail years of effort and piece-by-piece construction.

The process cannot be installed all at once, nor is it necessarily appropriate for all other companies. But nothing we do has a geographic or national basis; the sources of competitive success are the same in Japan, Germany, the United States, or any other strong manufacturing economy. A company that puts the pieces in place will see progress and results. We believe that planning will pay off if management implements it aggressively, that the results of the process will reward the intensity of the effort, and that people will respect and respond to tough challenges.

One final, basic point: never underestimate the cumulative impact of incremental change and the gathering forces of momentum. When you grind it out a yard at a time, you are in fact moving ahead. I can't say it will work for everybody, but at Emerson we view it as the only way to manage.

Charles F. Knight is the chairman and CEO of Emerson Electric Co., based in St. Louis, Missouri.

Why Measure the CEO's Performance

by C.E. Schneier, R.W. Beatty, and D.G. Shaw

Introduction

A recent survey (Sibson, 1990) of 644 companies found that only 14 percent bother to evaluate their CEO's performance via any systematic process. Evidence also suggests that, for CEOs, negative consequences (i.e., dismissal, drastically lower pay) associated with poor performance are almost non-existent (Jensen and Murphy, 1990). Finally, the relationship between CEO pay and company performance "is weakening" (Crystal, 1990; p. 94). Fifty-five percent of the variance in CEO pay is not accounted for by company performance, size, business risk, company geographic location, or even CEO tenure.

Without relevant measures of performance, clear evidence that there are consequences for poor performance, and a close linkage from performance to pay, shareholders do not know *how* they are paying arguably the person in the most critical position in their companies; *what* they are paying for, and *why*.

The purpose of this paper is to review the state of CEO performance measurement and management (PMM). We argue for a definition of CEO performance that transcends measurement of company financial outcomes. The role of the CEO has broadened. It must include, for example, the inputs to financial outcomes, such as articulating and communicating a vision for the company. We provide a perspective on what type of performance should be measured at the CEO level and how it can be measured. Examples from specific companies are cited

and discussed. A case study of a durable goods manufacturer is provided to illustrate our CEO PMM model.

Why Measure a CEO's Individual Performance?

A CEO's individual behavior influences, but is not the same as, his/her organization's performance. For any organization, the issue is not whether to measure CEO performance. It is what to measure, how to do so, and what to do with the results of the measurement. Financial performance of companies is, of course, always measured and the CEO's performance is hence inferred from financial performance. Organizational performance is not the same as the CEO's (individual) performance. As Figure 1 shows, a distinction can also be made between financial and non-financial performance. The items in the four cells of the figure do, however, influence each other. For example, increasing quality could impact budgets, which in turn could impact returns, which in turn could require elimination of staff, which could, in turn, affect "bench strength."

The interactive nature of Figure 1 would seem to complicate the CEO appraisal picture. However, the real issue for measuring individual CEO performance, as distinct from organizational performance, is to focus on what the CEO individually does or directs to be done or not to be done. Anything on the right side of Figure 1 could be part of the CEO's individual performance. The behaviors/decisions of the individual CEO all affect organization performance, but in varying degrees of immediacy and directness (see Figure 2).

	LEVEL OF PERFORMANCE MEASUREMENT*	
TYPE OF PERFORMANCE MEASURE	**Organizational:** How well the organization performs	**CEO (Individual):** What the CEO does/directs
Direct Financial	EPS ROE Revenue growth	Meet budgets Award stock options Add/eliminate staff
Non-financial	Product quality Customer satisfaction Corporate culture	Set strategic direction Develop "bench strength" Articulate values

* Illustrative, not Exhaustive

Figure 1: Organizational and CEO (Individual) Performance, Mutual Influences

CEO leadership is not the same as management. Organization observers and scholars (e.g., Zalesnik, 1977; Kotter, 1990) have differentiated between leadership and management. Management is rational, systematic, and planning oriented. Data is critical to a manager's success and the manager's many systems provide data. Hence, performance measurement can be a rational and orderly process, as comparing actual to budgeted results. Zalesnik (1977) explains:

> It takes neither genius nor heroism to be a manager, but rather persistence, tough-mindedness, hard work, intelligence, analytical ability and perhaps most important, tolerance and good will (p. 6). The influence a leader exerts in altering moods, evoking

	IMPACT ON ORGANIZATION PERFORMANCE*		
CEO INDIVIDUAL BEHAVIORS/ DECISIONS	**Indirect** (Culture)	**Direct** (Income Statement)	**Direct and Immediate**** (Balance Sheet)
	Communicating vision/values	Increasing prices	Repurchasing shares
	Setting succession criteria	Setting R&D budget	Decreasing dividend
	Personally providing recognition	Downsizing	Acquiring assets

* Illustrative, not Exhaustive
** Typically Involve Board

Figure 2: The Impact of CEO Behavior/Decisions on Organizational Performance

LEADERS	MANAGERS
Set direction	Plan and budget
Align people	Organize and staff
Motivate people	Control and problem solve

Figure 3: What Leaders and Managers Do (After Kotter, 1990)

images and expectations, and in establishing specific desires and objectives determines the direction a business takes (p. 9).

Nadler and Tushman (1990) include more traditional aspects of management (e.g., controlling, rewarding, structuring) in their notion of "transformation" leaders and Kotter (1990) argues that leadership "compliments" management. Based on the above descriptions, few would argue that management is more easily measured than leadership (see Figure 3).

Leadership "counts": organization performance is impacted by individual behavior. Leadership remains one of the most intensively researched areas in the management literature, with data emerging from thousands of experiments (see e.g., Bass,

1989, for a comprehensive review), as well as in-depth observations (see e.g., Vancil, 1987).

One of the most controversial streams of leadership research relates to the issue of whether and to what extent a leader impacts organization performance. A landmark 1972 study (Lieberson and O'Connor, 1972) found that mattered little, and was reinforced by subsequent research (e.g., Salancek and Pfeffer, 1977). Recent studies (e.g., Weimer, 1978; Thomas, 1988) have found that the results of the Lieberson and O'Connor research were artifactual. It is essentially dependent on the order variables were entered into the statistical analysis.

More important, however, for the purpose of this paper, recent work strongly supports the notion that leadership counts. As an individual CEO's decision-

Table 1: A CEO's Vision and Organization Performance: Examples from Some Visible CEOs
(Source: *Business Week*, April 1990)

CEO	COMPANY	VISION	ROE (%)*	INDUSTRY AVERAGE ROE (%)*	PERCENT GREATER THAN INDUSTRY AVERAGE
Bill Marriott	Marriott	Service	21.6%	9.2%	134%
Ray Vogelos	Merck	Invest in R&D for long term	44.8	23.8	88
Jack Welch	GE	Boundaryless, small company culture	18.9	15.8	20
Bob Crandall	AMR	Business traveler service	12.5	7.6	64
J.B. McCoy	BancOne	Customer service; new technology	15.8	10.3	53
Don Kearns	Xerox	Total quality	14.0	8.9	57

CEO RESPONSIBILITY	ILLUSTRATION
Chief Culture Change Agent/Catalyst	Jack Welch, GE "The winners of the nineties will be those who can develop a culture that allows them to move faster, communicate more clearly, and involve everyone in a focused effort to serve ever more demanding customers." (*Fortune,* March 26, 1990)
Chief Values Communicator	Robert Haas, Levi Strauss "It's the ideas of a business that are controlling, not some manager with authority. Values provide a common language for aligning a company's leadership and its people. My personal philosophy is to suboptimize business decisions. When you do that, suddenly the traditional hard values of business success and the nontraditional soft values relating to people start blending." (*Harvard Business Review,* Sep.-Oct., 1990)
Chief Organizational Architect	John Reed, Citicorp "We've come up with a way to deal with Japan, Europe, and North America as a seamless market with no geography, a truly global approach to corporate business." (*Harvard Business Review,* Nov.-Dec., 1990)
Chief Competitive and External Environmental Monitor	Alain Gomez, Thomson "A CEO has no specialty. An organization is neither an island nor inert. It is a living system interrelated to a set of wider systems. The CEO's task is to monitor how the company is attuned to the outside world (and how it is renewing itself internally)." (*Harvard Business Review,* May-June, 1990, parentheses added)
Chief Manager of Systems and Performance	T.J. Rodgers, Cyress Computer "Most companies don't fail for lack of talent on strategic vision. They fail for lack of execution . . . At Cyress, our management systems track . . . performance so regularly and in such detail . . . We don't go over budget—ever. (*Harvard Business Review,* July-August, 1990)

Figure 4: The Emerging Role of the CEO: Some Examples

making style, business strategies, and influence tactics are observed, differences in his or her organization's performance have been seen (e.g., Bennis and Nanus, 1985; Kotter, 1988; Peters and Austin, 1985). CEOs with a clear and well communicated "vision" for their organizations, translated easily into observable behavior, have been able to drive both culture change and resultant financial results (see Table 1).

Visible CEO behavior has a profound impact on the direction their companies take. For that reason, the performance that direction yields, a CEO's individual performance should be assessed.

The CEO role has broadened beyond financial and strategic decisions to chief values communica-tor and culture change agent. There have always been CEOs who set a change agenda. Recently, however, the emphasis on the (large company) CEO as secluded, unapproachable, and steeped in strategic and financial plans is giving way. By their own admission, many CEOs see themselves as strategic actors, not merely strategic thinkers, as architects of cultural change, and as the key single person who must articulate the vision and values of the company (see Figure 4).

Jack Welch of GE, Robert Haas of Levi Strauss, and Rod Canion of Compaq Computer are notable examples. These CEOs view their jobs as setting a cultural and change agenda, not just a strategic and financial one. They are sensitive to the power of

Table 2: Board Member Views of CEO Performance Measurement

	PERCENT OF BOARD MEMBERS RANKING CRITICAL TO CEO SUCCESS
QUALITATIVE PERFORMANCE MEASURES	
Establishing Strategic Direction	86%
Building Management Team	84
Leadership Quality	79
Providing for Succession	75
Implementing Strategy	64
QUANTITATIVE (FINANCIAL) PERFORMANCE MEASURES	
EPS Over Two to Five Years	64
Total Shareholder Return	56
Return on Invested Capital	41
Return Measure Trends	40
Return on Equity	33

* *Boards, Company Performance, and Executive Pay* (Princeton, NJ: Sibson & Company, Inc., 1988), n = 600+.

their behavior and the message it sends. They use their visibility, approachability, and actions to send their message.

For all the talk about keeping stock prices up and quarterly earnings growing, CEOs themselves view other, non-financial issues as important, according both to what they say (e.g., Table 1) and survey results. A 1990 Business International survey found that 53 percent of the CEOs see customer satisfaction as their greatest priority, with being a leader in quality second. In a 1989 Korn/Ferry and Columbia University survey, "strategy formulation" was the top ranking CEO skill needed in the year 2000, with "human resource management" ranking second. The chief concern of CEOs of large companies in a 1990 *Industry Week* survey was "quality."

Our research (see Schneier, 1991) shows that Board members rate the importance of four non-financial aspects of CEO performance above that of any of the financial aspects. Establishing a strategic direction and building a management team are the performance areas most often cited as critical or very critical to evaluating CEOs (see Table 2).

The State of CEO PMM

Is a measurement process used? For most large, publicly-held companies a CEO's performance is not separated from that of the (short-term) financial performance of the organization. The percentage of companies of various industries that do not use a formal appraisal process for their CEOs is very high (see Table 3).

What is measured? Company financial performance seems to be the most common actual CEO performance measure, although Boards and leadership experts (see e.g., Eccles, 1990) argue for a much broader set of measures, as discussed above. In cases where non-financial measures are used, they are not weighted as high as financial measures (see Table 4).

Table 3: Current Practice in CEO Performance Appraisal

INDUSTRY	PERCENT OF COMPANIES WITH NO FORMAL CEO APPRAISAL PROCESS
General Industry	86%
Durable Goods	83
Nondurable Goods	83
Services	91

* *Facts and Issues in Executive Compensation* (Princeton, NJ: Sibson & Company, Inc., 1990), n = 350+.

Some CEOs have made it difficult for their Boards to rely solely on short-term financial objectives as they have gone public with a non-financial agenda. Jack Welch of GE has made public (e.g., Tichy and Charam, 1990) his personal dedication to changing GE's culture via his Work-Out initiative. He has even reported progress on the effort of financial analysts. Jim Robinson of American Express changed the corporate bylaws to name himself Chief Quality Officer. (How effectively Mr. Robinson and the company performs in the quality arena may not easily escape the Board's eye at performance evaluation time.)

The CEO of Whirlpool has an appraisal system that includes both financial and non-financial measures. Scientific Atlanta's CEO has both financial and non-financial objectives on his appraisal screen and is assessed on strategic leadership and organizational changes.

Evidence is available indicating that CEOs could improve on the non-financial components of their job mentioned above. A recent survey reported in the *Wall Street Journal* found that 82% of the CEOs felt they effectively communicated strategy to their executive team. Less than one-third of the COOs and VPs who execute the strategies agreed. Nevertheless, organization-level, financial performance measures are the norm at the CEO level.

Top executives at several companies are evaluated on non-financial performance criteria. Ashard Oil uses safety records, Aluminum Company of America uses environmental sensitivity, and Chemical Bank uses customer rating of service. Reuben Mark of Colgate-Palmolive evaluates his subordinates on individual and qualitative, non-financial measures (e.g., developing woman and minority managers). Constantine Nicandos of Conoco measures environmental action. Paul Allaire of Xerox ties business to customer satisfaction. All these companies' CEOs would have a difficult time ignoring non-financial criteria at their own level, given the data base evaluations their direct reports provide.

Table 4: Weighting of CEO Performance Measures

INDUSTRY	PERCENT OF COMPANIES		
	Financial Measures Weighted More Heavily	Non-financial Measures Weighted More Heavily	Both Weighted Equally
General Industry	70%	2%	28%
Durable Goods	74	0	26
Nondurable Goods	73	5	22
Services	71	13	26

* *Annual Executive Compensation Report* (Princeton, NJ: Sibson & Company, Inc., 1990), n = 350+.

Is performance tied to compensation? A key to effective individual performance measurement systems is a link from the results of the assessment to rewards, including compensation (Lawler, 1990; Beatty and Schneier, 1988). As noted above, most CEO appraisal practices violate this condition (see e.g., Crystal, 1990). However, the relationship between CEO performance and pay requires some explanation. Most of the data supporting a weak relationship between CEO pay and "CEO performance" indicate organization-level and financial performance, not what an individual CEO does or does not do, as the primary performance criterion (e.g., Crystal, 1990; Jensen and Murphy, 1990).

The strongest correlate to pay was organization structure, not performance, in one study of 100 corporations over a four-year time period (Leonard, 1990). Companies with more layers paid more at the top. Crystal (1990) studied company financial performance, stock price volatility, company size, geographic location (i.e., Manhattan-base or not), CEO tenure, and industry pay levels. Unexplained variance in CEO pay was higher than the variance explained by the model's variables noted here. Jensen and Murphy (1990) studied the sensitivity of CEO pay changes on company performance in the 430 largest public corporations and found CEO pay relatively insensitive to changes in company performance.

Why the CEO Individual Performance Measurement Process Is Weak

Qualitative aspects of performance are more difficult to measure. Few would argue that earnings per share is more easily measured than "strategic leadership." Accounting and finance departments must collect and scrutinize financial data regardless of CEO performance measurement considerations, and they have perfected their craft. Companies are novices at measuring the less obvious aspects of performance.

Boards are seldom in a position to observe individual CEO behavior. As the late Harold Geneen of ITT pointed out, "How can they form a fair judgment if nearly all their information comes from the Chief Executive himself?" Particularly for outside directors, they rarely see the CEO in action except at board meetings.

Board members are often CEOs themselves: The fox is guarding the hen house. Confronting the CEO is not part of most Boards' culture or politics. Jensen and Murphy (1990) cite studies showing that in only 20 of 500 cases was a CEO actively fired for poor performance. There was little difference in dismissal percentages between high and low performing companies. Lockheed is an instructive case here. Despite obvious poor corporate performance (i.e., three-year average annual total return to shareholders = -1.9%), directors entrenched management (and themselves) further via stock ownership, a "poison pill" defense, and charter provision changes that "removed all accountability of the management to shareholders" (*Business Week,* April 16, 1990). Lockheed's board consisted of two former CEOs and of course the current CEO. None were likely to criticize the policies they developed. Many board members owe their prestigious and lucrative board seats to their relationship with the CEO, a fact tough to ignore at CEO appraisal time.

Interlocking directorates are commonplace. A CEO appraisal system too candid, too closely tied to a CEO's "style," too subjective, and which ties CEO pay too closely to company performance could be simply too easily copied at the board member's own company. This may not be perceived as a welcomed trend by many CEOs, often beneficiaries of rather insensitive appraisal systems.

Case Study: Measuring the Performance of the Head of a Durable Goods Manufacturer

The Business. A long-standing midwestern business (to be called "Transport"), with overseas operations and revenues in excess of one billion dollars, saw a change in the top job two years ago. Financial performance was unstable during the 1980s, with severe problems occurring in the recession of 1982 and a subsequent downsizing of half the exempt labor force. The late 1980s show Transport's workforce at 1500 exempt and 6000 nonexempt. The business manufactured a limited number of very large, technically complex products for the transportation industry, with one product group accounting for the vast majority of the revenue. Sub-

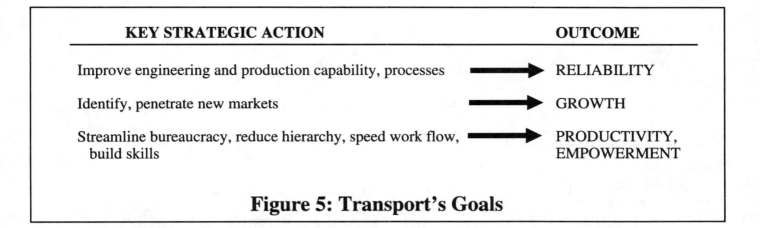

Figure 5: Transport's Goals

KEY STRATEGIC ACTION	OUTCOME
Improve engineering and production capability, processes	→ RELIABILITY
Identify, penetrate new markets	→ GROWTH
Streamline bureaucracy, reduce hierarchy, speed work flow, build skills	→ PRODUCTIVITY, EMPOWERMENT

stantial revenues also came from sales, service, and leasing.

The Business Issues. Over the last decade, Transport, partly because of its cash-poor position and hence low investment in development, lost its once significant technological competitive advantage. In addition, its inability to invest in plant and equipment, its outmoded production facility, and its failure to attract bright new engineering and manufacturing talent, hurt product reliability. Customers, themselves financially pinched, began to look not only at Transport's prices, but also their products' costs over the life of their use. Poor reliability drove those costs beyond that of the competition.

On the human resource side, years of downsizings and inadequate recruiting left the workforce shaken and insecure, with key skills missing. In short, Transport was a classic Rust Belt company with its once glorious past all but forgotten, hanging on to solvency by a thread. High start-up costs deterred competitors, and investors with deep pockets provided Transport much needed capital to continue operations.

The Business Objectives. The new business leader saw cultural, financial, and production imperatives (see Figure 5). The corporate culture was seen as the biggest obstacle to success (see Figure 6) and hence was the first target for change. However, it was obvious that culture change would be slow and customers and investors had little patience.

Developing Transport's Business Leader Performance Measures: Strategy Execution. The business leader saw both financial and non-financial goals as equally important. Relying solely on short-term, financial problem "treatments" (e.g., across-the-board budget cuts) could lower costs but would not fundamentally augment Transport's capability to compete. Longer-term, cultural "cures" had to be addressed as well. In arguing for a balanced approach, the business leader viewed his role as "Chief of Strategy Execution."

Strategy dictated a set of "Business Success Factors"—factors necessary to execute strategy and succeed as a corporation. Because these were at the organizational level, they were appropriate as the

Figure 6: Transport's Culture

THE CURRENT CULTURE	
Heros	Expend enormous effort
Way to Win	Lowered costs, reduced quality
External Customers	The enemy
Internal Customers	Insensitive
Suppliers	Source of cost savings
Reliability	Not at expense of cost
Management Style	Benign neglect, with fiefdoms
Communication	Give orders down, filter messages up
Conflict	Ignore
Cooperation	Within, not across, functions
Authority	Based on position/title
Accountability	To identify scapegoats
Failure	Blame others

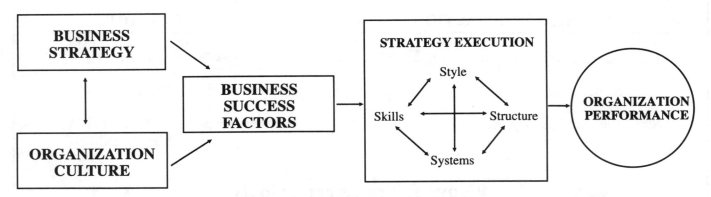

Figure 7: CEO Performance Based on Strategy Execution

performance measures for the business leader. Each of the four areas Transport deemed essential to execute strategy (see Figure 7). The business leader's major objective was to impact the "Business Success Factors" via leading the organization as it executed strategy.

For example, he changed the compensation and performance appraisal systems in the sourcing unit to recognize and reward choosing suppliers based on quality, not the historical measure of lowest price. He redesigned the organization structure to require specialists in engineering and manufacturing to work with those in marketing and sales to assure that what was sold could be built at the right margins and on time. He revamped the delivery system for skills development from training for functional expertise to process-mapping and continuous improvement. He defined the high-trust, candid, high discretion style he wanted, and practiced it himself. The resultant CEO appraisal system from a leadership in strategy execution perspective appears as Figure 8.

How the System Worked. The effectiveness of Transport's business leader PMM system must be evaluated on several levels. First, did individual and organizational performance improve? The business leader's subordinates were given a survey instrument to assess his behavior change. Marked improvements were noted by them after one year. Culture change was assessed via survey and focus groups, with market improvements seen even after 18 months. For example, 59% of those surveyed said they were using the process improvement tools

they had learned. Ratings of the leaders' communication style and effectiveness, as provided by their subordinates, showed considerable improvement. Product and process improvements were also notable. As an illustration, one key product component required an average of 8.6 hours of rework before process improvement and only 2.8 hours after the process was redesigned. Defects in the main motor of the product were reduced by 63%. Service response time went from 75% of responses within 14 days to 75% responses within 72 hours.

A second aspect of the new PMM system was whether the system had a positive impact on other, related systems. Because of the business leader's insistence on using both financial and non-financial performance measures at his level, a heretofore marginal performance management system throughout Transport was revitalized. New performance measures, based on Business Success Factors and the business leader's culture change objectives, were injected into the appraisal criteria of all managers.

These measures provided relevance and specificity, as well as higher performance hurdles for teams and individuals. Knowing the boss is taking appraisal seriously provides needed credibility for the performance management process at all levels. Since the business leader's annual incentive pay was linked to financial and non-financial appraisal criteria, tying performance to pay at all levels was more effective.

Did the system assist the organization in executing its strategy? Transport's organizational-level in-

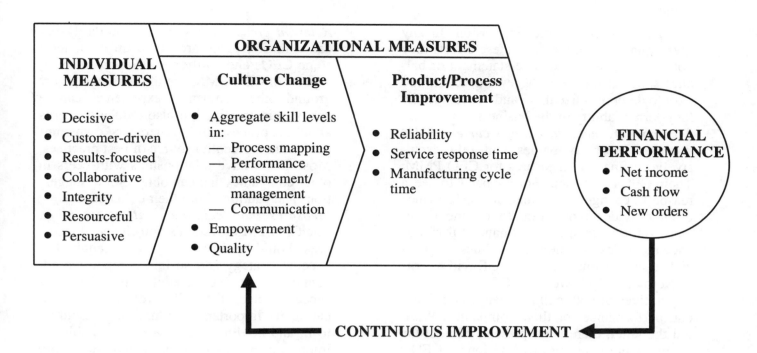

Figure 8: Transport's CEO Performance Measurement and Management System

(Specific measurement targets and methods were developed for each criterion; lists are illustrative, not exhaustive)

dicators in product/process improvement and financial performance indicated successful strategy execution. As Figure 7 shows, strategy execution is made possible by changes in structure, systems, skills, and style. At least in part because the business leader was being measured on a variety of criteria, changes in these four areas were made possible, if not imperative. For example, if the business leader is being measured on improvement and communication, his subordinates' style comes into question. As discussed above, each was changed to some extent, at the initiative of the business leader and others, in order to meet the performance targets.

CEO PMM Systems: Necessary Conditions for Success

At the best-run companies, CEO performance is more than just a numbers game. Companies that have broadened their CEO PMM systems beyond financial criteria have certain characteristics in common. Some of them are no doubt necessary for any PMM system to work, at any level in the company. Others are necessary for organization change to succeed. Still others are unique to the CEO position. Key CEO PMM success factors are:

1. *Board of Directors involvement.* It is the Board, or a Board Committee, that evaluates the CEO. Key Board accountabilities include their: (a) understanding of what should be measured in order for both the CEO and the company to succeed, (b) skill at the PMM process (e.g., data gathering, performance review), and (c) willingness to be candid and constructive regarding how well their CEO is doing.

2. *Linkage of individual CEO performance to consequences.* There is an obvious relationship between CEO individual behavior and performance and a company's performance. At least part of the CEO's rewards would be based on how well he/she does at the critical tasks of, for example, building "bench

strength" and communicating vision. In any given quarter, or even year, these efforts may not show up on the income statement or balance sheet. If they are not rewarded, it is too easy to de-emphasize them and hence hurt the long-term viability of the business.

3. *A compelling need to change current PMM practice.* Most companies still rely exclusively on financial measures for CEO PMM. Their CEOs and their Boards need to see a reason to change. Poor financial performance often provides motivation to fix the financials. Little interest in non-financial performance measures may be seen in times of financial crisis. Visionary CEOs like David Kearns of Xerox and Jack Welch of GE have seen the imperatives of both culture change and financial performance for their companies. Without the latter, there is no present, without the former, there is no future. A visionary CEO's passion, a strategic shift, a merger or acquisition, or a similar need is hence required to changed the CEO PMM status quo.

4. *Specific and quantifiable performance data from multiple sources.* In order to make CEO PMM work using non-financial measures, data must be gathered from subordinates, customers, board members, and other relevant constituents. A typical CEO has a penchant for data. Non-financial CEO measures will have little credibility with the CEO or the Board unless they are more than anecdotal. What evidence is there that strategy and values have been communicated, are understood, and are being acted upon? The CEO PMM system must provide accurate evidence on CEO performance. Without it, the Board will be loathe to confront its CEO or powerless to help him/her improve.

5. *Linkage to PMM systems below the CEO.* PMM at the CEO level is without a context or foundation unless it is carried out at levels below the CEO. To continue the example cited above, developing successors is something not only the CEO but other executives must do as well. If those below the CEO do not develop successors, too few candidates will be available high enough in the hierarchy for the CEO to develop.

6. *Relevant company best practices.* Partly because most Boards are made up of at least some CEOs and partly because non-financial aspects of CEO PMM are often breaking new ground, other companies' experiences can be not only instructive but also reduce concerns about the process. Board members' own companies are a potential source of best practices. Most CEOs have relationships with peers in other companies and can obtain some suggestions and cautions from their colleagues.

7. *Measures that facilitate strategy execution.* The CEO PMM system's non-financial measures should be driven by what is required to execute strategy and sustain competitive advantage. If product reliability is a "business success factor," the CEO's role in communicating its importance, committing resources to it, and holding executives accountable for improving it should be measured. A laundry list of generic executive "traits" is far less credible than a carefully developed, small set of measures that truly drive success in a specific organization. Like all members of organizations, the CEO's performance is continuously evaluated. The key decisions relate to: on what basis, according to what standards, by whom, by what mechanism, and for what purpose. The Board and CEO must ask and answer these questions. Quarterly company financial measures are necessary, but not sufficient. They rarely tell the whole story at the CEO level.

References

Annual Executive Compensation Report (Princeton: Sibson & Company, Inc., 1990).

Bass, B. M., *Stogdill's Handbook of Leadership* (NY: Free Press, 1990).

Beatty, R.W. and C.E. Schneier, "Strategic Performance Management Issues," in R. Schuler and S. Youngblood (eds.), *Personnel and Human Resource Management* (St. Paul: West, 1988), 256-266.

Bennis, W. and B. Nanus, *Leaders* (NY: Harper Row, 1985).

Bere, James F., *The CEO's Job: The Difference Between Motion and Movement* (Chicago: A. T. Kearney, Inc., 1986), 18.

Burchman, Seymour J. and Craig E. Schneier, "Assessing CEO Performance: It Goes Beyond the Numbers," *Directors & Boards*, 13,(2),15.

Crystal, Graef, S., "Seeking the Sense in CEO Pay," *Fortune,* June 5, 1989, 90–104.

Crystal, Graef S., "The Great CEO Pay Sweepstakes," *Fortune,* June 18, 1990, 94–102.

Deutsch, Claudia H., "Using Money to Change Executive Behavior," *New York Times*, May 20, 1990.

Dobrzynski, Judith H. and Eric Schine, "Lockheed's Lesson: It's Open Season on Yes-Man Boards," *Business Week*, April 16, 1990, 25.

Eccles, Robert G., "The Performance Measurement Manifesto," *Harvard Business Review,* January-February 1991, 131–137.

Howard, Robert, "Values Make the Company: An Interview with Robert Haas," *Harvard Business Review,* September-October 1990, 133–144.

Jensen, Michael C. and Kevin J. Murphy, "CEO Incentives—It's Not How Much You Pay, But How," *Harvard Business Review*, May-June 1990, 138–153.

Kotter, J. P., *A Force for Change* (NY: Free Press, 1990).

Kotter, J. P., *The Leadership Factor* (NY: Free Press, 1988).

Kotter, John P., "What Leaders Really Do," *Harvard Business Review*, May-June 1990, 103–111.

Lawler, E. E., *Strategic Pay* (SF: Jossey Bass, 1990).

Leonard, J. S., "Executive Pay and Firm Performance," in R.G. Ehrenberg (ed.), *Do Compensation Policies Matter?* (Ithaca: ILR Press, 1990), 13–29.

Lieberson S. and J. F. O'Connor, "Leadership and Organization Performance," *American Sociological Review*, 37, 1972, 117–130.

Nadler, D. A. and M. L. Tushman, "Beyond the Charismatic Leader," *California Management Review*, 33, Winter, 1990, 77–97.

"Pay Stubs of the Rich and Corporate," *Business Week*, May 7, 1990, 56, 108.

Peters, T. and N. Austin, *A Passion for Excellence* (NY: Random House, 1985).

Rodgers, T. J., "No Excuses Management," *Harvard Business Review*, July-August 1990, 84–98.

Salanick, G. R. and J. Pfeffer, "Constraints on Administrator Discretion," *Urban Affairs Quarterly*, 12, 1977, 475–498.

Schneier, Craig E., "Executing Strategy: The New Battleground in Business Competition," in C. E. Schneier (ed.), *Human Resource Strategies for the 1990's* (NY: American Management Association, 1990), 115.

Schneier, Craig E., "Measuring and Assessing Top Executive Performance," in M. Rock and G. Berger (eds.), *Compensation Handbook*, 3rd ed. (NY: McGraw Hill, 1990), 521–532.

Thomas, Alan Berkeley, "Does Leadership Make a Difference to Organization Performance?," *Administrative Science Quarterly*, 57, 1988, 388–400.

Tichy, Noel and Ram Charan, "Citicorp Faces the World: An Interview with John Reed," *Harvard Business Review*, November-December 1990, 135–144.

"Today's Leaders Look to Tomorrow," *Fortune*, March 26, 1990, 30–36.

Vancil, R. F., *Passing the Baton* (Boston: Harvard Business School Press, 1987).

Webber, Alan M., "Consensus, Continuity, and Common Sense: An Interview With Compaq's Rod Canion," *Harvard Business Review,* July-August 1990, 115–123.

Weiner, N. and T. A. Mahoney, "A Model of Corporate Performance as a Function of Environmental, Organizational, and Leadership Influences," *Academy of Management Journal*, 24, 1981, 453–470.

Zaleznik, Abraham, "Managers and Leaders: Are they Different?," *Harvard Business Review*, May-June 1977, 112.

The Executive Appraisal Paradox

by Clinton O. Longenecker, the University of Toledo, and
Dennis A. Gioia, Pennsylvania State University

Executive Overview

Executives perform the most uncertain, unstructured, ill-defined, and often the most important work in organizations. Common wisdom would suggest that people doing such jobs should be the ones supplied with the most effective feedback about their performance, simply because good, informative feedback helps them cope with the acknowledged demands of executive work. Therefore, one would expect the level of performance feedback to rise as one progresses up the organizational hierarchy. We found almost exactly the opposite to be true in many companies. Paradoxically, the higher one rises in an organization the less likely one is to receive quality feedback about job performance. In particular, we found that the executive review and appraisal process was often infrequently and haphazardly done, and that the underlying reasons for the poorly-conducted appraisals were traceable to a number of fallacious assumptions or myths about the nature of executives and their work. These myths not only hindered executives in the performance of their jobs, but also complicated their personal and professional development. In this article we identify and discuss six prevalent myths that contribute to the paradox of executive appraisal. We then offer a number of recommendations and suggestions that not only serve to counter the consequences of these myths, but also help to lay the groundwork for conducting constructive and comprehensive executive appraisals.

Article

"It just doesn't make any sense. The higher you climb the ladder in this organization, the less chance you have of getting feedback about your performance. The working rule of thumb is: 'the farther up you go, the stranger things get,' especially in the way are reviewed and rewarded...We seem to have time for everything else, but not time to give our top people the kind of reviews they need to help them develop."

This observation from an executive-level controller who had been with his company for 17 years is representative of the type of performance feedback received by most of the executives we have interviewed. With each promotion, reviews become less frequent, systematic, informative, and useful. At the executive level, there often is virtually no regular performance feedback other than superficial praise or criticism for some crisis.

The prevalence of this pattern suggests an apparent paradox in performance appraisal, i.e.: The higher that managers rise in an organization, the lower the likelihood that they will receive quality feedback on their job performance. For some obscure but apparently pervasive reason, executive appraisal seems to have become a taboo topic in many organizations.[1] Executives who arguably need more performance information because they are doing the most uncertain, unstructured, and generally the most important work in the organization, tend to receive the least formal feedback.

To some, this makes perfect sense. After all, the reasoning goes, people who are capable of making it to the top should not need frequent reassurances about their performance. They should be self-directed and self-reliant individuals with a high tolerance for ambiguity who can also keep their fingers on the pulse and read performance indicators as well as their bosses.[2] Therefore, senior-level executives should not need to waste time on a "nuisance task" like the appraisal of subordinate executives. It is inefficient, unnecessary, and maybe even demeaning to do so.

Despite the common belief that executives, of all people, should be able to fend for themselves, this view does not coincide with findings that indicate that executives want structured feedback as much as anybody else in the organization. It seems, instead, that executive-level people doing ambiguous jobs want unambiguous feedback about their performance of those jobs.[3] Given the typical level of competence of such executives, it would be shortsighted to argue that these people are somehow inadequate for their positions simply because they have a need to know how superiors perceive their performance. *Everybody* wants to know how he or she is doing, perhaps *especially* upper-level executives. Yet, the informal taboo against executives seeking out constructive feedback (and thus implying that they are somehow deficient) hinders even the best executives in their professional development.

Organizations currently spend millions of dollars on executive development and performance improvement programs.[4] Because executive work is becoming more complex, it would seem reasonable to try to design increasingly complex methods to boost executive performance. Our research, however, suggests that such a conclusion could be premature; in fact, just the opposite might be true.

> *Despite the accelerating pace of change and the burgeoning demands of executive work, a good vehicle for developing executives is already in place in virtually every organization, although it is likely to be myopically overlooked or woefully under-utilized. That vehicle is a properly conducted executive appraisal and review process. Although many organizations provide for such a process it is typically executed poorly.[5]*

Most books and articles either explicitly or implicitly treat appraisal as a lower-level, or at best a middle-management phenomenon.[6] Research on appraisal abounds, yet there is little consideration of executive appraisal. Despite well-worn maxims like "performance appraisal must start at the top,"

organizations appear to be ignoring their own folk wisdom.

There are a number of fallacies associated with executive appraisal that contribute to executives' failure to receive the performance planning, review, and feedback that they want. Our research suggests that the widespread disappointment with the quality of executive appraisals is traceable to a series of dysfunctional beliefs or myths surrounding the process. Taken together, they contribute to the paradox that those who could most use performance feedback to enhance their effectiveness are often the least likely to get it.

In this article we identify and discuss six prevalent myths that contribute to the paradox of executive appraisal. We then offer a number of recommendations and suggestions that not only serve to counter the consequences of these myths, but also help to lay the groundwork for conducting constructive and comprehensive executive appraisals.

Studying Executive Appraisal Through Depth Interviewing

We conducted in-depth, semi-structured interviews with eighty-four executives from eleven major organizations in manufacturing and service industries. All were managers of managers who averaged more than twenty-three years of corporate experience and fifteen years of executive experience. All together the executives had performance appraisal experience in more than 200 organizations during their careers. Twelve different functional areas were represented, including operations, marketing, finance, accounting, MIS, and human resources. All the organizations in the study had formal performance appraisal programs that included rater training and all (ostensibly) had requirements for the annual review of employees.

The tape-recorded interviews averaged one and a half hours each, and were designed to allow executives to discuss freely their perceptions and experiences with appraisals as both rater and ratee. The findings, observations, and recommendations in this article are based on a systematic qualitative content analysis of 118 hours of tape-recorded transcripts. The analysis was designed to group related observations of statements made by the executives. In stage one of the analysis, directly-quoted statements from each interview were transcribed onto cards. The transcription process yielded over 1700 cards with each card containing one statement or observation on a given topic. In stage two, each card was read by several judges and sorted into categories which dealt with aspects of executive appraisal (inter-rater reliability, 0.87). More than two thirds (or sixty-eight percent) of the executives had to address the same issue before it would be labeled as a finding. An additional step was used to enhance the reliability and validity of the research. In stage three, two research assistants independently assigned cards to the categories of the findings. They then tallied the number of cards in each classification group that supported the finding that had been identified in the second stage of the analysis. Overall inter-rater reliability for this step was 0.89.

The findings, which we came to label as myths, following the participants' own labeling, attempt to summarize the issues raised by these executives concerning their experiences with the executive appraisal process. Because this approach generated such rich detail and expressive content, we have included representative quotes, vignettes, and experiences from the participating executives.

Myths About Executive Performance Appraisal

The executive appraisal paradox is rooted in a series of dubious beliefs about executives and the nature of their work. A senior vice president made this telling observation: "Actually, very few managers fail because they lack technical skills or motivation. Rather, it usually has to do with the lack of a clear sense of direction and good feedback from above. There are a lot of myths floating around about how you manage a manager, and the way high-level people are reviewed is the obvious case in point." These myths have detrimental effects not only on subordinate executives and their aspirations, but also on senior-level executives who are responsible for their subordinates' performance. The myths turn out to be surprisingly common.

Myth #1: Executives neither need nor want structured performance reviews

If there is a central myth that leads to a lack of executive-level feedback, this is it. It is clear from our interviews that top-level executives often believe that their immediate subordinates have neither the necessity or desire for structured performance re-

views. This belief stems from a widely shared premise that the higher an individual's level in the organization, the lower *should be* the need for feedback. Given the competence of the people occupying executive-level slots, there is an implicit validity to this assumption. The paradox is that this is not the way the executives see it. *Every* executive we interviewed dismissed this common belief and said that systematic feedback in some form was crucial. As a division vice president put it: "Everybody wants regular and detailed information on how they are doing and what the boss thinks—good or bad—including executives. It's the number one thing that is going to help them grow."

A favorite, recurrent saying that we heard was "Any executive worth his [her] salt knows what the job entails." While this is true to a point, it is often somewhere short of where executives are comfortable and on track toward top-level development. The net effect of the assumption that executives neither want nor need formal reviews is to put the onus for professional development solely on the subordinate executive. This strategy is little more than a variant of another folk belief; that if you want someone to learn how to swim, throw them in at the deep end. In a high cost, high stakes game such as executive performance and development, that belief contributes to the failure of good people.

Myth #2: A formal review is beneath the dignity of an executive

A belief seems to have evolved that when one reaches the executive level a rite of passage is achieved, and one graduates beyond the obligation to endure formal performance reviews. Top-level executives sometimes see it as a symbol of status. To be subjected to a formal review is taken as a sign that one is still on professional probation. The fallacy here is the presumption that appraisal is necessarily a demeaning and aversive experience that managers mercifully can outgrow. Properly framed and executed, of course, an executive review can provide vital information instead of emotional tribulation and the perception of a degrading experience.

Naturally, appraisal at any level can produce anxiety. Some executives noted to us that there is both a "need to know, and a fear of knowing," tacitly acknowledging that just like everyone else, executives have anxieties about being appraised. *But,* they insisted that their need to know far outweighed their fear. They preferred to know where they stood.

Myth #3: Top-level executives are too busy to conduct appraisals

This myth came up as a recurring "excuse" by many of the interviewed executives. ("Well, I mean to do it, but it always gets cycled to the bottom of the 'To Do' list. You understand.") Because of executives' full schedules, this reason has a surface credibility. The excuses, however, soon turned into a suspicious litany, and we eventually got the impression that "too busy" was a smokescreen for some less mundane reason. A better translation of this myth, as related by a candid veteran, is: "Executive appraisal is a waste of time better spent on other things, like putting out fires." It was soon revealed that top-level executives responsible for conducting these reviews often believed that they were not worth doing, and therefore said that they did not have the time. The appropriate rejoinder came from an executive who had been burned by this attitude: "It seems like we have time for lots of things that are a lot less important than talking about improving performance and executive development. There should always be time for a process that contributes to higher performance and productivity, and paradoxically, the saving of time."

Myth #4: A lack of feedback fosters autonomy and creativity in executives

Another less prevalent, but certainly not rare, belief is that too much feedback and direction short-circuits the development of autonomy and creativity. Upper-echelon executives sometimes believe that withholding information builds character and forces young executives to figure out what information they need and what actions to take. So, they intentionally forego appraisal in the hope of fostering innovation. This approach to executive development is attractive because it affirms the admired notion of "pulling yourself up by your bootstraps." To some degree it can facilitate autonomy and creativity. There is ample evidence, however, that the same goal can be accomplished, and faster, with good feedback.

A general manager's recent history provides an instructive example. His excellent track record led to his promotion to general manager of a new division. In his previous position he received adequate performance feedback for his managerial job; as an executive, he received none. His new boss told him that part of his "executive seasoning" was to be creative and figure out what to do on his own. His boss also said that he was "philosophically opposed to the idea of appraising or second-guessing executives." Yet, in a little more than a year, a clash over marketing strategies emerged, because each was making different assumptions about the division's direction. Since he had never received any assessment of his ideas, plans, and goals the general manager was ignorant of the divergent strategies. His boss had second-guessed him. The general manager lost the unequal contest and was soon transferred. His comment: "A lack of performance feedback keeps people in the dark about how others view their performance. That breeds doubt and frustration, and maybe worse, allows little problems to fester into big ones."

Myth #5: Results are the only basis for assessing executive performance

It is an article of faith in many organizations that "results are the bottom line in measuring executive effectiveness." Therefore, department or division numbers should serve as surrogate measures of individual performance. By extension, executives should know how well they are doing simply by looking at the performance numbers for their operatio*ns*.

> *A strict results orientation for executives has a seductive simplicity about it, which is undoubtedly part of its attraction. But, although the bottom line is not an unreasonable standard to use for the evaluation of executive performance, it also is not a complete standard. It clearly focuses attention on job outcomes, yet it simultaneously ignores job process, which can be equally important to executive success.*

Exclusive use of a results-only standard does indeed weed out some low-performers, but it also compromises the development of other promising people who simply need feedback on process issues to succeed. As a division manager put it: "Sure, you have to get results; that's why we're in business. But, you also need to look at the road you took to get the results. You need feedback on process and style and the intangibles that you can't quantify. The hell of the matter is that the results-only evaluation is easy; it's also a cop out." As another VP observed, "Isolating on results is a formula for long-term trouble."

We heard several variations on the story of executives who made their numbers, but ultimately at significant cost to the company, and even to themselves. One example from the service industry concerned an executive who used hard-nosed methods to build his track record as a top corporate trouble-shooter, one who could turn divisions around. Recently, however, although he did shore up the bottom-line performance of one division, his severe tactics and caustic style nearly incited an employee rebellion. As a result he was called to headquarters and given an ultimatum to "improve your human relations skills right now, or else." It was the first time he had received any formal feedback other than praise. He currently is trying to recover from a derailment that he feels could (and should) have been avoided.

Myth #6: The comprehensive evaluation of executive performance simply cannot be captured via formal performance appraisal

Executive work often has an aura of mystery about it. Intuition, gut feelings, flashes of insight, and other non-measurable attributes are hallmarks of high-performing managers. Because these intangibles are seen as important facets of managerial work, top executives sometimes want the evaluation of executive performance to be considered as an intangible domain also ("I can't really tell you what makes a good executive, but I know it when I see it."). It is true that executive work is notably more ambiguous and uncertain than operational work, but it does not necessarily follow that standards for appraising that work cannot be developed.

Although it is difficult to demystify the way that effective executives actually work, it is important to try to de-mystify the standards for *judging* executive work. Flexible, but nonetheless specific, guidelines can be developed. Executives need to believe that some accepted ways of assessing their performance apply, or there will be a perception that rewards are not based on actual accomplishment. Rather, they are assumed to turn on some hidden, subjective, or even political, considerations that are seldom articulated.

A disgruntled victim of ambiguous performance standards recalled his exasperation: "You never really knew where you stood. You could do exactly what you thought you were supposed to do and get burned, or hit the right number in one column, screw up the rest, and be a saint. Performance at the upper levels *is* subjective, but sometimes it seems like it's kept that way for some suspicious reasons." In general, we found that performance standards were considered too poorly defined to be useful by the executives who had to live with them.

These six myths contribute to the paradox of executive appraisal. As a consequence of these dubious reasons for avoiding executive appraisal, we see organizations that simply (and incredibly) do no appraisal at all. Many others that conduct reviews do so half-heartedly, so they end up with a list of appraisal characteristics that reads like a bad script: the reviews tend to be infrequent, irregular, informal, and rushed. They also tend to lack specificity and fail to address the issue of performance planning adequately. As a result, they leave people foundering in a sea of uncertainty, often at a time when harried executives would very much appreciate any useful information they could get about their job performance.

Exhibit 1. Myths About Executive Performance Appraisal

Myth #1: Executives neither need nor want formal performance reviews

Myth #2: A formal review is beneath the dignity of an executive

Myth #3: Top-level executives are too busy to conduct appraisals

Myth #4: A lack of feedback fosters autonomy and creativity in executives

Myth #5: Results are the only basis for assessing executive performance

Myth #6: The comprehensive evaluation of executive performance simply cannot be captured via formal performance appraisal

Debunking the Myths: Doing Effective Executive Appraisal

It is not possible to design a "perfect" or "ideal" performance appraisal program. Although there are a variety of approaches, all have some advantages and disadvantages for the rater, the ratee, or the organization.[7] For any appraisal program to be of benefit to all parties, however, some important items must be in place. These include clearly articulated performance goals and standards, ongoing performance feedback, and an interactive feedback session between superior and subordinate.[8] Without these factors the benefits of the appraisal process are subverted. Although executive appraisals may differ in character, they do not differ in principle.

Given the findings that emerged from this study, there is a fair amount of room for improvement in the process. Because executive reviews are often poorly done, it may be suggested that exiting systems simply be scrapped in favor of installing some radical new system. (Or as one VP phrased it: "What do you want me to do? Call in an air strike and start over?") On the contrary, and perhaps paradoxically, in trying to right the wrongs associated with executive appraisal, there seldom is a need to install yet another new program to remedy an organizational problem. Every organization we studied had a performance review system already in place with some of the necessary characteristics of a potentially effective process. The main issues, however, have more to do with the assumptions (myths) that get in the way of using the existing system than with radically restructuring it.[9]

Organizations with effective executive appraisal almost invariably cite the involvement of top management as *the* dominant factor in the success of the process. Top managers need to articulate and enact the practices discussed below because senior executives are the key players in institutionalizing good executive appraisal processes as part of the organization's culture.

1. *Conduct a structured, systematic executive appraisal process*

Because of the misguided assumption that higher-level executives neither want nor need systematic reviews, executives and their organizations frequently translate this erroneous belief into an error of omission and make no provision for executive reviews at all. Of all the possible mistakes, this is perhaps the most serious. A senior VP with a reputation for developing managerial talent said succinctly: "That assumption can kill you. A formal, systematic approach is a prerequisite—formal, so that the process is taken seriously by all parties; systematic, so that it provides the executive with useful feedback and guidance." All effective executive appraisal programs share several central characteristics that provide for: 1) performance planning, 2) on-going informal feedback about performance, 3) periodic formal (written) reviews in conjunction with face-to-face appraisal interviews, and 4) established links between performance and rewards. The real trick is in adapting these fundamental features to the needs of individual executives. A manufacturing operations VP takes a broad view: "In many cases it means linking executive performance planning directly to strategic planning and the achievement of corporate goals."

2. *Incorporate performance planning, which is essential at the executive level, into the executive review and appraisal process*

Executive performance planning amounts to strategic planning for people. It is crucial for executives, especially as it relates to discussions of goals and responsibilities in the modern managerial environment of rapid change. A senior-level executive argued that "the more dynamic the job, the more you need good performance planning; it helps side-step activity traps that tend to capture executive time at the expense of effective action." A former director of the now defunct Coleco Industries specifically cited Coleco's failure to provide executive performance planning as one of the factors in its demise. Ideally, the process of performance planning should lead to a document specifying both parties' understandings about directions and priorities. A grassroots implementation of executive performance planning should include such actions as:

- Developing a flexibly framed description of the executive's mission, primary responsibilities, and secondary duties;
- Clarifying divisional/departmental goals and the executive's role in accomplishing those goals;
- Discussing management style issues as well as strategies for goal accomplishment;

• Agreeing upon what constitutes "successful" performance, given current strategic and operational goals.

A key issue for executives in this study was the need for communicating and clarifying expectations. An executive performance planning discussion needs to address more than just quantitative and financial objectives and P/L statements. These more broadly focused discussions reduce the likelihood of false starts, displaced goals, or the use of unarticulated criteria to evaluate performance. Good performance planning also helps take the trauma out of evaluating the executive's performance later, because it creates a mutually agreed-upon basis for his or her review, appraisal, and future management.

3. Make performance review and appraisal an ongoing process

Executives' descriptions of the ambiguity created by a lack of regular performance feedback included phrases like "never knowing where you stand," "being 'mushroom managed' (kept in the dark and fed manure)," and the old Watergate standard, "being left to twist slowly in the wind." These executives wanted on-going, specific feedback beyond a nominal yearly review. Instead, they were receiving a steady diet of executive-style feedback—either none at all, or that which was too general to be useful. Our participants provided a surprisingly short list of suggestions for senior executives as a way of giving meaningful, timely performance feedback to junior executives:

• Make notes on critical instances of effective and ineffective performance on the basis of personal, "hands-on" observation;

• Use the MIS to obtain regular financial and productivity indicators;

• Check the executive's performance with clients, customers, or other departments, to assess external relation and teamwork abilities;

• Use subordinate appraisals of executives to provide insight into management style strengths and weaknesses.

Of these, subordinate appraisal is probably the least used, yet it often tells the most about an executive's human resources management skills and operational process abilities; thus, it can provide an additional, triangulating view on executive performance.[10] A number of firms have implemented some form of (usually anonymous) subordinate input, either by making the process a required part of managerial appraisal or by conducting periodic surveys.

Once relevant performance data is obtained, however, the executives suggested regularly using mini-appraisals. One of the most frequently cited concerns of neophyte and even journeyman executives was the fear of taking executive action not understanding that their actions were considered to be a mistake by superiors.

Making mistakes might be acceptable; not knowing that they are mistakes is not. Naturally, the ambiguous executive environment breeds situations where criteria for such judgments are not easily established. And that is exactly the reason that executives want regular feedback, so that they can get on track, stay on track, or if necessary, get back on track.

A Group VP argued that "without giving people on-going feedback, it is easy for them to be derailed and not even realize it." Mini-appraisals monitor goals in light of changes in the operating environment, insure that they match corporate strategy, and provide corrective action prior to crisis. Use of the mini-appraisal is thus a "preventive maintenance" technique.

4. Focus on process as well as outcomes during the executive review

Bottom line issues are obvious candidates for discussion during a review, but according to the executives in this study, many executive appraisers never get beyond this topic. Process issues are more difficult to address, but are hallmarks of good executive mentors. Mentoring discussions about leadership style, organizational savvy, managing the ambiguity inherent in the job, and the many intangibles that go into executive work are all appropriate topics for an executive review (and also distinguish it from lower-level reviews). Executive work is not made up entirely of goal accomplishment, but also of learning *how* to accomplish goals and be effective.

A shipping firm executive captured his personal credo in the phrase: "You get what you measure." And we might add: "You measure what you value." If the organization values short-term results, that is what it will measure and get. If it values executive development, a different emphasis emerges. A good way of articulating this issue is in terms of "ends" and "means." Most would agree that successful performance depends on using appropriate means to achieve desired ends. Yet, most would also agree that recent American business history has been dominated by a selective focus on ends (with some notably deficient outcomes compared to international competitors who pointedly focus on means). Good executive development demands a significant re-orientation toward the valuation and measurement of executive process issues like communication, team-building, innovation, quality, mentoring, and subordinate development, as well as an emphasis on these issues as part of corporate culture.

In light of the swing toward strict results-based evaluative standards in the last decade, we recognize that a recommendation to focus more strongly on process issues may seem retrogressive. Yet the recommendation is based on the views of executives who have been living with the negative effects of results-only systems for years now. Perhaps it is time to ask if the pendulum has swung too far, and to consider a re-emphasis on executive process and style. Ironically, the focus on the bottom line tends to inhibit development of the ability to achieve the long-term bottom line results that everyone so badly wants. Striking a balance between means and ends, or processes and outcomes, seems a wiser strategy.

5. *Be as specific and thorough as possible in the executive appraisal*

The executive appraisals described in our interviews were typically informal, lacked specifics, were often hurriedly done, and were filled with nebulous language and non-performance issues ("Your style needs some polish"; "Your financials could be better"; "People have concerns about your loyalty to the division").

The executives who participated in our studies were, as expected, performing the kind of unstructured work typically associated with their positions. Yet, they said that they preferred to receive structured reviews of their performance despite the unstructured nature of their work. In part, this preference was expressed as a way to avoid what one described as a "non-review review"—one that was so informal and unstructured that the executive was not even aware that his review had taken place. A

project director told the story of a boss who once asked him how things were going, talked for five minutes about general issues concerning the job, and the next morning left the director's appraisal on his desk with a Post-it note saying "Please sign and return." That sequence ostensibly constituted his appraisal for the year.

Executive superiors were frequently portrayed as reluctant and uncomfortable giving appraisals and reticent in offering specific feedback on how to improve performance beyond the financials. Appraisals can be made more effective if the eclectic suggestions derived from the firms in our study are implemented:

- Avoid using a standard rating form (unless it includes factors that closely approximate the executive's actual work). Forms tend to force appraisals into categories that are not necessarily appropriate for executive performance;

- Have subordinate executives provide written self-appraisals focusing on achievements, areas needing improvement, and plans for development, to supplement (not substitute for) the senior executive's impressions;

- Use previously agreed-upon responsibilities, goals, and processes as the basis for the formal review;

- Focus the review both on specific, short-run goals and on long-run issues such as the processes used to achieve results;

- Avoid nebulous language when giving performance feedback; avoid political and/or non-performance issues as much as possible;

- Strengthen the link between performance and reward by citing specific reasons for any merit raises, bonuses, or perks;

- Allow time for the junior executive to air concerns and to engage in personal development discussions. The review is a forum for developing a blueprint for the coming year.

Whither Executive Appraisal?

A recent survey of more than 400 managers showed low levels of satisfaction with the review and feedback that they were receiving. Only twenty-five percent said that they were satisfied with the review itself; only twenty-seven percent were satisfied with the amount of feedback; and only thirty-four percent thought that the quality of feedback was adequate.[11] These kinds of statistics are telling, especially because they apply to one of the organization's most critical groups—its executives.

Although executive appraisal is a challenging and frequently delicate proposition, it is clear that executives benefit from systematic reviews. Appraisal has long been shown to be effective for letting people know where they stand, improving productivity, enhancing growth and development, and making training, promotion, and compensation decisions. There is no reason why, with appropriate adjustments, the same should not apply in principle to executives. Some of those adjustments might also involve providing financial incentives and rewards for senior executives who successfully aid their junior proteges via good review practices and who, by example, act as good role models for encouraging effective appraisal and feedback throughout the organization.[12] There is evidence from this project that the implementation of good appraisal practices is facilitated when senior executives are expected to demonstrate effectiveness in reviewing, appraising, and developing junior executives, *and* are rewarded for it.

Executive appraisal can help decrease executive job-role ambiguity despite the unavoidably ambiguous nature of executive work. It can be the key vehicle for communicating the firm's culture, values, and operating philosophy. It also gives executives a better feel for the firm's bigger picture, their goals within that picture, and their required actions in achieving those goals. In some significant sense executive appraisal might even be viewed as a fairly painless change intervention that orients the organization toward a concern with the professional growth and development of its executives.[13]

In light of the issues identified here, treating executive appraisal as an organizational taboo is simply short-sighted and dysfunctional. Perhaps one of the executives in our studies offered the most appropriate concluding comment on the paradox of executive appraisal:

"Many of us at the top are guilty of not focusing on what we are trying to do and how we are trying to do it. We can't plan for our executives' performance and we don't give or get regular feedback. We seem to ignore the people in the organization who could do the most with good personal performance information. In doing so, we perpetually make trouble for ourselves, and I really don't know why."

Endnotes

[1] See, for example, S.C. Aggarwal and V.S. Aggarwal, "The Control Gap at the Top," *Business Horizons,* May-June 1985, 27-31 for a discussion of the problems associated with not providing executives with performance feedback. Also see J.P. Kotter's book *The Leadership Factor* (New York: The Free Press, 1988), for a discussion of how appraisals are both used and neglected in the managerial ranks in a variety of U.S. organizations.

[2] In the article "What Makes a Top Executive," *Psychology Today,* 1983, 26-31, M.W. McCall, Jr. and M.M. Lombardo make a strong case based on interviews with executives that self-reliance and a high tolerance for ambiguity are the earmarks of executive level personnel. In addition, H. Vyterhoevens' "General Manager in the Middle," *Harvard Business Review,* September-October 1989, 136-145 suggests that top managers often do not know whether their performance is on track based on their superior's assessment.

3 For a detailed discussion of executive frustration with the appraisals they receive see C.O. Longenecker and D.A. Gioia, "Neglected at the Top: Executives Talk About Executive Appraisal," *Sloan Management Review,* Winter 1988, 41-47. Executives cited extreme frustration with the lack of structured feedback they receive on their performance.

[4] See R.H. Waterman, Jr.'s *The Renewal Factor: How the Best Get and Keep the Competitive Edge* (New York: Bantam Books, 1987) for a discussion of the approaches that organizations are using to enhance managerial performance.

[5] For an illustration of the problems of properly executing managerial appraisal see "Measuring the Unmeasurable: Setting Standards for Management Performance," by G. Ordiorne in *Business Horizons,* July-August 1987, 69-76 and H.J. Bernardin and L.A. Klatt, "Managerial Appraisal Systems: Has Practice Caught Up to the State of the Art?" *Personnel Administrator,* November 1985, 79-86.

[6] See A.M. Mohrman, Jr., S.M. Resnick West, and E.E. Lawler, *Designing Performance Appraisal Systems* (San Francisco: Jossey-Bass, 1989) and H.J. Bernardin and R.W. Beatty, *Performance Appraisal: Assessing Human Behavior at Work* (Boston: Kent, 1984) for these perspectives.

[7] For a discussion of these advantages and disadvantages see the well-known article by M. Beer, "Performance Appraisal: Dilemmas and Possibilities," *Organizational Dynamics,* 1981, 24-36.

[8] See L.R. Gomez-Mejia, R.C. Page, and W.W. Fornow, "Improving the Effectiveness of Performance Appraisal,"

Personnel Administrator, 1985, 30(1), 74-82 and E.E. Lawler, A.M. Mohrman, & S. Resnick, "Performance Appraisal Revisited," *Organizational Dynamics,* Summer 1984, 20-35.

[9] For a discussion of the importance of the appraisal process being viewed as a *system* instead of an event see M. Beer, et al., "A Performance Management System: Research, Design, Introduction, and Evaluation," *Personnel Psychology,* 1987, 31, 505-536.

[10] For two excellent discussions on the use and benefits of subordinate appraisal see H. Bernardin, "Subordinate Appraisal: A Valuable Source of Information About Managers," *Human Resource Management,* 1986, 25(3), 421-439 and H. Bernardin and R. Beatty, "Can Subordinate Appraisal Enhance Managerial Productivity?" *Sloan Management Review,* Summer 1987, 63-73.

[11] These statistics are reported by C.O. Longenecker in a working paper, "A Brief Look at How We Manage Managers," The University of Toledo, 1990.

[12] We are indebted to an anonymous reviewer for suggesting that senior executives would benefit from incentives and rewards for conducting good executive appraisals.

[13] We are also indebted to an anonymous reviewer for characterizing the executive appraisal process as a kind of change intervention.

Clinton O. Longenecker is an associate professor of management at The University of Toledo, and he holds a Ph.D. from the Pennsylvania State University. His research and writing focuses on management effectiveness, human resource management, and organizational development. He has published in a variety of journals including The Sloan Management Review, The Executive, The Journal of Vocational Behavior, The Journal of Business Ethics, *and* Business Horizons. *He is an active management consultant and trainer and has worked with over fifty organizations in the U.S. and abroad.*

Dennis A. Gioia is associate professor of organizational behavior in the Department of Management and Organization, The Smeal College of Business Administration, The Pennsylvania State University. His primary research and writing focus on appraisal dynamics and on the nature and uses of complex cognitive processes by organization members. His recent work has appeared in the Academy of Management Review, Academy of Management Executive, Journal of Applied Behavioral Science, Journal of Applied Social Psychology, Organization Studies, Organizational Behavior and Human Decision Processes, Sloan Management Review, *and* Strategic Management Journal.

How the Right Measures Help Teams Excel

by Christopher Meyer

Many executives have realized that process-focused, multifunctional teams can dramatically improve the way their companies deliver products and services to customers. Most executives have not yet realized, however, that such teams need new performance-measurement systems to fulfill their promise.

The design of any performance-measurement system should reflect the basic operating assumptions of the organization it supports. If the organization changes and the measurement system doesn't, the latter will be at best ineffective or, more likely, counterproductive. At many companies that have moved from control-oriented, functional hierarchies to a faster and flatter team-based approach, traditional performance-measurement systems not only fail to support the new teams but also undermine them. Indeed, traditional systems often heighten the conflicts between multifunctional teams and functions that are vexing many organizations today.

Ideally, a measurement system designed to support a team-based organization should help teams overcome two major obstacles to their effectiveness: getting functions to provide expertise to teams when they need it and getting people from different functions on a team to speak a common language. Traditional measurement systems don't solve those problems.

The primary role of traditional measurement systems, which are still used in most companies, is to

pull "good information" up so that senior managers can make "good decisions" that flow down. To that end, each relatively independent function has its own set of measures, whose main purpose is to inform top managers about its activities. Marketing tracks market share, operations watches inventory, finance monitors costs, and so on.

Such *results measures* tell an organization where it stands in its effort to achieve goals but not how it got there or, even more important, what it should do differently. Most results measures track what goes on within a function, not what happens across functions. The few cross-functional results measures in organizations are typically financial, like revenues, gross margins, costs of goods sold, capital assets, and debt, and they exist only to help top managers. In contrast, *process measures* monitor the tasks and activities throughout an organization that produce a given result. Such measures are essential for cross-functional teams that are responsible for processes that deliver an entire service or product to customers, like order fulfillment or new-product development. Unlike a traditional, functional organization, a team-based organization not only makes it possible to use process measures but also requires them.

How should performance-measurements systems be overhauled to maximize the effectiveness of teams? Here are four guiding principles:

1. **The overarching purpose of a measurement system should be to help a team, rather than top managers, gauge its progress.** A team's measurement system should primarily be a tool for telling the team when it must take corrective action. The measurement system must also provide top managers

with a means to intervene if the team runs into problems it cannot solve by itself. But even if a team has good measures, they will be of little use if senior managers use them to control the team. A measurement system is not only the measures but also the way they are used.

2. **A truly empowered team must play the lead role in designing its own measurement system.** A team will know best what sort of measurement system it needs, but the team should not design this system in isolation. Senior managers must ensure that the resulting measurement system is consistent with the company's strategy.

3. **Because a team is responsible for a value-delivery process that cuts across several functions (like product development, order fulfillment, or customer service), it must create measures to track that process.** In a traditional functional organization, no single function is responsible for a total value-delivery process, thus there are not good ways to measure those processes. In contrast, the purpose of the multifunctional team approach is to create a structure—the team—that is responsible for a complete value-delivery process. Teams must create measures that support their mission, or they will not fully exploit their ability to perform the process faster and in a way that is more responsive to customer demands.

A process measure that a product-development team might use is one that tracks staffing levels to make sure that the necessary people are on a given team at the right time. Another measure is the number or percentage of new or unique parts to be used in a product. While such parts may offer a performance advantage, the more a product contains, the greater the likelihood that there will be difficult design, integration, inventory, manufacturing, and assembly issues.

Having sung the praises of process measures, let me throw in a qualification: while such measures are extremely important, teams still need to use some traditional measures, like one that tracks receivables, to ensure that functional and team results are achieved. Functional excellence is a prerequisite for team excellence.

4. **A team should adopt only a handful of measures.** The long-held view that "what gets measured gets done" has spurred managers to react to intensifying competition by piling more and more measures on their operations in a bid to encourage employees to work harder. As a result, team members end up spending too much time collecting data and monitoring their activities and not enough time managing the project. I have seen dozens of teams spend too much time at meetings discussing the mechanics of the measurement system instead of discussing what to *do*. As a general rule, if a team has more than 15 measures, it should take a fresh look at the importance of each one.

Trying to run a team without a good, simple guidance system is like trying to drive a car without a dashboard. We might do it in a pinch but not as a matter of practice, because we'd lack the necessary information—the speed, the amount of fuel, the engine temperature—to ensure that we reach our destination. Companies may find it helpful to create a computerized "dashboard," which inexpensive graphics software has made easy to do. (See the insert "The Team Dashboard.")

The lack of an effective measurement system, or dashboard, can even prevent teams from making it much past the starting line. After companies first adopt the team approach, teams must typically prove to skeptical senior and middle managers that the power these managers have wielded can be handed to the teams without the business spinning out of control. A team can offer no such proof if it lacks the tools to track its performance.

What operations executive, for example, would be willing to let a new-product development team manage the transition from an existing product to a new one if the team did not have a measure that tracked old product inventory from the factory throughout the distribution channel? Without such information, the company might end up stuck with lots of an unsellable old product. And what development executive would be willing to hand over responsibility for a project if he or she did not see that the product-development team was able to track cost, quality, and schedule?

Many managers fail to realize that results measures like profits, market share, and cost, which may help them keep score on the performance of their businesses, do not help a multifunctional team, or any organization, monitor the activities or capabilities that enable it to perform a given process. Nor do such measures tell team members what they must do to improve their performance.

An 8% drop in quarterly profits accompanied by a 10% rise in service costs, for example, does not tell a customer-service team what its service technicians should do differently on their next call. Process measures, however, examine the actions and capabilities that contributed to the situation. Knowing that the average time spent per service call rose 15% last month and that, as a result, the number of late calls rose 10% would explain to the technicians why service costs had gone up and customer satisfaction and profits had gone down.

The most commonly used results measures in product development are schedule and cost. But the fact that a program is six months late and $2 million over budget doesn't tell anyone what went wrong or what to do differently. In contrast, tracking staffing levels during the course of a project—a process measure that might include not only the number of bodies but also the years of experience in major job categories—can radically affect a team's performance. Many product-development teams, for example, do a poor job planning exactly when they will need people with a certain functional expertise. Not having all the necessary people at a particular stage often leads to expensive and time-consuming efforts to fix problems that the right people would have detected earlier.

This is exactly what I saw happen at a company that had given a multifunctional team seven months to develop a consumer product for testing blood-sugar levels. The team began work on July 1 and had a February 1 target date for launching the product. Although the company had named the people from the critical functions who would serve on the team well before the effort got under way, Mary, the manufacturing representative, did not join the team until mid-August. By then, people from marketing and development engineering had already made some best-guess decisions about significant packaging and manufacturing issues. After one week on the team, Mary raised serious questions about many of those decisions, and the team decided to adopt her suggestions and retrace its steps.

Not only was Mary's arrival on the team very awkward, but also the program slipped by three weeks within the first two months.

A team's reliance on traditional measures can also cause its members to forget the team's goal and revert to their old functional way of working—or fighting—with one another. Consider the case of Ford Motor Company during the development of a luxury model in 1991. The project was one of Ford's first attempts to use multifunctional teams for product development. By and large, the team's measurement system was a collection of the individual measures that each function on the team (styling, body engineering, powertrain, purchasing, finance, etc.) had used for years.

Shortly before team members were to sign off on the car's design and begin engineering the body, a controversy developed over the door handle, which was different from the ones Ford had been using. One reason for the controversy was that each function made different assumptions about the relative importance of the factors contributing to the product's costs and competitiveness.

Members from the purchasing and finance departments feared that the handle would be too expensive. Their gauges were the cost of manufacturing the handle and its warranty costs. The people from design and body engineering responded that the handle's design was no more complex than that of existing handles. And because there was no basis for assuming that its warranty costs would be higher, they argued, the cost of manufacturing the handle should be the main issue in the cost debate. They submitted a bid from a vendor on Ford's approved vendor list as proof that the handle would be no more expensive to make. In addition, they argued, purchasing and finance were not giving enough weight to the importance of the handle's design in the overall design of the car.

The purchasing representative was still not satisfied about the warranty costs. He said that handles made by other approved vendors had had lower warranty costs than handles made by the vendor whose bid had been submitted. After a short shouting match, the design and engineering people gave up.

During the debate, no one asked the critical question: Would the new handle increase the car's ability to compete in the marketplace? Since the

The Team Dashboard

Spreadsheets are the most common format companies use to display their performance measures. But if a measurement system should function like a car's dashboard by providing a multifunctional team with the information it needs to complete its journey, why not actually construct a dashboard? The dashboard format, complete with colorful graphic indicators and other easy-to-read gauges, makes it much easier for a team to monitor its progress and know when it must change direction. A multifunctional team called Lethal, which designed and built a 2.5-inch disk drive for the Quantum Corporation in Milpitas, California, used the displayed dashboard.

Quantum had begun using multifunctional development teams only nine months before it established the Lethal team late in 1989. Lethal's core group included representatives from marketing, manufacturing, engineering, quality assurance, finance, and human resources. While Quantum was a strong player in the 3.5-inch drive segment, it had never made 2.5-inch drives. On top of this technical challenge, managers wanted Lethal to deliver the drive in 145 months—10 months less than similar projects had taken.

Larry, the team's principal leader, who came from engineering, was very skeptical about whether or not Quantum's past development practices would enable Lethal to reach its 14-month goal. When he asked leaders from previous teams what they would do differently, all said they would try to find a better way to detect problems early. The teams would gather all the right players, but too many problems still ended up being resolved in the functions. Larry recognized one reason for that situation: the teams had used measurement systems designed for hierarchical, functional organizations. He thought Lethal could do better.

When the team began trying to establish a schedule, its members quickly discovered that development engineering was the only function that had provided a complete schedule for performing its tasks. The others had only sketched out major milestones. In addition, individual team members were often unsure what the others' schedules meant, and none of the schedules had been integrated. Marketing had even gone ahead and set a date for the product launch without consulting development engineering!

After this revelation, the team members decided to spell out the details of all the functional schedules in terms that everyone could understand. They then integrated those schedules into one master product-development schedule, which product-development programs often lack.

In addition to this schedule monitor and a milestone gauge, the dashboard contains a variety of other results measures, which development teams typically use to track their progress in achieving the key strategic goals that will determine whether or not top managers consider the project a success. Lethal's goals included creating a product that could be manufactured at a targeted cost (tracked by the "Overhead" and "Bills of Materials" gauges) and had a competitive quality level (tracked by the "Product Quality" gauge). The dashboard also has results measures for tracking the product's success in achieving profit margin and revenue targets once it is on the market. But such results measures tell a team only where it stands, not why it stands there. To do the latter, Lethal adopted the first process measures used by multifunctional teams in the company.

Previous teams at Quantum had focused on developing the product and treated as secondary such tasks as developing the methods and equipment for testing. Only after teams discovered that early prototypes couldn't be adequately tested did those issues receive attention. To avoid such a bottleneck, Lethal adopted a separate process-development gauge for all the tasks involved in manufacturing, including testing.

A similar discussion resulted in a decision to include staffing gauges on the dashboard. People for areas like testing, manufacturing, and marketing had to be hired early enough so that they would be on board when the team needed them. If the team waited until the development of testing methods and equipment were supposed to start before hiring test engineers, the schedule could slip by at least six weeks.

Larry's motive for suggesting the employee-satisfaction gauge was simple: unhappy team members won't keep to an ambitious schedule. The position of the "Current" needle reflects the team leaders' opinion of the team's morale. The position of the "Last Survey" needle reflects the most recent survey of all team members. By forcing themselves to monitor morale,

Lethal's Dashboard

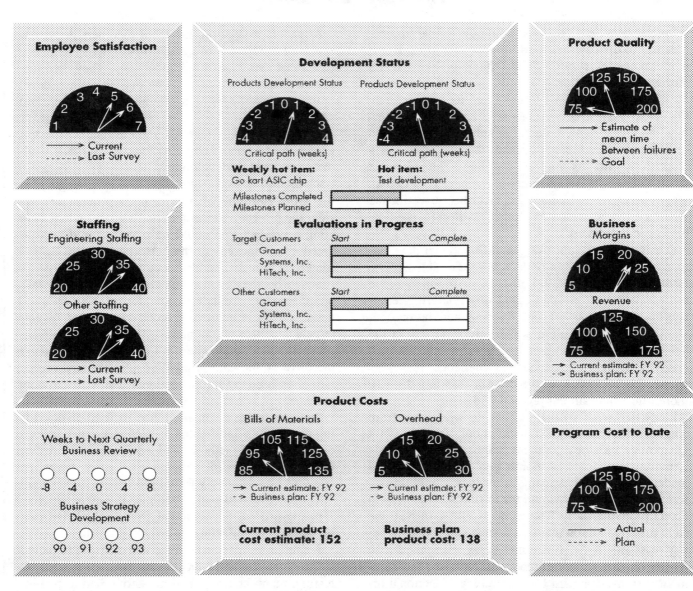

the leaders discovered that people were concerned about such things as the shortage of lab space and access to the workstations and were able to do something about those issues before they hurt morale.

The indicator lights in the lower left-hand corner of the dashboard were designed to ensure that the team allocated enough time to planning. While weekly team meetings were adequate for dealing with many issues, some, like product-launch planning, required more preparation. Because of the program's intensity, team members worried that issues that couldn't be solved quickly would eventually cause a bottleneck. Scheduling a half- or full-day meeting that everyone could attend would often take at least four weeks. John from marketing suggested that the team use the indicator lights as a reminder to schedule time for planning sessions.

The team quickly realized which gauges were not useful. John from finance argued that determining Lethal's expenses for the "Program Cost to Date" gauge was nearly impossible since the company did not have a project-based accounting system. Moreover, top managers rarely asked about an individual program's costs because they hardly varied from project to project. Since nobody on the team changed his or her behavior if the program-cost gauge dropped or increased, the team decided to eliminate it.

The team succeeded in getting potential customers for the 2.5-inch disk drive to approve the company as a qualified supplier in 16 months—2 months over the original target date but still 33% faster than previous teams. However, the drive took longer to move through the actual qualification phases than previous drives. The "Evaluations in Progress" gauges helped Lethal track its progress with potential customers but did not help the team discover a key problem until relatively late: Lethal's test procedures were more rigorous than those used by potential customers, which made it look as if the drives' failure rate was relatively high. On the basis of these data, potential customers would not qualify the company as a supplier.

Could a dashboard with different gauges have detected the problem early enough to solve it? Probably not. Like any performance-measurement tool, the dashboard is not a replacement for the decision maker.

Creating Process Measures

There are four basic steps to creating process measures: defining what kinds of factors, such as time, cost, quality, and product performance, are critical to satisfying customers; mapping the cross-functional process used to deliver results; identifying the critical tasks and capabilities required to complete the process successfully; and, finally, designing measures that track those tasks and capabilities. The most effective process measures are often those that express relative terms. For example, a measure that tracks the percentage of new or unique parts is usually more valuable than one that tracks the absolute number.

Here's how the parts and service operation of a Europe-based car company created process measures.

The warehousing function had traditionally measured its performance by tracking how often parts ordered by dealers could be filled immediately from the warehouse shelf. If a stock picker found a gasket on the warehouse shelf—meaning that it did not have to be ordered—that counted as a "first fill."

When the organization began using teams, it put the warehousing and the dealer-service groups on a multifunctional team charged with improving the total service process, from product breakdown through repair. The team reexamined the current performance measures and concluded that, from the dealer's perspective, the first-fill measure was meaningless. Dealers—and the final customers—didn't care where the part came from; they just wanted to know when they'd receive it. And just because a part was on the warehouse shelf did not ensure that it would get to a dealer quickly; the sloppy handling of orders and shipping problems could also cause delays.

Because the new team was responsible for the entire process, it mapped all the steps in the service cycle, from the moment the warehouse received a dealer's order to the moment the dealer received the part, and the time each step took. The team then identified its critical tasks and capabilities, which included the order-entry operation, the management-information system for tracking orders and inventories, warehouse operations, and shipping. The team created cycle-time measures for six to eight sub-processes, which helped the team see how much time was being spent on each step of the process relative to the value of the process. With this information, the team could begin figuring out how to reduce cycle time without sacrificing quality. The resulting changes included reducing the copies made of each order and the number of signatures required to authorize filling it. Within six months, the team was able to reduce the service cycle considerably. Not coincidentally, dealer complaints fell by a comparable amount.

model's distinctive styling was a critical competitive element, the new handle might have helped the vehicle capture enough additional customers to more than compensate for higher warranty costs. Adopting the old handle was not necessarily the best decision, and this last-minute design change, which in turn required other changes, added at least one week to the development process. The members of this product-development team were still thinking as they did in their functions, where nobody had an overview of what would make the product succeed in the marketplace.

What kind of measure could have helped the team avoid its win-lose battle over cost versus style? One possibility would have been a measure that incorporated several product attributes, such as product cost, features, service, and packaging, to enable the team to assess trade-offs. This may have helped the team realize that an undetermined factor—the proposed handle's warranty costs—should not have influenced the decision so heavily.

When cross-functional teams are being established, many companies do not institute a measurement system that supports the company's strategy, ensures senior managers that there won't be unpleasant surprises, and, last but not least, truly empowers the teams. Let me offer a generic process that most companies can implement. I'll start with the role of top managers.

In two articles on the *balanced scorecard* ("The Balanced Scorecard—Measures That Drive Performance," *HBR* January-February 1992, and "Putting the Balanced Scorecard to Work," *HBR* September-October 1993), Robert S. Kaplan and David P. Norton provide managers with a valuable framework for integrating a company's strategic objectives and competitive demands into its performance-measurement system. They urge managers to augment their traditional financial measures with measures of customer satisfaction, internal processes, and innovation and improvement activities.

What Kaplan and Norton do not explain is how such an approach can be applied to team-based organizations. I believe that it can, with one caveat: senior managers should create the strategic context for the teams but not the measures. Senior managers should dictate strategic goals, ensure that each team understands how its job fits into the strategy,

and provide training so that the team can devise its own measures. But to ensure that ownership of and accountability for performance remains with the teams, managers must require the teams to decide which measures will best help them perform their jobs.

For example, the managers of a multinational computer company established an ambitious strategic goal for all of the company's product-development teams to reduce their cycle times by more than 50% within three years. But rather than dictating how the teams measure cycle time, managers asked each team to select its own measures. To help the teams in this effort, managers provided training in cycle-time reduction and a very broad selection of measures from which the teams could choose.

Top managers and a team should jointly establish rules about when or under what circumstances managers will review the team's performance and its measurement system. A team should know at the outset that it will have to review the measures it has selected with top managers to ensure that they are consistent with corporate strategy and that it may have to adjust its measures. The team should also promise to renegotiate with managers any major changes in the measures made during the course of the project. As I will discuss later, measures should not be carved in stone.

The team and senior managers should also set boundaries, which, if crossed, will signal that the team has run into trouble serious enough to trigger an "out-of-bounds" management review. Such an approach keeps managers informed without disenfranchising the team.

During an out-of-bounds review, teams and managers must define the problem and decide what corrective action to take. The team must retain responsibility for calling and running the review and executing any decisions. It must be clear that the purpose of the reviews is for senior managers to help the teams solve problems, not to find fault.

Some product-development teams actually negotiate written contracts with senior managers at the start of a project. The contracts define the product, including features and quality targets; the targeted costs to the customer; the program cost; financial information like revenues, gross margins, and cost of goods sold; and the schedule. During the contract negotiations, management ensures that the overall program, including the measures, supports the company's strategy.

The contract also establishes rules for management reviews. For example, one company requires only two planned reviews. The first comes at the end of the design phase so that management can confirm that the product still meets the market need before the company invests in expensive tooling. The second review is after production is under way so that management can learn about and pass on to other teams any advances that the team has made, like designing a particular component to be manufactured easily, and can solve unforeseen production problems early on. During the entire design phase, the team is free to proceed without any contact with management unless it has broken or knows it will break its commitments on product features, performance, product and development costs, or schedule.

The main problem at most companies that now use multifunctional teams is that top managers use a team's measurement system to monitor and control projects or processes. Even if unintentional, such behavior will inevitably undermine the effectiveness of any team.

This is what happened when a Ford manufacturing plant turned to multifunctional teams to improve product quality but didn't change management's command-and-control mind-set.

The company grouped line workers from various functional areas into teams and trained them to collect and analyze data so that they could resolve quality problems on their own. But then came the mistake: the division managers asked quality engineers, who supposedly had been sent to assist the teams, to send a monthly report on the plant's quality and plans for improving it. In turn, the quality engineers asked the teams for their data.

Over time, the teams began to depend on the quality engineers to analyze the data and waited for the engineers' directions before taking action. The engineers recognized what was happening but felt caught in a bind because the division managers wanted them, rather than the teams, to provide the reports. Problems that the teams had been able to resolve on their own in a day or two began to require the involvement of the quality engineers and

twice the time. And the quality engineers asked for more engineers to help them support the teams.

The division managers became very frustrated. Given all their verbal support for empowering teams, they couldn't understand why the teams didn't act empowered.

When a group of people builds a measurement system, it also builds a team. One benefit of having a team create its own measurement system is that members who hail from different functions end up creating a common language, which they need in order to work as an effective team. Until a group creates a common language, it can't reach a common definition of goals or problems. Instead of acting like a team, the group will act like a collection of functions.

As a first step, the team should develop a work plan that can serve as a process map of the critical tasks and capabilities required to complete the project. The second step is to make sure that everyone understands the team's goals in the same way. Team members frequently start out believing that they share an understanding of their goals only to discover when they begin developing performance measures how wrong they were.

After the goals have been confirmed, the appropriate team members should develop individual measures for gauging the team's progress in achieving a given goal and identifying the conditions that would trigger an out-of-bounds review. In addition, each member should come to the next meeting with two or three gauges that he or she considers most effective for monitoring his or her functional area. In an attempt to push team members to focus on overall goals and the total value-delivery process as they develop measures, they should be encouraged to include process measures. (See the insert "Creating Process Measures.")

At the next meeting, each member should explain what his or her proposed measures track and why they are important. Everyone should make an effort to define any terms or concepts that are unfamiliar to others. One important rule is that no question is a "dumb question." So-called dumb questions are often the most valuable because they test the potential value of each measure in the most obvious terms.

Some measures will be either eliminated or agreed on very quickly. The hard work will be assessing those that fall in between. No final decisions should be made until all the gauges accepted or still in contention are tested as a unit against the following criteria:

- Are critical team objectives (like filling an order within 24 hours) tracked?
- Are all out-of-bounds conditions monitored?
- Are the critical variables required to reach the goal (like having enough skilled personnel to run an order-entry system) tracked?
- Would management approve the system as is or seek changes?
- Is there any gauge that wouldn't cause the team to change its behavior if the needle swung from one side to another? If so, eliminate it.
- Are there too many gauges? As I mentioned earlier, if a team has more than 15 measures, it should take a second look at each one.

After a team's measures have passed this test, the system is ready for the management review.

A team can preserve the value of its performance-measurement system by diligently adding and eliminating gauges, as required, during the project or task.

Measures that were relevant during the early stages in the development of a new product will undoubtedly become irrelevant as the product nears production. In most cases, teams realize that and plan for changes during the development of their measurement systems. But priorities often change during a project, which means that measures should be changed too. And sometimes measures prove not to be so useful after all and should be dropped. A team should also regularly audit the data being fed into its measurement system to make sure they are accurate and timely.

Managers are still in the early stages of learning how to maximize the effectiveness of multi-functional teams that are incorporated into their functional organizations. The same applies to the measurement systems used to guide both. As companies gain experience, they will discover that some specific measures can be used over and over again by different teams undertaking similar tasks or projects. But managers should be on their guard lest they do with performance-measurement systems what they have done with so many management tools: assume that one size fits all. Managers can systematize the process that teams use to create their measurement systems. They can also catalog the measures that appear to have been most effective in particular applications. But managers must never make the mistake of thinking that they know what is best for the team. If they do, they will have crossed the line and returned to the command-and-control ways of yore. And they will have rendered their empowered teams powerless.

Author's note: The author would like to thank Steven C. Wheelwright, who provided valuable guidance for this article.

Christopher Meyer is managing director of the Strategic Alignment Group, a consulting firm in Portola Valley, CA, that specializes in helping companies reduce time in knowledge-based work, such as product development, and design and implement multifunctional teams. He is the author of Fast Cycle Time: How to Align Purpose, Strategy, and Structure for Speed *(Free Press, 1993).*

Why to Go for Stretch Targets

by Shawn Tully

There's a musical management message in Frank Sinatra's bouncy 1959 hit "High Hopes," wherein an industrious ant confounds the skeptics by moving an entire rubber tree plant. That could serve as the new work song for industrial America. To a degree not seen since the Fifties, factories and labs across the U.S. are junking business-as-usual incremental objectives—moving a few more grains of sand—and striving instead to hit gigantic, seemingly unreachable milestones called stretch targets. From Boeing to 3M to papermaker Mead, managers and workers are aiming higher, working harder, and achieving more than they'd believed possible. Of course, there's a catch Sinatra never mentions: Employees are having to endure mounds, not anthills, of toil and trouble along the way.

Stretch targets reflect a major shift in the thinking of top management. Executives are recognizing that incremental goals, however worthy, invite managers and workers to perform the same comfortable processes a little better every year. The all-to-frequent result: mediocrity. In the words of Charles Jones of EDS's management consulting unit: "If you don't demand something out of the ordinary, you won't get anything but ordinary results." That's the rationale for stretch targets, which require big, athletic leaps of progress on measures like inventory turns, product development time, and manufacturing cycles. Imposing such imperatives can force companies to reinvent the way they conceive, make, and distribute products.

Why have stretch targets suddenly become the rage? The answer is that, despite the upswing in the business cycle, many companies now perceive that they must perform far better to prosper—or even, in the long term, to survive. Industries from paper to appliances face relatively bleak markets in which prices are falling inexorably, sales volume is growing slowly at best, and low-cost foreign competitors are crowding the market. Dwindling margins make it increasingly difficult for companies to earn their cost of capital. Eventually, they'll lack the money to buy new railcars or build the next generation of billion-dollar paper mills. Companies conclude that traditional ways of doing business are no longer good enough. That's when they reach for stretch targets.

CEOs embrace stretch targets with fervor. It's often the one subject that can turn a harried, taciturn boss into an impassioned chatterbox. "We're doing things we didn't think were possible," rhapsodizes Boeing CEO Frank Shrontz, a man not known for overstatement. Another evangelist is Jack Welch, CEO of General Electric: "We used to nudge the peanut along, moving from, say, 4.73 inventory turns to 4.91. Now we want big, stretch results like ten turns or 15 turns."

It's a good thing the bosses are so excited. Getting an organization to embrace wrenchingly difficult new goals—particularly in the absence of a crisis—can traumatize employees. Managers who can't stand the relentless new pace quit or get fired. Says Steven Mason, CEO of Mead: "A little over half the managers can adjust to stretch targets. For the program to work, the rest have to go." Mason adds that companies don't go for stretch targets unless they must: "It's unsubtle, painful, tough, and no fun."

Four masters of what may be called the art of stretch management—Boeing, Mead, 3M, and

CSX—rely to varying degrees on a set of nuts-and-bolts techniques.

- Honesty is the best management practice. To instill the sense of urgency necessary for radical change, a CEO must level with employees, explaining in clear, convincing terms why the company must either change or fall on hard times. The goals must ring true: Imposing arbitrary objectives is the quickest way to turn employees off. A stretch target, such as halving the time needed to produce a mainstay product, must derive unambiguously from the corporate goals.

- Employees must be convinced that they're not being asked to do the impossible. Benchmarking is a powerful persuader: showing that factories or labs at other companies—often in other industries—perform at levels that can never be achieved by incremental improvement. Seeing outsiders excel doesn't just teach managers how to, say, cut inventories; it is a potent psychological tool to enlist them in the crusade. If others can do it, they reckon, so can we. So powerful are the forces of pride and peer pressure that companies using stretch targets rarely view bonuses or other compensation incentives as key to the programs.

- Finally—and here's where stretch targets differ from old-fashioned top-down management by fiat that U.S. companies have spent years unlearning—the CEO has to get out of the way. The job belongs to managers in the field, workers on the plant floor, and engineers in the labs.

For CEO John Snow of CSX, the $9.5 billion-a-year railroad and shipping company, stretch targets were a natural extension of his business approach. The lanky Snow, 53, is a champion of management by economic value added (EVA), a form of analysis that calculates a combined charge to the business for debt and equity and then defines success as delivering returns that consistently exceed that hurdle. In 1991, CSX's return on capital hovered well below its capital charge in the range of 10%. Snow's bold goal: to make sure CSX would earn the full cost of capital by 1993 and exceed it thereafter.

As Snow foresaw, the goal forced managers to stare smack at the railroad's core problem—the fact that its multibillion-dollar fleet of locomotives and railcars sat loafing much of the time at loading docks and seaport terminals. Raising the company's return on capital would mean working the massive fleet far harder than had ever been attempted. Subordinates fretted that the task seemed impossible, but Snow refused to back off. He quips: "My son doesn't get better grades than I expect."

Having set the target, Snow got out of the way: "It's people in the field who find the right path." The strategy proved a winner. Since 1991, while handling a surge in business, CSX has eliminated from its rolling stock 20,000 of its 125,000 cars—the equivalent of a train stretching from Chicago to Detroit. That caused capital expenditures for supporting the fleet to shrink from $825 million a year to $625 million. CSX is now earning its full cost of capital.

Stretching infused CSX's $1.4-billion-a-year coal division with new life. The division now hauls slightly lower volumes with 31,300 hoppers than it did with 41,500 in 1991. That represents a more than $150 million reduction in capital. Now the division is aiming for 28,800 cars on higher volumes in 1995, another stretch goal.

Pete Carpenter, head of CSX's railroad business, decided that hitting such targets will require radical changes in the division, which up to now has run scheduling, sales, maintenance, and other functions spanning two-thirds of the country from its towering riverfront headquarters in Jacksonville, Florida. Result: a fascinating experiment in decentralization that is already yielding spectacular results.

Last year Carpenter dispatched five volunteers from Jacksonville to tiny Cumberland in the Appalachians, where they were to set up as an independent profit center in the business of hauling coal for customers in western Maryland. Ray Sharp, the new unit's president, says he gave up his comfortable post as sales manager serving the coal division's biggest customer, utility companies, without a second thought. "I was thrilled to be an entrepreneur," he says. "I knew we could run the business a lot better from the ground than from Jacksonville."

Conditions in Cumberland were primitive. Sandwiched in a ramshackle building next to a freight yard, Sharp and his team labored without secretaries for months. In the summer, weak air conditioning forced them to keep the windows open, allowing clouds of acrid diesel smoke from the locomotives to blow in. The pioneers padded around in gold shirts and Docksiders, and over pool and poker in the evenings, bonded into a feisty fraternity, exhilarated by their newfound independence from headquarters.

Carpenter wasn't coy about wanting quick results. He demanded that the region go from break even to a substantial profit within a year, and eliminate 800 of its 5,000 hoppers. "If you don't do it, we'll no longer need you up here," he told Sharp and his men. Carpenter didn't say if they could expect jobs back in Jacksonville.

The stretch target provided a spur. "I thought the goals were impossible," says Sharp. "But without them, we would have gotten comfortable and kept using railcars like they were free." The team quickly decided that hoppers and locomotives still spent too much time idle. "We'd look out our office windows at the tracks and wonder, 'Why aren't the cars moving?'" says finance director Peter Mills. The problem, the team finally realized, was the railroad's practice of running the longest trains possible—typically 160 cars. At the port terminal in Baltimore, hoppers often sat for two or three days until enough of them accumulated to form a train. At rail yards in the coal country, assembling a train of 160 hoppers could take the better part of a week.

The cause of the problem was a logjam at headquarters. Executives responsible for equipment utilization wanted to keep the hoppers busy by running shorter, more frequent trains. But they clashed with executives in charge of manning, who resisted shorter trains to hold down labor costs.

As head of a profit center, Sharp told the bureaucrats he'd gladly pay for extra crews in order to reap far bigger savings from cutting the fleet. Now his unit runs trains with as few as 78 cars, and hoppers never sit in Baltimore for more than a day. "I raise hell with headquarters to keep the cars moving," he says.

In just over a year, Sharp's group surpassed its stretch targets by cutting 1,000 of 5,000 railcars and 25 of 100 locomotives. It also mined more business, lifting volumes by 6%. The fleet reduction lowered depreciation and operating costs, causing profits to bubble. No wonder CSX has begun cloning the Cumberland unit in other regions.

The stretch target at 3M has been to vastly improve the creation of new products. That may sound

How to Stretch

- Set a clear, convincing, long-term corporate goal. Example: earning the full cost of capital.
- Translate it into one or two specific stretch targets for managers, such as doubling inventory turns.
- Use benchmarking to prove that the goal—though tough—isn't impossible, and to enlist employees in the crusade.
- Get out of the way: Let the people in the plants and labs find ways to meet the goals.

like just more of the same: The $14 billion-a-year company has long been renowned for product innovation. In its potpourri of 66,000 offerings, which include Post-It message pads, Scotch videotapes, and household sandpaper, 3M consistently met its goal: deriving 25% of its revenues from products introduced within the past five years.

Three years ago, however, L.D. DeSimone, the stocky, cheerful CEO, became convinced that the standard had lost its magic. Revenues from new products were flat, and 3M was facing grim market conditions that seemed unlikely to improve: Adjusting for inflation, it hasn't been able to raise prices since 1988. Worse, 3M's overall growth had almost completely stalled. Sales rose less than 1% in 1993 and profits only 2.4%, far from the 10% annual increases that DeSimone wants to see by the late 1990s.

In 1991, he unveiled a stretch target: Accelerate innovation to the point where 3M generates 30% of its sales from products introduced within the past four years, a 30-and-4 standard to replace the revered 25-and-5. Since new products grow far faster and generate higher margins than old ones, argued the CEO, the higher innovation rate would add the necessary octane to 3M's performance. Sporting a pink-and-gray paisley tie, his nickname DESI embossed on a laminated ID tag, DeSimone says simply, "We couldn't hit our growth targets without stepping up new products."

The goal sent tremors through 3M's campus-like R&D headquarters in St. Paul. It quickly became evident that sales of new products were flat partly because developers were wasting energy on too many small products similar to ones already on the market. Products were taking too long to progress from prototype to full production—as much as five years. DeSimone prodded his lieutenants to concentrate on products and the potential for big sales and launched a so-called pacing program to identify possible blockbusters in the lab and rush them to market.

Pacing helped break the R&D traffic jam. In 1992 the $5.2-billion-a-year consumer and industrial goods business earmarked 50 new products for the program; more than half have already reached consumers. According to the sector's president, Ronald Mitsch, the eight biggest products alone will generate $1 billion in annual sales by the late Nineties. Meanwhile, 3M is closing in on its targets for corporate growth. So far this year, sales are up 6% and profits around 12%.

What was the hottest product to come out of the pacing program? Scotch-Brite Never Rust soap pads, which might be described as a quantum leap in the science of scrubbing. Ordinary scouring pads, like Brillo and SOS, are made of steel wool that can leave rust stains on the sink and tiny metal splinters in dishpan hands. Never Rust, by contrast, is made from recycled plastic beverage bottles. It's a web of plastic fibers coated with fine abrasives. It won't rust or splinter. Having test-marketed small numbers of pads from a pilot plant in 1991, 3M was encouraged by the results; in January 1992 it made Never Rust one of the first products in its pacing plan. The result was the fastest product introduction in company history.

Almost immediately, division headquarters granted approval for a new plant, exclusively for Never Rust, in Prairie Du Chien, Wisconsin; construction crews broke ground in March 1992. The timetable was incredibly ambitious: It called for the plant to reach full production by November, and for 3M to launch the pads by January 1993. Workers started installing production equipment before the windows, bathrooms, or heating. When engineers hit a roadblock, they called on colleagues from all over 3M. Experts from the abrasives unit, for example trekked to Prairie Du Chien to help with a crucial process: coating the pads with fine particles of abrasive.

The plant hit full production right on schedule. Traditionally, 3M would have waited to make sure the machinery worked before developing a marketing plan; getting the product into stores nationwide would have taken another year. But Never Rust marketers had already been producing TV commercials and arranging promotions for months. The day the plant was finished, it started churning out pads and trucking them to supermarkets. The marketing campaign began with promotions in January and climaxed in a splashy nationwide launch in March. In the ensuring 18 months, Never Rust has made it onto a lot of sinks, capturing a stunning 22% of the $100-million-a-year U.S. market from Brillo and SOS.

Like CSX, Mead is clearing a path to profits in a bleak, capital-intensive business. When Mason, a 27-year Mead veteran, became CEO in 1992, the $4.8-billion-a-year papermaker was a cushy, complacent place to work. The boom-and-bust cyclicality of the paper industry offered easy rationalizations for poor performance. To many executives, paltry profits in the down part of the cycle were as natural as changing seasons. They simply waited for a windfall when business rebounded. Says Mason: "We accepted that our destiny was to be average."

Anything average rankles Mason, 58, a wiry dynamo who retrieves balls tirelessly on the tennis court. Says one lieutenant: "Perfection isn't good enough for him." Mason was convinced Mead was in jeopardy. He argued that it was folly to bank on a cyclical upswing, because overcapacity and foreign competition would soak up any increase in demand and make it impossible to raise prices. Mead, which had difficulty earning its cost of capital even in peak markets, now faced the prospect of living permanently below the bar. That was the formula for doom: Chronically low profits would ultimately rob Mead of the ability to pay for expensive new equipment it would need to compete. It became clear, says Mason, "we need to prosper even if prices don't come back."

He settled on using stretch targets after deciding that most management tools were either fads or too soft. In the 1980s and early 1990s he had watched Mead adopt and discard total quality improvement, management by objective, and continuous improvement. Of continuous improvement, he says, "we missed the point. We'd flutter up a little in performance and feel good about ourselves. But we really needed to jump to a new plateau."

In 1991, Mason delivered a brash plan: to raise long-term return on capital from 5% in 1992 to between 10% and 12% by the late 1990s. From that goal he derived a gritty stretch target using a formula adopted from GE that measures productivity as a ratio of revenues to costs adjusted for selling prices, raw material expense, and salaries. Says Mason: "The beauty is that it concentrates on things managers can control." By the new yardstick, Mead's performance looked pitiful. Productivity had risen an average of 0.3% a year. Based on that analysis, Mason set a target he describes as "reasonably unreasonable": a tenfold stretch to 3% productivity improvement in a year.

The toughest challenge for Mason was to convince employees that they needed to act. "In a crisis, you can do anything. But we had no wolf at the door. People wanted to wait until prices came back," he says. Mason sent managers to visit GE's appliance and light bulb divisions, businesses that earn brisk profits in mature industries with flat prices by relentlessly honing productivity. Some of the managers were inspired. With those who weren't, Mason fell back on autocratic stubbornness. "People would say, 'This is a different business; we're already low cost,'" he recalls. "I'd say, 'That's interesting. Your goal is 3%.'"

Since Mason tightened the screws, at least one-third of the 900 managers have left Mead. Those who remain have pushed the company to annual productivity gains of 2.6% over the past three years. Just as Mason had warned, a full-blown cyclical upswing has not materialized: Though paper industry sales are up, prices are barely rising. In the 12 months ended September 30, Mead has raised revenues 8% and earnings 24%. How does Mason react to the fact that Mead still hasn't hit its stretch target of 3%-a-year productivity gains? He has raised the target for 1995 to 4%.

Boeing has given itself stretch targets to overcome a major weakness few outsiders realize it has. In contrast to its sleek, sophisticated planes, Boeing's manufacturing process is shockingly primitive, cumbersome, and slow, a problem compounded, says CEO Shrontz, by veteran managers' mulish resistance to change. "We come from an incremental culture," says Shrontz. "I knew we could do far better in manufacturing if we really stretched, but managers kept saying 'Airplanes are different. They're far more difficult to make than other products.'" His lieutenants pointed out that Boeing was No. 1 in its industry and arguably far more efficient than other airplane makers.

For Shrontz, being the best in an inefficient industry wasn't enough. Boeing's toughest competition, he argues, isn't just Airbus Industrie but old aircraft that are still in use. The prices of new planes have climbed so high that airlines put off buying and keep old aircraft flying. Merely convincing airlines to replace any plane that is at least 20 years old would swell overall demand in the late 1990s by one-third, or some $14 billion a year. Boeing needs a share of that business to stay healthy in the long term, warns Shrontz: "Replacement business means the difference between slow growth and the strong sales needed to finance future models."

His straightforward solution: to lower prices so dramatically that it becomes cheaper for an airline to buy and operate new planes than to repair and operate old ones. In 1992, Shrontz set a stretch target: paring the cost of manufacturing a plane 25% by 1998. That would allow Boeing to raise the price of its 747-400, for example, currently about $150 million, far less than inflation, while adding new features, such as a new design on the wide-bodied 777 that makes it far easier than on previous models to reconfigure galleys and seats.

Shrontz set a second stretch target that complements the first: to radically reduce the time needed to build a plane—for the 747 and 767—from 18 months in 1992 to eight months in 1996. Speeding production helps cut costs by causing inventories to shrink. It's also a way to woo the airlines, by decreasing the risk involved in ordering a new plane. Up to now, doing so typically meant a two-year wait; with the short lead time, a United or Southwest can order as the business cycle takes off and roll the planes out while the recovery is in full flight.

Managers ultimately found the CEO's logic hard to resist. But Shrontz still had to convince them to adopt lean manufacturing techniques from other industries. Benchmarking helped: Compared with

GE, which turns its inventories in its heavy manufacturing operations at least seven times a year, Boeing's snail-like practice of turning its $8 billion inventory twice a year was embarrassing enough for the organization to strive for far better. To inspire his managers, Shrontz dispatched teams to study the world's best producers of everything from computers to ships.

Progress is already remarkable. Boeing now designs and builds each order of wide-bodied 747s and 767s in just ten months; 737s and 757s require just 12. Rather than simply tweak old techniques, the company is installing new approaches in almost every production phase.

The greatest gains came in the overhaul of Boeing's tortuous design process. Airplanes are the ultimate in customization. Each airline demands a unique configuration of galleys, lavatories, and seats, as well as engines, electronics, and landing gear. To avoid having to draw blueprints from scratch with each new order, engineers would scour cavernous archives for blueprints from past orders that matched portions of the new one. The engineers would then laboriously compile the new plans by copying parts of the old ones and adding their own modifications. The result was thick sheaf of blueprints that included hundreds of thousands of part numbers transferred by hand from the fading old plans.

As late as 1992, merely to design an order of 767s and procure the parts took a year of full-time toil by more than 1,000 engineers. To ensure that pipes and wiring ran properly through sections of the plane, Boeing would often create life-size mockups in plywood and plastic. When the planes finally went into production, mistakes would emerge by the dozen: Engineers frequently copied incorrect component numbers onto the new blueprints, causing slews of wrong parts to arrive at the plant.

The company is replacing that lumbering process with a huge computer library of parts and configurations for engineers to mix and match. Reconfiguring, say, the forward fuselage of a 767 takes weeks less than before. Production is faster too: The assembly plant receives the right parts; wiring and piping fit perfectly.

Boeing is making comparable leaps in other phases of manufacturing, such as parts production and final assembly—building big sections of the plane in parallel rather than in sequence, for example. To hit its stretch target in inventory turns, the company is bubbling with new ideas. One source of innovation is the Sheet Metal Center, a unit that makes 100,000 different parts a year, including the skins and frames that form the shell of an aircraft. Director Joe Peritore and his staff have invented a new ways of producing doors. Until recently, Sheet Metal supplied door parts in big bins to assembly division warehouses. Workers would spend hours sorting through the bins before the doors could be built. Now Peritore's team delivers door parts in ready-to-assemble kits directly to the assembly bays, totally bypassing the warehouses. "I no longer have to rummage through boxes to find the right part," says Doug Russo, who assembles doors in Renton, Washington.

Producing kits for entire modules shows how stretch targets draw the best ideas from the plant floor. Since 1993, Sheet Metal has cut stocks awaiting assembly from $270 million to $130 million. Now, Boeing is extending the kit concept to wing assemblies and other sections.

For many companies, reaching for heroic goals isn't an option, but a necessity. It takes a visionary boss like Shrontz or Mason to see the threat over the horizon and act before it's too late. And it takes adroit management to enlist the people on the factory floor who fashion airplane components, man the paper mills, hatch new products, and move the rubber tree plants.

III.
Developing a Performance Measurement and Management Approach

A. Overview of Alternative Approaches
Designing a Goal-Setting System to Enhance Performance: A Practical Guide
by Robert D. Pritchard, Philip L. Roth, Steven D. Jones, Patricia J. Galgay, and Margaret D. Watson
Managerial Performance Appraisal
by Michael Sokol and Robert Oresick
Managing Performance with a Behaviorally Based Appraisal System
by Douglas G. Shaw, Craig Eric Schneier, and Richard W. Beatty

B. Legal Implications
Appraisals Can Make—Or Break—Your Court Case
by David I. Rosen

C. Measuring the Effectiveness of the Performance Management Process
Failing Evaluations
by Katherine G. Hauck
Performance Reviews Get Mixed Reviews
by Michael A. Verespej

Designing a Goal-Setting System to Enhance Performance: A Practical Guide

by Robert D. Pritchard, Philip L. Roth, Steven D. Jones, Patricia J. Galgay, and Margaret D. Watson

Many organizations are making efforts to improve their employees' performance in order to increase productivity. Goal setting has been shown to be extremely effective in accomplishing this objective. While a great deal has been written about this technique, most of the literature is either very technical or consists of descriptions of organizations' successes with goal setting. Neither is especially useful to managers who want to utilize goal setting to increase motivation in their organizations. This article attempts to assist those managers by discussing in very concrete terms how one goes about designing and implementing a goal-setting system.

What Is a Goal-Setting System and Why Does It Work?

"Goal setting" means different things to different people. Some managers set goals that include, for example, developing the potential of all members of the organization, maximizing customer satisfaction, or achieving excellence in production. These are important issues for management, but they cannot be considered formal goals as we define them. Instead, they are organizational objectives that describe values or general organizational aims and priorities.

We use the term *goal setting* to refer to a formal program of setting numerical or quantitative performance goals for individuals or groups. For example, a production manager might set goals such as decreasing scrap by 5% in two months or increasing production by 2% this month. This process usually takes place in face-to-face sessions which are held on a regular, recurring basis. Results are normally reviewed after each performance period.

Goal setting has generally been very successful. Typical increases in performance range from 10% to 25%, and in some cases they have been even higher. And increases in performance as a result of goal setting have been found among many different kinds of workforces. These have included clerical personnel, logging crews, maintenance workers, production workers, salespeople, managers, engineers, and scientists.

Goal setting can increase performance for a number of reasons. First, because goal setting is based on regularly occurring feedback about performance, it allows employees to work "smarter." They know where to focus their efforts, they can correct mistakes, they can diagnose reasons for problems, and they know when a problem has been resolved. Goal setting also makes employees more accountable for their work, gives them a common level of performance to shoot for, and gives them a clear understanding of what is expected of them. In many goal-setting programs, moreover, goals—and each employee's success or failure in reaching them—are public knowledge. This provides added motivation to reach goals. And when employees do meet their goals, they receive recognition, feel proud, and are spurred on to new accomplishments.

Design Issues in Developing Goal-Setting Systems

In order to guide individuals through the process of designing a goal-setting system, we will provide answers to some questions that frequently arise in this regard. Many of these questions are similar to those that are often raised during the development of a feedback system.

The manager who has decided to develop a goal-setting system should assemble a team of individuals who will be charged with the design and implementation of the system. This group of individuals should include both supervisors and their direct reports. We urge the team who will be designing the system to review the following questions and answers, and to decide how to apply our suggestions to their specific organization.

What Should Goal Setting Be Based On?

Goal setting should be based on accurate measures of performance. Employees will try to maximize their performance on the work activities *that are measured*. Therefore, the quality of the measurement system determines in large part the success or failure of the goal-setting program. Measures that do not accurately reflect organizational objectives will lead employees to concentrate on doing things not helpful to the organization. Similarly if the measures fail to cover the entire job, some activities will often be ignored.

A complete guide to performance measurement is beyond the scope of this article. In short, however, many employers have achieved good results with the use of a four-step process to develop performance measures. First, organizational objectives need to be determined. Second, measures must be developed to quantify employee performance on these objectives. Third, an organization needs to integrate all the measures of objectives into a single index of performance. Finally, the measurement system must be implemented.

What Is the Relationship Between Feedback, Goal Setting, and Performance Measurement?

These three systems are all closely related: Good performance measurement is an absolute necessity for good feedback, good feedback is also a necessity for a quality goal-setting program, and the feedback allows employees to see how well they are performing and helps them set new goals for the future. Setting goals without establishing a way of measuring achievement is not effective. Thus designing a goal-setting system also involves designing a feedback system, and those participating in setting it up should keep in mind the following points:

- Managers, supervisors, and representative employees should all take part in designing the feedback system.

- A facilitator should be assigned to (1) make sure system development proceeds quickly, (2) see that all essential people are involved in the process, and (3) act as the moderator at design meetings.

- Feedback on the performance of individuals or small units is generally more effective than feedback on the performance of large units.

- Only aspects of the work over which the personnel have control should be included in the feedback system.

- Feedback should be delivered on a regular basis in written form. Meetings discussing past performance and planning future performance should follow distribution of the written reports.

- In addition to being given to the employees themselves, feedback reports should be given to managers at all levels who are involved in the feedback process.

- Feedback reports should include data on past performance, at least during the past few performance periods.

- Feedback should be private if it gives information on the performance of individuals, but public if the information is on group performance.

Because good goal setting requires good feedback—which in turn requires good performance measurement—the measurement system, the feedback system, and the goal-setting system must be consistent with one another. This means that in developing the goal-setting system, the design team must think through the other systems as well. The order of implementation of the systems is also important. We recommend that the performance measurement system be developed first. Next, a feedback system should be implemented and, finally, a goal-setting system should be added to the feedback system.

Further, the measurement and feedback systems must be designed so that the contribution of each individual section can be identified separately. The manager, for example, may want to know how different parts of an organization are achieving their respective goals. To determine this, the performance measurement system must be able to separate the performances of these different parts of the organization. In a typical case, a manager may want two repair departments to set goals on their quality of repair. If the systems are not designed to allow for such analysis, conducting this type of measurement and feedback may be costly and difficult.

What Type of Goal-Setting System Should Be Used?

Since goals can be set on a variety of different aspects of the work, the system design team must decide which factors will be the basis for goal setting. Two general approaches are possible. The first is *targeted goal setting*, which involves setting goals for a specific aspect of the work that needs significant improvement and must be given special attention. For example, suppose an equipment repair unit developed a serious backlog of repairs. After studying the situation, the manager determined that the problem was caused by a lack of personnel who were trained to perform the repairs. In this case, the goal-setting system might be limited to measures of how effectively the equipment repair unit trained its unskilled personnel to perform these repairs.

The second type of system is *overall goal setting*, in which goals are set to improve the unit's overall performance and not just its performance on specific aspects of the work. Although many of the issues and principles to be discussed are also applicable to the targeted goal-setting system, we will primarily explore the overall goal-setting system.

How Should Goals Be Measured?

Choosing the type of measurement index to be used is a key aspect of constructing a goal-setting system. We recommend using a single index of performance. It should measure all relevant aspects of performance, and more important aspects of performance should be weighted accordingly. Once this system has been developed, goal setting is a simple matter of specifying the level on the overall index that the unit wants to strive for.

Goal setting can still be accomplished without a single index of productivity. There are two alternative methods. First, goals can be set for each important aspect of the unit's work and the manager can keep track of the number of goals that have been met. For instance, if there were measures for 12 aspects of the unit's work, there would be 12 goals set, one for each area. A manager would then record how many of the 12 goals were met. This approach, although feasible, can become somewhat cumbersome to administer. For example, it can be difficult to set accurate goals for so many different areas. More troublesome, if the unit achieves some of the goals but not others, it is not easy to assess how well they did overall, particularly when comparing one period to another. If the unit achieved 8 of its 12 goals last month but only 6 of the 12 this month, it would seem at first glance that its performance worsened this month. In fact, however, this would depend on the relative importance and difficulty of the goals that were achieved.

A second alternative to a single index program is a system in which each area of the unit's work is assigned points for different levels of possible output. For example, suppose one measure for a quality control unit was the number of items inspected by the end of the week. If none of the items remained to be inspected, the unit would receive 50 points. If from 1 to 5 items remained to be inspected, the unit would receive 40 points; if from 6 to 10 remained to be inspected, 30 points; and so forth. An analogous point system would be developed for each of the unit's measures. A performance at the maximum realistically possible level in every area might result in a total point value of, for example, 550 points. Once this point system had been implemented, the unit's goal would be the number of points to be earned for a given time period. The unit might, for example, set a goal of 400 points for a given month. With this method, only one goal is set, and it is clear whether the goal is being met or not and whether the unit's performance is improving or not.

Another key issue to address in constructing a goal-setting system is employee control over performance. If a specific goal is set on measure of performance and the goal cannot be met because of factors beyond the unit's control, the goal loses its ability to motivate and, hence, its effectiveness. If some of the most important functions of the unit involve services or products that depend on other units or sources, then special indices of performance must be constructed that isolate the individual group's contribution. If this is not possible, management must consider the lack of control and set goals accordingly. One possibility in such a situation is to set the goal for the combined output of the units that do have control over the output.

Who Should Participate in Setting the Goals?

Employees and supervisors of the unit should be heavily involved in setting the goals. They should either set goals entirely on their own or set them and defend them to higher management.

Some of the literature advises that participation in goal setting by those who will be doing the work is not always necessary. We would argue in favor of their participation for two reasons. First, the employees and supervisors know their unique work situation and the problems they face on a day-to-day basis. Their participation will thus result in the setting of more appropriate goals. Second, employees' participation in the goal-setting process will increase their acceptance of the system, and their acceptance will increase the effectiveness of the system.

How Difficult Should the Goals Be?

Goals should be difficult but attainable. It is important that personnel accept the goals, so they should not be unacceptably difficult.

The meaning attached to the goals is another factor which determines how difficult they should be. In some goal-setting systems, the unit is expected to achieve the goals. The goals then become the minimum acceptable performance standard. If the goals are not met, unit members must explain why. In other systems, by contrast, the goals are seen as a

challenge to shoot for, rather than a minimum level of performance. Employees are not actually expected to achieve these goals.

These contrasting approaches create very different results. When the goals are the standard for minimum acceptable performance, they are relatively ineffective as motivators. If personnel exceed these minimum acceptable goals, they receive little recognition. If they fall below this minimum, they are criticized. Units usually respond to this type of system by setting future goals as low as possible and avoiding raising the goals, even if they have been exceeding them for some time.

By contrast, if the goals are seen as a challenge and the unit is not criticized for falling short of them, the system has very different results. Unit personnel set progressively higher goals, they increase them when appropriate, and the goals become a source of pride and positive feedback rather than a cause of criticism.

The design team must determine which approach to use. It is clear from the above presentation that we prefer the challenging goal approach, but organizational realities may preclude using it. Once the approach to be used has been determined, goal difficulty becomes a matter of judgment.

Should the Goals Be Public or Private?

Goals can be public (i.e., both the unit and higher-level management know what the goals are) or they can be private (i.e., set by the unit and not communicated to anyone else). The decision to use one type or the other should depend upon the desired results and the circumstances involved.

Public goals can be useful for several reasons. First, by allowing for public recognition, they often heighten the employees' awareness and motivation levels, increasing their efforts to achieve. Further, public goals can have a motivating effect on the rest of the organization. They often create competition among units, which strive to set and attain ever higher goals.

The private goals approach is less common, but it is sometimes effective in situations in which goals serve as the minimum acceptable standard of performance. As explained earlier, when employees are required to meet the goals, they may be quite reluctant to set challenging goals. Instead, they will set goals they know they can exceed. Keeping goals private sometimes serves to overcome this tendency. The unit sets challenging goals but does not communicate them to anyone higher up in the organizational hierarchy. The unit is not held formally accountable for achieving its goals and is not penalized or criticized for failing to do so. Yet the employees enjoy personal satisfaction when they meet the goals; thus the system provides motivation.

The logic of this approach lies in the fact that increased performance, not the achievement of a particular goal, is the ultimate objective of any goal-setting system. Therefore, focusing on the achievement of specific goals rather than on the level of unit performance is not effective over the long term. Moreover, whether the unit reaches its goals can be largely a function of the difficulty of those goals. In the private approach, the unit is held accountable only for its overall level of performance, not whether it has achieved any particular goal.

When choosing which system to use, the manager should weigh the potential positive and negative effects of each system. If the goals will not be treated as minimum acceptable performance standards but as sources of challenge, then the public system should generally be used. If goals will be minimums, the private system should certainly be considered. In any event, the employees and supervisors who will be doing the work and setting the goals should have a strong voice in making the decision.

For What Period of Time Should Goals Be Set?

The time period for goal setting should be based on the length of the job cycle and the availability of performance measures. The job cycle is the time required to complete one unit of work; it may be as short as a minute in a simple assembly job or as long as several months in managerial jobs. Goal setting should not be done more than once per job cycle, since if it were, information on completed units of work would not be available.

Conclusion

Goal setting can be a highly effective technique for increasing employee motivation to improve organizational performance. To make the most of the goal-setting system, the design team should carefully consider the various types of systems and develop the one that best suits the needs of the organization. Doing so should result in a highly effective goal-setting system.

Acknowledgment

This article is based in part on work done on Air Force Human Resources Laboratory contract F41689-83-C-0039. The opinions expressed here are those of the authors and should not be considered as those of the Air Force.

Selected Bibliography

Further information on practical issues in designing feedback systems can be found in Robert D. Pritchard, Philip L. Roth, Steven D. Jones, and Patricia J. Galgay's article, "Implementating Feedback Systems to Enhance Performance: A Practical Guide." A comparative analysis of feedback, goal setting, and incentive systems can be found in Pritchard's "Using Feedback, Goal Setting, and Incentive Systems to Enhance Organizational Productivity." Both are available from Dr. Pritchard.

Productivity and performance measurement are discussed in detail in Robert D. Pritchard, Steven D. Jones, Philip L. Roth, Karla K. Stuebing, and Steven E. Ekeberg's "The Evaluation of an Integrated Approach to Measuring Organizational Productivity." This manuscript is also available from Dr. Pritchard.

Several features are necessary for a successful goal-setting program. The following, which are more technical in nature than the present article, discuss these features: The necessity of feedback is presented by Miriam Erez in "Feedback: A Necessary Condition for the Goal Setting Performance Relationship" (*Journal of Applied Psychology*, Vol. 62, 1977). The necessity of commitment is covered by Erez and Isaac Zidon in "Effect of Goal Acceptance on the Relationship of Goal Difficulty to Performance" (*Journal of Applied Psychology*, Vol. 69, 1984) and in Edwin A. Locke, Gary P. Latham, and Miriam Erez's "The Determinants of Goal Commitment" (*Academy of Management Review,* Vol. 13, 1988).

For reviews of goal-setting research that look across a wide variety of applications and focus on characteristics of goal-setting programs, see Mark

Tubb's "Goal Setting: A Meta-Analytic Examination of the Empirical Evidence" (*Journal of Applied Psychology*, Vol. 71, 1986). Further reading on these topics can be found in Edwin A. Locke, Karyll N. Shaw, Lisa M. Saari, and Gary P. Latham's "Goal Setting and Task Performance: 1969—1980" (*Psychological Bulletin*, Vol. 90, 1981).

For a discussion of the effectiveness of setting goals on an overall index of performance, see Pritchard, Jones, Roth, Stuebing, and Ekeberg's "The Effects of Feedback, Goal Setting and Incentives on Organizational Productivity" (*Journal of Applied Psychology Monograph*, in press, 1988). For writing on typical increases obtained from goal-setting programs, see Latham and Locke's "Goal Setting: A Motivational Technique That Works" (*Organization Dynamics*, Autumn 1979).

A classic book on applying goal setting to organizations is Locke and Latham's *Goal Setting: A Motivational Technique That Works* (Prentice-Hall, 1984). A discussion of an updated application of MBO in modern organizations is given in *MBO Updated* (John Wiley and Sons, 1986) by Paul Mali.

Robert D. Pritchard is professor of industrial/organizational psychology at the University of Houston. He holds a Ph.D. from the University of Minnesota and is a Fellow of the American Psychological Association. His research interests include productivity measurement and enhancement, motivation, feedback, goal setting, and incentives.

Philip L. Roth is a Ph.D. candidate in the industrial/organizational psychology program at the University of Houston. His major interests are productivity measurement and the financial impact of productivity improvement programs on organizations.

Steven D. Jones is assistant professor of industrial/organizational psychology at the University of Tennessee at Chattanooga. He holds a Ph.D. from the University of Houston. He has worked in the areas of productivity measurement, feedback, and organizational effectiveness.

Patricia J. Galgay is a Ph.D. candidate in the industrial/organizational psychology program at the University of Houston. Her primary interests are goal setting and the psychometric characteristics of productivity measurement systems.

Margaret D. Watson is a Ph.D. candidate in the industrial/organizational psychology program at the University of Houston. Her main interests are productivity measurement and organizational effectiveness.

Managerial Performance Appraisal

by Michael Sokol and Robert Oresick

Introduction

Appraising the performance of managers is itself an important and challenging management activity. Its importance derives from the functions it serves. A systematic and equitable appraisal system provides information crucial for decisions about selecting managers and assigning them to appropriate jobs; for the allocation of rewards, both financial compensation and promotion; and for the development of managers (the information can indicate areas for feedback, further training, and planning a career path to include developmental assignments). Managerial performance appraisal is challenging because management is an inherently complex and various set of activities and because performance appraisal under the best of circumstances is problematic.

The problems posed by performance appraisal can be highlighted if one notices that appraisal is an evaluation of performance. That is, appraisal is the comparison of performance to some standards of adequacy or excellence. Logically, there are two distinct problems: how to determine what the performance actually was, that is, the measurement problem; and how to determine what the standards should be, that is, the criterion problem. Each of these will be considered in turn.

Techniques of Managerial Performance Appraisal

There is a spectrum of managerial performance appraisal techniques in use and a substantial litera-

ture corresponding to each. Fortunately, most of the prominent methods are discussed at length in other chapters in this volume, so when possible, the reader will be directed to them. Two other very helpful volumes are the contributions of Latham and Wexley (1981) and Meidan (1981). The purpose of this section is to describe the variety of appraisal methods and to highlight their respective criteria. Two surveys of managerial performance appraisal have been published recently. Eichel and Bender (1984) asked company representatives to rate the importance of appraisal methods; Lazer and Wikstrom (1977) surveyed the appraisal practices actually being used by corporations. Together these studies provide a picture of how several hundred American corporations appraise their managers.

Eichel and Bender (1984) group appraisal techniques into comparative, outcome-oriented, and absolute methods. They define "comparative methods" as those systems that compare people with one another, including ranking, paired comparisons, and forced distributions (e.g., placing people into categories to approximate a statistically normal distribution). They note that only 25 percent of their sample judged these techniques to be important; Lazer and Wikstrom (1977) also found that only 10 to 15 percent of their sample used these methods.

The comparative methods are relatively simple and natural, but they lack sensitivity and behavioral specificity, as Eichel and Bender pointed out. These techniques might be adequate for compensation or promotion purposes (e.g., bonuses for the top 10 percent), but they are useless for giving precise feedback to improve performance. Notice that these techniques use people as the criteria of evaluation.

By "outcome-oriented" methods, Eichel and Bender mean techniques that measure the outcomes of performance. These may be direct indices such as profit for the unit, increased sales, or reduced turnover; or they may be standards of or goals for performance set by the supervisor, by the manager, or through negotiation and mutual agreement of both parties. In the case of management by objectives, for instance, the goals are set in advance and appraisal after six months or a year is in terms of those goals. These methods have in common their reliance on products as criteria of evaluation.

Eichel and Bender found outcome-oriented methods to be judged important by 78 percent of their sample; and Lazer and Wikstrom found between 40 and 63 percent of their sample used such techniques, with higher proportions reported for appraisal of higher management levels. Eichel and Bender suggest that the prevalence of these techniques is probably the result of their objectivity and specificity—qualities whose absence in performance appraisals had been noted by McGregor (1957) in an influential article. On the other hand, direct indices such as profitability or increased sales are not unequivocal signs of managerial performance; for example, changes in the economy or the business environment may confound these measures. Furthermore, managerial accomplishments that are not measured in terms of these specific outcomes may be overlooked, and since the emphasis is on the products of performance, not the behaviors used to achieve them, information for coaching feedback and for developmental training and career planning is missing.

Eichel and Bender's last grouping is "absolute methods," where the focus is on what the manager actually did, not on how he or she compared to others or what the products were. In this grouping, then, behaviors are the criteria of appraisal and the criterion problem becomes the isolation of a set of behaviors that are to be valued. This technique includes assessment by the supervisor on the basis of (usually day-to-day and informal) observation and is written in a narrative essay. Despite its typically unsystematic and subjective nature, 73 percent of Eichel and Bender's sample rated it as an important method and 36 to 37 percent of Lazer and Wikstrom's sample actually used it.

Another technique used to assess behavior without direct observation is the appraisal interview, which is also typically used to give feedback on the results of appraisal (Lazer & Wikstrom, 1977). (See Wexley, chapter 6, for a discussion of this method.)

In the "critical incidents" technique developed by Flanagan (1954), information about behavior is collected according to a structured format, usually written, which is designed to document behavioral detail about episodes of effective and ineffective performance. Behaviors abstracted from these reports are thought to be critical to performance. About 58 percent of the Eichel and Bender sample rated this an important method, and 11 to 15 percent of the Lazer and Wikstrom sample actually used the technique. A major disadvantage of this approach is the large time investment necessary.

Time is saved (and objectivity may be enhanced) by the various rating systems for behavior. A checklist of some sort was rated important by 38 percent of the Eichel and Bender companies while between 8 and 13 percent of the Lazer and Wikstrom sample actually used them. More popular, in fact, probably the most widely used behavior-based technique, is the graphic or numerical rating scale (see Jacobs, chapter 2). About 58 percent of the companies Eichel and Bender surveyed thought it was important and 10 to 17 percent of the companies surveyed by Lazer and Wikstrom used it. Smith and Kendall (1963) advocated anchoring the scales behaviorally (BARS), but in the surveys just mentioned, only 23 percent judged this an important technique, and only 8 to 9 percent used it. (See the discussion of behaviorally anchored rating scales in chapter 3.)

Probably the most comprehensive method for getting at behavior is the "assessment center" introduced by Bray (1976). (See Byham and Thornton's presentation of this method in chapter 5.)

These "absolute" methods are commonly used in combinations with each other and with techniques from the other categories as part of a multimethod assessment. This is illustrated, for example, in the 1977 survey by Lazer and Wikstrom, which shows that exemplary companies use mixed approaches. (Lazer and Wikstrom's volume, incidentally, is especially useful because it contains several detailed case studies of companies' appraisal systems, including documents.) Absolute methods emphasize behavior; in this respect they are helpful for giving feedback and assessing training needs or developmental assignments. However, these techniques, assuming their validity and reliability, and assuming a multimethod system, all rest on the presumption that relevant and valid behavioral criteria have been established.

Criteria for Managerial Performance

From the preceding overview of managerial performance appraisal methods in use currently, it seems that they fall into three criterion categories, corresponding to Eichel and Bender's three methods of appraisal. Comparative methods are based on people, outcome-oriented methods rely on the products people produce, and absolute methods refer ultimately to criterion behaviors.

The criterion problem involves not only the types of criteria employed but also the processes used to establish and to define them. Although the determination of performance appraisal criteria is discussed by most authors, the discussion is typically only a passing prelude to a detailed exposition of the issues in the methods and techniques assessment. An outstanding counterexample, though, is Blumenfeld's monograph (1976), one of the most comprehensive discussions of the criterion problem and a good source of references to the literature.

Performance appraisal criteria can be discussed and evaluated according to several dimensions: functional utility, validity, empirical base, sensitivity, systematic development, and legal appropriateness.

First, functional utility is crucial. Performance is used for selection, compensation, and development; the criteria for performance appraisal may be more or less useful for each of these functions. An important aspect of functional utility is the acceptance by the manager of the appraiser's evaluation and feedback: the manager must see it as valid, fair, and useful.

Second, the criteria must be valid. Ordinarily, validity is understood to be a property of a measurement instrument or method, but the criteria also must be true. By extension from the measurement case, criteria can be face valid, content valid, or criterion valid. For example, earning a profit for a quarter could be a "face-valid" criterion. Since managers must direct the activities of subordinates, being able to persuade others is a "content-valid" behavioral criterion for their job. "Criterion validity" also applies to criteria themselves; for example,

using the comparative method, a company might establish a bonus for the top 10 percent of managers, as determined by a forced distribution. This criterion could be validated by showing that it was correlated to another important criterion, for example, profits (those top 10 percent of managers, say, headed units that showed the highest return on investment). This illustrates the important point that criteria ought not to be considered in isolation, a point forcefully argued by Ghiselli (1956).

Third, criteria may be empirical in the sense that the process employed to establish them utilizes empirical data to set thresholds and to revise and refine them.

Fourth, the sensitivity of criteria is also important. A criterion may be important to performance but may not differentiate levels, say, adequate from excellent performance.

Fifth, the determination of criteria may be more or less systematic. On the one hand, the criteria might be a rather haphazard conglomeration accrued over a particular historical period (characterized by a significant managerial and business change); on the other, they might be products of an explicit and systematic process, reevaluated periodically, and used in an integrated management process of selection, training and development, compensation, and promotion.

Finally, the criteria may be legally appropriate, where legality is broadly construed to include appropriate technical standards and social and organizational values (see Nathan & Cascio, Introduction).

These dimensions will be applied to the types of criteria to illustrate important considerations in the determination of appraisal criteria. Less is known about the current practices in determining criteria than about the methods used to appraise performance, so the following discussion can be taken as stimulus for thought and exploratory research by managerial appraisers.

People-based criteria. In general, people-based criteria have the most functional utility in selection and compensation, but they are sorely lacking in information for development. The validity of people-based criteria is typically face or content, but ideally, criterion validation would be important to establish. For example, should one hire the top ten nominations of paired comparisons unless those selected in this manner have been shown to be successful in the past or also have relevant abilities and skills? People-based criteria are, by definition, empirical, but empirical validation to other criteria would be desirable to refine and justify the thresholds, especially regarding sensitivity. People-based criteria can be adjusted to discriminate among various degrees of differences, but do those differences make a difference? And if one cannot demonstrate meaningful differences, what is the resulting legal or ethical position?

Product-based criteria. The functional utility of product-based criteria is considerably better than that of people-based criteria, primarily because in the case of performance standards or management by objectives, the goals set can be very close to explicit behavioral requirements and thus can direct behavior and serve as milestones for ongoing feedback. Often, however, the utility for feedback purposes is limited because the objective indices are a function of managerial performance and other factors such as the business cycle or performance of other units in the corporation. Some product-based criteria may have adequate face and content validity, particularly if they are expressions of company values or professional and legal requirements. For example, criteria such as low turnover, high profitability, and no lawsuits are compelling on the face of it. Other product criteria (especially those closely tied to behavioral expectations as part of a management by objectives program) raise selection issues very similar to ones encountered in the determination of behavior-based criteria, a topic addressed in the following section.

Behavior-based criteria. The family of behavior-based criteria is so large that they will be considered according to their sources.

One class of behavioral criteria is derived from legal, ethical, normative, and technical sources. They are less straightforward than might appear (see the Introduction for a fuller discussion). For instance, legal requirements, which may be the clearest case, are often difficult to interpret and to apply. Professional standards must be complied with, but standards vary in explicitness. What are the generally accepted practices in the diverse fields managers must direct? Adding to the complexity of the problem is the societal context that has an impact on these sorts of criteria. For instance, should an American company doing business in South Africa hire and promote according to the laws or norms of the United States? Should technical and safety standards in an Indian subsidiary conform to those of its parent organization in the United States? Legal and philosophical expertise may be required to determine such behavioral criteria.

The majority of behavioral criteria are probably set by the person who is most likely to be the appraiser, that is, the supervisor (Lazer & Wikstrom, 1977). The supervisor's determination of the criteria may be theoretical or observation based, or it may be intuitive, that is, a combination of both. In other words, the supervisors may have studied particular theories of management and decided to apply them. Or the supervisors may have performed the kinds of jobs the subordinates now do and extrapolated from their own experiences. Or they may observe and note what the successful (or well-liked) performers do. The major advantage of this type of criterion is its economy and the close control and participation it gives the appraisers/supervisors— they can transmit their expectations and develop, compensate, and promote accordingly. However, lack of systematic observation or empirical validation, political pressures, and other sources of bias hamper this approach.

To avoid the limitations of the immediate supervisor's perspective, outside experts can be consulted about the behavioral criteria. They may be peers or other supervisors in the company with similar responsibilities who can generate an inventory of desirable behaviors in a more systematic fashion and whose biases can be corrected to some extent by mutual discussion. But their knowledge may be limited and various forms of groupthink might influence the process.

The next possibility, then, is systematic research, either by in-house specialists or by outside consultants. The information base may include on-the-job observation, interviews with incumbents, off-the-job observation (e.g., assessment centers) and written reports (e.g., critical incidents). Both assessment centers and critical incidents are methods of assessment and methods of generating behavioral criteria, though they are probably used more frequently for the former purpose (see the discussion of assessment centers by Byham and Thornton in chapter 5). Such information can be analyzed to find criteria in the traits and abilities of people, in the behavioral requirements of the job, or in some combination of both. The personality assessment approach tries to identify the characteristics of good managers in general. There are clearly formidable psychometric problems here, but the most salient drawback is the recognition that managers actually perform, not in general, but in a particular job in a particular organization (see chapter 8).

Job analysis has not become a very sophisticated enterprise. Done well, it provides a systematic and empirically derived list of the behaviors required to accomplish the job. A comprehensive discussion of this type of analysis is given by Fine in chapter 1, so only two comments will be made here. First, the job of managing is so difficult to define across levels and industries and corporate climates that a job analysis probably has to be done on a case-by-case basis. Second, it is an open question whether the criteria resulting from the job analysis are capable of distinguishing adequacy versus excellence in the job.

Another important approach to the criterion problem, which combines a search for personality traits, skills, and so on, and the requirements of the particular job (though not a systematic job analysis), is through the identification of job competencies. Since this approach may be less familiar than the others mentioned thus far, a more detailed description will be given to illustrate it and the various desiderata expounded previously.

A Competency-Based Approach to the Criterion Problem

Defining managerial competence. The first step in deciding what would be assessed is defining what a manager does. Defining the jobs of a structural engineer, a software designer, an accountant, or an English teacher is a formidable task; establishing competencies and measures of them is difficult but possible. but managerial jobs are among the most wide-ranging in their scope and variation and thus are much more difficult to categorize.

What does a manager do? A number of management experts have tried to answer this question (Appley, 1969; Drucker, 1973; Katz & Kahn, 1978). In general, their definitions comprise descriptions of the various functions that managers perform; managers are asked to set goals, plan, co-

ordinate, make decisions, motivate others, and supervise the work of others. Katz and Kahn (1978) summarized the job of a manager as being concerned primarily with ensuring that the internal resources of an organization meet the external demands placed on that organization in such a way that everything runs smoothly. The actions that make one person better than another at carrying out this job are "managerial competencies."

A *managerial competency is a characteristic of an individual that underlies effective performance in a management position.* To make this definition clear, one must first understand what is meant by effective performance. Boyatzis (1982) argues that effective performance occurs when a job is carried out so that a specific, required outcome results from the performance of a specific action—an action that is carried out within the policies, procedures, and conditions of the organization environment. The key notion in this description is that specific actions lead to effective performance. In addition, what may be effective behavior leading to effective performance in one area will not necessarily work in another. For example, the same competencies that make one a good manager of a sales force in the computer industry are not the same as those that make one an effective manager of a manufacturing plant, though there may be some overlap. Similarly, what may be effective managerial behavior leading to effective performance in a middle-level manager is likely to be quite different than the qualities for success in first-line supervision or in upper-level positions. (Boyatzis, 1982, identifies core competencies across a range of managerial jobs.)

Different mixes of competencies are needed in order for workers to function in different organizations; in a managerial position, specific actions that are carried out are governed by underlying competencies because the job demands them. Thus effective performance can be defined as occurring when an individual's underlying competencies lead to behaviors that meet the job demands within the parameters of the organizational environment and when a specific desired result occurs.

If managerial competencies make the difference between an effective manager and an ineffective manager, then the next question is, What is a managerial job competency? A job competency is defined by Klemp and Spencer (1980) as an underly-

145

ing characteristic of a person that results in effective or superior performance in a job. They state that a competency can consist of a motive, trait, skill, aspect of self-image, social role, or body of knowledge that leads to effective performance.

A competency, then, can be any one of a set of notoriously elusive entities. Furthermore, a competency is generic in the sense that a single competency is manifested in several different behavioral indicators. For example, the competency "persuasion" might include persuading by appeals to the other's self-interest, the use of an influence network, and threats of sanctions.

Thus a more complete definition might be the following:

A managerial job competency is an underlying generic motive, trait, aspect of self-image, social role, or body of knowledge that is manifested in one or more particular behaviors that lead to effective managerial performance in a given job.

Determining competencies: A strategy. One method of establishing performance appraisal criteria for managers is based on the assumption that empirical research on a group of people who have been identified as superior performers in the organization under study will give the best information on what competencies are needed for effective performance. Thus these superior performers will define by their own behaviors the key competencies. This assumption directs us to the following tasks in the development of the performance appraisal criteria:

1. Selecting criterion groups
2. Collecting data on performance
3. Developing a competency model
4. Validating the model
5. Deploying the model for use in performance appraisal

Each will be discussed in turn.

Selecting criterion groups. The first step in the process of determining competency-based criteria is the selection of a sample of superior performers and a sample of merely average performers. The selection process is based upon three sources of information, whenever possible (i.e., as always, a multimethod approach is desirable): (1) a list of the managers who are considered to be outstanding performers by their supervisors; (2) ratings by incumbents themselves as to who are the best performers; and (3) measurable performance data on each incumbent from the organization's file. (Sources 1 and 2 employ comparative methods and people-based criteria, while source 3 reflects an outcome-oriented, product-based approach.) This process is intended to differentiate incumbents whose performance is characterized by excellence from those whose work is adequate or mediocre. The latter sample is selected to serve as a control group. The performance of this group provides baseline information for establishing the minimum, or threshold, competencies that people need to possess in order to carry out their jobs in an adequate manner. Thus the procedure seeks to build discriminative sensitivity into the criteria.

The selection process begins first by convening a panel of supervisors or, if there are too many supervisors, a specially chosen panel of experts. Once the purpose of the panel is explained, two experts are charged with identifying the hard (data-based) outcomes that they would expect to observe in the performance of a superior performer. For example, a superior sales manager might be expected to have salespeople perform at a certain level of profit, do their paperwork in timely fashion, show a low rate of turnover, support the overall efforts of the marketing plan, and exhibit a high rate of promotion (indicating that the manager is developing them professionally).

Some of the expected outcomes will be readily available in corporate files, but some either will not be available because the data have not been collected or cannot be assessed in the eyes of top management. Sometimes, the information has been collected but, for political reasons, is not available. The purpose of having the panel identify what the criteria for outstanding performance should be is threefold: (1) it tells what to look for and where to find it; (2) it transforms the implicit theories used by the group to judge individuals into explicit theories, which in turn gives the group a set of common criteria by which to compile a list of superior and average incumbents; and (3) it begins to build acceptance of the process both by the people who will be using the criteria and by the people who are viewed as experts in the organization and who are therefore opinion leaders. The actual number of incumbents selected may vary between sixteen and forty depending on the nature of the job, the number of incumbents, and the funding and time available.

Parallel to the panel's efforts, a list of all the incumbents in the job is compiled and sent to all those incumbents, who are asked first to identify those people they know and then to identify those they think are performing their job in a superior fashion. These data are then analyzed. The people who are known by a sufficiently large number of their peers and who are judged to be superior by 80 percent of those who know them are assigned to the superior group. The average group is defined as those people who are known by a large number of people and are judged to be superior by no more than 20 percent of the people who know them.

The three sources of data—the panel nominations, the peer nominations, and the outcome data—are then examined. Based on this examination, clearly average and clearly superior people are selected. Disagreements on classification at this point must be resolved by discussion; later, when the competency model is developed, empirical data can clarify the marginal and borderline cases. That is one of the advantages of an empirical approach: it can sharpen our powers of discrimination and uncover the underlying bases of people-based comparisons.

Aside from the obvious advantages of examining from three different perspectives what it means to be a superior performer, all three groups—the people who will use the criteria to evaluate others, the people being evaluated, and corporate headquarters—benefit because each has had input into designating the criterion groups on which the model for outstanding performance is based. This approach also reduces some of the biases that have plagued the selection of criterion groups, such as halo effects and the fact that peers and superiors rate on the basis of different information or criteria. Armed with a final list of superior and average performers, data can now be collected.

Collecting data on performance. One approach to data collection is to go to the people who are actually on the job and observe or interview them. This approach facilitates the construction of a competency model by providing a foundation of sound empirical information. Alternatively, the performance criteria can be based on a job analysis check-list or the perspectives of an expert panel. Both of these approaches are based on a somewhat biased picture of what it takes to carry out a job effectively. The job analysis checklist constrains the information that can be gathered by forcing people to fit their perceptions of the job into a set list of characteristics. The expert panel is constrained by the group process, which generally leads to a job description laden with socially desirable criteria and burdened with current theories of management rather than to an accurate description of what superior managers actually do on the job, that is, their competencies.

For example, one company discovered that its top managers routinely inspected the desks of their subordinates to ensure that phone calls were promptly returned and customer needs were met in a timely fashion. It is hard to imagine a group of experts coming up with a managerial model that suggests going through subordinates' desks as a sign of effective management. Yet this was the case, and if this corporation is interested in an accurate description of excellent managerial performance, it needs to assess the degree of checking its managers do of their subordinates' work. To obtain information about behavior at this level of detail and specificity, contact with the incumbent managers is imperative.

One strategy for solving some of these problems is to obtain a clear, detailed picture of how superior and average performers do their jobs through a data-gathering technique called the "behavioral events interview." (BEI, when applied properly, eliminates many of the difficulties mentioned above through its probing, which requires incumbents to describe what they do on the job and does not require them to make judgments about what is right or wrong, relevant or irrelevant to successful performance of the job. Nor does the interviewer have to interpret or evaluate. The analytic function of this competency-finding process is separated from the data-gathering phase.)

The BEI is based on the work of Flanagan (1954), who, while working for the Air Force, developed a methodology in which pilots were asked to write out what they did during a "critical incident," that is, a time when they were in some danger in the airplane. In this way he hoped to identify the key skills and abilities that helped pilots to survive. McClelland (1971) took up Flanagan's method of critical incidents and improved upon it in a number of ways. McClelland recommended that, rather than writing reports about their managerial critical incidents, the managers should be interviewed about high and low points of effectiveness so that an interviewer could probe beneath the surface for details of what actually happened during the incident; this retrieved more information than was usually obtained by writing, which is limited by people's motivation and expository writing ability.

The interviewer's primary job is to get interviewees to convey their critical incidents so the behaviors are described in sufficiently rich detail to form a data base for construction of a competency model. The interviewer's skill acts to focus those interviewees who philosophize about the theory of management on specific behaviors and (by building rapport) to elicit incidents from those individuals who have some resistance to giving information. The interviewer is able to inquire about thoughts and feelings as well as behavior, so important cognitive competencies can be identified.

The BEI differs from other types of interviews in two respects. The technique presses the interviewee for behavioral details, and the interviewer's job is to collect information, not to evaluate it. Other kinds of interviews either accept interviewees' vague generalities or require the interviewer to split attention between collecting and processing information (e.g., interpreting it or giving feedback). The only job of the individual conducting BEI is to find out what the interviewee did, said, thought, and felt at the time of the incident. The interviewer makes no value judgment, offers no emotional support, asks no leading questions to test out his or her own hypotheses about what it takes to do an outstanding job, and gives no coaching or feedback. The BEI interviewer is like a newspaper reporter interested only in getting a factual and accurate record of what actually took place. Because of this definite purpose, special training for BEI interviewers is necessary.

The interview itself comprises three distinct parts. The first is an explanation of why the interviewee is being interviewed. This part not only informs the interviewee about the nature of the project but also develops a feeling of rapport or comfort.

The next part of the interview is a request for the major duties and responsibilities of the incumbent. This step is designed to get an interviewee talking about the job on a general level, that is, to determine what the individual understands the job to be. Since this step is relatively free of probing, it allows the interviewee to state general theories and ideas about the job. The interviewer makes no judgmental comments and in general agrees with whatever the interviewee is saying, with the goal of building rapport and facilitating conversation. Together the first two parts may last ten minutes.

The third phase in the interviewing process is eliciting the critical incidents. This is the core of the interview and takes forty-five to ninety minutes. The interviewer asks the interviewee to think of a time when he or she felt particularly effective in the job over the last two years; this time period is suggested to ensure the interviewee will probably be able to remember the incident in sufficient detail. That is, interviewees are asked to pick a time when they felt good about their job performance—not when the supervisor thought they were performing well, and not when they met a company goal, but when they personally felt effective in the job. This step virtually guarantees that the incident conveyed will have the interviewee in a central role at a time when a number of competencies were needed. People are also asked to tell about personal low points on the job. By acquiring information about what the interviewees did during these high and low points, one is able to observe how they met with adversity and challenge when the demands of the job were greatest. The analysis will not contrast behaviors in high and low points, but behaviors in both high and low points of superior managers will be compared to such behaviors in average managers.

This tactic of asking for high and low points of felt effectiveness avoids one problem typical of observational studies of jobs. Observers end up watching the day-to-day functioning of an individual but not the key situations and behaviors that indicate superior performance or lack of ability, especially if they are relatively infrequent. Observational studies may work well for jobs with a great deal of repetitiveness, where job demands are stable and the environment changes slowly, if at all; but they are not very useful in assessing what it takes to be a manager in a dynamic, ever-changing business environment, which is the most typical circumstance of managers. One basic assumption of this approach is a variation of Pareto's principle: 20 percent of the individual's behaviors make 80 percent of the difference. Competencies, even relatively rare ones, seem to emerge most clearly in challenging situations when people are either very successful or are finally overcome by adversity. It is these episodes that people remember, and the BEI exploits this property of memory.

The BEI also differs from other types of interviews in the level of detail that is extracted from the interviewees. Eliciting rich behavioral detail is accomplished by a number of techniques: (1) interviewees are asked to translate all forms of jargon, buzz words, or technical language into ordinary English; (2) all statements that convey a host of behaviors are probed until the interviewee either gives an adequate behavioral description or states that no more details can be remembered—for example, "I convinced him" is not left standing but is probed for exact dialogue and the thought process underlying the persuasion—and (3) the interviewer strives to get the complete story on a single incident; that is, the interviewer tries to keep the interviewee on track by getting the person to narrate what he or she did in chronological order. The interview should include what led up to the incident, what the interviewee did, said, felt, and thought during the course of the incident, and the outcome. Between four and six incidents are collected per interviewee, evenly split between high and low points.

Finally, the interviewees are asked what they would look for if they were to be hiring a person for their job and what type of training they feel would make them more effective in the job. This step gathers some final insights, cements the alliance with the manager, and allows a transition out of the interview.

Developing a competency model. Transcriptions of the tape-recorded interviews form the data base for developing the competency model. Half of the interviews are used to form the "derivation sample," while the other half are put aside for use in the validation phase. Each of the interviews in the derivation group is read by at least two members of the team who will build the model.

The model-building team is made up of at least four individuals who have been trained in the BEI technique and have also participated in several other model-building sessions. They read the deri-

vation interviews and identify behaviors that result in the successful completion of a component of the job under study. Individual behaviors are recorded on index cards so that they can be easily sorted into different thematic groupings. The code number of each interviewee is also affixed to the card as well as the page number of the transcript where it was found. In this way, any one of the members of the model-building team can have easy access to the context in which the behaviors were exhibited. Each interview is read by at least two members of the team to ensure that behaviors are not missed and that each statement or interpretation of a behavior is accurate.

Next, the team members identify the overarching constructs that account for a number of behaviors they have seen across incidents and interviewees. As each theme is proposed, comments are solicited from all members of the team as to whether their experiences with interviewees can support or refine the theme. In this manner, all the behaviors that have been abstracted are clustered under thematic headings or they are discarded. A behavior is discarded when either no other behaviors like it have been found or it is recognized that it really isn't a behavior but only a hypothetical example or abstract concept espoused by the interviewee. Thus it is crucial to competency model building that the BEIs contain behaviorally rich information.

The next step in the process is refining and clustering the themes into competencies and their attendant behavioral indicators. This refinement is accomplished by crafting an accurate label that captures the essence of the motive, trait, skill, aspect of self-image, social role, or body of knowledge that has been displayed. Redundancies are eliminated and the behavioral indicators reworded to make them easily understood.

Validating the model. The competency model is then applied to the derivation sample of interviews. This is accomplished by having someone who was not involved in either the interviewing or the development of the competency model code each of the interviews. The coding involves recording any behavior that matches a behavioral indicator described in the competency model. The data from the coded interviews are then analyzed to test whether the superior performers differ statistically from the average performers on the coded provisional competencies. At this point, quantification is being introduced to obtain empirical feedback and to ensure discriminative sensitivity. Those indicators and provisional competencies that either have low frequencies of occurrence or do not statistically differentiate between the two sets of interviews (superior and average) are dropped.

The revised model is then applied to those interviews that were not used in the derivation sample, and the data collected are again tested statistically. Those indicators and the competencies that statistically differentiate the superior from the average performers are said to be cross-validated. Consequently, the model as a whole is refined and cross-validated.

Deploying the model. The validated competency model is the basis for a performance appraisal system, but it must be adapted, depending on the needs of the organization. These criteria can now be assessed by any of the measurement methods reviewed earlier. Appraisal interviews can be conducted by interviewers trained in the BEI format and evaluation can be based on the criteria defined in the model. The assessment center approach can be geared to elicit the competencies. The written form of the critical incidents report can be coded for the indicators. If ratings are preferred, a checklist of indicators or a BARS using the indicators is readily constructed.

Evaluation of the competency-based approach. The competency-based approach to the criterion problem has several advantages. Its functional utility is clear. The competencies are defined by behavioral indicators that are easily identifiable in performance records and so can be used for feedback and coaching. They are typically well-accepted by managers because the behaviors are clear and credibility is high, since many levels of the organization have had input into the process, including the superior performers.

The validity of the competency model is established. Face and content validity are obvious and criterion validity is documented when the competencies distinguish the criterion groups statistically.

The approach is clearly empirical—the whole model-building process is driven by the data; the indicators and competencies are derived from content analysis of the data and are refined by statistical analysis.

The sensitivity of the criteria is built-in, since the competencies are by definition those indicators that distinguish superior performers from merely adequate ones (who, by the way, in many organizations are quite good, just not excellent).

The process of establishing the criteria is very systematic, as shown above. It combines rational insight and analysis with empirical techniques. When possible, it uses multiple methods or criteria, and it enlists the efforts of many levels in the organization.

Legally, criteria generated in this fashion are probably as solid as one could get. They are clearly defined behaviors chosen precisely because of their relevance to the job; in fact, relevance to the job is documented statistically.

The major disadvantages are the expense and time required to execute a program like that just described and the blind spots inherent in the method. While the competency approach selects behaviors that distinguish superior from average performance, it neglects behaviors that are necessary for job performance but that do not happen to separate excellent performers. For example, the ability to understand a technical description for an engineering project may be essential for a manager of a chemical plant, but this ability may not be differentiating superior performers. Such threshold competencies need to be cataloged as well, which may require a more conventional job analysis. Legal and technical standards will also have to be addressed by another technique, with other expertise.

Despite these limitations, the competency-based approach incorporates many of the desiderata in the search for appraisal criteria. When complemented with the other approaches, it arguably represents the state of the art in managerial performance appraisal.

Future Directions and Needs

There are three major trends in the appraisal of managerial performance, extending from the current state of the art in rather direct ways: (1) there will be an increasing reliance on the use of observable and measurable behavior to evaluate a manager's performance; (2) performance appraisal for managers will be integrated into all decisions regarding their careers; and (3) technology in the form of computer-aided assessment techniques will make the performance appraisal of managers less labor intensive and less dependent on human judgment.

The performance appraisal of managers has been moving in two directions: from a "gut" level judgment by supervisors to systematic assessment based on measurable data, and from a focus on task or job analysis to an emphasis on competencies of a particular manager in a particular job. These two trends are closely related to one another; as our ability to define abstract human characteristics in behaviorally specific terms increases, the "art" of assessing managers will become increasingly a "science." This trend from the intuitive to the rigorously data-based appraisal methods and criteria is driven by two factors: the increased sophistication of the behavioral sciences and the press of social and legal challenges to the appraisal process. Neither factor shows any signs of diminishing.

As the recognition of the value of performance appraisal continues to grow, upper-level management will demand that more decisions be made using data generated by these techniques. Managers will be brought into organizations based on assessment interviews using criteria that also form the basic ongoing evaluation. Development, promotion or termination, job assignment, and compensation will all be part of an integrated, explicit, and relatively objective system.

Finally, like every other area of our society, performance appraisal will not escape computerization. The data base of appraisal will become more rich and yet more tractable. For example, with the advent of interactive video and computer systems, very sophisticated simulations can be designed and recorded in dramatic detail, and on-line feedback will be readily available. As the development of "expert systems" in the field of artificial intelligence extends into management, the best human judges and content analysts will be modeled in programs that will be available for use by the entire organization. The expertise will be spread around and costs in terms of time should decrease.

The future looks challenging, the future looks sophisticated, and the future for managerial performance appraisal looks assured.

References

Appley, L.A. (1969). *A management concept.* New York: American Management Association.

Blumenfeld, W.S. (1976). *Development and evaluation of job performance criteria: A procedural guide* (Research Monograph No. 64). Atlanta: Publishing Services Division, College of Business Administration, Georgia State University.

Boyatzis, R.E.. (1982). *The competent manager: A model for effective performance.* New York: Wiley.

Bray, D.W. (1976). The assessment center method. In R.L. Craig (Ed.), *Training and development handbook* (2nd ed.) New York: McGraw-Hill.

Drucker, P.F. (1973). *Management: Tasks, responsibility, practice.* New York: Harper and Row.

Eichel, E., & Bender, H.E. (1984). *Performance appraisal: A study of current techniques.* New York: American Management Association.

Flanagan, J.D. (1954). The critical incidents technique. *Psychological Bulletin, 51,* 327–358.

Ghiselli, E.E. (1956). Dimensional problems of criteria. *Journal of Applied Psychology, 40,* 1–4.

Katz, D., & Kahn, R. (1978). *The social psychology of organizations* (2nd ed.). New York: Wiley.

Klemp, G.O., Jr., & Spencer, L.M., Jr. (1980). *Job competence assessment.* Boston: McBer and Co.

Latham, G.P., & Wexley, K.N. (1981). *Increasing productivity through performance appraisal.* Reading, MA: Addison-Wesley.

Lazer, R.I., & Wikstrom, W.S. (1977). *Appraising managerial performance: Current practices and future directions.* New York: Conference Board.

McClelland, D.C. (1971). *Assessing human motivation.* New York: General Learning Press.

McGregor, D. (1957). An uneasy look at performance appraisal. *Harvard Business Review, 35,* 89–94.

Meidan, A. (1981). *The appraisal of managerial performance* (AMA Management Briefing). New York: AMACOM.

Smith, P.C., & Kendall, L.M. (1963). Retranslations of expectations: An approach to the construction of unambiguous anchors for rating scales. *Journal of Applied Psychology, 47,* 149–155.

Managing Performance with a Behaviorally Based Appraisal System

by Douglas G. Shaw, Craig Eric Schneier, and Richard W. Beatty

Communications Inc. (CI), a group of related high-technology and telecommunications businesses owned by one of the largest companies in the United States, had just completed one of their first business strategy planning cycles. The cycle culminated with not only an articulation of the group's mission and specific competitive strategies for each of their businesses but also statements of the values they needed to emphasize as an organization. Top management wanted to hold executives accountable for implementing the strategy. As a part of the action planning process, CI management hence committed to developing a management by objective (MBO) process within each of their businesses. Objectives were determined from the action plans, based on each executive's opportunity to affect key organizational results. Performance against objectives would be tied to the executives' compensation.

After working with the MBO process for a year, CI management became dissatisfied with it for three reasons. First, CI's top management found that while some of their managers delivered the results identified through the objectives, they "didn't like the way the results were achieved." For example, managers seemed to propose only the safest new projects, those that had been only modestly successful in the past. Few risks were taken because

managers were not willing to gamble on not meeting their objectives. Second, in the businesses that included all salaried employees in the MBO process, developing the objectives became more a required exercise than a useful management tool for implementing their business plans. Considerable time was spent arguing over the objectives, which were not well integrated into the strategy and action planning processes. Third, the values that were agreed to by the management team were not being reinforced by the MBO system.

After considerable discussion, CI's top management agreed that their MBO process had to be replaced, or at least augmented, by a process that better captured how and what performance should be measured. The process should be one that would hold people accountable for reinforcing CI's key values and would be a useful tool to track and measure performance accurately.

The values discussed in CI's first business planning cycle were narrowed to five most important values agreed upon by the top management team. CI management then developed a process for better integrating the organizational values into the management and appraisal process. First, each of the five values (do what it takes to get the job done, make timely decisions, take calculated risks, revise plans and adapt to change, serve clients' interests) was defined. Second, the values were communicated to all employees, along with the introduction of a process for linking the values to the responsibilities of all positions previously included in the MBO process. Third, small groups met to discuss the values and how they are (or could be) mani-

fested in their jobs. For each value they also developed examples of what exceeds, meets, and does not meet expectations would constitute for their jobs. After these examples were drafted, they were refined and consolidated to be used in the process of planning and appraising performance.

CI management preserved the objective-setting process for its executives, augmented by the process just described.

By measuring its executives on what was achieved and how it was achieved, the chief executive officer (CEO) had a performance planning and appraisal process that more accurately captured the performance he needed from his executives to grow and meet CI's competitive challenges. According to the CEO, the process was the key means of integrating the espoused values throughout the organization, which he believed was necessary to gain competitive advantage through each of the divisions' strategies. The values chosen to be reinforced were consistent with CI's rapidly changing, highly competitive marketplace. CI management overcame some of its earlier problems, such as taking a very narrow view of responsibilities, slow decision making, overanalyzing issues, and taking an overall management approach that was too conservative.

This case is a good illustration of why companies look for an alternative to objective setting for planning and appraising performance of executives, other managers, and nonmanagerial employees. In this case, the company chose a technique commonly referred to as behaviorally anchored rating scales (BARS) (see Schneier & Beatty, 1979; Beatty & Schneier, 1981) to assess performance, a process used to appraise individuals' performance in difficult-to-quantify job dimensions or factors. (These were CI's values in the case.)

Why BARS

In many cases, solely meeting objectives defined through an action planning process of a business's strategy does not adequately capture an executive's or manager's performance. (CI's predicament was similar.) Often the achievement of such objectives is not sufficient as a criterion for pay and promotion decisions, either because of the objective-setting process itself (e.g., were manager A's objectives as challenging as manager B's?) or because the

achievement of results could have been accomplished in a counter-productive manner.

For example, a manager could achieve a given financial objective by working a small group of people too hard, later resulting in unwanted turnover. But the manager might be promoted or rewarded through the pay program because he or she met objectives, hence sending the wrong message about desired behavior. To capture such nonquantitative aspects of performance, managers often use a nebulous criterion such as "Overall Job Performance," or a scale for "Managing Effectively" or "Interpersonal Relations" will be included, with adjectives (Outstanding, Average) at each scale value. Both allow evaluators to consider important aspects other than achieving objectives in appraising performance. While these scales may provide an evaluator with the needed latitude to appraise an individual's total contribution, they provide too vague a means of communicating expectations and providing feedback. In addition, such scales can be inaccurate, leading to inflated ratings (see e.g., Landy & Farr, 1983).

Also illustrated in the introductory CI case is another predicament of many managers using MBO: stretching the objective-setting process too far down in an organization. This can be an exercise in futility because of a position's distance from, or lack of control over, the results that are measured in an objective-setting process. In such cases, the objective-setting process itself becomes the goal rather than a tool to achieving the organization's goals. The consequences are a lot of wasted time and energy (see Bernardin & Beatty, 1984).

To address these issues with a practical technique, this discussion (1) defines BARS terminology, (2) reviews the process for developing BARS, (3) contrasts BARS to the other means of appraising performance, (4) describes how BARS can be used, and (5) provides guidelines for effective development and implementation of a BARS process.

Terminology

Three terms should be defined to understand BARS. *Dimensions* are broad categories of duties and responsibilities that comprise a job or number of jobs. A *scale* is a continuum of performance, ranging from the lowest to the highest level of performance. BARS use scales containing from as few

Figure 1. Example of a Behaviorally Anchored Rating Scale: Planning, Organizing, and Scheduling Project Assignments and Due Dates

7	[ ]	Excellent	Develops a comprehensive project plan, documents it well, obtains required approval, and distributes the plan to all concerned.
6	[ ]	Very Good	Plans, communicates, and observes milestones; states week by week where the project stands relative to plans. Maintains up-to-date charts of project accomplishments and backlogs and uses these to optimize any schedule modifications required.
			Experiences occasional minor operational problems but communicates effectively.
5	[ ]	Good	Lays out all the parts of a job and schedules each part; seeks to beat schedule and will allow for slack.
			Satisfies customers' time constraints; time and cost overruns occur infrequently.
4	[ ]	Average	Makes a list of due dates and revises them as the project progresses, usually adding unforeseen events; investigates frequent customer complaints.
			May have a sound plan but does not keep track of milestones; does not report slippages in schedule or other problems as they occur.
3	[ ]	Below Average	Plans are poorly defined; unrealistic time schedules are common.
			Cannot plan more than a day or two ahead; has no concept of a realistic project due date.
2	[ ]	Very Poor	Has no plan or schedule of work segments to be performed.
			Does little or no planning for project assignments.
1	[ ]	Unacceptable	Seldom, if ever, completes project because of lack of planning and does not seem to care.
			Fails consistently due to lack of planning and does not inquire about how to improve.

as three levels of performance to as many as nine. *Anchors* are specific descriptors of behavior attached to each level of performance used on a behaviorally anchored scale.

Figure 1 provides an example of a BARS scale for the planning, organizing, and scheduling dimension of a manager position. Note that the scale uses seven points, each accompanied by an anchor that describes different types of behavior. Figure 2 provides an example for the people development dimension of an executive's job.

Although two or more positions may share a job dimension (most managers could be rated on planning, organizing, and scheduling), the anchors on the scale may vary from position to position, given different roles and responsibilities. In other words, a job dimension can be exhibited differently for different jobs, leading to different anchors for the same dimension.

Developing BARS

Involving Raters and Ratees—The Systems Users

Although there are different approaches to developing BARS, involving incumbents of those positions for which BARS are being developed is critical to the success of the program. One of the advantages of the BARS performance appraisal process is the degree of specificity of relevant performance factors or dimensions. If incumbents are not involved in BARS development, the anchors could become too general and lose their meaning to job incumbents, therefore lessening the utility of the BARS.

A second advantage to involving job incumbents in the development of BARS is that there is likely to be more credibility in the appraisal process itself and its applicability if one has either been involved in its development or knows that one's peers have

Figure 2. Example of a Behaviorally Anchored Rating Scale: People Development

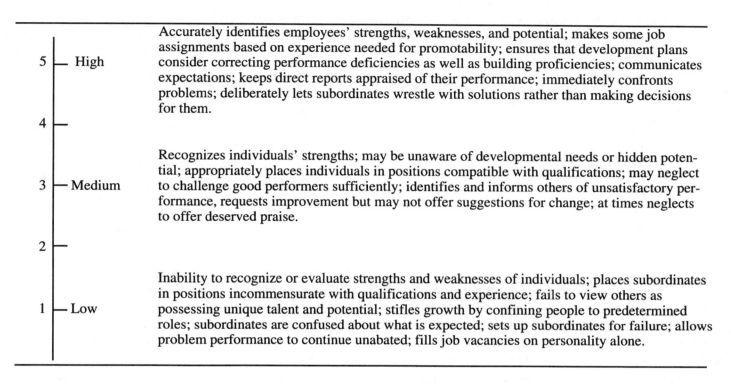

5 —	High	Accurately identifies employees' strengths, weaknesses, and potential; makes some job assignments based on experience needed for promotability; ensures that development plans consider correcting performance deficiencies as well as building proficiencies; communicates expectations; keeps direct reports appraised of their performance; immediately confronts problems; deliberately lets subordinates wrestle with solutions rather than making decisions for them.
4 —		
3 —	Medium	Recognizes individuals' strengths; may be unaware of developmental needs or hidden potential; appropriately places individuals in positions compatible with qualifications; may neglect to challenge good performers sufficiently; identifies and informs others of unsatisfactory performance, requests improvement but may not offer suggestions for change; at times neglects to offer deserved praise.
2 —		
1 —	Low	Inability to recognize or evaluate strengths and weaknesses of individuals; places subordinates in positions incommensurate with qualifications and experience; fails to view others as possessing unique talent and potential; stifles growth by confining people to predetermined roles; subordinates are confused about what is expected; sets up subordinates for failure; allows problem performance to continue unabated; fills job vacancies on personality alone.

been. In the introductory case, CI management expected to achieve a greater "buy-in" and understanding of the organization's values by having them examined as closely as they were in the development of BARS by the job incumbents.

Emphasizing Job Behaviors

Most people think of their jobs or their subordinates' jobs in terms of responsibilities or results rather than behaviors. For example, when describing a financial analyst's job, people will often think of responsibilities (e.g., data gathering) or outputs (e.g., monthly budget variance report). Rarely do people think of the financial analyst in terms of what the financial analyst actually does (e.g., soliciting input from the target audience regarding a report's utility). Behaviors can be used as descriptors or anchors describing various levels of performance. Nevertheless, when a financial analyst's performance falls short of expectations because reports lack needed data or analyses, a performance plan-

ning and appraisal process that concentrates on how the report is done (behaviors), rather than on the untimeliness of reports (results), can be more useful in improving the analyst's reports.

Once the intended uses of the appraisal system are determined (e.g., compensation, promotion), BARS can be developed by following the eight steps outlined below:

1. Determine the job or jobs for which BARS are to be developed. BARS can be developed for a single job (e.g., marketing managers) or for a group of similar jobs (e.g., managerial, executive, computer analyst). Then provide an orientation to BARS to all those participating in the process. The agenda should include why BARS are to be developed, definitions and illustrations of key terminology, an overview of the process, and a description of how the BARS will be used.

2. Job incumbents and their managers meet to identify the most relevant dimensions of the

job under discussion. It is helpful to provide a list of possible job dimensions as a basis for identifying the more relevant dimensions of a particular job. Lists of dimensions previously developed by others in the same job group can also be used as a starting point. However, the process should ensure that the dimensions decided upon for a particular job are truly the most relevant. Following are some examples of dimensions (Bray, 1976):

Oral communication

Leadership

Personal impact

Sensitivity

Flexibility

Independence

Work standards

Career ambition

Work involvement

Resistance to stress

Energy

Decisiveness

Planning and organization

Tenacity

3. Participants write job anchors for each job dimension defined for a given job. Participants should be given guidelines and examples before they begin drafting anchors. (Figure 3 provides a useful set of guidelines for writing anchors.) Anchors should not contain words such as *feel, think, know,* or other descriptors that cannot be observed. A useful process for

Figure 3. Suggestions for Writing Useful Behaviors

1. Use specific examples of behavior, not conclusions about the "goodness" or "badness" of behavior.

    Use This: This supervisor tells a secretary when the work was to be completed, the degree of perfection required, the amount of space it must typed within, and the kind of paper necessary.

    Not This: This supervisor could be expected to give very good instructions to a secretary. Instructions would be clear and concise.

2. Avoid using adjective qualifiers in the anchor statements; use descriptions of actual behavior.

    Use This: This supervisor understands employees such that the supervisor can repeat both the employee's communication and the intent of the message. They also make certain to talk in private when necessary and do not repeat the conversation to others.

    Not This: When supervising associates, this supervisor does a good job of understanding their problems. This supervisor is kind and friendly.

3. Avoid using anchors that make assumptions about employee knowledge about the job; use descriptions of behavior.

    Use This: This employee performs the disassembly procedure for rebuilding a carburetor by first removing the cap and then proceeding with the internal components, gaskets, etc. If in doubt about the procedure, the mechanic will refer to the appropriate manual.

    Not This: This mechanic knows how to disassemble a carburetor and will do so in an efficient and effective manner.

4. Avoid using frequencies in anchor statements; use descriptions of behavior.

    Use This: This officer performs the search procedure by first informing those arrested of their rights, asks them to assume the search position, and then proceeds to conduct the search by touching the arrested in the prescribed places. When the search is complete, the officer informs the arrested and proceeds to the next step in the arrest procedure.

    Not This: This officer always does a good job in performing in search procedure.

5. Avoid using quantitative values (numbers) within anchors.

    Use This: This accountant submits reports on time that contain no misinformation or mistakes. If discrepancies occur on reports from the last period, this accountant identifies the cause.

    Not This: This accountant could be expected to meet 90 percent of deadlines with 95 percent accuracy.

Figure 4. BARS Anchor Reassignment and Scale Value Worksheet

Instructions: Randomly order all anchors below in the left-hand column. Then put all of the job dimensions in the middle column. Ask participants to decide which job dimension each anchor most clearly illustrates by placing an "X" in one and only one job dimension column. Then participants note the degree the performance they feel is illustrated by each anchor by placing an "X" in one of the columns numbered 1 through 7.

| | Job Dimensions | | | | | | | Scale Values | | | | | | |
Behavioral Anchors	1	2	3	4	5	6	etc.	Excellent 7	Very Good 6	Good 5	Average 4	Below Average 3	Very Poor 2	Unacceptable 1
1.														
2.														
3.														
4.														
5.														
6.														
7.														
8.														
9.														
10.														
11.														
12.														
13.														
14.														
15.														
etc.														

developing anchors is to have each participant write two or more behavioral anchors for each point on the scale (write two anchors for each of the five performance levels on a five-point scale) for each dimension. These can be written on index cards. This step can be com-

pleted in a group, provided a reasonably sized pool of anchors (five to eight for each scale value) is developed by the group.

4. The participants reach a consensus on which specific job dimension each anchor best illustrates, regardless of the dimension for which

it was originally written. By distributing the deck of index cards containing the anchors to all participants and having each person identify each anchor's relevant dimension, the process identifies ambiguous anchors. If there is considerable disagreement as to which job dimension an anchor best illustrates (e.g., if more than 25 percent of participants disagree on the relevant dimension), the anchor is probably too ambiguous to be a useful behavior descriptor. A worksheet such as the one illustrated in Figure 4 can be used to link anchors and job dimensions. (The second half of the worksheet is used for step 5 in the development process.)

5. Participants determine scale values for all remaining anchors. In other words, each behavioral anchor is placed somewhere on a dimension's scale (1–5 on a five-point scale, 1–7 on a seven-point scale, etc.) by each member of the group. Group members hence individually determine the level of performance an anchor represents, regardless of the level for which it was originally written (see Figure 4 for a worksheet).

6. The final scale value is determined according to the mean scale value given to an anchor by the group. (The mean could be rounded to the nearest whole number.) Each participant's scale rating is averaged for each anchor, dimension by dimension. This can be done outside the group meeting.

It is important to look at the variance around the mean value given to an anchor by a group. If the variance is large, the group disagreed as to the anchor's placement. For example, a calculated mean of 4 on a seven-point scale could be derived from half of the participants rating the anchor as a 1 (lowest performance) and half rating the anchor as a 7 (higher performance), thus placing the anchor at the fourth point on the scale, indicating average performance. Yet the anchor was not rated as illustrative of average performance by anyone; hence it should be discarded. (A variation of this step is to conduct a group session to discuss each anchor's scale value and reach consensus.)

7. All anchors are arranged according to their calculated (or agreed-upon) scale for each dimension to prepare for the final step.

8. The group and then management review all the scales carefully to ensure that proper terminology is used. The group should also determine whether additional anchors should be used to clarify a performance level. (BARS are not meant to be exhaustive but rather illustrative. They cannot describe all possible behaviors for each job dimension and scale value.)

Since jobs and expectations frequently change, as do job incumbents, job dimensions and anchors should be reviewed by incumbents and their managers at least annually to ensure the relevance of the BARS. The annual review need not involve large numbers of people unless significant restructuring of jobs and expectations occurred. A critique soon after the completion of a performance review should be sufficient to modify any anchors or dimensions.

Legal Issues and BARS

Those involved in the development of a BARS system, or any other performance appraisal approach, should be aware of specific legal issues. Based on Title VII of the Civil Rights Act, guidelines for federal employees (*Uniform Guidelines on Employee Selection Procedures),* the Civil Service Reform Act of 1978 (especially section 430), and case law, those involved in designing a BARS appraisal process should ensure that it:

1. Uses specific performance criteria that are relevant to a job (critical work behaviors and outcomes determined through appropriate job analysis).
2. Communicates the performance appraisal standards to employees.
3. Relies on ratings that are not biased based on race, color, religion, national origin, sex, or age.
4. Draws on multiple ratings from different raters with direct knowledge of ratee job performance to reduce potential biases associated with a single rater.

For a more complete discussion of performance appraisal legal issues, see Schneier and Beatty (1984) and Burchett and DeMeuse (1985).

How BARS Differ from Other Appraisal Systems

The principal difference between most objective-setting processes and BARS is that while objectives focus on *what* people *achieve*, BARS provides a way to assess *how* results are achieved or *what people do* to achieve specified results. In the CI case, *how* results were achieved was at least as important as the results themselves because of CI's need to change certain managerial work processes and behaviors, such as decision making, risk taking, and teamwork. BARS can be a powerful tool for focusing individuals on what the organization believes are key behaviors or for changing certain aspects of an organization's culture, especially when linked to pay and selection decisions (see Beatty & Schneier, 1984).

An appraisal system must do more, however, than assess how work is performed or objectives are met. They do take time to develop, and it is sometimes difficult for job incumbents to write good behavioral anchors. BARS anchors are not completely observable and are open to interpretation, even if they do describe behavior. BARS are far from perfect. How do BARS stack up against a few commonly used appraisal systems in meeting other human resource management needs?

Table 1 compares how well BARS and three other common appraisal approaches meet different performance appraisal objectives. The three additional performance appraisal approaches are:

1. *Management by objectives,* in which specific, often quantifiable, objectives are set and individuals are rated whether they meet their objectives (see Odiorne, 1979; Locke & Latham, 1984).
2. *Forced distribution ranking,* in which individuals are ranked against others in the same department or job class, typically on a global measure of overall job performance; a specific distribution of scores is mandated, often to conform to a "normal" distribution (see Carroll & Schneier, 1982; Bernardin & Beatty, 1984).
3. *Personal trait scales,* in which individuals are rated for specified traits, such as energy, assertiveness, and ambition, but each scale is defined only with adjectives, such as *Excel-*

lent, Outstanding, or *Average* (see Carroll & Schneier, 1982; Bernardin & Beatty, 1984). It is obvious from Table 1 that forced distribution ranking and personal trait scales have severe limits when considering such uses for appraisal systems as providing performance feedback and identifying training needs.

Using BARS

Compatibility of BARS and Objectives

Although BARS have many uses (see Carroll & Schneier, 1982), their primary applications are in planning and appraising performance. BARS can be used as the only performance tool or as a complement to an objectives-based system. In the introductory case, CI used BARS *and* objectives for its top executives and only BARS for its lower-level employees (see Odiorne, 1979; Locke & Latham, 1984 for further discussions of objectives-based systems). Determining whether to use BARS in conjunction with objectives depends on several factors:

1. The degree to which business plans have been articulated and detailed in order to provide a basis for individual objectives.
2. The degree of control a person may have over meaningful objectives by virtue of his or her position responsibilities.
3. The degree to which results and objectives are a sufficient guide for planning and guiding performance.
4. The need to measure both results and the process by which results are achieved.

For Selection, Promotion, Development, and Compensation

Selection and Promotion. BARS can be used as a selection tool in a company's succession planning process (Burnett & Waters, 1984). Once critical job dimensions are identified for key positions included in the succession planning process, BARS can serve to identify those who perform well on the identified dimensions. Promotion or external selection decisions can be made more effectively once a position's critical dimensions have been defined. Candidates can be assessed against relevant dimensions in a number of ways (see Bray, 1976; Byham, 1980).

Table 1. Relative Ability of Performance Appraisal Methods to Attain Appraisal System Objectives

Performance Appraisal Objectives	Behaviorally Anchored Rating Scales (BARS)	Management by Objectives (MBO)	Forced Distribution Ranking	Personal Trait Scales
Feedback and development requires: Specific, behavioral terminology on the format Setting behavioral targets for ratees to work toward; participation of raters and ratees In development; job relatedness; problem-solving performance review, which ends with a plan for performance improvement Reduction of ambiguity/anxiety of ratees regarding job performance required and expected by raters/organizations	Very good to excellent	Fair to good	Poor	Poor
Measuring performance accurately requires: Lessening of rater response set errors (e.g., leniency, halo) Agreement with other performance measures not on the format (e.g., direct indexes, such as salary, sales volume) Reliability across multiple raters Flexibility to reflect changes in job environment; job-related criteria Commitment of raters to observe ratee performance frequently and complete format seriously The use of the same standards across raters	Good	Good to excellent	Poor to fair	Fair to poor
Rewards allocation requires: Ability to rank-order ratees or results in quantifiable performance score Facilitating a variance or spread of scores to discriminate among good, bad, fair, etc., ratees Measuring contributions to organizational/departmental objectives Perception of accuracy and credibility by employees	Very good to excellent	Good to excellent	Good to very good	Fair
Assessing training needs requires: Specifying deficiencies in behavioral terms Incorporating all relevant job dimensions Eliminating motivation/attitude and environmental conditions as causes of inadequate performance	Very good	Fair to good	Poor	Poor to fair

	Good (varies)	Fair to good	Fair to good (varies)	Poor to fair
A rationale for personnel decision making (e.g., identifying promotion potential, job assignments, demotions and termination, etc.) requires: Job-related critieria Job dimensions dealing with ability to assume increasingly difficult assignments built into form Ability to rank ratees comparatively Measurement of contribution to organization/ department objectives Assessment of ratee's career aspirations and long-range goals				
Validation of selection techniques requires: Job relatedness, comprehensive list of dimensions tapping behavioral domain of the job Systematic job analysis to derive criteria Assessment of interrater reliability Professional, objective administration of format Continual observation of ratee performance by raters	Very good to excellent	Fair to good	Poor	Poor

Source: Beatty and Schneier (1981).
Note: Each method's ability to attain the objectives would, of course, depend on several issues particular to each rating situation, such as rater biases, number of raters available, care taken to develop the format, or reward structure in the organization.

Training and Development. BARS can be used as a training and development tool for current positions and potential future positions identified through a formal or informal career planning process. BARS help identify the principal ways people can improve performance in their current position. Significant weaknesses identified by behaviors on the lower end of a behaviorally anchored scale can be addressed through relevant training and development programs. If a person is aspiring to a specific higher-level position, he or she can work toward developing the behaviors required to succeed at that position, as identified through the higher-level position's job dimensions and relevant BARS. Assignments, either permanent or part time, can be made to develop the needed skills.

Compensation. Results of BARS appraisals can also be used in making pay decisions. The specificity of BARS standards increases the directness and consistency of the performance-pay linkage (see Cumming, 1987, and McLaughlin, 1987, for discussions of linking pay to performance).

Ratings from BARS-based appraisals can be especially useful in determining appropriate salary levels. Most salary administration systems determine increases according to an individual's performance rating in combination with his or her current positioning in the salary range (in the lower, middle, or top third of the range). With uniform BARS for the same position being applied to all position incumbents, managers have a higher probability of giving consistent performance ratings and the appropriate salary treatment. Some appraisal systems, such as objectives-based systems, may not apply the consistent measurement standards that a BARS system provides. Often the level of rigor of objectives varies across incumbents in the same position and salary grade or level. These systems therefore may be more likely to result in uneven salary increase treatments.

Some incentive programs have an individual component, sometimes in addition to a company and/or division component, used to determine an award. The results of a BARS appraisal can, of course, be used as a determinant of individual incentive award adjustments (as can the achievement of individual objectives). Some managers have difficulty paying similar individual incentive awards to top people who both achieve their objectives yet do not have as equally good performance in their overall job responsibilities (as in the case at the beginning of this chapter). Tying BARS ratings, either alone or in conjunction with performance on a set of objectives, to the determination of individual incentive awards is an effective way of linking overall job performance to individual incentive awards.

Guidelines for Effective Development and Implementation of BARS

One concern with BARS is the amount of time needed to identify relevant job dimensions and develop appropriate behavioral anchors. A second concern is the difficulty people have in developing useful behaviors. BARS development can, however, be efficient. Using such aids as a list of possible job dimensions and useful examples of behavioral anchors can both facilitate and expedite BARS development. The key issue, however, is that time spent with design and development process of an appraisal system pays great dividends in its use. Once performance expectations are defined, behavioral performance feedback and performance problem solving are improved significantly because both raters and ratees know what is required to attain each rating level.

A third concern is having a large enough group of incumbents in a job to develop the number of anchors needed to develop a set of BARS. One supervisor and a single or a few subordinates could use BARS effectively. They do not need to use index cards, develop a pool of anchors, and calculate mean scale values. They simply need to discuss what different levels of performance would look like and come to an understanding as to what is expected.

Managers should remember that the real benefit of BARS (and any other performance appraisal process) lies in its developmental process and its use, not in its paperwork. No appraisal system, however well designed, solves problems of unwilling performance coaches, unskilled performance problem solvers, and/or biased performance raters (see Murphy & Constans, 1987; Landy & Farr, 1983).

To manage performance effectively, managers and their subordinates should determine what is important to measure. Forms serve as a guide to the communication required to manage performance. In the end, the degree of detail required should match the comfort level of the participants.

A final concern that should be addressed is the degree of commitment and accountability necessary to develop and use BARS effectively. There must be commitment to the process from a company's or division's influential managers. The commitment of the users of the system can be built through participation in the development of the BARS. In CI, the managers changed from resisting further use of the objective-setting process to enthusiastically using BARS as a useful management tool when they saw it meet their needs.

Accountability for managing performance is also required. One practical way to develop accountability is to rate each manager on his or her performance management competence. Once accountability is built, people will have a need to develop the requisite skills.

To make appraisal systems work, manage performance all year; don't just appraise it once a year. Appraisal systems fail all too frequently. Sometimes, as was the case with CI, the design was deficient—it did not provide a mechanism to measure *how* the objectives were accomplished and corporate values were reinforced by managers. BARS can help here. Often, however, the appraisal system is seen as a once-a-year *rating* of performance, not an ongoing process of *managing* it. The key to effective systems lies in their ability to measure what counts and their users' ability (and willingness) to operate them effectively (see Schneier, Beatty, & Baird, 1986; Schneier & Beatty, 1986).

Regardless of whether BARS are used alone or with objectives, there are certain fundamentals to ensure the effective use of any appraisal system. *Managers,* not staff professionals, must:

1. *Define the overall purpose or mission* of the relevant work group, department, or division and job. Why does this unit exist? Who are its "customers" (internal or external), and how does it serve them? How does this unit's work help meet organization-wide objectives? Why does each job exist? How does each job help accomplish the mission?

   The mission should be reviewed at least annually, based on new directions or emphases of the organization, as well as performance actually achieved in the prescribed time period. Overall unit goals or objectives can be derived from the mission (see Beatty & Schneier, 1984).

2. *Determine roles and responsibilities* of the unit members once their job's mission is determined. What roles and responsibilities are required to achieve the job's mission? How does each person help achieve the mission as he or she performs their job?

3. *Set performance expectations* by identifying a set of job dimensions (and relevant, illustrative behavioral anchors, to the extent necessary). These are the aspects of the job on which people should be rated. If outcomes or results should be evaluated (see the criteria for use of objectives cited above), specific, individual objectives must be set. Define a limited number of clear, measurable objectives. BARS can be used in conjunction with objectives.

4. *Monitor performance, solve performance problems, and provide performance feedback* during the performance period. Coaching, counseling, and solving performance problems are required throughout the year, not just at year end. The goal is to eliminate surprises at the assessment step, for both managers and subordinates.

5. *Evaluate performance* based on data collected on performance against expectations (both process and results), and communicate it to ratees with clear examples that support the evaluation. Ask "customers," peers, and even subordinates, who have relevant data.

Figure 5. A Performance Management Model: An Ongoing, Management-Driven, Participative Process

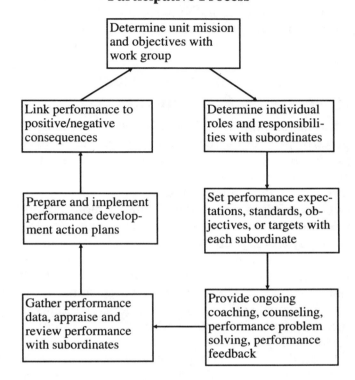

6. *Define performance development action plans* to address improvement opportunities identified in the previous step. Both ratees and their managers should be held accountable for meeting these targets. Training, self-development, job rotation, closer supervision, and expanded responsibilities are all options here.

7. *Link performance to specific consequences* (e.g., salary increases, incentive awards, and promotion opportunities). Most companies talk about merit pay and pay for performance, yet very few have effective systems (see McLaughlin, 1987). A prerequisite to paying for performance is a viable mechanism for identifying, defining, and measuring performance, as well as a committed and skilled group of managers.

Figure 5 illustrates a performance management cycle (see also Schneier, Beatty, & Baird, 1987).

Managers who follow these seven steps are likely to develop a performance management *process,* not merely an appraisal *form,* that effectively improves the performance of individuals, and therefore departments, units, divisions, and the company as a whole.

Compelling Business Needs: A Necessary Prerequisite

Having a compelling business need for managing performance is, above all other factors, the principal driver for having a performance management system that works (Peters, 1987). In the introductory case, CI's compelling need was to turn the *modus operandi* of management into a more action-oriented, risk-taking mode in order to increase the company's competitive advantage. There are many examples of companies turning to an active performance management process to help it achieve important goals. GE's emphasis on customer service (Trachtenberg, 1986) and American Express's measurement of departments' impact on customers (Uttal, 1987) are two examples.

In addition to having a strong business need, other factors, noted above, are necessary to ensure the effectiveness of a performance management system. However, these factors (identified below) are more likely to be addressed once the compelling business need is clear. The key factors are:

1. *Management commitment* to the performance management process (summarized in Figure 5).
2. *Accountability* for managing performance, reinforced through pay and promotion decisions.
3. Addressing performance management *skill development,* made easier once the needs are recognized through management accountability for the process.

Unless a performance appraisal approach such as BARS is linked to specific business needs and addresses them, the process will have limited utility and appeal and will fall into disuse. After all, the ultimate purpose of any appraisal system is to improve organizational performance via effective individual appraisal, development, and rewards.

References

Beatty, R.W., & Schneier, C.E. (1981). *Personnel administration: An experiential skill-building approach.* Reading, MA: Addison-Wesley Publishing Company.

Beatty, R.W., & Schneier, C.E. (1984). Strategic performance appraisal issues. In R.S. Schuler & S.A. Youngblood (Eds.), *Readings in personnel and human resource management.* St. Paul, MN: West Publishing Co.

Bernardin, H.J., & Beatty, R.W. (1984). *Performance appraisal.* Boston: Kent Publishing.

Bray, D.W. (1976). The assessment centers method. In *Training and development handbook.* New York: McGraw-Hill.

Burchett, S.R., & DeMeuse, K.P. (1985). Performance appraisal and the law. *Personnel,* 62 (7), 29–37.

Burnett, R.S., & Waters, J.A. (1984). The action profile: A practical aid to career development and succession planning. *Business Horizons,* 27 (3), 15–21.

Byham, W.C. (1980). Starting an assessment center the correct way. *Personnel Administrator,* 27–32.

Carroll S.J., & Schneier, C.E. (1982). *Performance appraisal: A systems approach.* Glenview, IL: Scott Foresman & Company.

Cumming, C.S. (1987). New directions in salary administration. *Personnel,* 64 (1), 68–69.

Landy, F.J., & Farr, J.F. (1983). *Measurement of work performance: Methods, theory & applications.* San Diego: Academic Press.

Locke, E.A., Latham, G.P. (1984). *Goal-setting: A motivational technique that works!* Englewood Cliffs, NJ: Prentice-Hall.

McLaughlin, D.J. (1987). Pay for performance: A perspective. *Compensation and Benefits Management,* 3 (2), 37–41.

Murphy, K.R., & Constans, J.I. (1987). Behavioral anchors as a source of bias in ratings. *Journal of Applied Psychology,* 72 (4), 573–577.

Odiorne, G.S. (1979). *MBO II: A system of managerial leadership for the 80's.* Belmont, CA: D.S. Lake Publishers.

Peters, T. (1978). *Thriving on chaos: A revolutionary agenda for today's manager.* New York: Alfred A. Knopf.

Schneier, C.E., & Beatty, R.W. (1979). Developing behaviorally-anchored rating scales. *Personnel Administrator,* 24, 59–68.

Schneier, C.E., & Beatty, R.W. (1984). Designing a legally defensible performance appraisal system. In M. Cohen & M. Golembiewski (Eds.), *Public personnel update.* New York: Marcel Dekker.

Schneier, C.E., & Beatty, R.W. (1986). How to construct a performance appraisal system. *Training and Development Journal,* 40 (4), 38–42.

Schneier, C.E., & Beatty, R.W., & Baird, L.S. (1986). Creating a performance management system. *Training and Development Journal,* 40 (5), 74–79.

Schneier, C.E., & Beatty, R.W., & Baird, L.S. (1987). *The performance management sourcebook.* Amherst, MA: Human Resource Development Press, Inc.

Trachtenberg, J.A. (1986). Shake, rattle and clonk. *Forbes,* 138 (1), 71–74.

Uttal, Bro. (1987). Companies that serve you best. *Fortune,* 116 (13), 98–116.

Appraisals Can Make—or Break—Your Court Case

by David I. Rosen

Employees who have been demoted, discharged, disciplined or denied promotions and pay increases increasingly turn to the courts and regulatory agencies for relief from what they see as arbitrary actions by their employers.

The judgment often goes against the employer because the employee is able to:

- Produce records of consistently favorable appraisals showing that there had been no real warning of trouble

- Show that *no* formal appraisals criticizing performance were received

- Prove that the employer's appraisal system is inherently biased against members of a protected class

It's difficult enough for a company to defend a case in which an employee who previously has received generally fair and accurate appraisals is discharged for a justifiable reason. It's even tougher if the reason for the discharge is less than noble or if previous evaluations didn't reflect the employee's real faults. When both the reason *and* the appraisal record are questionable, dismissal of an employee can be nearly impossible to justify legally. Although faulty evaluations can undermine the best of cases, they can be the final blow to the case that's weak at the outset.

Documentation is crucial. Fair and impartial performance appraisals that document the intent to help rectify problem areas help defend companies against wrongful discharge claims and similar

charges. Explicit documentation of honest appraisals is especially important in the case of employees who are protected by major antidiscrimination laws dealing with disability, age, race, religion, national origin or gender. For example, although Equal Employment Opportunity Commission (EEOC) regulations were written having employment and placement tests in mind, they also apply to performance appraisals and require that any measurement made to distinguish between employees be valid and administered fairly. An employer must document that these requirements have been met.

Other agency regulations and court decisions have laid down further requirements including:

- Tool measuring performance is linked directly to job requirements

- A good score means good performance

- The test reliably predicts future performance

- The appraisal is a valid measure of motivation and intelligence

Problems stem from subjective judgments. Performance appraisals also should be objective. Supervisors must make some subjective judgments, however, and human judgment is subject to many errors. Among them are:

- Grouping everyone's ratings unreasonably *toward the high end* of the scale, to curry favor with employees

- Allowing the *halo effect*—a favorable judgment on one quality—to overshadow other problem areas

- Allowing *personal bias* to affect the evaluation

Taking into account *how the appraisal will be used.* For example, if the evaluators know the appraisal results will be used only to set salaries, they might unconsciously give higher ratings. By contrast, if the evaluator believes that by giving a severely negative evaluation he or she might gain approval to terminate a problem employee, the appraisal might be harsher than warranted.

Resolution often depends on good faith. If any of the above occurs and an employee is terminated, he or she may file suit for wrongful discharge (based on rulings of many courts indicating that employees have the right to be treated fairly). When such a suit has been filed, its resolution often has depended on whether the supervisor acted fairly and in good faith.

To find out if the worker was treated fairly, ask yourself: 1) Has the employee been evaluated objectively and impartially in accordance with a sound performance appraisal system; and 2) Did the dismissed worker's previous appraisals show a history of satisfactory service?

An appraisal form that reflects good job performance may undercut the legitimacy of the employer's later decision to fire the worker and may subject the decision to question. If an objective appraisal system has been established closely related to the job requirements, however, and if a consistent, good faith effort has been made to judge workers by it, those efforts usually will be rewarded with a finding in the company's favor.

Companies also may face an employee's claim that he or she has been defamed by untruthful statements made in an evaluation that harm his or her good name and reputation, or cause termination, a lower-than-expected salary increase, a missed promotion, or failure to be hired by a new employer. However, if an evaluation is truthful and the supervisor acted in good faith, believing the evaluation to be a fair and accurate reflection of the employee's job performance, a defamation suit by the employee is unlikely to succeed.

An employer also may be vulnerable to a negligent retention or retraining claim if an employee who gets an unsatisfactory job evaluation is retained in employment, but no corrective action (like retraining) is taken, and he or she causes injury to a third party. If an evaluation is thorough, and the employer acts upon the results of the evaluation by removing from the payroll any worker who poses a risk to the safety and health of others, a negligence claim is less likely to arise. A breach-of-contract claim also may be filed against an employer that doesn't adhere to a written appraisal policy setting forth specific procedures that it pledges to follow. In addition, employers frequently lose discharge arbitrations in unionized shops in which evaluations are either nonexistent or are inconsistent with the positions taken by the employer in the presence of the arbitrator.

An appraisal system must be properly used. It becomes obvious that a sound appraisal system, fairly administered, can be an important element in the defense of nearly any type of contested discharge case. No matter what line of argument a former employee's attorney might consider, the use of a good appraisal system can be an important index of fair dealing and good faith. If good cause must be shown, the appraisal system can reveal this as well.

However, the appraisal system must be even-handed and properly used to be effective as a defense. A quick review at the annual appraisal hour won't suffice. The appraisal record should show the results of an honest evaluation that fairly reflects the employee's actual ability, including both strong and weak points. Appraisal systems that use subjective criteria aren't necessarily unfair, but they will draw extra attention from courts and enforcement agencies, compared with systems that use objective, numerical rating methods. If strictly followed, the guidelines below will help shield a company from legal problems arising from performance appraisals:

- Regular, written appraisals should be conducted for all employees
- Supervisors should be trained thoroughly on proper evaluation procedures
- In preparing evaluations, supervisors should apply consistent, explicit and objective job-related standards. To keep bias out of the appraisal process, work performance—not the person performing the job—should be judged
- Evaluation should be prepared on a timely basis and never back-dated or altered after the fact

Making a Case for Accurate Appraisals

Performance appraisals have become a necessary defense in suits filed against employers by terminated employees. Faulty appraisal systems, however, can contribute to employer liability. Here are some examples:

- An African-American female manager successfully sued for race discrimination following her discharge, which had been a part of a work force reduction. The employer's stated reason for selecting the woman for discharge was her tendency to criticize other people, which prevented her from achieving management's goals of building morale and promoting employee team spirit. The court held that the stated reason for dismissal was a pretext for discrimination because the discharged employee had received consistently good performance ratings and two merit raises. Her only negative ratings were a part of a set of evaluations that she never had seen. Also, management had pressured the employee's supervisor to lower her ratings on the negative evaluation after deciding to discharge her. *Norris v. Hartmax,* 54 FEP Cases 1099 (5th Cir. 1990).

- While he was still employed, an employee complained to his immediate supervisor that he was a victim of age discrimination. Within a few months, the supervisor fired the employee for unsatisfactory job performance. Just before the employee's dismissal, his supervisor evaluated his job performance negatively, causing the company to believe that it would have an ironclad defense in an age-discrimination suit. Testimony at the trial, however, revealed that the supervisor had lowered the worker's performance appraisal deliberately without his knowledge after he had complained about age discrimination; subsequently the supervisor had deluged the employee with job assignments. The judge, refusing to set aside a $450,000 jury verdict, concluded that the jury could have inferred reasonably that the supervisor purposely had set the employee up for failure, hoping to have a pretext for firing him. The doctored performance appraisal was the smoking gun. *Dominic v. Consolidated Edison Co. Of New York,* 652 F. Supp. 815 (S.D.N.Y.1986).

- An employee was terminated, after 23 years of employment, because of his poor attitude, lack of cooperation and lack of leadership. The company's policy stated that an employee could be discharged only if given notice of job performance deficiencies and an opportunity to improve. Moreover, the company had a written policy of annual performance review, part of the purpose of which was to apprise employees of supervisor dissatisfaction with the job performances. The evaluation performed immediately before the employee's discharge didn't disclose any dissatisfaction, even though,

at the time of the evaluation, the supervisor was actively considering terminating the employee. The court held that the employee could sue his former employer for "negligent evaluation" as described by Michigan law. *Chamberlain v. Bissell, Inc.,* 547 R. Supp. 1067 (W.D. Mich. 1982).

- The U.S. Drug Enforcement Agency's (DEA) evaluation procedures had a disproportionate impact on African-American special agents, adversely affecting their status as employees. Evidence established that African-American agents systematically were rated lower than white agents and thus were less likely to receive promotions and choice job assignments. Because the DEA failed to provide supervisors with any written instructions on how to evaluate agent performance, and because virtually all supervisors conducting the evaluations were white, the rating criteria used were highly subjective. Further, the DEA failed to establish that its evaluation system was related to job performance, or that it served any legitimate business need. *Segar v. Civiletti,* 508 F. Supp. 690 (D.D.C. 1981).

- A discharged employee brought suit against his former employer for "breach of contract" as defined by New York law. The employee alleged that, at the time he was hired, company officials assured him that he could be terminated only for serious mistakes and that the performance evaluation procedure, described in detail in the employee handbook, would be used to determine the existence of just cause. The court held that these alleged assurances, if believed by a jury, would constitute an express limitation on the right to fire an individual who would otherwise be an employee-at-will. *Sivel v. Reader's Digest Inc.,* 2 IER Cases 1880 (S.D.N.Y. 1988).

- An African-American team leader sued a federal government agency for race discrimination after her supervisor rated her lower on her performance appraisal than the same supervisor had rated four white team leaders. The court found in favor of the employee and directed the agency to give her the same performance rating as her white peers. The court determined that the employee's supervisor had rated the team leaders in a "subjective, inexperienced, imprecise and unfair" manner, and had allowed subjective and extraneous factors to determine the outcome of the woman's evaluation. The court held that the agency's failure to implement a fair and objective performance system for the team leaders raised an inference that it intended to discriminate on the basis of race. *Tyson v. Levinson,* 52 FEP Cases 350 (D.D.C. 1990).

- An audit system should be established to guard against inflated appraisals and to ensure that evaluations are conducted in an unbiased manner

- Before an evaluation is communicated to the employee, it should be reviewed and approved by another manager

- Evaluations shouldn't be malicious

- Evaluations should be truthful

- Evaluations should be candid but constructive

- Problem areas should be detailed and documented. Supervisors should be specific and take the time necessary to write out comments

- The employee should be given the opportunity to respond to a negative performance evaluation by giving his or her version of the facts. This will help smoke out potential future legal claims and involve the worker in the appraisal process

- When an employee's performance has been appraised as substandard, specific goals—agreed upon by the employee—should be developed to improve deficiency areas. Appraisals are most effective when they contain a compliance timetable and secure the worker's commitment to comply

- An employer should be able to prove that an employee received the evaluation, either by having the employee sign for it or by having the employee's receipt witnessed by another supervisor

- Evaluations shouldn't be limited to hourly and rank-and-file employees; where appraisal systems are instituted, they should be applied throughout the organization

- Circulation of evaluations should be restricted to those in management having a need to know

- In considering termination based on unsatisfactory job performance, earlier evaluations should be scrutinized to find out if the employee was informed of the performance deficiencies and if the evaluations are consistent with the stated reasons for the employee's dismissal

By being aware of the legal problems that may arise from the use of its performance appraisals and the steps to take to avoid litigation, companies can make their performance appraisal reports a part of their defense and not a source of liability.

David I. Rosen is a partner in the New York City-based law firm of Clifton Budd & DeMaria.

Failing Evaluations

by Katherine G. Hauck

The '80s are over. And one thing that appears to have bitten the dust along with the decade is the old-fashioned, once-a-year, paternalistic employee performance evaluation.

And it deserved to die, says Sandra Price, manager of strategic planning and projects at Intel Corp., a microprocessor company based in Santa Clara, Calif. Conducted for workforce management or salary review purposes, or out of sheer annual habit, the old-fashioned employee evaluation is "manager-dependent and hierarchical," she claims.

Price reports to Intel's vice president of human resources, and for the last several years has been directly involved in the company's implementation of an all-new performance assessment system. What Intel has done with its 5,000 headquarter's employees for three years, and now with an additional 20,000 employees worldwide, is heavily involve each of them in his or her own evaluation and development planning. "This doesn't quite describe it," Price admits, but the system Intel uses is "more negotiated."

More negotiated. Interactive. Development driven. Arriving at words to describe performance management—the practice now supplanting performance evaluation at some progressive companies—is as difficult as arriving at the practice itself. Craig Dreilinger, director of the Dreiford Group, management consultants in Bethesda, Md., says his firm witnessed "so many efforts that tried to give an accurate measure of somebody's performance in a way that was developmental, and that the employee and supervisor could buy into—and failed." They turned down performance evaluation consulting jobs for five years after concluding nothing worked.

That's where Nancy Thacker, corporate director of personnel for Litton Industries, a 52,000-employee technology company, is right now.

Thacker manages HR function at Litton's Beverly Hills headquarters. She feels torn between working with Litton divisions that have formal-but-flawed evaluation structures; not having a structure for the largely executive population with which she works; and knowing that "having none doesn't work," but worrying that once you've put something on paper, you've created a "legal document...something they could use for wrongful discharge."

In trying to develop an evaluation structure to fill the void at Litton's corporate division, Thacker says, she has "looked at the forms and practices of at least six different companies, and saw none I really liked."

Walking a Tightrope

Disliking evaluation forms is just the tip of the iceberg. According to Kathryn Craft Rogers, deputy HR manager for the Lawrence Livermore National Laboratory, Livermore, Calif., "The real challenge is walking that tight-rope of giving good data to people that will help them develop their careers, while at the same time, providing adequate documentation...to justify human resources decisions," such as whom to promote, transfer, or give raises to.

HR professionals say boobytraps riddle standard evaluation methodology. A prevalent one is the "halo effect"—the tendency to find better appraisals higher up the ladder. The term is also used when a person who receives an initial outstanding performance rating basks in that glow even when performance later lags.

"Actually, it can be a halo or horns," Roger notes, "depending on what that first impression was."

Reviewers not only have difficulty with objectivity, but with giving constructive feedback, particularly criticism. The result is "rating creep: a gradual, false up-tick in performance rating to avoid the negative," explains Renee Booth, regional director of human resources, planning and development for Hay Management Consultants in Philadelphia.

Thacker believes the threat of litigation further intimidates managers into accentuating the positive. Patrick Moran, assistant director for human resources at the Brandywine Hospital and Trauma Center, which has 1,250 employees in Coatesville, Pa., cites other causes.

One is the blinding kinship that develops between people who have worked together for a while; second is that "Evaluators are like salespeople: You can teach them to be more aware of the employee's contribution, but the good ones are born, not made."

Indeed, managers who attain supervisory posts rarely receive ongoing evaluation training, and some companies struggle to ensure that both sides understand the significance of a given grade, according to Ken Rohner, director of personnel for Schlumberger Technologies in New York City. In the commonly used A-to-E alpha rating system, Rohner points out, the majority of workers fall into the C category.

"C is a good rating, but if you're just out of college and used to getting A's, a C feels bad. We try very hard to tell managers not to give B's so people won't get upset. But there's always that 10 percent that may be off-base, even in the most objective system I can think of."

Upset is unavoidable in the face of what Moran calls "the critical incident effect." He finds that any incident occurring just before appraisal time can overturn a year's performance—good or bad.

But was that incident due to the employee? "It's hard for managers to know what's really within an employee's control," notes James Kisela, vice president of human resources for the Vanguard Group, a family of mutual funds in Wayne, Pa. He knows that "fairness requires looking carefully." But do managers consistently make time for analysis?

In her consulting practice, Booth has repeatedly discovered that most employees do not think so.

"Employees generally don't believe managers can evaluate their performance," she says. "They don't trust that the traditional performance appraisal system measures their true contribution to the organization."

More Responsibility

Back in the '80s, when management by objective was extremely popular, companies complied with the law, giving employees a right to respond to their appraisals, but didn't care if they disliked the way they were evaluated.

But Kathleen Guinn, a Hay consultant in Pittsburgh, believes that today's total quality management ideals, in which the employee takes more responsibility for decisions and expects to have more control, "has taken big chips out of the paternalistic relationship between managers and employees."

For example, Schlumberger's use of performance management techniques is reflected in a hybrid form called the performance appraisal and development plan. This form works both backwards and forwards, to assess actual performance and future potential. It combines subjective and objective elements, such as efforts to develop the company's cultural base and performance against objectives, and it combines top-down assessment with mutually determined goals and milestones.

Both the supervisor and worker set expectations in the first step of the plan, and there are two interim appraisals and an annual review. The review uses an alpha system of performance codes. A is outstanding; B, well above normal expectancy; C, normal expectancy; D, development needed; and E, significant development needed.

In the annual review, both the supervisor and the worker discuss succession planning and complete a form that spells out how prepared the worker is to replace a given person, identifies any impediments, and notes the development status of his or her potential replacements in the succession pipeline.

In total, Schlumberger's performance appraisal and development plan, including the succession planning form, consists of three pages of writing and filling in the boxes, and one page to define terms.

Moran has tried numerous ways to structure the review process, from doing regression analyses that weight each aspect of performance with mathemati-

Intel's Appraisal System

Intel Inc., a microprocessor company in Santa Clara, Calif., has a comprehensive appraisal system. Sandra Price, a manager of strategic planning and projects, describes it:

"In addition to getting a formal, annual review written to their file, managers meet to rank workers against peers performing similar jobs. A good ranking group is 10 to 30 people, and each individual is ranked on his contribution to the department, the division, and organization. A 'ranking manager' runs the meetings where this takes place, keeps people on track, maintains objectivity, and drives the output—a ranked list.

"Before managers go into the meeting, they fill out a short evaluation form to make their approaches similar. It captures what happened during the year—the individual's accomplishments.

"As part of the ranking process, workers go through a rating that measures how they did against the requirements of their job. After surveys found that a five-level rating system equated too closely to an A, B, C, D, E system, in which C isn't viewed as positive, we changed it to three simple ratings—outstanding, successful, or improvement required.

"We also evaluate performance trends—how an individual is trending against their peers. Are they moving faster? Taking new responsibility? Equal to peers? About as expected? Slower? This trend evaluation is a new element designed to give people as early notice as possible when their performance starts to slow down.

"Intel also conducts focals—a point in time when we evaluate an employee's individual performance contribution to the group development needs for future growth and appropriate compensation.

"We use past performance to project the future and ask the employee to decide with the manager what areas they need to improve or want to concentrate on over the next year. Improvement relates to defined objectives—we're an MBO company. Do they have the skills and knowledge that enable them to meet objectives and grow as they desire? The worker and the manager agree to the skills that are required and together devise a plan that will use both formal and informal learning systems to help the worker succeed.

"We leave it up to the manager as to how often they meet and discuss progress, and we place the responsibility for improvement on the employee. They own that."

Price, an attorney, believes the comprehensiveness of Intel's evaluation process is one reason why the company has "for its size been relatively untouched by litigation related to wrongful termination."

---

cal value, to imposing forced ranking salary administration groups, to conducting month-by-month writeups that really diminish halo and critical incident effects. All of these are notoriously time consuming.

But basically, he insists, all jobs come down to four elements—the worker's direct responsibilities, contribution to the unit's agenda, quality (thoroughness and accuracy), and timeliness. Moran separates a salary review from a developmental review. He thinks the best systems are those that emphasize frequent, frank, two-way communications derived from the quality circle movement.

For example, after agreeing on the things that will be evaluated, both the boss and the worker conduct an appraisal. It's in discussing those areas where their judgments differ that understanding takes place, he says, noting "Managers don't always know what an employee is doing, or what his strengths and weaknesses are."

Peer Review

Indeed, review by others is a major tenet of performance management. "In addition to your supervisor, five of your peers rate you and five of your clients (or interfacing workers) rate you," explains Dreilinger. "If you're a manager, add five of your subordinates."

Known as a 360-degree review, its validity is based on the premise that "the people who are most qualified to conduct a performance review are those affected by it," he says.

Guinn thinks 360-degree review also ties in with the market-driven company. "Performance expectations must be generated from customer expectations, not job descriptions," she adds.

The Vanguard Group doesn't use 360-degree review, Kisela says, but they do have interdisciplinary teams of workers now modifying evaluation forms to assure that the language used really does describe the jobs at hand. "The main job is communication," he says.

Virginia Lord, a consultant with Philadelphia-based Right Associates, agrees. The communication in performance management brings about earlier discussion of problems, which brings, she says, surer resolution and "a chance for the worker to demonstrate added capability that can be the basis for promotion."

It also builds teamwork and truer understanding of workers' strengths. "I ask my direct reports, 'What obstacles have you confronted that you need my help with?' to move the project along without implying they couldn't handle it," Lord says. "With some jobs, you can evaluate people on the basis of knowledge and pay for competency, rather than what they do day to day."

And what's new about any of this, asks Lawrence Livermore National Lab's Rogers? A good supervisor "has the ability to articulate what the expectations are that the individual will be evaluated against; has good coaching and monitoring skills so they can observe how the employee could be more effective; and can communicate those suggestions to the individual in a way they can understand and do something about it," she says.

"A good evaluator is someone who has established rapport with the people who work for him or her all along, so when they sit down to review in a summary way, there are no surprises."

At the lab, Rogers says, they add "a second level of review to assure that the standards being applied in any given work unit support the standards of the larger organization and are consistent from one department to the next." This is a common defense against litigation.

According to a survey by the Wyatt Co., nearly 12 percent of all director's and officer's liability claims related to wrongful termination in 1990. In the last two survey years, this claim category has led all others.

Jury Verdict Research Inc. of Horsham, Pa., reported last year that about 52 percent of recent jury awards for wrongful discharge exceeded $250,000.

Between 1986 and 1988, the Washington, D.C.-based Bureau of National Affairs reported a 64 percent victory rate in the courts by employees alleging wrongful termination.

But this threat could have a positive impact, too. As a routine measure, Rogers says, "Review practices, see what other companies do, ensure that performance objectives are truly job related, and ensure that the process is fair, and based on fact."

Performance Reviews Get Mixed Reviews

by Michael A. Verespej

In this era of worker empowerment, employees are gaining more control over their own jobs. So you might expect one offshoot to be companies having an easier time reviewing performance in a fashion that employees find acceptable.

Guess again.

Although there's only a slight variation in the numbers from a previous IW survey conducted in 1987, there's no doubt that employers have not been listening to their workers. And employee dissatisfaction with the performance-review process is higher than it was when IW conducted the earlier survey.

For example, in 1987 only 11.8% of the respondents said their companies conducted reviews semiannually, even though the largest percentage of IW readers (47%) felt that semiannual reviews would be best. Despite that suggestion, the number of respondents whose companies conduct twice-a-year reviews has fallen to 10.1% in this survey—and the number of IW readers who prefer semiannual reviews has risen to 52.4%.

In 1987, 20% said reviews were very effective. That fell to 18% in this survey, and, at the same time, the number of readers who feel that reviews are a waste of time rose from 6% to 9%. Another 22% now say reviews are not very effective (it was 22.2% in the previous survey). An even higher percentage—48.8% versus 43% in 1987—say reviews often crumble into second-guessing sessions.

And the same problems remain. To wit, the review is only as good—or as bad—as the manager who conducts it; there is no consistency among reviews across a corporation; there is little relationship between the performance review and salary increases; the reviews crumble into second-guessing sessions almost half the time, and too often focus on an employee's performance in the last few weeks, rather than the preceding 12 months.

One manager in the aerospace industry claims not to have gotten a written review in 16 years. Another says he spent five and a half years at Westinghouse before he got his first review. And—this should come as no surprise—many say politics plays too large a role in a performance evaluation.

"Reviews can be enormously helpful—if done honestly and fairly," says one Chicago manager. "But most companies don't do it properly. Reviews are usually unfair to the employee, biased by politics and personality, and rarely, if ever, based on measurable criteria."

"Reviews become more of a popularity contest, rather than an evaluation of capability or performance," says J.C. Accountius, supervisor of quality assurance-engineering at Texas Instruments' Sherman, Tex., plant.

Adds R.D. Thorson, a micrographics manager for Rockwell International in Cedar Rapids, Iowa: "Too many reviews are based on friendship and favoritism, rather than productive workmanship."

Another problem: Many workers feel reviews are structured to "justify predetermined salary or position changes," says an engineer at Plessey Electronic Systems in Wayne, N.J. It's the same sentiment echoed by managers at GE, American Cyanamid, Mack Truck, International Paper, and Rohr Industries.

Even if companies actually use performance reviews to determine a worker's salary increase, few managers are confident in the abilities of their fellow managers to conduct a review in a professional, competent manner.

"Most managers have not been trained in how to give performance reviews," says a plant manager in Hanover, Pa. "They should be trained to review, and be reviewed upon their ability to review. But since they are not measured on how well they review their people, the message to them is that it is really not very important."

The negative tone that often overrides many review sessions also annoys workers. "Reviews often turn into a bashing session where all of a worker's bad points are touched on, but the good points are forgotten," says a manager in Chicago.

"I've always felt that at review time an effort is made to find the *one* mistake of the year, and no effort goes into pointing out the achievements," adds Wayne Hartlich, operations supervisor at Wigwam Mills Inc., Sheboygan, Wis.

As a result, reviews often *de*motivate employees, says Frank L. Messersmith, chief of production and engineering for the U.S. Defense Dept.'s Defense Logistics Agency in Santa Clara, Calif. "In general, performance reviews are destructive and counterproductive. They are *worse* than a waste of time."

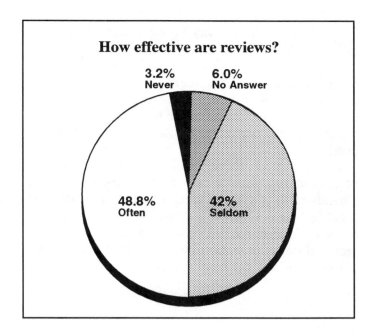

How could reviews be made useful? IW readers certainly don't lack for suggestions.

"Keep away from a standard format," suggests one senior manufacturing engineer. "Tailor the review to meet the type of communication that is needed to help both the person being reviewed and the company."

Many others, including a Goodyear Tire & Rubber Co. manager in Topeka, Kans., suggest that there be more peer review. "Those above you, your peers, and those who work for you should all have input into the review," he says.

And reviews would be more useful, says a manager at Corning Glass, if "future development needs—not just ancient history"—were discussed.

Adds Ron Melcher, sales engineer at the Brecksville, Ohio, operation of AIP Inc., a supplier of piercing equipment to the metal-stamping industry: "Performance reviews should not be a report card, but a growth and developmental tool for both managers and employees. And it should include the perspectives of peers, subordinates, and customers."

Finally, a good number of IW readers feel that if managers did a better job of communicating on a daily basis, there wouldn't be much need for a yearly review.

"Performance reviews too often look only at last week or yesterday," says an engineer at Sundstrand

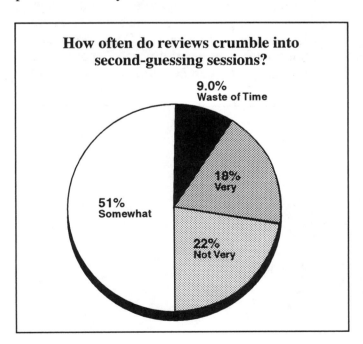

Corp., Rockford, Ill. "Day-to-day feedback is much more effective."

"You need to talk to each employee daily," says John Laymon, vice president of manufacturing at Rexair Inc., a vacuum-cleaner manufacturer in Cadillac, Mich. "Congratulate them as often as it is deserved, and criticize or suggest change as often as needed."

In other words, there's still no substitute for simple, ordinary communication. As a manager at the Chamberlain Group's storm-door manufacturing plant in Nogales, Ariz., asserts: "Reviews are useful tools if done conscientiously, but day-to-day contact and communication between the manager and employee is still the best 'review.'"

LOOK OUT, MANAGERS!
Employees want to review you.

The next two emerging issues in performance reviews—based on the write-in comments of IW readers—will be peer review and review of *managers* by their employees.

Possibly triggered by IW's query as to whether companies should insist that managers review all employees (90% thought they should), many took the opportunity to take that idea one step further.

"Employees should also review the managers so that management can see how their effectiveness is viewed by those they manage," asserts a senior chemist.

Adds an engineer at Ford: "Managers need a performance review from the bottom up. That view is often quite different from the one from the top down."

Or, as a materials supervisor for Harris Corp., Novato, Calif., notes: "Why not have managers reviewed by their employees? It could open some eyes!"

And many IW readers said they'd like to see peer reviews. "Part of a person's review should be done by subordinates or the person's 'internal' customers, or both," says James Stabe, purchasing manager at Kyocera America Inc., San Diego. "Co-workers and subordinates are generally more perceptive than managers when performance reviews are done."

IV.
Managing, Appraising, and Developing Performance

Interviewing:
Key to Effective Management

by Joseph P. Zima, GMI Engineering & Management Institute

Chapter 9
The Goal-Setting Interview

The motivation, the potential for development, the capacity for assuming responsibility, the readiness to direct behavior toward organizational goals are all present in people. Management does not put them there....The essential task of management is to arrange organizational conditions and methods of operations so that people can achieve their own goals best by directing their own efforts toward organizational objectives.

Douglas McGregor
The Human Side of Enterprise

Objectives

Upon completing this chapter, you will be able to:

- explain why mutual goal setting is beneficial to both the individual and the organization

- follow the steps essential to the development of meaningful objectives

- identify characteristics of meaningful objectives

- rewrite vague or poorly defined goals in objective, measurable terms

- deal with the tendency of employees to set unrealistic objectives whether too low or too high

- prepare properly for the goal-setting interview
- follow the most appropriate strategy for setting objectives
- conclude the goal-setting interview effectively

The next three chapters will deal with developmental interviews. The term *developmental* (as used here) means an experience that leads to the personal growth of individual employees as they contribute to organizational objectives. Developmental interviews include goal or objective setting, problem solving, and appraisal. These three interviews are linked by the concept of "management by objectives" (or "management by results"), which was pioneered by Peter F. Drucker in his book, *The Practice of Management*. He wrote that a business must be managed by setting appropriate objectives for the enterprise. He recognized that the objectives should communicate the key results that the organization expects to attain as well as the plan that is needed to achieve those objectives. People at all levels of the organization must know what the organization is trying to accomplish and how their jobs contribute to those overall objectives.

Managing by objectives is generally intended to be applied at all management levels, from top managers to first-line supervisors. Below the management level, employees normally do not have the degree of freedom of action, authority, or decision-making responsibility that would allow them to commit their future activities. Management by objectives, however, is being applied more and more at all levels of the organization.

What Is Managing by Objectives?

Managing by objectives is a management approach to planning and evaluation. Specific goals are established for a designated length of time for each manager, supervisor, or employee. These goals then become a part of the results each person must achieve if the overall objectives of the organization are to be met. The actual results are then measured against the established or expected goals to which each employee has committed. When properly implemented, managing by objectives can become a total management system, by which positive achievements can be planned and upon which activities can be concentrated that offer the greatest opportunity for payoff.

Three major values should emerge from an effective management by objectives program: (1) planning becomes a highly disciplined activity, (2) employees become involved and motivated by participating in the planning process, and (3) a more solid basis is provided for the appraisal process.

Steps in Managing by Objectives

There are four basic steps in a managing by objectives system:

1. *Each employee reviews his or her job responsibilities and determines the key results* to be reached during a particular period of time ahead (usually six months or a year). The proposed targets or goals emerge out of a review of key job responsibilities.

2. *Supervisor and employee confer about the goals proposed by the employee.* During this step, the supervisor also proposes goals or targets for the employee to consider. The final result is a *negotiated* set of goals for the subordinate to work on for the specified period.

3. *Supervisor conducts periodic progress reviews with each employee.* The progress reviews, which should be built into the plan, provide an opportunity for discussion, consultation, and problem solving between supervisor and employee. The supervisor and employee can determine if satisfactory progress is being made and whether the goals are realistic. Where satisfactory progress is not being made, the two parties can explore the causes of the condition, attempt to solve the

problem, or set a new course of action, if necessary. The periodic review provides an opportunity for goals to be added, modified, or eliminated. A major benefit of periodic reviews is that communication between supervisor and employee is emphasized.

4. *Supervisor conducts an appraisal with each employee.* At the end of the time period, the supervisor and employee review the employee's accomplishments on those goals established for the period. The employee must be able to respond to the following questions: Were the agreed-upon goals reached or not? If they were not achieved, what went wrong? Notice how the emphasis is on goals and not on personalities.

When the cycle is completed, new goals and objectives are established for the next period of time.

Managing by objectives has taken on increased importance in American industry over the past few years, particularly in light of the move toward the more participative or employee-centered management styles in many organizations. Such a participative philosophy is embodied in the goal setting, problem solving, and appraisal interviews. If management and employees can sit down together to define the job, negotiate mutual objectives, create a problem-solving climate, and engage in constructive feedback on a regular and frequent basis, employees will more likely be committed both to the job and to the organization.

This chapter will focus on the goal-setting or objective-setting interview. Clear goals and objectives are important to getting results, and the most important consideration in management is getting results.

Many organizations have implemented results-oriented management programs. Significantly, however, fewer have gotten the results they expected. Although most managers understand the importance of setting clear goals and objectives, many lack the necessary skills to translate those objectives to the people who will determine, in large part, whether the goals are met.

Some of the objectives of this chapter are to help managers:

1. provide an overview and rationale for involving employees in the goal-setting process

2. determine the important steps in establishing objectives

3. assist their employees in defining areas of responsibility and exploring personal and organizational expectations
4. assist their employees in setting realistic objectives that clearly state the results expected of them
5. assist their employees in developing performance measures that can be used as guides for managing their own areas of responsibility and as standards for evaluating their own contributions

Conventional Goal Setting

The conventional process of setting objectives is one whereby objectives are established by upper-level management and then imposed on the lower levels of the organization. This process is based on the assumption that only higher levels of management have the broader knowledge necessary for planning, which is true to some extent. Upper levels of management *should* set the overall organizational objectives including certain aspects of performance such as overall production goals, costs, profit margins, new plant construction, long-term planning, and so on.

One theory of management, Theory X, maintains that employees basically dislike work and must be controlled, threatened, and closely supervised to get them to make a contribution to the organization. Managers operating under these assumptions simply establish both organizational and personal objectives for their subordinates. Once established, managers either tell or sell these objectives to their subordinates. There are, however, some problems with this approach. When objectives are externally imposed on employees, genuine commitment is seldom achieved. Resulting behaviors are more likely indifference, passive acceptance, resistance, or even hostility.

Mutual Goal-Setting Rationale

In attempting to overcome negative employee attitudes, some managers and entire organizations have been trying an approach based on mutual goal setting. With this approach, upper-level management sets only the overall objectives of the organization, leaving room for self-direction and input on the part of those at lower levels on how those goals might be reached. This is the process of mutual goal setting between management and employees.

There are two major kinds of organizational planning. The first involves planning by a central group, who determines in detail what each division or department will do. The detailed objectives are then communicated to the different units throughout the organization. The second kind of planning is where the central group communicates what are believed to be desirable objectives to each of the different units. Each of the units then is asked to determine how it can contribute to reaching the objectives. The important theoretical consideration between the two kinds of planning is that in the second form there is an implied assumption that employees will accept the responsibility for self-direction and self-control. When employees participate in setting both personal and organizational objectives and have some say in how their performance will be measured, they will be more committed to taking responsibility for their own performance. This objective-setting approach is consistent with modern management concepts of participation and employee-centered leadership.

An employee-centered manager assumes that properly motivated employees will exercise a high degree of self-discipline and control, actively seek responsibility, respond creatively to job challenges, improve overall decision making, and better use the organization's human resources. This approach to management could be characterized as Theory Y, in contrast with the Theory X style discussed earlier.

Why does setting one's own objectives result in greater involvement and commitment? One explanation is offered by Abraham Maslow's Hierarchy of Needs (Fig. 9.1). According to Maslow, every individual has five need levels which must be satisfied in order, starting with the lowest and most basic. The most basic are physiological needs (food, oxygen, rest, shelter), which are survival-oriented. Second-order needs include security and safety, characterized by such things as stable employment and environment, satisfactory income, and so forth. Third-order needs include the desire for love and belonging, social activity, and group membership. Status, recognition, prestige, competence, and independence fall under the fourth-order need, esteem.

The highest-order need, self-fulfillment, concerns the individual's need to become all that she or he is capable of becoming.

The critical thing about this need hierarchy is that money can satisfy only the two lower-order needs. The higher-order needs are more complex, and it is generally agreed that money alone cannot satisfy them. The objectives-setting approach to management assumes that employees, when properly motivated, will exercise a high degree of self-control and actively seek responsibility because they are satisfying their higher-order needs.

Establishing Objectives

Having provided a rationale for involving employees in the goal-setting process, the next step is to describe the process of establishing organizational and personal objectives. There are three basic steps in determining objectives, whether they are for the organization or the individual.

1. *Identify areas of responsibility or activities that are critical to success.* These are frequently referred to as *key result areas* and may include, for the company, such factors as profitability, market position, product development, social responsibility, and so forth. For the individual they depend on occupation, but in the case of a purchasing agent, for example, they might include such things as cost saving or value analysis, price control, nego-

tiation, vendor performance, relations with other departments, and so forth.

2. *Identify performance measures for each area or activity.* For example, if production is a key result area, performance measures could include quantity, quality, costs, equipment utilization, and so forth. Or in the area of vendor performance in our purchasing agent example, measures might be lead time requirements, shipping times, or reject rates.

3. *Define and quantify the objectives.* For example, in the area of market position, with share-of-the-market by sales as the performance measure, a firm might set an objective of increasing its share by 5 percent in the next 12 months. Or with reject rates as a vendor performance measurement, a purchasing agent's objective might be to reduce fastener rejects from 2 percent to 1.8 percent over the next three months, without disturbing other measures of vendor performance.

Meaningful objectives for an individual must meet certain conditions if they are to be acceptable and effective. They should be:

1. related to the needs of the business and should support organizational goals
2. clear, concise, and realistic
3. measurable and quantifiable whenever possible
4. guides to action; they should state what is to be achieved
5. ambitious enough to offer a challenge so that a person can be proud when he or she achieves them

The ability to conduct an effective goal-setting interview requires that the manager understand the importance of developing clear, measurable objectives or goals.

The Language of Managing by Objectives

A primary barrier to conducting effective goal-setting interviews is the inability of both supervisor and subordinate to state explicit objectives. To help in establishing clear objectives, four words or concepts used in managing by objectives need to be defined. They are *objectives, goals, plans,* and *accountability.*

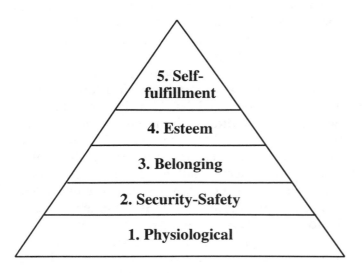

Figure 9.1 Hierarchy of needs

Objectives. Objectives define the results to be achieved if the organization is to be successful. Top management sets the overall objectives it wants to achieve, which may include goals for a 6- or 12-month period or even a five-year plan or longer. These objectives are the starting point for setting objectives throughout the organization. Managers and supervisors at lower levels of the organization can formulate their own goals only if the overall organizational objectives are clear.

Goals. Goals constitute a set of specific objectives. Once the overall organizational objectives have been formulated, managers must think through the specific objectives that they and their subordinates must accomplish. These specific objectives then become the goals that support the achievement of the overall organizational objectives.

Plans. Plans include tasks, steps, activities, and projects that be completed in order to achieve the goals. The goals specify *what* is to be achieved, and the plans specify *how* they are to be achieved. Within limits, employees are free to choose the plan that they think will be most effective in reaching the established goals.

Accountability. Accountability means that a person is responsible for achieving certain results and is often determined by referring to the individual's job description and key job responsibilities. People can be held accountable only when they understand their responsibilities and the measures of acceptable performance. Once the results that are expected from employees are defined, then measures of acceptable performance must be developed.

Developing Measurable Objectives

Too often objectives are phrased vaguely and in unmeasurable generalities. Judging one's progress toward vague goals is most difficult. Thus an ability to state goals and objectives clearly is a very valuable skill. Goals can be stated in terms of quotas, percentages, return on investment, cost reduction, increases, standards, targets, deadlines, volume, and so on. Goals can be classified into four general categories: (1) routine-work goals, (2) problem-solving goals, (3) innovative goals, and (4) personal-development goals.

Routine-Work Goals. Every organizational member is charged with certain well-defined duties, re-

sponsibilities, or tasks. Examples include inspecting, supervising, writing reports, purchasing, scheduling, manufacturing, and so on. These are the duties that individual members must carry out if the organization is to be successful. There must also be methods of measuring how well these duties are being performed.

Problem-Solving Goals. Problem-solving goals can be defined as any individual commitment to bring about needed improvements or to minimize or eliminate barriers that may be blocking achievement of daily job responsibilities. These could include high absenteeism, poor quality, high scrap rates, inefficiency, high turnover, high sickness and accident claims, missed schedules, and so on.

Innovative Goals. Innovative goals are goals that are directed at creating opportunities for change and improvement. Innovative goals go beyond the responsibility of carrying out routine duties and involve the development of new methods, new structures, new approaches, introduction of new technology and new systems, and so on. Ingenuity and creativity are encouraged in meeting innovative goals.

Personal-Development Goals. Personal-development goals are goals that employees set for themselves. They are goals that enhance individual growth through increased formal education, technical training, or other developmental experiences. Individuals may set goals to take a specific class or attend a training seminar with the intent of preparing themselves to take on added responsibilities or make up for a self-perceived deficiency. These are examples of personal development goals.

Writing Goal Statements

A major problem in establishing goals is that they are often stated vaguely and in unmeasurable generalities. Judging one's progress toward vague objectives is most difficult. Thus an ability to phrase and write goals and objectives in clear language is a most valuable skill.

Well-written objectives should satisfy four major criteria:

1. They should state goals, or targets, as *explicitly* as possible.
2. They should be *feasible* in light of economic and business conditions.
3. They should state *specific time frames.*

4. They should be stated so that progress toward them can be *measured.*

In addition to the four criteria just mentioned, goal statements should typically begin with the word *to* followed by an action word such as *maintain, improve, reduce, complete, install, schedule, issue,* and so on. Action words are used because the achievement of a goal must come as a result of some action.

Following are some examples of vaguely phrased objectives, each of which has been rewritten as a more measurable objective.

---

1. Vague form: To improve myself professionally during the next year.
   Measurable form: To attend two national seminars of the Society of American Engineers, January 12 and August 17. To present a paper at the August 17 conference dealing with heat transfer experiments now being conducted. To submit application to City University Graduate School for fall evening classes by the registration due date of May 31.

2. Vague form: Improve communications between Labor Relations and my department.
   Measurable form: To establish, by June 30, a new grievance form to be used in conjunction with Labor Relations specialists for purposes of informing front-line supervisors of actions taken in grievance cases.

3. Vague form: Meet Occupational Safety and Health Act standards in my department.
   Measurable form: To issue to all employees by February 15, one set of ear-protection head phones and safety glasses with side shields.

4. Vague form: To make our department the number one department in the plant.
   Measurable form: To have my department above the plant average of 91 percent efficiency (productivity versus direct and indirect labor costs) by the end of the current model year.

5. Vague form: To do a better job in handling employee suggestions.
   Measurable form: To reduce the backlog of suggestions by the end of the calendar year so that the response time from initial submission of the suggestion to written response is one month or less.

Following are some examples of areas of responsibility and their measures, for various types of jobs.

Supervisor

Responsibility	*Measure*
Maintain line output at standard rate	Average output, weekly
Ensure a steady work flow	Work waiting to be completed represents 30 minutes' work at standard rate
Have sufficient crew on hand to ensure standard production	All workstations fully staffed and operating at a rate of 95 percent

General Supervisor

Responsibility

Maintain section production output at standard

Maintain low reject rate

Have sufficient crew on hand to ensure standard production

Keep accidents to a minimum

Measure

Compute daily variances: compute weekly average

Percentage of total output

Necessity to place supervisors on the line at not more than four hours per week

Lost time due to accidents per available labor-hours per week

Plant Manager

Responsibility

Return on total investment

Investment control:

(a) Inventory

(b) Accounts Receivable

Management development:

(a) Training replacements

(b) Training programs—seminars—formal schooling

(c) Loss of key personnel

Measure

After-tax profit as percent of investment

Turnover (cost of goods sold—inventory value)

Days of sales outstanding

How many persons and how often

How many persons and how often

How many persons and how often

Sales Manager

Responsibility

Order processing and freight costs

Overall profitability

Advertising expense

Prospecting calls

Measure

Actual dollars; percent of gross sales

Actual dollars; percent of net to gross sales

Dollars per quarter; percent of budgeted dollars

Total per quarter, per salesperson; total per selling territory

Purchasing Manager

Responsibility

Fast processing of all POs

Ensure low unit cost

Prepare purchase contracts

Evaluate bids

Measure

Average process time, weekly

Number of vendors contacted, number of bids evaluated (per PO, per month)

Average time to prepare (computed quarterly)

Average time to evaluate (computed quarterly)

Safety Director

Responsibility

Establish and continually improve safe practices

Verify that safety rules are adhered to by the plant personnel

Conduct safety training classes for plant employees

Evaluation of main causes and sources of accidents

Measure

Number of reviews of present practices per month

Number of plant visits per month; number of reports of findings prepared per month

Number of days per quarter

Frequency of evaluation of accident reports; number of accident reports; number of safety meetings held with plant management per quarter

Once managers understand the process of establishing and writing clear, measurable objectives, they are ready to schedule goal or objective setting interviews with their subordinates.

Conducting the Goal-Setting Interview

Purpose. The broad objective of the goal-setting interview is to encourage employees to establish objectives for themselves that will promote both organizational and personal progress. The manager can also learn about employees' expectations and how they see their job responsibilities. Research in industry has indicated that there are significant differences in the perceptions of supervisors and subordinates when they are asked to describe their duties and responsibilities and then to establish priorities. The goal-setting interview can help the manager and subordinate share their understandings and perceptions of how they see one another's responsibilities. A good deal can also be learned from the goal-setting interview about employees' expectations and aspiration levels. The manager who is skillful at conducting a goal-setting interview can also teach and inform employees about how higher-level management sets organizational goals by asking the employees how their personal and departmental goals complement those of the larger organization.

Situational Factors. The skillful and sensitive manager must also be aware of any situational factors that may affect the goal-setting interview. First, the employee may never have been asked to set goals before. Thus calling the employee in for a goal-setting interview could create a great deal of anxiety for the employee, particularly in the cases of organizations whose management styles have been paternal or authoritarian. In most paternal or authoritarian organizations, employees are dependent upon higher-level management for their setting of goals. Another important situational variable may be the difference of experience and position between the manager and the employee. What may seem to be very reasonable goals to the manager may not seem so to the employee. He or she may be reluctant or unwilling to accept the manager's expectations. There is also the problem of over-enthusiastic employees who set their goals too high.

When goals are set unrealistically high, the employee is almost certain to fail. The manager should try to stretch the employee, but also make certain that the goals are reachable.

Preparation. These are some of the situations with which the manager should be prepared to deal. A very important step is to forewarn the employee about the goal-setting interview. Tell the employee at least a week in advance to prepare for the interview. Effective goal setting takes good planning. If I were to ask you right now to cite some specific personal objectives for six months from now, could you do it? Probably not without some adequate planning time. Managers should also begin to cite some of the objectives that they would like to see their employees set. Those objectives should meet specific criteria: first, they should be *attainable,* employees should have the training and experience that would allow them to reach their goals; second, the goals should be *justifiable,* both in terms of the organization's objectives and in terms of the employee's job description. These two criteria are very important. If not satisfied, the employee may see the goals as unfair, while the manager may see them as unreasonably low.

Finally, the goals must be *clear* and *measurable.* This objective cannot be stressed too much. To deal in vague generalities is easy. Most employees want to improve and most organizations want to be profitable. These objectives are too vague and must be made more specific. Wherever possible, goals and objectives should be quantifiable and measurable. If the goals cannot be quantified, at least some objective method must be found to determine when in fact the goals have been met.

Following is a Job Objectives Form (Fig. 9.2) that can be used by both managers and employees to prepare for the goal-setting interview. An overall survey of job responsibilities, taken prior to establishing specific goals, might help ensure that key result areas have not been overlooked and that important priorities have been considered.

Strategy. In conducting the goal setting interview, the manager should use a combination of directive and nondirective strategies. The manager's primary interest should be helping the employees plan their jobs in such a way that both personal and organizational goals will be achieved. While the superior has veto power by virtue of her or his position in the organization, it should be exercised only when it becomes absolutely necessary.

Figure 9.2 Job objectives form

Job Objectives Form		Name _____	
General responsibility _____		Date: _____	
# Key Result Areas (Duties, Responsibilities, Goals, Objectives)	Measurement Factors (Quantity, Quality, Cost, Time, Efficiency, Yield, Scrap, Production, etc.)	Time Allocation (Completion Dates; When? What? With Whom?)	Remarks (Progress Reviews, Obstacles, Priorities, Areas of Improvement)

The manager's job is to guide the employees in the development of their goals, to help in the articulation of those goals, and to help in establishing the criteria for measuring their progress toward those goals. The manager should be helpful rather than authoritarian. He or she is the resource that the employee can call upon.

When the goal-setting approach is first used, employees typically set goals that are too low or too high. (This approach permits employees to learn by experience rather than by simply telling them where their planning is unrealistic or inadequate.) Managers usually have more information and experience in goal setting than their employees and should help employees set realistic goals. There is a delicate difference between guiding and directing. Remember, employees' commitment to their objectives is often proportional to their degree of involvement in establishing those objectives.

In a typical approach to goal setting, the manager should ask employees to do some thinking and planning about their objectives before the interview. Using a form such as the Job Objectives Form (Fig. 9.2), employees should make up a list of objectives or targets and specify the means or methods by which they expect to meet those targets. Managers should also make up a list of targets and objectives for each of their employees before the goal-setting interview. The goal-setting interview would then consist of both the manager and employee sharing and exploring their perceptions of the employee's responsibilities and goals. The manager, of course, must use just the right amount of directiveness and nondirectiveness in the interview. Much will depend on the relationship that has been established between the two parties. If a comfortable give-and-take exists between the manager and the employee, the setting of objectives should proceed well.

To get the employee to examine the consequences or implications of setting goals that are unrealistically high, the manager frequently may need to use a series of hypothetical probes. To deal with the opposite problem in which the employees set their goals too low, the manager must ask the employee to consider past performance data or related job projections in a specific job area. The important issue is to lead the employee to considering these implications or consequences rather than simply imposing them. A strategy that is too directive may fail because employees may not see the objectives as their own. A strategy that is too nondirective may result in goals that are set either below or beyond the employee's capability. The proper strategy, then, is an artful blend of directive and nondirective techniques. Remember, the final result of the interview should be a negotiated, merging set of goals toward which the employee will direct his or her efforts in the six months or year ahead.

Close. Finally, the interview must be effectively closed. In closing the goal-setting interview, the manager should make certain that all the goals that have been agreed upon are stated clearly and are reasonable. Specific time frames should be established for each objective. Also, the employees should know the criteria that will measure their progress toward their goals. Some benchmarks may help monitor progress. For example, if the employee has set a six-month goal, where should he or she be in two months, or four months? Finally, the employee should be assured that the manager is available for further consultation and problem solving, particularly if changing conditions or unforeseen circumstances make necessary a modification in the objectives.

As a final check in assessing the objectives you have developed, measure them against a form like the following:

Measurable Objectives Checklist

	Yes	No
Do the objectives support organizational needs and goals?	_____	_____
Do the objectives state *what* is to be done, rather than *how* to do something?	_____	_____
Are the objectives clearly stated in language that is free from distortion or misinterpretation?	_____	_____
Are numbers, statistics, and quantifiable terms used wherever possible?	_____	_____
Are the objectives feasible in light of current (or highly predictable) business and economic conditions?	_____	_____
Are the objectives challenging but reasonable?	_____	_____
Do the objectives cover a specific time period?	_____	_____
Are benchmark times set, with corresponding progress states defined?	_____	_____
Can progress towards meeting these objectives be reliably measured?	_____	_____
Does the employee have the ability and authority necessary to accomplish the objectives?	_____	_____

An Example of a Goal-Setting Interview

Background. Harry Edwards is vice-president, staff services, for a manufacturing company with 20 plants in the midwest. Edwards was brought into the company three years ago by the president, who felt that the staff functions of the organization needed strengthening. One of the president's major concerns was the Personnel Department. He felt that the management needed a lot of help and guidance in fulfilling its responsibilities, particularly in relation to the government's guidelines in affirmative action. Harry has just returned from a management seminar on managing by objectives and is determined to make the philosophy work in his company.

June Rinaldo has just been moved up to Director of Personnel Administration. Harry has called June to have a meeting where they will discuss the job responsibilities of the Personnel Director and establish some goals.

Harry: ...And that's why I wanted to have you in, June. I asked you to bring along a written statement of the major responsibilities of your job, as you see them. I don't want to define your job for you. If I did that, it wouldn't be your job. Of course, I don't expect that we will necessarily see eye-to-eye on everything either. I take for granted that we at least share one common purpose: to make this company the best that it can possibly be.

June: Well, I appreciate the confidence you've shown in me Harry, and I welcome the opportunity to have some say regarding my job responsibilities. As you suggested, I started with the formal job description and then added a list of my own. I must admit that setting goals and targets is a lot harder than I thought. So, where do you want me to start?

Harry: Well, let's start with what you consider to be your major role or function.

June: I suppose I see my job primarily in an advisory capacity. I see Personnel responding to the human resources needs of the company as identified by the executive committee.

Harry: In your estimation, how good a job has the committee done in identifying those needs?

June: Well, I suppose with all the problems they've been having, they really haven't had much time to deal with the areas that I think are important.

Harry: What are some of those areas?

June: I've got a list of six major priorities. The first is absenteeism; we've really got a problem there. Second is white-collar dissatisfaction. Third, we need an evaluation of our compensation system; fourth, evaluation of our affirmative action goals; fifth, a quality of work-life program; and six, I'd like to see some employee participation groups—based on the Japanese quality circles.

Harry: Sounds like a pretty heavy list of priorities. What do you expect to accomplish in dealing with absenteeism, for example?

June: Well, I'd like to cut absenteeism in half and go after some of those sickness and accident claims.

Harry: Well, that would be fantastic. But what we need to do here June, is to set down some specific goals so we can monitor and measure our progress toward meeting them. A question you might ask yourself is, "How do I know when I'm doing a good job in an area?"

June: Oh, okay. In other words, you want some definite numbers or targets to shoot for.

Harry: Yeah, that's right. Let's take each of your priorities one at a time and take a look at them. What I'd like us to come up with after this meeting is a set of goals that are clear and reasonable—by that I mean reachable. Each goal should also have a particular time frame specified, and each goal should be measurable so that we can tell when and whether it has been achieved. Okay?

189

June: Okay, I think I got ya.

Harry: Okay. Let's take a look at the absenteeism problem. That's one we've got to do something about soon before it really gets out of control. What would be a realistic goal to shoot for in that area?

June: Well, I'd like to cut it in half.

Harry: How realistic is that given the constraints that we have?

June: Well, I guess I'd be happy if we could cut it by a quarter of what it is now.

Harry: Even that is very optimistic. How much time do you think you will need to reduce it by 25 percent?

June: Well, we're coming into a heavy holiday period, and hunting season is just around the corner.

Harry: You think you'll need some time to make a real dent in the problem.

June: If we could reduce absenteeism by 25 percent by the same time next year, I think that would be pretty good.

Harry: Okay, let's write that down as one of your objectives. The specific objective is to reduce overall absenteeism by 25 percent by July 1 of next year. By the way, aren't there some plants where the absenteeism is way out of line with the rest of the division?

June: Yeah, the Metal Fabricating and Hardware plants are way out of line. They're the ones that are really messing up the statistics. Maybe I should concentrate in the Metal Fab plant and the Hardware plant. Okay, let's change the objective to read: "To reduce overall absenteeism by 15 percent by July 1 of next year, with particular emphasis in the Metal Fab and Hardware plants where I'd like to reduce absenteeism by 25 percent."

Harry: Yeah, now we're talking about a specific goal that you could work toward. Okay, what about the area of sickness and accident benefits claims? What can be done in that area?

June: First of all, we need to do a lot more follow-up. I think we need to initiate a program of regular telephone calling and field visits to identify the most flagrant offenders. Those insurance costs are taking a sizable chunk out of the budget. We also need to establish better relationships with area physicians. I'd like to see our company physician do more in this area.

Harry: What kind of objectives do you see setting there?...

In this goal-setting interview Harry is helping June to sort out her responsibilities and to set some specific goals. The manager must make certain that the employee does not set unrealistic goals. Harry has also indicated that he and June will probably not agree on everything. Harry's style is moderately directive. He is trying to make certain that June establishes a number of goals by identifying and dealing with each of the goals separately. After each goal is identified and discussed, a statement regarding each goal will be developed that is clear, reasonable, has a specific time frame, and is measurable.

Harry is getting June to consider the implications of her goals by asking questions. He is attempting to blend the directive and nondirective techniques. Now let's look at how Harry might close this interview with June.

Harry: There's one other area that I think we need to work on and that is the area of university contacts. We are in an area of several universities, and I'd like to see us make better use of their resources in a consulting capacity as well as using some of the students to do some research in filling their course requirements. That would also give us a chance to look at some prospective employees.

June: I agree, there are some good possibilities. I've got some contacts over at the schools that I need to follow up on.

Harry: Well, I think we've pretty much explored your major job responsibilities, and I see you playing a more active selling role rather than simply reacting to requests from other parts of the organization.

June: Sounds good to me. I'm glad I've got your support.

Harry: We had a chance to a least rough out some major objectives. I'd like us to get together next week and review and tighten up the objectives we've established for the next six months and talk about some ways that I can support you in reaching those goals.

One area we haven't had time to explore is the area of your personal goals. In other words, think about the kinds of training and developmental experiences you would like to have over the next year or so, and we'll take a closer look at those. Okay?

June: Sounds good. Should I plan on the same time next week?

Harry: Yeah. This time look pretty good to me right now.

In closing the interview, Harry reviews the major content of the interview and emphasizes his perception of June's role. Sometimes the process of goal setting may take several interviews. In this interview, Harry and June have roughed out some major organizational objectives, and Harry has asked June to meet with him again the following week to review those objectives and to take a look at some personal objectives that she would like to establish.

Summary

This chapter dealt with the objective, or goal-setting, interview. The goal-setting interview is consistent with modern management concepts of participation and employee-centered leadership. When employees are encouraged to take responsibility for their own performance by participating in the goal-setting process, they will be more involved and committed to those goals. Establishing goals or objectives involves three basic steps: (1) identify areas of responsibilities or activities that are critical to organizational success such as profitability, market position, product development, social responsibility, and so on; (2) identify performance measures for each area or activity (in production, for example, performance measures could include quantity, quality, costs, etc.); and (3) define and quantify the objectives.

Well-written objectives should satisfy four criteria: they should be *explicit, reasonable,* have a *specific time frame* for completion, and be *measurable.* In conducting the goal-setting interview, the manager should use a combination of directive and nondirective strategies. Remember, employees' commitment to their objectives is often proportional to their degree of involvement in establishing those objectives.

A Constructive Criticism Primer

by Daniel Goleman

An engineer presented a plan for developing new software to the vice president of his high-technology company. With his team, the engineer waited expectantly, hoping for praise and encouragement; the plan was the result of months of work.

But the reaction from the vice president was harsh. "These specifications are ridiculous," he said. "They haven't a chance of getting past my desk." Then, his voice thick with sarcasm, he added, "How long have you been out of graduate school?"

"The engineer was crushed," said Dr. Hendrie Weisinger, a psychologist at the School of Management at the University of California at Los Angeles, who tells the story. "For two weeks, he could think only about his humiliation in front of his team. He hated the vice president and worried over his future. He thought of leaving the company."

Dr. Weisinger—whose book "The Critical Edge: How to Criticize Up and Down Your Organization and Make It Pay Off" was published earlier this year by Harper & Row—offers the tale as an example of the most common errors managers make in giving criticism. "The worst way to criticize is with a blanket statement, like 'You're really screwing up,' without offering the person some way to do things better," said Dr. Weisinger. "It leaves the other person feeling helpless and angry."

Dr. Weisinger is one of several psychologists studying the fine art of criticism, which, they say, is typically approached with far too little finesse, if it is practiced at all. Yet failing to let people know when they are faltering is, of course, a recipe for disaster.

An artful critique can be one of the most helpful messages a manager can send. "It's how the manager delivers a criticism that determines whether its effects will be productive or disastrous," said Robert Baron, a professor of psychology and management at Rensselaer Polytechnic Institute in Troy, N.Y. The hallmarks of artful criticism include being

---

Criticism: The Good and the Bad

Constructive

Specific: The manager says exactly what the person is doing wrong, such as, "This is what I didn't like, and why."

Supportive: Gives the sense that the criticism is meant to help the person do better.

Problem-solving: Suggests a solution or offers to help find a way to improve things.

Timely: Gives the message soon after the problem occurs.

Destructive

Vague: Offers no specifics, but makes a blanket condemnation, such as, "That was a lousy job."

Blames the person: Attributes the problem to personality or some other unchangeable trait.

Threatening: Makes the person feel attacked, such as, "Next time, you're through."

Pessimistic: Offers no hope for change or suggestion for doing better.

---

specific, making no threats, placing no personal blame—and being timely. The key, said Dr. Baron, is that the person receiving the criticism feel that he or she is "being helped to do better."

"Giving criticism is one of the most important jobs a manager has," Dr. Weisinger said. "But it's also one of the most unpleasant tasks managers face, and one of the most often put off."

That delay can be costly. A supervisor's failure to give an employee timely criticism led to a $250,000 claim for wrongful termination, said Laurie Dutcher, director of human resources at the Capital Area Community Health Plan, in Latham, N.Y.

"She was fired because of a terrible absentee record, but she didn't feel her performance was lacking in any way," Ms. Dutcher said. "For years, her supervisor had put off telling her that she was remiss. We find that story often, with a manager being too uncomfortable giving criticism to let employees know when they are failing."

Also, when managers let their dissatisfactions build up without saying anything at all, she said, the result is likely to be an outburst. "Too often, a manager just blows up," said Dr. Baron. He encourages managers to "give negative feedback as needed, regularly, and in small chunks, with suggestions for how to do the job better."

If a manager realizes he or she has offered criticism that is destructive, Dr. Baron urges an apology. "You've damaged the relationship, and you have to get in there and repair things," he said.

But many managers do not recognize their criticism as destructive. Dr. Weisinger said that the engineer, still feeling bitter, approached his boss two weeks later, and asked: "What were you trying to accomplish?" The vice president was astonished, said Dr. Weisinger. "He simply hadn't realized how he was coming off."

If criticism is being delivered ineffectively, Dr. Baron has found, the person receiving it simply makes excuses but does not change, is defensive and may simply avoid the critic.

"The sign your criticism is skillful," he said, "is that the person changes as you desired."

Coaching and the Art of Management

by Roger D. Evered and James C. Selman

The "manager" is viewed variously as a team captain, parent, steward, battle commander, fountain of wisdom, poker player, group spokesperson, gatekeeper, minister, drill instructor, facilitator, initiator, mediator, navigator, candystore-keeper, linchpin, umbrella-holder, and everything else between nurse and Attila-the-Hun. We ask you to view the manager as a coach, and as a creator of a culture for coaching. Our proposition: good coaching is the essential feature of really effective management which, in turn, generates the context for good coaching.

The view of the *manager as coach* and *as creator of a culture for coaching* is a new paradigm for management. By paradigm we mean the set of assumptions, everyday truths, and conventional wisdom about people and how they work in organizations. The prevailing management paradigm focuses heavily on control, order, and compliance, with the consequence that people become objectified, measured, and expended. Coaching, on the other hand, focuses on discovering actions that enable and empower people to contribute more fully, productively, and with less alienation than the control model entails.

The article addresses the issue of shifting from coaching as a possible tool or technique within the prevailing paradigm of management, to a new paradigm in which the process of creating an organizational culture for coaching becomes the core managerial activity. We are convinced from our work that a management paradigm based on building an organizational context for "coaching" can readily outperform the existing management paradigm based on "control." The key is to let go of the "managing equals controlling" mindset, and take on a "managing equals creating a context for coaching" orientation.

We view coaching not as a subset of the field of management, but rather as the heart of management. We contend that when managers are truly effective, coaching is necessarily occurring. We suspect that skillful coaching may be the essential difference between the ordinary and the extraordinary manager. If that is so, then it is worth taking a closer look at the essential managerial task of creating an organizational environment in which coaching and being coached can occur continuously. First let's clarify what we mean by "effective management."

The essence of truly effective management remains as elusive as the essence of art. We recognize and appreciate it. We can even explain it *after* the fact. But we don't seem able to generate it intentionally. Certainly we can paint "by-the-numbers," but great paintings can never be created that way. Does anyone seriously believe they can generate high performance when they manage "by the numbers"?

Yet conventional wisdom holds that managers become more effective when they learn the prescribed techniques, rules, and principles. Mere knowledge has only limited impact on managerial performance. The presumptions that we can know, prescriptively, what produces performance and that we can control all these factors and variables are the principal barriers to increased performance. Effective managers know that performance comes from enabling and improving what is there rather than controlling it.

Effective management remains essentially an *art*—the art of "getting things done through people." Thinking of management as an art (rather than a set of techniques) is potentially more fruitful because it recognizes management as more than a set of explicit techniques. Management as art implies inventiveness rather than mere conformity, practice rather than mere prescription, wisdom rather than mere knowledge.

When we focus on what actually goes on when a manager is being effective, five points become clear:

1. Observing a truly effective manager in action is much like watching an artist at work.
2. Managers who attend to what is actually going on outperform those who try to apply remembered techniques, canned prescriptions, and rational models.
3. Work results spring from the quality of the communication (speaking and listening) between managers and their people.
4. The effectiveness of management flows from the level of partnership that is created between managers and the people with whom, through whom, and by whom the job gets done and the results are generated.
5. Effective managers are skillful in generating and empowering organizational climate.

The Managerial Context for Coaching, and the Coaching Context for Managing

Much of "the art of getting things done through people" is actually a sensitivity to, and skill with, the climate, environment, and context in which the work gets done. The popular management textbook, *Principles of Management*, begins with the following statement: "Managing is defined here as the design or creation and maintenance of an internal environment in an enterprise where individuals, working together in groups, can perform efficiently and effectively toward the attainment of group goals."

Reduced to its barest essentials, management may be viewed as a people-based art that focuses on creating and maintaining a climate, environment, and context which enable/empower a group of people to generate desired results, achievement, and accomplishments. Coaching, as we use the term, refers to the managerial activity of creating, by communication only, the climate, environment, and context that empowers individuals and teams to generate results.

The context of managing influences, and is influenced by, the relationship between the manager and the managed. Each is largely determined by the beliefs and assumptions of the prevailing culture that we find ourselves in, and which none of us consciously designed. In American society the relationship between the manager and those managed occurs within a context that includes concepts such as authority, hierarchy, order, specialization, division of labor, job security, ownership rights, compliance, control, and several other "blueprints" for how we "should" relate to each other at work. The aggregate of these operating concepts comprises a paradigm that might be called "control-order-prescription" ("c.o.p."), which makes up the underlying design for much of the present-day managerial thinking and relating. In this context, managers act out core managerial beliefs, such as being in charge, controlling others, implementing the owner's orders, prescribing behaviors and events, maintaining order, gaining and exercising command and control, and discarding the noncompliant.

Contrast this with an alternative paradigm in which the underlying conceptual foundation and commitment of management is to empower and create, a paradigm that might be called "acknowledge-create-empower" ("a.c.e."). In this paradigm, the core managerial beliefs have to do with rethinking our thoughts, aligned purpose, commitment to accomplishment, collaboration, involvement, mutual support, individual growth—in short, *enabling the people in a group or team to generate results and to be empowered by the results they generate.*

The distinction between these two paradigms has been described as "domination" versus "cooperation," "control-oriented" versus "involvement-inducing," "compliance driven" versus "vision-led," or "command" versus "commitment." Whatever the transformation from one mode to the other is called, the idea of shifting from a control-order-prescription paradigm that increasingly does not work to an acknowledge-create-empower paradigm that works (when the manager allows himself or herself to let go of the control paradigm) is clearly "in the wind."

While discussion of the contrast between these two paradigms is not new, the implementation of an organizational culture that calls for "a.c.e." has eluded many, perhaps all, who have attempted the shift. Coaching provides an action path for generating the shift from "c.o.p." to "a.c.e."

Coaching is the name we give to management of and within an acknowledge-create-empower paradigm. It requires a major shift in the thinking of both managers and the managed. This definition of "coaching" is not identical with the ordinary use of the term.

What Is a Coach?

The Everyday Meaning of Coaching

A dictionary definition of "coach" is "one who instructs, trains, or guides players or performers (or teams thereof) in some particular activity or endeavor." This is okay, although it does not capture how the term is currently used in organizational literature or what we mean in this article. In general terms, however, coaching is a widely accepted way to produce performance improvement. Coaches are used by *individual* players to improve personal performance (as in tennis, golf, fencing, ice skating, skiing, and car-racing) or by *teams* to improve team performance (as in football, basketball, and rowing). Public speakers and performing artists also work with coaches.

The Familiar Management Meaning of Coaching

The advantages of coaching have not gone unnoticed by corporate managers who realize that: (1) individuals and teams generally perform better with a coach, (2) superior individual and team performance in business readily translates into productivity and profits, and (3) the quality of coaching makes a big difference in the results produced.

Coaching first appeared in management literature during the 1950s. It was viewed as part of the superior's responsibility to develop subordinates through a sort of master-apprentice relationship. The coaching often took the form of a boss "coaching" an employee, most notably at the time of the annual review, thus within the context of a hierarchical relationship and implied job threat. The articles on coaching at this time stressed the value of training supervisors in coaching skills to improve an employee's work skills. Coaching became synonymous with job skills development, in contrast with counseling, which dealt with an employee's personal problems that interfered with job performance. The mid-1970s saw the appearance of articles attempting to translate sports coaching into managerial situations. Since 1980 coaching appears in the literature as a training technique in the context of management development.

Recent management coaching literature contains several new elements. Articles now connect coaching with mentoring, career development, management development over a long time period, and generating team (versus individual) performance. The most recent discussions center on the creation of a climate for coaching and use of a consultant as managerial coach.

Much of business's focus on coaching has been in translating sports coaching into techniques for business management, especially techniques to motivate people, train them in job skills, or improve management development. In nearly all cases, the orientation is that the "superior" is acting as a coach who "directs" the players (or teams) to higher levels of performance. In other words, most attempts to translate coaching into managerial applications take place within the control-order-prescription paradigm.

Translating the techniques of sports coaching directly into the world of business management seems to us insufficient. Of far more value is a study of the *context of committed partnership* in which sports coaches operate. There has been little examination of coaching as a new management paradigm. If the coaching relationship could be viewed in other than superior-subordinate, employee-improvement terms, it might provide a breakthrough.

As an illustration of the limits imposed by the superior-subordinate, control-and-order type of thinking, imagine the breakdown in day-to-day performance if one attempted to coach a little league championship game by "controlling" the actions of the players from the sidelines. Imagine a coach prescribing action without regard to what was actually happening in the game. At best one would get conformity and compliance, and at worst a mutiny. It is inconceivable that the team could win the game; if it did, the suppressed mood of the team would in all likelihood leave the participants wondering whether it was worth it.

The New Management Meaning of Coaching

Coaching is the name we give to management of and within a paradigm of acknowledge-create-empower. Coaching implies actively attending to a context that allows the communicative process between player/performer and coach to be effective. *In this context, a coach is someone who has an ongoing, committed partnership with a player/performer and who empowers that person, or team, to exceed prior levels of play/performance.*

The Commitment to Coaching and to Being Coached

Let's take a comprehensive look at coaching as a new distinction for management. This requires a major shift in thinking on the part of both managers and the managed.

Most people have experienced working with a coach. Many consider their relationships with a valued coach as being among the most important and empowering in their lives. Why then is coaching so missing in management? If one compares the way one relates to a coach with the way one relates to a manager the reasons become clear.

Those who go to a coach generally are open to improvement, eager to learn from mistakes, and willing to try a new approach. People do not normally try to "look good" for a coach, or to convince him/her of how much they know, or what fine performers they already are. Contrast this with the way people commonly relate to a manager. Most often they hide or justify mistakes, attempt to "look good," and listen defensively rather than openly.

When people work with a coach, they commit to producing a result, such as improving the level of performance. They *demand* whatever the coach can provide. *One of the basic principles of effective coaching is that no one can be coached in the absence of a demand for it. And in the world of control-oriented management, there is very little demand either for being coached, or for that matter being managed.* The demand for coaching shows

up naturally and automatically in an environment of committed partnership-oriented management.

In almost every field of human endeavor where performance is crucial, coaching is an integral part. The more outstanding the players, the more likely they are to have an ongoing and committed relationship with a coach. (Coaches rarely are able to outperform those they coach.) Coaches share a commitment to improving the players' performance, but from a different perspective. They have a different view of the action and a different role to play in the game. Their role is fundamental because no person can observe himself or herself in action.

If there is a demand for coaching in almost every arena where high performance is valued, what is within our management culture that precludes coaching as a normal, empowering part of organizational work life? Why don't managers have an ongoing relationship with a coach? Why don't they spend more time coaching the teams they manage? What can be done to have coaching be an integral part of organizational lives?

There are three aspects of the culture of management within which most of us work that may account for the absence of a demand for coaching:

1. *Managers believe they already know how to manage.* Contemporary management culture is presumed to be knowledge-based, and managing is regarded primarily as *knowledge driven.* People succeed in most organizations as a function of what they know, or more precisely, what they and others believe they know. In contrast, coaching is almost exclusively *action-results driven.* Although coaches may be knowledgeable, their knowledge is always in the background of their relationship with the players and of whatever is apparent in the moment of play or performance. In the foreground the players' actions generate the results.

2. *Managers may be more committed to control, authority, order, prediction, and power than they are to producing results.* Contemporary management culture seems to reward control-order-prescription management and to produce compliant, political, or "looking good" behavior, as distinct from behavior and actions that produce results. Although managers say they are committed to results, it's quite

possible that they rationalize their commitment to control by presuming that more control/authority/order/power will produce more or better results. Clearly, no effective coaching can occur if the "player" is focused on scoring points with the coach instead of producing results on the field.

3. *Managers actually may not feel responsible for the poor results produced by their group.* Contemporary management culture is ambivalent regarding the responsibility of individual managers for their team's results. Being "not responsible" is excused in two ways. First, circumstances can often explain away undesired results and hence deflect a manager's responsibility. Second, a manager's job is commonly conceived of as holding others responsible, implying (erroneously) that "therefore, I'm not responsible."

Possibly the greatest differences between traditional management and coaching are in responsibility and commitment. In traditional management, for example, it is the manager's job to motivate. In coaching, motivation is the player's responsibility. In management, managers work constantly to get employees "to buy into" management's initiatives. In coaching, the players bring their commitment to the task to the coach rather than derive commitment from the coach. In management, responsibility is usually a matter for negotiation. In coaching, responsibility is a privilege.

In a management culture that rewards individual managers for seeing themselves as already knowledgeable, oriented toward control-order-prescription and able to readily blame circumstances (including other people) for the poor group performance, there can be little demand for either coaching or being coached. In a management culture based on partnership for achieving results and on commitment to collaborating in accomplishing new possibilities, a demand for coaching and being coached is always urgently present.

To get significantly more performance from a system, there needs to be an organizationwide demand for coaching. And that requires us to learn how to transform our thinking from "attempting to control others" to "empowering others." In short, if we are interested in *large* increases in system performance, we shall have to commit ourselves to shifting the prevailing management paradigm from "controlling" to "empowering."

The Essential Coaching Relationship

The critical difference between managements within the two alternative paradigms (control versus empowering) is in the fundamentally different contexts of relating in which coaches and managers work.

In a c.o.p. environment, the bottom line relationship is that management decides and the managed implement. This is true even if the decisions are wrapped in warm and fuzzy management systems such as "participatory management" or "employee involvement." People are "resources" to be used. The "resources" perform all sorts of impersonal functions or roles. People are referred to as *labor,* the *workforce, hands, employees,* or merely as *man-hours.* In other words, people are related to as objects, or machine parts that need to be maintained (motivated), fixed (developed), and eventually upgraded (retrained), or replaced (outplaced). Although there is nothing intrinsically limiting in the use of labels, these reflect the nature of the core at-work relationship: impersonal, functional, mechanical, and disposable.

In contrast, coaching occurs in an action-oriented, results-oriented, and person-oriented relationship between coach and player/performer. The terms commonly associated with coaching are notably person-oriented: player, actor, performer, singer, artist, team leader, captain. These terms describe people rather than objects, doers rather than objects to be acted upon. The language of coaching reflects a relationship which is essentially action-oriented, enabling, and growth-inducing.

Coaches in the a.c.e. paradigm simply have a different relationship, and hence a different job in the relationship, from that of the traditional c.o.p. paradigm manager. The coach's job is to spot the player/performer's "blind spots," with the sole objective of providing whatever is needed for the player/performer to excel beyond prior limits. The presumption of the relationship is that people have limits (barriers) which may be surpassed through mutual commitment (partnership) of *both* the coach and the player/performer.

Exhibit 1
The Coaching Relationship in Generic Terms

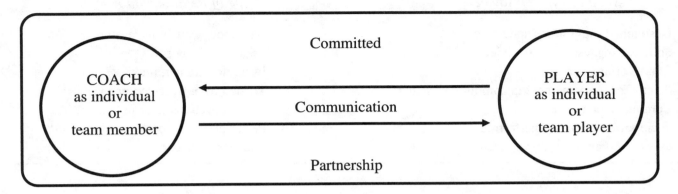

Communication in a partnership committed to accomplishment

Coaching enables the player/performer to see something about his playing/performing which he does not see and would not otherwise be able to see. What the coach enables the player to see and improve upon makes a difference in the results produced. Without coaching, the player/performer is limited merely to honing the prevailing level of play/performance. Small incremental improvements are feasible, but the level of results remains constrained by the way the player/performer habitually interprets things. Coaching makes possible a reinterpretation of actions so that a quantum shift in results can quite naturally occur. A good coach continuously produces these shifts in results—shifts that the player/performer could not have achieved on his or her own.

"Coaching" as a New Distinction

It's time to pull together what we currently know about coaching and its pertinence for management. What follows is based primarily upon our direct experience of coaching and being coached, especially in the setting of consulting with a variety of organizations and managers. Additionally it's based on our observations of great coaches, and to a lesser extent on the published literature.

What are the essential elements or characteristics that define "coaching" as distinct from anything else? The phrases below are not meant to be mutu-

ally exclusive components. Each expresses a different way of grasping the core of coaching.

1. Partnership, mutuality, relationship
2. Commitment to producing a result and enacting a vision
3. Compassion, generosity, nonjudgmental acceptance, love
4. Speaking and listening for action
5. Responsiveness of the player to the coach's interpretation
6. Honoring the uniqueness of each player, relationship, and situation
7. Practice and preparation
8. Willingness to coach and to be coached
9. Sensitivity to "team" as well as to individuals
10. Willingness to go beyond what's already been achieved

At the heart of a.c.e. coaching is the *relationship* between coach and player.

In generic terms, the coaching relationship may be as represented in Exhibit 1.

The beneficial effects of coaching on a player's performance derive almost solely from the nature of the coach-player relationship and the communication (speaking and listening) that occur within that relationship. (Research into coaching is likely to be most fruitful in exploring the qualities of this speaking-and-listening between coach and player.) A manager may be either the coach (to an organiza-

Exhibit 2
Kinds of Advice and Their Sources

Level and Type of Advice	*Type of Relationship Involved*
1. Unsolicited suggestions and advice	Neighbor, acquaintance, stranger
2. Solicited suggestions and advice	Friend, colleague
3. Course of instruction	Instructor, trainer, tutor
4. Responses from an ongoing committed-listener	Trusted friend, mentor, counsellor
5. Committed partnership	Sports coach (team or individual)
to empower the player/performer	Performing arts coach
to exceed previous levels of accomplishment	Management coach

tional player or players) or an organizational player (with his or her own coach or coaches).

The coach's job is *not* primarily to give information, although some information-giving is involved. As a rule, a coach is *not* an expert player. (Arnold Palmer, Steffi Graf and Brian Boitanno perform much better than their coaches ever will.) Technical expertise frequently is less relevant than the ability to enable or empower the player to go beyond the current level of performance. An insight into the player, in all his or her uniqueness, far outweighs the mere delivery of information. Coaching is *not* especially concerned with resolving personal or psychological problems, except perhaps peripherally. And a coach is *not* simply another term for an advisor or good buddy, although a mentor relationship probably resembles most closely the kind of coaching relationship described here. A mentor, in an organizational setting, usually refers to a trusted friend or counsellor who gradually teaches the novice the organizational ropes. A coach, in contrast to the above, is centrally concerned with the way the player is seeing and interpreting the play.

We need to explicitly note that we are not concerned in this article with "good relationship" in the sense of being friendly, liked, or comfortable with. A "good relationship" between manager and worker, in this human relations sense, is not essential to producing excellent results—the acid test of management effectiveness. Thus being "nice" is not a relevant component of coaching. One can readily think of effective sports coaches who were anything but nice.

Many kinds of advisory relationships are commonly called coaching. Exhibit 2 contrasts coaching with other advisory relationships. Only level 5 constitutes coaching as we conceive it.

Characteristics of a Great Coach

The thesis of this article was first presented publicly in October 1987 at a management seminar that featured five star coaches:

- *George Allen* has had more than 30 years of coaching professional football teams. His record of 116-47-5 ranks as the second best in the history of the NFL among coaches who coached for more than a decade. He turned the perennial losers, Los Angeles Rams and Washington Redskins, into champions almost overnight. He never had a losing season, was the NFL Coach-of-the-Year four times, and twelve of his assistant coaches went on to become NFL head coaches.

- *Red Auerbach,* a legendary figure in the field of professional basketball, became coach of the Boston Celtics at the age of 24. He subsequently was their general manager and president. When Red retired, he had accumulated the extraordinary record of 1,037 wins for the Celtics, and he won the NBA Championship in nine out of his last ten coaching seasons. He is credited with building both the Celtics team and their remarkable organization. He has the unique distinction of being named Coach-of-the-Year and Executive-of-the-Year in the same season.

- *Tim Gallwey* was a national amateur tennis champion and a successful tennis coach. He's also the author of *The Inner Game of Tennis,* which became the best-selling sports book in history. The book and his coaching are based on his personal discoveries of what produces "peak performances," which he termed "the inner game process." Known as a "coach's coach" in individual sports, his primary laboratory is the tennis court, where the practicality of his theory has been clearly and dramatically demonstrated. Tim has just completed *The Inner Game of Work;* he consults with major corporations around the world.

- *John Wooden's* career as a college basketball coach is unparalleled. His record with the UCLA Bruins is unequaled, having achieved ten NCAA Championships (seven of which were consecutive). His Bruin teams also won 88 consecutive games, a still unbroken record for any collegiate sport. He continuously turned raw freshman talent into championship teams. His entire college record over 29 years is a staggering 81% (677-161). John was college Coach-of-the-Year six times, and is the only person inducted into the National Basketball Hall of Fame as both a player and a coach.

- *Werner Erhard,* the sometimes controversial founder of "est," focused much of his work in the past decade on coaching, both as a coach and as one being coached. His research and studies into coaching have included thousands of hours of being formally coached in a variety of disciplines, culminating in a comprehensive theory and technology for implementing principles of coaching in the workplace.

The group shared several qualities. Each was noticeably soft-spoken, articulate, humble, charming, witty, respectful of others, direct in speaking, and dedicated to his profession and players. Noticeably missing was any tendency to take credit for successes or to blame others for mistakes. They seemed to be non-punitive. They showed almost no interest in records and statistics and seemed focused on what it takes to win the next game. They also were tough-minded and intolerant of anything less than the best from themselves and their players. Not one of the coaches was punitive of errors by their players. What spoke loudest was their quality of authenticity.

It became clear from the discussion, however, that these qualities alone do not account for the coaches' superior performance. They did reveal common practices they followed when coaching with those they coached that might shed more light on the factors behind their success. Although no list of do's and don'ts can accurately pinpoint what actually underlies great coaching, here are some commonalities:

1. *Be clear it's a game, and that the point is to win.* Each of the coaches regarded the game as a canvas on which to express his talents and abilities. To produce the best work, he dealt with the full spectrum of human concerns, issues, and possibilities.

2. *Be ethical within the rules of the game, but don't let the rules limit your thinking.* Each coach developed new features of playing where others saw no such possibility. For example, George Allen conceived the "special team" in football, and Red Auerbach created the "sixth man" concept in basketball. Allen's concept of the special team, used in situations like kickoffs, punting, and field goals, was revolutionary because it was the first time a coach began using certain players exclusively in these situations. The sixth-man concept was unique because it meant withholding the use of a key player as a starter and using that player in substitute positions.

3. *Be committed to the players, and generate a personal stake in the success and well-being of each individual.* Amazingly, these great coaches continued to keep in touch with almost everyone they had ever coached.

4. *Be focused on the development of each player.* One coach underscored this point by saying he never asked a player for more than his best and never allowed players on a team to compete with each other.

5. *Be uncompromising in one's discipline to preparation and practice.* Each coach genuinely enjoyed the process of preparing for a game and practicing, functions that constitute a coach's primary workplace.

6. *Be committed to the possibility that there are no absolute limits to the performance of either an individual or an organization.* These coaches believe that improvement is always possible.

7. *Be in continuous communication with the players, the owners, the public, and the competition.* Coaching occurs within the context of interaction amongst all those who have a stake in the game. Success is never an individual accomplishment.

8. *Be personally responsible for the outcome, but not in a way that robs the players of their being fully responsible.* Validate the players' efforts when they lose, and point to what was missing when they win. Never blame the players for poor results, and be generous with acknowledgment.

9. *Be honest, talk straight, and model the qualities that you demand from the players.* If you want respect, trust, dedication, commitment, and responsibility from the players, then you must model these qualities.

10. *Be aware of the overall team picture and what is occurring in all aspects of the game that impact the team.* No individual performer can outperform a team. John Wooden noted that only once since 1950 has basketball's championship team also had the league's highest individual scorer. "You win as a team, and you lose as a team."

11. *Be uncompromising in attention to details.* Breakthroughs in performance come from having perfected the little things. Handle everything up front, put nothing under the rug, and complete all pieces of the work.

12. *Be a teacher.* Each saw his job as teaching. John Wooden still considers himself a teacher first; only secondarily is he a coach.

13. *Be a learner and listen acutely.* One common trait of all the coaches was their regard for their own coaches and their commitment to continuously expanding their own coaching abilities.

14. *Be your word.* Do what you say you will do, and don't dwell on past failures.

15. *Be oriented to what is happening right now and focus on winning the next game.* When that game is over, focus on the next opportunity.

16. *Be in love with the game and the privilege of being a coach.* The panelists agree that without love of the game and love of their players, a successful outcome is not possible.

So What Is Coaching?

Earlier in this article we stated that we see coaching as much more than a handy sports analog for managers, or as a technique for doing more of what is already possible within our contemporary culture of management. Following is a summary of some of the things we've learned about "coaching" and what can be seen from the perspective of generating a new context for managing.

1. Coaching is a comprehensive and distinctive way of being related to others in an enterprise. The source of accomplishment in coaching derives from the particular kind of relationship that constitutes coaching.

2. Coaching provides a player/performer or team with the possibility of dealing with what is not seen, or even seeable, from the prevailing paradigm. Great coaches communicate in a way that allows a player of a team to "see" the game differently than from the perspective of action. In doing so, it provides a possibility for action not available in the absence of coaching.

3. Coaching as a way of being and relating at work can provide managers with a way of developing themselves and others in what has customarily been explained away as the "art" of management.

4. Coaching is "missing" as a way of being and relating in most organizations. Consequently little or no attention is given to developing the skills and qualities of effective coaching in various management development programs.

5. Coaching is "missing" by virtue of our cultural blindspots or paradigm that we have termed our control-and-order structure of thinking.

6. Coaching is a two-way process, which suggests that being a great coach also includes being a great coachee.

7. Coaching produces results solely through a medium of communication. The actions of coaches are found in what they say (either orally or non-orally) and in the quality of their listening (or noticing). Coaches impact action "in the game" by how they listen and what they say.

8. Coaching is driven by commitment, both the commitment of the coach and the commitment of the players. Coaching lives in the relationship between committed individuals who are working to accomplish something together.

9. Coaching is a dyad, like leader/follower or director/actor. Coaching cannot be separated from the actions of the partner in the relationship, yet it is distinct within a "whole" consisting of both the coach and the player/performer.

10. Unlike other types of supportive relationships (counsellor, friend, instructor, trainer, mentor, etc.), coaching calls for a high degree of interpersonal risk and trust on the part of both the coach and the person who is coached. This risk always exists where there is a mutual commitment to the possibility of a breakthrough in performance.

11. Coaching generates new possibilities for action and allows for breakthroughs in performance.

12. Coaching calls for rethinking and transforming our traditional models of management, organization, work, and society. As a field, management has evolved in a hierarchical model of organization. Coaching requires a more interrelated and dynamic vision of organization based more on relationship, commitment, purpose, and results than on role, hierarchical position, prescribed order, and authority.

Creating an Organizational Culture of and for Coaching

In addition to studying the model of great coaches, what can a manager do to become a wiz-ard at coaching in a business context? The answer, of course, is paradigm-dependent. In the prevailing management paradigm of control, the answer is likely to be almost technical: What causal action produces what specific effect? But in the new management paradigm of coaching, the proper response is to *listen,* especially *for commitment and for the possibility of action out of that commitment.* Listening is the primary means for providing the necessary context for commitment, possibility, and relevant action. Putting listening ahead of control, instead of control ahead of listening, is in itself the shift we have discussed in this article.

What can management do to bring about the paradigm shift? A variety of approaches are being used. The following steps constitute one scenario that has proven successful.

1. *Educate people in the parameters of effective coaching* by examining what factors currently limit action in the organization and exploring the possibility of creating a new organizational way of relating. This has been done effectively in workshops led by effective coaches who have experience in developing other effective coaches. The education phase usually involves serious thinking about the nature of organization, communication, commitment, and what shapes managers' perceptions of situations they encounter.

2. *Commit to undertake a specific project* having a specific timetable and an unpredictable or "beyond business as usual" result. A computer software organization, for example, may decide on a project to reduce errors by 50% while increasing productivity by 200%. Commit to having this project be the "laboratory" in which the effective coaching skills will be developed and practiced.

3. *Determine the "players" in the project* as well as those who also will have a stake in the project's outcome, or who will be tangentially involved. These may include "bosses," vendors, regulators, unions, or community groups. Then *clarify the commitments cf the players* to each "stakeholder" as well as specify the roles or support required from the stakeholders.

4. *Declare who will be the coach in each project relationship and what the person or persons*

being coached is committed to accomplishing. As the project unfolds, coaching rapidly ceases to be confined to a fixed role and becomes a dimension of all interactions.

5. *Be prepared for "breakdowns" as the project progresses.* A natural consequence of commitment in a coaching relationship is that the coaching (if successful) always uncovers barriers to the next level of performance. The more one is coached, the more one develops tolerance for breakdowns which are recognized as the "raw material" from which evolve subsequent breakthroughs in performance.

6. *Allow the day-to-day actions of the project to emerge from openings (new possibilities) that occur naturally in conversations with a coach.* Continuously look for new actions that are in line with the players' commitment and intended results. An effective coach listens for commitment, observes behavior, and interacts with the player to close the gap.

7. *Validate and acknowledge accomplishments and breakdowns as opportunities to regenerate the originating commitment to the project.* For example, one pitfall that may often emerge during the development of a strong coaching relationship is that when breakdowns do occur, what comes into question is the relationship, and hence communication, with the coach. Frequently this takes the form of the player blaming himself or herself ("I let the coach down") or blaming the coach ("I did what he said and it didn't work; he is a bad coach"). Both of these natural responses must be acknowledged and worked through, as they shift the relationship from one of possibility and empowerment to one of assessment and domination.

8. *Complete everything as you go along.* Push nothing under the rug, and no matter what the circumstances, look forward. At the conclusion of the project, or at interim phases, *tell the truth about whether you accomplished what you intended,* and choose to regenerate or revoke the commitment.

Summary: Revising Our Thinking About Management

Until recently, coaching has been viewed as a tool, or technique, for improving the efficiency of a particular operation, developing specific management skills, or ameliorating a problem situation. Sports coaching seems to be the origin of much of the talk about coaching in business organizations. We do not view coaching in this light. We see coaching as a profound challenge to our customary ways of thinking about management. In our formulation, coaching is a way of relating and communicating that transcends all sports and performing arts, not merely something transported from one arena to another. It is independent of the particular game or field in which it is played. And, once more, it is *not* a technique!

Our current understanding of the power of the coaching relationship suggests that it represents a fundamental shift in our current thinking regarding managerial effectiveness and presents us with the possibility of extraordinary increases in managerial effectiveness, if we are willing to put at risk some of our habitual ways of thinking about management.

What's involved is a paradigm shift from traditional concerns with hierarchical authority, order and control, and motivation by job insecurity, to one that is based on partnership for achieving results, and commitment to collaborating in accomplishing new possibilities rather than maintaining old structures.

The paradigm shift foreshadowed by the coaching relationship is represented in Exhibit 3. In this article we have alluded to the team aspects of coaching. There are, of course, major organizational implications of coaching that we have not been able to develop here. Exhibit 3 reminds us that there are also profound societal ramifications of taking the coaching relationship seriously.

A skeptical reader may feel we are overstating the case for the alleged power of coaching and that we have not demonstrated how to put the idea into practice. We would remind such a reader that no paradigm has ever been generated that had a guaranteed workable formula for putting it into practice.

Exhibit 3
Comparative Ways of Thinking About Management

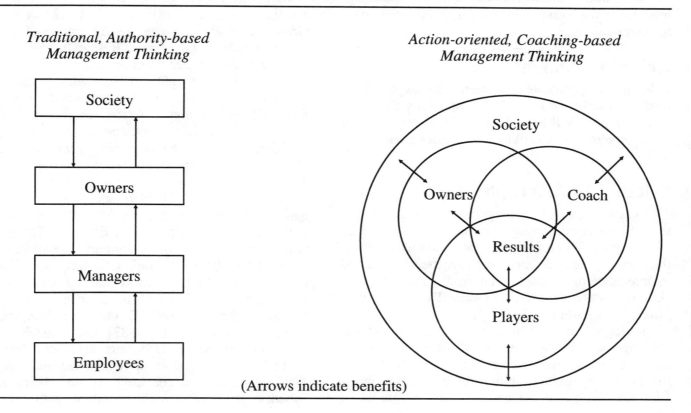

Traditional, Authority-based Management Thinking

Society → Owners → Managers → Employees

Action-oriented, Coaching-based Management Thinking

Society / Owners / Coach / Results / Players

(Arrows indicate benefits)

The prevailing paradigm of American management, which is based on the premise that managerial effectiveness derives from attempting to control the behaviors of employees, has been notably poor at demonstrating the validity of that idea—despite at least eight decades and many millions of research dollars spent in trying to.

The paradigm that has conditioned us to think that increasing managerial effectiveness can be achieved by specifying behaviors is, from our experience, bankrupt. Why is corporate America so stuck with attempting to control and more precisely specify employee behavior to improve effectiveness, productivity, and competitiveness when the evidence is so contrary? *What's missing is people committed to achieving excellent results and empowered by management; and that's precisely the focus of coaching.*

Coaching is not a new concept in the history of human relationships. Coaching should not be seen as another "new" answer for managing, but rather as a reminder of what really counts in management, organization, and work. It *does,* however, offer something radically new for present-day management—a revision of our thinking about human organization and a fresh approach to breakthroughs in performance in areas that have become stagnant or unproductive.

Thoughtful managers have been looking for a way to pinpoint the skills that make the elusive "art" of management appear so natural in "great" managers. Coaching captures these essentials in a way that enables people to shift their thinking from a traditional paradigm of control/order/prescription to a paradigm designed for acknowledging and empowering people in action. It creates a new context for management, one that fosters a genuine partnership between managers and employees so that both can accomplish more than currently can be imagined from the perspective of our traditional management culture.

Acknowledgment

We deep appreciate the many colleagues who read early drafts of this article, especially Bob Tannenbaum and Will McWhinney. Their constructive criticisms greatly contributed to the development of this article.

Selected Bibliography

The statement that "management is the art of getting things done through people" is attributed to Mary Parker Follett in the 1920s. And the statement that "Managing is defined here as…the creation and maintenance of an internal environment…" is from Harold Koontz and Cyril O'Donnell's *Principles of Management,* 4th ed., 1968.

The definitions and functions of "coaching" and "management" have some important things in common. In fact sports coaches are often called "field managers" by owners and front office personnel. Both coaching and management are people-based arts, and both focus on getting something done through the actions of others by a communicative process. Good coaching and good management both depend on the quality of communication.

The word "coach" was first used in the modern sense of a sports coach in the 1880s (referring specifically to one who trained a team of athletes to win a boat race). Previously (beginning in the 1840s), the word "coach" was used colloquially at Oxford University to refer to a private (vs. university) tutor who prepared a student for an examination. But the very first use of the word "coach" in English occurred in the 1500s to refer to a particular kind of carriage. (It still does.) Hence the root meaning of the verb "to coach": to convey a valued person from where he or she was to where he or she wanted to be.

The earliest efforts to explore coaching as a management function seem to come from the work of Myles Mace in the 1950s. He conceived of coaching as a worthy and acquirable management skill.

His work is well worth reading. See "On-the-Job Coaching," by M.L. Mace and W.R. Mahler, in *Developing Executive Skills* (Eds. H.F. Merrill and E. Marting, AMA, 1958); and M.L. Mace's *The Growth and Development of Executives* (Harvard Business School, Division of Research, 1959).

There is little other literature on coaching that is really noteworthy until 1978, when Ferdinand Fournies' book *Coaching for Improved Work Performance* (F. Fournies & Assoc., Inc.) was published, which stimulated renewed interest. See also Hawdon Hague's *The Organic Organisation and How to Manage It* (John Wiley & Sons, 1978). Then see "Coaching—A Management Tool for More Effective Work Performance," by G.E. Allenbaugh (*Management Review,* May 1983); "Coaching: Turning a Group into an Effective Team," by G.K. Himes (*Supervision,* January 1984); "Developing Employees Through Coaching and Career Management," by L.M. Shore and A.J. Bloom (*Personnel,* August 1986); "The Manager's Role as Coach and Mentor," by C.D. Orth *et al.* (*Organizational Dynamics,* Spring 1987); and "Coaching for High Performance: the Manager as Coach," by C.R. Bell (*SAM Advanced Management Journal,* August 1987). (Articles on coaching are now being published in the management literature at the rate of approximately twenty per year.)

Probably the best available statements yet on coaching are by Tom Peters in Chapter 18 of *A Passion for Excellence*—Tom Peters and Nancy Austin (Warner Books, 1985); and by Dennis Kinlaw in *Coaching for Commitment: Managerial Strategies for Obtaining Superior Performance* (University Associates, Inc., 1989).

Finally, it is interesting to note that Frederick Taylor might have written the last paragraph of the preceding article, except that in place of the word "coaching" he would have used "scientific management." The critical difference lies in the degree to which people in organizations, both managers and employees, are empowered. "Coaching" is explicitly designed to empower, whereas "scientific management" has an 80-year track record of disempowering people at work. Hence Taylor's vision of a genuine partnership in the workplace was never realized.

Roger Evered is professor of management at the Naval Postgraduate School in Monterey, California. He teaches strategic management, organizational change, leadership, and managerial communication. His area of research is on the nature of managerial action. He has written numerous articles and book chapters on action research, strategic management, organization transformation, and epistemological issues in management research.

Evered has 16 years of practical experience with large engineering companies, including McDonnell-Douglas (Missiles and Space Systems), Bristol Siddeley Aero Engines (England), Renault (France), Klein, Schanzlin & Becker (Germany), and General Motors (England). Before joining the Naval Postgraduate School in 1979, he held academic positions at the University of Michigan, U.C.L.A., Penn State University, and the University of Illinois.

He received his B.Sc. in mechanical engineering and D.I.C. in thermodynamics from the University of London, England, and an M.S. in management and a Ph.D. in organizational science from U.C.L.A. He is also past president of the Western Academy of Management.

James C. Selman has specialized for the past 18 years in organization design, productivity improvement, and human resources development. Until 1977 he worked as a management consulting partner for Touche Ross & Company. In that capacity he was responsible for designing and managing major engagements in the public and private sectors, including projects for multinational corporations, the U.S. Congress, and the White House. He has also worked as an independent consultant in formulating and executing organizational and institutional strategies relating to water pollution, drug abuse, and energy.

In 1984 he co-founded Transformational Technologies, Inc., a franchise system of more than 70 independent consulting firms. He resigned as CEO in mid-1988 to form Selman and Associates so he could work more closely with client organizations and further his research into the fundamental principles and abstractions that govern organizational performance. He is a recognized leader and authority in this field.

Mr. Selman graduated in social psychology and philosophy from the University of Oklahoma and did post-graduate work at the University of Florida. He is a certified member of the Institute of Management Consultants. He has published and spoken widely on the subjects of organizational transformation and management productivity.

360-Degree Feedback as a Competitive Advantage

by Manuel London and Richard W. Beatty

This article examines the status of 360-degree feedback in organizations. How to optimally use feedback from multiple constituencies as a competitive advantage is discussed. Differences between traditional performance appraisal and 360-degree feedback are elucidated. Elements of designing and implementing an effective 360-degree feedback program are explored: content, employee involvement, item type, format, relevance, implementation, using results for evaluation and/or development, including managers' self-assessment, and the form and content of the feedback. A research agenda on 360-degree programs is charted. © 1993 by John Wiley & Sons, Inc.

> The total quality management movement and current literature on progressive performance management practices advise incorporating peer, subordinate, and customer reviews into the appraisal process. Very few organizations, however, rely on these "360-degree" programs.
>
> Towers Perrin (1992)

As the Towers Perrin report indicates, there is much lip service paid to 360-degree feedback (programs of performance ratings from subordinates, peers, customers, and suppliers as well as supervisors, or a subset thereof) in organizations. In prac-

tice the emphasis on total quality management to increase or regain a firm's competitive advantage is fueling the use of 360-degree feedback as a popular management tool for providing feedback to leaders and managers. What is implicit in the Towers Perrin finding is that even when 360-degree feedback is implemented, more often than not it is more accurately described as 270-degree feedback, because a major data source—the next and ultimate customers of a work unit's efforts—is not included. We will use this expansion of the concept—the involvement of customers (Ulrich, 1992) as well as including subordinates (as "the customers of managerial work")—to help us rethink how 360-degree feedback may be used to add greater value to leadership development and organizational effectiveness.

The concept of adding value is an important concern from an organization's perspective and needs to be addressed before current usage of 360-degree systems is discussed. By adding value, we mean contributing relatively directly to a firm's competitive advantage, where competitive advantage is defined as providing a product or service perceived by its customers as adding value and doing so in a way that is unique and difficult for a competitor to readily duplicate (Ulrich & Lake, 1990). There are many potential ways 360-degree feedback can add to a firm's competitive advantage, such as providing better customer-based data on products and processes designed to serve the customer. Such data does not only help to improve existing customer processes, but also to provide "customer intelligence," such that a work unit serving the customer can better anticipate its customers' needs and can provide *unique* products and services over time that make the firm the customer's preferred provider. When such customer-based data are combined with data on leader behavior as seen by subordinates (and perhaps customers), such "feedback" often creates the discrepancies that energize focused change. Indeed, the combined data may not only tell leaders *what* needs to be done to improve the performance of their work units, but also how this might be accomplished through alterations in their own behavior, for example, in improving teamwork, risk-taking, candor, innovation, and empowerment (depending on the design of the data collection effort).

Considerations in 360-Degree Practices

Research has shown that 360-degree feedback can enhance communications and performance (Bernardin & Beatty, 1987). It is often used to initiate leadership training programs by supplying guidance for developmental purposes (e.g., Center for Creative Leadership). In some organizations feedback is used solely for development; in others, it serves as input for merit evaluation and compensation adjustment (McEvoy & Buller, 1987; London, Wohlers, & Gallagher, 1990).

The 360-degree approach recognizes that little change can be expected without feedback, and that different constituencies are a source of rich and useful information to help managers guide their behavior. For instance, a subordinate's perspective likely will be distinctly different from that of the supervisor, who is traditionally charged with evaluating a *manager's* performance. Subordinates observe, and are affected by, managerial behaviors and decisions in ways which are not always evident to supervisors, especially leadership behaviors the "Boss" may seldom see demonstrated by the manager. In fact, supervisory feedback may primarily reflect the performance of the manager's work unit, rather than leadership behaviors. That is, the supervisor may draw inferences from the performance of the work unit as opposed to actually observing a manager's behavior. This is the classic *what* vs. *how* issue in evaluating managerial performance (Schneier & Beatty, 1977), and both are important as will be shown later. Thus, a 360-degree feedback program formalizes input to the manager from the "customers" of their work (i.e., those who are to be served), especially their subordinates. Such "how" data about leadership skills of managers may not other-

Figure 1. Leadership and 360-degree feedback: Data sources and measurement dimensions

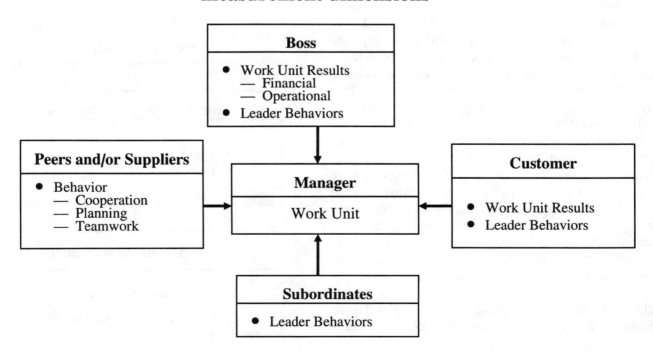

209

wise be obtained from what is arguably the best source—those whom they lead.

Even in organizations using 360-degree programs for managerial appraisal or development, these programs are often carried out in the absence of a strategic context and are not focused upon contributions to a firm's competitive advantage (Schneier, Shaw, & Beatty, 1992). We urge the expansion of the concept to broaden the measures commonly used to evaluate managerial performance; they are shown schematically in Figure 1. At least four possible data sources are represented [supervisor, subordinates, peers (or suppliers), and customers], as well as the potential facets of performance upon which managers have traditionally received feedback. These include work unit measurements such as financial (e.g., return on investment, profitability, costs) and operational measures (e.g., speed, productivity, quality, or customer service) in addition to their performance in terms of behaviors in the areas of leadership and communication, participation, teamwork, etc.

The role of manager exists within the context of a business strategy (Fig. 2). That role is designed to execute the strategy with the resources allocated—financial, material, and human (Schneier et al., 1992). In today's organizational parlance, such resources are to be marshaled to realize the business's vision (e.g., strategic intent) and to develop the desired performance culture (values), such as teamwork, innovation, risk-taking, etc. Managerial execution of strategy involves designing appropriate work structures (including job design), producing customer value, building appropriate workforce competencies, behaving in a supportive and effective leadership style, and aligning basic systems, such as financial, material, information, and especially human resource systems (e.g., appraisal, selection, rewards) to enhance organizational performance. Therefore, to be comprehensive, any measure of managerial effectiveness must include not only contribution to organizational performance through measures of business success (such as financial and operational), but must also include leadership behaviors that are aligned with the business strategy (e.g., empowerment, teamwork, developing employees, etc.).

The process of developing effective 360-degree feedback involves several key, interconnected steps

focusing on measuring the "right work" and feeding the results to managers. The steps include establishing and communicating the purpose of the ef-

Figure 2. Leadership and strategy execution

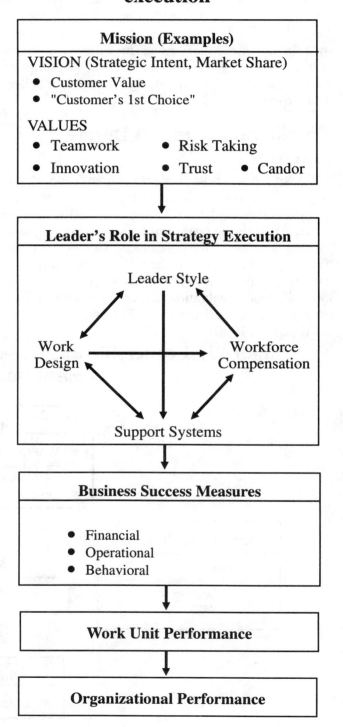

210

fort, developing the content and format of the survey (the most commonly used method, although alternative methods of feedback such as focus groups are also used), establishing a report format and procedures for distributing results, facilitating the use of the results by managers, and following up to assess progress/improvement. The process may involve training and motivating raters in observing, judging, and recording managerial behaviors as well as training leaders and/or facilitators to interpret and use feedback to direct and motivate improvement (Kluger, 1993), to reduce uncertainty (Ashford, 1986) about desired leadership behaviors and work unit results, or to clarify interpersonal dynamics of customer-supplier relationships. Thus, 360-degree feedback can become a powerful organizational intervention to increase awareness of the importance of aligning leader behaviors, work unit results, and customer expectations, as well as increasing employee participation in leadership development and work unit effectiveness.

In his 1991 letter to shareholders in the GE Annual Report, Jack Welch explicitly addressed the importance of leader behaviors. He argued that effective leaders must not only achieve work unit results but also the desired leader behaviors. Figure 3 is a matrix depicting the decision process used to assess who, of four management types, gets promoted at GE. Welch has declared that GE "cannot afford management styles that suppress and intimidate" subordinates (as cited in *The Wall Street Journal,* 1992). The article goes on to say that:

> Even some executives at the highest levels of the company in recent months have been found wanting under these measurements and have been reassigned or signaled to seek work elsewhere. "An easy call," [Welch says is the] leader who "delivers on commitments—financial or otherwise—and shares the values of our company."

Leaders who miss commitments but share the values "usually get a second chance, preferably in a different environment" within the company, he declares.

The fourth type is "the most difficult for many of us to deal with. That leader delivers on commitments, makes all the numbers, but doesn't share the values we must have. This is the individual who typically forces per-

Figure 3. GE leader assessment

Lo   RESULTS   Hi

	Lo RESULTS	Hi
Hi VALUES	Type 2 Second Chance	Type 1 Easy Decision
Lo	Type 3 Easy Decision	Type 4 Difficult Decision

formance out of people rather than inspire it: the autocrat, the big shot, the tyrant. Too often all of us have looked the other way, tolerating these 'Type 4' managers because 'they always deliver'—at least in the short term."

[A GE] spokesman confirmed that "several" executives were ousted in 1991 based on the leadership guidelines.

Similarities and Differences Between 360-Degree Feedback and Performance Appraisal

There is a large body of literature on performance appraisal (supervisor evaluation and feedback) processes and practices, but little has been devoted to the relationship among the various components of 360-degree feedback (e.g., the relationship between leadership effectiveness, supervisory ratings, work unit success, and customer satisfaction). We attempt to model the relevant processes using the image theory of Mitchell and Beach (1990) to explain image formation and evaluation (raters gathering and interpreting information, and managers receiving and reacting to feedback). We believe this approach can improve understanding of the relationship between leader behavior and work unit results from the perspective of the organization and the customers of a work unit.

Appraisals of managers (supervisors rating subordinates) and 360-degree feedback both involve reports of behavior, as well as judgments of performance based on work unit results. Both can use rating scales, and thus be subject to traditional issues of data validity and bias, for example, response consistency, leniency, halo, and stereotyping (Borman, 1974).

In 360-degree feedback, rating scales can be identical for all raters or can be customized to reflect the unique features of each relationship. For instance, upward feedback (subordinates rating their supervisor) may consist of items that focus only on the manager-subordinate relationship. In organizations that do not share Jack Welch's view that it is important for managers to achieve results in ways consonant with the organization's values, the manager's relations to subordinates may have little influence on supervisors, who focus primarily on work unit's results as the largest determinant of the manager's performance. For example, some organizations have loosely defined customer service positions that are used to create customer value by almost any means possible, requiring an empowering leadership; whereas some firms may have strategies that by their very nature create turnover (e.g., low labor cost strategies). The relevance of measuring leadership behaviors in the former is great, in the latter irrelevant.

There are also differences across organizations in terms of the leadership styles (i.e., values) supervisors believe best represent what is needed by subordinates from their managers. Figure 4 summarizes the dimensions measured by several major firms, as well as by a consultant, that use subordinate feedback to leaders. Of these firms, only IBM uses subordinate appraisals for evaluative purposes as opposed to "for feedback only." (IBM also did not include customers, which might have been very useful in anticipating the environment they face today.) Ordinarily, subordinates are asked to rate leadership dimensions primarily.

There are other major differences between performance appraisal and 360-degree feedback. First, performance appraisal is conducted primarily for evaluation and has organizational consequences, such as pay treatment and opportunities for job as-

Figure 4. Dimensions subordinates use to evaluate managers in selected organizations

Company	Teamwork	Leadership	Coaching	Integrity	Innovation	Sensitivity	Decision Making	Problem Identification	Communication	Performance Observation	Job Knowledge
IBM	✓		✓	✓		✓					
BP	✓	✓	✓		✓	✓	✓	✓	✓		
Tenneco	✓		✓		✓					✓	✓
Amoco (Production)	✓	✓	✓		✓		✓		✓		
PDI's Profiles	✓	✓	✓	✓		✓	✓			✓	

signments, transfer, and promotion. Performance appraisal is not ordinarily geared to improving work unit performance or leader behavior. Second, although performance appraisal nominally has a developmental component to improve weaknesses and enhance strengths, this aspect is often incidental and suffers because the focus of managerial evaluation is on the performance of the work unit. Since supervisors are accountable for the contributions of their subordinate managers' work units, they may be less concerned with leadership behaviors which they may seldom observe. Because development efforts focus on behavior change, the expectation that supervisory ratings of work unit level performance would be directly related to changing managerial behaviors is unrealistic (McEvoy & Beatty, 1989). Thus, traditional performance appraisal may be less than adequate in development and career planning.

In traditional performance appraisal, supervisory ratings are often the sole source of evaluative data. When 360-degree feedback data are input in the evaluation process, no single component is likely to be the sole source of evaluation. When data are gathered primarily for developmental purposes (especially peer, subordinate, and even customer surveys), they are usually used *only* for developmental improvement efforts. Feedback data may or may not be shared with the manager's boss, which is not problematic in situations where the manager is charged to make primary contributions through work unit results, and *how* they are achieved is best left to those responsible for the work. Thus, the supervisory rating still remains the only evaluative data used by the organization. Sometimes, the feedback data are shared with subordinates on a voluntary basis. These observations on sharing the data appear to be consistent with Kluger's (1993) recommendations.

Unlike supervisory ratings, 360-degree feedback recognizes the complexity of management and the value of input from different sources (Becker & Klimoski, 1989). For instance, subordinates are excellently positioned to view and evaluate leadership behaviors. Indeed, they may have more complete and accurate information about many leadership behaviors than supervisors have. It is axiomatic that managers should not be rating behaviors they do not observe, and often leader behaviors exhibited in

the manager-subordinate relationship are not observed by the boss. Examples abound: the extent to which the managers structure work, provide performance feedback, foster a positive working environment, provide necessary resources, arrange training, and support employee development. Yet the quality of manager-subordinate relationships may be crucial to the success of the work group. The same argument can be made for ratings from other "customers" of the manager's work—peers and internal and external customers.

Unlike supervisory appraisal, 360-degree ratings from multiple sources permit testing of consistency of leader behaviors and reliability of the information gathered. When subordinate capabilities and job demands are reasonably similar, one would expect a manager to behave similarly with most, if not all, subordinates. As a corollary, one would expect subordinates to agree in their ratings of the manager. When subordinates' capabilities and jobs differ, and the jobs are not interrelated, the manager might be expected to behave differently with different subordinates. Then, although the range of ratings among the subordinates in the work group may vary, these ratings would nevertheless supply useful feedback even though the data could not be averaged because of this variation. These principles apply to peer, customer, and supervisor relationships as well. Peers are more likely to agree with each other when they observe the colleague in the same context. On the other hand, peers who interact with the manager for different reasons at different times may perceive the manager differently. Likewise, the supervisor may also provide yet another perspective in terms of opportunities to observe.

Managerial behavior can vary by constituency because role expectations may differ with respect to each constituency, whether upward, downward, or laterally. Managers may strive differentially to create a favorable impression upwardly, exhibiting greater concern to create a good impression with supervisors, who control pay and promotional opportunities, as well as resources, at the expense of subordinate perceptions of, say, integrity (e.g., "cooking the books" for upper management or preparing a presentation that obfuscates the reality of what is actually going on). In manager-subordinate relationships in which, for historical reasons, creating a favorable impression with subordinates has been de-emphasized in favor of simply getting work done to specification regardless of others' perceptions, implementing 360-degree feedback programs can be particularly useful where managerial style actually works against the achievement of work unit goals.

The perspective of internal and external customers provides yet another potentially useful insight into how and why image management is important in all relationships. In this case, it is easier to ensure that accuracy and leniency questions are properly framed for the context. Figure 5 is a sample internal survey that takes into account these concerns. That is, the customer may not always be right or consistent in evaluating the performance of a work unit and its leadership. But if the work unit (supplier) wishes to retain the customer, it must work at clarifying its customer's expectations and change where necessary, whether through image management (in the sense of customer education and training) or substantive change. By simultaneously measuring expectations versus performance, the focus effectively shifts from the weight to be given the rater to the effectiveness of the manager and the work unit in responding to ever-changing customer requirements, as Figure 5 reveals. Such an approach might also be used to identify the organization's "active learners" (Center for Creative Leadership, 1992)—those who are able to anticipate and respond to supervisory, subordinate, and *customer* needs, as well as take the initiative to operate on their environment, impact results, and maintain a perpetual state of professional growth.

Risks and Rewards of 360-Degree Feedback

Feedback has a number of potentially beneficial spin-offs for an organization. First, as mentioned earlier, it can call attention to important performance dimensions heretofore neglected by an organization, in the process of conveying organizational values. It may also be a useful intervention to enhance two-way communications, increase formal as well as informal communications, build more effective work relationships, increase opportunities for employee involvement, uncover and resolve conflict, and demonstrate respect for employee opinions on the part of top management. Because 360-degree feedback requires an element of reciprocity between managers and raters as sources of feedback, reinforcement, and improved satisfaction of customers, it can provide greater job and employability security because employees who create greater value for customers ultimately create greater value for themselves as employees.

Feedback is consonant with, and can also contribute to, other organizational initiatives to improve work process quality. Such initiatives often focus on interpersonal relationships between and within groups, and 360-degree feedback is consistent with, and fosters, participative cultures. Even though managers may ultimately be evaluated on work unit outputs, information about managerial behaviors can help develop and ultimately improve outputs.

There are costs associated with 360-degree feedback: time and money for preparation and implementation (e.g., explaining the purpose and training managers on how to use the feedback). It adds complexity to the appraisal administration process, requiring distributing the forms to the proper individuals and collating the data, perhaps entailing the use of sophisticated computer programming and outside help. There are potential risks to raters, and the process may generate tension between the manager and those who provide ratings (Hautaluoma, Jobe, Visser, & Donkersgoed, 1992). The process also establishes expectations that behavior will change, carrying the seeds of unmet expectations. Further, it may set up potential conflict by highlighting the need to be "different things to different people." In addition, the process not only generates a considerable body of information to integrate, but it can also become the vehicle for selective perception and information distortion. Because of its very nature—its use of more significant others than traditional supervisory ratings—360-degree feedback raises the stakes for a manager, placing increased pressure on self-concept and goals. As a result, negative information becomes more powerful and difficult to deny, especially when raters agree; and easy to distort or perceive selectively, especially when raters disagree.

Designing 360-Degree Systems

There are, of course, a variety of ways to design a 360-degree feedback instrument, collect the data,

Figure 5. Sample internal customer feedback survey for an accounts payable department

	What level of service should be provided Accounts Payable?	What level of service do you receive from Accounts Payable?
SERVICES PROVIDED	**Expectations**	**Performance**
	High .... Low	High .... Low
Processing of vendor invoices	7 6 5 4 3 2 1 NA	7 6 5 4 3 2 1 NA
COMMUNICATION	**Expectations**	**Performance**
	High .... Low	High .... Low
Tells when service will be performed	7 6 5 4 3 2 1 NA	7 6 5 4 3 2 1 NA
Listens to customer	7 6 5 4 3 2 1 NA	7 6 5 4 3 2 1 NA
Provides updates/follow-up	7 6 5 4 3 2 1 NA	7 6 5 4 3 2 1 NA
Explains procedures/services/results	7 6 5 4 3 2 1 NA	7 6 5 4 3 2 1 NA
Seeks feedback	7 6 5 4 3 2 1 NA	7 6 5 4 3 2 1 NA
RELIABILITY	**Expectations**	**Performance**
	High .... Low	High .... Low
Provides service that is promised	7 6 5 4 3 2 1 NA	7 6 5 4 3 2 1 NA
Consistent in service delivery	7 6 5 4 3 2 1 NA	7 6 5 4 3 2 1 NA
Dependable	7 6 5 4 3 2 1 NA	7 6 5 4 3 2 1 NA
Takes responsibility for their service	7 6 5 4 3 2 1 NA	7 6 5 4 3 2 1 NA
Accuracy	7 6 5 4 3 2 1 NA	7 6 5 4 3 2 1 NA
FLEXIBILITY/CREATIVITY	**Expectations**	**Performance**
	High .... Low	High .... Low
Use of alternative methods to meet customer needs or solve problems	7 6 5 4 3 2 1 NA	7 6 5 4 3 2 1 NA
Adaptable to special situations	7 6 5 4 3 2 1 NA	7 6 5 4 3 2 1 NA
Employees can make decisions when normal operating procedures do not apply	7 6 5 4 3 2 1 NA	7 6 5 4 3 2 1 NA
KNOWLEDGE/UNDERSTANDING	**Expectations**	**Performance**
	High .... Low	High .... Low
Understands how their efforts relate to overall service	7 6 5 4 3 2 1 NA	7 6 5 4 3 2 1 NA
Understands customer needs	7 6 5 4 3 2 1 NA	7 6 5 4 3 2 1 NA
Knows how to provide requested service	7 6 5 4 3 2 1 NA	7 6 5 4 3 2 1 NA
Sensitive to client needs	7 6 5 4 3 2 1 NA	7 6 5 4 3 2 1 NA
Advice and consulting	7 6 5 4 3 2 1 NA	7 6 5 4 3 2 1 NA
ACCESS	**Expectations**	**Performance**
	High .... Low	High .... Low
Can talk to someone to get questions answered	7 6 5 4 3 2 1 NA	7 6 5 4 3 2 1 NA
Convenient office hours	7 6 5 4 3 2 1 NA	7 6 5 4 3 2 1 NA
Someone available to provide service	7 6 5 4 3 2 1 NA	7 6 5 4 3 2 1 NA

report, and use the results (Bernardin & Beatty, 1987; London et al., 1990). We focus here on item content, involving employees in developing items, item type and format, relevance, implementation (accompanying instructions, training, etc.), use of the results (whether for evaluation and/or development), inclusion of managers' self-assessment, and the form and content of the feedback.

Content

Like performance appraisal, 360-degree feedback ratings should be made on performance dimensions strategic to organizational success and thus by definition relevant to the job. Job analyses are then one way to determine appropriate content. But in some cases managers may need to be evaluated on behaviors that have not heretofore been considered a part of the current formal job design. For example, in the process of an organizational change effort, top management may announce a new vision of the types of leaders they wish to reward and advance (perhaps, those who increase management democracy, employee empowerment, teamwork, customer focus, etc.). These forward-looking behavioral aspects can be captured on the feedback scales.

Involving Employees in Program Design

A useful technique to capture these forward-looking behaviors of organizational change efforts is to involve a group of knowledgeable employees to identify and generate behavioral statements as a part of content development. This process opens up two-way channels of communicating, generating insights on leader behaviors that may perhaps have been invisible to top management and in the very process of involving employees strengthening the link between 360-degree feedback and the organization's strategies and visions. The process also tends to engender increased commitment to the 360-degree process, as it communicates the importance of the desired behaviors, thereby enhancing the value of the process to the organization.

Item Types and Format

Feedback ratings are made on a set of items likely to be familiar to the raters. Items can be general (for instance, asking about managers' characteristics and abilities) or specific (asking about behaviors within the manager-subordinate, peer, or customer-supplier

relationships). Questions posed can request an evaluation ("How well does the manager do X...?") or a frequency estimate ("How often does the manager do Y..."?). Content generally reflects elements of leadership, work group relationships, or manager-subordinate relationships that are easily understood and tied to experiences with the manager. They are the sorts of things one would expect to rate or be rated on; they are consistent with organizational and personal values. The rating format for specific items apparently has little effect on rating accuracy, as is the case with performance appraisal (DeNisi, Cafferty, & Meglino, 1984).

Item Relevance

Issues of relevance generally focus on the extent to which the items reflect prototypical managerial behaviors. The more the items represent prototypes, the more salient the items will be to the rater (Cronshaw & Lord, 1987). The rating process then becomes a simple compatibility test (i.e., "Does the ratee fit the prototype?"). Compatible ratees will be given high ratings and incompatible ratees will be given low ratings. Items that are ambiguous or that don't reflect the prototype will be in the middle. However, prototypical managers may not be what are desired by organizations experiencing rapid, turbulent change. In such circumstances organizations may wish to break prototypical roles and involve managers in developing new customer-focused and employee empowering roles. Thus the item relevance may come from customers and employees in relation to a supervisor's efforts in meeting customer requirements.

Implementation

The 360-degree feedback process itself must be clear, with participants understanding the intended use of the results. Accordingly, instructions should be unambiguous, and training should be provided to explain the purpose of the ratings, how data will be aggregated, and how results will be fed back. As in performance appraisal, training tends to reduce rating biases by sensitizing employees to common rating errors (leniency, halo, central tendency, etc.).

Care must be taken to ensure rater anonymity. This means guarding the results, probably by using a third party outside the formal organization to analyze the data and prepare feedback reports. Such reports are usually computer-generated, but may also involve transcribing written comments to disguise handwriting. In some organizations managers do not receive subordinate ratings when the number of peers or subordinates is small (e.g., for Amoco, three or less) because of the risk of revealing the identity of the raters through the numbers alone. That anonymity is fundamental is not only a common-sense observation but is also supported by research findings. In a follow-up survey of subordinates several months after they had provided upward feedback to managers (London et al., 1990), they were asked in an interview, "Would you have rated your boss any differently if feedback had not been given anonymously"; 24% of the 53 subordinates replied yes.

Frequency

Ratings are likely to be done annually. Of course, this does not preclude managers from seeking informal feedback. The introduction of 360-degree feedback often facilitates managers seeking feedback more frequently. As programs of 360-degree feedback develop over time, they tend to create an environment where feedback is regarded as less threatening to all employees and as a valued tool for individual and organizational development, especially as employees and managers become familiar with the process and see its effects on managerial and organizational development.

Uses

How 360-degree feedback is used influences the seriousness with which it is regarded and how quickly it becomes an integral managerial tool. Some organizations integrate 360-degree feedback results with performance evaluation. Others treat supervisor, upward, and/or peer feedback as separate performance criteria, with managers expected to reach or exceed threshold ratings (for example, favorable ratings from subordinates). Managers who do not achieve the threshold may then be placed on a probation or "needs improvement" list that requires showing improvement the next year.

Some organizations use 360-degree feedback solely for development. Managers receive a report but are not required to share the results with either their boss or subordinates. Guidance or counseling sometimes supplements the feedback. This ap-

proach emphasizes the role of development within organizations, and 360-degree feedback is sometimes a vehicle to reemphasize the importance of development, especially during organizational change efforts. Using peer and/or subordinate ratings for evaluation requires greater sensitivity, because managers are more likely to be put on the defensive and to respond to feedback by criticizing the validity of the data, an issue that is usually less critical in the developmental context. However, using feedback for development only can impede the effective use of the results unless there is a requirement for the manager to be responsive to the feedback. Therefore, a useful introductory strategy might involve a two-step process, employing 360-degree feedback for development for several years before using it as input to supervisory evaluations and decisions about pay and promotion.

Whether 360-degree feedback is used for appraisal or development can affect subordinate attitudes about the feedback process and perhaps about the nature of the results themselves. In the upward feedback follow-up survey referred to earlier, 34% of subordinates said they would have rated their boss differently had the feedback been used for the manager's performance appraisal (London et al., 1990).

The ground rules of administering 360-degree feedback vary. Work unit participation can be mandatory or voluntary. The feedback procedure can also vary in directness of the relationship between raters and manager. For instance, the manager can seek out feedback directly from subordinates or peers; a third party might prepare a summary report of ratings; or a group meeting might be held with subordinates or peers during which the manager discusses the results. Hautaluoma, Jobe, Visser, and Donkersgoed (1992) investigated employee attitudes about these various approaches, as well as whether feedback results should be used for development or evaluation. The subjects were 222 subordinates and their managers from two departments of a large firm in the photographic industry. Most favored an approach that incorporated the advantages of a formal policy requiring upward feedback use and a strong developmental purpose, but no direct contact between manager and subordinate. Moreover, the survey revealed the importance of organizational context, as employees who rated their trust in the company higher were more likely to perceive benefits of participation. In addition, these employees recognized that one of the main benefits of the 360-degree feedback process is in producing a sense of participation in important decisions, increasing beliefs of fairness about supervisors' evaluations, increasing accuracy of evaluations, and resolving conflicts.

Self-Assessment

Feedback ratings are often accompanied by managers' self-ratings on the same items on which they are rated by their subordinates, peers, and customers. Self-ratings help focus the manager's attention on the results and build motivation in establishing the direction of self-development efforts (Meyer, 1991; Bassett & Meyer, 1968). Self-appraisals are often used for employee development (Campbell & Lee, 1988), although performance appraisal research has shown that self-appraisals generally disagree with supervisor appraisals (Harris & Schaubroeck, 1988; Mabe & West, 1982). The disagreement could stem from differences in attributional processes with self-ratings subject to a strong self-serving bias (for instance, the tendency to attribute negative events to external causes and positive events to internal causes) (Levy & Foti, 1989; Levy, 1991). By and large, we have found that self-ratings in 360-degree feedback facilitate behavioral change because managers can compare their self-perceptions directly to how a great many others see them. The weight of numbers often forces managers to reconsider self-concepts when the ratings are seriously discrepant, although there is still room for misinterpreting, discounting, or ignoring feedback. In practice, we have found self-ratings are a useful vehicle in focusing attention on discrepancies as well as similarities between self and others' perceptions, and identifying gaps in perceptions. The discrepancies demand resolution of some kind (rationalization, changing self-perceptions, or altering behaviors).

Report Format

The format of the 360-degree feedback can affect how results are internalized and applied. Several variants have been used. One is a narrative statement summarizing the results. Another is a statistical summary with average ratings reported across items or perhaps with average results for clusters of items. Measures of average variation are sometimes included to reflect agreement among subordinates (e.g., average range or variance). Some organizations use a more elaborate report format than an item-by-item listing, adding mean subordinate rating, the highest and lowest rating, the norm for the department or organization (the average rating for the item across managers rated), and the manager's self-rating. The more detailed the report, the more specific the information for guiding behavior change.

Summarizing data by averaging items across predetermined factors usually produces a more reliable, meaningful, and useful format. We have found that the more detailed the report, the more interpretation required, increasing the likelihood that the manager's biases will affect the interpretation. The more detailed the report, the more managers focus on results that match their self-perceptions and ignore results that contradict their self-perceptions (Kahneman, Slovic, & Tversky, 1982; Fischoff, 1988). People are reasonably good at estimating measures of central tendency (e.g., Peterson & Beach, 1967), and this principle likely extends to estimating on average how well one is perceived by subordinates. Therefore, showering a manager with statistics makes the process potentially threatening to his or her self-concept because of the fear of negative results. The managerial response under such circumstances is more likely to be a deterioration in judgment, and a resort to self-defense and biases (Fischoff, 1988). Reports that summarize data on statistically derived factor analyses provide reliable, more easily digestible data without losing distinguishing information.

In summary, we believe that when employees are involved in the design of the feedback process, the uses and consequences are clear, the ratings are anonymous and nonthreatening, self-assessments and group norms are included, and the report format is clear: (a) The rater's evaluation will be more accurate (there will be a positive relationship between attribution of characteristics to the manager and the evaluation) and (b) the manager will be better able to incorporate feedback into an evolving self-concept (there will be a positive relationship between the feedback and image acceptance).

Conclusion

As 360-degree feedback grows in popularity, further research will be needed to improve and facilitate the process. Besides testing how the components of 360-degree feedback relate to managerial response to feedback, there are other areas that need to be investigated for improved practice. Research is needed on different types of 360-degree feedback processes (e.g., different methods of design and implementation, as well as different rating and reporting formats). Differential outcomes between use for development and/or evaluation should be explored. Investigation of 360-degree feedback in terms of organizational culture is needed to determine measures of short-term and long-term effects of 360-degree feedback on work groups, customer relationships, and organizational culture. The effects of varying interpersonal relationships and characteristics on rater agreement and manager acceptance of feedback should be studied. Research is needed on image formation and acceptance processes. Managers' self-concepts and raters' prototypes of managers and leaders should be identified, especially as the roles continue to evolve. Ways to clarify and differentiate these images should be investigated (e.g., by involving subordinates, peers, customers, and managers in generating relevant behaviors to be rated).

As practitioners experiment with interventions to improve the acceptance of 360-degree feedback processes and results, its long-term effects on management style and behavior change should be investigated. Multiple criteria of 360-degree feedback success should be measured, including employee acceptance of the process, managerial acceptance and use of results, change in managerial behavior, and changes in work group and organizational relationships.

Finally, and perhaps most importantly, the linkage of the potential components of 360-degree appraisal with obtaining and sustaining a firm's competitive advantage requires significant research attention. As noted, most efforts on 360-degree feedback efforts are not reported in an organizational or strategic context. The inclusion of external and internal customers (and perhaps suppliers) can provide insight into the leader–behavior–work–unit relationship that may help identify the leadership energy, roles, and behaviors essential for organizational survival.

Understanding this relationship and using 360-degree data feedback to improve work unit results, leadership competency and performance, and customer success in doing business with the firm can indeed make 360-degree feedback a source of competitive advantage.

The authors express appreciation to Drs. Gerrit Wolf, Robert Boice, Jeff Ewing, Helaine Randerson, and Jerry McAdams for their contributions and constructive comments on earlier drafts.

Manuel London is Deputy to the President of the State University of New York at Stony Brook and Professor and Director of the Center for Labor/ Management Studies in Stony Brook's Harriman School for Management and Policy. He is the author of several books, including Managing Careers, Developing Managers, Career Management and Survival in the Workplace, Change Agents: New Roles and Innovation Strategies for Human Resources Professionals, *and* Managing the Training Enterprise. *Dr. London earned his MA and Ph.D. degrees in industrial and organizational psychology from the Ohio State University. He previously worked for AT&T and taught at the University of Illinois at Urbana.*

Richard W. Beatty is Professor of Industrial Relations and Human Resources in the Institute of Management and Labor Relations at Rutgers University. The author of several books, including Personnel Administration, The Performance Management Sourcebook, Performance Appraisal: The Assessment of Human Behavior at Work, *and* The Productivity Sourcebook, *Dr. Beatty earned his MBA from Emory University and Ph.D. in organizational behavior and industrial psychology from Washington University.*

References

Ashford, S. J. (1986). Feedback seeking in individual adaptation: A resource perspective. *Academy of Management Journal, 29,* 465–487.

Bassett, G. A., & Meyer, H. H. (1968). Performance appraisal based on self-review. *Personnel Psychology, 21,* 421–430.

Becker, T. E., & Klimoski, R. J. (1989). A field study of the relationship between the organizational feedback environment and performance. *Personnel Psychology, 42,* 343–358.

Bernardin, J. H., & Beatty, R. W. (1987). Can subordinate appraisals enhance managerial productivity? *Sloan Management Review,* 28(4), 63–73.

Borman, W. C. (1974). The rating of individuals in organizations: An alternative approach. *Organizational Behavior and Human Performance,* 12, 105-124.

Campbell, D. J., & Lee, C. (1988). Self-appraisal in performance evaluation: Development versus evaluation. *Academy of Management Review,* 13, 302-314.

Center for Creative Leadership. (1992). *Tools for developing successful executives.*

Cronshaw, S. F., & Lord, R. G. (1987). Effects of categorization, attribution, and encoding processes on leadership perceptions. *Journal of Applied Psychology,* 72, 97-106.

DeNisi, A. S., Cafferty, T. P., & Meglino, B. M. (1984). A cognitive view of the performance appraisal process: A model and research proposition. *Organizational Behavior and Human Performance,* 33, 360-396.

Fischhoff, B. (1988). Judgment and decision making. In R. J. Sternberg, & E. E. Smith (Eds.), *The psychology of human thought* (pp. 155-187). New York: Cambridge University Press.

Harris, M. M., & Schaubroeck, J. (1988). A meta-analysis of self-manager, self-peer, and peer-manager ratings. *Personnel Psychology,* 41, 43-62.

Hautaluoma, J., Jobe, L., Visser, S., & Donkersgoed, W. (1992). *Employee reactions to different upward feedback methods.* Presented at the Seventh Annual Meeting of the Society for Industrial and Organizational Psychology, Montreal.

Kahneman, D., Slovic, P., & Tversky, A. (1982). *Judgment under uncertainty: Heuristics and biases.* New York: Cambridge University Press.

Kluger, A. N. (1993). *A meta-analysis of the effects of feedback interventions on performance.* To be presented at the Society for Industrial and Organizational Psychology, San Francisco.

Levy, P. E. (1991). *Self-appraisal and attributional judgments.* Paper presented at the Sixth Annual Meeting of the Society for Industrial and Organizational Psychology, St. Louis.

Levy, P. E., & Foti, R. J. (1989). *Reactions to performance feedback as a function of attributional and performance discrepancies.* Paper presented at the Meeting of the American Psychological Association, New Orleans, LA.

London, M., Wohlers, A. J., & Gallagher, P. (1990). 360 degree feedback surveys: A source of feedback to guide management development. *Journal of Management Development,* 9, 17-31.

Mabe, P. A., & West, S. G. (1982). Validity of self-evaluation of ability: A review and meta-analysis. *Journal of Applied Psychology,* 67, 280-296.

McEvoy, G. M., & Beatty, R. W. (1989). Assessment centers and subordinate appraisals of managers: A seven year longitudinal examination of predictive validity. *Personnel Psychology,* 42(1), 37-52.

McEvoy, G. M., & Buller, P. F. (1987). User acceptance of peer appraisals in an industrial setting. *Personnel Psychology,* 40, 785-797.

Meyer, H. H. (1991). A solution to the performance appraisal feedback enigma. *Academy of Management Executive,* 5, 68-76.

Mitchell, T. R., & Beach, L. R. (1990). "...Do I love thee? Let me count . . ." Toward an understanding of intuitive and automatic decision making. *Organizational Behavior and Human Decision Processes,* 47, 1-20.

Peterson, C. R., & Beach, L. R. (1967). Man as an intuitive statistician. *Psychological Bulletin,* 68, 29-46.

Schneier, C. E., & Beatty, R. W. (1977a). An empirical investigation of perceptions of ratee behavior frequency and ratee behavior change using behavioral expectations scales. *Personnel Psychology*, 30(4).

Schneier, C. E., & Beatty, R. W. (1977b). Predicting participants' performance and reactions in an experiential learning setting: An empirical investigation. *Proceedings of the Association for Business Simulation and Experimental Learning.*

Schneier, C. E., Shaw, D., & Beatty, R. W. (1991). Performance measurement and management: A new tool for strategy execution. *Human Resource Management,* 30, 279-301.

Towers Perrin. (1992). *What's new in employee pay.*

Ulrich, D. (1992). Strategic and human resource planning: Linking customers and employees. *Human Resource Planning,* 15(2), 47-62.

Ulrich, D., & Lake, D. (1990). *Organizational capability.* New York: Wiley.

Welch, J. (1992). General Electric Annual Report, 1991, as cited in *The Wall Street Journal.* February 14, 1992.

360° Feedback Can Change Your Life

by Brian O'Reilly

You've been X-rayed, CAT-scanned, poked, prodded, and palpated in all the most embarrassing places. Now a kindly professional you've never met is about to pull up a folder with your name on it and tell you what he or she found.

Only it's not your lower intestine that's about to be discussed but something even more personal: you. Your personality. The way you deal with people. Your talents, your values, your ethics, your leadership. And the folks who did the poking and temperature taking weren't anonymous technicians but a half dozen or more of your closest colleagues at work.

You, pal, are about to be stripped naked by an increasingly popular human resources device aimed at improving your on-the-job performance: feedback from co-workers—also known as 360-degree feedback and multi-rater assessment.

Here's how it works. Everyone from the office screwup to your boss, including your crackerjack assistant and your rival across the hall, will fill out lengthy, anonymous questionnaires about you. You'll complete one too. Are you crisp, clear, and articulate? Abrasive? Spreading yourself too thin? Trustworthy? Off-the-cuff remarks may be gathered too. A week or two later you'll get the results, all crunched and graphed by a computer. Ideally, all this will be explained by someone from your human resources department or the company that handled the questionnaires, a person who can break bad news gently. You get to see how your opinion of yourself differs from those of the group of subordinates who participated, your peer group, and the boss.

The results won't necessarily determine your pay, promotions, or termination. At least, not yet. The technique as it's now applied doesn't work well for that. When it is designed to provide information that you can use to become a better manager, scores from your handpicked pals or from randomly chosen associates typically turn out remarkably similar. But when used as the basis for formal performance evaluations, things change. Friends pump up your score, rivals become remarkably lukewarm, and that staff boob you keep reaming out cuts you dead. Mark Edwards, president of Teams Inc., a feedback company in Arizona, says he doesn't know of any major company that relies primarily on 360-degree feedback for evaluations. But his firm is working on ways to weed out slanted responses, and he says lots of clients are intrigued by the idea of using feedback for appraisals.

Even if it doesn't find its way into your personnel file, make-you-better feedback can still hurt. Though it often contains pleasant news, feedback can be surprising, powerful, and uncomfortable stuff, as conversations with a dozen feedback recipients—ranging from corporate CEOs and division managers to second-tier supervisors—reveal. What probably wounds deepest are bad reports about interpersonal skills. If your buddies think you're lousy at budgeting, no huge deal. But several feedback experts singled out "untrustworthy" as the most devastating single criticism for most people. "Bad listener" stings. Word that your judgment and thinking are subpar will rattle almost anyone too, says Susan Gebelein, a vice president at Personnel Decisions Inc., a big human resources consulting company in Minneapolis. "Those are core competencies," she says.

What's most interesting about feedback isn't the pain it causes, the mechanics of its operation, or its growing popularity. It is the huge variety of unpredictable comments—and potential learning—that it delivers. Most people are surprised by what they hear. Only a fraction of managers have a good grasp of their own abilities. Those with certain kinds of blind spots are routinely judged less effective by co-workers.

One boss thought he was a fabulous writer. His underlings suffered in silence as he routinely criticized their reports and corrected their grammar, but they never mentioned their discomfort to one another. At feedback time, they all mentioned that they thought he was a mediocre writer and wished he would quit bothering them. He was supremely embarrassed, apologized, and stopped.

The president of Raychem, a $1.5 billion electronics and electrical equipment company in California, says he didn't get any major surprises about himself but he was intrigued to learn that he wasn't fooling his subordinates either. They told Robert Saldich he wasn't good at contingency planning. His reaction: "Shucks. I haven't been hiding here."

One manager learned that he had two annoying traits, recalls consultant Edwards: He stood too close to people, and little bits of spit flew from his mouth when he spoke. A very bad combination. He began keeping his distance and got speech therapy, and his career prospects improved dramatically.

Joe Malik, manager of a team of engineers at AT&T, got nicked for his vigorous temper. That was not a big revelation—he was already working on correcting it. But he was startled to learn that when his direct reports asked him about the company's plans for the group, he often scrunched up in his chair. His subordinates thought he was being evasive. "I was just trying to come up with the answer," he says. "If I were being evasive, I would have said I couldn't answer."

Most revealing to Malik was that his subordinates expected things of him he'd never imagined. "I found out I need to articulate the vision and mission of our little unit. I was surprised. Not because I prided myself on my visioning, but because we're a heads-down organization working on networking products for the phone system. But people want to know where we're going and whether the managers' heads are screwed on right, and what I aspire the business to be."

There are plenty of all-too-common complaints and familiar patterns that surface in feedback too. Many companies are using feedback for cultural change, to accelerate the shift to teamwork and employee empowerment. Bosses who charged up the corporate ladder by controlling everything and barking like a drill sergeant often get an earful from eagerly critical underlings.

Kim Jeffery, the CEO of Nestle's Perrier operation in the U.S., didn't need feedback to know he was a demanding manager. It had been his style on purpose. "Our company style resembled the lion-tamer school of management," he says, referring to relations among top executives. "You keep them all on their own platforms and deal with them as individuals. Because if you don't, they'll kill each other and the lion tamer." The technique had worked for his predecessor, but after a year and a half on the job, Jeffery realized that he needed a new style. "The company was growing and maturing. And I wasn't getting the kind of input from managers I needed to make good decisions." He brought in Alex Platt, a Connecticut psychologist who works with business leaders, to handle feedback questionnaires and conduct interviews with senior executives.

Jeffery's subordinates revealed that his elevation to the presidency had made him a far more frightening figure to them than he'd been before. His temper and occasional "public whippings" of senior managers were tolerable when he was head of sales and marketing but terrifying when he had the ultimate authority to fire anybody.

He was amazed. He had grown up in modest circumstances and disdained the pomp and ceremony he associated with many top execs. "I thought I was seen as a regular guy," he says. "I didn't realize the impact of my words on people." Some managers told him that they were so intimidated, they weren't coming to him with problems and ideas. "I was mad at myself when I heard," Jeffery says. "I know the right way to do things." He says he's better now—fewer outbursts and more effort to get managers working together—but not perfect. "With one or two lapses, I'm told I've done very well."

Jerry Wallace, an up-and-coming manager at General Motors, was surprised by his feedback too. "There were a couple of 'wows,'" says Wallace, who recently became head of personnel at a Saturn assembly plant in Tennessee. He discovered he isn't nearly as flexible as he thought. His subordinates said they were frustrated because he sometimes made them follow prescribed processes without finding out whether there were better ways of doing things. "I was sure I was very flexible," he says.

But the message that hit Wallace hardest was a common one: excess control. "The strongest message I got was that I need to delegate more," he says. "I thought I'd been doing it. But I need to do it more and sooner. My people are saying, 'Turn me loose.'"

For some control freaks, it takes massive doses of feedback before the lights finally come on. The Center for Creative Leadership, a nonprofit research center in Greensboro, North Carolina, puts on week-long feedback programs. In addition to getting questionnaire results from co-workers back home, 20 participants eyeball one another during simulated exercises and deliver unvarnished opinions about what they see. Wallace, who participated last August, says another manager at CCL finally saw how domineering he was and painfully realized the consequences. "He said, 'No wonder nobody wants to be on a team with me, and why I have to do everything myself.'"

Okay, so you're into control, but everybody knows that you're only a curmudgeon on the outside, that you really have a warm, fuzzy spot in your heart for everyone. You might be that way, but don't be too sure everybody—or even anybody—knows.

Marc Breslawsky, head of the 8,000-employee office systems division at Pitney Bowes, didn't expect much from the feedback process, but he was curious about what employees thought of him. He found out that they viewed him as a man with little warmth who made cold, hard business decisions. "I assumed they knew I was pleased," he says. "I didn't pat people on the back. I didn't say thank-you. That wasn't my style. And if I had something difficult to discuss with someone, I didn't temper it by discussing their good parts. They felt I didn't care about them."

His behavior, unfortunately, was infectious. "A lot of people saw me like that, and they treated their people that way." Now he's virtually a poster boy for feedback. "I started telling people what they do

well and being more open in my discussions, and the results have been amazing." Teamwork is up, he says, and the time it takes to develop new products has been cut in half. Like many top bananas who experience big benefits from feedback, he wants his managers to go through the process too.

Similar news awaited Donald Boudreau, an executive vice president in charge of branch banking at Chase Manhattan Bank. Disciplined, demanding, smart, sometimes intimidating, not a back patter. Most surprising of all: "Almost universally, people said I didn't have a sense of humor." He disagrees, but understands why people might think that: "I have one, but apparently I hide it."

Any doubts about the accuracy of the feedback were dispelled when Boudreau asked his wife what she thought. Ouch. "She said they got it right." He approached subordinates and asked for help. They told him to back off a bit. "If I wanted people to discuss ideas with me without feeling they were getting a personal evaluation, I had to change." He doesn't crack bawdy limericks to warm things up at staff meetings now and doesn't sound as if he ever will. But when he criticizes a subordinate for poor performance, he tries to go back "and make sure the person doesn't see it as career terminating."

Both Breslawsky at Pitney Bowes and Boudreau at Chase got some special insight from peers. Boudreau learned that taking a strong position in a meeting with peers and a boss can get under the skin of the peers. They understood that such a stance can often be appropriate advocacy, he says, but that "sometimes it looks like you're running for office." Breslawsky's feedback was even more pointed. Says he: "They said sometimes I seem to be shooting at them."

How do managers rate themselves? Only about a third produce self-assessments that generally match what co-workers concluded. Another third—called "high self-raters—have an inflated view of their talents," says Ellen Van Velsor, a researcher at the Center for Creative Leadership. The remaining third rate themselves lower than co-workers do.

An oversize ego, it turns out, is murder in a manager. Almost invariably, the high self-raters are judged the least effective by co-workers, says Van Velsor. And yet, for reasons she can't entirely explain, high self-raters are more common high up in organizations than down low. "It could be that the higher they go, the less feedback they get, so their view of themselves gets distorted. Maybe they're being judged by a higher standard. And maybe they're just more self-confident than managers who don't reach senior positions."

Van Velsor says that on effectiveness, the self-doubters actually get better scores from co-workers than do the other two groups. She figures they probably work harder and rely more on others. But Paul Connolly, president of Performance Programs Inc., a feedback firm in Connecticut, thinks the strongest managers are the ones who size themselves up about right. Says he: "People with a good sense of their influence and effectiveness will use it to their advantage. The ones with the low self-image make people scurry around and waste a lot of effort."

Clearly, feedback is not a panacea. Whether it permanently improves the managerial and leadership ability of those who get it is hard to pin down. Even Walter Ulmer, retiring president of CCL, agrees that measuring its effectiveness is difficult. William J. Miller, a research supervisor at Du Pont, helped install a feedback process for 80 scientists and support people several years ago. "A high or low score didn't predict a scientist's ability to invent Teflon," says Miller. "But what feedback did was really improve the ability of people to work in teams. Their regard for others, and behaviors that were damaging and self-centered, are what changed." Says Gebelein at Personnel Decisions: "Feedback delivers its wallop and generates changes depending on what a person and the organization value. If they care about relationships with others, it will have an effect in that area. If they emphasize management planning, it will have an impact there."

A few conditions are crucial for feedback to make a difference. Obviously, the person has to want to change. When a feedback recipient yawns at people trying to help and asks for an audiotape to play in the car instead of a multistep improvement plan, "we know not a lot will happen," says one counselor. Jeannie Rice, manager of buildings and property information at Vanderbilt University, spent a week at CCL. She says a few fellow attendees seemed determined not to change. "Their attitude was, 'I'm a butthead and I'm proud.'"

To make the most of the process, experts say you should talk over the results with everyone who participated. At CCL, Rice learned that her thick Southern accent made her seem soft at first, but that colleagues called her "demanding, blunt, critical, and opinionated." When she returned to Vanderbilt, she sat down with staffers who had sent their anonymous comments to CCL. "A lot of them said, 'I didn't say that,'" she says with amusement. But it triggered a long discussion. "They said things like, 'Well, you used to be that way.'"

Ideally, your boss will have already had training from human resources personnel on how to respond when you come for help. But with or without the boss, pick a small number of shortcomings to fix and decide on a few concrete remedies. A lousy listener? Find out which staffers are considered good at listening, and make it a point to watch them at work. Call a few staff meetings where your primary objective is to keep your mouth shut as much as possible. Ask a colleague to keep an eye on you and signal when you start slipping up.

Exhausted just at the thought of all that self-improvement? Don't hold your breath waiting for feedback to go away. Its use is still expanding. Increasingly, chief executives are using the feedback process to promulgate their own special vision of the company to the troops. Says Peter Wentworth, director of management development at Warner-Lambert: "There's an old saying that you treasure what you measure." Therefore, when CEO Melvin Goodes articulated the corporation's values two years ago, "rather than press it into Lucite and stick it on the wall, we built a 360-feedback process around it." Now the drug company's employees grade one another on such traits as creativity, candor, and speed of action.

A similar program exists at AT&T's business products division. Any manager supervising three or more people has to go through an evaluation every year pegged to the company's values statement and must share the results with colleagues both up and down. Says Patricia Russo, head of AT&T's Global Business Communications Systems unit: "I think we're just beginning to see the power of this." So far, the feedback on feedback is positive.

Can Subordinate Appraisals Enhance Managerial Productivity?

by H. John Bernardin, Florida Atlantic University, and Richard W. Beatty, Rutgers University

Although the subject matter is elusive, and the objective is not always within reach, "improving managerial effectiveness" remains a pressing concern for the business community. The authors propose what might seem to some a radical approach to producing competent managers—giving subordinates a "voice" in formal performance evaluation of their bosses. Although management's initial reaction may be negative, the authors believe that properly implemented and monitored subordinate appraisals can be a meaningful source of feedback for all involved—supervisors, subordinates, and the organization at large.

Organizations spend millions of dollars on training programs and assessment procedures to improve management effectiveness. Yet, according to a recent survey on managerial assessment procedures, few companies use one of the most practical and efficient methods for diagnosing management problems and improving performance: subordinate appraisals.[1] Given that virtually every definition of management has to do with achieving results through *people,* subordinate appraisal gives employees an opportunity to provide a unique and critical perspective on a manager's performance. Although research is limited, that which does exist is quite positive. In fact, subordinate appraisal may

be one of the best-kept secrets only because organizations have not chosen to publicize it.

There are three compelling reasons to support the formal use of subordinate appraisals. First, subordinates are a valid source of information because they are often in a good position to observe and evaluate managerial performance on several dimensions, especially leadership. Second, because appraisals are often collected simultaneously from several subordinates, multiple assessments are potentially more accurate than the most commonly used supervisor-only rating. Third, a formal subordinate appraisal system is compatible with employee "commitment" and "involvement" models that are gaining greater support today.[2] When properly implemented, subordinate appraisals should enhance worker job satisfaction and morale.

It may be no coincidence that IBM, a company frequently cited for its commitment to and involvement with its employees, has been using such appraisals for over twenty-five years. Walton discusses the importance of providing employees a "means to be heard on such issues as production methods, problem solving, and human resource policies and practices."[3] The use of a subordinate appraisal would not only enhance perceptions of "employee voice" policies and labor-management relations, but would also provide insight into how managers are behaving in accordance with the new management philosophy of commitment and participation. According to Walton, "The commitment model requires first-line supervisors to facilitate rather than direct the workforce, to impart rather than merely practice their technical and administrative expertise, and to help workers develop the ability to manage themselves."[4] Viewed in this context, subordinate appraisals seem particularly useful in helping an organization through the transitional stages of adopting a commitment/participative style of management, because subordinates are in the best position to judge the extent to which such requirements are fulfilled.

Through our study of IBM, RCA, Syntex, Libbey-Owens-Ford, and a highway patrol, we show how these companies incorporated subordinate appraisals into their overall corporate performance appraisal systems to help improve managerial effectiveness, evaluate and promote personnel, change corporate culture, implement strategic planning, reduce costs of promotion decisions, and reassign workloads. For example, we describe how Syntex, a multibillion-dollar manufacturer of chemical compounds, uses these appraisals to develop its managers. Libbey-Owens-Ford, on the other hand, uses them as a way of changing managerial behavior in order to further corporate strategic plans.

While subordinate appraisals can create problems, we believe the problems can be resolved or avoided by carefully implementing appropriate monitoring procedures. These problems, in fact, may not be unique to subordinate appraisals, but may be common to performance appraisal systems in general. Through our case studies, we note the problem areas and offer solutions.

The Value of Subordinate Appraisals

Researchers have long recognized the value of subordinate evaluations. The most widely used and studied questionnaire on leadership style, the Leader Behavior Description Questionnaire, asks subordinates to describe their managers' behavior. Numerous studies have shown significant relationships between the questionnaire and traditional measures of managerial effectiveness (e.g., the bosses' ratings, group effectiveness) and productivity output measures (e.g., turnover, absenteeism, and grievance rates).[5] Also, Likert's "Profile of Organizational Characteristics," which was the empirical basis for his "System IV" model of managerial effectiveness, includes several key questions re-

garding subordinates' attitudes toward their managers. Research has demonstrated positive correlations between these responses and hard evidence of organizational effectiveness.[6]

In further support of the claim that subordinates are a legitimate source of information for measuring managerial performance is the frequent use of subordinate evaluation in management development programs. The Administrative Systems Center at Florida Atlantic University in Boca Raton, for example, requires that supervisors and managers submit subordinate appraisals prior to a manager's arrival at the center. These appraisals serve as a basis for training and development intervention. Managers are extremely interested in these appraisals and consider them one of the most valid sources of feedback.

In a study of managers at the U.S. Geological Survey, over 45 percent of the managers indicated that subordinate appraisals would be a "valid" or "highly valid" source of performance assessment. Likewise, over 80 percent of the subordinates felt their evaluations would be useful and legitimate.[7]

In considering the use of subordinate appraisals, it is important that specific purposes first be clarified. Some appraisal systems are designed to improve or develop individual managers, while others attempt to measure performance for specific personnel actions (e.g., promotions, merit-based pay). Our position is that subordinate appraisals can serve both purposes.

IBM

Perhaps the strongest support for subordinate appraisals comes from those companies that have been quietly using the method for years. In the early 1960s IBM incorporated such an appraisal system into its elaborate annual employee opinion survey, which is an integral part of the IBM management system. The survey questions are designed to provide "feedback to managers as a basis for improving working relationships with their subordinates." Employees are asked to indicate how well their bosses set performance plans, handle disciplinary problems, provide feedback on performance, anticipate and deal with workload issues, explain key business decisions, and emphasize quality. The surveys are distributed to all full-time employees and are completed voluntarily and anonymously by over 90 percent of them. The Personnel Research Department carefully studies all of the responses.

The most important areas of concern are average ratings, the variance in ratings across subordinates, the norms for similar managerial situations, and the relevant written responses. Based on the results, a specific action-plan is developed for each manager, and feedback is provided by trained personnel.

IBM has explicit and uniform guidelines for the administration and interpretation of the opinion surveys: Corporate personnel offices in Armonk, New York, provide detailed guidance on administration, feedback, data consolidation, and reporting procedures to all U.S. divisions and subsidiaries. Among the most important guidelines are the following.

- All members of departments should be surveyed to "enhance the manager/employee relationship through the feedback and action-planning process."

- Corporate personnel develops all core items of the survey, and the items that form the core questionnaire are to be asked in all of the surveys.

- Specific procedures for assuring the anonymity of respondents are enforced. For example, there has to be a minimum of eight people before response distributions are presented, and a minimum of five people for the presentation of mean responses for each item. Demographic data analysis is done only for large groups (e.g., job function, division, or facility). Employees are also advised not to answer any demographic items if they are concerned about identification. Finally, all written comments are edited for personal identifiers.

- Employees are given explicit directions for completing the survey on company time, while appropriate safeguards are enforced to preserve anonymity. In the case of group administration, a personnel professional must be present and the management of the unit being surveyed should not be present.

- Careful, unambiguous directions are provided on how to submit the completed answer sheets and on how the answer sheets are to be transcribed and inputed.

- First-line managers are required to present the complete survey results to all employees as soon as the surveys are scored.

It is not difficult to understand the importance IBM places on the subordinate appraisal system when one considers its long history of guaranteeing employee involvement and job satisfaction. Considerable research exists on the reluctance of employees to communicate their problems and concerns upward when there is no formal vehicle for doing so. The institutionalized survey-feedback system at IBM is the vehicle and ensures that employees' pressing concerns are heard by top management. Major personnel decisions within the company are linked to subordinate appraisals and action plans. Obviously IBM puts great stock in the information gained from this method. Interviews with IBM supervisors and managers indicate strong support for the survey method and subordinate appraisal as a performance-feedback tool.

RCA

RCA relies heavily on subordinate appraisals for making personnel decisions. The Talent Inventory (TI) program, which has been in operation at RCA for over twelve years, is used to evaluate over 7,500 managers in nine major RCA businesses. This multiple assessment approach calls for ratings by five to seven individuals within a manager's "work network," including the manager's supervisor. The manager also submits the names of all persons who are qualified raters, including subordinates. The actual raters are selected from this group based on the frequency and significance of contact between each potential rater and the manager. It is required that one or two of the raters be subordinates. Like the IBM system, raters are anonymous (preliminary survey data indicated that 88 percent said they would not be candid if their identity were known). The selected subordinates are asked to rate how well the manager performs several critical functions. For example, they rate to what extent the manager "solicits and utilizes input about personal and career goals," "looks for ways to improve existing systems," "establishes timetables and goals to measure success of a project," "delays taking action on urgent requests," and "overdelegates to the point of losing control." A composite assessment is derived from these ratings, and the variance in responses across raters is carefully analyzed.

In a 1973 survey evaluating the TI program, 94 percent of the managers indicated that they liked the system as a whole and that they preferred multiple feedback assessments to the traditional supervisor-only approach. A 1985 survey of the program continued to reflect this highly positive attitude. This is remarkable given that performance appraisals are factored into major decisions such as promotions and merit pay. In fact, the program is considered the main vehicle for managerial assessment and development at RCA, and subordinate appraisal is a critical component of this process.

RCA also uses subordinate evaluations for managerial training. A month and a half before managers are scheduled to attend the corporate-sponsored "coaching and counseling" training program, the subordinates of the participating managers fill out a lengthy questionnaire regarding their managers' performance. The completed evaluations are mailed directly to corporate headquarters and an in-depth assessment of each manager is prepared based on the aggregated subordinate appraisal. This feedback is then used to construct an individualized coaching and counseling training program for each RCA manager.

Syntex

There are cultural behaviors that are the accepted norms of an organization. For example, in some organizations, unsparing honesty, the use of first names, an open-door policy of walking into someone's office without knocking may be considered healthy, important, and fully acceptable. In others, even within the same industry or within other units of the same company, such behavior might be inappropriate and viewed as aggressive, damaging, nosy, and overindulgent. What we see at work is the culture; that is, "How we do things around here." Astute managers are those who diagnose a culture early and operate within its context: they move effectively from one cultural behavior to another and not only manifest the appropriate behaviors, but also coach other managers on the behaviors appropriate in each context. On the other hand, some managers, especially new ones, may be unable to diagnose and adopt the set of cultural behaviors or

performance norms required to be effective within the organization.

In response to Syntex's rapid change in holdings—which created a complex organization with multiple demands and diverse management practices that produced behavioral inconsistencies in meeting corporate goals—the company established and presented to its managers worldwide a set of principles and practices that would help them fulfill their responsibilities and create the "desired" new culture. Syntex assumed that the existing culture was determined by the managers' behaviors and the consequences of their actions. In order to change its culture, Syntex's top management decided to initiate changes in managerial behavior by including in its management development efforts a purposeful statement of *how* the organization should manage its business.

The then-chairman George Rosenkranz and president Albert Bowers determined that it was not sufficient to simply use classroom theory and techniques to develop effective managers, and, therefore, proposed that, on a more fundamental level, each manager be given an explanation from a corporate executive about what it means *behaviorally* to be a Syntex manager. The resulting fifty-four principles and practices were set forth in a document called *Managing at Syntex* (MAS) and fell under the headings of corporate objectives, planning and budgeting, leadership, interactions with upper management, interactions with colleagues, interactions outside Syntex, and career management. For example, under "planning and budgeting," one principle is to "convert plans into specific, time-bound goals." Another is to "involve your people in developing plans prior to finalizing goals." Drs. Rosenkranz and Bowers themselves stated in the preface that they were "committed to implementing the MAS practices and to determine on a personal and group basis where improvement is needed. We certainly have room to improve and it is our hope that each manager will join us in a renewed effort to raise our personal level of management performance through better implementation of principles and practices of management at Syntex."

Managing at Syntex was implemented through a training and self-auditing process, starting with the top-management group and continuing through the organization worldwide. Training, auditing, and action planning took place in a two-day workshop in which all managers participated with their management team.

Today, as people are promoted into management or hired from the outside, they are immediately introduced to MAS principles in a one-day workshop: this is critical to making the system a way of life. The first follow-up activity to the original two-day MAS program is the individual Management Practices Analysis, which is designed to help a manager assess his or her managerial actions in relation to MAS principles. The process involves feedback from boss, peers, and *subordinates* on how well the manager's actions measure up to these principles. Based on this analysis, a specific individual development plan is drawn up to help the manager enhance his or her managerial effectiveness.

Financial rewards are also commensurate with how well managers carry out MAS principles in their daily work. At one time, Syntex had a management incentive compensation program that gave bonuses to employees based on their achieving traditional organizational goals. The plan has since been modified to assess and reward employees not only on how well they perform against specific budget, program, or project goals, but also on how well they conform to MAS behavioral principles. Managers earn *no* bonus if performance relative to MAS principles is not achieved. Likewise, an individual can live up to MAS principles, not accomplish certain goals, and still receive a bonus, albeit reduced. Underlying these rewards is a positive financial incentive based on both *what* managers accomplish and *how* they accomplish it.

Even though Syntex established a management performance system that consciously reinforces its culture, it is not without problems and disappointments. Few managers live up to all of the established principles and practices all of the time. Managers whose MAS performance is unsatisfactory are usually obvious to employees who work with them, and their failure to measure up raises questions to upper-management's commitment to the principles. Thus top management must frequently express support for the program: Higher-level managers whose "numbers were satisfactory" but whose management practices were not, have after appropriate counseling, been terminated based on

subordinate appraisals. People at Syntex are reminded that these principles and practices represent a set of ideals to which managers should strive: Employees are urged to demonstrate patience in the learning and behavioral change process.

Libbey-Owens-Ford

In the fall of 1984, Libbey-Owens-Ford (LOF) began a "performance planning and appraisal" program to train its managers to implement the corporate strategic plan by linking strategic planning to management performance planning. The Management Education Department, also known as the management development department, was made responsible for the training process. Historically, most company managers focused on performance appraisals only during the formal performance review process, without giving further thought to managing performance throughout the rest of the year. In other words, managers had not been trained to consciously and strategically manage their human resources to achieve corporate goals. With the introduction of this program, however, the management development group's responsibility (i.e., their strategic objective) was to develop skill-ready managers who could accomplish corporate strategic plans through effective management. This was a significant responsibility because most personnel development functions are not perceived as central to the organization's strategic planning efforts, let alone given a unique opportunity to affect the organization's strategic planning process and, ultimately, corporate productivity.

The program was initiated by requesting that managers receive feedback from subordinates concerning their performance management skills. Subordinate feedback was based on the following criteria: achieving strategic-performance planning linkages, gaining employee commitment, setting work unit goals, negotiating individual performance goals and standards, observing employee performance, documenting employee performance, giving feedback and coaching employees, conducting formal performance reviews, and rewarding performance with pay.

The managers were then sent to a two-day training workshop where they were required to develop measurable work outcomes and work standards for themselves and their subordinates, and to tie the standards in with the strategic plan of each operating unit. During the workshop, managers were asked to present their performance plans and subject themselves to criticism from peers, supervisors, and subordinates. They were also required to develop skills that would help them measure employee performance, such as accurately observing and documenting what constitutes good performance behavior. Finally, they were asked to participate in performance-review role plays to evaluate subordinate progress in achieving specific corporate goals.

One of the most powerful measures of the strategic management efforts at Libbey-Owens-Ford is subordinate assessment of the manager's improvement in the trained skills. In other words, managers are expected to change their supervisory behavior; in turn, subordinates are expected to evaluate their managers' behavioral changes. This "check-balance" system helps managers improve because the subordinate feedback survey clarifies managerial performance expectations. Here, the potentially most powerful measure of management effectiveness is the actual year-to-year improvement of each unit in accomplishing its strategic goals.

State Patrol

In 1979 the state patrol faced the imminent retirement of many high-level officers. The new chief was going to make eleven promotions to major, thirty-one to captain, and forty-six to lieutenant within the next two years, all created by retirements and forecasted attrition.

Historically, the organization used assessment centers to select its managers. Typically assessment centers are a one-to-three-day evaluation of personnel who are asked to perform a number of work simulations. A team of trained assessors observes the participants and makes evaluations on skill categories that are related to the position under study (e.g., decision making, adaptability, leadership, communicative skills). While most assessment centers are used to assist organizations in making selection and promotion decisions, others are designed to train and develop personnel. The chief was supportive of the centers since he himself had been selected through this process and had skipped the rank of major in his promotion to chief. Still, he was concerned about the time and cost of assess-

ment centers. Furthermore, he had always wondered about the relationship between assessment centers and specific performance evaluations found in the management-by-objective (MBO) type of performance appraisal system, which the patrol had used for several years. He like the MBO system because he felt it gave him enough flexibility to accomplish the strategic change requested by the governor. Intrigued by the idea that subordinates might have as good a perspective (if not better) as assessment centers regarding managerial performance, the chief wanted to explore the use of subordinate appraisals vis-à-vis assessment centers.

The patrol's new personnel manager was summoned by the chief and asked to design a "bottom-up" performance appraisal system to assess each manager as part of a broader survey of organizational performance. He was also asked to determine and compare the costs and accuracy of predicting officer performance using assessment center data, subordinate assessments, and historic performance appraisals. The chief was adamant that the dimensions assessed by subordinate appraisals be the same as those used by the assessment center to predict managerial success. The results indicated that subordinates proved to be better predictors of subsequent supervisory performance than the assessment center at approximately one-twentieth the cost.[8] In fact, for the critical dimensions of interpersonal skills and leadership, potential subordinate ratings outpredicted the assessment center substantially.

How Accurate Are Subordinate Appraisals?

When subordinate appraisals are viewed as a source of information for personnel decision making, such as promotions, key questions arise. For example, to what extent are subordinate appraisals considered to be more valid than other assessment procedures, and how do subordinate appraisals add validity to the more common methods? Also, are subordinate appraisals superior to assessment centers in predicting subsequent performance? Do they add unique and valuable information? Unfortunately, only the one public-sector study cited directly addressed this key question. This study found higher validities for subordinate appraisals than for the highly touted assessment center approach in predicting managerial performance. Moreover, the combined use of subordinate appraisals with assessment center data was found to be superior to either approach used independently. Although further study on relative validity is certainly needed, these results support the theory that subordinate appraisals serve a useful purpose in personnel decision making. It should be noted that one of the major reasons why assessment centers have proven to be effective across a variety of settings is because they use trained multiple assessors to measure managerial performance.[9] Thus training subordinates to observe managerial performance fulfills this critical component of the performance assessment procedures.

Studies have found significant but moderate relationships between subordinate and supervisory ratings, with higher correlations on some managerial dimensions than on others.[10] These findings reflect a position that subordinates not only share a common perspective with superiors on some managerial dimensions, but also offer a unique and important perspective on other aspects of the manager's performance. Another study found few significant correlations between subordinate appraisals and managers' self-ratings.[11] Managers who perceived themselves to be effective at "providing clear instruction and explanation to employees when giving assignment" were not perceived as such by those persons supposedly on the receiving end of the instructions!

If nothing else, these findings illustrate the value of subordinate ratings for feedback purposes. While most findings support some convergence between subordinates and superiors in the ratings of managers, the moderate levels of correlation illustrate that subordinates have a valuable and unique perspective on several dimensions that they should be in a good position to observe.

Another line of support for the use of subordinate appraisals comes from a recent survey of managerial appraisal practices. Although fewer than 8 percent of all organizations surveyed use subordinate appraisals, those that do rated their appraisal systems as being more effective than those organizations that do not use them.[12]

What Areas Should Subordinates Appraise?

A survey of managers at a major international company not only supports the use of subordinate appraisals but also offers guidelines on which managerial dimensions subordinates are actually qualified to rate. Forty-five upper-level managers were first asked to study the definitions of ten managerial performance dimensions based on the work of Henry Mintzberg.[13] After some discussion and clarification of the definitions, each manager was then asked to indicate the extent to which each of the role descriptions for the managerial job *below* them best describes effective managerial performance. Table 1 presents a summary of the ratings from this question. Five of the ten role descriptions had average ratings at 4.00 or higher, indicating that managers believed the descriptions were predictive of success "to a fairly large extent" or higher. This result, of course, comes as no surprise. What was surprising, however, were the responses to the questions about the best sources of information about the role descriptions. The same managers were asked to indicate the extent to which they themselves, or subordinates, were qualified to evaluate the manager's performance. Table 2 presents a summary of the ratings to those questions. For two of the descriptions (leader role and information disseminator), superiors regarded subordinates as more qualified than themselves to evaluate the manager. For six of the ten descriptions, managers regarded subordinates as qualified to rate performance *at least* to a moderate extent.

This result is quite remarkable given that none of these managers had ever been involved in a formal subordinate appraisal system. While the managers certainly "did not give away the store" regarding their own role in evaluating their subordinate managers, it was clear that subordinate input was considered valuable for certain managerial roles. The data in Table 2 clearly indicates that in terms of predicting managerial success, subordinate ratings were regarded as potentially valid predictors. This result supports what experts on performance appraisal have been saying for a long time. The most valid appraisal systems are those in which more

Table 1. To What Extent Do You Feel Each of the Role Descriptions for the Managerial Level Below You Is Predictive of Managerial Success at Your Present Level?

0 — Not at All
1 — To a Very Limited Extent
2 — To a Limited Extent
3 — To a Moderate Extent
4 — To a Fairly Large Extent
5 — To a Great Extent

Role Description	Mean Rating
1. Organizational Representative	2.9
2. Leader	4.0
3. Liaison	3.5
4. Environment Monitor	4.1
5. Information Disseminator	3.3
6. Spokesperson	3.0
7. Entrepreneur	4.2
8. Crisis Handler	4.0
9. Resource Allocator	4.2
10. Negotiator	3.8

than one rater is used. In addition, the case law regarding performance appraisals and personnel decisions strongly supports the use of more than one rater whenever performance judgments are made to promote, demote, discharge, or determine merit pay.[14]

The Obvious Question

Given the positive tone of this article up to this point, perhaps an obvious question might be, "Then why haven't more organizations tried subordinate appraisals?" There are three major reasons. First, top-down performance appraisal, by far the most common approach, is more compatible with the most dominant U.S. management styles and the strict separation of managerial and nonmanagerial functions. Second, there has been very little writing on the subject by either academics or practitioners in support of subordinate appraisals. Third, the initial reaction to the idea spawns a plethora of concerns. For example, when the forty-five managers surveyed were asked to consider subordinate appraisals in their organizations, they generated a list of major concerns. The most important were: managers will focus on just trying to please subordinates; the authority of the manager will be challenged; subordinates lack the ability to rate managerial performance; managers will not stand for subordinate appraisals and quit their jobs; the hardest working, more productive workers will rate their managers the lowest because they are "pushed"; and subordinates will be paranoid about telling the truth. While these are legitimate concerns, there is no empirical evidence to indicate that such problems are inevitable; in fact, some evidence indicates that these problems can be avoided with proper administration.

In light of the well-documented problems with traditional appraisal systems, many managers regard subordinate appraisals with equal suspicion. For example, subordinates of an automotive company division, who operated under a fairly autocratic style of management, expressed a near unanimous suspicion that the "truth" about certain managers would come back to haunt them in the end. As a result, several subordinates admitted to falsifying their responses and portraying their managers in a more positive light. Obviously, the lack of trust can completely invalidate the subordinate appraisal process and vitiate the actions to be taken based on the ratings.

For now it seems that subordinate appraisals are more easily implemented, administered, and maintained where participative styles of management are firmly ingrained. High levels of trust across organizational levels—a characteristic of participative models and "commitment" strategies—not only enhance the process of developing and institutionalizing the approach, but also increase the probabilities of receiving more valid data.

Prescriptions to Follow

Despite the low acceptance of appraisal systems, a number of prescriptions have evolved to increase the probability of their acceptance and effectiveness. The excellent track records of IBM, RCA, and Syntex attest to the prescriptions' usefulness in enhancing managerial performance.

Table 2. To What Extent Are You/Your Subordinates Qualified to Evaluate Managerial Performance in Each of the Following Areas?

0 — Not at All
1 — To a Very Limited Extent
2 — To a Limited Extent
3 — To a Moderate Extent
4 — To a Fairly Large Extent
5 — To a Great Extent

	Mean Rating	
Role Description	Managers	Subordinates
1. Organizational Representative	4.1	1.5
2. Leader	2.9	4.2
3. Liaison	3.9	3.0
4. Environment Monitor	3.9	3.2
5. Information Disseminator	2.8	3.8
6. Spokesperson	4.8	2.5
7. Entrepreneur	3.3	2.9
8. Crisis Handler	3.8	3.6
9. Resource Allocator	3.5	3.2
10. Negotiator	4.2	1.8

- The *objectives* of the program should be carefully and meticulously developed. Questions to be asked should include: "Why do we want to use subordinate appraisals?"; "What will we do with the results?"; and "Who will have access to the information?"

- The personnel/human resource department should have tight *administrative control* of the program, because of the potential for problems with this approach. A detailed plan for distribution and data collection should be developed and field testing should be conducted. All employees affected by the system should receive clear directions as to the purpose of the procedure. Several weeks prior to the evaluation, a memorandum explaining the controlled data-collection procedures should be circulated. Also, a "hotline" should be set up to clarify any troubling procedural matters during the period of actual administration. The personnel department should receive all completed ratings directly from the rater rather than from the manager. If the organization already has a formal appraisal survey method in place, the subordinate appraisal items could be incorporated into the survey, provided that other conditions for data collection are met. A cover letter of endorsement from a high-ranking official (outside of personnel) should accompany the material. Employees should be granted company time to complete the survey forms. Rater training programs may be used to inhibit some of the most common rating errors.

- Complete employee *anonymity and confidentiality* should be ensured. A minimum of five subordinates should participate in order to foster confidence in the anonymity of the system. The ratings should be averaged and variances studied carefully. It is critical that subordinates feel that their anonymity is preserved. All handwritten comments should be destroyed after they have been transcribed. Since it will take several iterations of the method before confidentiality reaches a high level, questions having to do with subordinate identification (e.g., demographics, location) should be avoided initially. IBM spent ten years experimenting with its opinion surveys before it fully institutionalized them.

- When personnel decision making is the major purpose, subordinate appraisals should be incorporated into a *multiple-rater* system. While subordinates are in a good position and are qualified to evaluate several managerial dimensions, they may be unqualified to judge managerial performance (e.g., budgeting), especially if they are not managers themselves. An abbreviated form of job analysis could be used to identify the dimensions to be rated by subordinates. One method identifies those critical dimensions for which it is possible for the subordinate to observe or gain direct knowledge of the outcome of carrying out a particular task or behavior. The Appendix presents a sample survey format identifying those items in a subordinate-appraisal system that provide useful feedback for supervisors and managers. This type of job analysis may determine that only superiors should rate certain dimensions (e.g., planning and budgeting), while superiors and subordinates should rate others (e.g., interpersonal skills and leadership). Managers making personnel decisions (e.g., promotions) would then have a larger and more comprehensive package of evaluative materials.

- Make the items to be rated as *specific* as possible. Every effort should be made to avoid rating psychological traits such as judgment, attitude, dependability, and initiative. Behavioral items such as those presented in the Appendix or described in RCA's *Talent Inventory* or Syntex's *Managing at Syntex* are preferable from both a legal and psychometric perspective. In addition, if the data is to provide useful managerial feedback, ratings on items such as "provides clear performance standards" and "sets realistic timetables for the completion of work" are far more meaningful to a manager than a "3" on a 7-point scale on "initiative."

The latter type of "feedback" has never been shown to improve performance.

- The complete system should be *field tested* on a sample workforce to ensure that all evaluation components are in good working order. Statistical analysis of the item ratings should be performed in order to identify, amend, and eliminate problematic items. Interviews with subordinates and managers regarding the procedures would also provide useful information.

- The data should be *interpreted cautiously* at first. It would be helpful to initially collect data strictly for purposes of constructing norms for the most common managerial situations. While interpretation of the results is possible without establishing norms, interpreting a manager's ratings in the context of another manager's ratings in a similar situation is a far more prudent approach, particularly if such data will be used for personnel decisions. The personnel department should analyze subordinate ratings as a function of factors that are beyond the control of the manager. For example, a cut in a supervisor's budget may affect a subordinate's appraisal of that supervisor, despite the fact that the budgetary cuts were beyond the supervisor's control. To the extent that personnel can identify such external factors, more valid measurement and interpretation can be realized: A computerized appraisal system now available provides a method of statistically correcting ratings for extraneous factors, which are beyond the control of the person who is being rated.[15] If the data is to be used strictly for feedback, rigorous norm development and the search for correlates are not nearly as critical.

- Subordinate appraisal data should be interpreted only in conjunction *with other information* (e.g., outcome/results data, other rating sources). Just as organizations should never place 100 percent weight on assessment center data, subordinate appraisals should be properly weighted and interpreted vis-à-vis all sources of valid information. While the mean of subordinate data based on five or more independent raters is probably a valid assessment of managerial performance—regardless of the detail in administrative procedure—there are occasions when such data is more a function of some type of rating bias. Great discrepancies between subordinate appraisals and other managerial-performance data would be "red flagged" for such occasions.

- *Fast turnaround* is important for the system to work, particularly if feedback is the primary or only purpose of subordinate appraisals. Such feedback should get to the managers quickly (within four weeks). Thus, personnel may need extra staffing for this critical period of time. Sophisticated data processing (e.g., direct entry, optical-scanning sheets) is critical for large-scale operations. Managers above those being appraised should serve as the major vehicle for feedback and action planning in order to correct acknowledged problems. Sessions involving the superior manager and the subordinates are very helpful in clarifying the results of the appraisals. Training materials as well as training programs, perhaps via videotape, should be available for providing feedback and conducting such meetings. The personnel department should be responsible for the training.

- The personnel department should *monitor the system* carefully if the data is to be used for personnel decisions. Like any performance appraisal method used to make personnel decisions, data should be analyzed for adverse impact against groups covered under Title VII of the 1964 Civil Rights Act and the Age Discrimination in Employment Act. Significantly lower ratings for female or minority managers should also be examined to ensure that proper procedures were followed.

Conclusion

Management's initial reaction to formal subordinate appraisals is often unfavorable, particularly in organizations where autocratic management styles are dominant. Many of the problems discussed are thought insurmountable or at least a rationale for not considering the idea. Yet, organizations like IBM, Syntex, and RCA put great faith in the method and have been using it for some time. The

limited research available on the technique is also supportive. There is a growing interest in the subject as well. The Federal Aviation Administration, for example, is installing an agencywide subordinate appraisal system for all supervisors and managers. Several other organizations are presently experimenting with the approach as well.

It is time to take a more critical look at subordinate appraisals and to consider their advantages relative to the more popular and less controversial approaches to managerial assessment. When properly implemented, subordinate appraisals can be a valuable source of information. The data can provide an excellent "warning" signaling potential problems, such as the turnover of key personnel, intergroup conflicts, and downturns in productivity. In addition, the approach may yield data for important personnel decisions, such as merit pay, promotions, and transfers.[16]

At the very least, the approach provides feedback to managers that they would not ordinarily receive.[17] A 1984 study documented the isolation and insulation of upper-level management. It was found that upper-level management received little valid performance criticism and that subordinates felt uneasy about "telling it like it is."[18] The researchers concluded that isolation "impedes criticism that an executive could use in an effort to develop and perform his role even more effectively." A formal subordinate appraisal can increase the probability that management will learn "what's really on the minds of the employees." One researcher referred to the "delusionary system" under which managers and subordinates usually communicate. Such systems are not likely to foster growth in the relationship or to improve organizational effectiveness. Subordinate appraisals offer an opportunity to gather valid information while fostering communication across organizational lines.

Appendix: Sample Survey

- Sample question: *To what extent can subordinates provide useful feedback on various managerial or supervisory positions for purposes of improving managerial performance?* In your rating on each item, consider the following factors: the clarity/ambiguity of the item; whether subordinates are in a position to observe the behavior described; whether subordinates are qualified to make a valid rating; and whether the item is specific enough to guide the supervisor. Use the following scale to make one rating for each item:

0   not at all
1   to a little extent
2   to some extent
3   to a moderate extent
4   to a great extent

Sample items to be rated:

- Develops and/or reviews annually job elements (critical and other) and performance standards.
- Discusses job elements and standards with employees during the rating period.
- Objectively evaluates employees' performances against existing standards during at least one periodic progress review.
- Objectively evaluates employees' performances for a final review within the rating period.
- Takes action to recognize positive performance.
- Takes action to correct performance deficiencies and to deal with conduct and discipline situations.
- Manages resources and workload, schedules, and position to balance utilization of employee skills and potential with operational requirements.
- Determines training needs and, with employee, develops a formal or informal plan to meet job performance requirements.
- Counsels employee on attainment of job performance objectives.
- Counsels employee on full utilization of potential in present position, and if employee desires, on feasible career goals.
- Informs employees of organizational plans and programs that impact their work lives.
- Seeks input from employees on organizational plans and programs.

- Raises employee concerns to higher management.
- Promotes employee participation and provides resources to the participative process.
- Delegates decision-making authority and considers employees in the decision-making process.
- Implements appropriate employee recommendations.
- Prevents, resolves, or elevates disputes and grievances in a timely manner.
- Exhibits a working knowledge of the negotiated agreement. Applies provisions of a negotiated agreement correctly and uniformly.
- Maintains a positive and collaborative approach to labor-management relationships.
- Communicates and reinforces EEO policy and programs.
- Gives equal consideration to women and other minority groups when taking the following actions that are within the supervisor's authority: recruitment, selection, training, recognition, promotions, and assignment of work.
- Fosters a nondiscriminatory environment where employees are accepted regardless of race, color, sex, age, religion, handicap, and national origin. In other words, takes action against reported or detected instances of offensive or hostile jokes, language, slogans, or posted material, unwanted physical contact, or suggestive remarks.
- Attempts to resolve discrimination complaints at the lowest level.
- When warranted, recommends disciplinary action for persons responsible for discriminatory acts.

A rating format such as the following could be used:

a.   clearly outstanding
b.   appreciably better than satisfactory
c.   consistently satisfactory
d.   some improvement needed
e.   considerable improvement needed

References

[1] H.J. Bernardin and L.A. Klatt, "Managerial Appraisal Systems: Has Practice 'Caught-Up' with the State of the Art?" *Personnel Administrator* 30 (1985): 79-86.

[2] V. Nieva, D. Perkinds, and E.E. Lawler, "Improving the Quality of Life at Work: Assessment of a Collaborative Selection Process," *Journal of Occupational Behavior I* (1979): 1-10; R.E. Walton, "From Control to Commitment in the Workplace," *Harvard Business Review,* March-April 1985, pp. 77-84.

[3] Ibid.

[4] Ibid.

[5] S. Kerr and C. Schreisheim, "Consideration, Initiating Structure, and Organizational Criteria: An Update of Korman's 1966 Review," *Personnel Psychology* 27 (1974): 555-568.

[6] J.P. Campbell et al., "The Measurement of Organizational Effectiveness: A Review of Relevant Research and Opinion" (San Diego: Contract #0022-72-C-0023, NPRDC, 1974).

[7] H.J. Bernardin, "A Performance Appraisal System," in *Performance Assessment,* ed. R. Berk (Baltimore: Johns Hopkins University Press, 1987), pp. 277-304.

[8] G. McEvoy, R.W. Beatty, and H.J. Bernardin, "Unanswered Questions About Assessment Centers," *Journal of Business and Psychology,* in press.

[9] H.J. Bernardin and D. Bownas, *Personality Assessment in Organizations* (New York: Praeger, 1985).

[10] M.K. Mount, "Psychometric Properties of Subordinate Ratings of Managerial Performance," *Personnel Psychology* (Winter 1984): 687-701.

[12] Bernardin and Klatt (1985).

[13] H. Mintzberg, *The Nature of Managerial Work* (New York: Harper & Row, 1973).

[14] H.J. Bernardin and W.F. Cascio, "Performance Appraisal and the Law," in *Readings in Personnel/Human Relations,* ed. R. Schuler (St. Paul, MN: West Publishing, 1987).

[15] J.S. Kane, "Performance Distribution Assessment," in *Performance Assessment,* ed. R. Berk (Baltimore: John Hopkins University Press, 1987), pp. 237-274.

[16] H.J. Bernardin and R.W. Beatty, *Performance Appraisal: Assessing Human Behavior at Work* (Boston: Kent-Wadsworth, 1984).

[17] M.F.R. Kets de Vries, "Managers Can Drive Their Subordinates Mad," *Harvard Business Review,* 57 (4): 125-134.

[18] R.E. Kaplan, W.H. Drath, and J.R. Kofodimas, "Power and Getting Criticism," *Issues and Observations* 4: 1-8.

H. John Bernardin is Professor of Management and Director of Research at the College of Business and Public Administration, Florida Atlantic University. Dr. Bernardin has written extensively on the subject of performance appraisals and is the coauthor of Performance Appraisal: Assessing Human Behavior at Work.

Richard W. Beatty is Professor of Industrial Relations and Human Resources at the Institute of Management and Labor Relations, Rutgers University. He is the coauthor of the award-winning book, Personnel Administration: An Experiential/Skill Building Approach. *He has authored numerous articles in the human resource management area.*

Turning the Tables: Underlings Evaluate Bosses

by Joann S. Lublin

Robert E. Allen, AT&T Corp.'s chairman and chief executive, recently changed his ways. The reason: His lieutenants didn't like the passive way he ran the management executive committee.

Mr. Allen says he now spends more time drafting the committee's agenda, airs his opinions freely during its meetings and pushes the group harder to make clear-cut decisions. Still, getting written feedback from his senior executives made him uncomfortable initially. "Nobody likes to be told that they are not performing at the maximum level," he concedes.

From chief executives to first-line supervisors, bosses across the nation increasingly find themselves judged by those they lead. In 1992, subordinates critiqued their superiors at 12% of 897 U.S. companies surveyed by consultants Wyatt Co. The figure "is a lot higher than that now" and may reach 30% in five years, says David Campbell, a senior fellow at the nonprofit Center for Creative Leadership in Greensboro, N.C.

To keep a competitive edge, "we should do a better job of making sure our supervisors are leading properly," says Paul Green, a performance-improvement manager at Dow Chemical Co.'s chemicals and plastics group. "Some individuals will find they don't have that ability," he adds. The chemical group's 235 top executives recently solicited feedback from their subordinates and others within the group.

Upward appraisals are often part of a broader "360-degree feedback" process. Executives discover how well they are doing from detailed questionnaires that are also completed by colleagues, customers, higher-ups and themselves. The feedback—generally anonymous—includes such topics as the manager's ability to take charge, coach workers, delegate responsibility, manage conflict and communicate clearly. The costly process typically serves as a personal-development tool rather than a factor in pay decisions.

So far, there is little evidence that such efforts make people manage any better. And the use of subordinate feedback can be even trickier than gathering feedback from peers.

But proponents contend that subordinates can provide valuable insights into a superior's talents and shortcomings. AT&T's Mr. Allen shares that view. He sought an upward appraisal in early 1993, soon after the telecommunication giant drafted "Our Common Bond," a new set of corporate values. The questionnaire "dealt with how my leadership style was or wasn't connected to our values," he says. "I rated myself slightly lower" in certain categories than executive committee members did, he recollects.

The dozen executives agreed or disagreed with about 30 statements concerning Mr. Allen's leadership. An example: "My manager does not 'shoot the messenger.'" Another: "My manager encourages people to learn from one another." An internal consultant helped Mr. Allen interpret the results and run an executive committee session at which he requested more specific improvement ideas.

Mr. Allen sought the feedback again earlier this year. This time, he says, his lieutenants told him he was managing the agenda better, though "they wanted still more of my active participation in the discussion." Over the past year, nearly 68,000 AT&T managers have received upward appraisals, alone or as part of a 360-degree feedback, a spokesman says.

Mr. Allen says he will keep using upward appraisals until he concludes they're a waste of time. He now knows the kind of leadership his subordinates seek, he says, "but I am not doing it as well as they want me to do it yet."

On the other hand, many bosses cringe at the idea of being judged by underlings. Some fear workers will use the process to settle a score or make personal attacks.

When a senior Citicorp executive sought confidential, written feedback from his 60 employees a few years ago, he quickly guessed that a completely negative essay came from one particular poor performer. "There were smears about me personally," the executive recalls.

The bank executive soon stopped doing upward appraisals, viewing them as useless popularity contests. "The people who work for you are not qualified to comment on your ability to lead or not to lead," he says. In December, the executive lost his job after a power struggle with his own boss. "We do not have upward appraisals as part of our ap-praisal process at this point," a Citicorp spokesman says.

While most companies say they won't use subordinate reviews to penalize a manager in terms of pay and promotion, managers don't always believe that. As a result, some executives "coach" their lower-level employees on how to complete the feedback forms—or even buy them lunch that day.

The accounting vice president of a midsize utility became dismayed after a subordinate-feedback survey suggested that he wasn't doing enough to develop his workers. But the rankings improved markedly in a second survey eight months later. The vice president had "made it clear that if the profile didn't improve this time, he was going to change some staff members," remembers Dr. Campbell, then a consultant for the utility.

Threats of retribution sometimes backfire. An unhappy supervisor at a Phoenix engine unit of conglomerate AlliedSignal Inc. complained to his subordinates after they rated him poorly on his interpersonal skills. (At the time, the unit directly linked 360-degree feedback to managers' pay—a practice that it has since abandoned.) Subordinates tattled about the supervisor's complaints, and he "got a lower merit raise" than most colleagues, says Craig Chapman, an AlliedSignal human-resources director. The man was later demoted from his supervisory position and subsequently left the company.

How To Do Peer Review

by Gloria E. Bader and Audrey E. Bloom

More than 40 years ago in the coal mines of South Yorkshire, England, the concept of the peer review process was born. These productive and safe mines exemplified a balance of social, technical, and economic working conditions. According to Eric Trist and Fred Emery of Tavistock Institute, the miners were the high-performing teams of the day.

Because the miners were dedicated to a common task, the work group became the focus of change. Internal regulations were essential to the miners. They monitored and helped each person achieve group goals. They increased their skills and learned the social and economic aspects of their work.

The work groups inspired the concept of sociotechnical systems that provides the basis for understanding peer review today. Contemporary performance management systems emphasize the following:

- ongoing communication (particularly of performance expectations)
- timely, constructive feedback
- pay for performance
- a "no surprises" approach to performance reviews

Many systems also encourage self-appraisal and personal goal setting.

Today's flat organizations demand those characteristics and ongoing refinements in their performance management systems. Whether performance improvement is spurred by total quality management goals, by new organizational structures, or by a renewed focus on customer service, peer review is a natural strategy to employ.

Consider the experiences of one senior executive. When faced with the unworkable prospect of requiring each of his managers to prepare and conduct 125 to 150 performance evaluations, the executive searched for time-saving options.

The executive chose to turn over the design of a new process for performance data collection and analysis to several high-level staff members, except in cases in which the performance was marginal or corrective action was required.

The executive's management team formalized a fledgling peer review effort in three phases:

- implementing consistent procedures across the department's five work units
- training for the appraisers and appraisees
- conducting and evaluating pilot projects throughout the process

Peer review is the evaluation of work performance by peers or colleagues of equal rank against established performance criteria or competencies. More broadly, as part of a larger accountability and reward system, peer review is an untapped and underutilized tool for responding to the performance pressures of the 1990s. It is a process many organizations will adopt.

Introducing Peer Review

What does it take to design and implement a peer review process? It involves hard work, collaboration, patience, and above all, careful planning.

There will be obstacles. People will react to the process with a variety of feelings and concerns. Many employees will recognize its value, but will have some degree of fear and tension about the peer review process—for example, fear that their input, as peers, could result in personnel actions of some kind.

People might fear that their feedback will jeopardize a co-worker's salary increase or promotion. They may fear that the system will be abused by revengeful co-workers. How comfortable employees are with the peer review process depends on the history of the work unit, the degree to which it has developed as a team, and the trust group members have in each other and in their leaders.

Several other pitfalls can set you back (see the box on this page). This is where careful program design and planning for pitfalls and rough spots is well spent.

It is critical to base innovative (and potentially controversial) peer review strategies on an established, objective evaluation process. A performance management system that is not supported by written policies, objective criteria, and clearly communicated competencies is likely to fail.

Early in the design process, it's best to work with a task force of three to six colleagues to keep the discussions focused. This group should outline the desired benefits, the overall goals of the peer review program, and the group's preliminary objectives. During these discussions, the group should try to reach agreement on broad issues.

Encourage members of the task force to speak informally with the employees (end users of the process), managers (implementers), and administrators. Remind them to keep these discussions light and exploratory. They should listen to concerns and doubts as they gather support for the concept. The plan's strength depends on how completely its design and objectives address everyone's concerns.

The next step is designing a performance management system. Such a system is derived from the organization's mission and business objectives. It ensures that criteria-based performance standards for managers and employees are on solid ground. A well-established, criteria-based performance management system is the best foundation for peer review.

Evaluate your current system's specific procedures for performance review and evaluation, and consider what aspects of the existing methods are most valuable to the organization's managers and employees. Pinpoint strengths and weaknesses.

The design of the peer review component can take advantage of, rather than compromise, what is already working. At the same time, a peer review

Peer Review Pitfalls

Fortunately, the following peer review pitfalls can be avoided through proper preparation, design, and training.

- the initial time commitment required on everyone's part
- the difficulty of keeping the performance input anonymous, especially in smaller work units or departments
- the inappropriate use of peer review input in corrective action situations, not informing peers as to the kinds of decisions their input may be used to support
- the failure to clearly draw the line at the point where, for example, the review moves from being used as input into a development plan, to becoming the primary source of data for a major personnel decision
- the tendency of some people to perceive peer review as an opportunity to get even with someone
- the tendency of reviewers to remember isolated or recent incidents or to balloon incidents out of proportion
- the tendency for a peer or co-worker to save feedback for when he or she will be a peer reviewer for a performance appraisal, rather then delivering feedback when it is needed.

process might compensate for some of the existing program's logistical flaws. For instance, in an organization in which employees work off site or in shifts, a peer review system can compensate for managers who rarely get the opportunity to see employees in action.

You should also evaluate how (and how well) expectations for performance are communicated to people. Are performance standards—the "by when, how much, and to what degree" of a performance—included in position descriptions? When a position description calls for an employee to practice excellent communication skills, does the employee understand exactly what that means for his or her position?

If such expectations are unclear to the employee, they will be unclear to peers who attempt to evaluate the employee's performance. Unclear or abstract performance expectations increase the subjective nature of the process and jeopardize system improvements.

Determining whether position descriptions define performance tasks rather than personal characteristics is important to the peer review design process. A peer review process is doomed if it does not allow you to observe specific behaviors objectively. The point of starting a peer review process is to increase the validity of evaluations, not to increase the number of subjective opinions.

Early exploratory discussions may reveal that some forms of peer review are already being used. If so, identify the current methods and assess people's feelings and opinions as to how well they are working. Collect samples of feedback and input tools that are being used.

Finalizing the Objectives

The task force must reach a consensus on the objectives before delving into procedural issues. Clear objectives will make the next phase infinitely easier. As you discuss procedures, keep in mind that you can add, subtract, combine, or refine objectives.

Writing objectives may not be the most creative activity of the design process, but it may be the most critical. Base the objectives on the needs discovered during the task force's preliminary discussion and analysis.

You'll find that down the road, a tight, focused, credible list of objectives is invaluable. Such a list can prevent the task force from becoming disoriented or bogged down in procedural details. The list of objectives is also an excellent communication tool. A clear set of objectives conveys the message that the task force is focused and clarifies the benefits of the process to others. A few examples of objectives for a peer review process are as follows:

- to improve the quality of performance input by systematically incorporating performance feedback from multiple sources
- to deliver performance feedback on an ongoing basis in a manner that is comfortable for

all employees, that maintains strong interpersonal relationships, and that builds the work team

- to reduce managers' performance evaluation work loads
- to raise appraisers' levels of professionalism and accountability to the work team
- to raise appraisees' levels of professionalism and accountability to the work team

Developing Guidelines and Procedures

Now that the preliminary objectives have been clearly outlined, it is time to expand the task force into a full-fledged planning team. You'll want to enlist the cooperation and input of others, including staff members and colleagues who are skeptical. The planning team's role is to conduct further research, to propose guidelines and procedures, and to develop prototypes of tools to be used.

The Menu of Peer Review Options (see following box) presents a good beginning, but it is not an all-inclusive list of procedural options. In the box, options are presented as questions or issues that require design decisions such as, "Who will participate?" and "How will employees be prepared for participation?" The challenge of this phase is to assess which options best support the overall objectives.

Menus of such options can be easily translated into questionnaires or surveys for distribution to employees, managers, and administrators. For example, the question, "How will a manager's input be weighed relative to peers' input?" can be framed as a multiple-choice item on a questionnaire, as follows:

Relative to a manager's input, a peer's input should count—

- A — half as much
- B — a fourth as much
- C — equally
- D — in some other ratio (specify)

Ask different questions of different groups. Introduce the survey carefully. Let respondents know that you are seeking their opinions in order to establish their needs and to evaluate and improve the

Menu of Peer Review Options

A variety of options should be considered during the peer review design phase. System planners should ask various questions pertaining to the following areas of concern.

Range of performance to be evaluated

- Should all areas of performance or all performance standards be evaluated, or should peer review evaluate only selected performance areas or standards?

- Should peer input be used for a professional development plan?

- Is it practical to use peer input for both performance categories and a development plan?

Participation options

- Will participation in the peer review process be required or optional?

- Under what circumstances, if any, would a manager's evaluation override the peer review?

- How should evaluators be selected, by employees, by managers, or at random?

- Should peer review include nonprofessional staff?

- How often should any given peer be asked to participate?

Procedures

- Will the peer's name be linked with the input?

- How will the supervisor or manager's input be weighted relative to the peers' input?

- How will the input be synthesized if multiple peer sources are used?

- Will peer review be combined with some form of self-appraisal?

- How or when will the peer review process itself be piloted and evaluated? How will new employees be oriented and integrated into the system?

- When or how often will peer input be collected—Once a year for formal evaluation? At reviews where pay or promotion is not discussed? At frequent, informal, one-on-one feedback sessions between peers?

Training and orientation

- How should training and orientation be presented—As a one-time special event? In phases, beginning with employee orientation? As an ongoing segment of staff meetings?

- Who will conduct the orientation and training?

- Should training and orientation be mandatory or optional?

- How should employee training be conducted?

- What should be included in training for the employees (peers) and for the reviewees?

- Should training include procedures, interpersonal skills (giving and receiving constructive feedback), or both?

Tools

- Should the peer review process use mission and values statements linked to performance input?

- Should the process depend on position descriptions and performance standards?

- Will reviews take the form of verbal input, written input, or both?

- Will forms and guidelines be used to integrate peers' input with managers' input and with self-appraisal input?

preliminary design. The more you involve people during the design phase, the more readily they will accept the final program.

After collecting and interpreting the data, the planning team should address the options, category by category, to develop written guidelines and procedures for implementation. Later, a proposal to senior management that incorporates the planning team's objectives, recommendations, and draft guidelines becomes useful as a communication tool and a training guide.

Other key concepts to consider during the development phase:

- When a performance evaluation system is based on objective, criteria-based standards, the questions posed to peers should correspond as directly as possible to the standards.

- Peer review should be an ongoing process rather than a yearly event. With appropriate preparation and training, peer feedback on a day-to-day basis should become a program goal.

- The peer review process should complement a self-appraisal process.

Once the development phase is complete, you're ready to produce a well-planned orientation and training program.

Well before introducing the peer review process, consider the plan's orientation and training requirements from two perspectives: the logistical and procedural perspective, and the standpoint of the interpersonal communication skills required to support effective peer evaluation.

You'll need an orientation to the new process, its procedures, and its ground rules. Anticipate such questions as, "What if the peer doing my review is trying to get back at me for something?" "I want feedback, but what if my peers are uncomfortable telling me what they really think?" and "What if I disagree with what my peer is saying?"

If the planning process is thorough and if you select peer review options that match the group's needs and issues, you should have little difficulty responding to such concerns.

Allow plenty of time for the orientation. Prepare handouts that outline the process, its objectives, its benefits, and guidelines for participation. Describe both the parts of the performance appraisal process that will remain the same and the parts that are new. Cover the range of concerns, from the big picture ("Why are we getting into this anyway?") to the details ("Who tells the peer that my performance evaluation is coming up?").

Rather than communicating the program solely through a memo or a newsletter, hold workshops that allow face-to-face participation. You might choose to combine the introduction of procedures with specific training in how to give and receive feedback.

Recognize the importance of skill-building in ensuring a constructive process. It is a good idea to return to the objectives, because they may suggest training requirements.

For example, the objective, "To deliver performance feedback on an ongoing basis in a manner that is comfortable to all employees and that maintains strong interpersonal relationships and builds the work team," may remind you that employees need training in general communication skills, and more specifically, in giving and receiving feedback. Coordinators may require training in team building, negotiation, and conflict management.

Piloting the Process

A pilot period, during which employees are encouraged to provide feedback on the process itself, further serves to reduce tension and refine procedures. Employees need to know that the process is open to improvement.

The pilot phase is the ideal time to test printed forms, draft evaluations, and input tools. Print only limited quantities of these materials until the final changes are complete. Use the pilot period to present any additional interpersonal-skills training that is needed to support the process.

Experience and patience will play a factor in the success of your peer review process. The longer people work at it, the more comfortable they will be with the peer review process and the more they will recognize its value.

Gloria Bader is president of The Bader Group, 4615 48th Street, San Diego, CA 92115.

Audrey Bloom is an instructional design consultant, at Box 881208, San Diego, CA 92168.

Reviews From Peers Instruct—and Sting

by Sue Shellenbarger

Preparing employees for performance reviews these days sometimes resembles group therapy.

Eastman Chemical Co. workers practice boosting one another's self-esteem. Honeywell Inc. employees discuss how to get along with one another. Workers in a Baxter International Inc. division struggle to criticize one another honestly.

All are part of a trend toward peer appraisal—having co-workers, rather than bosses, deliver performance reviews. Once limited mostly to a few manufacturing operations, peer appraisals are spreading to white-collar employees at hundreds of companies. Driven by the movement to leaner, less hierarchical organizations, some employers are including peers in efforts to collect "360-degree feedback." Others are gathering peer appraisals from self-directed work teams.

But as the trend accelerates, employers are finding peer appraisal is "a very difficult process with all sorts of sticky things attached," including getting employees to be honest and then dealing with the fallout, says Sam Modoono, a senior consultant in Boston for the Hay Group.

At its best, peer appraisal can solve problems bosses can't. An employee at Honeywell's air-transport systems unit was stirring up trouble by gossiping on the job and pitting co-workers against one another, and she shrugged off bosses' criticisms, says Barbara Lykins, an operations resource manager for the unit. After teammates told her in peer

appraisals that her activities were poisoning the work atmosphere, she quit the company. The rebuke "forced her to address" the problems she was causing, Ms. Lykins says.

But honest criticism from peers is hard to get. Though research shows peers often have the best information about co-workers' performance, they may not give it freely. Some may attack a peer they dislike. Others pull punches to spare a co-worker's feelings or career.

After Baxter's information-technology unit decided last year to start peer appraisals, an employee task force agreed that the appraisals should determine pay raises and that anonymous negative feedback shouldn't be allowed.

The result: almost uniformly positive reviews for everyone. "Everybody was very gun-shy. We ended up with fairly distorted...feedback," says Barbara Harmon, the unit's director of human resources. "This may have been the most uniform year of [pay] increases that we have had." Next year, the task force won't tie pay and appraisals so closely, stressing feedback as a self-development tool.

Employees often need to learn not only trust but also new interpersonal skills. Many of the abilities needed "are rooted in family dynamics, in what people learned growing up and in all their relationships to conflict and authority," says Dennis LaMountain, a senior consultant with ODT Inc., an Amherst, Mass., feedback systems concern.

Honeywell's air-transport systems unit has spent three years training its employees to deliver constructive criticism. Before workers at Eastman Chemical's Tennessee Eastman unit can even begin to evaluate peers, they must go through one to two years of "capability development" courses, including up to 10 workshops on leadership, building self-esteem in co-workers, listening, asking for help and encouraging one another.

Still, at many companies the notion of giving helpful criticism clashes head-on with the corporate culture. Mr. LaMountain worked with a manufacturing company whose middle managers were so used to attacking each other that their meetings were "kind of like the old Roman games," he says. "Somebody got in the middle of the arena, and another played lion and tried to gobble them up. They thought that made people tough."

In fact, though, Mr. LaMountain says, most employees were afraid to open their mouths. He worked with team members to get them to listen better, play back others' ideas to make sure they had heard them right and work through the pros and cons of one another's suggestions. Then he told them to go home and practice on family members.

Even with training, criticism from co-workers can raise strong emotions that are hard to handle in the workplace. One employee at Honeywell's air-transport systems unit got "mad as hell" when team members criticized him for working overtime without consulting the team, says Tom Grace, a technician specialist on the team. Team members were angry themselves and "got tough," pointing out that the man's behavior was jeopardizing the team's goal of reducing overtime. But with a team leader reminding everyone to stick to the rules—including avoiding personal attacks—the man saw the point and changed his ways.

Some companies shield employees from one another by having a consultant interpret peer ratings. Many add an extra layer of protection by making the feedback anonymous. But both steps, while helpful at first, can blunt the impact. Unless a manager or coach follows up with employees, "a large percentage of people are going to look at [the feedback], find it interesting and ignore it," says Brian L. Davis, senior vice president of Personnel Decisions Inc., Minneapolis.

And if feedback hits hard, most employees will figure out who delivered the punch anyway. Mr. Grace was surprised to learn that an anonymous co-worker thought he should "improve people skills." He tracked down the person who wrote the evaluation and asked him what he meant. "Well, when you're crossed, I figure I had better get out of the way," the worker said—a response that Mr. Grace says he found both surprising and helpful in seeing "how I come across."

246

When You Absolutely, Positively Have to Give Better Service

by Shlomo Maital

Nature itself seemed to conspire against Federal Express, the global overnight package and document delivery firm recently chosen for the Malcolm Baldrige National Quality Award. Soon after the company's bold, billion-dollar merger with Flying Tiger International in August 1989, Hurricane Hugo blasted across the Carolinas and wreaked havoc with the company's pickups and deliveries. Then the San Francisco earthquake wrecked the Bay Bridge and Federal Express's delivery vans couldn't get packages across. Not to be outdone, the Mount Redoubt volcano erupted in Alaska, generating a huge dust cloud that stranded five Federal Express 747s in Anchorage. Finally, just before Christmas, the worst cold wave in 50 years struck Memphis, the company's U.S. air hub, bursting water pipes and damaging Federal Express's computers.

All of this, in five months.

How did Federal Express deal with this onslaught of natural disasters, which trimmed its quarterly profits by about 80 percent? If you are a service company, if your corporate slogan promises quality service, and if your competitors are breathing down your neck, you sink much of your remaining profits into a costly, ongoing quality improvement program. Which is precisely what Federal Express did.

Federal Express and a growing number of service companies are religiously applying the "zero-defect" quality improvement philosophy that origi-

nated with manufacturing firms. They are willing to sink huge amounts of labor and capital into providing better service, because they know their survival depends on it. Christopher H. Lovelock, a professor of marketing at the International Institute for Management Development in Lausanne, Switzerland, has just completed a case study of Federal Express's efforts to improve quality. The study has important lessons for the entire U.S. service sector, which accounts for 60 percent of the U.S. gross national product, two-thirds of employment, and a badly needed export surplus.

Service, as defined by Federal Express, is "all actions and reactions that customers perceive they have purchased." Service quality measures the gap between what customers think they will receive and what they actually get. The key to higher service quality is measurement. What you cannot concretely measure, you cannot effectively track, alter, and improve.

In his study, Lovelock documents how Federal Express—working closely with Organizational Dynamics Inc., a Massachusetts consulting firm—built a service quality index, called SQI (pronounced "sky"). Early on, Federal Express realized that a company whose slogan is "when it absolutely, positively has to be there overnight" cannot afford even a 98 percent success rate. Many companies have adopted just-in-time inventory strategies, which bring parts and materials to their plants precisely when they are needed. For these firms, late delivery can be disastrous.

So, rather than use success or failure rates, SQI takes a dozen different service failure events, counts them daily through Federal Express's far-flung operations, weights each according to the aggravation it causes customers—Fred Smith, the company's founder, calls them a "hierarchy of horrors"—and then tots up a day-by-day "golf score," the lower the better. A missed pickup or lost package gets a weight of "10"; a missing "proof of delivery" is assigned a weight of "1." A dozen quality action teams, most headed by a vice president, work to locate spots where SQI hits bunkers and sand traps and then eliminate them. The company's management bonus is based on achieving SQI goals.

Because of the hurricane-earthquake-volcano-cold snap mishaps, Federal Express missed its goal of a daily-average 125,000 SQI points. (If everything went wrong with all 1.25 million packages handled daily, the index would total 40 million.) During the computer shutdown at Christmas 1989, SQI soared to more than 600,000. But natural disasters and shrinking profits failed to deter Federal Express from continuing to invest heavily in quality improvement. As many other companies have learned, boosting product quality often has no immediate measurable return on investment. The goal is often to reduce or prevent customer defection, and the imputed income gained by keeping customers is too hypothetical to appear in current accounting systems.

The rewards, however, are massive. "Companies can boost profits by almost 100 percent by retaining just 5 percent more of their customers," claim Frederick Reichheld and W. Earl Sasser Jr. in a recent *Harvard Business Review* article. In the credit-card business, they note, where you lose half your customers each year, each one is worth $20 in profits, because customers don't stay around long enough to justify the high cost of acquiring them. But when only one in 20 defect annually, each customer is worth $525—26 times more.

This year Federal Express will spend more than $200 on each of its 86,000 employees for quality initiatives. Thomas R. Oliver, a senior vice president, talks about the "courage gap"—the guts managers need to continue spending on quality improvement when the costs are large and the benefits unclear. "I want to insure that last year's interest in quality doesn't get preempted by this year's interest in cutting costs," Oliver says. The message is: If you think raising service quality is expensive, try mass defection of customers to your competitors.

In high service quality environments, such as Federal Express's, customer relations are particularly challenging. Employees need a high degree of sophistication to meet customers' needs. A significant industry has sprung up to teach such skills. According to Grace Major, head of Sigma International Inc., a service quality training company, major telecommunications and computer firms typically invest $250 annually in such training for each of their front-line personnel.

By their nature, most services are less price-sensitive than consumer goods. That means customers will pay a premium for top quality. But all too often, operations and production management—not customers—define "quality." And while manufacturing firms can differentiate their products through design and packaging, service companies compete by improving their relations with customers. Naive "give the customers everything they want" approaches are unrealistic and rarely work; they usually end up promising far more than can be delivered.

Service improvement demands extensive, expensive use of technology in order to update and modernize the complex machines and methods that meet customers' needs. Most firms won't accept new technology if the equipment that embodies it has failure rates above 8 percent (meaning, for example, that handheld Supertracker bar code readers used to track packages would be rejected if inoperative one day out of every 12). Federal Express has a different policy. Its threshold is 20 percent; even equipment that is "down" one day out of five may be adopted. Problems are overcome by large-scale redundancy—when first introduced, spare Supertrackers were kept in Federal Express delivery vans, in case the cantankerous one in the driver's pocket conked out.

In the tradition of user-generated innovation, Federal Express pesters high-tech equipment suppliers to conceive and supply ever-newer devices, and even designs its own hardware in some cases. This builds on the common-sense principle that new technology works best when it is designed and used by people intimately familiar with how the company works.

Ron J. Ponder, a former business school professor and now a senior vice president of Federal Express, has been a key figure in the U.S. quality movement. "You can view technology as a wave in the ocean, washing in debris," says Ponder. "Most people concentrate on the debris that floats in. That's where I think they mess up. I view the technology as the wave itself, not the individual things that are brought to shore. We knew what we wanted to do 10 years ago, but the technology wasn't there. So we were waiting for the wave and constantly prodding manufacturers to create what we needed as the wave rolled in."

Ponder embraces new technologies, such as massively parallel computing (computers that tackle different parts of a problem simultaneously, instead of one step at a time) and RISC (reduced-instruction-set computing), as they appear on the horizon. This enables Federal Express computers to handle more business in less time, at lower cost and with fewer errors.

There are three kinds of service delivery, Lovelock says—services that process people, objects, and information. For each, marketing and quality improvement differ. "When you get a haircut, you can see the value added," he says. "But for many services, such as preventive medical care, this is not readily apparent." Lovelock recommends that for such "credence services," companies try to document the long-run outcomes of their services and relate their costs to the payoffs. What happens, for instance, if the oil in a car is not changed frequently enough? What is the cost of added wear to engine parts?

Models of quality should be based on the needs and concerns of customers, Lovelock asserts. For some services, this can be a real challenge. In air transportation, the competitive thrust was once: "We will get you there in one piece and on time." Today, it has become: "We will get you there in comfort, ready to do business." Airlines learned from their business customers that comfort is a dominant factor in choosing carriers.

How good are American service providers, compared with their foreign counterparts? "The best are top rate," says Lovelock. "But the average service providers are simply not good enough." His view is echoed in a recent *Sloan Management Review* article by Leonard L. Berry, Valarie A. Zeithaml, and A. Parasuraman. "There are examples of companies in the United States delivering superb service and profiting from it," they write. "But these are the exceptional stories; in most companies, quality service is still a soft idea, an elusive goal, or a low priority." They offer three prescriptions: Encourage customers to complain and make it easy for them to do so; make timely personal communications with customers a key part of the strategy; and encourage and enable employees to respond effectively to customer problems.

Federal Express is now eyeing the rich $1.5 billion European market. In 1989, it had a meager 10 percent European market share, trailing DHL (50 percent) and TNT (25 percent). One reason: Its service quality there lags. A 1989 survey by *Commercial Motor,* a British trade magazine, found Federal Express scored only half as high as competitors UPS and TNT on service in delivering identical packages from Newcastle to Stuttgart. The company is working hard to find remedies.

Lovelock plans to document Federal Express's global strategy for a future case study. Here is a small but weighty piece of evidence, suggesting Lovelock's new study will describe a burgeoning success.

Parked near the runways at Memphis is a fleet of snowplows, painted in the corporate purple, orange, and white colors. Their steel blades gleam incongruously in the bright Tennessee sunshine. Federal Express bought the costly equipment in 1988 after a heavy snowstorm in Memphis clogged runways and delayed takeoffs and landings. The fleet of plows is used on average one night every two years.

"When we need it, we really need it," a company official told Lovelock.

Look for more service providers to reach the same conclusion. When customers need reliable, top-flight service, they really need it—and increasingly, only companies that work and spend to provide it will prosper.

PC Program Lets Machines Help Bosses Manage People

by Walter S. Mossberg

Good managers spend a lot of their time developing and evaluating their employees, but there isn't much commercial computer software to help them do so.

Plenty of programs for managing projects involve tracking certain activities of particular employees for limited periods. But many managers need a program centered on people, not projects, that would help them oversee employees' development, spot problems early, prepare for performance reviews, and schedule raises and other rewards.

Avantos Performance Systems, Emeryville, Calif., has come up with such a product, an unusual and impressive $245 program called ManagePro that runs on IBM-compatible personal computers in conjunction with Microsoft's Windows software. ManagePro is so useful that, by itself, it may provide the justification some managers have needed to start using Windows on their PCs. Owners of Apple's Macintosh machines will get their own version of ManagePro in the spring.

Dreamed up by a couple of former management consultants, ManagePro is designed to let managers track their employees' progress against goals, both companywide and individual, set by the bosses.

The program has two linked main modules, for goal planning and people planning. In the goal-planning module, a user establishes objectives for the company or department, and then assigns supporting goals to particular employees or groups.

For instance, a staff member may be handed a task like processing customer complaints faster in a certain office, which may be part of an overall company goal to raise customer satisfaction to 90% by a given date. Or she may be assigned a personal goal, such as learning a new computer system.

In the people-planning and development side of ManagePro, users view the business from a personnel angle, looking at employees and teams to see how they are doing against these goals. Here the program prompts managers periodically to offer feedback and coaching to each employee, and to reward success or flag failure. Supervisors can establish a schedule for interim and formal performance reviews, which ManagePro will remind them to conduct. The program makes the reviews easier by documenting previous feedback and progress against goals.

ManagePro also offers a built-in "adviser," a collection of people-management tips and strategies written by personnel consultants, which bosses can tap for help in particular situations. The "adviser" suggests providing plenty of recognition for employee successes; for between pay raises, it proposes rewards like sports tickets or dinner for two. The program also comes with a book on managing people.

The software's design is elegant. It has no complicated commands to memorize. Instead, every screen and function is available by clicking with a mouse on bright, clear icons or by selecting plain-English commands from menus. The various screens for viewing data are color-coded and otherwise marked so you always know where you are in the program. The software comes with a clear manual, and a 30-minute on-screen tutorial gets users up and running.

The goals module of the program lets you define and review goals in three ways: by an outline of the hierarchy of goals; by a timeline that shows the schedules of goals; and by a "status board." This last resembles an organizational chart, with boxes and lines, but it automatically colors each goal green, for "on track," yellow for "behind" or red for "critical."

The people-tracking portion of the program has an outline view and a status board, with similar color-coding. But this module is even richer, permitting entry and checking of employee's progress, feedback, pending reviews, recognition and more.

The linkages among the various screens and modules are particularly impressive. If you establish a new goal in the goals module, it shows up automatically in the people module as being associated with the staffer to whom it was assigned. And you can "drill down" from any screen to see underlying details of goals and employees' records.

The program contains a calendar and an "action list" for scheduling things. It also can print out beautiful reports on all aspects of your staff and goals.

ManagePro can be easily configured to suit the needs and tastes of its users. You can set it to display only the goals or just the people module, or to operate in a simplified fashion within each module, offering fewer screen and features. You can change the terminology for measuring employees' progress, customize various forms for entering data, and more.

The program has only one serious drawback: It's slow. Even on a PC with a speedy 486 chip, I found ManagePro sluggish in bringing up new screens and windows. The problem isn't fatal, but Avantos acknowledges it needs fixing, and says it aims to speed things up in version 2.0, due out in the spring.

There are a couple of lesser problems. ManagePro lacks a function for entering an employee work schedule; the company says it is considering adding one. Finally, the program may be hard to find. It is sold by a few mail-order houses, but isn't on many store shelves yet.

It's worth investing some time to locate a copy of ManagePro, because it does what good software should do: It helps people use their computers to do their jobs better without forcing them to become computer experts.

A Solution to the Performance Appraisal Feedback Enigma

by Herbert H. Meyer, University of South Florida

Executive Overview

It is hard to dispute the value of the ubiquitous formal performance appraisal programs used in almost all large organizations. In theory, these programs should serve important organizational objectives. Each employee should be evaluated at least annually and be given feedback to communicate how he or she is performing. In practice, however, most managers find these feedback interviews distasteful. Unless constrained by some sort of administrative pressure, like a subordinate sign-off requirement, managers are likely to ignore the responsibility.

The traditional manager-to-subordinate performance appraisal feedback interview is becoming anachronistic in our culture. The appraisal feedback interview is a very authoritarian procedure—a parent-child type of exchange. Most modern organizations are moving away from authoritarian management toward an involvement-oriented working environment. A performance review discussion based on the subordinate's self-review fits an involvement-oriented climate much better than the traditional top-down performance review discussion. It also has the advantage of forcing the manager into a counseling mode, rather than serving as a judge. Research has shown that performance review discussions based on self-review prove to be more productive and satisfying than traditional manager-initiated appraisal discussions.

Article

To say that the performance appraisal feedback problem has been an enigma for managers and personnel specialists is probably a glaring understatement. Formal programs to evaluate and document the job performance of subordinates and then provide feedback to the respective subordinates have been around at least as long as there have been personnel departments in organizations. The appraisal and feedback program is one of the psychologists' and personnel specialists' popular topics in the personnel literature. There have been literally thousands of articles on this topic in journals in the personnel field during the last seventy-five years. Most of these articles generally applaud the virtues of the performance appraisal and feedback process, lament their lack of success, then present suggested solutions to the program. This format has not changed much over the years.

Problems experienced with performance appraisal programs are myriad. Significant evidence has shown that most managers find the program onerous and distasteful. The following scenario depicts a situation that many managers have probably faced in dealing with the performance appraisal feedback problem:

Jane Novak was preparing for the annual performance appraisal review discussion scheduled with Henry Buckner. She remembered the unpleasant experience she had in a similar discussion a year ago. Henry's performance since that discussion had been tolerable, but mediocre at best. While there were many aspects of the job where Henry's performance could be improved, she planned to focus on only two or three areas where improvement was especially needed.

Last year in her first appraisal discussion with Henry, he reacted very defensively to any suggestions she made for improving performance. He was especially annoyed by the fact that the overall rating she had assigned was only "Very Satisfactory." In fact, he appealed the rating, but fortunately Jane's boss supported her judgment. Customarily, most professionals in the company were rated as either "Outstanding" or "Excellent." While distributions weren't published, it was generally known that only a small percentage received ratings below "Excellent" on the scale. Yet, Jane couldn't in good conscience rate Henry above "Very Satisfactory," which was the midpoint on the scale.

Jane hated to conduct these annual review discussions, especially with those for whom she couldn't justify an "Outstanding" overall rating. The discussions often seemed to do more harm than good. Her relationships with Henry, for example, has been strained since their annual review discussion last year.

Is Jane's experience with the annual performance review discussion unusual? Do her reactions indicate that she is a poor manager? The answer to both questions is no.

Experience with appraisal programs shows that unless administrative pressures are applied to ensure that people are appraised and feedback given, the programs invariably die out very rapidly. Managers just do not carry out the process, even though departmental policy may call for it. Most organizations have found that a subordinate sign-off procedure must be used to guarantee that appraisals are completed and feedback is given.

Is Appraisal Feedback Useful?

Starting about 30 years ago at G.E., we carried out an intensive series of studies on the performance appraisal and feedback process. Followup surveys showed that the majority of employees expressed more uncertainty about the status of their performance in their managers' opinions after a performance appraisal interview than before. Evidently, in many cases the manager's formal feedback was discrepant with the informal signals they had been receiving about his or her view of their job performance. As Dave DeVries observed in a newsletter published by the Center for Creative Leadership a few years ago, most people get the feedback they consider to be really reliable in indirect, obscure ways. They judge the boss's mood, talk with the boss's secretary, note whether or not they are invited to important meetings, whether or not their opinion is sought on important matters, and so on.

A great deal of evidence, from our General Electric research and that reported in the literature, has shown that there is a strong tendency to distort appraisals toward favorable reviews when feedback must be given. For example, the federal government introduced a merit pay plan for mid-level employees about ten years ago. A rating of "fully successful" or better is needed to qualify for a merit increase. A recent study showed that 99.5 percent were eligible.[2]

Managers learn through unpleasant experience that negative feedback not only results in the employee having negative feelings, but it also too often results in deteriorated rather than improved performance. Consequently, because of this positive distortion, subordinates may get misleading information which is often inconsistent with administrative decisions such as salary actions, promotion, and demotions. Such distorted ratings sometimes cause trouble when the manager wants to fire a poor performer. The manager may decide that a certain employee who has consistently performed inadequately should be demoted or fired. Yet, the record may show that this employee's performance has been consistently rated as "very satisfactory."

Few "Good" Programs

Surveys of companies with appraisal programs have repeatedly revealed that few are satisfied with its performance appraisal program. A survey of 200 large companies conducted by Psychological Associates showed that 70 percent of employees said they were more confused than enlightened by the performance appraisal feedback they received. Similarly, an American Society of Personnel Administrators survey concluded that less than ten percent of companies have reasonably successful performance appraisal programs.

A recent nationwide survey of 3,500 companies showed that the most frequently mentioned human resource concern was the organization's performance appraisal system. Based on another survey reported in *Industry Week,* the author summarized that, "The handling of performance reviews is little short of disastrous—a periodic agony thrust on both bosses and subordinates."[3]

In a recent article in *Personnel Management,* after an exhaustive study of appraisal programs in the public sector the author observed, "The chances of failure in operating appraisal schemes far outweigh the chances of success. Many organizations have failed. Many others have systems which have degenerated into sterile paper chases, satisfying personnel departments' thirst for forms and justifying their existence but contributing little to the quality of organizational performance. Appraisal in practice tends to become a grand annual convulsion, more of a bureaucratic colossus than a means of insuring continuing development of people."[4]

R.E. Kopleman, in his book *Managing Productivity in Organizations*, noted that most managers regard the performance appraisal interview as a fundamentally unpleasant situation—one to be avoided, postponed, or handled hurriedly.[5] A similar conclusion was reached by Napier and Latham based on their survey of appraisal programs in practice. They found that most appraisers saw little or no practical value in conducting performance appraisal interviews. No potential positive or negative consequences were generally foreseen, unless negative information was fed back and in those cases, the appraiser usually experienced aversive consequences.[6]

Why Are Programs Retained?

If the results of appraisal and feedback programs have been so negative, why have they persisted? Why do we keep butting our heads against the wall and continue the search for a solution when the quest for this utopia seems so hopeless? I am sure we persist because the idea seems so logical, so common-sensible. Appraisal and feedback should serve important administrative and developmental objectives.

Feedback regarding job performance seems necessary to justify administrative decisions, such as whether a salary increase is awarded and the size of the increase, or whether an employee should be transferred to another job or scheduled for promotion. Feedback should contribute to improved performance. The positive effect of feedback on performance has always been an accepted psychological principle.

It is also well established that feedback designed to reinforce or alter behavior is most effective if provided when the behavior occurs. Daily coaching is more valuable for this purpose than a once-a-year discussion. However, most personnel managers insist that their managers schedule an annual, formally documented review to ensure that every employee gets at least some feedback about his or her job performance. This annual feedback interview is intended to provide a clear message to employees about their performance and to motivate them to improve.

Split Roles

In some organizations, administrative feedback, such as communicating planned salary action, is separated from motivational and developmental feedback. Norman Maier, a noted industrial psychologist, recommended this more than thirty years ago. He ascertained that when the supervisor appraises a subordinate for administrative purposes, he or she is serving as a judge. If the supervisor is to effectively motivate a subordinate and provide guidance for development, he or she must serve as a counselor. Maier maintained that being both judge and counselor is incompatible. A person being judged is likely to be defensive. For counseling to be effective, the employee must be receptive to advice and suggestion, not defensive.[7]

One of our G.E. studies in which almost 100 actual appraisal interviews were observed, supported Norm Maier's contention.[8] Managers were required to communicate a salary decision and suggestions for performance improvement in the same interview. We observed that subordinate's defensive reactions were so common, and the ego involvement in the salary decision so powerful, that attempts to counsel the employee about needed performance improvement were mostly futile.

Our recommendation that salary action appraisal and motivational and developmental appraisal be accomplished in separate programs has not been widely accepted—at least not in the United States.

Surveys show that in most organizations, both types of appraisals are covered in the same interview. Evidently this is not true in Great Britain where a recent survey of appraisal practices in large companies revealed that appraisals for the two different purposes were separated in 85 percent of the responding companies.[9]

Based on my experience, I still maintain very strongly that appraisal for the two different purposes should be separated. I will focus here principally on motivational and developmental appraisal discussions. How can the process be more effective? I think the answer is to change our approach to the process.

Control versus Involvement-Oriented Management

The traditional workforce management approach is to achieve efficiency by imposing management control over workers' behavior. However, it is becoming clear that a control-oriented approach to management is less effective. Our culture has changed. To remain competitive, organizations must elicit the commitment of employees at all levels. Commitment is not likely to be engendered in today's employees by interacting with them in a control-oriented manner. Employees want to be respected, to be in the know, involved, and to be treated as important individuals rather than as "hands."

The conventional approach to performance appraisal and feedback is certainly consistent with the control-oriented approach to management. It fits perfectly in a bureaucratically run organization. It is incompatible with an involvement-oriented management style.

A Changed Approach

The traditional approach to appraisal—where the manager completes an evaluation form and meets with the employee to communicate the appraisal—is becoming *anachronistic* in our culture. Performance appraisal conducted in the traditional manner is highly authoritarian. When a manager sits down with an employee for an appraisal, there is no doubt about who is the "boss" and who is in the subordinate or dependent role. It is a *parent-child* type of exchange.

Our culture has been moving away from authoritarianism for at least the last fifty years. Few people like a dictatorial boss and no one wants to have his or her dependence accentuated. People want to be involved, respected, treated as equals and for this reason, involvement-oriented management has become popular. Most performance appraisal programs are inconsistent with this management style.

The Use of Self Appraisal

The conventional approach to performance appraisal is sometimes appropriate when the subordinate is dependent on the supervisor—for new employees, trainees, or perhaps for people in highly structured jobs. It is not appropriate, however, for most employees. It is certainly inappropriate for professionals and administrators. For employees who are not in an obviously dependent role, an appraisal discussion designed to serve communication, motivation, and development purposes should be based on the subordinate's *self appraisal.*

About twenty years ago, Glenn Bassett and I conducted another study at G.E. which demonstrated that appraisal discussions between manager and subordinate based on the subordinate's self-review, were significantly more constructive and satisfying to both parties than those based on the manager's appraisal. It also resulted in significant improvement in job performance. Even though these discussions also communicated a salary decision, focussing on the subordinate's self-review was definitely more favorable.[10]

Advantages of Self-Review

Self-review has several advantages. First, it enhances the subordinate's dignity and self-respect. The employee is not forced into a dependent role. Second, it places the manager into the role of counselor, not judge. Third, it is more likely to elicit employee commitment to any development plans or goals formulated in the discussion. That is, the subordinate is more likely to develop a feeling of ownership in plans and goals which he or she helped to create.

A fourth and major advantage of the self-review approach to the appraisal discussion was mentioned previously. That is, discussion based on the subordinate's review of his or her own performance is likely to be more satisfying to both parties and more productive than is the more traditional manager-to-subordinate review. Indeed, a number of studies seem to support that satisfaction with appraisal discussion results is strongly related to subordinate contribution and participation in the discussion.[11]

The biggest problem with this approach is that it violates traditional mores regarding the proper relationship between boss and subordinate. This is probably why the results of our experiment on self appraisals have not been widely applied. Certainly, supervisors participating in appraisal discussions based on subordinates' self-review have to some extent lost the value of their acquired credentials as the "superior."

Another disadvantage of self-review is the self-serving bias expected to inflate the self appraisal. However, research has shown that this "leniency error" can be minimized by orienting the self analysis toward self development rather than appraisal for administrative purposes. In fact, self-reviews have proved to be superior to supervisory reviews in identifying individual strengths and shortcomings.[12]

Eliminate the "Grading"

To improve the value of a feedback discussion based on self-review, the "grading" aspect should be eliminated. Assigning a numerical or adjectival grade, such as "satisfactory," "excellent," "adequate," "outstanding," or "poor" to overall performance or specific performance tends to obstruct rather than facilitate constructive discussion.

In addition, I recommend eliminating the formal grading aspect of a performance appraisal program used for administrative purposes. Most people in business find grading somewhat demeaning. It treats a mature person like a school child. The administrative action taken, such as the amount of salary increase or a promotion will communicate an overall appraisal better than will a grade. Recognition can certainly be given and improvement needs discussed without necessarily assigning grades to performance.

Content of the Discussion

Usually, formal performance appraisal discussions are scheduled annually. The major purpose is to provide a periodic summary of job performance and future possibilities. This discussion, if based on self-review, will provide the supervisor with the *subordinate's perspective* of the job, goals, problems, and responsibilities. Specifically, this annual discussion might cover:

(1) Overall progress—an analysis of accomplishments and shortcomings.
(2) Problems encountered in meeting job requirements.
(3) Opportunities to improve performance.
(4) Long range plans, opportunities—for the job and for the individual's career.
(5) General discussion of possible plans and goals for the coming year.

If a goal-setting program is being used, such as Management by Objectives, this annual review discussion is not the best place to establish detailed job goals for the year. To be effective, a goal-setting program must be a continuous process. Several meetings may be needed to propose, negotiate, and agree on goals. Review discussions should be held more than once a year. In many jobs, quarterly reviews may be appropriate, while in other jobs progress review discussions may be needed monthly or weekly.

The Supervisor's Role

Even though the subordinate has the lead role in the annual review discussion, the supervisor is not passive. The supervisor should prepare by noting the points he or she would like to make and how to present them. Actually, the supervisor is in a better position to give the employee recognition and suggest changes in activities or behavior when reacting to instead of initiating all input. The supervisor's role becomes that of "counselor" rather than judge or "the boss."

Need for Training

If self-review is adopted as the medium for an annual review, it will not obviate the need for training. Training supervisors to handle this type of discussion could be valuable. It need not be any more extensive than the training given for conventional appraisal programs. I can envision, for example, a behavior modeling training program which covers such topics as how to deal with an overly favorable self appraisal, an unrealistically self-deprecating review, an important problem or development need not brought up by the subordinate, and so on.

In addition, employees will need guidance on how to prepare for and conduct a self-review discussion. As a minimum, instructional materials, perhaps in the form of a brief manual, should be provided.

How Will Administrative Decisions Be Made?

Performance appraisal programs are often used as the basis for compensation and promotion decisions. If the type of performance review discussion proposed here is directed only to communication and development objectives, how should those administrative decisions be made and communicated?

As indicated earlier, I strongly believe that appraisal for development should be separated from appraisal for compensation or promotion. The annual discussion based on a self-review is designed to stimulate self development and to open communication channels to improve the working relationship between supervisor and subordinate. A performance appraisal discussion in which salary and/or promotion decisions are communicated does not provide a desirable climate for achieving communication and development objectives.[13]

Administrative decisions pertaining to merit raises or promotions are too important to the organization to be made by supervisors alone. Few supervisors are all-seeing, all-knowing persons. They have their own idiosyncrasies, failings, biases. In some cases, a supervisor may hide an especially effective employee to ensure continued achievement of his or her unit's objectives. Sometimes a supervisor is threatened by an unusually effective subordinate.

An administrative decision, such as on merit pay or promotion, almost always constitutes a zero-sum game. If differentiations are made, for each winner there must be one or more losers. Identifying the winners is extremely important to the organization as a whole, and therefore these should be organizational decisions, not decisions made by individual supervisors.

A growing trend in large organizations is to use an "annual human resources review" procedure to appraise the performance and potential of all em-

ployees. Peer-level managers in each division meet as a team with their manager to discuss the performance and potential of all employees who report to them. Using a team of people to evaluate individual performance provides a broader perspective in appraising employees than individual assessment. It not only provides a more comprehensive and objective evaluation of each employee's performance, potential, and development needs, but it also minimizes the effects of individual biases based on distorted emphases, prejudicial viewpoints, and limited perspectives.

Even though some of the managers in this process may have minimal exposure to some of the employees, they can contribute by insisting that judgments are backed by objective and behavioral evidence. After all, each participating manager has an important stake in the process. If another manager's employee is identified as a winner, one or more of his or her "winners" might become losers.

Appraisals resulting from a team meeting of this kind are more likely to be accepted by employees. It is more difficult to challenge an appraisal formulated by group consensus. Moreover, when a supervisor communicates a merit pay decision to a subordinate, it is less likely that their working relationship will deteriorate. This is not the case when a merit pay decision is made by the supervisor acting alone.

The annual human resources review process has additional benefits that more than justify the investment of time. Each participating manager will become thoroughly familiar with the responsibilities and performance characteristics of each employee in the department. It may clarify expectations regarding responsibilities of specific individuals or positions. It often defines and solves departmental workflow problems. The participating managers may formulate strategy and action plans for more effectively using human resources to achieve department objectives.

Summary

I think the administrative and developmental objectives of the performance appraisal process should be addressed in separate programs. To achieve communication, counseling, and development objectives, I believe very strongly that our traditional top-down approach to performance appraisal is anachronistic, passé, and obsolete. It is a parent-child type of exchange that is inconsistent with cultural values that have evolved in modern organizations. It often proves to be an embarrassing experience for both parties involved and it accentuates the dependent role of the subordinate. This relationship is appropriate only in a control-oriented management environment. Effective organizations are moving away from the control-oriented approach toward an involvement-oriented climate designed to elicit commitment on the part of employees at all levels. Even the term "subordinate" is eschewed in modern organizations.

In most organizations, if supervisors are constrained to use the traditional supervisor rating and feedback approach to the annual review discussion, it would be better to abandon the program altogether. Conversely, if one concedes that it is desirable for supervisors to have some sort of annual review discussion with each of their direct reports, a discussion based on self-review can be valuable and constructive.

Endnotes

[1] See David DeVries comments in the June 1978 Center for Creative Leadership Newsletter regarding his survey of 1,450 managers on their experiences with the communication of performance appraisals.

[2] This finding was based on a federal government study which was cited in an article entitled, "Grading 'Merit Pay'," in the November 1988 issue of *Newsweek*.

[3] The four survey results described here were cited in an article entitled, "Performance Review: Examining the Eye of the Beholder" by Berkeley Rice in the December 1985 issue of *Across the Board* (a journal published by the Conference Board in New York).

[4] J. George, "Appraisal in the Public Sector: Dispensing with the Big Stick," *Personnel Management*, May 1986, 32-35.

[5] R.E. Kopelman, *Managing Productivity in Organizations: A Practical, People-Oriented Perspective* (New York: McGraw-Hill, 1986).

[6] N.K. Napier and G.P. Latham, "Outcome Expectancies of People Who Conduct Performance Appraisals," *Personnel Psychology*, 1986, Vol. 39, No. 4, 827-837.

[7] Normal Maier's 1958 book on this subject, *The Appraisal Interview: Objectives, Methods, and Skills,* published by Wiley, is still widely used in training programs and frequently referred to by writers in the field.

[8] This study was reported in a 1965 *Harvard Business Review* article entitled, "Split Roles in Performance Appraisal." A shortened version of the article was republished in 1989 as an *"HBR* Retrospect," since the original 1965 article was one of *HBR*'s ten best-selling reprints.

[9] This finding was reported in a 1985 article in the British journal, *Personnel Management*. The article, by H. Murlis and A. Wright, was entitled, "Rewarding the Performance of the Eager Beaver."

[10] This study was reported in a 1968 article in *Personnel Psychology* entitled, "Performance Appraisal Based on Self-Review." Incidentally, recently a student, P.R. Simmons, in our Ph.D. program in industrial/ organizational psychology at the University of South Florida, replicated this study with a few modifications for a dissertation project. His study sample consisted of clerical workers. I would expect their jobs to be fairly highly structured, so that perhaps the traditional top-down approach to appraisal might be appropriate. As an added twist, he obtained a measure of the degree to which each of the participating departments was run in a democratic or authoritarian manner. He found the self-review approach to appraisal to be especially effective in democratically run departments. Subordinate motivation to improve performance and supervisor satisfaction with the results of the appraisal program were significantly more favorable under the self-review condition.

[11] The positive effects of subordinate participation in appraisal discussions have been documented in a number of articles relating to performance appraisal, including: D.J. Campbell and C. Lee, "Self-Appraisal in Performance Evaluation: Development Versus Evaluation," *Academy of Management Review*, 1988, Vol. 13, No. 2, 302-324; D.M. Herold, R.C. Liden, and M.L. Leatherwood, "Using Multiple Attributes to Assess Sources of Performance Feedback," *Academy of Management Journal*, 1987, Vol. 30, No. 4, 826-835; J.M. Ivancevich and J.T. McMahon, "The Effects of Goal Setting, External Feedback, and Self-Generated Feedback on Outcome Variables: A Field Experiment," *Academy of Management Journal*, 1982, Vol. 25, No. 2, 359-372; R.L. Dipboye and R. de Pontbriand, "Correlates of Employee Reactions to Performance Appraisals and Appraisal Systems," *Journal of Applied Psychology*, 1981, Vol. 66, No. 2, 248-251; C.C. Manz and H.P. Sims, Jr., "Self Management as a Substitute for Leadership: A Social Learning Perspective," *Academy of Management Review*, 1980, Vol. 5, No. 3, 361-367; R.J. Burke, W. Weitzel, and T. Weir, "Characteristics of Effective Performance Review and Development Interviews: Replication and Extension," *Personnel Psychology*, 1978, Vol. 31, No. 4, 903-919; H.H. Meyer, "The Annual Performance Review Discussion—Making It Effective," *Personnel Journal*, October 1977; and M.M. Greller, "Subordinate Participation and Reactions to the Appraisal Interview," *Journal of Applied Psychology*, 1975, Vol. 6, No. 5, 544-549.

[12] The superiority of self-reviews over supervisory appraisals for self-development purposes was well documented by Paul Mabe and Stephen West in a June 1982 article in the *Journal of Applied Psychology* (Vol. 67, No. 3), which

presented a summary of the results of 55 studies in which self-evaluations were compared with other measures of performance. In a similar survey of research on self appraisal, George Thornton found that self appraisals showed less "halo" than ratings made by supervisors. In other words, subordinates rating their own performance identified specific strengths and shortcomings better than did their respective supervisors. This study was reported in an article entitled, "Psychometric Properties of Self-Appraisals of Job Performance," in the Summer 1980 issue of *Personnel Psychology* (Vol. 33, No. 2).

[13] The study referred to in endnote 8 showed quite clearly that the supervisor's role as "judge" in communicating an administrative decision, such as a scheduled merit raise, created an almost impossible climate for providing counseling or development planning effectively. More often than not, the subordinate's evaluation of his or her supervisor actually declined as a result of the dual-purpose appraisal discussion. This was probably because in the great majority of cases, the planned administrative action communicated, such as the size of the scheduled merit raise, fell short of the subordinate's expectation.

Dr. Meyer, Professor Emeritus at the University of South Florida, came to the university in 1973 to organize and direct a new Ph.D. program in industrial/organizational psychology. Before that, Dr. Meyer directed a personnel research program on the corporate staff of the General Electric Co. for more than twenty years. In this role, he and his staff carried out a large number of research and development projects on a variety of topics pertaining to human resources management. Among these projects were several studies of the performance appraisal process. Dr. Meyer received the Ph.D. degree in psychology from the University of Michigan in 1949.

Performance Review: Examining the Eye of the Beholder

by Berkeley Rice

Looking back over the years of research assessing systems of performance appraisal, Frank J. Landy, a psychologist at Penn State University, admits that he has grown discouraged. Landy concludes that all the attempts to "build a better mousetrap" by experimenting with new types of rating scales or controlling sources of bias have been disappointing. Even when those attempts succeed at reducing error, he says, the improvements in accuracy are often so small as to be merely cosmetic.

"After more than 30 years of serious research," says Landy, "it seems that little progress has been made in developing an efficient and psychometrically sound alternative to the traditional graphic rating scale.... One major conclusion to be drawn from this research is that there is no easy way to get accurate and informative performance data."

Though review systems remain fairly crude instruments for evaluating performance—and there is even widespread disagreement about what they are supposed to accomplish—few companies appear ready to abandon them. Because of constant pressure to increase productivity, the evaluation of employee performance has become a critical issue to industry.

"In spite of the criticisms," says Andrew Grove, president of Intel Corporation, the Silicon Valley electronics firm, "I remain steadfast in my conviction that if we want performance in the workplace, somebody has to have the courage and confidence to determine whether we are getting it or not. We must also find ways to enhance what we are getting."

Because of the general dissatisfaction with current performance-review systems, industrial psychologists have conducted hundreds of studies to identify sources of error, bias, and confusion, while management consultants and companies have been experimenting with a variety of new approaches. Some of the research has produced valuable insights into the mental processes involved in performance review, and some of the experiments look highly promising.

According to this approach, the perceptual and cognitive differences among raters may affect their ratings as much as or more than the nature of the rating scale itself. In fact, these cognitive processes and resulting biases may be impervious to any changes in the "system" of evaluation or the structure of the rating scale.

Cognitive researchers often cite studies on eyewitness testimony that demonstrate the fallibility of human observation and memory. Relying on videotapes of people's descriptions of staged "accidents" and other situations, these studies have revealed the unconscious tendency to "reconstruct" past events based on cognitive biases, stereotypes, and other unrelated or subsequent information. Compared with recalling a few crucial details about an accident viewed only days before, the evaluation of managerial performance after six months or an entire year represents such an awesome task that one should not expect a high level of accuracy.

Like witnesses at a busy intersection, whose vision may be hindered by weather conditions or traffic, managers must often base their judgments on only fragmentary evidence of their subordinates' performance. Though they may think they're basing their evaluations on the six months or one year under review, studies of short- versus long-term memory indicate that such ratings are based primarily on the most recent observations.

Cognitive researchers have discovered a variety of ways in which managers unconsciously categorize or stereotype employees, ways that interfere with accurate judgments of their actual performance on the job. Once established, these categories act like filters, distorting observation and recall of a subordinate's behavior. A supervisor is thus likely to notice behavior that confirms his previous opinion of a subordinate, and ignore or forget behavior that conflicts with it. A star employee whose performance declines may continue to receive evaluations based on his previously good behavior; one who makes a serious effort to improve may be condemned by his previous reputation for mediocrity.

According to Jack Felman, professor of management at the University of Florida at Gainesville, these mental stereotypes or categories are difficult to shake because much of any manager's ability to monitor performance is unconscious, or automatic. "To the degree that the behavior of an employee is consistent with the supervisor's expectations," says Feldman, "it is noted and stored automatically. Only when the behavior departs from expectations—as when an employee thought to be competent at a task turns out not to be—does the supervisor begin to pay conscious attention to the subordinate's behavior."

Given this unconscious process, once an employee has been mentally categorized as competent, incompetent, or average, observation and recall of his behavior will be automatically governed by the characteristics of that category. When evaluation time comes, if the supervisor cannot recall any specific information relevant to a critical judgment, the category or stereotype will unconsciously provide it, even creating imaginary examples of illustrative behavior. According to Feldman, such "false memories" are particularly likely to occur when a supervisor has many subordinates to evaluate, and little time or opportunity to actually observe them on the job.

This categorical information processing may be governed not only by such obvious factors as age, sex, race, and attractiveness, but also by stereotypes about certain kinds of jobs. Thus some managers may evaluate the performance of all sales people by the degree to which they fit the traditional image of the fast-talking, aggressive "go-getter," and all bookkeepers by the image of the cautious, meticulous "grind," whether or not the qualities that those images convey are suitable for the particular job.

Another form of cognitive error endemic to performance reviews can be explained by "attribution theory." According to this theory, now well established in social psychology, people tend to attribute their own actions to situational factors, whereas observers tend to attribute them to personal factors. For example, a worker doing poorly on a job might attempt to justify his performance by citing lack of supplies, unpredictable or excessive work load, difficult co-workers, or ambiguous instructions. That man's supervisor, however, is more likely to attribute the employee's poor performance to his lack of ability or motivation.

The same cognitive process affects the way managers appraise their own performance. In one study of a group of middle-level managers, most cited lack of ability or motivation as the cause of unsatisfactory performance by their own employees. But when asked to explain occasions when they had received unsatisfactory reviews themselves, only 20 percent attributed their own poor performance to such personal factors. Most cited factors "beyond their control."

Personal relations can also affect such causal attributions. When evaluating a well-liked subordinate, managers are more likely to attribute successful performance to personal competence, and blame failures on external or mitigating circumstances. With a disliked employee, the reverse attribution will occur. The employees may receive more credit or blame than they actually deserve.

The discovery of how such cognitive processes affect performance review has shaken the field of management psychology, according to Frank Landy. "Eight years ago we would have given plenty of prescriptive advice about how to do an accurate review," he says, "but most of it would have been wrong. The bad news is that there's simply no easy way to do performance review. As appealing as the notion of a precise method of appraisal is, it's never going to be possible to measure such complex behavior in any absolute way. Managers in each company are going to have to get personally involved in developing their own systems.

"The good news," says Landy, "is that we've discovered that a lot of that stuff about rating scales and evaluation formats is really trivial. The particular format just doesn't seem to make much difference. There is no one 'right' way to do it. There are dozens of ways. You just use whichever method feels right for your company. It may not be very accurate, but the degree of error won't make much difference."

Whatever it's called—review, appraisal, evaluation, or rating—most companies conduct some form of regular performance review. But few, apparently, do it well. In a survey of nearly 200 companies by Psychological Associates, a human-resources consulting firm, 70 percent of the employees reported that their review sessions had not given them a clear idea of what was expected of them. Only half said their bosses helped them set job objectives; only one in five reported any attempt by the boss to follow up the review during the year. A survey of 265 major corporations by Drake Beam Morin, another consulting firm, found general dissatisfaction with existing performance-review systems because of such problems as inflated ratings, unclear criteria, and subjective standards.

"Probably less than 10 percent of the nation's companies have systems that are reasonably good," laments Ronald Pilenzo, president of the American Society for Personnel Administration. In many companies, according to *Industry Week,* the handling of performance reviews is "little short of disastrous—a periodic agony thrust on both bosses and subordinates." For both, the result is often mistrust, misunderstanding, and confusion.

One basic source of confusion about performance-review systems is the lack of agreement on their purpose. Are they designed merely to evaluate performance, or to critique and improve it as well? Should they be used primarily to determine salaries and prospects for promotion, or should they serve as a means of training and career development? Should they focus on behavior or results? Should they be held once or twice a year, quarterly, or more often? And finally, just whom is the review supposed to help, the employee or the supervisor? No appraisal system can accomplish all goals, and conflicting purposes will often undermine attempts at effective evaluation.

Research has shown, for example, that the purpose of an appraisal can have a significant effect on individual ratings. When the review is to be used as the basis for decisions on salaries, promotions, or layoffs, ratings are generally much more lenient than when they will be used only for "career development."

One of the chief complaints about performance reviews is that they are unfair to employees. They are often based on personality traits or such vague qualities as reliability, initiative, or leadership, which are difficult to measure objectives. Many standardized, or "canned," appraisal forms use criteria that are not relevant to the particular job under review. Other standard forms provide a quick and superficial checklist that leaves no room for individual evaluation.

Another common criticism of performance reviews is that they put the employee in a defensive position. The usually one-sided discussion, dominated by the boss, creates a kind of parent-child relationship. Such reviews often turn into lectures or harangues, ending with the boss telling the subordinate that "it's been great to have this open exchange of views."

It may come as a surprise to employees who feel threatened by an upcoming review, but many of their bosses find them equally burdensome. They, too, grumble about vague criteria and the irrelevance of standardized review forms. They also complain that reviews require too much paperwork, don't leave room for individual judgment, and don't lead to improved performance.

Many managers feel they need more information in how to conduct reviews, but few companies offer such help. Robert Lefton, president of Psychological Associates, which conducts company training sessions, readily admits that the performance review is a tough job—"the equivalent of walking up to a person and saying, 'Here's what I think of your baby.' It requires knowing how to handle fear, anger, and a gamut of other emotions, which a lot of managers aren't comfortable with."

Over the past decade, the quest for more accurate appraisals has led to a greater emphasis on specifically job-related criteria, and on supposedly objective or quantifiable ratings. While this effort has produced numerous studies and a variety of new appraisal techniques, the field has hardly achieved scientific precision.

Still, employers have a lot of reasons for not abandoning the quest for greater precision, not the least of which is the need to defend against employee lawsuits charging discrimination or wrongful discharge. "Under the EEOC's Uniform Guidelines," says J. Peter Graves, a Redlands, California, consultant who specializes in this field, "a company must now be able to defend personnel decisions based on performance reviews by showing that those reviews are objective, job-related, and unbiased."

In many cases, they can't. In a number of recent decisions, courts have found the review process too subjective and unrelated to the specific job, and therefore potentially illegal if used in determining promotions, raises, or layoffs.

Until quite recently, most of the research on performance review focused on the rating format and the biasing effect of various nonperformance factors, such as race and sex. But numerous studies on the effects of sex have produced no consistent pattern of bias, although several studies have demonstrated that occupational sex stereotypes can affect performance appraisal. Women working at jobs that are generally perceived as typically or traditionally masculine tend to receive lower ratings than men of comparable ability in the same jobs.

Research on the effects of racial bias has produced a fairly consistent pattern: White supervisors do tend to give higher ratings to white than to black subordinates, while black supervisors tend to favor blacks. But while such bias may be statistically significant, it generally has only a slight effect on the actual ratings. The same holds true for age, education, and other personal or psychological characteristics of the raters and the rated.

One of the chief sources of error in performance reviews lies in the rating format itself. Appraisal forms vary markedly from one company to another, and even among similar divisions of the same com-

pany. At Allstate Insurance, for example, review forms for managerial employees are two pages, and are limited mainly to actual performance. At Reynolds Metals, they run seven pages, and also cover developmental factors, personal improvement plans, career interests, and a section for self-assessment.

By far the most widely used system is still the traditional numerical or graphic rating scale. For each trait or skill being evaluated, the scale may be marked simply by numbers, say from one to ten, or by such vague adjectives as "unsatisfactory," "below average," "average," "above average," "outstanding." (Xerox, for one, has a slightly more explicit version of the same set of categories: "unsatisfactory," "less-than-expected level of performance," "expected level," "consistently exceed expected level," and "exceptional performance.")

In a vain attempt to achieve more precise measurements, many companies have adopted numerical rating scales ranging from 10 up to 100. Research has shown, however, that five to nine categories seem to produce the most reliable ratings. Having fewer than five doesn't provide enough room for clear distinctions; having 10 or more brings no meaningful increase in accuracy.

The real problem with any system of graded ratings, according to Robert Guion, an industrial psychologist and editor of *The Journal of Applied Psychology*, is that "you get fairly valid ratings when you look mainly for the extremes of outstanding or very poor performance. But when you look closely at the middle or average range, the objectivity tends to disappear."

That middle range, of course, is where the great majority of ratings usually fall. The reason for this, according to many psychologists, is what they call "central tendency error" or leniency, a natural reluctance to assign low ratings to poor performers. (As one manager puts it, "You don't want to inflict pain.") Several studies have shown that when supervisors know that their subordinates will see the ratings, or that they will have to confront them with the ratings in a "feedback session," they tend to be more lenient. This may be perfectly human, but it doesn't lead to valid appraisals.

Some companies try to prevent central-tendency error, or unreasonable leniency, with "forced-distribution" systems. These set minimums or maximums for the percentage of ratings in each category: No more than 10 percent of one's subordinates, say, can be rated outstanding; no more than 50 percent, average. Many supervisors, however, object to the imposition of such arbitrary limits. Besides, who can say what the distribution curve for such ratings should really be?

Another common source of rating error is the so-called halo effect, by which the "good guy" gets consistently and perhaps undeservedly favorable ratings on all dimensions. The opposite effect can produce unfairly low ratings when there's "bad chemistry" between the subordinate and his supervisor. In both cases, the ratings are the result of general impressions of the employee as a person, rather than measures of specific abilities.

Because of growing dissatisfaction with traditional rating scales, and the search for more objective methods of appraisal, many companies have adopted some form of "behaviorally anchored" rating scales, known as BARS. To create a BARS scale, companies must first conduct a formal job analysis to determine what kinds of behavior constitute proper and improper performance for specific tasks or for "critical incidents" that typify each job. These behavioral descriptions are then used to define, or "anchor," the ratings on the scale. For example, for an item such as "perseverance," a BARS scale might offer choices ranging from "Keeps working on difficult tasks until job is completed" to "Likely to stop work on a hard job at the first sign of difficulty."

Many companies have adopted some form of behavioral-rating scale, even though they may not call it by that name. Some use an actual behavioral scale, while others insist on behavioral examples to back up numerical ratings. Such job analyses are often conducted by outside consultants, but many industrial psychologists feel that the participation in this process by the employees themselves, as well as their supervisors, leads to more realistic job descriptions. Besides, their very involvement in the process should make them more aware of what is considered good work behavior, and thus help them improve their performance.

Advocates of BARS—particularly the consultants who do a thriving business with it—claim that it's a great leap forward. Critics, however, point to several drawbacks. The lengthy job analyses and complex scale construction require a major investment of a company's time and money. A scale designed for use in one department may not be applicable to another. In fact, separate scales may be necessary for each job category within the same department, since the requirements for good performance may differ markedly.

Comparative studies have found that despite its behavioral specificity, and resulting increases in reliability and validity, the BARS method produces only minimal improvements in appraisals, often not enough to justify the major investments of time and money required. Besides, while BARS scales are suitable for jobs involving observable and easily measurable behavior, such as production or clerical work, they are less useful for managerial positions, in which performance cannot easily be reduced to specific or observable behavior. In such jobs, complex judgment may be more important than measurable behavior, and thus not easily reduced to items on a six-point scale.

For jobs of this type, many companies have adopted "management by objectives," or MBO, which focuses on results rather than behavior. As practiced today, MBO usually means that supervisors and their subordinates sit down at the beginning of each year, or every six months, and agree (often in writing) on specific goals. At the end of the set period, the subordinates' performance is evaluated in terms of how well they have met those objectives. MBO has become popular at the managerial level because it can be tailored to the requirements of individual jobs, and because subordinates learn in advance which specific goals will be used to measure their performance.

In practice, however, appraisals based on management by objectives can be just as open to claims of unfairness as other systems of performance review. One weakness is the difficulty of setting firm goals six months to a year in advance when performance may be vulnerable to unforeseen factors outside the employee's control: economic conditions, labor problems, price increases, and so on. Even more important, perhaps, is the fact that the method's very individuality makes it difficult to compare the performance of one subordinate with that of another—which is, after all, one ostensible purpose of performance review.

Dos and Don'ts for Reviewers

However imperfect, performance reviews will continue to be a necessary duty for most managers. Fortunately, along with all the criticism and research, there is also plenty of advice around on how to conduct them. Herewith, a brief, selective summary of tips given in the dozens of books and articles on performance review.

- Decide in advance on what you want to achieve: evaluation, criticism, training, coaching, morale-building, greater output. Don't let one goal interfere with another.

- Don't wait until the review itself to let your staff know what you expect from them. Let them know early on exactly what the job requires, what specific goals, standards, and deadlines you expect them to meet, and how you plan to evaluate and reward their performance. Then, when review time comes, there shouldn't be any unpleasant surprises or misunderstandings.

- For use at review time, keep a written log or journal throughout the year, in which you enter detailed accounts of individual performance—good or bad—on typical tasks during "critical incidents."

- The review should not be a one-way street. Let employees talk about their own performance and problems. See whether they have a realistic estimate of their abilities.

- Go over your written evaluation with each employee. Find out whether they feel that your ratings are fair. They don't have to agree with you 100 percent, but if they strongly disagree, they're likely to be less motivated to improve their performance. It's worth exploring the reasons for their disagreement.

- Keep the review focused on the particular individual's performance. Show that you care about him and his career. Otherwise, the employee will get the message that the review—and perhaps his performance—doesn't really matter.

- When critiquing an employee's performance, make sure you also do some stroking. Reinforce good habits with praise. Be constructive in your criticism. Don't simply tell someone that he's "not aggressive enough." Point out how he can improve, with specific examples.

- Whenever possible, try to base your judgments on observable behavior, not general opinions or impressions. Even when rating personality or character traits, try to recall specific examples of such traits in actual practice on the job.

- Critique the behavior, not the employee. Keep the discussion on a professional level, not personal. Avoid confrontation.

- Be fair, but don't be afraid to give honest criticism when necessary. Most employees don't want a meaningless pat on the back. They want to know where they stand, and how they can improve.

- Listen. Numerous surveys of employee attitudes reveal the feeling that "management doesn't care what we think." The review is your chance to get valuable feedback from your own subordinates about their jobs or company policy.

- Don't play the role of therapist during the review. If personal problems are affecting an employee's performance, be supportive, but be careful about getting involved. Suggest outside professional help is necessary.

- Explain how the goals you set, and thus the employee's performance, contribute to department or corporate objectives. In this way, the review can help build morale and loyalty.

- Don't wait until the next performance review to keep employees informed about how they are doing. Follow up on each review periodically with informal progress reports or "mini-reviews." Keep up a continuing exchange so that you'll both spot problems before they become serious.

- Use the occasion of a review to get an informal opinion of your own performance. Encourage your staff to tell you about any of your own habits that make their work unnecessarily difficult, or what changes you could make that would help them do their jobs better.

—B.R.

Studies, surveys and experiments at a number of U.S. companies have pointed up plenty of ways to improve performance reviews. Selig Danzig, a management consultant, had a few suggestions based on a recent study at General Electric. Danzig found that managers were much more satisfied with GE's appraisal process than were the employees being evaluated. The employees complained that they hadn't been allowed to express their own views about their performance reviews, and that personality factors had weighed too heavily in the ratings.

Danzig recommends that companies limit the number of functions that they expect the appraisal to achieve. Managers, he says, cannot effectively play the often conflicting roles of judge, critic, and coach. Another source of confusion, he feels, is the attempt to discuss salary and performance at the same review session. Employees tend to focus their attention on the money rather than their performance. To make the review process more interactive, Danzig suggests appraisal-training programs in which both managers and their subordinates take part.

Most companies include some training in performance review for new managers, but after that they are usually left on their own. A few companies, such as IBM, do offer periodic refresher training on review procedures for all managers.

Although some companies are trying to incorporate the latest cognitive research into their appraisal-training programs, Kevin Murphy, a psychologist at Colorado State University, feels that these mental processes are so complex and so unconscious that it will be exceedingly difficult to eliminate or even modify them in training. He recommends that companies instead train managers to become better observers. Managers, he says, should learn how to gather and record supporting evidence, how to discriminate between relevant and irrelevant information, how to do selective "work sampling" when direct observation is necessarily infrequent, and how to decide which aspects of job performance can really be measured.

According to psychologists who have studied the MBO method of appraisal, companies that have adopted some version of it should try to keep their systems as flexible as possible, to allow for individual difference in jobs. At University Research Corporation, a management-consulting firm in Chevy Chase, Maryland, MBO is based on an annual work plan that covers specific duties, targets, and goals. The plan is formulated jointly by employees and their supervisors, a process that often takes two or three sessions. Each person keeps a copy, and reviews it periodically throughout the year in case it needs revision. "We recognize that jobs change, tasks end, and performance expectations are often modified," says Gary Jonas, the president of University Research Corporation. "The system has to accommodate our dynamic and changing work environment."

Whatever the appraisal method, one of the major complaints from employees is favoritism in the ratings. At Intel Corporation, Andrew Grove takes personal pride in a review system that has built-in safeguards against such biases. Once a supervisor has filled out the review form on an employee, it goes to that supervisor's boss who must approve the evaluation. "Being one level removed," says Grove, "he can put the employee's performance in broader perspective. A second check takes place when the personnel representative assigned to each department must approve the reviews of each of its employees. If he detects signs of favoritism, he calls them to the attention of the supervisor's manager. As a final check, supervisors meet with their peers at review time and compare the ratings of all their subordinates. Any supervisor who has had contact with another's subordinate can question his evaluations."

Grove recognizes that Intel's system of checks and balances is not foolproof, and that it requires a good deal of time on the part of his managers. But if it increases everyone's confidence that they'll get a fair appraisal, and "if the effort expended contributes to an employee's performance," then Grove considers it a worthwhile investment.

Another way that companies are trying to promote fairness in performance appraisals is to solicit reviews from subordinates as well as from supervisors. When Levi Strauss had to lay off nearly 10 percent of its work force last year, it used such a process to help identify candidates for dismissal from a pool of 2,300 white-collar employees. Each was rated in comparison with colleagues by his immediate boss, two other superiors, two subordinates, and two employees from outside the department, and was permitted to see the evaluations.

Although this novel approach rarely led to any surprising reevaluations, it did help to assure both those who were laid off and those who were retained that the selections were made as fairly as possible. While she calls the new process "very useful," Susan Thompson, Levi Strauss's director of human resources, cautions that it was "only one component" in identifying layoff candidates, and that it has not been incorporated into the company's regular system of performance review.

Despite all the recent research and experiments with different types of performance reviews, there is still considerable dispute between researchers and managers on how to conduct them. David DeVries, a management psychologist at the Center for Creative Leadership in Greensboro, North Carolina, has a foot in both camps. "There's no one system that works for every company," he tells the 100 or so executives who come to the center each year for his one-week seminar on performance appraisal. "What we try to do here is show what the options are, and how the companies' own managers can generally design a system more appropriate for them.

"Because everyone knows that most performance reviews aren't very good, most companies are always revising their appraisal forms or their entire systems, hoping to solve the problem," says DeVries. "That's good for the management consultants, but for the managers who have to do the reviews, it's a real pain in the ass."

DeVries cautions against dropping such traits as integrity, initiative, optimism, energy, and intelligence just because they are highly subjective, and therefore psychometrically suspect. "In business," DeVries points out, "those traits are very important, subjective or not. Executives make personnel decisions based on them all the time. If they do, then those traits should be evaluated, and we researchers can't afford to ignore them.

"There's an inherent level of subjectivity in any appraisal system. You can try to manage it, but you can't make it go away. This does not mean that companies should simply ignore performance appraisal, or let their managers do what they want. It's important to reward your top performers, and to make it clear to the others why they're being rewarded. And it's equally important to distinguish the poor performers. If you don't, it demoralizes those who are really trying hard.

"A good performance-appraisal system can help managers do this, but it must be taken seriously by the managers, by the employees, and by the company. It must be the basis for deciding who gets ahead and who doesn't."

Berkeley Rice is a journalist specializing in management. His article is based on one that appeared recently in Psychology Today.

Chutes and Ladders: Growing the General Manager

by Thomas V. Bonoma and Joseph C. Lawler

How do you make a junior manager into a competent middle manager? And how do you turn that competent middle manager into a top-echelon leader? Recent discussions of corporate leadership have tended to focus on issues like global vision and technological innovativeness. These are essential—but so are such timeless qualities as sensitivity, credibility, confidence, and the capacity to think analogically. Many firms fail to nurture these qualities in tomorrow's leaders. This failure can be remedied, according to the authors, by paying close attention to junior managers' assignment paths. They offer a systematic review of what qualities are essential for "up and comers," what qualities are essential for senior-level managers, and how assignment routing can best be used to develop those qualities.

Perhaps the most shopworn advice ever offered to top managers is this: "Choose your people wisely; then manage them well." Unfortunately, the choosing and the managing are often themselves the problem. Guiding managers and potential leaders on a career path often resembles the child's game of "Chutes and Ladders"; they are moved up, down, and around on the basis of organizational need or political convenience—*not* on the basis of their own developmental needs. Not surprisingly, when management training and development is governed

arbitrarily, or worse, left ungoverned, candidates often fail to realize their potential.[1]

This situation is a cause for real concern. By all accounts, the top manager's job is becoming more difficult. Not only are there the age-old problems of running the business, setting strategy, and improving performance. In addition, there is a host of new challenges, ranging from retaining or regaining basic competitiveness, improving the ability to execute strategic initiatives, and responding to the demands of a global marketplace.

What triggered our attention to assignment paths was a recurring observation that most CEOs are regularly forced off the grand road of strategy for forays into the brush to fight tactical fires not caught in time by subordinates. No CEO is stronger than the organization's weakest manager, and it is axiomatic among the top executives we know that 80 percent of their time is spent on problems created by 20% of the people under them. We call these time-consuming subordinates "weak links," not because of any personal weaknesses they may have, but rather because the problems they create or cannot solve pull the CEO away from visionary and strategic concerns.

Is there a way to better select, train, motivate, and find assignment paths for subordinates? A way that will create executives able to run significant portions of the business, free up the CEO for strategic tasks, and build a stable of future leaders? We think there is.[2] The theory is simple. Picking the right people and fostering their development in the right way makes for better subordinates. Here "development" means using jobs and task assignments to test and strengthen junior managers' weaknesses and to prepare the best of them to run the company.

Let us look first at what senior managers must do to find the subordinates best able to replace them. In this examination, we will develop two "screens" managers can use; one differentiates "up-and-comers" from the remainder of the managerial pack, and the other identifies general management candidates among the pool of up-and-comers. Finally, we will present developmental assignment paths that can help minimize weak links in the general management structure.

How Top Managers Get Made

Figure 1 presents normal paths of progression toward the top manager's job.[3] It also shows the qualities that up-and-comers and general managers need to have. We would like to emphasize five points related to this diagram.

- *The managerial jobs triangle is not symmetrical.* Line jobs that involve customers and products or services on the low end, business unit responsibilities in the middle, and multiple business responsibilities on the upper end are a more direct path to leadership strengths than are staff jobs. Staff jobs are essential, however, both to the organization and to some aspects of becoming a general manager.

Line jobs may be the most direct path to the CEO office, but staff jobs have earned many managers a second look. Indeed, Sears and Roebuck, which was long thought to have the best managers in retailing, regularly sent potential senior managers zigzagging from headquarters to the field to headquarters and back again. There is much that is appealing in this method, though we are more of the apprenticeship school of thought—if you want to make a shoemaker, it is a good idea to give the kid some leather, nails, and an anvil.

- *The CEO's most important tasks involving junior managers are selecting, training, motivating, and assigning them to various jobs.* Most training and motivating done by senior management revolves around assignment patterns, because senior managers do not have the political latitude, time, or inclination to select managers from outside more than occasionally. Company cultures more often than not value internal promotion, not external hiring; so, by

necessity, most development must be done with already-selected managers.

Compensation and training are equally constrained. Compensation in most organizations is restricted to certain well-worn, and not necessarily motivational, pathways that represent a kind of "organizational average" for all the firm's managers. Regarding training, it is our experience that most relevant training done by managers of managers is done on the job.

Since selection, compensation, and training are often more or less fixed for development purposes, most of the junior management development job revolves around the crucial notion of assignment patterns. Good assignment paths will reinforce a manager's strengths, remove weaknesses, and produce a better senior management candidate. Bad paths produce managers with serious, and sometimes firm-threatening, shortcomings that often don't appear until the incumbent has a senior job where the pressure is intense and the costs of failure are high.[4]

Advice from academic experts, compensation consultants, and headhunters tends to center on the variables of selection, motivation, and training. The CEO who listens closely can become an expert in picking people from the outside, designing incentive compensation schemes, or spending millions on training seminars, without ever considering the most critical variable of all, who gets what job with what purpose.

- *Senior management can employ two different "screens" for the pool of managerial candidates. The first screen distinguishes the up-and-comers from the remainder of the management pack.* These up-and-comers are the candidates that middle and senior managers believe contain their replacements.

The up-and-comers screen is applied to lower- and middle-level managers. It is the barrier between functional expertise and general management training. It consists of four separate traits that determine upper-middle managerial potential.

- *After the first screen has been applied, a general management screen can be used on the remaining candidates.* This screen measures distinctly different characteristics. While the up-and-comers screen looks for management po-

Figure 1
What Top Managers Do Developmentally

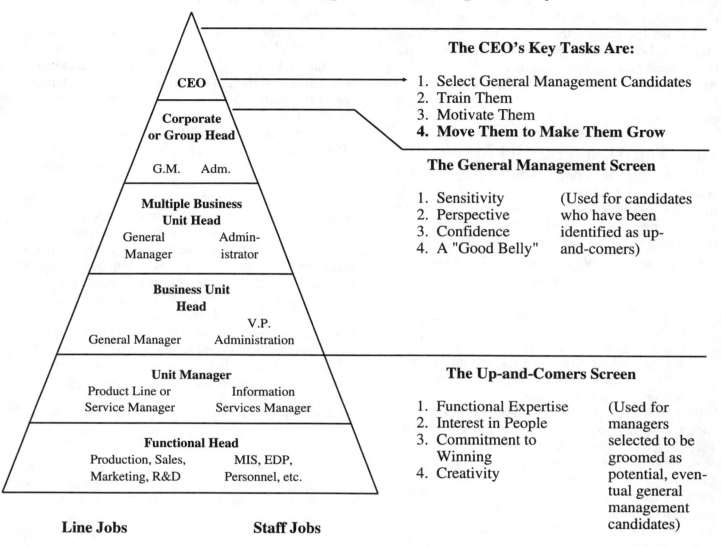

The CEO's Key Tasks Are:

1. Select General Management Candidates
2. Train Them
3. Motivate Them
4. **Move Them to Make Them Grow**

The General Management Screen

1. Sensitivity   (Used for candidates
2. Perspective   who have been
3. Confidence   identified as up-
4. A "Good Belly"   and-comers)

The Up-and-Comers Screen

1. Functional Expertise   (Used for
2. Interest in People   managers
3. Commitment to   selected to be
    Winning   groomed as
4. Creativity   potential, even-
    tual general
    management
    candidates)

tential, the general management screen looks for leadership ability.

The final point to be learned from Figure 1 is this.

* *The sequence, flow, and strategic use of job assignments develops or retards the very qualities that senior management is seeking.* Fortuitous or well-thought-through assignments let managers develop as far as their abilities will take them. Inopportune or thoughtless assignments do the reverse; they retard or end development. It is essential to

learn to make such assignments in a useful way and to identify the traits needed if senior managers are to better the firm in the next generation.

The Up-and-Comers Screen

It is a rare day when a savior appears from outside who can make up for all the internal development that has not been done in a company. So management's first job is to identify junior managers who have real potential. In our experience, the "perfect" candidate has four qualities: functional expertise, interest in others, commitment to winning, and creativity (see Figure 2).[5]

Functional Expertise

Whether because of training, experience, character, or all three, some managers can be called functional experts early in their careers, and some never achieve this status. It is our experience that the manager without functional expertise cannot and will not be developed further by senior management. In a sense this pattern is paradoxical, since the journey toward general management consists of becoming less of a specific expert. But those who are chosen for general management development nearly always have a low-level functional expertise.

The history of one top manager is illustrative. An expert woodworker who had graduated from Rhode Island School of Design started his own woodworking shop. After a few years of slow growth and no benefits, he joined a small business as a supervisor in the wood shop. He challenged the organization to change its woodworking shop practices, and soon gained management confidence because of his technical skills and creative problem solving in this "backwater" area. This attention allowed him to get involved in new product design and in marketing.

In just three years he was named president of this same small firm. After spending a few years developing his general management skills, he left to join a West Coast retailer as president; he now spearheads one of the most exciting, fastest-growing retail concepts in the country.

The specific business area of functional expertise is irrelevant: accounting, sales, production, and finance are all suitable, though one firm's culture may make accountants especially visible to middle and upper management, while in another the marketers are on a "fast track."

Sometimes, but only rarely, this credibility can be attained from formal education. The CPA degree is one that earns respect for functional competence, as do certain engineering degrees. According to most executives, the MBA degree does not. But even narrow academic expertise can lead to larger opportunity under the right circumstances. One CPA we know started in the back room on the books; his performance there led to assignments in accounting, finance, and strategic planning. Now he is head of manufacturing. His own abilities gradually increased his credibility, but the first chance came from functional soundness.

Junior managers in many corporations do not get the experience they need to prepare them for the

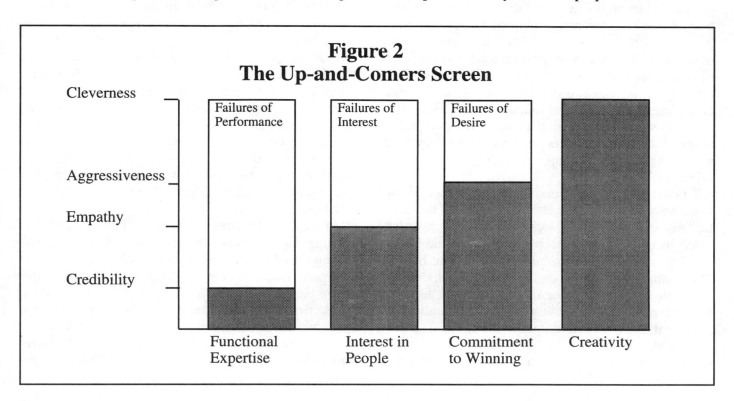

Figure 2
The Up-and-Comers Screen

next rungs on the ladder. Sometimes this happens because a candidate seeks too much variety from too little experience. More often, candidates are victimized by senior managers who either value rapid movement over sound functional expertise or cave in to demands from young Turks for rapid advancement. Juniors are often their own worst enemies, mistaking the first five years of a career for the career itself, and forgetting that rapidity at some stages may stall a career later on. Those who have paid their dues gaining functional expertise may find it difficult to respect those who have not. When general managers succumb to pressures from fast-track juniors, they risk the juniors' careers and the firm's future. A successful career in general management is analogous to climbing a ladder—skipped rungs almost always create a safety hazard for the whole crew.

When junior managers fail to gain sufficient, concentrated functional expertise to be credible, we call these "failures of performance." The usual lot of such managers is a short-circuited career.

Interest in People

Some managers realize that successful management has more to do with governing the efforts of others than it has to do with tasks, policies, or programs. Other promising candidates never make this leap, either because assignment patterns keep them in jobs where success depends on their own efforts or because they are simply more interested in tasks than in individuals. Managers who do not shift their primary focus from tasks to people cannot become candidates for the general management ranks. They learn at some point that they can't do everything alone. The best managers we know are savvy with numbers *and* with people. Neither skill can be faked for long.

When managers are unable to make this transition, we speak of "failures of interest." The functionally expert manager who remains more interested in tasks than in people will in all likelihood wind up as the head of a business function, but not of a business. Where he or she *is* promoted, disaster can follow, as one major retailer recently learned. Having promoted a genius-level merchandiser to president, the firm found itself with millions of dollars in shrinkage because the president was more occupied with merchandising than with managing

all his people, including the "lowly" store managers.

Commitment to Winning

The third requirement to clear the up-and-comers screen is a commitment to winning. Much has been said recently about management's overcompetitive ethic, its "go for the throat" way of doing business. In our view, most firms have exactly the opposite problem. Many managers (perhaps *most* managers) simply do not have a competitive will to win. They are either grateful for the status quo, or they are so busy trying to gain political leverage that they mistake looking good for winning.

If American competitiveness is down, the main reason is that our junior managers' commitment to win in the marketplace is also down. Their functional expertise is insufficient. In addition, they bring too little desire and "fire in the belly" to the office. They concern themselves with office politics rather than doing a great job, and fail, when they do, because they did not want to win badly enough to reduce the staff by 30 percent, the expenditures by 35 percent, and the market prices by 50 percent in order to gain a dominant share.

Overcompliance is often encouraged and even demanded by superiors. This is always the case when mistakes are not tolerated by superiors, for a junior who is not making mistakes is not doing enough. One director of R&D we know was concerned about the possibility of a serious static charge in bottles of cleaning fluid, even though a top management directive had said that "everything was all right." He graphically demonstrated it was *not* all right by taking his boss to the supermarket and opening two cases of the product. The first forty-one bottles did nothing—but the forty-second knocked him, and the vice president, into the opposing aisle of bleach! The filling procedures were changed.

In many companies we have worked with, middle management is now akin to civil service employment—predictable, safe, and completely unchallenging. This situation occurs partly because people have been taught that management is a ticket to limos, first class travel, and unscrutinized costs, but in larger part because of assignment patterns chosen by the seniors and *their* lack of commitment to winning. Where failures of desire stem from poor assignment choices, managers don't hone their abilities in a way that will give them the confidence to take on large, businesswide challenges in the future. Where the failures come from character, all is lost for this candidate.

Creativity

The final, most sought after, and rarest criterion for membership in the up-and-comers group is creativity. Many candidates have functional expertise; quite a lot have shifted their focus from tasks to people; and a good number are committed to winning. But only a few work creatively. In some cases, this constitutes a character flaw. In most cases, however, it is the result of what candidates have been exposed to. In many corporations, creativity is not found because it is not rewarded.

At a staff meeting one of us attended recently, the junior managers in each of the firm's five key functions were asked to make presentations on "critical flaws in the business"—a risky but innovative assignment. One after the other, four juniors rose to suggest there *were* no flaws in production, sales, marketing, or R&D. The fifth person, a bookish and shy finance manager, tentatively suggested that perhaps accounts receivable could be improved if, instead of waiting sixty days for the formal computer report, management was willing to call known delinquent accounts on the phone. He thought this might save the firm several hundred thousand dollars annually. The man's boss reacted as if someone had assaulted his daughter—he expressed outrage, pain, and denial, and then he summarily dismissed the suggestion.

One of us has written at length on the relationship of management skills and the firm's structures to eliciting good marketing performance.[6] Bonoma's study of good marketing practices suggested clearly that the culprit in many marketing failures was the structures that routinized and semiautomated the marketing job. These structures were often inappropriate to the problem or the environment facing the firm. The accomplices to these marketing failures were the managers themselves, who should have been sufficiently creative to go around the systems and get the job done despite systemic shortfalls.

Regardless of the business function, where systems and structures replace creativity, "formula" solutions will work at best for only some problems,

and then only some of the time. Managers who circumvent structural shortfalls using creative interventions improve both their own skills and the firm's practices. They are our most creative general management candidates, though they sometimes live at the border of what their seniors think is acceptable practice. Managers who blindly follow structural rules so that they can become "one of the pack" often get their wish: they *become* one of the pack. We call these failed candidates "failures of familiarity," for they have elected the familiar instead of seeking the creative.

Top managers clearly dislike end runs, nonconformists, and people who refuse to play by the rules. But most of these same top managers dislike poor results even more than they dislike rule breakers. One marketing manager overspent his budget on a national dealer organization meeting by 25 percent; the overrun was not pre-approved by his superiors. He had done what he felt was necessary to make the meeting a success. Orders booked at the meeting exceeded those booked in previous years by 50 percent. This manager walked a fine line, but the results were so good he was praised rather than punished for his execution.

Ideal up-and-comers, then, have developed four key traits. First, they have functional expertise in one area. Second, they have learned how to work with, motivate, and lead others. Third, they are committed to winning. And finally, they are willing to abandon conformity and embrace the dangerous but rewarding world of creativity.

Even if these characteristics are well developed, the junior manager has only bought a ticket to the show, not a seat in the front row. From the pool of up-and-comers, top management must weed out all those who cannot clear a second, tougher set of hurdles. We call this the general management screen.

The General Management Screen

Figure 3 shows the general management screen. Across the bottom are the four characteristics needed to advance to the top of the organization: sensitivity, perspective, confidence, and a "good belly." Across the side are the skills these traits provide: empathy, analogical wisdom, a bias to act, and the right instincts. The boxes contain descriptions of how a candidate may fall short of developing these key characteristics and skills. We look at each.

Sensitivity

The up-and-comer is required to translate an interest in people into genuine *sensitivity* to others. Where this is successful, it breeds empathy, or "the capacity for participation in another's feelings and ideas." Where it is not successful, we have a failure to develop empathy, and probably a candidate who should not get to the middle, much less the top, management ranks.

The dictionary definition of empathy quoted above is remarkably complete. Good general managers are able to *participate* in how another might feel or think; this capacity allows them to get subordinates to work for them, suppliers to deal with them, and customers to critique their products in ways other managers cannot. Note that participating in how another might think or feel is not the same thing as *capitulating to* or even *endorsing* another's feelings or ideas. Empathy simply means the capacity to participate in the processes that got the person from point A to point B, no matter how unbelievable, disagreeable, or powerfully wrong B might seem to be.

We are both friends with the president of a $500-million consumer products business who has these skills; they seem to rub off on the people he associates with. We have seen many aggressive marketing people go to work for this man; within a short period of time, they are emulating his behavior. His style is almost a cliché—he is a good listener; he makes eye contact when people talk with him; and he encourages them in their ideas more often than not. In short, he truly seems to care. Good subordinates get powerfully excited working for someone who cares about their careers.

We consider sensitivity to others, and the empathy it breeds, as the starting point for managerial wisdom. Without it, no amount of perspective will allow the candidate to learn the lessons needed to run a company. But it is only the starting point, for sensitivity *without* perspective breeds poor general management candidates who can empathize with their charges, but who do not have enough experience to solve problems.

Perspective

Managers gain *perspective* when they have had enough assignments with enough different people in enough diverse settings to be not only empathetic, but what we call "analogically wise"—wise in both familiar and unfamiliar situations. Our CEO friend's credibility is not based just on his ability to listen and empathize. It is also based on his ability

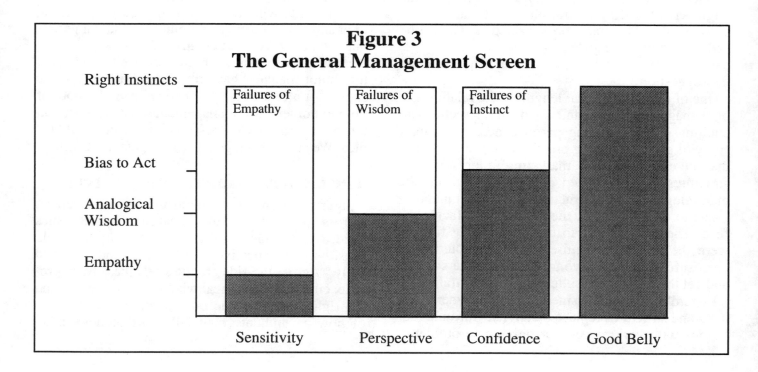

Figure 3
The General Management Screen

274

to draw on past experience to ask the kinds of questions that spark insight in subordinates. Good managers do this all the time.

Wisdom comes from sensitivity, which is the ability to participate in what you're living, and from perspective, which is having enough life experiences that you can draw on a storehouse of situations from which generalizations can be made. Perspective without sensitivity is useless, for the insensitive general management candidate is unable to learn, no matter how diverse the job assignments may be. Sensitivity without perspective is not quite as useless. While it is true that the candidate will be unable to create a storehouse of experience analogies, what the candidate *does* know may be enough for a senior staff or line position, where skills can be focused on similar problems. Perspective without sensitivity, though, creates broad-ranging weak links.[7]

Nowhere is enforced perspective development more evident than in case learning, which is the process of confronting able individuals with a massive number of business problems over a two-year period as they pursue their MBAs. One of us is the victim of this process as practiced at the Harvard Business School; the other has been the victimizer of almost 2,000 students at the same institution. While neither of us would contend that the process of analyzing cases is as valuable as *living* them, we do believe that confronting three business problems a night for two years gives students a remarkable business foundation. Case analysis builds perspective, develops the habit of searching for alternative solutions, and provides an inventory of problems on which to base the search. But until students or strategic planners must implement recommendations, they will not develop the sensitivity to an organization that general managers need.

For most managers, of course, perspective and analogical wisdom come not from simulations but from the diversity and developmental appropriateness of their job assignments. Each business problem is a case study with its own peculiarities. The perspective needed to join the top management team develops with each new assignment—first to manage a plant where stopped up toilets and materials waste are key problems, then to do a staff job where analytical skills are paramount, and then to

run a small division where the candidate must be a *general* manager.

Whether in simulation or actual experience, the principle is the same—perspective develops because a candidate is dumped in enough situations to be able to generalize when confronted with a new problem. It is wisdom gained from analogy, and it is a key currency of the firm's top managers.

Some candidates will learn from their assignments, and some will not. But some assignments *permit* learning to occur, and many other assignment paths are too slow; they are just holding patterns for the manager in question. This person cannot do as well as the manager whose superiors put some thought into developmental challenges. Candidates who have not developed perspective, but who rise in the organization anyway—"failures of wisdom"—are likely to be weak links who cause, rather than solve, problems for top managers.

Confidence

The third important characteristic for tomorrow's top managers is *confidence,* expressed in the "bias toward action" that Tom Peters writes about.[8] Confidence is a justified reliance on one's own judgments, even when these are not confirmable by current information. To the manager pondering a major decision, only so many studies and discussions are useful. Eventually, he or she must decide to do the thing or not. Those who are able to move ahead on the basis of their own experience, judgment, and beliefs have confidence; those who are paralyzed by the analysis do not.

The president of a small business we know was faced with a variety of strategic choices. What he chose was probably less important than choosing *something,* and doing it well. Last time we talked to him, he was still evaluating his alternatives, and losing his shirt. He was simply not sure how to pick the best direction, so he decided to keep looking. What was lacking was not information, but the "bias toward action" that comes from confidence.

The president of another small business was closing in on the end of the fiscal year, and feared he might fall short of a profit commitment to his parent firm. The business had never done a special promotion before, but this officer reviewed his inventory position, collected the names of customers who were most likely to buy a slow-moving line, discounted the line 10 percent, and had a mailing out within a week. He made that profit commitment, reduced inventories, and built customer loyalty as well.

It is possible, of course, to be excessively confident yet lack sensitivity or perspective. People like this are dangerous, for they know no fear, but they have no basis for making the right decisions. However, unlike lack of confidence, excessive confidence is usually treatable: if one or two profound and visible mistakes occur and the candidate survives them, ordinarily the problem is solved.

A "Good Belly"

The final, most important characteristic for would-be top managers is what we call a *good belly*, or good instincts. It is a "soft" characteristic that undoubtedly results from experience, but is not strictly definable as the result of experience. Without it, all the sensitivity, perspective, and confidence in the world will come to naught. With it, large gaps in perspective can be patched up, and confidence is a great deal easier to come by.

Belly is the willingness to trust gut judgment when there is little else to inform decisions. Someone with a good belly and confidence will trust his or her own judgment even in the face of evidence pointing another way.

The CEO of a medium-sized firm asked one of his division heads to take a look at a potential acquisition. The homework was done carefully and included numerous financial, store audit, and market-based analyses. The division head concluded that it was inappropriate to buy the firm in question. The CEO did the same analysis, but included one other piece of information; he talked directly with the owners. The business was bought despite the other analyses, because the CEO's instinct told him the owners would fit in well and would make the concept work. The new division is now one of the most profitable in the corporation. *That's* belly.

The executive vice president of one of the largest and fastest-growing mail order companies in the U.S. also has good instincts. It is a product-driven business in the apparel and hard-goods segments. The company's success comes from picking new products with uncanny accuracy and from marketing expertise that is second to none in the industry.

But, as anybody in the fashion or toy business can tell you, there is just no way to know what is going to sell next season. As this manager said to us, "You just have to *feel* it." Monitoring trends, analyzing statistics, knowing the customer—all of this helps, but having a feel for the business is even more important.

The very best general management candidates have a recurrent, strong sense of what to do and which way to go. They are not right *all* the time, but as long as they are right much of the time, they will do well.

Assignments for Growth

Once top management has found its up-and-comers, the critical task is to develop the four general management characteristics in the shortest time possible. The primary means to this end is the use of assignment paths. Careful diagnosis of the missing elements in the up-and-comer under consideration will suggest assignment parameters. Figure 4 shows ways to address promising candidates' weak points.

Building Sensitivity

The insensitive executive's preconceptions and biases need to be challenged. Lack of sensitivity is so fundamental that it will completely short circuit a career if it is not remedied once and for all. Managers can often learn sensitivity by being confronted in the new job with different kinds of people and realities. For the executive suffering a mild form of the disease, a "perspective" treatment, like an international assignment or a functional reversal, may do a world of good. Putting a staff person on the production line as a shift supervisor can work marvels; so can putting a financial person in a sales branch for six months. Consumer package goods companies regularly train their assistant product managers by requiring them to spend six months selling in the field. There is nothing quite like seeing a buyer react to a sales program conceived by a marketing desk-jockey for sobering up recruits. This sort of "reality dosing" should be a regular part of all managerial work.

However, such short-term moves will not work if the candidate is more than mildly insensitive. When the problem is severe, a more radical assignment path may be in order. Perhaps if a rival was pro-

Figure 4
Eliminating Weak Links through Assignment Paths

	Challenges	Examples	Supervision	Styles	Frequency/Next Moves
"Belly"	Unpredictable, unanalyzable problems and tasks.	• New venture in un-related business • Touchy labor relations • Chancy turnaround • Potential "kill" decision	• Hands-off; at a dis-tance; act, then report. • Low process feedback, but high outcome feedback.	Socratic	Another one. 2–5 years
Confi-dence **Candidate Lacks...**	Problems and tasks where anxieties can be worked out through the expen-diture of effort, leading to heightened pre-dictability.	• Produce extension in known market • Organization/cost reduction • Turnaround of a unit that has been grossly mismanaged (easy to fix)	• Suggestions; moder-ately high input if sought. • Low process feed-back, but high out-come feedback at very frequent intervals.	Counseling	Another until candidate is convinced; then assign for "belly." 1–3 years
Perspec-tive	Highly diverse, unfamiliar tasks and challenges where candidate has absolutely no experience.	• Cultural reversal (international assignment) • Functional reversal (R&D to production or sales) • Skills reversal (en-gineering to sales) • Perspective reversal (line-staff)	• Challenging, counseling. • High process feedback, low outcome feedback.	Mentoring	Rapid repe-tition of these assignments at this level; then test for confi-dence. 6–18 months
Sensitivity	Challenges that violate precon-ceptions and biases. Confrontations with different kinds of people and realities.	• Any of the above, plus • Role reversal (promotion of rival) • Failure experience	• Challenging, confrontational. • High process feedback, high outcome feedback.	Directive	Slow repetition of assignments at this level; then test for perspective. 3–12 months

moted and became the insensitive manager's super-visor—or if the manager was allowed to experience a powerful but not career-threatening failure that was attributable to his inability to work well with others—then radical changes would occur. While these recommendations would not win many "good personnel" awards, they can be medicines of last re-sort for an otherwise talented up-and-comer who simply will not be sensitive to others.

A highly insensitive manager needs challenging, confrontational feedback. Having a supervisor closely monitor the manager's behavior, down to the style of a memorandum or the conduct of a staff meeting, is probably useful. Only the most direct intervention will have a chance of success, for the disease makes it hard for the person to hear *any* feedback constructively. We have a sense that fail-ures of sensitivity are prone to quick wins or quick losses; a rapid series of assignments of the sort described here every three to twelve months should do the job. Then perspective can be tested in the next assignment.

Building Perspective

The candidate considered lacking in perspective needs assignment treatment similar to the one described above. However, for this weak link, the goal is not shock treatment but a more gentle assignment diversity, provided over a longer period of time. The best approach is to throw candidates into various geographic and functional areas where they have no experience. The managerial style should again be challenging, but oriented toward counseling rather than confrontation.

The problem with bright, aggressive, high-potential management candidates is that they usually don't know what they don't know. A mentor can help the candidate integrate current experiences with background ones. More rapid assignment changes (six to eighteen months) are especially useful, since the goal is to develop breadth, not depth. One pattern we have seen work well is a series of "special project" assignments, where the candidate is sent now to R&D, now to a foreign subsidiary, to help straighten out problems.

Building Confidence

For the manager lacking in confidence, the best approach is to assign problems and tasks in which anxieties can be worked out through effort, and in which the expenditure of that effort leads to predictability. There are many such jobs in the managerial ranks, though they are not often used developmentally. For instance, putting a highly able up-and-comer with confidence issues in charge of a product extension in a known market, or of an organizational cost reduction, is the kind of assignment in which high effort frequently leads to success. The anxiety level of the candidate will make the expenditure of this effort easy; as long as the problem is correctable and shows the results of work, the candidate will shine.

Unfortunately, the increasingly matrixed structures of corporations in the 1970s and 1980s make it harder for senior managers to find project or product work in which the growing executive can manage a small piece of the business without endangering the whole. Where people and results are interdependent, it is difficult to give developmental assignments that allow for individual initiative and a chance to succeed in a clear-cut way. As one vice president of a major office products manufacturer put the matter to us:

> Our problem is that we have no small businesses or stand-alone entities in this $10 billion company. The consequence is that our managers are never developed to be general managers; only the president has profit- and loss responsibility, so there is no opportunity to practice. When someone gets promoted into the top management ranks, he or she has a lot to learn very quickly about running a business. Some make it; some don't.

The developmental challenge is to build *job-related* confidence, not self-confidence. For all the rigidity imposed on their most able managers, the consumer package goods companies develop job-specific confidence very well with their product management systems. Becoming first an assistant, then an associate, then a product manager of a small brand precedes reclimbing the ladder all over again on a larger brand. The assignment path carefully ingrains "learning how to learn," in Harry Harlow's famous phrase. The challenge for the recently promoted is not how to learn about a new segment, but rather how to apply what is generalizable from the last job to the next one. The confidence-building process is subtle, but important.

The developmental risk is mistaking self-confidence for job-related confidence. The manager who has done well on previous tasks often develops tremendous self-confidence. If much of that confidence is based on the benefits of a structured environment, where solid ruts make performance easy, promotion to a less structured task can be disastrous. The junior is convinced (and convincing) about his or her ability to handle the new tasks—and unable to acknowledge difficulty when it arises.

The best management style for this concern is a pure counseling one, where the supervisor serves largely as a nondirective question-asker and suggestion-giver. Input is given if sought, but low process feedback ("What should I do?") is given candidates in order to make them develop these assessment skills on their own. While process feedback ought to be low, outcome feedback ("How am I doing?") should be high. The problem is that these candidates do not yet believe in themselves *in the job context;* this lack of confidence is best rectified by repetitive confirmation that effort and judgment lead to success. As Figure 4 shows, a somewhat slower path (one to three years) is in order with these assignments; the assignment should be repeated at slightly broader levels until the candidate no longer has confidence problems.

Building Good Instincts

Assignment paths to develop "belly" are undoubtedly the hardest for senior management to come up with—yet they do exist. These jobs should have unpredictable parameters and unanalyzable problems, where the decision is going to rest on gut judgment. These issues need not be of firm-threatening magnitude; many smaller-sized issues of this nature face the firm every day. Figure 4 shows some examples; others might include handling a tricky decision on firing a low-level subordinate, chairing a task force to see which of two facilities that need to be integrated moves, or handling a small product development venture in an unformed market.

Product or project management builds the judgment and confidence that lead to a good belly. Goals are carefully defined, a timetable is set, and then the manager is left alone. He or she quickly learns to call the shots and work without a net. The supervisory net is there, though; a mentor should test assumptions, probe rationales, and ensure that progress is occurring.

The supervision for this weak link should be at arm's length; this forces the candidate to develop and then rely on his or her own judgment. Supervision should be Socratic—that is, illuminating questions may be posed, but the problem should always be turned back to the junior manager. Assignments should last from two to five years, because the relevant instincts take time to develop.

Eliminating Weak Links

The key tool top managers have for forging stronger subordinates is how these subordinates are assigned to jobs. Often assignments are made because of current openings, need, or happenstance, rather than with any attention to the developmental path that might best help an up-and-comer. If top

managers spend most of their time fighting fires and managing around weak links, they should remember that they themselves forged the chain that keeps breaking. Where there are too many weak links, we can be sure that not enough time is spent on strategy, and also that top management has not really used the most powerful tool there is for developing the next generation of senior managers...assignment paths.

References

1 There is a burgeoning literature on careers, career management, and even a little work on assignment pathing that began to appear in the organizational behavior discipline in the late 1970s and early 1980s, though the academic reader will be surprised to learn that "career" does not appear in the index of the *Handbook of Industrial and Organizational Psychology* (Chicago: Rand-McNally, 1976).
Much earlier work left the implications of career pathing to be inferred from leader behavior. For instance, see R.L. Katz, "Skills of an Effective Administrator," *Harvard Business Review,* September-October 1974, pp. 90–102; or R.J. House, "A Path Goal Theory of Leader Effectiveness," *Administrative Science Quarterly* 16 (1971): 321–329.
Later work on this topic does address career systems and even career stages directly, but seldom assignment pathing. See, for example:
J. A. Sonnenfeld and M.A. Pieperl, "Staffing Policy as a Strategic Response: A Typology of Career Systems," *Academy of Management Journal* 13 (1988): 588–600;
J.A. Sonnenfeld, *Managing Career Systems* (Homewood, IL: Richard D. Irwin, 1984); or
E.H. Schein, *Career Dynamics: Matching Individual and Organizational Needs* (Reading, MA: Addison-Wesley, 1978).

2 The thoughtful manager will want to read Katz's "Skills of an Effective Administrator" (see reference 1), where he argues that human, conceptual, and technical skills are the key ingredients of a successful leader. Originally Katz argued that all these skills were trainable. When his article was reprinted in 1974, he said he was no longer sure that basic conceptual horsepower could be developed on the job; perhaps it was something that "should perhaps be viewed as an innate ability" (p. 101). This is remarkably similar to our own understanding of what raw materials need to be brought to the job.

3 See also Schein's three-dimensional model of organizations. E.H. Schein, "The Individual, the Organization, and the Career: A Conceptual Scheme," *Journal of Applied Behavioral Science* 7 (1971): 40. Schein uses a more sophisticated model than ours that covers many business

subfunctions, like production and marketing, as growth paths toward top management; he argues that inclusion in the centrality of business issues and rank are two dimensions on which job functions and managerial development can be cut.

4 See: D.T. Hall, *Careers in Organizations* (Pacific Palisades: Goodyear Press, 1976); or D.T. Hall and Associates, *Career Development in Organizations* (San Francisco: Jossey-Bass, 1986).

5 Frankly, we are not sure in what measure the candidate must bring these traits, and to what degree they can be "brought out" by management experiences. Certainly, the truth is some mixture of the two, but we do not hope to settle the nature-nurture controversy here. Katz (1974) identifies three out of four skills as key ones for the effective administrator. When he originally wrote (1955),

perhaps commitment to winning was not at issue. It is now.

6 T.V. Bonoma, "Marketing Subversives," *Harvard Business Review,* November-December 1986, pp. 113-118.

7 The consulting business tends to breed great perspective but little sensitivity. Consultants are valuable because their breadth of experience can be useful in analyzing situations and making action recommendations, but they rarely consider the consequences of dealing with the individuals who will be affected by recommendations.

8 T.J. Peters, *Thriving on Chaos* (New York: Alfred A. Knopf, 1987).

Great Leaps in Career Development

by Morgan W. McCall Jr., Michael M. Lombardo, and Ann M. Morrison

He watched from the helicopter door as laborers clutching chain saws were lowered into the jungle below. For several days the snarl of the saws rose up from the canopy, until at last a landing area large enough to accommodate a helicopter had been cleared. This constituted the ground breaking for a new plant on the Amazon. It was indicative of difficulties to come.

He was responsible for everything—2,000 laborers, costs, results. He had to deal with a hostile government in a language he had learned only after arriving there. He had to fight disease, contend with political riots, and stand by as his meticulous plans were dashed by capricious officials. Yet, despite these adverse circumstances, the plant got built and is in operation today.

Quite an experience. The stuff of learning by doing. But what, in fact, did this manager learn from his assignment in the jungle? "Oh, part of it was that you really find out if you can manage when you lock up with a foreign government, because they can tell you to go to hell in a second. Other things? I don't know, so many I can't describe them, but overwhelmingly a sense that, if I could survive this, nothing would ever hurt that way again."

We interviewed or surveyed 191 successful executives from six major corporations who described for us more than 600 developmental experiences in their careers—experiences that made lasting changes in the way they manage. The Amazon assignment was one of 34 start-ups in which a manager had to bring something new into existence.

Other executives we interviewed grew in their careers by switching from line job to headquarters positions, by turning around troubled divisions in "fix-it" assignments, or by taking what we call a "leap in scope," a massive increase in responsibility.

Many researchers agree that job challenge, and specifically difficult assignments, are indeed an important teacher of up-and-coming executives. In their long-term study of AT&T executives, Douglas Bray and his associates found relationships between early demanding jobs and later management success. John Kotter of the Harvard Business School found that the companies with the best reputations for good management make extensive use of job challenge to develop their executive talent. (See *Across the Board,* March 1988.) In this article we will describe in detail the kinds of assignments that challenged the executives in our study and what they say they learned as a result.

The executives we studied were well into their careers, in their early to middle 40s on average. In recalling the experiences that had made lasting changes in them, most drew from a period of more than 20 years. Because we asked them to describe only three assignments from their long careers, we are confident they chose turning points in their growth as executives.

Special Projects and Task-Force Assignments

Executives told us about three general types of project assignments: trying out new ideas or installing new systems; negotiating agreements with external parties, such as joint-venture partners, unions, or governments; and troubleshooting a problem-filled situation such as a major accident or plant closing. Regardless of the type, each project assignment could have been labeled: "This is a test." Could managers learn a new skill on the run? Could they cope with groups of people they'd never worked with before? Could they do it quickly? Could they handle the pressure of visible success or failure?

Also, regardless of type, the lessons from project assignments fell into two broad categories: learning how to handle ignorance (which may represent a first for a technical or functional expert) and learning how to get others to cooperate without having authority over them (which can get exceedingly difficult as the stakes get higher).

Managers found that they couldn't be experts on everything. Many began their careers in a technical or functional specialty, such as engineering, law, or finance, and rose because of their technical excellence. Project assignments propelled them into a world in which their old skills may not have meant much, and others may have known more than they did.

One executive, for example, was put on a secret acquisition team to buy out a supplier of computer parts. He knew little about acquisitions, and because of the secret nature of the project, he could not openly ask for desperately needed information. Yet, when he began to suspect something wasn't right with the deal, he broke off negotiations— against the advice of his senior management. Later, the company that had almost been acquired went abruptly out of business, and the executive's judgment was vindicated. He had taken the risk of opposing senior management in an area where he was a novice and had learned valuable lessons—not only about his ability to handle new situations, but also about the importance of standing up for himself and his analysis.

Project assignments like this one placed managers at a fork in the road. The easy path would have been to rely on habit and become worn out trying to become an instant technical expert. After all, technical expertise had guaranteed success so far, and it would have been easy to see such expertise as the right choice again. The other path was to rely on the skills of others, giving up the illusion of mastery.

One executive who took this latter, more challenging path described his experience this way: "I was a marketing guy sent to start up the first computerization project our company had ever attempted. In those days, adding machines were our most sophisticated tool. I walked in, not really even knowing what a computer was, and faced this group of computer fanatics ready to revolutionize our operations. Maybe my ignorance saved me— how could I posture when I knew nothing? Anyway, this is what I said: 'Let me tell you guys three things. One, you've got a leader who knows nothing about computers and a lot about marketing, so we've got a lot to learn from each other. Two, I'm not afraid to say I don't know and ask stupid questions, and don't you be either. Third, let's not worry about our differences. Let's see what we can do to set up this system, and while we're at it, let's move the art of marketing 20 years into the future.'"

As sensible as this may seem, managers usually choose the easy path. It's more comforting to stay with what they know or immerse themselves in the technical details of a new field, falling back on the ultimate defense of the mediocre manager: Take no action until all the information is in. This approach assumes that it's a manager's responsibility to be the expert, master the content of the assignment, and direct others accordingly—a technical manager for all seasons, a walking encyclopedia of business brilliance. Some might call this arrogance (and it may be, partly), but more often such a belief results from fear of giving up control, of being exposed as a nincompoop—or, worse, being wrong with everyone watching.

Yet the test of a project assignment is not to see if a manager can master a new field in six months. The true test is: Can you *manage* something new without having to *master* it first? Can you be a quick study and learn to ask the right questions, grasp the basics, and work with others to get the job done?

The second major lesson of project assignments grew out of this need to work with and through others. Lacking the expertise, yet charged with the responsibility, managers had to find some common ground—they had to learn to understand the other person's point of view.

The marketing manager charged with the computerization project had to get excited about computers and what they could do for the corporation, and he had to inspire the computer buffs to think of every possible application, not just the general administrative and accounting applications they were charged with. By putting together two separate areas of expertise—marketing and computers—they came up with one of the first computer-driven, market-research packages. "The key all along was to make it clear that we were in this together. I rarely pulled rank, even when I disagreed with them," the manager explained. "After all, if they didn't know more about what they were doing than I did, we were all in deep trouble."

One way or another, the managers we studied learned that to get things done they had to be able to work with others over whom they had little authority or control. Furthermore, they learned that having authority and control was not the issue: persuading others through patience and understanding was. Sometimes leadership boiled down to stopping, asking questions, and listening to other points of view. Concern for those views and melding them into a common goal were what paid off.

Mastering Ambiguity at Headquarters

Some of the managers we studied were plucked, even pushed, into one- or two-year assignments in corporate staff roles. All had been in operational jobs where they were responsible for some bottom-line numbers. With the switch to a staff assignment they were suddenly on alien turf. They were usually relocated to corporate headquarters and reported to or worked with executives several levels up from themselves, even while struggling with a new technical area. The areas assigned were commonly in planning and financial analysis; less often they were in general administration, research-and-development management, training and human resources, or productivity improvement. The stated purposes of these assignments were to teach the managers other sides of the business, help them understand corporate strategies and culture, and expose them to executives who ran the company.

For managers accustomed to finite jobs with finite accountabilities, staff assignments produced anxiety. This was partly because the assignments were conceptual rather than tangible, and strategic rather than tactical. But above all, staff assignments were frustrating, because managerial performance couldn't be measured by the method managers had

come to know and respect—the bottom line. The two main lessons to master in line-to-staff switches were: learning to cope with ambiguity and understanding corporate strategy and culture.

"I had never been in a position with no bottom line before," one executive recalled. "Although it was intellectually demanding, I had trouble with its sterility—all those numbers were dehumanizing. I did not enjoy the job, although working with the top brass was exciting." Many managers didn't enjoy their time at corporate headquarters, perhaps because they didn't feel that they were accomplishing anything tangible. They persuaded, recommended, and occasionally saw things done at their behest, but they were not performing a concrete job. Perhaps worse, there were no sales figures, production charts, or profit statements to assure them that they were in fact doing a good job.

The managers we studied learned that gathering and synthesizing information was the key to dealing with these ambiguous situations. Like the managers in project assignments, those who switched to staff jobs learned to rely on others, ask questions to find out what was most important, and tackle new technical areas piece by piece. Yet once the new information was assimilated, the picture was still incomplete—because it was of what *might* be. This scenario, with all of its uncertainties, usually became the basis of a report or presentation to top management. Even for the confident, it was unnerving to walk into a room full of executives and expound on topics barely known six months or a year before. The intellectual challenge, coupled with the obvious testing, drained them.

But the presentations counted for something. Whatever the topic, major decisions might be made, and whatever was said had to be crisp, accurate, and insightful. "Information is the executive medium," one manager said. "You'd better be accurate, and you'd better believe in what you're saying. It's okay to say, 'I don't know,' but it's not okay to back off a point you've carefully prepared—then people begin to wonder what you're doing there if you have no point of view."

As managers looked back on these presentations, they drew a lesson: the importance of constructing a point of view and of having the courage to present it. The very act of doing this reduced their anxiety and changed their view of ambiguous situations.

The ambiguity of not knowing became less something to be feared and more something to be accepted. "Ambiguity just is," said one executive. "You're never going to have all the information, but you have to act anyway." In the course of developmental staff assignments, the managers said they picked up significant technical expertise and began to understand how business must respond to external conditions—customers, competitors, government regulators, and Wall Street analysts. Responding and adapting to changes from the outside involved some science and some guesswork. Successful strategies hinged on raising the chances of success a bit by playing out different scenarios, dreaming up options, and working on problems from new angles.

Although these managers didn't as yet set the strategies, they came to realize the attitudes necessary to do so. Strategies were guesses at the future by fallible human beings. "In financing an acquisition," one chief financial officer said, "financial models can eliminate the bad ways, but you're still left with five or so alternatives. There's no computer model that's going to predict the future for you. So finally, as always, it boils down to human judgment."

In learning about strategy, managers learned about business possibilities. But just which business possibilities were viable depended on the culture of the corporation itself, its attitude toward risk, and how it treated its employees. It was in seeing how the corporate culture operated that managers found out what was truly possible in their particular environment.

This understanding of what was possible was dominated by two factors: the nature of the company's business and the attitudes of the dominant people who ran it. A stable company in a stable business was unlikely to have a culture that encouraged heavy risks. A culture in which the norm was to talk everything over and get everyone's agreement before acting was not likely to be conducive to taking quick, decisive action.

As with other developmental assignments, a year or two on the corporate staff helped managers make a mental transition, in this case from thinking tactically to thinking more strategically. They came to see the broader context in which decisions are made and learned that one of the roles of an executive lay in constructing strategies for dealing with uncertain future events.

Start-Ups and Fix-Its

If projects and staff assignments taught methods of leadership by persuasion, line assignments carried with them lessons of power and accountability. These were down-and-dirty jobs, hands on, action oriented, with real bottom lines, and sometimes involved managing casts of thousands. Looking at what these executives had to do, it is understandable that many of them were critical of people who had never had to make the bottom line.

Three major kinds of line assignments emerged as the firing line for leadership in the traditional taking-charge sense: starting something from scratch, turning a business around, and managing an operation of larger scope. Each type of assignment carried with it a somewhat different set of implications for career development; each offered its own special panoply of lessons.

The challenge of starting from scratch was easy to define: Build something from nothing. This something might include plants, product lines, new markets, or subsidiaries. In such start-up operations, managers may have been plagued with all manner of adversities beyond the job itself. The managers we interviewed built towns in the wilderness; created policies; confronted social, political, and cultural problems they initially knew nothing about, and coped with some of the harshest weather on earth.

In the midst of this, they were usually loosely supervised. "I was sent overseas to create a new market for a product," one executive said, "given carte blanche and absolutely no guidance. I had to find an office, hire people, and build a market from scratch while I carved profit-and-loss responsibility for a core business."

Many of the developmental start-up assignments were outside of the United States, leaving the managers geographically isolated and often viewed with suspicion by the local population. Sometimes they found themselves trying to build a staff from scratch, hiring inexperienced workers who couldn't speak English, or trying to make an efficient team out of antagonistic, wary groups.

Other disadvantages were occasionally present as well. Sometimes the corporate office was skeptical of the new operation or considered the business a secondary one. Sometimes the job carried a stigma: "An overseas assignment is a graveyard in this company."

The focus of the managerial challenge in starting-from-scratch assignments was almost singular: survival through individual leadership, an advanced course in how to stand alone. This and the sheer number of demands put a premium on individual initiative. The urgency, lack of structure, and frequent inexperience of the staff resulted in using whomever and whatever was available to solve problems. Strategies that would slow down progress weren't considered viable, no matter how sensible. Any reflective pauses would have to come much later.

Four strong lessons stood out in from-scratch assignments:

- Out of chaos managers learned how to identify what was important and how to organize themselves to get it done.

- Creating a staff taught them how to select, train, and motivate subordinates.

- Successfully making it through the assignment taught them that they could survive. This raw endurance carried with it increased confidence and willingness to take risks.

- They learned firsthand just how much leadership matters and how lonely the role can be.

Not all of the start-ups were as demanding as building a new plant in the Amazon. Instead of starting with absolutely nothing, some began with a facility or, more simply, rolled out a new product. As the degree of challenge decreased, so, too, did the power of the lessons. At their toughest, start-ups were a jolt of adrenaline, described by one executive as "the purest time of my life." And, when the assignment was over, unlike many jobs they had held, the managers left behind something permanent, something they had created. For some managers, there would never be another job like it, and indeed some never could adjust to a subsequent job at corporate headquarters.

Troubled operations, even disastrous ones, are commonplace in the business world: units rocked by fraud and scandal, teams that are the laughing-stock of the company, groups with no financial con-trols, divisions that lose money year after year, and businesses whose profits plunge precipitously. Being sent in to turn around an operation—fix it!—was a frequently cited developmental experience.

Learning from fix-its came from being tough and persuasive *and* being tough and instrumental. "When I was a kid, I thought that most decisions were a matter of choosing right over wrong," one manager said. "I'm still looking to make a decision like that. It seems that all my decisions are between two goods or two bads."

In fix-it assignments, managers had to make tough decisions, decisions that would inevitably result in human pain. One manager we interviewed closed a plant in Iran during the 1979 revolution, another had to fire an entire department in 15-minute internals. "It was kinder than letting people sweat it out for days until their turn came," he said. His other choice was between trying to change the operation against overwhelming resistance or letting it wallow until most of those involved would have been fired or demoted anyway.

So managers had to be tough, but they needed to be persuasive at the same time. One manager who inherited an ailing financial function as part of a fix-it assignment was faced with the fact that the man who ran finance was not performing well. But he'd been with the company for 40 years. He was a decent fellow whose skills had simply become obsolete. Did the manager dump him unceremoniously or give him a chance to save face? The manager realized that just because a new financial system and new reporting relationship had been decreed didn't mean they were going to be implemented as written. *What* was going to happen was a given; *how* and with what degree of cooperation it would happen was up to the people involved. So even though it might have been easier to dismiss everyone who didn't seem to fit in, the truth was that he was going to have to work with people one way or another.

In coming to this realization, he grasped that it was possible to tear something to bits without tearing up the people involved. He could explain what was going to happen and why, listen to their worries and fears, supply them with facts, and even concede that they might have a better idea. Although a few people might have to be dismissed, it was better to work with those you inherited. Many times all they lacked was direction, control systems, and standards that made sense to them.

The ultimate lesson was straightforward. Organizations could be torn down by decree, but building them back up was another matter. Authority wasn't much help in getting people to work together. People needed to believe that they were moving toward something better and the change would be worth it in the long run. The managers learned that they had to live with their people once the changes were over.

The dark side of fix-it assignments was that the executive could develop a hard-boiled attitude toward people. The pressure from upper management was immense, changes had to be made, and the time was limited—six months to two years on average. Managers found that it was sometimes necessary and sometimes simply easier to order rather than consult or to fire rather than develop.

The managers we interviewed confronted fraud, gross negligence, abuses of sick leave and vacation, and widespread cheating on expense accounts. They inherited units that were millions of dollars in the red and confronted hostile unions. Often their choice was between firing a few people or waiting until the ax fell on the entire group. As a result, the assignment could be psychologically brutal. "Letting people go is never easy, no matter how justified," said one manager. As their skins thickened, calluses could form over emotions as well.

Some managers focused narrowly on systems, standards, and how to get people to do a job quickly. Rationalizing these actions later was easy—if the fix-it succeeded. They had saved jobs and turned a troubled division into an inspiring place to work. All the numbers looked good. Maybe they were promoted. But they paid a price for this success. Some, particularly those who became fix-it specialists, made themselves more or less immune to caring.

The essential tension of fix-its (tear down and build back up) required contradictory behavior. The managers had to have, on the one hand, a thick skin, confronting problems and taking action, and on the other, the ability to persuade and control, dealing with groups over which they had no control or situations in which authority didn't matter. Unlike a start-up, in which a manager could "do it

right the first time," the turn-around required strategic pruning and making the best of what was left.

A Leap in Scope

We found that a fix-it was quite different from a start-up, and both were different from managing a large operation that was basically doing okay. But when a new assignment involved an increase in responsibility that was both broader and different from anything a manager had previously known, it was what we call a leap in scope. Here is how one executive described such a leap: "Prior to [the] assignment, I was running a division of about $80 million a year in sales. This was a billion-dollar-a-year business. This was quite a jump for me, into a business that I knew absolutely nothing about. I didn't know the product. I didn't know the customers. I was terrified. Absolutely terrified.

"My boss's boss told me that I was running a new ship. He said that what I ran before was a rowboat and this is the Queen Mary. In a rowboat, you make a little correction to the rudder and the boat immediately responds. The Queen Mary doesn't respond to the rudder as quickly. You have to have a lot of patience, or you'll make some big errors."

Executives in our study described scope changes of three basic kinds: promotions in the same function or area, promotions into new functions or areas, and lateral moves. Such moves could be massive (a promotion two levels into a different business, for example) or modest, but an increase in scope always meant a relative increase in the number of people, dollars, and functions to manage.

Learning from leaps in scope depended in part on the size of the change. The larger the leap, the greater the challenge and learning. Even a more modest shift, however, could to some degree teach how to develop subordinates and how to think like an executive.

Executives may have said that they knew how to delegate, but it wasn't until they faced a job that was much too big for them to handle alone that many of them discovered what that really meant. Like any other adult learner, the managers learned something when they needed to. Only when they had total responsibility ("I was in charge of everything corporatewide") did much purposeful development of others take place. There wasn't any choice.

But the problem was greater than this. In addition to developing people that the managers could trust to run the operation for them, they also faced the issue of creating a challenging climate where people had the room and the resources to continue developing. To do this, the managers had to make sure people knew the strategy behind the specifics so that they knew what was expected of them and why. "If you expect 15 percent growth, tell them why that number was chosen," one said. These successful managers shared information across units and functions, even information that their subordinates seemingly didn't need to know to do their jobs. Who were they to say what connections, what ideas, what ramifications might result from sharing the strategy?

Because they couldn't keep their arms around it all and *had* to let others run things, the managers behaved differently than in previous jobs. They had to tolerate mistakes, and efficiency that was perhaps 90 percent of what they thought it should be. Increasingly, they learned to "manage by remote control"—staying informed, prodding, pushing, asking lots of questions, but not doing. Much of their job became clearing the way so that people could get their work done—supplying information and money and buffering them from interference.

Responsibility was theirs as always, although it took on a different form. Responsibility for doing the job was replaced with responsibility for seeing that systems and work processes were set up so that it got done. Their control over what was done lay in their ability to figure out what was important.

Most of the managers used clichés and catch phrases to symbolize what they thought was important, but the best of them actually lived those slogans. If they believed in "close to the customer," they spent lots of time with customers; if they raved about quality, they were willing to pay for it and change practices to make it better. If costs were a problem, they didn't fly off to faraway resorts in the corporate jet. As their role became increasingly symbolic, they learned that being closely watched by corporate staff was nothing compared with being closely watched by *everyone* in their operation. Did they talk about caring and never thank their secretary? Did they trumpet innovation and dump all over new ideas? Did they herald aggressiveness and fold the first time someone threatened a lawsuit?

Congruence was important. Consistency was important. Setting goals and then driving themselves and everyone else toward them was important. Their people didn't expect them to be omniscient or do it all, but they did expect them to lead, push indefatigably, and be out there showing some guts.

Nothing could be further from the executive's life than the serene boardrooms and polished desks often portrayed in the media. More than 40 studies of managerial work dating back to the 1950s have shown that "executives just sort of dash around all the time." Executives work on many problems simultaneously, endure numerous interruptions, and manage hundreds of contacts who weave in and out on a regular basis. Little time is spent giving orders; more often the job is one of juggling problems and cajoling others as a series of events streams by. The managers we studied knew that controlling their time or the problems that appeared was something they could direct only up to a point.

With increasing scope, executives had to learn to be comfortable with events running without them. They could prod, insist, structure, emphasize the importance of a few priorities, tear apart faulty logic, and see what happened. They had gotten where they were by relying on themselves; now they learned to rely on, develop, and manage others. This was no small transition.

Risk Beats Repetition

It may be that something can be learned in any job, but none of the executives in our study mentioned going into a stable, predictable business loaded down with policies or directives as a major learning event. They seldom described lateral transfers or promotions within the same unit—both common moves for promising young managers—as having been turning-point jobs after the early work years. Job rotations per se—such as switching from one marketing role to another in a different division; brief exposure stints in different functions; or simple promotions, such as going from plant controller in a small operation to plant controller in a larger one—go only part of the way toward being truly developmental.

Even though such moves might offer exposure to new business topics, or different people or groups or products, they are essentially more of the same. It would seem that neither exposure without accountability nor small increases in responsibility are as valuable to executive development as diversity in assignments. Jobs that demand dealing with sudden, unexpected changes or call for skills the manager doesn't have are most important to development.

The essence of development is that diversity and adversity beat out repetition every time. The more dramatic the change in skills demanded, the more severe the personnel problems, the greater the bottom-line pressure, and the more sinuous and unexpected the turns in the road, then the greater the opportunity for learning. Unappealing though it may seem, shocks and pressures and problems with other people are the best teachers.

Morgan W. McCall Jr. is a senior research scientist at the University of Southern California; Michael M. Lombardo is at the Center for Creative Leadership in Greensboro, NC; and Ann M. Morrison is director of the newly opened San Diego office of the Center for Creative Leadership.

Do Your Workers Really Merit a Raise?

by Ira Kay

The effort to control salaries has become a critical problem for companies competing in the global marketplace. Some are pursuing a solution that may seem extreme: severely paring or even abolishing the annual salary increase.

While to many this may appear hopelessly reactionary—or even downright unAmerican—the almost-automatic ratcheting up of employees' salaries every 12 months has been common practice only for the past 25 years or so, spurred on by cost-of-living adjustments built into union contracts. More important, the philosophical underpinning of the annual merit increase—to reward and motivate better performance—is buckling under the weight of economic necessity and the absence of firm evidence that such increases usually have much impact on employees' work.

In a typical "merit" program, the spread between salary increases for the best performers and for the just-average is too narrow to be meaningful. Our most recent data, based on a survey of 459 companies, show top performers averaging 7.7% increases while satisfactory performers average 4.7%. What appears on the surface to be a discernible difference, however, turns into just $20 per week after taxes for a $40,000 employee—hardly enough to fuel a family of four at the local McDonald's.

In a larger survey, drawing from 2,100 companies, my company found that most employees and employers think their performance appraisal systems need major improvement. But supervisors frequently are reluctant to address performance issues

straight on. Common wisdom is that the top two on the list of "hardest things for a manager to do" are fire an employee and give a performance review—but not necessarily in that order.

There is also little or no empirical evidence to show that merit-increase programs are generally effective in improving individual performance or the company's financial performance. Our own data find no correlation between profit growth and the size of salary-increase budgets. But though profits may go up or down, pay levels march inexorably upward.

A company with $50 million in sales will raise fixed costs by about $5 million to fund a 5% merit increase. In an average year, after taxes, this represents more than 10% of net profit. In a poor year, much more.

Of course, some merit-increase programs work well. But these have become the exception. And once employees lose confidence in the process, it is extremely difficult to win them back.

How can companies extricate themselves from the merit-increase morass? There are several new approaches already being tried. All have a common goal: to reduce or replace the fixed salary increase with performance-based rewards.

These rewards must be constructed to pay out significantly more than the typical merit increase if performance is high, and less than the typical merit increase if performance lags. The measure by which the reward is determined may be performance of the company as a whole; results for a small group or unit; an individual set of objectives, or a combination of these.

As with any change, management and employees alike may develop a long list of reasons to cling to the existing system. Understandably, the prospect of putting significant amounts of money at risk—the basis of any incentive system—is quite risky for those below the mid- to upper-management level.

These realities argue for systems such as the one my company helped install at Du Pont Co.'s fibers department in Wilmington, Del. Over the course of three to five years the department will award lower-than-usual merit increases. In exchange for accepting salaries and wages lower than they otherwise might have expected, employees have been given the opportunity to earn bonuses as high as 18% of their salaries—12 percentage points more than they would have received under their traditional merit-increase program. This bonus is based on outstanding performance—as measured by quantifiable results. Target performance would yield a 6% bonus, an amount equal to the average increase under the traditional program. Preliminary employee reactions have been positive, and profits continue to rise.

Such performance-based programs are not guaranteed to work magic, engender instant employee commitment, or turn around an ailing company. As when any other new ingredients are introduced into the management mix, groundwork and communication are vital.

For instance, in an environment where employees do not express trust in their management, most new compensation plans will fall flat—unless, of course, the company first works to change that perception or provide some quick compensation gain associated with the new plan.

In some cases, misguided performance-based compensation programs may actually undermine employee-management relations. A chemical-company subsidiary of a major oil company had two incentive plans: a profit-sharing plan for all employees, and a management incentive plan. Unfortunately, the two plans had different measuring rules: The profit-sharing plan paid off for gross operating margin, while the management incentive plan was based on "return on equity" and had a different threshold amount for payout. In 1989, the profit-sharing plan did *not* pay out, while the management plan did (although below target levels). This created tension between employees and management. The CEO is ensuring that 1990 performance measures and payout levels are better synchronized.

Employees must know how the plan works and why it was instituted. Periodically, this communication must be reinforced. The process must be managed on a year-round basis, and not just through an annual multiplication exercise.

People certainly still have the right to fair pay and just rewards for their contributions as employees. But in cost-constrained times, with world-wide competitive pressures growing every day, performance-based pay systems merit greater consideration as the vehicle that can best link employee value to employer returns.

Mr. Kay is managing director of compensation consulting for the Hay Group.

Strengthening the Pay-Performance Relationship: The Research

by George Milkovich and Carolyn Milkovich

Just as Jack Nicklaus would not tour today's highly competitive international golf circuit using clubs designed for an earlier era, today's organizations are not likely to compete with compensation programs designed for past years. Shortened product life cycles, fierce price competition, an emphasis on quality, shifting regulations, and the need for global operations are changing the way organizations are managed.

Compensation management is also changing. Nowhere is this more evident than in performance-based pay. Creatively managed compensation systems can dramatically enhance a company's ability to compete. They can also improve employee relations. Conventional approaches are accused of being bureaucratic and of institutionalizing mediocrity. Gainsharing, stock options, merit awards, and decentralized decision making are often cited as new pay approaches that are more appropriate for today's workforce. But can these new approaches help companies gain a competitive advantage and foster creativity, quality improvement, and productivity while controlling costs? Can they support new business strategies? Or will they, in turn, become bureaucratic burdens, part of the tyranny of institutions that retards performance rather than supporting it?

New approaches run the risk of simply replacing traditional conventions. Companies may implement the new plans with conviction, but even though conviction is probably necessary for any plan to work, it is insufficient. Findings from research provide information that managers can use in addition to their beliefs, experiences, and convictions as a basis for decisions. Research can help direct them to changes that make sense for their organizations. This article examines what recent research tells us (and doesn't tell us) about performance-based pay.

Creative Change

Pay communicates. When a company changes its compensation system, it is conveying information about what it expects of its employees. New knowledge and behaviors may be required to take the company in new directions. For example, changing job evaluation factors to emphasize product quality or customer relations makes a statement about the company's values and business directions. But change can also be more radical. For example, a company may abandon traditional pay structures in favor of a structure based on skill attainment or place some portion of pay at risk by tying it to certain performance targets.

Change may be evolutionary or revolutionary. Merck, for example, has an evolutionary approach. The company maintains that it makes performance-based pay decisions in the same way it develops drugs: It builds on a base of knowledge and practice and spends considerable effort improving both. IBM has also chosen an evolutionary approach. Pressured by fierce world-wide competition, it has decentralized and globalized its operations. Changes in IBM's compensation systems support these efforts.

Polaroid has taken a more revolutionary approach. It reduced its workforce from 18,000 to 8,000 in less than three years and changed to a company-wide knowledge-based pay system to reward the new behaviors required in the reconfigured organization.

Merrill Lynch is another revolutionary. In an effort to reduce turnover among stockbrokers, it recently revamped its pay system to reward longevity. Now, stockbrokers who meet certain performance standards and stay with the company for ten years are rewarded with a bonus payment of $100,000. And instead of paying branch managers solely according to their offices' productivity, the company now bases part of their pay on how effectively they train new brokers to meet clients' needs. The objective of these changes is to provide incentives for both brokers and clients to stay with the firm over the long term.

Whether evolutionary or revolutionary, changes in a company's performance-based pay plan influence the lives of individual employees and potentially, the profitability of the company. Because change can also be difficult and disruptive, such decisions are not made on a whim. In most companies, the decision to change the compensation plan is guided by many factors. Managers' experiences and beliefs are often important. Many companies benchmark or follow what competitors are doing. Union Carbide, for example, adopted a profit-sharing plan shortly after DuPont announced one. Although DuPont subsequently dropped its plan, Union Carbide's continues.

Increasingly, companies are making decisions on the basis of deliberate strategies. They are deciding which compensation decisions are critical to the success of the business, and they are acting accordingly. Compensation becomes part of the overall business strategy. The company's business philosophy, the nature of the workforce required to accomplish the company's business goals, and external conditions—such as tax laws, union pressures, and health-care costs—all drive compensation decisions. A strategic approach shifts the focus from administering a plan effectively to ensuring that the plan helps the business compete.

Which Compensation Decisions Matter?

Although the literature on business strategy is well developed, research on strategies in human resources, particularly compensation, is more recent. Renae Broderick asked compensation managers in 200 major firms to identify which compensation issues they believed were critical to the success of their organizations. One of the most frequently given responses was "how to link pay with performance." The competitive pay position of the company, the pay structure, the way the plan was administered, and the overall role of compensation in human resources strategy were also identified as critical issues.

Broderick concluded that compensation policies vary in the degree to which they affect the success of employees and organizations. It seems logical that those issues that were identified as critical are the ones that should be tailored to fit a firm's industry, market conditions, and workforce.

It's Not How Much, But How You Pay

Building on the idea that one size does not necessarily fit all, Barry Gerhart and George Milkovich (one of the authors of this article) examined how performance-based pay fits into a compensation strategy. They analyzed six years of pay information on approximately 16,000 top- and middle-level managers in more than 200 organizations. Companies in the sample were fairly typical of the Fortune 500: In 1985, average head count was 34,378; managerial based salary was $71,155; and the average return on assets, measured as net income divided by assets, was 6.1%.

Gerhart and Milkovich found persistent and stable patterns of differences among organizations in both the percentage of pay that was variable and the percentage of managers eligible for bonuses and incentives. These differences could not be explained by differences in industry, size of the organization, or job. They attributed these results to a deliberate pay strategy.

Further, these pay strategies were related to subsequent financial performance. A 10% increase in the size of the bonus was associated with a 1.5% increase in return on assets the following year. A 10% increase in the number of managers eligible for bonuses was associated with a 0.20% increase in return on assets the following year. The percentage of pay that was variable was more strongly related to profitability than was the level of base pay. Therefore, they concluded, developing a pay strategy is more a matter of choosing how to pay, not how much.

Just because base pay was not related to a firm's performance did not mean that there were no base pay differences among firms. There were. These differences, however, could be explained almost completely by the industry, size of the organization, and job variables, whereas the differences in patterns of variable pay could not.

The weak relationship between base pay and profitability was probably due to the fact that the firms in the sample tended to have similar base-pay levels. Pegging base pay either above or below the market may jeopardize competitiveness. In contrast, incentives, bonuses, and other forms of variable pay provide flexibility. For example, deemphasizing base pay and emphasizing incentives can conserve cash for a rapidly growing firm. Tying pay to productivity can reduce risk for firms with fluctuating product demand and high labor costs. Variable pay can be tailored to unique circumstances more easily than base wages can. The research indicates that successful organizations make deliberate choices that enable them to link their compensation policies to their business strategy. Consequently, the mix of pay options that results is an important part of the company's overall compensation strategy.

Choosing the Right Mix

If choosing a mix of compensation alternatives is so important, which mix matches which business strategy? George Milkovich, Barry Gerhart, and John Hannon addressed this question by combining the pay data described above with employer financial data. A sample of 110 firms was characterized as "research intensive" on the basis of the companies' ratio of research and development spending to sales; their research and development spending per employee; and their total research and development spending. These firms displayed a recognizable pattern of compensation practices that included high base pay ($75,561, compared with $67,810 in the

rest of the sample), higher ratios of bonuses to base pay (21.7% compared to 19.3%), and more frequent use of long-term incentives. Fully 78.5% of the managers in the research-intensive firms were eligible for long-term bonuses, compared with only 57.3% percent in the other companies.

How does this compensation pattern of high base pay and generous use of bonuses complement a business strategy? Use of a high base may attract the best talent; a high bonus-to-base ratio may focus employees' attention on outcomes; and long-term incentives may encourage people to stay with the firm long enough to reap the payoffs of their research. Because the long payback period for research and development expenses makes employee retention an important issue in high-technology firms, a compensation strategy emphasizing long-term employment of the right people supports a business strategy that emphasizes research and development. Some caution is required, however. This strategy is designed to attract and retain the best and brightest research and development talent; it does not weed out weak performers. Because employees are encouraged to stay, these firms risk becoming overstaffed. Consequently, firings, retirements, layoffs, transfers, or other separations may also be needed.

So the research supports the notion that compensation strategies can contribute to the organization's success, most likely by communicating and reinforcing the performance required by the business

---

EXHIBIT 1
Does Performance-Based Pay Matter?

	Level of Performance Measurement	
	Individual	*Group*
Added in to Base	Merit	
Not Added In	Awards Piece Rates Commissions	Gainsharing Profit Sharing Stock Options
	Bonuses	

strategy. An emphasis on how you pay, rather than how much you pay, offers greater flexibility, and is therefore a key dimension of a pay strategy.

Pay-for-Performance Plans

The variety among performance-based pay plans is almost as great as the number of work behaviors they seek to encourage. In an effort to understand the current state of knowledge regarding performance-based pay, the National Academy of Science assembled a team of experts from industry, academia, and government. These experts categorized the wide variety of available plans using the two dimensions shown in Exhibit 1. The first is the level at which performance is measured—that is, does individual performance or group performance determine payment? Group measures may be based on the performance of a team, facility, division, or corporation.

The second dimension is the way that performance payments are made. For example, traditional merit plans emphasize individual performance. The merit increase is added onto base pay, and subsequent increases are calculated using the new base. For plans that do not add into base, payment can be triggered by either individual performance (as is the case with sales commissions and piece rates) or group performance (as with gainsharing and profit sharing). These performance-based pay plans are loosely grouped under the heading "variable pay." The question is, what does the research tell us about the effects of these various plans? Beliefs, experience, and a tad of wishful thinking are all rolled into the rhetoric regarding their effectiveness.

Merit Pay

Merit pay is the most widely used plan for managing performance, yet its effects on employee behavior and organization performance are virtually unstudied. A survey by Robert Bretz, George Milkovich, and Walter Read found that 95% of the Fortune 100 organizations use merit pay. The message of merit pay is that individual employees matter; that is, they can make a difference in our firms, and that difference is valued and recognized with pay. According to a study by Lee Dyer, most managers believe that merit pay fits into an overall human resources systems that emphasizes meritocracy as the basis for making pay and promotion decisions.

Merit pay typically combines individual performance evaluation with corporate-wide guidelines that translate a specific performance rating and position in the pay range into an increase percentage. These guidelines control costs and ensure consistent treatment across organizational units. The bulk of research on merit pay has focused on ways to improve the accuracy and reduce the subjectiveness of assessments of individual merit. Critical incidents, management-by-objectives, and behaviorally anchored rating scales are some of the approaches. Unfortunately, most of this research is of only marginal use to managers, in that it often overlooks subsequent effects on employee performance. The Bretz survey revealed that two separate perspectives on performance appraisal exist. On one side are researchers honing measurement devices to eliminate errors. On the other side are managers who view performance appraisal as a communication, reinforcement, and motivation tool. While all of these managers are certainly concerned with the accuracy and fairness of the measurement, of greater concern is how employees feel at the end of the appraisal process and how these feelings affect their subsequent work behavior. So while researchers despair of the Lake Wobegon model used in many organizations—everyone is "above average"—managers continue to use traditional merit plans as a device to communicate and reinforce positive behaviors.

There is little research that examines merit pay directly or its effect on performance. Studies of job satisfaction and performance indicate that these may be positively affected by merit pay, but other studies equivocate. And few studies control for factors that might mediate merit pay's effects, such as the size of the merit budget or the tenure of the workforce.

Is Merit Mismanaged?

Given the widespread use of merit pay, why aren't there clear-cut research results showing substantial effects on performance? The answer may lie in the way merit pay is frequently managed. First, the design and administration of most merit plans call for yearly performance evaluations and pay adjustments. This long time frame makes it hard for employees to connect today's pay with behavior that occurred months ago. In addition, an annual increase results in only a small change in a weekly paycheck. Hay Associates reports that over the last few years, annual merit increases have hovered around 5%, while variable pay plans have been paying closer to 18%. A 5% increase on a $40,000 base comes to $38 before taxes in a weekly paycheck; if taxes are around 30%, the new paycheck is only $27 higher than the old paycheck. An increase of $27 lacks the psychological impact of an 18% bonus, which would be $4,700 after taxes.

A second problem is the size of the differentials among performance levels. Many managers in the Bretz, Milkovich, and Read survey reported that the difference between the pay increase for employees whose performance was average was not enough to motivate performance at a higher level. Assume that employees who perform at a fully satisfactory level are given a 5% increase, and those who perform at an exemplary level are given 8%. Those who rate 8% will receive, after taxes, only $15 more per paycheck than their co-workers whose work is average. Even if employees were absolutely certain that extra effort on their part would lead to a higher performance rating (a certainty that not all employees possess), the extra $15 might not be perceived to be worth the effort.

So the weekly impact of 5%, or even 8%, may seem inconsequential. However, the extra $27, $38, or $53 recurs every week in every year that the employee stays at the job. Few employees or managers seem to realize the financial impact of rolling increases into a base. If a $40,000 employee receives 5% increases every year, after 10 years the new salary is $62,000. The total cash paid to this employee in the 10 years is $503,116. In addition, costs for benefits tied to wages, such as pensions, Social Security taxes, and life insurance, have also increased. Do employees realize that merit increases need to be viewed in the context of their entire career, as the beginning of an income stream? Or do they view the increase as just "a measly $28"? For the same $503,000, the firm could have kept base pay at $40,000 and given a 26.8% bonus every single year.

Obviously, this is an oversimplification. Few firms will hold base pay constant for a decade. But the example illustrates how payout procedures and the lack of realistic communications can dilute any motivational value that merit pay may potentially have. There is a growing belief that merit pay is mismanaged: Too much money is going to too many people with too little effect on their performance or productivity. The heart of the problem lies in the way merit pay is managed—as a cost control, not a motivational mechanism. If performance motivation, rather than cost control, were an objective, then more attention would be devoted to designing merit grids that motivate employees.

Individual Incentives

Individual incentive systems, such as commissions or piece rates, avoid the pitfalls of performance evaluation by using objective measures to calculate pay. Although an incentive payment may be larger than a merit increase, there is also the downside risk of no payout at all.

Properly structured incentive plans meet many of the conditions that psychological theory requires for pay to affect performance: The accomplishment of performance goals requires behaviors and conditions that are under the control of the individual, the payment is clearly linked to goal achievement, and the payment is big enough to justify the effort required to reach the goal. These three issues—line of sight, clear message, and meaningful increases—are crucial to the success of an incentive plan.

Research shows that increases in productivity of up to 30% can be obtained through the use of properly structured incentives. Unfortunately, most of this research was conducted in artificial settings in which college psychology students did simple tasks such as proofreading or sorting colored objects. In real-world situations, the unintended negative effects of imposing individual incentives are well documented. Studies in retail sales, for example, have shown that employees won't bother doing job tasks such as restocking displays if these tasks are not the basis for payments, even though they are part of the job. Some will even sabotage coworkers by hiding the most salable merchandise. Sears auto centers in several states were recently accused of selling unnecessary auto repairs—the result, according to Sears, of the Sears incentive pay plan for mechanics. Numerous studies have documented clashes between high producers and other members of a work group. Such clashes appear to be motivated by fear of new, higher performance standards or even of job loss. Individual incentives appear to work best when they are applied to structured jobs where employees work mostly by themselves. But the lesson we seem doomed to have to relearn is that incentives motivate behavior—both ethical and unethical.

Where employees trust management to set fair standards and do not fear losing their jobs, individual incentives can have a positive effect on individual performance. But few jobs completely fulfill the conditions that psychological theories require for individual incentives to affect performance. Most work is complex, and most tasks interdependent. Thus it is not surprising that surveys of compensation managers report tremendous interest in group incentives to influence group performance.

Group Incentives

Generally, there are two basic types of group incentive plans: gainsharing and profit sharing. The typical gainsharing plan focuses on production cost savings as the performance measure at team or facility levels. A portion of the difference between current production or labor costs and average costs in the past is paid out quarterly to members of the team or unit. Profit-sharing plans focus on changes in profitability as the performance measure. A portion of profits (diversion or corporate) above a targeted level is distributed among employees, generally as a percentage of base salary. Gainsharing and profit sharing are similar in many ways, but administration of the plans differs in ways that may influence their effects on performance.

Gainsharing

A number of case studies and surveys report impressive increases in performance connected with the introduction of gainsharing. There are only a few controlled studies, however. From the late 1950s to the early 1970s, published reports consisted of technical information written by advocates. By and large, they agreed that the introduction of a gainsharing plan initially increased employee suggestions for work improvements, reduced costs, led to improved quality, and fostered more cooperative employee-management relations.

Surveys in the 1980s were equally enthusiastic, but flawed. One reported, for example, that 70% of those firms that had some form of gainsharing credited the plans with improved productivity. Unfortu-

nately, the survey asked managers only for their opinions; no data on productivity were reported. In another survey of 36 firms conducted by the U.S. Government Accounting Office (GAO), managers at 13 firms with sales of less than $100 million indicated that their financial situation improved by 17.3% as a result of gainsharing, while 11 firms with sales of more than $100 million indicated that their results improved by 16.4% percent. But even though the precision of the statistics is impressive, the GAO received financial data from only 24 of the 36 firms, and only 9 firms claimed to assess formally the results of their plans.

Recent research has been conducted under better-controlled conditions. Michael Schuster conducted a five-year study of the effect of gainsharing on 28 plants with complex, interdependent jobs. He found that significant gains in productivity occurred immediately in half the plants and continued throughout the study period. Those plans where improvement did not occur were hampered by infrequent bonus payouts, poor union-management relations before and during the study period, and a lack of employee input into the plan design and production standards. Schuster concluded that employee involvement in the design and administration of a gainsharing plan is crucial to its success. John Wagner studied a foundry's productivity data for four years before and six years after a gainsharing plan was implemented. He found that productivity improved at a faster rate after the introduction of gainsharing and that labor costs and grievance rates were reduced.

But there is negative evidence as well. A study of a gainsharing plan at AT&T found that some individuals became less productive. The employees who were least productive before the plan was implemented improved their performance after the start of the plan, but the most productive employees apparently reduced their efforts. Does this matter? In some cases, no. If the work allows for little range in performance, then the diminished productivity of some high performers may be offset by the overall increase in productivity. In other situations, however, the productivity loss can be devastating. "Outlyers" may provide the creative spark that inspires, leads, and motivates. If three members of the Los Angeles Kings hockey team each play 10% better, for example, it is still uncertain if they can offset a 30% decline in Wayne Gretzky's performance. Nevertheless, Wagner's and Schuster's data offer the best documentation that gainsharing can result in increases in productivity that can be sustained over a long time. Both researchers caution, however, that gainsharing must be part of an overall approach to human resources that is built on solid employee relations and that emphasizes employee participation in decision making.

Profit Sharing and Bonus Plans

An often-noted problem with profit sharing and bonus plans as a motivational tool is the "line of sight" argument: Very few employees see a direct connection between their behavior and their firm's profits. Forces inside the organization (e.g., decisions by executives to relocate facilities or revamp product lines) as well as outside (e.g., changes in exchange and interest rates) weaken the link between individual work behavior and corporate profits, particularly for lower-level employees. Nevertheless, advocates of profit sharing point out other potential benefits, notably improved employee commitment to and understanding of the firm's business.

Disentangling the effects of a profit-sharing plan from other determinants of profitability, such as marketing and manufacturing, is difficult at best. Research on this issue is emerging, however. The Gerhart and Milkovich study discussed earlier concluded that managerial bonuses and profit sharing can affect corporate performance. The next step is to discover where and in what kinds of organizations profit sharing and bonus plans are most effective.

Employee Acceptance of Variable Pay Plans

From the employees' perspective, pay is a major determinant of economic well-being—and more. It can also affect social standing and psychological well-being. Employees therefore seek an economically secure base. The reaction of employees to a variable pay plan is probably related as much to their own financial needs as to the specifics of the plan.

In examining employees' acceptance of variable pay plans, two characteristics are salient: *leverage* and *level of risk.* Leverage is the ratio of variable pay to base pay. The leverage that is appropriate may differ among employee groups and among organizations. Executive pay, for example, is typically more leveraged than that of other employees. Executives also tend to have greater confidence that their performance is linked to the organization's performance.

The risk is the probability that an employee will get an increase commensurate with effort. Many executive pay plans are highly leveraged but relatively risk-free—that is, the probability of payoff is very high. Again, different risks may be more appropriate for different employee groups. Employees in variable pay plans may well experience periods when there are no payouts. The effect on participants throughout the firm, particularly rank-and-file and administrative employees, must be seriously considered.

Lincoln Electric's plan illustrates some of the questions that must be considered in evaluating leverage and risk. Lincoln Electric pays base wages that are competitive relative to the company's labor market. In addition, all Lincoln Electric employees are eligible for its profitsharing plan. The plan is a highly leveraged one: Employees have the potential to double their base. The probability that the profit-sharing plan will pay off is also relatively high because of Lincoln Electric's unique market position. Hence, the degree of risk for employees is less than it would be under different market conditions.

It is essential that employees in profit-sharing plans be kept informed of conditions, economic or otherwise, that are likely to affect the payout. Critics of profit-sharing plans note that many plans do not inform employees of the chances of reaching or exceeding the payout target. Furthermore, many plans require employees to give back a percentage of their base pay in order to enter the plan. A portion of their pay is thus placed at risk. Too often the degree of risk is unexplained and not under the employees' control. Some suggest that these were the fundamental weaknesses that caused DuPont to withdraw its much publicized profit-sharing plan in 1990, the second year of a three-year pilot program.

Many employees are not in a position to manage a risky financial portfolio of such personal importance. Evidence suggests that employees begin the count on variable pay regardless of the likelihood

EXHIBIT 2. Designing a Pay-for-Performance Plan

The following principles, objectives, and design standards provide a framework; each organization can tailor the specific pay-for-performance programs that are compatible with its environment.

Overall Principles

Pay-for-performance programs should...

- Be designed to ensure that all units' programs meet overall corporate policies, thereby supporting the overall philosophy and intentions of the firm.
- Offer decentralized units within the firm the operational flexibility to strengthen pay for performance in ways that take into account their unique circumstances while simultaneously adhering to corporate personnel policies and strategy.

All pay-for-performance programs must...

- Adhere to the philosophy of a meritocracy.
- Ensure fair employee/labor relations.
- Improve the firm's quality of services and operations.
- Support corporate personnel strategies and philosophy.
- Be consistent with and supported by the appropriate corporate compensation system.
- Be cost effective/affordable.
- Maintain/enhance the reputation and legitimacy of the firm.

Specific Program Objectives

Each unit's pay-for-performance program must be designed to...

- Help improve the unit's quality of services and performance.
- Sharpen employees' focus on unit purposes and results.
- Contain costs/enhance affordability.
- Support fair labor/employee relations.
- Take advantage of the unit's unique features.
- Adhere to and be consistent with corporate personnel policies.

Program Design Standards

To ensure a technically sound design, companies should follow these design standards:

Objective(s)	Make objectives specific yet flexible.
Measures	Specify appraisals, measures, and results to measure objectives.
Eligibility	Specify which employees are eligible, which are not, rationales, etc.
Funding	Examine how the plan will be funded and its effects on labor costs.
Data Sources	Detail information systems that exist or need to be developed to support measurements.
Labor/Employee Relations	Specify how employees and/or their units will participate in the plan.
Payouts	Specify the nature of payouts, timing, etc.
Simulation of Scenarios	Give a detailed analysis of payouts/nonpayouts and anticipated effects under various conditions.
Modifications/Termination	Consider how the program will or can be adapted and/or terminated as conditions change.
Dispute-Resolution Procedures	Specify how issues will be handled.
Communications/Expectations Management	Consider how employees and manager will understand and react to the plan; anticipate effects on employee satisfaction. Communicate how participants can influence achievement.
Administration	Consider ease of administration and administrative roles and responsibilities.
Fit with Total Compensation	Keep in mind that pay-for-performance programs are part of a total compensation approach. Ensure that these programs are not conceived in isolation from rest of the firm's pay system.
Evaluation of Effects	Detail how the effects of plan on the unit's mission will be evaluated.
Measurements	Ensure that these are known and understood by participants. Make them as simple as possible. Ensure that documentation enables examination or audit.

of receiving it. They undertake financial obligations consistent with their earnings potential, rather than with the realities of the company's economic situation. Because employees usually can hold only one job at a time, they cannot minimize risk through diversification. John Zalusky of the AFL-CIO point out that "banks that hold mortgages and utilities that provide services do not adjust monthly bills to fit changes in worker income. Until they do, it is unlikely that workers will ask their unions to change their approach to variable pay packages."

Ensuring Equity and Fairness

Despite the rhetoric, most variable pay plans seem to be designed to reduce or control labor costs. The emphasis seems to be to make greater proportions of compensation a variable rather than a fixed expense. But many of the plans' provisions suggest that they are implemented to secure concessions: to remove cost-of-living adjustments, to secure wage rollbacks, to eliminate wage increases, to implement two-tier pay structures, or to provide workers with lump-sum payments so as to avoid increases that roll into the base.

While advocates emphasize that variable pay plans link pay to performance, in practice this link is often a challenge to create. Several conditions must be met, including a constructive relationship with employees; fair, understandable criteria for measuring performance; a plan for providing employees with honest feedback; simple, easily understood mechanisms for payouts (or nonpayouts); and some means to handle the inevitable changes that are required. Exhibit 2 highlights the design principles for a successful pay-for performance plan, and includes specific objectives and standards for judging the soundness of a plan.

It is also important to remember that these plans are only part of a total compensation system, which is part of an overall human resources management system. A pay system that is consistent with the company's approach to managing human resources communicates the organization's philosophy and values and strengthens the link between behaviors and rewards. Performance-based pay plans can benefit employers and link their financial success with that of employees, but not unless managers give serious thought to both the company's business situation and employees' needs. Then, employees are more likely to feel that they are receiving equitable returns for their efforts, and managers are more likely to see greater success for the organization.

George T. Milkovich is the Catherwood Professor and Research Director at the Center for Advanced Human Resource Studies, ILR School, Cornell University. He recently chaired the National Academy of Sciences Committee on Pay for Performance and the Congressionally appointed Committee on Strengthening the Relationship Between Pay for Performance. He is the co-author of Compensation, *the most widely used text in the field. Carolyn Milkovich is a free-lance writer and editor specializing in human resources management issues. She contributes frequently to writing projects at the Center for Advanced Human Resource Studies at Cornell University.*

When Pay at Risk Is a Risk Worth Taking

by Diane J. Gherson

Now that more than one-third of major companies have implemented a group incentive program somewhere in their organization, these organizations are beginning to define the conditions under which pay can exceed market rates (Towers Perrin 1994). One often hears the following refrain: "From now on, we'll be requiring some pay at risk." By putting pay at risk, organizations are attempting to guarantee a suitable return on their investment in compensation.

The problem lies in defining "pay at risk." Although some organizations use the term to describe a variable pay program, the two are not necessarily synonymous. Many variable pay programs merely layer an incentive on top of base salary. Employees in this kind of program are not "risking" anything in the true sense of the word. Their pay may vary year to year, but it will not fall below an established base, even in the event of poor performance.

Even in the "new pay" literature, the terminology is not consistent. One variable pay expert includes all performance-based pay in his definition (Lawler 1990); two other experts exclude "add-on" programs, which offer rewards in excess of base salary for superior performance, from their definition (Schuster and Zingheim 1992).

Ironically, far from instilling a risk/reward stakeholder mentality, labeling the add-on approach as "pay at risk" simply heightens the sense of entitlement among employees. Because organizations usually communicate employees' new "target"

compensation, these employees are likely to see the incentive as a basic part of the total yearly package. A good example is at many of the Regional Bell Operating Companies ("Baby Bells"), where "pay at risk" often is used to describe an add-on program that has been in place for several years. Employees at these organizations expect to get every penny of their "at risk" pay every year.

For the purposes of this discussion, a pay-at-risk program is defined as a program in which a portion of the base pay that employees expect becomes contingent on business performance. This definition includes current base pay and "expected" merit pay. Generally, merit pay budgets are linked to changes in market conditions (Heneman 1992). Under a pay-at-risk arrangement, this deal changes. If performance is good, employees may earn more than the market, but if performance is poor, their earnings may drop below market levels.

Add-on incentive plans continue to be implemented more often than pay-at-risk plans at a rate of about four to one. Although about 35 percent of U.S. companies have variable pay programs covering the nonsales, nonexecutive work force, only about 8 percent of U.S. companies use their incentive plan to replace all or a portion of their salary-increase programs (Towers Perrin 1994). Nonetheless, the number of companies experimenting with pay at risk is growing at an annual rate of 15 percent (Towers Perrin 1992–94).

Pay at risk is an emotional issue for most employees. Even if an organization has communicated its strategic vision effectively and everyone has bought into that vision, employees can react negatively when comfortable entitlements are taken away. In place of these entitlements, employees are asked to make a personal investment in the business. This works only if employees can supply their own source of security—i.e., confidence that their team has a good chance of succeeding. Such confidence only is engendered by a management style that empowers employees and a business in which employees truly can make a difference. Drawing on the experiences of numerous organizations that have had success and failure with pay at risk, three factors should be in place for such an approach to work. (See Figure 1.)

Four basic types of pay at risk are in use today. (See Figure 2.) At one extreme, the individual experiences a pay cut. At the other extreme, the merit budget is cut and the individual's sense of risk is less direct.

Cutting Base Pay

In the most extreme form of pay at risk, base pay is cut and employees essentially are asked to earn it back, betting their own money on business outcomes. If the organization or individual exceeds performance targets, employees receive some multiple of the foregone base pay in a lump sum. If targets are not met, employees lose the pay cut.

In recent years, a few Fortune 500 companies have joined the ranks of smaller organizations that use this form of pay at risk for all employees. A leading office products company characterized the cut as a "salary buy-in" to its new incentive plan. In the second year of the plan, senior management pay was cut 7.5 percent, and pay was reduced 5 percent for all other exempt employees. For each group, the potential upside was set at two times the pay cut.

Where It Works

The pay-cut approach can work well in a sales function because there is a clear "line of sight" between the goal—increased revenues—and the actions and behavior required to achieve that goal. Sales representatives generally have clear-cut sales objectives for their assigned territory, they are measured individually against those objectives and they have a fair amount of control over what they do. Each of these line-of-sight factors is critical to the success of this kind of pay-at-risk plan.

In addition to line of sight, the goals must be perceived to be achievable. A 1992 study of 250 sales organizations by the Krannert Graduate School of Management at Purdue University found that turnover of sales staff was not affected as much by the percentage of pay at risk as by the level of uncertainty associated with bonus payouts. Turnover rates shot up as soon as the chance of receiving a bonus dipped below 51 percent (*Sales & Marketing Management* 1994). Schuster and Zingheim argue that while a threshold percentage might not always

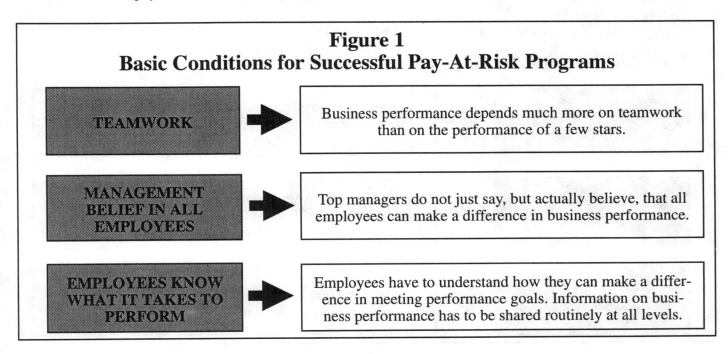

Figure 1
Basic Conditions for Successful Pay-At-Risk Programs

TEAMWORK → Business performance depends much more on teamwork than on the performance of a few stars.

MANAGEMENT BELIEF IN ALL EMPLOYEES → Top managers do not just say, but actually believe, that all employees can make a difference in business performance.

EMPLOYEES KNOW WHAT IT TAKES TO PERFORM → Employees have to understand how they can make a difference in meeting performance goals. Information on business performance has to be shared routinely at all levels.

be necessary in add-on plans, at-risk plans should have a minimum certainty for bonus payouts to increase the perceived achievability of goals (Schuster and Zingheim 1993).

Line of sight and perception of goal achievability often are difficult to achieve when group performance is involved. Thus, a pay cut in conjunction with a group incentive plan may not be an appropriate choice for many organizations unless broad-scale job losses pose an imminent threat.

Even when corporate survival is in question, most employees (including senior management) tend to react negatively to pay cuts. An interesting exception to this pattern occurred at a major oil company when the Alaska pay premium was cut significantly and merit pay was eliminated. One important reason for employee acceptance is that incentive payments have averaged more than 18 percent annually since the plan's adoption two years ago.

A start-up operation (such as a "greenfield" company or site) can be in the fortunate position of implementing the pay-cut approach without the danger of damaging employee relations. This is because the organization explicitly can define the employer-employee compact right from the start as consisting of below-average base pay with the opportunity to earn an incentive. Because the organization can invite new or transferred employees to join under these terms, it is not likely to be on the defensive because its work force will accept risk as part of the package for which it signed up. General Motors Corp.'s Saturn division successfully persuaded workers to move voluntarily from Detroit to Tennessee to enjoy a higher standard of living and to participate in a new workplace where risk is part of the compensation package (Wallace 1993).

The Risk/Return Ratio

Employees want a good return on their foregone money, and focus group feedback at organizations considering pay at risk suggests that a 2-to-1 ratio is generally the minimum acceptable potential return. If employees give up $2,000 of their salary, they should have at least an opportunity to realize $4,000 if performance conditions are met.

Although this return may appear quite high, especially compared with returns from other investments, keep in mind that employees are foregoing

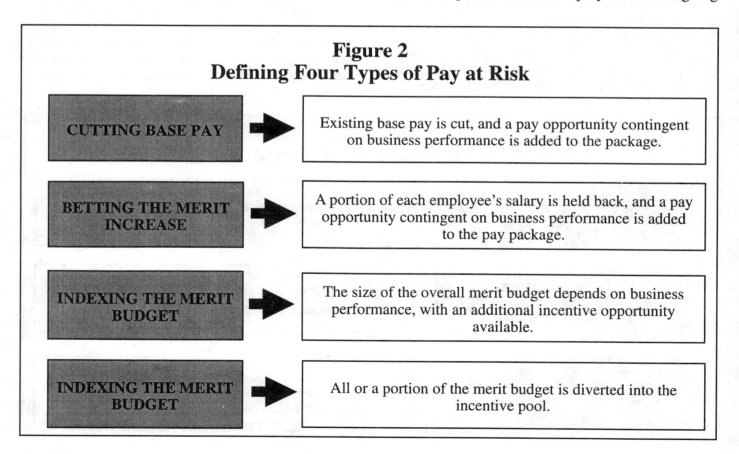

Figure 2
Defining Four Types of Pay at Risk

CUTTING BASE PAY	Existing base pay is cut, and a pay opportunity contingent on business performance is added to the package.
BETTING THE MERIT INCREASE	A portion of each employee's salary is held back, and a pay opportunity contingent on business performance is added to the pay package.
INDEXING THE MERIT BUDGET	The size of the overall merit budget depends on business performance, with an additional incentive opportunity available.
INDEXING THE MERIT BUDGET	All or a portion of the merit budget is diverted into the incentive pool.

the opportunity to receive the compounded value of the amount at risk over time. Schuster and Zingheim have calculated that a $40,000 employee who receives 2 percent less than a peer in a single year will experience a cumulative earnings loss of 11 percent (or $4,333) after five years and a cumulative earnings loss of 40 percent (or $16,019) after 15 years. With the benefits impact factored in, the cumulative differential after 15 years increases to 51 percent (Schuster and Zingheim 1992). A study conducted by ARCO in 1989 analyzed the present value and benefits impact of a 5-percent merit increase during a typical employee career and concluded that the equivalent lump-sum amount is 30 to 40 percent of base salary. By these standards, a 2-to-1 ratio is conservative.

Betting the Merit Increase

The second type of pay at risk ties directly to individual merit pay. Under this approach, employees forego all or part of their regular annual merit increase in return for the promise of an incentive contingent on specific performance goals.

The most famous example of this approach is DuPont's "Achievement Sharing Plan," which was discontinued in 1991. The plan covered 20,000 employees in the company's Fibers Department. Under this plan, employees could receive up to three times their pay at risk. In 1989, employees received 3.6 percent of salary for 1988 performance in exchange for giving up 2 percent of future merit increases in each of the following three years. The total pay at risk would have been 6 percent of base pay after three years (McNutt 1990).

How did the 2-percent foregone merit increase actually work? At the time of each salary increase, DuPont employees received two numbers from their supervisors: the merit increase they would have received without pay at risk and their actual merit increase under the new plan. In most cases, the individual employee put 2 percent at risk each year. This was not true for lower performers. Because the first 1 percent of every merit increase was reserved for the employee, those employees receiving increases under 3 percent put less than 2 percent at risk, and their payouts were discounted accordingly. In summary, the plan caused the lower performers to take on less risk in the early years.

In contrast, American Express Travel Related Services used an approach that caused all employees to assume equal risk each year. A pilot incentive plan was introduced in 1993 to selected line groups at two operating centers covering 2,800 employees. (The plan since has been extended to more than 10,000 employees in most operating centers.) The pilot operating centers used merit-increase grids that were uniformly 1 percent lower than those of the nonpilot operating centers. If the team met all of its performance goals, it earned the 1 percent; if the team exceeded its goals, it could earn up to four times the amount at risk. In this situation, all employees have equal risk because the merit grid forces supervisors to reduce all merit increases by 1 percent.

A problem experienced by organizations using pay at risk is ensuring equity for intracompany transfers and new recruits. Employees who transfer or are hired into a pay-at-risk division will arrive with the advantage of a full merit increase and yet have access to the incentive plan. Most organizations address this issue by "slowing down" these individuals' merit increases to ensure internal equity. At DuPont, for instance, transferring employees were asked to take an immediate pay cut or to have their pay transitioned to 6 percent at risk over a three-year period.

Where It Works

In many ways, betting the merit increase is the ideal form of pay at risk because it provides a tangible sense of risk to each employee without diminishing actual earnings. Several conditions must be in place for the concept to work:

- *An effective merit process.* The supervisor must not "back into" a performance rating to create a meaningful increase for competent performers. The result will be that higher performers assume a disproportionate share of the risk.

- *A meaningful risk multiple.* As in the case of the pay cut, individuals must believe the reward is worth the risk. A 2-to-1 ratio represents the minimum risk/return ratio.

- *A well-accepted team concept.* The foregone merit increase must be earned by a group, not by an individual. This requires a general acceptance that the team makes a difference to company success, not the individual "star" performer.

- *Incentive measures with good line of sight.* Individuals must believe that they can make a different in meeting the goals or they will resent the foregone merit and will view the deal as a punishment rather than a bet.

Indexing the Merit Budget

The third type of pay at risk is perhaps the most common, and it is in the early stages of implementation at numerous Fortune 500 operating companies. Under this approach, business performance rather than competitive practice explicitly drives the size of the merit budget. If the organization or unit meets or exceeds performance targets, it earns a competitive merit budget. If it does not meet targets, the budget is frozen or halved. This provides the downside risk to employees that offsets the upside opportunity of an incentive plan.

The downside risk, however, is not unlimited. As a safety valve, most of these plans have a "basement floor" clause, whereby a merit budget kicks in to prevent organization pay rates from dropping below a certain market level (such as 90 percent of market). In many cases, this downside cap is matched by an upside cap on the incentive.

In some respects, organizations have been applying the indexing approach for some time in the form of periodic freezes and end-of-the-year cuts to the merit budget. The real difference now is that the organizations openly are communicating the way the merit budget is handled. When they are carried out in secret, budget cuts may be seen by employees as an after-the-fact punishment. Explained in advance, before the performance year starts, an at-risk merit budget can represent the opportunity to be rewarded for a job well done. The secret approach reinforces the entitlement syndrome (i.e., "they took away my pay increase"). The open approach, in contrast, can help promote a genuine stakeholder mentality.

At a division of a major oil company, if performance falls below a minimum threshold, the merit budget is zero. If performance is at target, the merit budget is half the company norm and the division funds a 2-percent incentive pool. At higher performance levels, the merit budget matches company norms and the incentive pool is funded up to 12 percent of payroll. In this case, the indexing approach provided the division with the flexibility to introduce variable pay without upsetting the perception of internal equity elsewhere in the company.

Figure 3
How Merit Indexing Can Hurt Higher Performers

Example of a Company With 12-Percent Incentive Caps	The Higher Performer		The Below-Average Performer	
	Salary Increase	Risk	Salary Increase	Risk
Traditional (no risk) Program	8%	0%	2%	0%
At-Risk Program				
Year One (0% Budget)	0%	8%	0%	2%
Year Two (2% Budget)	6%	2%	1%	1%
Total Risk Taken	—	10%	—	3%
Total Upside Opportunity	12%		12%	
Risk/Potential Return Ratio	1:1.2		1:4	

Dealing with High Performers

The exciting aspect of this form of pay at risk is that it explicitly communicates that payroll must meet a required rate of return. The downside, as with the other forms of pay at risk, is that high performers tend to get hurt the most. (See Figure 3.)

For example, suppose an organization installs a program with a group incentive opportunity capped at 12 percent. Under the traditional merit program, a high performer would receive an 8-percent increase and a below-average performer would receive 2 percent. During the first year of the program, performance does not warrant a merit budget. During the second year, the organization halves its merit budget to 2 percent. The high performer receives a 6-percent raise while the low performer gets 1 percent. In this case, the high performer has "risked" 10 percent (8 percent in the first year and 2 percent in the second year) while the below-average performer has risked only 3 percent. At the same time, the potential upside for both employees is the same. Unfortunately, this outcome can increase turnover among the group of employees that struggling organizations can least afford to lose.

This problem may be temporary. As more organizations introduce pay at risk, the importance of competing for talent on a base salary basis may diminish. For the moment, with only 8 percent of U.S. companies offering pay at risk, these organizations must act defensively.

One way to alleviate the negative impact on high performers is through a "dual fund" approach. Figure 4 shows how one company explicitly earmarked its merit funds for high performers. This enhanced the ability of the high performers to recoup the pay they risked in previous years. In another company, the design involved an increase in the differentiation between high performers and average performers. The design team determined that the chance of not funding the merit budget is 50 percent. Under the merit distribution guidelines, the high performer would be risking 8 percent every two years, or 4 percent annually. The average performer risks 4 percent every two years, or 2 percent

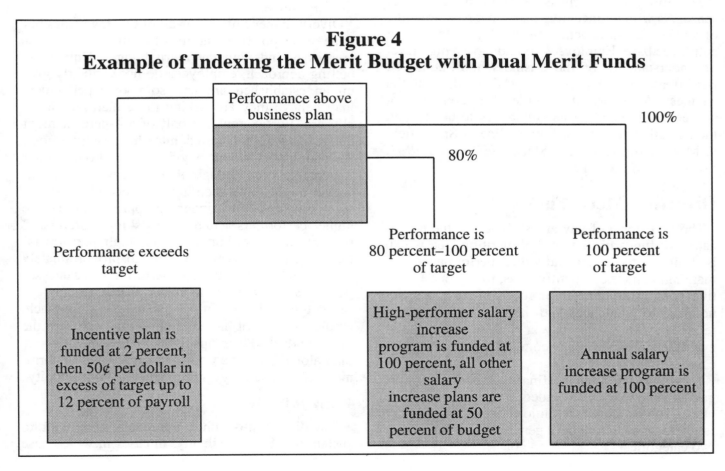

Figure 4
Example of Indexing the Merit Budget with Dual Merit Funds

Performance above business plan

100%

80%

Performance exceeds target

Performance is 80 percent–100 percent of target

Performance is 100 percent of target

Incentive plan is funded at 2 percent, then 50¢ per dollar in excess of target up to 12 percent of payroll

High-performer salary increase program is funded at 100 percent, all other salary increase plans are funded at 50 percent of budget

Annual salary increase program is funded at 100 percent

annually. In the years when the merit budget is paid out, the high performers receive double the normal differentiation between high and average performers.

Where It Works

The indexing approach requires an arsenal of alternative rewards and recognition vehicles to ensure that high performers feel valued and recognized. Even with these vehicles, the company or division runs the risk of losing key talent if pay levels fall too far below market. For this reason, a "basement" clause, specifying how far salaries can fall below market, is essential.

In addition, the indexing formula should be clear and understandable to all employees. Without reliable peer benchmarks and good communication of company financials, the indexing approach can be perceived as a "take-away" rather than as a collective gamble.

The performance index typically is set at the aggregate company or profit-and-loss level. This means low line of sight is likely in the traditional sense. As with all incentive plans that have low line of sight, success depends on the "eyesight" of the employee base. Employees should have a high level of understanding of the business and should be treated as—and act as—true stakeholders in the business. A celebrated example of a company that succeeded in enabling its employees to understand their relationship to the bottom line is Springfield ReManufacturing Corp. (Stack 1992, Case 1993, Lough and Mackay 1994).

Diverting Merit Funds

The final form of pay at risk involves the reallocation of funds from a normal merit budget, which is designed to reward individual performance and maintain market competitiveness, to a group incentive pool. This transfer of funds often is not announced to employees and therefore is sometimes referred to as "silent" pay at risk. In reality, however, the risk generally becomes known to employees.

This approach often is a financial necessity for organizations with self-funded employee incentive plans. The economic conditions for diverting merit funds to an incentive pool generally fall into one of two categories:

- *Above-market pay levels.* In this case, the organization is not in serious danger of losing valued talent.

- *Insufficient incentive funding.* The typical target payout for a group incentive plan is about 6 percent of base salary (McAdams and Hawk 1992). In some cases, an organization's stretch goals are inadequate to fund this kind of payout. As an example, consider the avionics division of a Fortune 500 company: with 1,300 employees and a payroll of $75 million, the division is forecasting a $15-million profit. The division wants to share with employees half the gains in excess of the profit target, but it would have to generate a profit of 30 percent above target to be able to fund a 3-percent payout to all employees. Faced with a choice between reinforcing the entitlement syndrome and financial survival, many organizations in industries as diverse as aerospace and health care are reducing pay competitiveness in the short run to provide a meaningful incentive.

Diverting merit funds has all of the downsides but none of the positive features of betting the merit increases or indexing the merit budget. Unlike the betting approach, employees do not explicitly give up an established amount, so poorer performers may believe they are risking more than they actually are. For example, if half of a 4-percent merit budget has been diverted into the incentive pool, the poorer performers may feel cheated out of their 2 percent, even though their deserved merit increase might have been zero. A second disadvantage compared to the indexing approach is that the higher performers actually are risking more than 2 percent. In lower-budget years, high performers' merit increases typically are disproportionately lower than those of average performers because supervisors may attempt to ensure that most employees get something. Unlike the indexing approach, employees do not have the opportunity to earn the merit budget. Their upside is in the variable pay plan alone. Thus the traditional individual opportunity is supplanted by a group incentive opportunity.

Where It Works

The diversion-of-funds approach is difficult to sustain if it is done silently. In cases in which base

Figure 5
Conditions for Pay at Risk

	Pay Plan Feature	Organization Characteristics
Cutting base pay	• Individual measures/excellent line-of-sight • Perceived goal achievability • Good risk/return ratio	• Greenfield site/new company • Imminent threat of job loss
Betting the merit increase	• Disciplined performance-merit linkage • Good line of sight • Good risk/return ratio	• Pilot sites/units within company not adapting • Acceptance of team concept
Indexing the merit budget	• Reliable peer performance benchmarks • High-performer retention vehicles • Recognition vehicles • Perceived goal achievability • Good risk/return ratio • "Basement" clause	• "Open book" approach to sharing of financial information with employees • Employees treated and behave as stakeholders
Diverting merit funds	• Base pay already above market • High-performer retention vehicles • Recognition vehicles • Perceived goal achievability • "Basement" clause	• Economics of company understood by employees • Financial survival at stake • Employee belief in company future • Employee conviction they can make a difference

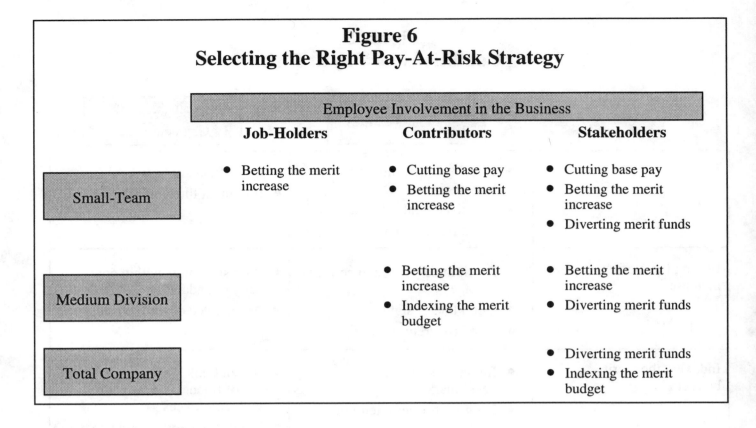

Figure 6
Selecting the Right Pay-At-Risk Strategy

	Employee Involvement in the Business		
	Job-Holders	**Contributors**	**Stakeholders**
Small-Team	• Betting the merit increase	• Cutting base pay • Betting the merit increase	• Cutting base pay • Betting the merit increase • Diverting merit funds
Medium Division		• Betting the merit increase • Indexing the merit budget	• Betting the merit increase • Diverting merit funds
Total Company			• Diverting merit funds • Indexing the merit budget

pay already is above market, an organization is better off communicating this instead of simply freezing merit budgets. In cases in which financial performance cannot justify a market-based merit increase budget, a company is wise to explain the economics of the situation and the conditions needed to return to market pay levels. This requires sharing financial data with employees on an ongoing basis. Employees should understand clearly the economics of the business, believe in the organization's future and possess the conviction that they can make a difference as a group. As with the index approach, the organization should find ways to recognize and value its key performers, and it must indicate how far below market it is prepared to go before letting a merit budget kick in. If these conditions are not in place, the organization runs the risk of losing key talent and retaining a group of disgruntled employees.

How to Select the Right "At-Risk" Strategy

Pay at risk can work either with line-of-sight goals or employee involvement. In many ways, employee involvement is nothing more than aggregate line of sight. The conditions for success for each of the four pay-at-risk approaches is shown in Figure 5.

In general, if employee involvement is moderate—with employees contributing above and beyond their jobs but not yet acting and thinking like owners—then pay at risk should only be considered if employees have a very clear line of sight. The pay-cut or betting-the-merit-increase approaches are the most appropriate under these conditions. If employee involvement is high but incentive goals are at the organization level, the indexed-merit-budget and diversion-of-funds approaches are viable options. If an organization can offer neither line of sight nor an environment of high employee involvement, it should not consider pay at risk. (See Figure 6.)

One way to ascertain whether sufficient employee involvement or line of sight are present is to survey employees. Using a five-point scale (ranging from "strongly agree" to "strongly disagree"), a helpful survey question is: "I believe I (or my team/work unit) can make a difference in the size of the payout." It is important to note that not everyone has to strongly agree; in fact, this will almost never happen. The key is to have buy-in from the majority of employees. The wise design team will attempt to get all the organization's opinion leaders on board before rollout, either through informal discussions or through the use of formal teams. These opinion leaders can be instrumental in bringing around mainstream employees.

It is also important that managers be prepared to ignore the "noise" from resisters, although this kind of management tenacity often is hard to come by. One way of testing management tenacity is to discuss "what if" scenarios with the top management team before the plan is rolled out. The "double loop" exercise developed by Harvard professor Chris Argyris is a particularly effective approach (Argyris 1994). This technique forces normally undiscussable issues regarding resistance to change out into the open through a written role-playing exercise.

The dilemma for human resources professionals is that many of the conditions for the success of pay at risk are beyond their control. Although their senior managers want to convert the work force from entitled jobholders to true stakeholders, they may not have created the right environment for the shift. Typically, organizations have to evolve from treating employees as input ("do your job") to contributors ("help us save money") before they can create the conditions necessary for stakeholdership ("we all add value").

If an organization cannot meet all the conditions required for successful implementation of pay at risk, it is better off with a traditional pay-increase program. At best, such a program helps create a loyal work force that can be converted to committed stakeholders when the time is ripe. At worst, it communicates what employees already know: that they can count on the security of some basic pay in-crease for doing their jobs. In a world of change, employees can take some comfort in that.

References

Argyris, Chris. "Good Communication That Blocks Learning." *Harvard Business Review*. July-August 1994. 77-85.

Case, John. "A Company of Businesspeople." *Inc.* April 1993. 79-93.

"Do Sales Commissions Equal High Turnover?" *Sales and Marketing Management*. January 1994. 40.

Heneman, Robert L. *Merit Pay: Linking Pay Increases to Performance Ratings*. Boston: Addison-Wesley, 1992.

Lawler, Edward E. III. *Strategic Pay*. San Francisco: Jossey-Bass, 1990.

Lough, David A., and Drew Mackay. "A Testimonial from Springfield ReManufacturing Corp. CEO Jack Stack: Motivating People Through the Income Statement and Balance Sheet." *ACA Journal*. Autumn 1994. 3(3): 104-111.

McAdams, Jerry L., and Elizabeth J. Hawk. *Capitalizing on Human Assets*. Scottsdale, Ariz.: American Compensation Association, 1992.

McNutt, Robert P. "Sharing Across the Board: DuPont's Achievement Sharing Program." *Compensation & Benefits Review*. July-August 1990. 17-22.

Schuster, Jay R., and Patricia K. Zingheim. *The New Pay*. New York: Lexington Books, 1992.

-----. "The New Variable Pay: Key Design Issues." *Compensation & Benefits Review*. March-April 1993. 33.

Stack, Jack. *The Great Game of Business: The Only Sensible Way to Run a Company*. New York: Doubleday, 1993.

Towers Perrin. *Salary Management Survey*. New York: Towers Perrin, May 1994, April 1993, April 1992.

Wallace, Marc J. Jr. "Interview with Saturn President Richard G. 'Skip' LeFauve: Work Design, Teams and Rewards at Saturn Corp." *ACA Journal*. Spring/Summer 1993. 2(1):6-13.

Diane J. Gherson is a Principal in Towers Perrin's Los Angeles office and heads the firm's national employee incentive practice. She has 12 years of consulting experience in compensation, change management and business strategy. Before joining Towers Perrin, Gherson consulted with The Hay Group. She also has worked in strategic plan-

ning at MAC/Gemini, and in organization effectiveness and compensation at Shell Canada Ltd. She has a B.A. in political science and economics from the University of Toronto and an M.S. in industrial and labor relations from Cornell University. She has completed course work toward a doctorate in organization behavior at MIT Sloan School of Management.

Bonus Pay: Buzzword or Bonanza?

by Howard Gleckman

At first glance, Luling, La., seems like the last place you would expect to find a workplace revolution. Little more than a wide spot on a back road between New Orleans and Baton Rouge, Luling is a testing ground for a dramatic shift in the way workers are paid. At a modest-size Monsanto Co. chemical plant here, managers and workers have been struggling to find ways to link employee pay to some measure of company success. First, they tied worker bonuses to plant safety. That was risky: It might have encouraged coverups of accidents. Then, they linked pay to the plant's overall success. Workers hated that, because they had no control over what happened in someone else's product line.

Now, after eight years of false starts and potentially dangerous turns, the folks at Luling think they may have gotten it right. They have tied most of a 5% to 10% bonus to results at individual units. And they now reward workers for helping to prevent accidents—for example, by attending training programs.

"LIKE WILDFIRE." The Monsanto plant is in the vanguard of a gathering movement in Corporate America to push incentive pay down the line. Some proportion of pay for top managers has long been tied to corporate performance, of course. But now, a growing number of companies are asking rank-and-file workers to put a portion of their pay on the line. The schemes are varied: They may link compensation to company track records, unit performance, team success, or individual achievement. But they all have a key element in common: By offering big incentives when things go well but withholding

raises, or even cutting pay, when things so sour, they're demanding that workers share in the risks and rewards of doing business.

There's a new urgency to these efforts: With inflation low and international competition strong, traditional, automatic merit pay increases are increasingly a memory. At the same time, though, companies are asking workers to do more, work harder, be more creative, and take part in decision making. And they're promoting huge changes in the workplace, such as the shift to teams. Tying pay more closely to performance is one of the few ways companies can increase rewards to employees in a world of fierce cost pressures. If they're designed and managed properly, performance-based compensation plans will more than pay for themselves in productivity gains. "We've gotten back everything we've paid, plus," says Luling plant manager Tony L. Corley.

A new survey by consultants Hewitt Associates shows that nearly two-thirds of midsize and large companies have some form of incentive pay for nonexecutives, up from 50% just four years ago. The consulting firm Towers Perrin reports that, among companies of all sizes, such schemes increased by 40% in the past two years alone. And Towers figures that the average bonus payout this year will exceed 7% of base pay, even as the pool for traditional merit raises is expected to fall below 4%. "Performance-based pay is growing like wildfire," says Robert W. Hall, director of new programs at the Association for Manufacturing Excellence.

The trick, of course, is doing it right. Some of the nation's most progressively managed companies have recently had problems with their own pay-for-performance programs. At chemical giant DuPont

311

Co., for example, a 13-member task force spent two years designing a widely celebrated "Achievement Sharing" plan for 20,000 employees in its fibers division. The program made 6% of salary contingent on the entire division's annual profits. But when a business downturn made the division fall short of its profit goals for 1990, the company pulled the plug rather than withhold pay from a workforce that had been shrunk from 27,000 in the early 1980s. "Morale was a factor," says Robert P. McNutt, manager of new compensation and benefit initiatives for DuPont. "People were working harder because of the earlier downsizing."

DuPont's misstep illustrates a key lesson in performance-based pay: Workers must know that their individual toil can affect overall performance goals. That means pushing incentives deep into the corporation—even down to work teams. The same message also came through loud and clear for Monsanto. It originally tied pay to the overall performance of the Luling plant, which produces a wide range of chemicals. The goal met strong resistance from employees who felt the targets were beyond their control. "People didn't feel they had an impact," says Bruce Swaim, an electrical technician. So in 1992, the bulk of every worker's bonus was tied to the performance of groups of just 50 to 60 employees, rather than to plantwide achievement. "Once you feel some sort of ownership, it works well," says Gina Maney, a traffic manager.

WARY WORKERS. That's why Monsanto now has more than 60 separate programs at various operations around the world. "Each one is different," says Barry Bingham, the company's director of compensation. "It's been built from the bottom up." By contrast, Bingham admits, failed plans were almost all pushed on units by corporate headquarters. "Every one that was screwed up was designed in St. Louis."

New research supports the view that small is beautiful. Todd Zenger, a management professor at Washington University in St. Louis, concludes that performance gains increase by roughly 20% for each step down the organization. "Size matters a lot," he says. "Incentive plans attached to smaller groups, be it departments instead of divisions, or divisions instead of entire corporations, tend to be more effective."

To succeed, new pay plans must also be phased in gradually and carefully explained to often wary workers. American Express Co., for example, rolled out an incentive pay plan on July 1 for the 10,000 employees in its consumer-card and consumer-lending groups. But for a full year before the rollout, AmEx ran a closely monitored pilot program. "People who are used to having fixed compensation can be insecure about not knowing what they will earn in a year," says Jill Kanin-Lovers, senior vice-president for worldwide compensation and benefits. "You can't just slap this on an organization."

The pilot was a big success—especially because about 98% of the 1,500 employees gained payouts of up to 4% of their base salaries. "I got to distribute some of the checks, and it was like lottery day," recalls Lorin L. Brown, a team leader at an American Express operations center in Phoenix. But the company also discovered that it needed to work harder to communicate the plan's goals to employees and to simplify it, basing payouts on three measures instead of six. The criteria are now customer satisfaction, employee productivity, and shareholder wealth creation.

FICKLE CUSTOMERS. Companies also need to be willing to revise their performance goals as circumstances change. Xaloy Inc., a small manufacturer of plastic-extrusion equipment in Pulaski, Va., has been tinkering with its incentive targets since adopting a bonus plan in the mid-1980s. Those targets can be remarkably specific: For example, faced with a serious production snafu at its southwest Virginia plant this year, the 300-employee company refocused the plant's bonus program to target the foul-up. The incentive system helped get the whole plant involved in solving the problem, says President Walter G. Cox Jr. "We even had people from data processing out on the shop floor."

Of course, a plan can't succeed unless it measures performance accurately. That's fairly easy for manufacturing facilities, which have tallied output, quality, and safety for years. But for services, figuring performance can be tough. Like American Express, GTE Corp. has made customer satisfaction a key component of its incentive plan. It has devised a dual-bonus system, which applied to about 25,000 telephone operations workers in Texas, California, and Florida. A key component: surveys that measure customer approval.

But customers can be fickle—and their attitudes highly subjective. That's why some union officials are questioning such links. Workers more easily accept compensation plans that provide bonuses or base-pay increases for learning additional skills. At Black Box Corp., a Pittsburgh-based marketer of computer-network and other communications devices, workers can nearly double their pay in the same job. For instance, Black Box pays starting order-entry clerks $17,000 to $20,000. As they boost their product knowledge, their pay rises to $25,000 to $28,000. Those who improve skills even more—learning another language to handle international sales, for example—can make up to $35,000 plus a bigger profit-sharing bonus.

Black Box provides formal in-house training and will pay for continuing education. But the decision to boost skills—and pay—belongs to the employees. "They can dictate their own earning powers to a great degree," says Black Box President Jeff Boetticher. And the payoff for the company? "The more skilled the workforce, the higher the level of customer satisfaction," he says.

Xel Communication, based in Aurora, Colo., is using incentive pay to foster its move to teams. The maker of telecommunications transmission equipment paid its 300 workers an average of $500 each in profit-sharing in the last quarter. Another component gives workers a chance to earn an additional 50 cents per hour for each new task they master. The key for Xel, though, is its team-based compensation. Each unit shares a bonus based on meeting a quarterly goal, such as improving on-time delivery. The average reward is 4.5% of payroll, with top teams earning up to 10% and lagging groups getting nothing.

UNAMBIGUOUS. Employees are generally positive. William R. Walker, an assembler on one team, loves the group-based bonus: "It gives people more incentive to work harder to better their team." Still, Terri L. Mudd, a member of another team, has her doubts: "I don't know how fair that is. You can work very hard and your team does poorly and your increase is not as much as it should be."

The payoff for Xel seems unambiguous: Average production time has been slashed from 30 days to 3, and waste as a percentage of sales has been cut in half. "The pay system doesn't stand alone," says

How to Make Performance Pay Work

Set Attainable Goals

Incentive pay works best when workers feel they can meet the targets. Tying pay to broad measures such as companywide results leaves workers feeling frustrated and helpless.

Set Meaningful Goals

You can neither motivate nor reward by setting targets employees can't comprehend. Complex financial measures or jargon-heavy benchmarks mean nothing to most.

Bring Workers In

Give them a say in developing performance measures and listen to their advice on ways to change work systems. Phase pay plans in gradually so employees have a chance to absorb them.

Keep Targets Moving

Performance-pay plans must be constantly adjusted to meet the changing needs of workers and customers. The life expectancy of a plan may be no more than three or four years.

Aim Carefully

Know what message you want to send. Make sure that new scheme doesn't reward the wrong behavior. Linking bonuses to plant safety, for example, could encourage coverups.

Julie A. Rich, vice-president for human resources. "It's only a support of the teams."

And that, perhaps, is the bottom line. Performance pay can't replace good management. Throwing cash at a frustrated or bored worker solves nothing. But as part of an overall management system that aims to bring out the best in its workers, incentive pay can be more than the latest fad. It can be another step on the road to higher productivity and more competitive companies—in Luling and elsewhere around the world.

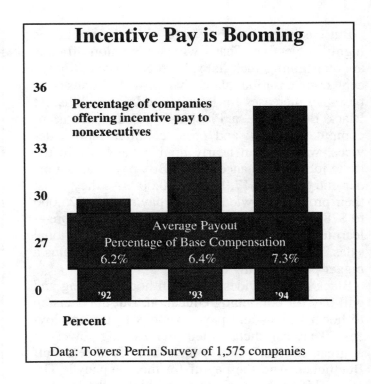

Incentive Pay is Booming

36

Percentage of companies offering incentive pay to nonexecutives

33

30

Average Payout
Percentage of Base Compensation

27

6.2%   6.4%   7.3%

0   '92   '93   '94

Percent

Data: Towers Perrin Survey of 1,575 companies

V.

Successful Implementation of the Performance Measurement, Management, and Appraisal Process: Case Studies

Cyanamid's New Take on Performance Appraisal

by Saul W. Gellerman and William G. Hodgson

In one form or another, performance appraisals have been with us more than 50 years. Few would quarrel with the notion of linking pay to performance, thus rewarding good work and (the employer hopes) giving mediocre performers an incentive or a goad to do better next year. If those who fail to perform quit, the organization benefits.

Still, performance appraisal systems remain endlessly controversial. For one thing, many (if not most) achievers are motivated at least as much by pride or the desire to excel as they are by the hope of better pay. Critics also claim that poor ratings tend to demotivate inferior performers rather than to spur their improvement. Moreover, these poor performers often don't quit; many hang on for years and years. Then there's the sometimes thorny question of how to measure performance. Finally, many managers regard with distaste the obligatory, one-to-one meetings with subordinates to talk about results versus expectations.

At American Cyanamid Company, a performance appraisal system called "progress reviews" had been in operation for more than a decade when, in 1984, the company decided to take a hard look at it. The reviews were part of the merit-based salary administration procedure.

The evaluation grew out of an effort launched by CEO George J. Sella, Jr. to change the company's culture. In a survey, its executives had used these words to describe Cyanamid: conservative, bureaucratic, and not sufficiently people oriented. While giving it high ratings for integrity and dedication to research and development, they had wished it had "a looser structure," stirred "more creativity," and exhibited more "willingness to take risks."

In response, Sella set $1 million aside for an "innovation fund" to support projects that might improve the quality of life for the company's employees.

A project that got under way at the same time was a different approach to the much-criticized performance appraisal scheme. Undertaken in the Medical Research Division, it was adjudged a success and a similar plan has been adopted for all 11,500 salaried Cyanamid employees in the United States.

In effect companywide only since 1986, the new tack is still on trial. But there's no question of its success among the knowledge workers in the Medical Research Division.

This alone may have great significance in view of the growing numbers and importance in organizations of workers who make their living mainly by interpreting information. (About one out of eight people in the labor force is now in that category, and their proportion is growing fast.) Satisfying the desire for recognition and advancement of these professional or quasi-professional employees often conflicts with the preference of the organization's bureaucracy for uniform and easily administered procedures, like the performance appraisal.

Reprinted by permission of the authors, "Cyanamid's New Take on Performance Appraisal," by Saul W. Gellerman and William G. Hodgson. *Harvard Business Review*, May-June 1988. All rights reserved.

Acute Dissatisfaction

At Cyanamid, under the old system, salaried people whose performance was judged to be best received an *O* (for "outstanding"), which entitled them to the highest raises. Most others received one or the other of two rankings: *X* ("excellent in several major areas"), or *R* ("achieves expected results"). Approximately 20% of the employees in a given unit were supposed to be rated *O*; 40%, *X*; and 40%, *R*. Subdividing these categories were plus and minus qualifiers, for example, *X+* and *X-* on either side of *X*. There was also a fourth rating, *N* (for "needs improvement"), rarely given. Thus there were ten possible ratings.

Division administrators of the plan customarily awarded ratings more or less in keeping with the 20-40-40 guideline. This also affected salary increases, which were set according to a range in each category. The biggest raises went to employees who won *O* ratings but who stood low in their salary ranges. The fixed distribution of rewards tended to flatten out the pay raises of those who had earned the same ratings for a period of time.

Scientists in Cyanamid's Medical Research Division, asked for their reactions to the system, offered acid comments, including these:

"The progress reviews do illustrate some aspects of how my superior rates me, but I know damned well that it's also influenced by quotas."

"My work could be outstanding year in and year out, but if one other person in my group was outstanding, I would be denied such a rating."

"Until it's my turn, I can't get a better rating no matter what I do."

"I don't take it seriously. It's a Mickey Mouse numbers game. My superior and I just laugh at it, and we get through it as quickly as we can."

"Evidently there is an effort to fit the people within a section to a bell curve so they can dole out raises and not go over the budget. But as a scientist I know that a bell curve should be applied only when a population is large enough; and these departments are very small."

Among Cyanamid managers, the procedure had advocates and detractors. The advocates held that although it suffered from many of the usual flaws inherent in performance appraisal, its central purpose—to reward and encourage excellence—was simply too important to be sacrificed. Others thought that too often rewards seemed correlated with education and length of service. And further, that the system created apathy and a sense of futility among employees receiving lower ratings whose performance, if measured against their job descriptions rather than against each other, was entirely satisfactory. To the critics, the worst aspect was the demotivating effect of an *R* rating, which was generally regarded as a stigma.

Cyanamid's personnel department often heard complaints from managers who felt uncomfortable handling the progress reviews. Supervisors were required to identify and discuss aspects of an employee's performance that needed improvement. They dreaded this task. They often felt forced to dwell on trivial shortcomings that ordinarily would be overlooked or on habits that were unlikely to change. And managers shrank from the duty of comparing an employee's performance with that of others in the same department. Many complained of having to face the resentment of employees who got *R*s.

Clearly, the company was ready for a change.

Divisional Trial

The Medical Research Division carried out the experiment in two of its sections, each employing roughly 70 people, over a two-year period. These sections were chosen because they were the most comparable in the division with respect to size, mission, job characteristics, demographics (especially education and length of employment), and salary distribution. Both sections do experiments and laboratory analysis; both include employees in about the same proportions at the bachelor's, master's, and Ph.D. levels, as well as managers at these levels.

The first step was to establish a baseline of attitudes and perceptions for both groups by means of a questionnaire. This survey found that the two groups were comparable in their almost uniform dislike of the progress reviews, particularly in their antipathy toward the predetermined distribution of ratings. One section now became a control group and the other an experimental group.

While the control group continued under the old system, the experimental group was introduced to a new plan that had these features:

- It had only three possible performance ratings.

- It assumed that most employees, most of the time, perform somewhere within a broad range of acceptability, and that while fine distinctions within this range are possible (like above or below normal expectations), making them is neither necessary administratively nor desirable motivationally. This broad range of expected performance levels was designated G (for "good").

- It assumed that occasionally, but not inevitably, someone's contribution so greatly surpasses the usual range of performance that no reasonable observer would include it within the normal expectations for the particular function. This is not simply a matter of improving on the performance of one's peers but of exceeding the demands of the job itself. Such performance is often a matter of both luck and pluck, of not only being in the right place at the right time but also of seizing opportunities and exploiting them creatively. This category of performance was called E (for "exceptional").

- Finally, it assumed that performance is sometimes unacceptable and that unless an employee makes a prompt, pronounced, and lasting improvement, he or she should no longer be considered qualified to hold the job. This is not a mere matter of being the poorest performer in one's group but of failing to fill the requirements of the job. This category of performance was designated U (for "unacceptable").

- It called for no recommended distribution. Since the E and U categories had narrow, stringent definitions, few (or even, occasionally, no) employees would get either rating. By far the greatest number would ordinarily be rated G. The distribution depended on how many employees' work fit the three descriptions.

The system simplified the salary procedure. All employees rated G and E were awarded raises based only on their positions in the salary range. The Es also received lump-sum bonuses equal to fixed percentages of their salaries. Those rated U received no raises.

In the revised progress review interviews, supervisors were expected to compliment subordinates on their strengths and accomplishments, and refer to shortcomings only if they were serious (as in the case of the Us) or were clearly within the employees' power to change through improved effort or attention. The purpose was to make the meeting an ego-supporting instead of ego-damaging experience. The theory was that workers who felt good about themselves would perform better, or at least view their circumstances in a more favorable light, than those who had to defend themselves against what they might see as attacks.

The new system simplified the managers' task. Determining ratings was easier and, more important, the communication of the rating decision was easier. No longer were some employees stigmatized when their work was actually acceptable.

But the program also had its costs. The better performers among the Gs (and for that matter the worse performers) were lumped with the others in that big group. Moreover, employees who excelled were not necessarily rewarded differently from their peers. Division officers feared that these features would cause those whose work had been superior to lose their drive to excel. One purpose of the experiment was to determine if this would occur.

Happy Results

Following expectations, the vast majority of the members of the experimental group scored G in the appraisals. The distribution of performance ratings in two years was this:

	1985	1986
Exceptional	10%	13%
Good	87	87
Unacceptable	3	0

In measuring the reactions of the two groups over one- and two-year intervals, the division used the same survey as the one that established baseline attitudes toward the progress reviews. The results showed a much more favorable attitude developing toward the experimental procedure. Supervisors noted that their subordinates were complaining less.

The responses of the experimental group to a series of statements, four of which are shown in the

Encouraging Results from Surveys of the Two Groups

Statement: Under the progress review system, the factors on which the overall evaluation of my work is based are clearly defined and relevant to my job. (Percentages of "undecided" responses are omitted for all four statements.)

| | Experimental Group | | Control Group | |
	Yes	No	Yes	No
1984	16%	34%	28%	38%
1985	37	24	28	34
1986	55	18	21	35

Statement: On balance, the progress review gives a fair appraisal of my overall performance.

	Yes	No	Yes	No
1984	41%	33%	31%	28%
1985	43	21	22	33
1986	63	18	24	32

Statement: Under the progress review system, the relationship between my performance appraisal and my salary increase is clear and logical.

	Yes	No	Yes	No
1984	29%	42%	34%	51%
1985	30	39	17	61
1986	36	26	17	65

Statement: As far as I can tell, the advancement of other employees in my department during the past year has been primarily on the basis of ability and accomplishment. (This question was inadvertently omitted in 1985.)

	Yes	No	Yes	No
1984	26%	21%	31%	44%
1986	51	26	32	32

insert, indicate a growing perception of the performance review system as being less arbitrary. This contrasts sharply with the control group's attitude.

Can the responses of the experimental group be attributed to a "Hawthorne effect"—the brief surge in favorable attitudes that often follows changes in long-standing procedures? We doubt it. Such an attitude would not last two years. The experimental group became more favorably disposed later in the trial period. Nor is it likely that the negative trend in the control group reflected envy of the experimental group, since the existence of the study was not widely known outside the experimental group.

These results imply that views about compensation among comparably paid groups of professional workers depend less on salary levels than on the perceived fairness of the system for determining pay. They may also be a reaction to a simpler, more easily understood way of assigning salary increases.

A happy benefit for managers was a reduction in time spent preparing for the interviews with subordinates: an average of about six hours each under the old review system compared with about three hours for the experimental group's supervisors. One reason, no doubt, was the change from sessions full of negative comments to anticipation of more pleasant meetings. Whereas, for instance, some 80% of subordinates were reported by their superior in 1984 to be critical of the matching of performance ratings to the recommended distribution, the experimental group's supervisors reported that 85% of their subordinates expressed satisfaction about the *absence* of such distributions.

After two years of exposure to the new system, the most favorable views toward it came from the Ph.D.s—despite the advantages they had enjoyed under the previous system. This reinforced their claim that they were motivated more by professional pride than by money. One of them wrote in response to a survey question: "For me, the work ethic, my professional pride, and drive are stronger motivating factors than salary increases. But a poor salary increase could be a demotivator."

The Medical Research Division groups were small and unrepresentative of the company as a whole, so it is necessary to interpret the results cautiously. But they are internally consistent. They imply that, at least with highly educated workers, performance appraisal systems that are designed to support rather than deflate egos bolster motivation and promote acceptance of a salary administration system, at no greater financial cost whatever.

Cyanamid Buys It

Without waiting for the end of the experiment in the Medical Research Division, and in a sense anticipating its results, Cyanamid introduced in 1986 new progress review systems for all its salaried workers domestically. The new systems have these characteristics:

- There is no recommended distribution.

- There are three possible ratings, S ("superior"), Q ("quality"), and N ("needs improvement").

- Specific objectives are emphasized, with sign-off by both employee and supervisor on annual performance objectives.

- The employee is involved in the performance planning process, particularly in setting up a training and development plan.

The experiment in the medical group confirmed management's judgment in designing those features. But in fairness it must be said that the company would have made these moves even if the trial had not confirmed their worth.

Cyanamid's experience with its new system has been largely positive, but of course it is still new. Early reactions indicate it is considerably more effective and helpful for supervisors and subordinates than the previous system. Some personnel managers have expressed a preference for further differentiation within the broad Q rating; but for the present, top management has decided to keep the system intact while acquiring more experience with it. So far, available evidence indicates that it is broadly applicable to salaried workers of all kinds, not just scientists, and that it represents an improvement over the previous system for all such groups.

The new performance appraisal system has not been without its critics, either in its trial mode or now. Some thought that the Medical Research Division program, however popular with employees and supervisors, was overly egalitarian and would ultimately discourage the most capable people from striving to excel. Others feared that the lack of emphasis on employee shortcomings during progress review interviews would gradually entrench sloppy or inefficient habits. The experiment furnished no evidence to support these fears, but if they would eventually prove to be true, they would have to be reckoned as costs to be weighed against the benefits of the system.

At first glance, the different method of administering salaries may seem to have broken the link between pay and performance (and to have done so without damage to the organization); within the broad group of Gs—87% or more of the total, as we noted—raises were based not on performance differences but on the position of one's salary within a range.

The traditional system, however, may actually have broken that link more than the new one has, by rating workers' performance against each other rather than against the expectations implied in their job descriptions, and by making finer distinctions between acceptably performing people than can be justified.

The experiment recognized that in companies that hire selectively, promote on the basis of superior performance, and reassign or dismiss on the basis of inadequate performance, the distribution of performance does not follow a bell curve but is skewed disproportionately toward superior performance. Therefore, expectations must be similarly skewed; presumably, most people will turn in results that fall within a broad range of acceptability, and only a few will either exceed or come up short of that range.

By eliminating the implied stigma of inferiority that inevitably follows when most others are rated superior, the new system has restored the perception of a link between pay and performance for those whose performance had in fact been quite acceptable. It has not created a new stigma for those formerly rated as superior because they too preferred being rated against the expectations for their jobs rather than against other workers in jobs not necessarily similar to theirs.

Two main lessons have emerged thus far from the Cyanamid experience. First, motivation is more important than administrative convenience. Second, professional pride can be a powerful motivator and should not be discounted in considering how changes in performance appraisal and compensation systems will affect the productivity of knowledge workers.

Saul W. Gellerman is dean of the Graduate School of Management, University of Dallas. An industrial psychologist, he headed his own consulting firm from 1967, when he left IBM, to 1984, when he assumed his current position. William G. Hodgson is director of research service for the Medical Research Division of American Cyanamid Company. He installed and oversaw the experiment described in this article.

Interview with Dennis Dammerman, Chief Financial Officer, General Electric Company

Interviewed by Deborah C. Shah

Shah: Mr. Dammerman, I know you've done a good deal of thinking about the issue of performance measurement over the last few years. I wondered, therefore, what general conclusions you have come to?

Dammerman: Any discussion of performance measures is going to focus first on financial measures. That is, in part, because finance, as a function, has been very dominant in American industry. For instance, if you were to look at who the heroes of the eighties were, they weren't the inventors or the doers, they were the financial wizards—individuals doing deals on Wall Street. Individuals focused, in a very analytical way, on results—net income, return on sales, return on equity, cash flow.

By the way, this is in marked contrast to Japan. There, engineers, inventors have a much more prominent place. Perhaps that's why one study I've seen showed that, in Japan, they have fifty-seven direct workers per accountant while here in the United States that figure is eighteen.

And that's not because the finance function is bad. Financial measures clearly give us a way of communicating to ourselves and the rest of the world about how we're doing. Especially, in a business as diverse as GE, they give us a common language and help us to maintain the very high performance standards that have made our company successful for nearly 100 years.

However, the emphasis on financial measures has had some unintended consequences. For one, it has focused much of our attention on only one constituency—Wall Street. These are the people for whom traditional financial measures have meaning. At the same time, we haven't had as much focus on some of our other, critical constituencies—customers, employees, community. Financial measures help very little when you are trying to meet the needs of these constituencies, and it is very hard to talk to these groups solely in terms of profitability, that is, how much money you make from each thing you sell.

At GE, therefore, the finance function is expected to take the lead in developing the measures that help us gauge where we stand with our customers, our employees, and the communities in which we work and do business.

That's not to say that we are in the process of coming up with a GE-wide Customer Satisfaction Index. That makes no sense given the businesses we're in and the customers we're trying to serve, but we are putting new emphasis on measuring customer satisfaction in each business. And at the Corporate Executive Council (an executive committee composed of the heads of each of GE's businesses and major corporate staff functions), we ask each business leader to tell us something about what's happening in their business with regard to customer satisfaction.

We also want to know what's happening on the employee front—what's happening with cycle times, with community involvement, and environmental concerns. We expect each business leader to focus on all of these aspects of running a business. And each GE business has its own tailor made ways of measuring their progress. It's not qualitative measures or quantitative measures. At GE, you've got to have both.

Shah: That's one of those paradoxes that you and Jack Welch, Chairman and CEO of GE, have talked about so frequently?

Dammerman: Yes, managing for the short term and the long run; focusing on qualitative as well as quantitative measures; being hard-headed and soft-hearted. The notion that it's a lot of different things and all those things at once.

For instance, it took over 10 years for our MRI product to make a profit, and we've spent billions of dollars on the GE 90 engines. We employ more than 500 Ph.D.s in our Corporate Research and Development organization. These are examples of taking the long-term view. We're always looking for places to make strategic investment, to make the right trade-off between price and share, but we still hold each and every business leader accountable for today's results.

Shah: But aren't there some theorists now who would argue that if you get the qualitative things right, if you reduce cycle time, focus on meeting or exceeding customer requirements, then financial success will follow?

Dammerman: Yes, there are some who would argue that view. But I believe that requires a leap of faith that we are not ready to make. We are not going to apologize for focusing on financial success. We've had 46 quarters of continuous growth and profitability. We continue to outperform corporate America, and we aren't going to let up on that.

But I believe a strong corporation must focus on several things simultaneously. For instance, I made a speech not so long ago in which I shared the Corporation's ten number-one priorities, not our top-ten priorities, but our **ten number-one priorities**—each equally important—each essential to our survival.

Shah: Is there some danger that an emphasis on softer issues could go too far?

Dammerman: Perhaps. If you were to attend our Corporate Executive Council and look around the room, I believe you would see individuals who today share the values I've mentioned. But thirty years ago, that wasn't necessarily the case. Indeed, one of the reasons we're even around that table today is because we are each reasonably aggressive people. And certainly, in our youth, we had an edge, an aggressive approach to our work that may have been inconsistent with some of the people values we espouse today.

Over time, however, we gained self-confidence and matured. We deal more effectively with people who work with and for us. But my point is, we weren't always like this. And it's important for us to work with talented young people who also have an edge. If, in the course of our appraisal and development process, we find somebody with great strength, with the right drive and business acumen, who nevertheless has an edge, we should try to understand why they have an edge and what they can do about it. We have to provide the counseling and feedback I talked about before or risk losing some very capable people. In addition, if we don't develop all our people, we risk homogenizing the company and losing the value of diversity.

Shah: Many of the measures you mentioned, particularly in association with financial performance, focus on end results or outcomes. A great deal of emphasis these days at GE is on process or how something is accomplished. What measures are being used to evaluate process, and how important is it, in your view, for a company to have process measures?

Dammerman: Process is very important, in our view, to business success, and we are particularly concerned with cycle time, that is, how long it takes to accomplish something. In particular, we are scrutinizing cycle time with respect to our order-to-remittance process and our new product development process. There is ample evidence that each of these is linked directly to competitive strength.

In our case, we have to go business by business. We have to map each process and benchmark the time required. That is, we have to compare cycle time to where we've been in the past, but we also have to compare ourselves to the best in the world. In addition, we have to anticipate customer expectations, not just today, but down the road. Only where we can gain or maintain cycle time advantage can we hope to outperform others in the industry.

But I'm not really talking about anything the competition doesn't also know and isn't also focusing on. They understand cycle time and the advantages it gives you. So we must constantly evaluate our own performance and look for ways to make continuous improvement.

Shah: What is your role as Chief Financial Officer in developing these measures?

Dammerman: As each business begins to identify for itself the appropriate drivers to be measured and evaluated, we can establish some standards; that is, ways to look at cycle time, ways to evaluate existing data. We can serve as a repository for best practices, and we can provide the corporate primer, if you will, on how to proceed. We can ensure that wherever cycle time is being used throughout GE, the concepts are uniform, and the approach is similar. We can create a template for how to look at these factors and some definitions around terminology.

But it is crucial that we avoid establishing a single measure. For instance, requiring all GE businesses to measure customer satisfaction in the same way and report it regularly to the Corporate level; I'm particularly sensitive to that one. After all, each of our executives is running a very large business. If customer satisfaction is not on their screen every day, then they're not really running their business effectively. They don't need me or Jack Welch to insist that they focus on their customers.

Shah: Is that true for some of the softer issues we were talking about earlier? Do you have to measure people on diversity or the environment, for instance? Do you make it an explicit part of their incentive compensation?

Dammerman: Historically, at GE, we haven't given specific, objective weightings in bonus determination to factors like diversity or environment. However, there is a very large subjective factor in each individual's incentive compensation, and we make the importance of these issues very clear—in management meetings, in written communication, in every interaction the CEO has with leaders in the organization.

We have an approach, here at GE, which we call "loose-tight." For instance, we spent over two billion dollars this year in plant investment. And not one individual appropriation went to the Board of Directors. That's because approval levels are very high. We understand what business managers are spending the investment for, and we trust their judgment. They know their businesses best. We, at Corporate, simply manage the total dollar pot and its allocation to specific businesses based on their strategic needs, their growth cycle, etc.

On other issues, however, we take a tight approach. We want to know specifically what managers are doing with respect to the environment, with regard to employees, with ethical issues. We need to make sure, at a Corporate level, that as we strive to outperform Corporate America, to create the greatest cost and asset productivity we can, that we don't take shortcuts in getting there. Outperforming the competition at the expense of these other issues won't serve us well in the long run. While we're striving for productivity and profitability in the short term, we have to be continually moving in the right direction on our values as a corporation.

Shah: You strive to create a dynamic tension for people so they have to do all things well.

Dammerman: That's right.

Shah: What processes do you have in place to ensure that this is happening?

Dammerman: We have several. In the early summer we begin with a Strategic Review of each business. We sit down with the leadership of each business and discuss the direction the business is taking, the competitive arena, the investment opportunities. In every case, we also discuss where the business stands with respect to its customers, to the environment, and the issue of speed I mentioned before. And let me tell you, those are very challenging sessions. A few months later, each business returns for a budget or operating plan review. Again, we return to issues like customer satisfaction, environmental responsibilities, cycle time. But this time, we are looking at much more specific plans for achieving shorter term goals.

Shah: You've mentioned benchmarking and best practices several times. How important is that?

Dammerman: It is essential; it's probably the one piece of advice I would give someone who really wanted to leverage the use of measures. No matter what you're doing, somebody's always doing at least a piece of it better. You have to find those companies or functions and share information. You have to say, "I know you do this pretty well, but we do this other thing pretty well; let's compare notes." That's been a real change at GE, beginning to look outside for good ideas. And once you get in the mode of learning what other people are doing, you find the insights you gain are very powerful. Indeed, your entire "head set" changes.

Shah: What about your own staff? Do you find yourself establishing specific measures for their performance?

Dammerman: Well, I have two very different kinds of organizations reporting to me. For the staff areas, for example, Financial Reporting and Analysis, I use very qualitative measures and I rely heavily on feedback from the businesses. They are, after all, our customers. Years ago, the Audit staff had a measure on the cost savings they generated, but that really isn't of value.

Fortunately, we have a culture here at GE, where nobody worries about picking up the phone and telling me, "You know, this person on your staff really screwed up." or "They really did a good job." I factor that kind of feedback into my assessment of key staff executives all the time.

For the operating areas like our large Payroll and Accounting Centers, I use the same kind of measures a business would use. We set specific goals each year based on benchmarking best practices. We are concerned with issues like cycle time and asset productivity. We have measures of customer satisfaction. These are the factors I use to assess the success of each of those operations.

Shah: Any other advice for companies who are focusing on the measures issue?

Dammerman: I think I would advise them not to search for a single best measure. For instance, it doesn't do you any good to have the fastest cycle time in the world for making buggy whips or even the best customer ratings. You know, the one remaining buggy whip customer in the world can be very happy with how you're serving him. It doesn't do you any good if you're falling behind in terms of product development, if you're not paying attention to change in your marketplace. Suddenly, you have the fastest cycle and the best customer satis-

faction for producing and supplying the wrong thing. You always have to have your eye on several variables, and you always have to keep your eye on the future. It's very tempting to pull the latest idea off the shelf—one process, one measure, one issue. I think we've learned that business is more complex, and you have to focus on more than one things at a time to be the best.

Dennis D. Dammerman, Senior Vice President and Chief Financial Officer for General Electric Company, has had a long and distinguished career. He joined the company's Financial Management Program in 1967 after graduating from the University of Dubuque. He subsequently held positions with the Corporate Audit Staff and the Lighting Business Group. In 1976 he joined GE Capital Corporation as Manager—Corporate Financial Analysis and in 1978 was named Manager—Operations Analysis for the Consumer Products and Services Sector. He returned to GECC in 1979 as Vice President and Comptroller and in March 1981 was named Vice President and General Manager for the Commercial Financial Services Department. In September 1981, he was named Vice President and General Manager of the Real Estate Financial Services Division.

He was elected to his current position in March 1984 becoming one of GE's youngest senior executives. Today his responsibilities go far beyond Finance to include Corporate Information Technology, Licensing and Trading, Real Estate as well as leadership of GE's businesses in Brazil and Mexico.

Dennis is a member of the Financial Executives Institute, the Council of Financial Executives and a former member of the Financial Accounting Standards Advisory Council. He has twice been named best Chief Financial Officer by his peers and last year was cited as one of Business Week's *best managers.*

Deborah Shah, President of Management Partners, has worked for more than a dozen years with senior management in industry on issues of organization effectiveness. Her firm assists organizations undergoing significant strategic change to implement total quality management and to design the human resource programs and practices essential to success. Ms. Shah counts among her clients some of the world's largest and most dynamic companies—AT&T, Chase Manhattan Bank, American Express, Volvo of North America, and Bristol Myers. From 1989 to 1991, Ms. Shah served as a member of General Electric's WORK OUT! design team. This seven-person steering committee directed a corporate-wide, multimillion-dollar effort to eliminate wasteful work practices and instill speed, simplicity, and self-confidence throughout the organization. Prior to founding Management Partners in 1987, Ms. Shah held progressively more responsible human resource positions at Chase Manhattan Bank and the National Broadcasting Company. An honors graduate from Barnard College, Columbia University, Ms. Shah holds an MBA from Harvard University School of Business Administration.

Peer Review Drives Compensation at Johnsonville

by Shannon Peters Talbott

At Johnsonville Foods, employees are talking about each other. But they aren't gossiping near the watercooler or spreading rumors in the lunchroom. This talk is encouraged by management: It's peer review.

More than a decade ago, as part of an improvement effort, Johnsonville Foods incorporated a team structure into its work environment. Within this framework, open communication and co-worker feedback became vital to the functioning of the business. As employees learned to work together as part of high-performance teams, they began to incorporate the essentials of peer review into their day-to-day jobs.

Today, Johnsonville's employee feedback isn't informal, as it was in the 1980s. Instead, the Sheboygan, Wisconsin-based sausage manufacturer uses a structured peer-review process in practically all areas, including not only performance, development and dispute resolution, but also compensation.

Peer review's move into the compensation arena began four years ago at Johnsonville, with the company's approximately 400 hourly employees, or *members*. Tim Lenz, an employee in Johnsonville's manufacturing facility, was one of many who were frustrated with the company's hourly compensation strategy.

"There really wasn't a system anymore," says Lenz, who's now assistant coordinator for Johnsonville's Riverside, Wisconsin, plant. "When I came to the company in 1979, we had several wage scales for positions throughout the facility. These slowly deteriorated, and it had gotten to the point where no one knew how to get a raise."

Leah Glaub, member services (equivalent to human resources in many companies) coordinator at Johnsonville, agrees that the company's hourly compensation strategy wasn't ideal: "We had a system in which the squeaky wheel got the oil." Glaub says, "People would pick up different responsibilities, then go to their coaches and get salary increases. There wasn't really an established system, and this caused frustration among people."

A team of employees leads the design process. Instead of simply complaining about the haphazard process, Lenz decided to do something about it. In 1990, he went to the vice president of manufacturing and proposed that a group of employees work together to rethink the hourly compensation system. The vice president not only approved Lenz's suggestion, he also agreed to work with the team as needed throughout the design process.

Having obtained this support, Lenz hung a note on the plant bulletin board, inviting other employees to help him try to improve the hourly compensation system. He says that approximately 12 people signed up to help. After several introductory meetings, eight of these volunteers made the commitment to be members of the hourly compensation design team.

During one of the initial meetings, the team members decided that they needed some assistance from member services. "We invited a member of our company's (HR) department to join the team, be-

328

cause we knew that those skills would be necessary, and knowledge about compensation would help us determine the right system for our company," says Lenz. Because the team members had little or no expertise in the compensation area, this HR person (later replaced by Glaub) was able to conduct initial research for the team and gather useful data to assist them in the compensation system's design.

As part of the research process, team members also conducted focus groups of employees at Johnsonville to determine their needs and expectations, benchmarked other companies to evaluate different types of compensation systems and talked with consultants to generate ideas.

Lenz says that one particularly helpful research project was a site visit and one-day seminar on skill-based pay sponsored by Aid Association for Lutherans, a fraternal benefits society in Appleton, Wisconsin. This seminar helped the team determine what type of compensation structure would work within Johnsonville's culture, he says.

Cumulatively, this research led the team to develop four primary philosophies for Johnsonville:
1) Employees need to know exactly what they have to do to get a raise.
2) Employees should have responsibility for compensation. They should be able to request a pay increase when they feel they're ready.
3) Employees should be involved in the review process.
4) Base pay should equal the average market rate based on traditional internal and external values.

Once these goals were articulated, the team set about to meet them. But this didn't happen overnight. In fact, because the team met and discussed the project only once every two weeks on average, the final proposal wasn't introduced until 1992. "If I were to do this again, I'd like to see the team move faster," says Glaub. She adds that part of the problem was the team's determination to introduce a flawless program: "Sometimes, you can't just sit there and [try to] make something perfect. You just have to go try it out and then start tweaking it from there."

The process was a long one, but the result was strong. After two years of work and cooperation, the team members presented management with a compensation system that directly responded to the four philosophies they had established for Johnsonville.

Lenz says that as a whole, the senior ranks approved of the team's proposal. Because he had kept management updated along the way and because the vice president of manufacturing worked with the team off and on throughout the process, there weren't any surprises during the final presentation. "A few were skeptical, but the majority were supportive," Lenz says. Therefore, after presentations to employees and a vote by all members of the work force, the new compensation system was introduced.

Peers review performance to determine pay increases. Overall, the compensation system is what Lenz describes as "pay-for-performance." Although grounded in a traditional evaluation structure—a point factor—it's also heavily reliant on a peer-review process.

The system centers around *result blocks* for each of approximately 80 positions. These blocks each comprise as many as 15 separate criteria, which highlight the key requirements for each job. Lenz says that most positions have two or three result blocks that are completed in progression, but some positions have as many as five. "Our belief is that you start out with the tasks that you must accomplish to do the basic parts of your job," he says. "These make up the first result block. Once you know how to do these tasks, you progress to the skills you need to know to perform at a higher level. Finally, you go on to the results that you should be able to achieve because of the competencies that you have."

Going along with this belief is a philosophy that people should be paid for what they do, and shouldn't be restricted from learning and growing. Therefore, the company sets no limits on how quickly employees can move through their result blocks. "If someone is doing the job, we don't want to hold them back," Glaub explains. "We want to pay them what the job's worth." She adds, however, it takes employees months—and sometimes years—to work through most of the blocks: "If you have them set up right, people are going to be challenged and won't test through them too quickly."

When employees are ready to be evaluated on a result block, they must follow specific steps. On the bulletin board in each plant, there's a form to initiate this compensation change process. When an employee feels prepared to "pass" an evaluation of all eight to 15 results, he or she fills out the form, which includes the employee's name, title and team, as well as the result block to be evaluated. This completed, the employee passes the form on to his or her supervisor, or *coach*.

Together, the employee and supervisor select some of the employee's peers who already have completed the result block being evaluated and also are in a position to see the employee's work on a regular basis. These employees—plus the employee's team leader and supervisor—become the peer-review team. Glaub says that usually this number comes to four or five, but "it depends on the job and how many people that person really interacts with day to day."

For each result in the block, there is a different measurement—evaluations that range from written quizzes to timed demonstrations. "They're supposed to be as objective as possible," says Glaub. "We really are looking for proof of new competencies." She admits, however, that some results—especially in the highest result blocks—need to be quite subjective in nature. "For example, I have payroll coordinators on my team," she explains. "One of the things that they have on their last result block is that they must make meaningful contributions to project teams." Understandably, "meaningful contributions" aren't easily measured. Therefore, the peers reviewing the result block must analyze the employee's past meeting participation and come to a consensus on whether he or she met the criterium.

Glaub says that for most supervisors, this peer-review process is refreshing. "They get a lot of input," she says. This makes the performance review and salary decision easier: "The decision isn't based only on their observations—it's based on a number of different people's observations. They feel more like facilitators and less like judges."

But what do employees think about it? Lenz says that they like having more control over their salary increases. "We don't have the good-old-boy system anymore," he says. "People, for the most part, don't mind honestly evaluating their peers, because that means that they will be evaluated fairly, too, when it comes time for their result-block test."

Glaub says that if employees are uncomfortable participating in the peer review, she does what she can to make it easier for them. "If someone is having a tough time, we make them responsible for an area that's easier to measure so that they don't feel they're getting into personal issues," she says. But—in the end—peer review is required of everyone. "Since the 1980s, we've been a very team-oriented company," Glaub says. "People are used to giving a lot of feedback and being involved. If it's uncomfortable for some people, they have to get used to it if they want to work here. That's just the way we operate."

Monthly contract fulfillment determines individual bonus. As the hourly team was completing its task, another team of approximately 35 employees began looking at Johnsonville's bonus system. Working closely with Glaub and the member services department, the team developed a monthly companywide bonus system that also requires that employees talk openly with—and about—their peers.

According to this plan, Johnsonville employees follow designated steps to receive their bonuses. The process begins with all teams, salaried members and coaches writing six-month contracts, stating their six-month goals and the ways they plan to meet them. The goals must fall into the framework of four overriding company *endstates;* a noticeably better product, outstanding financial results, outstanding customer service and outstanding people.

In addition, the six-month contract contains professional-development goals. These ensure that each employee continually is challenging himself or herself to learn more and provide increasing value to his or her customers, says Gene Rech, southwest regional sales coach for Johnsonville. "If you aren't at fair market value, you want to work on the skills that will get you there," he says. "If you are already at fair market value, you should include actions that will move you further ahead." Glaub says that these professional-development actions vary greatly from job to job and month to month, but examples might include reading a specific book or learning a new computer skill. "It's any action that will help you to move your position forward," she explains.

At the beginning of every month, each employee writes a contract that includes his or her actions that will help accomplish that month's goals—and eventually, the six-month goals as well. "The whole purpose is to help people focus, prioritize and manage their time," Glaub says. "The contracts really keep [employees] moving on long-term actions."

To obtain feedback on this performance, individual employees select three internal *customers*—or people who will be affected by the employee's work—as feedback providers each month. Through the company's electronic bulletin board system, employees send their contracts to the three customers. At the end of the month, these customers respond through surveys that provide detailed information on employees' performance.

Employees also post their contracts to a company-wide bulletin board so anyone can read others' monthly goals and actions and comment on them. "We realize that people have more than three customers each month," Glaub says. "This allows for more feedback from others who may be interested. People do get comments on their contracts through this system."

Glaub says that the company teams meet at the beginning of the month to review contracts and ensure that the employees' goals are attainable. "It's the team members' role to say up front, 'Hey, I think it would work out better if you focused on some different activities,'" she says.

At this same meeting, the team discusses the customer feedback from the previous month's contracts. "If you do something for someone and the team thinks you could have done it better or differently, you'll receive feedback that will help you improve your performance next time," Glaub explains. Lenz adds: "If there was an honest effort and constant communication, then we use the attempt as a learning experience." This isn't always the case, however. "If you don't complete a project, your team may not give you your whole bonus," Glaub says.

This is an important aspect of the system. As it's set up, bonuses—which are based on the company's performance—are distributed monthly to teams as a whole. Each individual has a bonus *target* for the year, which Glaub says usually makes up 10% to 25% of an employee's base pay. However, the monthly responsibility for dividing the bonus is left to the team members, who must decide collaboratively if the individual members have fulfilled their

VITALS

ORGANIZATION
Johnsonville Foods

TYPE OF BUSINESS
Specialty sausage manufacturer

HEADQUARTERS
Sheboygan, Wisconsin

OPERATIONS
Two processing facilities in Wisconsin and one in Connecticut; one slaughter facility in Wisconsin

EMPLOYEES
600

MEMBER SERVICES COORDINATOR
Leah Glaub

YOU SHOULD KNOW
Before Johnsonville Foods changed its hourly compensation system, the design team presented its proposal to the employees at each of the company's locations. After each presentation, the team distributed ballots and asked employees to vote on the change. Although the team's goal was to obtain a simple majority vote, more than 80% of the employees voted in favor of the result-block system.

contracted obligations. "Sometimes, employees come in below target at the year's end; sometimes they get 110% of their targeted bonus," Glaub says. "The target is established so individuals can measure their performance against a pre-established dollar amount."

Glaub says that in the event that contracts aren't complete, the team usually knows before the month's end. "Team members are supposed to come tell us halfway through the month if they're having some difficulties or if something came up of higher priority," Glaub says. "In those instances, the customers must say that it's OK that the member didn't finish the work [and fulfill the contract]." Usually, in these circumstances, Glaub says the employee will continue to work with the same customer the following month.

Lenz says that there have been cases in which team members didn't receive the bonuses expected: "We've had team members who lost some of their dollars because they didn't fulfill some of their contract obligations." This is rare, however. Why? Not only is there a financial incentive to complete tasks, but the contract also encourages hard work. "You're making a commitment when you write your contract, so you have to plan well and organize your time to get your work done," Glaub says. "People don't like to go to others and say, 'I didn't get finished.'"

The peer-review process builds bonds between workers. As Johnsonville enters its third year of peer review for compensation, everyone agrees that the benefits are evident. For management, the process alleviates some of the pressure caused by performance reviews and salary decisions. And for employees, it creates structure and needed challenge. "It can be stressful because the bar always is raised, and you can't get into those comfort levels where you can just coast," Lenz explains. "But, there's always a lot expected of you, and your contributions are valued. Plus, everyone knows what needs to be done to get a salary increase."

In addition, Rech says that there's a better bond between employees as a result of the review process. "People know what's being done throughout the areas. Everyone knows what others are working on, and each member is accountable to his or her peers." Overall, says Rech, the peer-review structure improves employee communication regarding job descriptions, work flow, accountability and productivity. Or, in other words, peer review helps this sausage company create more than one type of link.

Performance Appraisal with a Difference

by William H. Wagel

When Merck & Co., Inc.'s performance began to lag behind the other leading drug companies a few years ago, management decided to examine potential causes. Some of the causes, such as unfavorable foreign exchange rates, the increased cost of doing business, and several disappointing new-product introductions, were obvious. Others, however, required a deeper search for solutions.

A task force, known as the employee relations review committee, was therefore created to review the company's policies and practices. Chaired by Steven M. Darien, vice-president of employee relations, the task force interviewed a cross-section of 300 employees in groups of 10 to 15 at five major company sites. In addition, the task force visited other companies acknowledged as leaders in progressive human resources practices, spoke to noted academicians, and thoroughly reviewed available literature. However, the employee interviews served as the major source of information.

"Management was extremely interested in learning what our own employees thought of Merck policies and practices and how employees thought we could improve our work environment," Darien said. "The employee relations review committee's study confirmed that our written policies are in the forefront of the employee relations field. It also clearly revealed a number of areas where improvements could and should be made. The committee's recommendations were directed at maintaining a

positive and productive work environment in the future."

Among the 50 recommendations made by the committee were proposals for improving the company's performance appraisal system and salary administration program. The committee suggested that the performance appraisal system for exempt employees be revised to make better distinctions between performance levels of employees and to improve consistency among divisions and departments. The committee also suggested that the salary administration program be revised to provide more substantial increases to outstanding performers and lesser increases to employees not performing as well. To further recognize outstanding performers, the committee recommended the use of a variety of financial and nonfinancial rewards beyond those provided through the company's regular salary administration program.

Focus on Performance

In response to the employee relations review committee's finding that managers did not adequately distinguish between various levels of performance, the company developed a new performance appraisal and salary administration program, which was first pilot-tested in several divisions of the company and is now being used throughout the organization. Commenting on the philosophy behind the program, Darien said, "Even organizations noted for their overall excellence, such as top universities, professional football teams, or world-renowned opera companies, must find ways to provide special rewards for their best performers—

those who contribute above and beyond their peers."

Under the company's old appraisal system, approximately 97% of Merck employees had been grouped within a very narrow band of ratings. As a result, salary increases failed to reflect differences in performance levels, especially for employees who accomplished exceptional results during a given year. Therefore, the old numerical 13-point rating scale (1 through 5 with pluses and minuses) was replaced by five rating describers (see Exhibit 1). A sixth category called *progressing* (PR) is used for rating the performance of employees who are new to the company or new to positions that are significantly different from their previous positions.

In addition, the new system has revised and expanded performance definitions for three major areas of performance: specific job measures and ongoing duties, planned objectives, and management of people. The third category, management of people, was added for all managers and supervisors because the employee relations review committee had found that employees and managers at all levels of the company believed that managers were primarily

Exhibit 1. Exempt Performance Rating Definitions

Performance Ratings			Performance Definitions		
Rating		*Distribution Target*	*Specific Job Measures and Ongoing Duties*	*Planned Objectives*	*Management of People*
EX	Exceptional within Merck	5%	Far above Merck peers Capitalized on unexpected events to gain superior results	Made significant break-throughs or exceptional achievements	Outstanding leader Exceptional development/recruitment of people Superior communications
WD	Merck standard with distinction	15%	Clearly superior to Merck peers in most respects Took advantage of unexpected events to achieve unusually good results	Objectives met and many exceeded	A clear leader among Merck peers Top quality people recruited/developed Excellent communications
HS	High Merck standard	70%	Comparable to Merck peers Made use of unexpected events to achieve very good results	Objectives met	A very good leader Hires very good people/develops people as well as peers Very good communications
RI	Merck standard with room for improvement	8%	Work is not quite as good as Merck peers Contended with unexpected events	Most objectives met Some shortfalls	Adequate leader Hires good people Satisfactory communications
NA	Not adequate for Merck	2%	Work clearly inferior to Merck peers Did not fully cope with unexpected events	Missed significant objectives	Poor leader Communications could be better

PR	Progressing	Not applicable	Typically this employee is new to the company or in a significantly different assignment. Normally this rating would apply only during the first year in the new job.

compensated for their technical ability but were not always recognized or rewarded for their managerial ability.

A distribution target for performance ratings was created to help managers rank employees according to their performance and in comparison with the performance of their peers. Thus performance evaluation under the new system is a two-step process: First, an employee's performance is measured against objectives and ongoing duties, and then his or her performance is compared with the performance of other employees in the same area of the company.

As Arthur F. Strohmer, executive director of staffing and development for human resources, explained: "Under the company's old numerical appraisal system, employees were evaluated in terms of *absolute* definitions of performance. As a result, only about 1.5% of employees met the absolute definition of a '5' rating. The new system requires divisions to identify 5% of employees whose performance ranks in the top performance category *relative* to their peers, and then 15% for the next performance category, and so on."

Rewards for Achievement

Merck has also made some key changes in salary administration. For each category of performance and for each position within a salary range, a salary-planning guideline specifies the range of the increases that may be given and the frequency with which they may be given. Compa-ratio targets are emphasized to guide supervisors in assessing the long-term impact of merit actions and to ensure that an employee's salary is properly positioned within his or her salary range on the basis of sustained level of performance over several years.

The key objective of this system is to provide considerably higher increases for the company's best performers. For employees who consistently outperform their peers, the compa-ratio targets also serve to properly position those employees' salaries at the high end of their respective salary range.

To determine Merck's overall compensation levels, the company participates in an extensive variety of salary surveys each year. The primary survey used for determining salaries is the annual Hay Associates Compensation Comparison. The amount of money allocated for merit increases is designed to keep salaries competitive with those offered at top-paying companies and is a function of external competition as well as the company's own success.

A Significant Improvement

When the new performance appraisal and salary administration program was first pilot-tested at three Merck divisions, employees were cautious about it. However, most of them have now concluded that, fairly administered, it is a significant improvement over the old numerical system. The new program enables managers to give more financial rewards and recognition to employees who are truly contributing to the organization. It also seems, in the words of one employee, "more business-oriented" and reflects "a more mature relationship between supervisor and employee."

William H. Wagel is an associate editor for AMACOM's Human Resource Periodicals.

335

In Search Of Six Sigma: 99.9997% Defect-Free

by Brian M. Cook

The *Oxford English Dictionary* defines the word "quality" as "degree of excellence." And these days in industry, getting away from the word is almost impossible. Experts on world-class manufacturing say a company can't survive without it. And the people at Ford are constantly telling us, via their television commercials, that Quality is Job 1.

The question is: What does quality in industry mean? Does it mean having a finished product that's the best that can be made? That's not all of it, says Motorola Inc., the giant electronics group headquartered in Schaumburg, Ill. It offers what it calls a better definition: A product almost completely bereft of defects.

That philosophy is being increasingly echoed across a whole range of industrial companies in the U.S. Motorola and others are not only directing their energies at making their products defect-free; superior quality also means getting everything right—from the invoices, through internal and external communications, sales support, and down to the level of janitorial services within the company.

Most experts believe this "total" approach to quality—which involves trusting the members of the workforce and educating and training all of them (including top management)—will be essential for competing properly in world markets.

Following a recent survey of world-class manufacturers, which resulted in a report titled "Operational Principles of the 1990s," Gregory M. Seal, national director for manufacturing consulting, and

Craig A. Giffi, senior manager, both of Touche Ross & Co., Cleveland, said: "Quality has become a clear prerequisite to competing in the 1990s. Quality will be treated as a commodity. Those without it will not play in the markets. Superior quality will no longer differentiate competitors, but instead will validate a company's worthiness to compete."

And they're talking not only about quality as perceived by the manufacturer. Vital to the success is the quality seen through the eyes of the customers, who may sometimes be the workers themselves. Says the Touche Ross duo: "The concept of internal customers, while simple in nature, appears to be an indicator of the orientation of world-class competitors."

And there is a big difference between "good" quality—say, parts or products that are 95% or 98% defect-free—and the level of quality that provides a global competitive edge.

When Motorola, for example, won the coveted Malcolm Baldrige National Quality Award in 1988, it was in the early stages of an ambitious plan that by 1992 would, hopefully, achieve what may be the ultimate: Six Sigma Quality—99.9997% defect-free products, or 3.4 defects per 1,000,000 in its product line.

Talking to Motorola and other companies that have set their sights on such high quality perfection, it becomes clear that improvements in quality don't come through managerial edict. The message is that management must provide leadership.

Motorola watchers credit that company's success to the energy and vision of ex-Chairman, now chairman of the company's executive committee, Robert Galvin. He made quality the No. 1 item on the agenda at board meetings even before talking about financial matters—and he thus turned the whole subject of quality into a crusade.

"You don't just turn to the VP of Quality and tell him you want him to lead the crusade," agrees Jack W. Packard, chairman and CEO of Elco Industries Inc., Rockford, Ill., a manufacturer of industrial fasteners which is in the midst of a program that has set zero defects as its goal. "You, as top manager, have to lead."

Crusade is actually a very appropriate term for what has to occur to attain the highest achievable quality. There are many ways to do it, but there are also many pitfalls and problems.

One that immediately springs to mind is managing change. Management in particular has to be ready to accept that what has gone before in terms of quality performance is not good enough.

Complacency is a definite danger. Management has to learn to sustain the level of intensity at all times, says Mr. Packard. David Luther, senior vice president and corporate director of quality at Corning Inc., Corning, N.Y., adds that management must keep the momentum going, once a quality drive is initiated, by making everything appear new and exciting.

There is *no* one path to quality glory. Different companies adopt different approaches, but the end result is the same: The target is perfect quality.

For Motorola, winning the 1988 Baldrige Award was quite an achievement, considering that in the early '80s the company was reeling from the Japanese attack on its television and car-radio businesses. In 1981 the company embarked on a five-year program to increase productivity tenfold. It pretty much succeeded in this endeavor, but then it decided to go for the gold and seek a 100-fold improvement by the early 1990s.

In 1987, as part of this process, Motorola invested $44 million in employee training and education. The crusade was truly underway.

Today, the company's semi-conductor, automotive-electronics, cellular-radio, and pager businesses are competing favorably worldwide, including the Japanese market. Its net sales in 1989 reached a record $9.2 billion. The company's employees are being urged to embrace the perfect-quality credo—anticipating customer desires and

having the solution by the time the client is aware that there is a need for one.

The company's managers literally carry printed cards bearing the corporate objective of "total customer satisfaction." Corporate officials and business managers wear pagers so that they can quickly respond to customer inquiries. And they regularly visit customers' businesses to find out their likes and dislikes regarding Motorola's products and services.

All of this information, together with data from customer surveys, complaint hot lines, field audits, and other customer feedback measures, guides Motorola's planning for quality improvement and product development.

A participative-management process that emphasizes employee involvement at all levels has also been a key factor in Motorola's quality push. Such efforts have brought impressive results. For example, cycle times in the subscriber-cellular-telephone operation have been reduced by two-thirds. And pagers produced at the company's Boynton Beach, Fla., plant roll off the assembly line just two hours after assembly begins—one-twentieth of the previous cycle time—and are four times as reliable.

As well as asking for Six Sigma reports at directors' meetings, management is tying quality improvements to workers' pay. Performance reviews and bonus incentives play a role. New employees risk dismissal if they don't meet quality standards after a 90-day probation period.

Customer satisfaction is atop the pile. If a salesperson gets more than one complaint per 2,000 orders each quarter, he or she loses a 10% sales bonus.

So how does management control quality in a large and diverse company that has about 100,000 employees working in 53 plants worldwide? Mr. Galvin and CEO George Fisher appointed Richard Buetow, a former engineer at the company's Communications Sector, as vice president-director of quality. What he needs he gets. He has the full attention of both Mr. Galvin and Mr. Fisher. Reporting to him are more than 50 vice presidents of quality from all the Motorola divisions, although their first allegiance is to the general manager of each facility.

Mr. Buetow says there are three principal elements to his job: leading from the top, teaching, and auditing. The leading part he describes as counseling management on how to approach the subject; where the thrusts should be.

The teaching involves training and making sure that everyone gets the same message. In this regard, the company ensures that each employee gets at least 40 hours of training annually at what the company calls Motorola University.

The auditing function, meanwhile, takes note of policy- and goal-setting, and the commitment must be top-down in nature. There must be active participation from the CEO and COO for it to succeed. And at Motorola, senior managers of each plant meet eight times a year to review the progress made toward Six Sigma.

Motorola is already reaping rewards. Mr. Buetow estimates that during 1989, when the company reported $9.2 billion sales, $480 million was "saved" or came about as a result of the Six Sigma program of defect reductions.

This shows, he says, that once the proper measurement has been adopted, and everyone understands the goals, the investment needed is not large. As the 1989 results show, quality can be free, and it does pay dividends.

Mr. Buetow concedes, though, that even in the midst of a quality drive, companies do have flat spots. But he adds that the better a company gets, the more ways it finds to improve quality. The quality search becomes a never-ending process, with teamwork playing a major part.

The moral? Says Mr. Buetow:"You have to keep ahead of the competition. If quality goes down, costs go up. The opposite is also true." So it seems that going after higher quality is a form of cost containment. Higher quality is achieved by setting goals, making sure all the statistical tools are available, and using available technology to help define the proper design and manufacture of new products. Engineers designing new products at Motorola have to estimate the defect rate of all new or future products. The rule is "no handoff"—in other words, don't make it someone else's problem.

All of this is being achieved at a time when the public-education system is in crisis. Motorola has spent about $5 million to date to teach basic reading, writing, and math skills to those workers who do not have them. Mr. Buetow estimates the company will spend $35 million in this area during the

next five years or so. And this, more than anything else, is seen as a major problem for many companies seeking to attain high-quality products in an ever-increasingly competitive world market. But they may, like Motorola, have to solve it themselves.

What does Mr. Buetow advise someone in his shoes at another company to do about starting up a quality drive? Laughing, he responds: "Buy a lot of airline tickets." With 53 Motorola plants across the world, Mr. Buetow spends about half of his time traveling and meeting with management and quality people to discuss Six Sigma progress.

Elco's Mr. Packard believes that his company's uninterrupted profitability since its founding in 1933 will continue to be the result of providing high-quality products. The company, which makes metal and plastic fasteners for the automotive, construction and consumer do-it-yourself markets, employs some 1,600 people, who work in facilities in Rockford, Ill., Logansport and Mishawaka, Ind., and Goodlettsville, Tenn.

Zero defects is the company's ultimate goal, and its march toward that target has resulted in Ford's "Best-In-Class" and "Q1" awards, and General Motors' "Mark of Excellence Award"—the first time a fastener company has won this.

Elco's philosophy on the subject of quality is summed up in these words: "We shall continually strive for excellence in all that we do. We shall set our goals to achieve total customer satisfaction by delivering on-time products and services that conform to the requirements 100% of the time. Our name must represent quality and service to our customers and ourselves."

Mr. Packard has put himself at the forefront of the company's drive for 100% quality. This spring, management spent 30 hours in discussions of "managing change." He says it's like "asking people to do what you yourself are prepared to do." That, he says, is then cascaded through the organization.

"Listening to the customer" is another major aspect of the company's approach, along with the belief that quality is the most important product it makes. Uniform control, a more practical approach, is what Elco says it has to offer its customers. This means, says the company, that every aspect of its business—from needs analysis and design engineering to production and just-in-time shipping—is "housed under one roof" and therefore controlled by one quality ethos.

This has been backed up by an aggressive capital-expenditure program, employee training, and the implementation of Company-Wide Quality Control (CWQC). The company views CWQC as total quality integration: quality of management, human resources, work being done, work environment, and quality of product and service.

Total quality integration also means employee participation, human resources management, statistical process control, and education and training at all levels and in all areas. (Each employee averages 22 hours of classroom education annually, which represents an outlay of 1% of annual sales.) Quality is built in every step of the way, from pre-production planning to shipping.

Another factor that cannot be forgotten is the supplier. Without high-quality parts, all efforts to increase quality can be for naught. Adhering to this approach, Elco has built up a preferred list of vendors over the years. Says Mr. Packard: "Purchasing has not operated in a vacuum. We are willing to pay for a part at what on the surface looks like a higher price. But in the long run it costs less because your final product is better."

During the course of the drive for higher quality, Mr. Packard visited the company's competition in Europe and Japan to see how they handle quality. He brought back ideas on how to compete. One was the formation of Making Things Better teams. These teams—there are now 50—along with formal suggestion systems, have been responsible for more than 1,000 quality-improvement ideas. The results include: manufacturing queue times reduced 57% over a two-year period; nonconformance costs slashed by 52%; and shippable on-time percentages increased from 85% to 97%.

Mr. Packard is proud of what has been achieved, and believes that Elco is well on the way to attaining its 100% quality goals. He plans to meet with all employees soon to help provide that extra push.

Those in the know say that the next company likely to win a Baldrige Award is Corning. In 1983, Chairman James Houghton launched a major quality drive that involved setting aside $5 million for education of the company's worldwide workforce and the creation of a director of quality.

"No one at the time knew what he was talking about," comments Mr. Luther, Corning's director of quality. But they do now, because in the intervening years Corning has built a quality program that has enabled it to train all of its 28,000 workers. Corning's training program has been translated into six languages, but it has one set of clear strategies. These constitute the underpinning of the whole program.

The principal focus is on leadership. The program also involves the customer, training, employee involvement, communications, and finally, quality processes, tools, and measures.

On the first point, Mr. Luther says a company cannot succeed in any quality pursuit without the involvement of the top executives. Their participation will permeate the whole organization.

On the second point, the customer, he says the whole exercise is pointless unless a company *knows* what the customer wants—instead of *thinking* it knows. "You have to get at what it is the customer is saying," he says.

As it does at both Motorola and Elco, training plays a major role in the Corning quality effort. So does teamwork. Everyone is paid according to training levels. Everyone from top management down is involved in teams. And everyone has a key to the plant door. Trust is a very important factor at Corning.

Underscoring the company's commitment to employee involvement, new hires are encouraged to bring their families to orientation sessions. This approach is apparently having its effect; team participation has doubled in the last three years.

Then there's communications. Attention is paid to what workers have to offer. Climate surveys are taken. And the response has grown to the point that the company gets some 18,000 suggestions annually, compared with about 400 in 1982.

Finally, the company's focus on quality processes and the like translates into Six Sigma-like quality. Attempts to increase productivity and attain high-quality performance have to be accompanied by telling workers why it is important, says Mr. Luther. The essentials are setting goals, ensuring that people have the tools to carry them out, and having the right statistical measurements to gage progress.

Despite the obvious advances being made in the search for perfect quality by a growing number of

U.S. companies, there is still a lingering doubt about the outcome.

Does management have what it takes to lead its workers into a completely new way of making products that involves truly transferring some of the control to shop-floor workers? How many companies would, like Corning, give each worker a key to the plant door?

In the process of trusting machine operators and assembly workers to inspect their work, personnel such as supervisors and quality inspectors may go the way of the dodo. And so, there is likely to be much resistance.

But, come what may, U.S. manufacturers should heed the words of a Motorola worker: "There's someone out there who *will* do it if I don't."

Strategic Performance Measurement and Management in Multinational Corporations

by Randall S. Schuler, John R. Fulkerson, and Peter J. Dowling

For multinational firms, operating as global businesses with global workforces, the challenge of managing diverse operations in diverse environments has never been greater. The need to maintain appropriate consistency and coordinate vastly separated operations presents unique challenges. These simultaneous loose-tight requirements of managing business operations significantly increase the difficulty level.

In the area of international human resource management it means the identification and development of strategic international human resource actions that will prove a global consistency of purpose. Strategic international human resource management takes on particular importance in the areas of performance measurement and management in multinational corporations (MNCs). This article focuses around the three components of strategic international human resource management: interunit linkages, internal operations, and competitive requirements. Previous literature is reviewed within this framework, and the work of Pepsi-Cola International is used as an example of how MNCs manage some performance measurement and management issues. © 1992 by John Wiley & Sons, Inc.

Introduction

As the area of human resource management has expanded and become more linked with the strategic needs of the business, human resource actions are characterized as *strategic* human resource management (Schuler, 1992; Wright & McMahan, 1992). Strategic human resource management is defined as all those activities affecting the behavior of individuals in their efforts to formulate and implement the strategic needs of the business. Typically strategic business needs arise from decisions and intentions to guide the organization through a sea of turbulence and competitive pressures for the purposes of survival, growth, adaptability, and profitability (Hamel & Prahalad, 1989).

A similar phenomenon is occurring in the area of international human resource management, namely, the linkage of international human resource management with the strategic needs of the business and thus the development of strategic international human resource management (SIHRM). Reasons for this development include the recognition that human resource management is critical to business strategy implementation (Hambrick & Snow, 1989; Lawler, 1984; Sherwood, 1988); that there are common human resource demands that transcend national boundaries in managing human resources, for example, those associated with advanced manufacturing systems and competitive strategies targeting quality improvement (Jelinek & Goldhar, 1983; Wickens, 1987); and that the significant sharing of business experience and education is creating a worldwide workforce with more commonality rather than less (Reich, 1990).

At the same time that these vents are driving the development of strategic international human resource management, they are also giving a broader definition and focus to the field than is typically associated with international human resource management. The impact of this development is particularly evident in the area of strategic performance measurement and management. Describing this impact is the major focus of this article. The focus of strategic international human resource management is addressed first.

Strategic International Human Resource Management

Our definition of strategic international human resource management is simply: *all those activities affecting the behaviors of individuals in their efforts to formulate and implement the strategic needs of the international business operation* (Schuler, 1992). For multinationals (MNCs), major strategic business needs include being concerned with: (a) interunit linkages of the MNC (Doz & Prahalad, 1986), (b) internal operations (Schuler, Dowling, & DeCieri, in press; Evans, 1986), and (c) competitive requirements (Punnett & Ricks, 1992). While the importance of each of these three is expected to vary with the type of MNC (Punnett & Ricks, 1992; Garland, Farmer, & Taylor, 1990; Phatak, 1992), these three major strategic needs of MNCs allow for the development of a basic framework for describing strategic international performance measurement and management in MNCs.

Strategic International Performance Measurement and Management

A key component of strategic international human resource management is the development of strategic international performance measurement and management. Performance management is a critical business driver that can help produce business results. If viewed as a strategic tool, performance management can be a powerful addition to management action. The distinction between what is a strategic human resource action and what is not strategic is based on whether or not the activity is being explicitly done to support the strategic needs of the business (Foulkes, 1986; Hamel & Prahalad, 1989). Thus a US MNC's efforts to develop performance appraisal forms in Australia is a strategic activity if it is explicitly being done in concert with the firm's strategic intentions and directions to improve individual performance.

This approach, rather than being new, is really consistent with the treatment by Pucik (1985) and Evans (1986). In essence, this approach represents an alternative to distinguishing human resource activities being done at operational, management, and strategic levels (Fombrun, Devanna, & Tichy, 1981). It also recognizes that all employees can be involved in activities that have a direct connection with the strategic intentions, directions, and interests of the MNC.

Because this article is concerned with the strategic aspects of MNCs that relate to performance measurement and management, it touches upon the performance and behaviors of all employees. The three major components of strategic international human resource management: interunit linkages, internal operations, and competitive requirements are discussed, highlighting the current issues and dilemmas. An example is provided describing one US MNC firm's approach to strategic performance measurement and management that addresses some of these issues and dilemmas.

Interunit Linkages: The Role of Performance Management in Business Unit Coordination and Control

Interunit linkages have been a traditional focal point for the discussion of international human resource management generally and performance measurement and management more specifically (Pucik & Katz, 1986). The focus of these discussions has typically been around the themes of control and variety, in particular, how to facilitate variety and how to control and coordinate that variety (Doz & Prahalad, 1986; Bartlett & Ghoshal, 1987). Discussions have focused on: (a) factors impacting MNC employee performance (particularly expatriate managerial performance, (b) constraints on unit-level appraisal in MNCs (Pucik & Katz, 1986), and (c) criteria used for measuring, appraising, and managing performance of employees. Basically these topics have been addressed within the context of MNCs exporting people to distant and different locations and/or exporting the entire HR function itself and specific practices such as performance appraisal *en masse* to other parts of the world (Fisher, 1989).

The assessment of expatriate performance demands an understanding of the variables that influence an expatriate's success or failure in a foreign assignment. The three major variables include the environment (culture), the task (job requirements), and personality characteristics of the individual (Pucik, 1985; Dowling & Schuler, 1990).

Environment. The cultural and/or living environment has an impact on any job, but it becomes of primary importance in the success or failure of the expatriate. As environments vary greatly, the potential for successful performance also varies. Some environments can yield a relatively easy adaptation by an expatriate, while others impose tremendous difficulties. Many factors that can be expected or taken for granted in one's home country simply may not exist in the host country. It is also likely that expatriate managers and their families will have some difficulty adjusting to a new culture, which, in turn, may impact on the manager's work performance. This difficulty in cultural adjustment should be taken into account when assessing the speed with which an expatriate masters a new job (Davidson, 1984; Mendenhall & Oddou, 1988).

Task. In attempting to predict how well an individual will perform in the expatriate assignment, consideration must be given to the general type of job assignment and job requirements. The specific work tasks an expatriate must perform vary widely. Hays (1974) categorizes the general types of expatriate assignments or tasks into four groups:

- The *structure reproducer* carries the assignment of building or reproducing in a foreign subsidiary a structure similar to that which he or she knows from another part of the company. He or she could be building a marketing framework, implementing an accounting and financial reporting system, or establishing a production plant, for example.

- The *technical troubleshooter* is the individual who is sent to a foreign location to analyze and solve a particular operational problem.

- The *operational expatriate* is the individual whose assignment is to perform as an acting element (well defined) in an already existing, ongoing business proposition.

- The *chief executive officer* has the assignment of overseeing and directing the entire foreign operation.

As various categories of job assignments are examined, it becomes clear that the abilities of the individual sent to perform a particular job must match the assignment demands. Most MNCs are able to obtain a reasonably accurate assessment of an individual's basic capability for the job, in terms of the task involved, from performance evaluations prior to the expatriate assignment. Many individuals and firms rank job ability as the primary ingredient relating to their expected probability of success in the international assignment. Certain types of tasks, however, require significantly more interaction with a local culture than others.

The difficulty of an assignment increases when task, environmental, and/or cultural variables are interrelated. The process of establishing a new marketing system or operating as a chief executive officer, for example, may depend heavily on an individual's ability to interact effectively with the local culture and environment. On the other hand, a technical troubleshooter may require considerably less cultural flexibility to operate efficiently in a foreign environment. Clearly, job assignments and tasks that require an ability to relate effectively to the local culture place a greater demand on the social and cultural skills of the individual.

Personality Factors. Personality factors also play a role in explaining an international manager's ability to adapt to a foreign environment. Much of the expatriate effectiveness literature is concerned with assessing personality variables. As the environment and the job may be largely predetermined, the selection of the individual is one of the few decisions under the full control of the MNC. Personality variables, in particular personal and cultural flexibility, appear to play an important role in helping to increase the probability of successful performance of international managers (Daspin, 1985).

In summary, the environment, the assignments or tasks, and the individual's personality are important variables in expatriate performance. The circumstances of a particular assignment will dictate which factors are of primary importance. Of course, staffing international operations with host country nationals (HCNs) and third country nationals (TCNs) reduces the potential negative impact of cultural or environmental factors. But regardless of the source of the MNC manager, there will still be performance variables which must be managed through performance appraisal and management.

Constraints and Strategic Performance Measurement and Management in MNCs

In developing a strategic performance measurement and management system for managers of MNCs, there are five major constraints or features of an international organization that affect appraisal. While they primarily impact the MNC's appraisal of each unit in their international operations, these constraints also have the potential for affecting the performance of the unit's individual managers. Thus performance measurement and management systems for MNC managers need to address the following constraints.

Whole versus Part. To pursue a competitive global strategy, a MNC must focus simultaneously on global performance and subsidiary or regional market performance. In the long run, the sum of short-term, optimal, subportfolio investments does not necessarily lead to optimal, long-term performance for the MNC as a whole. An organization may use short-term, local profit-maximization strategies due to local competitive pressures which it ordinarily would not use on a global basis.

Noncomparable Data. Frequently, the data obtained from one subsidiary may not be directly applicable to another. For example, notions of what constitutes appropriate marketing copy can vary widely from one country to another; import tariffs can distort pricing schedules; and local labor laws may make workforce reductions difficult at plants which are producing at below capacity. These factors make objective appraisal of subsidiary performance more complicated.

Volatility of the International Environment. The economic or political volatility under which subsidiaries operate may require varying definitions of what constitutes success. It is important to reconcile the tension between the need for universal appraisal standards with specific objectives in local subsidiaries.

Separation by Time and Distance. Judgments concerning the fit between long-term MNC strategy and activities in subsidiaries are further complicated by the physical distance, time-zone differences, and frequency of contact between the corporate head-office staff and subsidiary management. Developments in sophisticated worldwide communications systems such as fax machines do not substitute fully for "face to face" contacts between subsidiary managers and MNC corporate staff. It is often necessary to meet personally with a manager to truly understand the problems or issues managers must face. For this reason, many MNC corporate HR managers spend a considerable amount of time traveling in order to assure understanding and communication of the human resource strategies.

Variable Levels of Market Maturity. Without the supporting infrastructure of the parent company, market development in a foreign subsidiary may be slower and more difficult to achieve than in the home country where established brands can support new products, and new business areas can be funded by other divisions. As a result, more time may be needed to achieve results than in a fully developed domestic market.

Criteria Used for Performance Appraisal of International Employees

Now that the variables likely to influence expatriate performance have been described, the criteria by which performance is to be appraised and evaluated can be discussed. These criteria generally are a function of the nature of the specific type of expatriate assignment (such as Hays' categorization), the stages of international business development, and the international HRM philosophy or approach of the MNC.

The approach of the MNC to human resource management influences which criteria are used and who sets the standards. With a strict global approach, standards are set and administered by parent country nationals (PCNs). A drawback of this approach is that it fails to take advantage of local variety and diversity. With a more localized approach, standards are largely determined and administered by host country nationals (HCNs) at the local level. This may have the drawback of not allowing a MNC headquarters the level of coordination it may want, but may allow the local flexibility to meet market demands and changes.

As the stage of international business development changes, appraisal criteria also change. For example, a change in focus from technology transfer to a more strategic approach with longer-term objectives requires a considerable change in emphasis with regard to performance appraisal. The type and relevance of performance criteria also may vary according to the level of control or decentralization exercised by the parent over the subsidiary.

Pucik (1985) has suggested that in order to properly evaluate a subsidiary's performance, a set of parallel accounts adjusted for the influence of financial differences may need to be maintained, or new measures of control may need to be developed, that are less susceptible to the influence of factors such as exchange-rate fluctuations, cashflow and liquidity, and transfer pricing.

Another alternative would be to evaluate a manager on the basis of subsidiary performance using achievement of long-range goals rather than short-term measures such as profit or return on equity. A strictly results-oriented approach, however, does not consider the way results are obtained and the behaviors used to obtain these results. The Foreign Corrupt Practices Act has prompted an increased use of behavioral as well as results data in MNCs to appraise the performance of the expatriate manager. Broadly defined behavioral criteria are also becoming popular with MNCs desiring a global managerial workforce. It appears that familiarizing managers with one set of behavioral performance criteria makes it easier to move and adjust to different international settings (Fulkerson & Schuler, 1992).

In summary, this discussion on interunit linkage issues and their implications for strategic performance measurement and management systems suggests that there are many factors which impact the performance of expatriate managers (and nonmanagers) running or operating foreign operations. Because of this complexity, it can be difficult to make fair evaluations and comparisons of managerial contributions.

The evaluation of performance under widely varying operating conditions is faced by many MNCs. Pepsi-Cola International, like other MNCs,

faced the problem of matching strategic business focus with ample latitude for local initiation and creativity.

Pepsi-Cola International (PCI) is the international beverage division (outside of North America) of Pepsico, Inc.; its brands are sold in over 150 countries and it faces the challenge of matching the demand for high standards of individual performance with the needs of a globally diverse workforce in a highly decentralized organization that can be most successful when its strategic activities are coordinated on a worldwide basis. Pepsi-Cola International is meeting this challenge by providing a foundation of human resource practices that are modified to meet country-specific requirements. The design of human resource practices starts with the basic assumption that the improvement of individual and organization performance, along with a coordinated, yet decentralized approach to the businesses, are the desired outcomes (Fulkerson & Schuler, 1992).

In 1985, there was some confusion about what it took to be individually successful in Pepsi-Cola International. There was no shared value system or vocabulary for describing individual performance. For example, in the socialist countries the concept of individual performance was practically nonexistent, whereas in Germany it carried meaning similar to its meaning in the United States. The business was developing and growing at a rapid rate, and the pressures on individual managers were considerable. As a consequence, a "Success Study" was launched.

With the full support of the Division President, a study was initiated, in cooperation with the Center for Creative Leadership, to determine what factors might be associated with individual performance success across many markets and nationalities. Because the study was aimed at identifying the factors that contribute to the success of the business, it was clearly a study in strategic performance measurement and management. The study team looked at 100 successful and 100 not-so-successful managers from different functional specialties and from different nationalities. The factors that emerged from the study are shown in Exhibit 1.

The impact of the results of the study on building common values was remarkable. The greatest impact was to focus people for the first time on a common vocabulary for discussing individual performance and development. Prior to the study, it had been difficult to articulate dimensions of performance in a consistent, globally acceptable way.

Through the study, Pepsi-Cola International developed a multinational vocabulary that could be used to unite people from many different cultures and countries. For example, "Handling Business Complexity" might translate differently in China than it does in France. In China it might mean that you get a product produced and to the loading dock. By contrast, in France it might mean being concerned with marketing, distribution, and merchandising, in addition to getting a product produced and to the loading dock. Though different in meaning, the outcome is the same: generating sales in the local environment.

Thus while "Handling Business Complexity" translates differently, the intent or behavioral outcome remains the same regardless of the language or culture. The business issues addressed by the success factor "Handling Business Complexity" is getting an individual to figure out what needs to be done, regardless of country, and to chart a course of action. This turned out to be the most important success factor, and one that could be universally understood from behavioral and business perspectives. While the Success Study provided much needed focus on describing strategic performance measurement and management issues, it also pointed out the need for revision in many of the other specific HR programs and processes being used at PCI to coordinate the globally diverse operation.

In terms of interunit linkages, PCI's strategic performance measurement and management system offers a way of facilitating variety and yet retaining some degree of uniformity for control and coordination. The system also moves attention away from just "producing good numbers" in its far-flung operations. The system recognizes that many factors such as market conditions and stages of economic development will have a differential impact on performance. Performance standards and criteria, being interactively developed, might best be described as reflecting a more global orientation (Heenan & Perlmutter, 1979).

In other words, the strategic performance measurement and management system at PCI serves as a

---

Exhibit 1. PCI Success Factors for Performance Measurement and Management

1. Handling business complexity: Figuring out what needs to be done and charting a course of action.
2. Drives results orientation: Focusing on an outcome and driving for completion.
3. Leads/manages people: Directing the work of and motivating others.
4. Executional excellence: Putting ideas into action.
5. Organizational savvy: Knowing how the organization works and how to maximize it.
6. Composure under pressure: Staying focused in the international pressure cooker and still getting things done.
7. Executive maturity: Always acting with maturity and good judgment.
8. Technical knowledge: Understanding and applying technical knowledge.
9. Positive people skills: Knowing how to get along with people from all cultures.
10. Effective communication: Knowing how to communicate cross-culturally.
11. Impact, influence: Being able to get things done when faced with obstacles.

Adapted from Fulkerson, J.R., & Schuler, R.S. (1992). Managing worldwide diversity at Pepsi-Cola International. In S.E. Jackson & Associates, *Diversity in the workplace. Human resources initiatives.* New York: Guilford Press.

---

tool for attaining the strategic objectives of the business as well as meeting the needs of the local environment and local manager. In fact, the movement away from using expatriates makes such a system more critical. It was seen as a necessary tool to meld the diverse operations across many cultures into a focused, global, yet decentralized operation.

Strategic performance measurement and management system at PCI assists in managing the *manag-*

ers of its diverse operations; it assists these managers in focusing on results. In so doing, the performance management process also assists in balancing results and process regardless of the culture in which a MNC may be operating.

Internal Operations: Thinking Globally and Acting Locally

The second major strategic business need of MNCs is concern for the human resource management activities within each geographic location (unit), which becomes critical as MNCs strive to integrate an otherwise global set of diverse businesses. Headquarters wants to have some ability to coordinate operations, yet it recognizes the reality of local cultural imperatives (Adler, 1991). In these efforts to deal with local cultural imperatives, MNCs quickly become involved with internal operations of foreign units. This overlap of the issues pertinent to both internal operations and interunit linkages reflects the complexity of MNCs seeking to operate in globally coordinated yet decentralized ways. This is certainly evident in the discussion of balancing imperatives. Further specific impact of this balancing act on internal operations is played out as performance measurement and management need to be aligned with other human resource practices within the unit (Adler, 1991; Schneider, 1988; Latham & Napier, 1989; Adler & Jelinek, 1986; Child, 1981; Enz, 1986).

Balancing Business Imperatives with Cultural Imperatives

The cultural imperative here addresses the local culture, economy, legal system, religious beliefs, and education. The cultural imperative is important in SIHRM because of its impact on acceptable, legitimate, and feasible practices and behaviors (Adler, 1991; Schuler et al., in press); acceptable in terms of: "Can we appraise workers in the same way worldwide and thereby differentiate them, according to performance?"; legitimate in terms of: "Are there any legal statutes prohibiting us from formally appraising?"; feasible in terms of: "While the society is hierarchical, authoritarian, and paternalistic, can we empower the workforce to appraise its own performance in order to facilitate our competitive strategy of quality improvement?"

All three components of the cultural imperative are important for MNCs to consider in decisions about: (a) what behaviors to address, (b) which performance measurement and management tools to use, and (c) which tools can be used within the local units. Because questions about which tools to use are also influenced by the MNC's need for worldwide coordination and control (the administrative imperative), it may be necessary to balance the needs of the cultural imperative with those of the administrative imperative (Doz & Prahalad, 1986).

Key themes in balancing the imperatives include: the sensitivity to determine the need for balancing imperatives, the balancing of the imperatives of the need to manage the business consistently for control and coordination with the need to benefit from the variety of local differences, and the awareness of the necessity of identifying and aligning several international human resource management activities.

Balancing the Global with the Local

Performance measurement and management is a major SIHRM practice that MNCs have used to help coordinate and control their far-flung global operations (Pucik & Katz, 1986; Dowling & Schuler, 1990). Traditional MNCs have sent parent country nationals or expatriates abroad to ensure that the policies and procedures of the home office were being carried out to the letter in foreign operations (Punnett & Ricks, 1992). As costs became prohibitive and career issues made these assignments less attractive, MNCs turned to third county nationals and host country nationals to satisfy international staffing needs (Heenan & Perlmutter, 1979).

While this approach may have solved the staffing need, it raised concern about its ability to satisfy the administrative imperative for coordination and control. As Pucik and Katz (1986) argued, MNCs could react by: (a) establishing rules and procedures for employees to carry out or (b) socializing the employees to think and behave like expatriates. Of course these pure types might rarely be found as MNCs seek to find the most appropriate fit to the circumstances. For example, under conditions of rapid change, high uncertainty, and the need for information to be gathered and utilized, firms would more likely help employees have a greater understanding of the political, social, and cultural environment. Under conditions of stability, certainty, and the need for technical information to be utilized, firms would more likely be found establishing more consistent processes and procedures (Pucik & Katz, 1986).

But MNCs rarely find either one set of conditions or another, so combinations of the two approaches were common. Because socializing has a tendency to reflect the culture and norms of the parent firm, this process tends to be biased (Pucik & Katz, 1986). Thus the ability of the firm to maximize variety was compromised. This was particularly so as the MNC engaged more third country nationals and host country nationals in preference to expatriates, individuals who would be expected to have a full understanding of the corporate culture.

Although use of TCNs and HCNs is extensive, discussions in the literature minimize the issue of appraising the performance of HCN and TCN managers. This reflects the scarcity of research on the topic and the general lack of an acceptable way to address the situation (Mendenhall, 1989; Morgan, 1989). In practice, US MNCs have tried using the same appraisal form on HCNs and TCNs (and expatriates if they are not heading the subsidiary) as on their domestic employees without translation from English or the same form translated to the appropriate language. Both approaches have drawbacks: The use of English-worded forms may not be readily understood by HCN and TCN managers and their employees (nor do they easily apply to all jobs in all situations). Even when the forms are translated and then returned to the home office, they still may not be readily understood by the domestic staff. Any objectives of the performance measurement and management system are thus thwarted.

The practice of performance appraisal itself confronts the issue of cultural applicability (Adler, 1991). Performance appraisal in different countries can be interpreted as a signal of distrust or even an insult. As a consequence, MNCs may have been hesitant about doing performance appraisals of their HCN and TCN employees. Of course MNCs, desiring to recognize, yet also take advantage of variety, want to coordinate distant operations. Thus the top

management of MNCs desire to establish a method for them to appraise distant operations while at the same time allowing for the expression of cultural differences. Here is how PCI's system of strategic performance measurement and management addresses this dilemma.

Strategic Performance Measurement and Management within PCI

As Pepsi-Cola International has grown, senior business and human resource management executives from headquarters and local field operations meet regularly and travel extensively to understand how organization performance can be improved. Both formal and informal meetings and discussions surface needs and stimulate a search for performance management solutions.

Whether formally or informally generated, data used to develop and drive the development of human resource practices, such as strategic performance measurement and management, generally come from the individuals who are running the business. Regular climate surveys are conducted by the local operating units to find periodic improvements in their performance and in other management practices. Surveys are also conducted as a regular part of managerial and leadership training programs. Individuals are regularly asked to comment on the needs of the business, on the organization, and on how to improve the performance of individual managers.

Because this is done at the local level, the surveys can be translated into the local language and modified to fit local conditions. The primary actions taken on the basis of the results are left largely up to the local HR staff. Survey results in the United Kingdom are likely to be different from those in China, and their actions will be different. But even if the results were the same, the actions may be different. For example, if the survey results revealed a need for more entry-level workers, the operations in the United Kingdom might begin an advertising campaign in the local newspaper. In China, the local operation would first go to the local government and discuss the matter.

This philosophy of asking employees and localizing management is a cornerstone of the development of Pepsi-Cola International's strategic performance measurement and management practices.

It stands to reason that in a truly diverse work environment, the local manager is the most knowledgeable expert as to what will or will not work. For example, when it was necessary to redesign the human resource planning process, over 70 managers from across the world were interviewed to gather suggestions on what would help them run their units more effectively. It was these same managers who initially suggested that the process needed to be more focused on individual and organization development. Using an outside consultant, an internal team (of both HR and business managers), with the assistance of senior management, built general consensus that preserved local human resource decision making while retaining a common framework for all of Pepsi-Cola International. While it was agreed that all units would embrace the philosophy of performance improvement and instant feedback, they could adapt this to their own local conditions.

PCI addresses the balance between cultural imperative and administrative imperative with common HR policies that serve as guidelines used by local units in developing tools for performance measurement and management. In general, a core guiding philosophy of PCI is a continuous pursuit of "High Standards of Performance."

Instant Feedback. For purposes of illustrating how an HR policy serves as a guide in developing specific performance measurement and management tools, here is how a portion of PCI's "High Standards of Personal Performance" applies across 150 nations in which PCI operates. This portion is called "Instant Feedback." Stated simply, the principle of instant feedback says that if you have a problem or an idea about any aspect of the business or about an individual's performance, the organization demands that you raise the issue appropriately and discuss it maturely. Instant Feedback is at the base of a chain of feedback systems designed to improve and maintain high levels of personal performance.

Because Pepsi-Cola International is fundamentally a feedback driven organization, this feedback policy is mirrored in every tool used to measure and improve performance. The original vehicle that delivered this message was a twenty-minute video tape on Instant Feedback. The tape used dramatizations and explanations to explain how Instant Feedback is now a part of the everyday vocabulary of Pepsi-Cola International. It is heard when someone

with an issue or problem says to another individual, "Let me give you some Instant Feedback." With travel schedules, frequent phone contact, and constant time zone pressures, Instant Feedback has become a shorthand for getting to the point and communicating clearly.

There are differences, but Instant Feedback can be modified to fit any country. The successful delivery of Instant Feedback requires some fitting to local cultures. Americans use it because it fits the fast-paced American way. In Asian cultures, feedback may be tough and direct, but it should never be given in public. Canadians will say that Americans are too direct, and some Europeans will say that Americans are too demanding and critical. In some Asian cultures, there is a lot of headnodding during Instant Feedback as if signifying agreement, but it really only signifies that the message has been heard. Some Latins will argue very strongly if they do not agree with the feedback, and some nationalities (e.g., India) will insist on a great deal of specificity.

The important point is that the Instant Feedback message can be delivered in any culture. The focus of Instant Feedback is always how to improve business performance and is not directed against cultural styles. While total cultural neutrality is not possible, Instant Feedback says that it does not really matter *how* you do it as long as you do it. In the process, however, PCI balances the cultural and administrative imperatives.

In addition to Instant Feedback, four other individual performance management tools Pepsi-Cola International employs are listed in Exhibit 2. In all cases, the intent of each tool is to improve individual performance *vis-à-vis* business objectives. For example, Pepsi-Cola International has a workshop on performance management that is designed to help managers and employees understand how and why performance management is a competitive advantage and why it can help assure individual success. This performance management workshop, delivered by local staff, takes the concept of Instant Feedback as a starting point and links the feedback tools together. The intent is to assure that performance management occurs in a manner that is as culturally neutral as possible and linked with the strategic needs of the business. The performance management workshop may be delivered in the local

349

language, and attendees are encouraged to find ways to apply the principles in concert with local customers and culture.

Coaching. Coaching differs from Instant Feedback in that coaching is a series of Instant Feedbacks designed to improve a large chunk of behavior. Coaching can be scripted to improve larger chunks of knowledge that cannot be learned on one trial. Both Instant Feedback and Coaching are then combined to provide data points that are used in preparing the annual written performance appraisal.

Accountability Based Performance Appraisals. Pepsi-Cola International is a pay-for-performance company. This means that compensation is always tied to results. A written performance appraisal is required before compensation adjustments can be made. The appraisal may be written in the local language, but no matter where or how it is done, the language of appraisal is focused on the individual's performance against assigned accountabilities. The appraisal form also requires a specification of areas for improvement within each separate accountability. To make the appraisal as culturally neutral as possible, accountabilities are specified in terms of what must be accomplished. For example, a good accountability statement might read: "Achieve a 15% sales growth for the year." The accountability does not specify the methods by which the accountability is achieved. That is left up to local management judgment. The performance management system requires that an appraisal must be done and that it must be very specific in terms of what was good and what needs improvement. Beyond that, local operating conditions dictate the content. To provide guidance and consistency, the headquarters develops models that the local field locations can adopt and adapt. For example, the PCI headquarters staff has developed models for performance management, selection, and management development. The local operations are expected to adopt and adapt these models, knowing that they still are held accountable for accomplishment of business objectives.

Finally, there is common people management accountability in managerial appraisals. This linkage and reinforcement assure that people management is part of individual compensation and is constant across the Pepsi-Cola International system. The components of the people management account-

---

Exhibit 2.
PCI's Performance Measurement and Management Tools

What	Frequency
• Instant feedback	Daily
• Coaching (performance management)	Event-driven
• Accountability based performance appraisals	Yearly
• Development feedback	Yearly
• Human resource planning	Yearly

Adapted from Fulkerson, J.R., & Schuler, R.S. (1992). Managing worldwide diversity at Pepsi-Cola International. In S.E. Jackson & Associates, *Diversity in the workplace: Human resources initiatives.* New York: Guilford Press.

---

ability and the behaviors that can be adapted to local conditions associated with each component are as follows:

- *Conducting Performance Appraisals:* Managing a diverse organization requires that a manager do a thorough job of evaluating performance. A portion of a manager's personal compensation is dependent on doing a good job of evaluating the performance of others in a culturally neutral manner.

- *Conducting Personal Development Discussion:* Development of skills is a cornerstone of a pay-for-performance organization. Managers must seek ways to develop their subordinates using available performance management tools and have regular feedback discussions.

- *Implementing Development Plans:* It is not sufficient simply to have had a discussion about development issues, a manager must follow-up to be certain the plans have been implemented and have brought about the desired outcomes.

- *Attracting/Hiring Superior Talent:* The growth of local country talent is critical to future business growth. It does not matter if the search is for a Chinese or a Nigerian, the manager has the responsibility for attracting and bringing talent into the organization.

- *Providing Instant Feedback/Coaching:* These are an integral part of a manager's responsibilities, regardless of location. Once again, however, adaptation to local culture is recognized.

- *Fostering Teamwork:* This aspect of managerial behavior helps build the cooperation and sharing of knowledge that are key parts of Pepsi-Cola International's management style. A manager must share the credit for accomplishments and find ways to energize the cultural synergies that exist.

- *Building Bench* (Succession Development): The ultimate objective of bringing talented individuals into the organization is not satisfied unless they are developed and prepared for greater responsibility. In a performance-driven organization, there must always be a payoff and Bench Building is one of those payoffs. Without a bench of talented individuals there is no organization continuity. In a sense, each manager has a continuing responsibility to leave behind even better and more capable people.

- *Managing/Building Executional Excellence:* At the bottom line of maintaining high standards is a relentless focus on delivering results. All the management in the world counts for nothing unless the results are delivered. It is this constant focus on getting things done that helps minimize cultural differences.

The culture of Pepsico and Pepsi-Cola International is action oriented. Managers within the system believe that national cultural differences can be used as a force for strength if producing results is always the shared goal. Maintaining high standards means that managers understand that Arabs attack a problem in a slightly different manner than Americans or Japanese. However, the focus on high standards produces a mindset that says "Let me hear what you think or how you believe this should get done, and then we will combine the best of both our ideas to produce a culturally creative way of solving our mutual business problems."

Development Feedback. With a pay-for-performance appraisal system, it was apparent to all managers using the system that specifying areas for improvement would drive development. It is one thing to tell someone that something needs improvement and quite another to explain how that improvement can and should be accomplished. Pepsi-Cola International and a number of other Pepsico divisions employ a development feedback process to aid in driving strategic performance management and development.

Basically, the process requires an individual employee to complete a rating form to assess how well they believe they are doing against a set of success factors. After the self-ratings have been completed, the employee's supervisor rates the employee on the same success factors. The employee and supervisor then have a development discussion that is relatively free of accountability content. In effect, the pay increase decision has been completed, and the purpose of this discussion is to focus on personal development issues. Put another way, the performance appraisal is focused on what has happened in the past, while the development feedback discussion is focused on the future. The content of the discussion revolves around the skills that need to be improved or gained to assure continued success on an individual basis. From this discussion, a development plan is crafted, and future career prospects are discussed. For example, if technical knowledge needs development, then the specific knowledge and skills that need improvement are delineated, and programs for improvement may be suggested.

This entire performance management and development feedback effort can be conducted in any language and in any culture. The development action plans can be implemented in the context of the country or business where the employee works. The completion of the development feedback discussion serves to meet the continuing goal of building a feedback driven culture. The discussion with the employee is open and candid, regardless of nationality, and is free to include a wide range of development issues. The objective is to improve careers and performance in the most culturally acceptable manner possible. Culturally, differences are reflected in performance management and career development activities. For example, in Japan career progression generally follows from seniority first with performance being a lagging variable. In the United States and, to a lesser extent, Eastern Europe, performance seems to matter most and seniority, unless reflective of job-related experience, is the lagging variable. Thus these cultural differences get reflected in the career activities as the local field operations are left to adapt the common HR practices to their conditions.

Human Resource Planning. The performance management and development feedback process also serves another goal: The results of that feedback become the primary document for the human resource planning process.

The human resource planning process is a business tool used to plan organizational and individual growth. The organization side of the process drives and defines the human resource actions needed to achieve business plans. From an individual perspective, the human resource planning process is focused on assuring individual development and providing yet another opportunity for feedback to the individual employee on personal growth issues. The same document used for the development feedback process is used in the human resource planning process, and the same performance rating used in the performance appraisal is used in the human resource plant. The linkage is very tight, but the communication process is open in the performance management, employee development, and human resource planning system. The intent is to open up the process to the individuals involved to build trust and to allow the process to be used as a development tool as opposed to a judgment device.

Development and personal growth would appear to be universal human needs, and when a human resource system taps into those needs and is relatively uncomplicated, it stands a better change of working across cultures. Again, there are differences. In Asian cultures where relationships between the individual and organization are longer term and seniority-based, career development activities are played out combining these longer termed and seniority-based aspects with performance. In contrast, in Western cultures career development activities are carried out largely by performance, thus career

advancement in Western nations is more rapid than in Asian nations.

Not only does the PCI approach to strategic performance measurement and management address the issue of balancing imperatives for local unit managers, it also provides those managers direction and guidance in aligning performance appraisal with other SIHRM activities. These activities have their primary impact on the employees working for the local managers within the local unit.

Aligning Performance Measurement and Management with Other SIHRM Activities

Increasingly, professionals and academicians envision the need for simultaneous existence of several international human resource management activities. That is, just being concerned with the strategic performance measurement and management practices is not going to serve any MNC very well in its efforts to attain its strategic objectives. Being concerned with all the SIHRM practices simultaneously, while certainly better, is not enough. What is necessary is the development of a set of SIHRM practices and activities that are internally consistent. A full action set includes an SIHRM philosophy, SIHRM policies, and SIHRM practices.

Statements of SIHRM philosophy or people culture are about how people are to be treated within the organization regardless of worldwide location. While general, they have the ability to proscribe limits on the actual treatment of individuals regardless of location. This is done through its top-down impact on other SIHRM activities as shown in Exhibit 3. When these are consciously and systematically linked to the strategic business needs of the MNC, they are appropriately regarded as strategic international human resource management activities (Schuler et al., in press). PCI has crafted general statements of SIHRM philosophy to assist the coordination of all its HR activities. Examples include:

- Empowering people to drive the business from the closest point to the market

- Developing the right skills to be the best in the business

- Building career opportunities

- Building teamwork

Exhibit 3. Aligning and Balancing Strategic International Human Resource Management Activities	
Contribution	
• Expresses how to treat and value people	• **Human resource philosophy** expressed in statement of business values and defining of people culture
• Establishes guidelines for action	• **Human resource policies** expressed as shared values (guidelines)
• Motivates needed role behaviors	• **Human resource practices** for leadership, managerial, and operational employee role behaviors

Adapted from R.S. Schuler, "Strategic Human Resource Management: Linking People with the Strategic Needs of the Business," *Organizational Dynamics,* Summer 1992.

• Helping people succeed by building an environment with high integrity, strong and consistent values, and continuous improvement

Armed with an SIHRM philosophy, MNCs are able to further define how employees are to be treated. Strategic international HRM policies help to specify the meaning of the philosophy. At PCI, SIHRM policies also are referred to as statements of shared values.

Briefly stated, the HR policies at PCI refer to:

• Leadership
• Balancing Teamwork and Individual Achievement
• High Standards of Personal Performance
• Career/Skill Development

From these policies or shared values come more specific SIHRM practices. These are the human resource activities that directly impact employees, for example, types of strategic performance measurement and management tools and forms of strategic training and development. There are many choices among the array of SIHRM practices. And because they, as the other SIHRM activities, influence the behaviors of individuals, they need to be selected systematically to be aligned with the other activities.

While the nature of this alignment is less than precise, it begins with the questions such as "What role behaviors do we really need from employees in the organization?" The answers are influenced by factors including the local conditions and the desires and goals of top management. In essence, these factors are treated as imperatives for determining needed role behaviors. The questions that need to be addressed include: "What specific SIHRM practices will stimulate and reinforce these behaviors, that is, carry the message of what role behaviors are needed and rewarded?" "What policies and philosophies are consistent with these practices that are needed?" "Are these philosophies and policies consistent with each other and with the desires of the organization, namely, top management?"

At PCI these questions have been answered through a very interactive process that recognizes the validity of both imperatives. In fact, it also incorporates the imperatives that derive from the nature of the competitive strategy and the technology being utilized.

As global firms such as PCI deal with the need to balance the administrative and cultural imperatives in designing their strategic performance measurement and management tools and deal with consistency in alignment, they increasingly find that they also have to be aware of the imperatives of competitive requirements (Schuler et al., in press).

Competitive Requirements Vis-à-Vis the External Environment: Competitive Drivers for MNC Performance Management

The third major strategic business need of MNCs is that which is related to being competitive in the global economy. Key competitive thrusts and direction are summarized in statements of competitive strategy regarding quality improvement, cost reduction, innovation, flexibility, and speed (Porter, 1985; Peters, 1987).

As MNCs have become more global and the standards for competitive success heightened, they also have tended to become more interdependent. Decisions on competitive thrust and direction, therefore, influence all operations, regardless of location. Increasingly the success of these decisions rests upon managing employees systematically, that is, with a conscious awareness of the associated people-related needs and the strategic international human resource activities necessary to address those needs (Dowling & Schuler, 1990). This discussion centers on the theme of matching human resource management practices with competitive strategies in a systematic and internally consistent manner.

Models linking competitive strategy and human resource management practices have been identified elsewhere (Schuler & Jackson, 1987). These models have developed topologies of human resource practices for different competitive strategies such as innovation, quality improvement, and cost reduction. The rationale for the specific human resource practices is based upon employee role behaviors necessary because of the strategy (Beatty, 1989). Basically, these models have been applied to the domestic (i.e., US) environment. MNCs, however, are faced with the need to apply human resource practices in several locations of the international environment.

There is some evidence to suggest that a common approach to managing human resources is a key component of competitive strategy. Case studies from England (Scullion, 1991); Japan (Pucik, 1992); and Australia (Dunphy & Stace, 1991) point to the existence of a common set of needed employee role behaviors for quality improvement and a common set of human resource practices for those behaviors. For example, the employee role behaviors and human resource practices shown in Exhibit 4 have been found in the NUMMI plant in Fremont, California, the Honda plant in Marysville, Ohio, the Nissan plant in Sunderland, England, and the Mitsubishi plant in Adelaide, South Australia. Exhibit 4 illustrates two significant points: (a) there are common performance measurement and management practices in firms pursing a competitive strategy of quality improvement (Dobbins & Crawford-Mason, 1991), namely use of process criteria, longer-term-oriented criteria, some group-based criteria, and participation of the final set of tools; and (b) there is a need to align certain other HR practices with the performance measurement and management practice to stimulate and reinforce the needed employee role behaviors.

These employee role behaviors are based on basic characteristics of the business. Exhibit 4 illustrates those behaviors needed from employees in a quality improvement manufacturing environment. The general characteristics of this type of environment include:

- Just-In-Time Inventory
- Just-In-Time Working
- Commitment
- Team-Orientation
- Multiskilled—Technical, Process, Interpersonal
- Flexibility
- Trust, Harmonious Employee Relations
- Horizontal and Vertical Communications
- Egalitarianism
- Distributed Leadership
- Responsibility for Customers
- Standard Operating Procedures
- Continuous Improvement
- No-Fault Policies

Exhibit 4. Role Behaviors and Human Resource Practices

Quality Improvement Employee Role Behaviors
- Predictable, repetitive behavior
- Intermediate term focus
- Some cooperative behavior
- High concern for quality
- High concern for process
- Preference for responsibility
- Modest flexibility to change
- Modest tolerance for ambiguity
- Broad skill application
- High job involvement

Key Human Resource Management Practices
- High participation
- Explicit job analysis
- Narrow career paths
- Mostly process criteria
- Mostly longer-term criteria
- Some group criteria
- Some employment security
- Egalitarian pay
- Extensive training
- Cooperative labor management relations

- Reduction of Job Grades and Classes
- Rewards for Small Improvements/Suggestions
- Supplier and Customer Involvement
- Site Visits, Comparisons, Benchmarks

Even within quality improvement manufacturing operations there is variety in terms of these employee characteristics and human resource practices. This variation reflects in part cultural and technological imperatives (Dobbins & Crawford-Mason, 1991; Lengnick-Hall, 1986; Lei & Goldhar, 1990). Again it is important for MNCs to recognize and facilitate imperatives at the local level (viz., cultural and technological differences that may exist at the local plants and offices) and at the same time to satisfy the imperatives of the administrative needs for control, coordination, and competitive strategy.

The PCI approach to performance measurement and management specifically, and all other SIHRM practices more generally, appear to do just that. Because of the strategic business needs of MNCs presented here, however, this approach seems to require the most attention. Comments and observations carrying any scientifically based rigor would make a substantial contribution to an understanding of this competitive strategy imperative. A more extensive understanding of this imperative would facilitate the process of balancing the imperatives of culture, administration, technology, and competitive requirements. It would also further the process of

evaluating the contribution that strategic performance measurement and management can make in MNCs.

Contribution Assessment:
HR as a Business Partner

The international human resource department of an MNC can demonstrate its contribution to the organization in many ways. As HR departments seek to become partners with the organization in providing strategic direction, they are being proactive in providing evidence of their contributions.

While there are many criteria or standards against which the contributions of HR departments can be assessed, they can be grouped into two categories: (a) doing the right things, and (b) doing things right (Walker & Bechet, 1991).

Doing the right things means that the HR department does things which are needed in order for the organization to be successful. In essence, is the department helping the organization be more successful in areas such as competitiveness, profitability, adaptability, and strategy implementation? Is it facilitating the work of line managers and the employees in their efforts to contribute to the maximum of their potential consistent with the strategic needs of the business?

Doing things right means that the HR department does the right things as efficiently as possible. Of course, the organization wants to use the best performance measurement system, but it wants to do so at the least cost possible. The HR department wants to facilitate the work of the line managers in their performance measurement and management efforts, but they do it in a way that maximizes the benefit and minimizes the cost.

Within each of these categories of criteria against which to assess departmental contribution, there are many more specific measures that can be used. For example, within doing things right, measures of assessment for performance measurement and management include:

- distribution of performance ratings
- percent of objectives that are clear and well-written
- extent to which stated development activities are implemented
- extent to which management and employee self ratings coincide
- average rating history/trends by unit/function (Walker & Bechet, 1991)

Within the area of doing the right things, the strategic aspect of performance measurement and management, measures of assessment include:

- knowledge of the organization's strategy
- knowledge of the line managers' HR needs
- development of performance measures that are consistent with the firm's strategy
- degree of HR's involvement in the strategic planning process
- quality of interunit linkages regarding the balance of diversity and control
- alignment of performance measurement practices with other practices and activities and with the competitive strategy
- balancing of the administrative, cultural, strategic, and technological imperatives

While both categories of criteria are important to a MNC like Pepsi-Cola International, it is the second category that is most relevant to strategic performance measurement and management: The firm regularly assesses its international human resource operations. Managers and employees worldwide are included in the assessment which is actively monitored by frequent international travel, telecommunications, and meetings.

Performance Measurement and Management as a Management Tool

In part, the frequent assessment of the performance measurement and management system helps account for its apparent effectiveness. Another view might suggest that an even more likely reason for success is how the system is perceived; at Pepsi-Cola International, the performance management system is viewed not as an HR tool as much as it is a business building tool. As a business building tool, line managers own the system and use it with their people. HR sees its involvement as part of a business building program and consequently wants the line managers to own it. While no system is without imperfections, the perception of performance measurement and management as a business-oriented, line manager system seems to help account for the current effectiveness at Pepsi-Cola International.

Summary

As multinational firms seek to enhance their levels of competitiveness, they are attempting to maximize their use of human resources. A major component of this utilization drive is the systematic linkage of human resource management activities with the strategic needs of the business. For MNCs this amounts to the development of strategic international human resource management.

An essential activity in strategic international human resource management is strategic performance measurement and management. As with the other activities, strategic performance measurement and management is relevant at three points for MNCs. The first is the interunit linkages. These linkages are those connecting the far-flung operations of the MNC into a cohesive whole that maximizes diversity while facilitating coordination. The second is the internal operations of the international locations. The need is for balancing administrative imperatives and cultural imperatives and aligning all the HRM activities within the location. The third point to be made is the need to serve the imperative of competitive strategy by linking the needed international human resource practices with the competitive strategy of the MNC in all its worldwide locations.

In this article the role of strategic performance measurement and management in each of these three points was discussed. This approach was used as a framework for organizing the materials in this article as well as for reviewing previous research. To provide additional support and substance for this conceptualization of strategic international performance measurement and management, the experience of Pepsi-Cola International was used as an example.

This presentation was intended to illustrate the importance and the complexity of systematically linking international human resource management activities to the strategic business needs of MNCs. It also illustrated the need to understand and incorporate the multi-imperatives that MNCs confront in strategically measuring and managing the performance of all their employees worldwide.

The authors wish to thank Susan Jackson, Stuart Youngblood, Steve Kobrin, and Mark Mendenhall for their helpful comments.

Randall S. Schuler (Ph.D., Michigan State University) is Professor, Stern School of Business, New York University. His interests are international human resource management, organizational uncertainty, personnel and human resource management, entrepreneurship, and the interface of competitive strategy and human resource management. He has authored and edited over 25 books, has contributed over 20 chapters to reading books, and has published over 70 articles in professional journals and academic proceedings. Presently, he is on the Editorial Board of International Journal of Human Resource Management, Human Resource Management, Asia Pacific HRM, *and* Organization Science. *He is a Fellow of the American Psychological Association. Professor Schuler has been on the faculties of the University of Maryland, Ohio State University, Penn State University, and Cleveland State University. He also worked at the United States Office of Personnel Management in Washington, D.C. and has done extensive consulting and management development work in North America, Europe, and Australia.*

John R. Fulkerson (Ph.D., Baylor University) is vice president of organizational and management development for Pepsi-Cola International. He started his career working for an internationally focused branch of the US government where he was responsible for the assessment and development of high-ability staff officers. He then was a principal in a Dallas-based consulting firm that offered a wide range of organizational psychology services. Subsequently, he was the vice president of personnel for a Texas bank holding company. In his current role, he is responsible for the coordination of programs and organization effectiveness interventions for the International Beverage Division of Pepsico. He directs Human Resource and Organization Development activities that impact organizations and people managing Pepsi-Cola business in some 150 countries.

*Peter J. Dowling (Ph.D., Flinders University) is Professorial Fellow and Associate Director of the Graduate School of Management at Monash University. Previous teaching appointments include the California State University at Chico, the University of Melbourne, and Cornell University. He has also worked for the Postmaster-General's Department and the Royal Australian Air Force. His current research interests are concerned with the cross-national transferability of HRM practices and the HR implications of European integration in 1992. Professor Dowling has co-authored two books (*International Dimensions of Human Resource Management *with Randall Schuler, and* People in Organizations: An Introduction to Organizational Behavior in Australia *with Terence Mitchell, Boris Kabanoff, and James Larson). He has also written or co-authored over 25 journal articles and book chapters. He serves on the Editorial Board of* Human Resource Planning Journal *and is the Editor of* Asia Pacific Journal of Human Resources. *He is currently Vice-President of the Australian Human Resources Institute.*

References

Adler, N.J. (1991). *International Dimensions of Organizational Behavior, 2nd ed.* Boston: PWS-Kent Publishing Company.

Adler, N.J., & Jelinek, M. (1986). Is "organizational culture" culture bound? *Human Resource Management,* 25(1), 73-90.

Bartlett, C., & Ghoshal, S. (Fall, 1987). Managing across borders: New organizational responses. *Sloan Management Review,* 43-53.

Beatty, R.W. (1989). Competitive human resource advantages through the strategic management of performance. *Human Resource Planning,* 12(3), 179-194.

Child, J. (1981). Culture, contingency and capitalism in the cross-national study of organizations. In L.L. Cummings and B.M. Staw (Eds.), *Research in Organizational Behavior, Vol. 3.* Greenwich, CT: JAI Press, pp. 303-356.

Dapsin, E. (July, 1985). Managing expatriate employees. *Management Review,* 31-37.

Davidson, W. (Fall, 1984). Administrative orientation and international performance. *Journal of International Business Studies,* 11-23.

Devanna, M.A., Fombrun, D., & Tichy, N. (Winter, 1981). Human resources management: A strategic perspective. *Organizational Dynamics,* 51-67.

Dobbins, L., & Crawford-Mason, C. (1991). *Quality or Else: The Revolution in World Business.* Boston: Houghton-Mifflin.

Doz, Y., & Pralahad, C.K. (1986). Controlled variety: A challenge for human resource management in the MNC. *Human Resource Management,* 25(1), 55-72.

Dowling, P.J., & Schuler, R.S. (1990). *International Dimensions of Human Resource Management.* Boston: PWS-Kent. Materials from Chapter 4 are adapted for use in this discussion of interunit linkages.

Dunphy, D., & Stace, D. (1991). *Under New Management: Australian Organizations in Transition.* Sydney: McGraw-Hill Book Company.

Enz, C.A. (1986). New directions for cross-cultural studies: Linking organizational and societal cultures. In R.N. Farmer (Ed.), *Advances in International Comparative Management, Vol. 2.* Greenwich, CT: JAI Press, pp. 173–189.

Evans, P.A. (1986). The strategic outcomes of human resource management. *Human Resource Management,* 25(1), 149-168.

Fisher, C.D. (1989). Current and recurrent challenges in HRM. *Journal of Management,* 15(2), 157-180.

Foulkes, F.K. (1986). *Strategic Human Resource Management.* Englewood Cliffs, NJ: Prentice-Hall.

Fulkerson, J., & Schuler, R.S. (1992). Managing worldwide diversity at Pepsi-Cola International. In S.E. Jackson (Ed.), *Diversity in the Workplace: Human Resource Initiatives.* New York: Guilford Publications. All the materials on PCI are adapted from that chapter.

Garland, J., Farmer, R.N., & Taylor, M. (1990). *International Dimensions of Business Policy and Strategy, 3rd ed.* Boston: PWS-Kent Publishing Company.

Hambrick, D.C., & Snow, C.C. (1989). Strategic reward systems. In C.C. Snow (Ed.), *Strategy, Organizational Design and Human Resource Management.* Greenwich, CT: JAI Press.

Hamel, G., & Prahalad, C.K. (May-June, 1989). Strategic intent. *Harvard Business Review,* 63-76.

Hays, R. (1974). Expatriate selection: Insuring success and avoiding failure. *Journal of International Business Studies,* 5(1), 25-37.

Heenan, D.A., & Perlmutter, H.V. (1979). *Multinational Organizational Development.* Reading, MA: Addison-Wesley.

Jelinek, M., & Goldhar, J.D. (Summer, 1983). The strategic implications of the factory of the future. *Sloan Management Review,* 29-37.

Latham, G.P., & Napier, N.K. (1989). Chinese human resource management practices in Hong Kong and Singapore: An exploratory study. In G. Ferris, K. Rowland, and A. Need, *Research in Personnel and Human Resource Management, Vol 6.* Greenwich, CT: JAI Press.

Lawler, E.E., III (1984). The strategic design of reward systems. In R.S. Schuler and S.A. Youngblood (Eds.), *Readings in Personnel and Human Resource Management, 2d ed.* St Paul, MN: West Publishing Company.

Lorange, P. (1986). Human resource management in multinational cooperative ventures. *Human Resource Management,* 25(1), 133-148.

Mendenhall, M. (1989). Personal conversation with first author, August 17.

Mendenhall, J., & Oddou, G. (September-October, 1988). The overseas assignment: A practical look. *Business Horizons,* 78-84.

Morgan. P. (1989). Personal conversation with first author, August 17.

Phatak, A.V. (1992). *International Dimensions of Management, 3rd ed.* Boston: PWS-Kent.

Peters, T. (1987). *Thriving on Chaos.* New York: Alfred A. Knopf.

Porter, M.E. (1985). *Competitive Advantage.* New York: The Free Press.

Pucik, V. (1992). Human resource practices in large Japanese firms. Working paper, Cornell University.

Pucik, V. (1985). Strategic human resource management in a multinational firm. In H.V. Wortzel and L.H. Wortzel (Eds.), *Strategic Management of Multinational Corporations: The Essentials.* New York: John Wiley.

Pucik, V., & Katz, J.H. (1986). Information, control and human resource management in multinational firms. *Human Resource Management,* 25(1), 121-132.

Punnett, B.J., & Ricks, D.A. (1992). *International Business.* Boston: PWS-Kent.

Reich, R.B. (January-February, 1990). Who is us? *Harvard Business Review,* 57-64.

Schneider, S. (1988). National vs. corporate culture: Implications for human resource management. *Human Resource Management,* 27, 231-246.

Schuler, R.S. (Summer, 1992). Strategic human resource management: Linking the people with the strategic needs of the business. *Organizational Dynamics,* 18-32.

Schuler, R.S., Dowling, P.J., & DeCieri, H. (in press). Strategic international human resource management. *Journal of Management,* special yearly issue.

Schuler, R.S., & Jackson, S.E. (August, 1987). Linking competitive strategies and human resource management practices. *Academy of Management Executive,* 207-219.

Scullion, H. (1991). Human resource practices in British firms. Unpublished working paper, University of Newcastle.

Sherwood, J.J. (Winter, 1988). Creating work cultures with competitive advantage. *Organizational Dynamics,* 5-27.

Walker, J.W., & Bechet, T.P. (June 11-14, 1984). Defining effectiveness and efficiency measures in the context of human resource strategy. Fourth Biennial Research Symposium.

Wickens, P. (1987). *The Road to Nissan.* London: MacMillan.

Wright, P.M., & McMahan, G.C. (1992). Theoretical perspectives for strategic human resource management. *Journal of Management,* 18(2), 295-320.

Capitalizing on Performance Management, Recognition, and Rewards Systems

by Craig Eric Schneier

In today's business environment, complex factors—including the demands of a global economy, the need to downsize to increase efficiency, the constant threat of takeovers, and the pursuit of lost markets—call for carefully conceived organizational change. Many change efforts focus on performance and reward systems—those processes that determine what is expected of people (performance standards and performance appraisal) and what people can expect in return (compensation, recognition, and rewards).

A company's performance management, recognition, and reward (PMRR) system is a critical element in the success of any large-scale change. Yet such systems are often paper-pushing exercises that fail to become forces for cultural change. Recent national surveys have found that more than half of U.S. workers admit they could improve their productivity significantly, but apparently have little reason to do so: Only one in five believes a link exists between performance and rewards.

Too many companies' performance management and rewards and recognition systems do not really work (see Exhibits 1 and 2). Performance management often means no more to a manager than completing an annual appraisal form. Thirty-five percent of companies are dissatisfied enough to revise

or replace their systems each year. Reward and recognition systems fare no better. At least 75% of companies have experimented with a new system in the last five years.

Six predominant reasons account for the failure of PMRR systems to drive change: (1) the absence of a compelling strategic business reason to change, (2) a lack of top management support and actual involvement, (3) a company's failure to forge a direct link between performance and rewards or recognition, (4) a system owned by human resources staff units, not its users—employees and line managers, (5) emphasis on an annual event, not a continuous process, for managing performance and allocating rewards and recognition, and (6) an implementation strategy that relies too heavily on classroom programs and too little on on-the-job orientation and training.

This article examines one company's efforts to avoid these common mistakes and make the PMRR system work. That company—*Pratt & Whitney* (P&W)—implemented a broad cultural change in an effort to improve quality and regain its technological edge.

Pratt & Whitney's Competitive Environment

A leading manufacturer of aircraft engines, P&W has a long, rich history of technological innovation and market leadership. As one of United Technologies' larger companies, it is vital to its parent's suc-

---

Exhibit 1
Are Performance Management Systems Working?*

70% of workers have no idea of their supervisors' performance expectations.

64% of companies do not train their managers on how to manage or appraise performance.

75% of workers and managers admit they could be *significantly* more effective in their jobs.

64% of managers want better communication and feedback from their managers.

70% of workers say they have never had a meaningful discussion with their manager about performance.

---

*Data based on national surveys reported in the business press.

Strengthening PMRR

Top company and human resources executives recognized early on that for Q+ to succeed, the company needed a PMRR process that was sound, consistently and equitably administered, and compatible with the target culture and strategy. The first step in improving performance was to define desired performance—in terms of customer service levels, productivity indices, or product quality. Then performance expectations or targets needed to be communicated to each person. Performance deficiencies needed to be addressed, and causes of poor performance removed. Finally, to sustain high performance the company had to properly align and differentially administer rewards on the basis of performance. In essence, performance had to be carefully and deliberately managed.

P&W's existing systems for managing and rewarding performance needed improvement: Performance appraisal was seen as an exercise necessary to generate the paperwork for salary increases, the performance category labels (for example, "outstanding") were inconsistently applied, and the average rating was skewed toward the lenient side.

A Q+ corrective action team was formed to address this problem. Ten line managers, representing P&W's four divisions and administration, were

cess. With 45,000 employees located primarily in Connecticut and southeastern Florida, its financial health has a major impact on several communities.

In the mid 1980s, rising costs and increased competition were eroding P&W's technological and, hence, competitive edges. In addition, the government, a major customer, was exerting pressure for cost control. In response, P&W developed numerous strategies including a large-scale effort to improve quality and, in the process, transform the P&W culture. Management knew that creating an effective PMRR process was critical to achieving a successful culture change.

P&W's lead program aimed at broad-based culture change was called Q+. The Q+ initiative focused on improving all aspects of the company through problem diagnosis, participative involvement, corrective action teams, executive and managerial action, and continual review. It emphasized customer requirements and supplier relationships and involved the full hierarchy of all line units and staff support functions.

Exhibit 2
Are Reward and Recognition Systems Working?*

3% of base salary separates average from outstanding employees.

33% of managers would rather work in another organization where they could receive better recognition.

81% of workers say they would not receive any reward for productivity increases.

60% of managers feel their compensation will not increase if their performance improves.

49% of workers say the best way to get ahead is to "know the right people."

---

*Data based on national surveys reported in the business press.

Exhibit 3
The Pratt and Whitney Performance Management, Recognition, and Reward Process

The Manager's Role

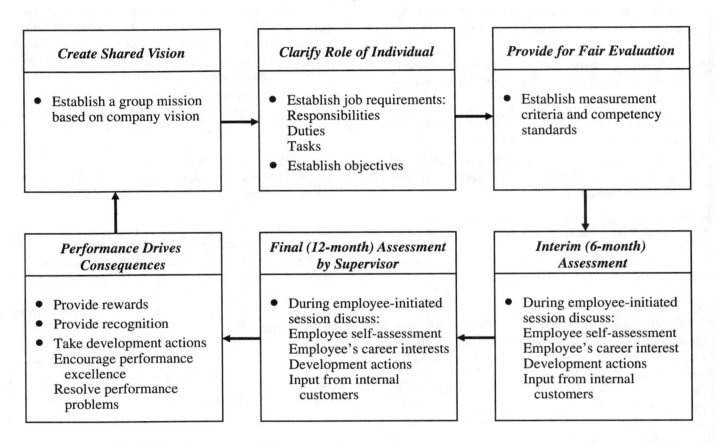

chosen as team members because of their technical and managerial experience and competence. They reported to a steering group of top human resources and Q+ managers and, ultimately, to senior management.

The team operated within the Q+ guidelines and adhered to Q+ values—participation, data gathering, and long-term solutions. Their charter was not to design a PMRR system using any specific technique, but to investigate the needs and problems of employees and managers at all levels and present preliminary ideas to as many people as possible for feedback. This extensive data-gathering and feedback process helped the team uncover real issues

and, most importantly, transferred ownership of the recommendations to the users.

The data-gathering effort generally reinforced top management and the team perceptions that the PMRR process was not a viable vehicle for driving the change required. Most managers used a process that did not promote the concept of performance-based compensation. A survey indicated that while pay was considered adequate, it was not closely linked in employees' minds with performance. Other shortcomings pointed to the need for skill building in performance management and resolution of various performance and reward issues. Improvements had the potential to build a performance-driven culture and assist the company in implementing strategy and improving performance.

Building Managerial Ownership

In designing a new PMRR process, the team came to understand fully the difference between performance *appraisal* (a rating of performance once a year) and performance *management* (the managing of performance all year long). It developed a process structured around managers' roles and responsibilities (see Exhibit 3).

P&W's new performance management cycle begins with a determination of the mission of each group or unit—the reason the unit exists. Then appropriate roles and responsibilities—what people do—are specified. Next, performance standards—how well people must perform—are set. The interim and final assessments that follow include input from those with whom the employee has worked throughout the cycle. Finally, consequences, both positive and negative, directly follow the appraisal.

The cycle emphasizes ongoing managerial tasks. It is not driven by the personnel or human resources department, because managing performance is clearly managers' work. Employees participate in the entire process. The full cycle is important, not just the final appraisal. Forms, rules, and procedures are a means, not an end.

The Competencies

An important feature of the new process is the following set of management "competencies" derived from P&W's culture, mission, and values: Leadership competencies include a manager's ability to (1) create a shared vision, (2) empower others, (3) develop people, and (4) recognize merit. Personal competencies include his or her (1) ability to satisfy the customer, (2) technical expertise, (3) initiative, (4) commitment and contribution to quality, (5) commitment to teamwork, and (6) ability to build effective relationships.

Various management groups developed support behavioral examples for each competency at three performance levels (see Exhibit 4). The competencies clearly signal that P&W is now measuring, evaluating, and rewarding each manager's work process and behavior, as well as the technical skills he or she applies and the results obtained. Evaluating people on the competencies and linking the evaluation to consequences builds accountability for managing effectively, as well as for obtaining

Exhibit 4
Key Leadership Competency: Ability to Recognize Merit

Exceptional Manager

Is a leader in drawing high performance from employees and recognizing them for it. Is aware of each employee's level of contribution and supports continued growth through many forms of recognition.

Fully Competent Manager

Assesses accurately the accomplishments of employees, differentiates between performance levels, and communicates candidly regarding performance. Makes compensation decisions that reflect clear distinctions between levels of performance achieved. Spends time in the work area interacting with employees, inquiring about day-to-day activities and providing specific, timely performance feedback. Effectively uses formal and informal recognition actions. Maintains group performance. When warranted, takes appropriate action with poor performers through corrective action plans, firing employee when necessary.

Developing Manager

Is becoming more aware of the importance of employee recognition and feedback, and is increasing in ability to be involved in the accomplishments of employees on a regular basis.

Exhibit 4 (continued)

Rewards and Recognition at Other Companies

An Insurance Company

A large insurance company with more than 30,000 workers has continually moved toward a more innovative, participative culture. Traditional performance hurdles were raised in all parts of the organization; hence, linking pay directly to the attainment of unit business objectives and to individual and group performance made sense. Features of the company's reward and recognition system now include the following:

1. *Performance bonus.* Total budget of 2% of eligible employees' salaries; 50% participation rate; $1,000 average award.
2. *Employee recognition.* Noncash (that is, theatre tickets, dinners); 75% participation rate; designed to increase commitment to specific objectives.
3. *Skill-based pay.* Pay increases for identifying, mastering, and using skills, not required for functional responsibilities; those in $20,000 to $57,000 pay range participate.
4. *Gainsharing.* Productivity improvements (quality and quantity) measured and tracked; gains shared equally by employees in a group or office.
5. *Self-developed rewards.* Units given opportunity to design their own incentive compensation systems, which can differ from companywide systems.
6. *Lump-sum salary increases.* Employees can elect to receive 100% of their merit increases for two years as lump sum; nonexempt employees with five or more years' service eligible.

Employee surveys indicate significantly higher morale and motivation and a stronger relationship between performance and rewards.

A Restaurant Chain

A rapidly growing restaurant chain had a clearly defined market niche. With superior service and more than 40 units well placed in expanding metropolitan areas, all looked well. But turnover of managers was 45%. For very long hours and a host of headaches, they were paid an average of $26,000. The problem was not just the *level* of pay, but the basis for the pay level. Size of store, not performance, drove salary.

The performance-based reward system. Because growth was strategically important for the chain to develop national name recognition, deter competitors, and attain economies of scale in purchasing and services, it decided to provide an incentive for sales above a targeted level. Food and labor costs could not stray outside of targets. Things worked fine for a time. Then fast growth required managers to move from small to larger stores, often before their incentive plans could really pay off. The emphasis on sales came at the expense of customer service. The time to serve customers increased steadily, and store cleanliness declined; competitors began to infiltrate the market. Despite better training, better systems, better machines, and higher wages for the hourly people, the service problems drove down sales.

The equity plan. Simply put, the store manager's job, even with incentives, was a real pain: long hours, weekend work, labor shortages, personnel problems. Top management realized it needed to make the gain worth the pain. That meant providing a base salary and tying incentive compensation to controllable profits (that is, profit minus rent and depreciation). Managers of larger stores had some advantage, but small store managers could gain significant incentive pay by holding down labor costs and shrinkage. Because the sales volume goals were still there, the incentive to provide excellent service to maintain a customer base was strong. A portion of the monthly bonus went into a reserve fund, to be paid out when employment contracts expired. Turnover plummeted. Average compensation for managers rose from $26,000 to $75,000 in just over one year. Sales increased 40%.

A Utility

One of the country's largest utilities diversified into nonregulated businesses. Faced with increasing competition, it had to sharpen its marketing orientation and skills. New business strategies meant new job responsibilities and a premium on innovation. But merit pay policies had become entitlements, with almost automatic annual increases for modest performance levels. Managers were reluctant to reduce or withhold increases for fear of being accused of taking rewards away. Employees saw no relationship between company performance and pay.

Exhibit 4 (concluded)

A new system was installed with two lump-sum vehicles: an individual merit plan and a group incentive plan. Considerable line management and employee involvement characterized the developmental process.

Individual Merit Plan

1. Eligibility: 25%.
2. Minimum award: 3% of salary.
3. "Immediate" payment of award.
4. Special documentation of outstanding performance required.
5. Awards are equal percentages of base compensation across pay grades.

Group Incentive Plan

1. Target award based on financial performance measure (for example, return on assets).
2. Amounts from 0% to 250% of target available.
3. Plan funded via a portion of annual salary-increase budget.
4. Units/departments receive budgets but amounts to each team vary according to performance.

Performance appraisal. The existing performance appraisal system provided ratings that were neither well documented nor able to differentiate people on the basis of their performance. The system was retained but the need to document performance and explain reward decisions to those who did and who did not receive awards made raters view the system in a new light. With some skill building, the old system began to work just fine. Performance ratings spread out over the scale, documentation was more fact-based, and feedback became more useful.

---

desired results. The competencies also specify behaviors necessary for the organization to build and sustain the new culture.

Ratee Participation and Performance Development

The new PMRR process at P&W also measures each person's key job requirements (major responsibilities) and specific objectives, if appropriate. Ratees provide written self-assessments during both the interim and end-of-period reviews. Developmental needs and action plans are also stressed during these reviews, and a corrective action plan is mandated for substandard performance. The process promotes narrative-type assessments based on demonstrated behaviors and actual accomplishments, rather than numerical ratings. Once the employee's assessment has been completed, his or her performance is linked to various consequences via the recognition and reward system.

Recognition and Rewards

Data gathering conducted at P&W had indicated that recognition vehicles were under-utilized, as were team rewards, and the link between pay and performance was weak. An investigation of rewards and recognition devices used in the divisions had revealed numerous excellent practices, but also weaknesses: little consistency, little recognition for truly outstanding performance, and too long a separation between performance reviews and receipt of rewards.

In revamping the reward process, the team was mindful of P&W's need to operate more effectively and reduce costs. It developed the following reward and recognition vehicles, which capitalize on both the motivating potential of noncash rewards (revealed by P&W's own survey) and the low cost of such rewards: (1) salary increases (accruing to base salary), (2) bonuses (not accruing to base salary), (3) verbal recognition and praise, (4) appreciation

Exhibit 5
Strategy for Successful Implementation

Critical Condition	P&W Action
1. Top-management involvement	Top management allocated resources, personally stressed PMRR's importance to employees, and participated in the training and use of the process.
2. Employee ownership	Line management and employees provided input in the design, reviewed the drafts, and were thoroughly briefed on the system's workings.
3. Human resources system integration	Those responsible for related human resources systems, such as promotion, training and development, and employee relations, were brought into the process.
4. Supervisor skill building	Training to build PMRR skills was carefully planned and executed by line managers with the assistance of professional trainers and consultants.

awards (for example, tickets to local events), (5) Eagle Awards (for example, a weekend trip or the equivalent in cash), and (6) P&W Special Awards (cash).

The P&W recognition and reward process has five objectives: to reward high performers, to reward teams, to have a budget-neutral cost impact, to communicate effectively the link between performance and rewards, and to be perceived as fair. Distribution of rewards is left largely to the supervisor's discretion, with the caveat that awards must quickly follow performance.

Salary Increases

The PMRR process now places more pay "at risk": Pay is not guaranteed, but tied to performance or contribution. Supervisors are instructed to consider what overall pay levels, not merely increase amounts, are appropriate given an employee's performance. In addition, they have broad latitude in basing increases on performance and salary positions within a pay range. Supervisors re-

ceive annual guidance on the *range* of possible increases, rather than on fixed amounts or percentages.

While P&W does consider the impact of the external market and the range position of a given salary in determining increases, no strict formula exists linking increase size to performance rating or range position. A particularly critical reward element for P&W is the bonus, which allows sizeable rewards for those employees high in the pay range who perform exceptionally. This strategy differs significantly from the typical "merit matrix," which often denies sizable increases to those most deserving of rewards—seasoned, experienced, top-performing employees who are pushing the maximums of their pay ranges.

The performance-reward link is now much stronger, thanks to the new P&W process. Supervisors give certain rewards, such as verbal praise and trips, almost immediately following the performance contribution. Accountability for timely rewards is built into the system through the "recog-

Exhibit 6
Business Strategy Drives Managerial Behavior and Rewards

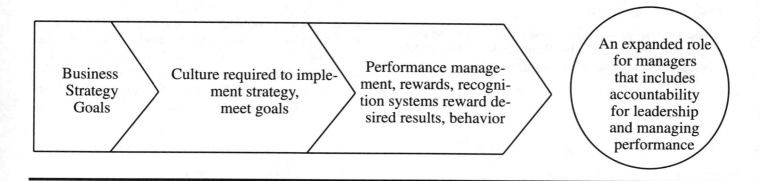

nize merit" leadership competency. Supervisors must also make and communicate pay decisions within four weeks of the annual performance review. The actual reward is received within another two weeks. Rewards are contingent on both performance results and behavior—that is, on *what* was achieved and *how* it was achieved. Poor performance is addressed by a corrective action plan, which calls for specific actions if deficiencies are not overcome.

Avoiding Implementation Pitfalls

While the new PMRR system is appropriate given P&W's culture and strategy, and it is based on sound principles and theory, improper use would mean failure. Four conditions are considered critical to successful implementation: (1) top-management involvement, (2) employee ownership, (3) human resources system integration, and (4) supervisor skill building. The actions P&W took to meet these conditions are outlined in Exhibit 5.

Training

The P&W team and senior management view the PMRR project as both a major cultural change and a process, not merely as another program. Training is therefore designed to build skills that are critical to managers' success in the new Q+ culture.

The process begins with managers attending a brief workshop to obtain an overview of the process and their responsibilities and accountabilities. Managers then work with employees, practicing the re-

quired skills and using the PMRR system to manage and reward performance continually. Ongoing assistance is available to managers from specifically trained staff teams. Follow-up training sessions deal with issues managers face as they use the process. Top management, aware that lasting change requires constant attention, has committed to ongoing skill development.

PMRR's Part in Changing Corporate Culture

The P&W PMRR process was conceived as part of a mechanism to induce a major cultural shift in the organization. As such, it led to a business-driven redefinition of management's role and accountability. Managers now strive to be effective leaders who develop and manage their employees' performance. Many managers had already viewed their roles this broadly, but P&W decided to make this leadership role more explicitly.

For most organizations, the PMRR process is an important and often overlooked vehicle for change. It accommodates the business and cultural needs of an organization in transition. Yet a well-structured PMRR system—at both P&W and other companies—can only succeed under certain conditions: The system must be tied to compelling business and cultural needs that call for immediate action (see Exhibit 6); the performance-management process that defines and measures performance must be linked to recognition and rewards; managerial

PMRR skills need to be developed on the job; and managers must be held accountable for making the process work.

Acknowledgement

The author would like to acknowledge the assistance and support of the Pratt & Whitney PMRR task force and corporate communications.

Craig Eric Schneier is managing principal and national director, human resource and organization effectiveness practice, for Sibson & Company. He has 17 years' consulting experience and has been an advisor to several management consulting firms, including Arthur Young and Booz-Allen & Hamilton. He received his doctorate and master's degrees from the University of Colorado and held a tenured professorship in management and human resources management at the College of Business and Management, University of Maryland.

Teamwork Developed a Successful Appraisal System

by Ron Sorensen and Geralyn McClure Franklin

Human resources increasingly has become an important element in any organization's success. As a result, professionals are being pressured to manage effectively and report on employee performance. Just as accounting systems document financial performance and production reports show factory output, appraisal systems must reflect employee performance. Although difficulties arise with any appraisal process, proper design and implementation can provide significant benefits.

The Forest Division of Temple-Inland Forest Products Corporation formulated a successful performance appraisal system that dealt with typical problems. A representative committee of employees took part in the design and implementation phases, an approach that is expected to be used more often during the 1990s.

After completing a review of its salary administration system, the company undertook an initiative to implement a performance-based pay scheme for salaried employees in each division. Temple-Inland is a highly decentralized organization, and each division was left to its own devices to determine how to design and implement its appraisal system.

Developing any one system to meet the needs of such a diverse group of employees is quite challenging. A majority of the division personnel also had no previous experience with a formalized appraisal system. Overall, opinions were mixed re-

garding the value of a formalized process, with much skepticism over what type of system to develop.

The decision was made to formulate the performance appraisal system using a representative committee of divisional personnel, a group that became known as a resource team, chaired by a member of the upper management group and facilitated by the management program coordinator. Efforts were made to gather team members from as many areas of the division as possible to maximize expertise and improve representation throughout the division.

Three months were allotted to develop a workable system. Team members were encouraged to collect opinions from, and report results to, their operating areas between team meetings.

The plan for operating the resource team relied on very basic problem-solving techniques: defining the desired goals or outcomes; generating alternatives to achieve the goals; and selecting the most appropriate alternatives.

The first positive aspect of the resource team approach became evident during the goal-setting stage. Although members understood the reasoning behind the team, and that the appraisal system originated from a performance-based pay goal, the general opinion was that any system with this as the primary goal would not realize its full potential. Members instead agreed that the appraisal system should serve as a primer for increased communication between employees and supervisors, and for identification of employee development needs. In essence, the system should help employees do their jobs better through improved definition and communication of job responsibilities and managerial expectations, not simply reward workers who do well. Administering salaries, identifying promotions and documenting poor performance were recognized as benefits but were considered secondary to developing employees.

The actual system design varied considerably from the original notion of a performance-based appraisal system once employee development became the system's primary outcome. The focus shifted from a system based on individual traits and skills to a more job-specific system based on actual responsibilities. The implementation and training plans also were expanded to higher levels to allow for the improved managerial skills required to operate such a system effectively.

The team reviewed several types of appraisal systems. These included ones used by other divisions within the company, as well as systems in place at other companies. Much attention was directed at the following three appraisal characteristics: evaluation frequency, evaluation criteria and system flow within the organization. The broad representation of the resource team was beneficial at this point. Members shared their experiences and improved the decision-making process.

Evaluation Frequency

After looking at systems with annual and biannual review cycles, the team determined that a quarterly review cycle would be the most advantageous. Members realized a major limitation to the appraisal idea: annual appraisals can degenerate into "dumping" sessions during which managers bring up performance problems they failed to mention during the year.

To comply with employee development and "coaching" goals, the team believed that a shorter time between review cycles was necessary. This decision offered an excellent example of how the employee development goal influenced system design. A primary goal of a performance-based system probably would not have led to the decision to use quarterly reviews.

The time needed for system administration also was a major concern, particularly due to the selection of a quarterly review cycle. A substantial amount of paperwork often can cause a decline in appraisal quality and system compliance. Fortu-

nately, the quarterly review cycle did not add paperwork.

Managers and employees were expected to review progress in major performance areas each quarter. Employees could express concern regarding their supervisor's expectations and concerns about progress in key areas, as well as goal attainment. The end result was that when the final quarterly review occurred, and ratings were actually issued, there would be no surprises.

Evaluation Criteria

Team members believed that the system should focus as much as possible on specific, measurable performance criteria. Instead of rating performance in general skills categories, such as communication or professionalism, specific skills and responsibilities should be drawn from each employee's job analysis. For appraisal purposes, these responsibilities were termed key performance areas (KPAs). As a general rule, the team suggested eight to 10 KPAs on each appraisal form, each focusing on major result areas.

Performance standards relating to quality, quantity, time and cost were to be developed for each KPA by the supervisor and employee at the beginning of the appraisal cycle. Thus, specific job responsibilities, along with supporting standards, served as the basis for the appraisal interview discussion.

Considerable team debate centered around the number of rating categories. Systems that had five or more rating categories appeared to result in appraisers using only a few of the available categories. The team agreed that as the number of rating categories increased, so did the likelihood for misuse and confusion.

Therefore, team members decided that the following three evaluation ratings were sufficient: 1—Needs improvement; 2—Meets and often exceeds requirements; 3—Consistently exceeds requirements.

Although the team recognized that such a scale could cover a broad range of performance, especially in the second rating category, members did not think that further differentiation of the categories was warranted. The "needs improvement" category would indicate that specific development needs were in order.

In addition to the KPA portion of the appraisal document, an annual goals section was included. Individual development goals could be established at the beginning of each year, and progress checked on a quarterly basis and finally included in the rating process at year's end. The inclusion of the goals section was intended to provide every manager with individual control to design a development plan for each employee. Goals could be included to add extra emphasis to improving performance in a given KPA area, acquiring new skills or achieving personal development.

System Flow

All forms and documents were to be kept between the immediate supervisor and the employee for the first three quarters of the year. During the fourth quarter, when ratings actually were assigned to KPAs and goals, completed forms would be circulated to the employees' second-level supervisors. The purpose here was twofold. Distribution to second-level supervisors allowed the system to impact on promotional opportunities because this level often determines promotions. Involving second-level superiors also provided a quality-control function. Completion of quarterly reviews could be monitored, and any abuses could be investigated. Ultimately, this second-level review would provide a means of motivation for the immediate supervisor to complete the appraisal review process thoroughly.

After completing the system design, the resource team began work on implementation. An independent consultant was hired to assist in program design and delivery, as well as to critique the proposed system. Team members requested that they be able to review the training process and evaluate its potential success in achieving the stated objectives.

During the first year of operation, the system worked much better than expected, considering the division's lack of experience with performance appraisals. Much of this favorable opinion was generated by the positive momentum provided by the significant training effort. In addition, resource team members served as effective spokespersons for the system. Members gave presentations during training sessions that explained the system's design and overall purpose.

Fine-Tuning the Process

The experience of using a resource team proved so positive that the company decided to use the same team to evaluate system operation and recommend any adjustments for the second year. The team found that most appraisers were dissatisfied with the use of only three ratings. They argued that a supervisor was somewhat limited in the amount of feedback that he or she could give an employee, especially in cases of substandard performance. In turn, the rating categories were revised to include the following: 1—Needs improvement; 2—Meets minimum requirements; 3—Meets and often exceeds requirements; 4—Consistently exceeds requirements.

Supervisors indicated that the addition of a "meets minimum requirements" rating would give them leeway to encourage improvement in a performance area without issuing the lowest available rating, which carried the connotation of no effort or totally unacceptable performance in a KPA.

Ron Sorensen is employee development coordinator for Temple-Inland Forest Products Corp., Diboll, Texas. Geralyn McClure Franklin, Ph.D., is an associate professor of management at Stephen F. Austin State University, Nacogdoches, Texas.

The Call For Full Disclosure

by Bill Birchard

One way to stir up senior executives these days is to ask them to share operating-performance data with investors and bankers. You'll hear a lot of griping from them about blood-thirsty plaintiffs' attorneys on the prowl for class-action securities lawsuits. You'll also hear concerns about sensitive competitive information falling into rivals' laps and, if you listen closely, rumblings about shareholders sticking their noses where they don't belong.

But say "full disclosure" to the people running Whirlpool Corp., and the first sound they hear is the ringing of cash registers. To underscore the link between operating skill and appealing returns for shareholders, executives from the $7.5 billion Benton Harbor, Michigan, appliance maker begin presentations to analyst meetings with details on such topics as product and service quality, brand loyalty, brand share, and trade-partner satisfaction. The standard review of financial results comes second. "When a company's future turns on productivity gains and customer intimacy," insists chairman and chief executive officer David Whitwam, "the last thing you want to do is downplay the correlation between financial and operating performance. What good is an operating strategy anyway, if it can't withstand public scrutiny?"

Michael Callahan (who, as we went to press, had left the CFO slot at Whirlpool to become CFO of FMC Corp., in Chicago) also believes in taking the bull by the horns. "You really must approach performance measurement the other way around," he told *CFO*. At Whirlpool, in fact, Callahan sought to prove that "if you can meet tough operating goals, the financial results will follow."

It's no coincidence, Callahan argues, that for the past three years, Whirlpool has been riding a wave of successful international expansion. Revenues and operating profits, meanwhile, have gained solid ground. Return on equity, which stood at 5 percent in 1990, topped 14 percent last year. Over the next five years, the company is hoping to give shareholders total investment returns that will place it among the top 25 percent of large, publicly traded U.S. companies.

Throwing Open the Books

Clearly, the top people at Whirlpool stand out of the mainstream of current management thinking. All fall, some of America's largest companies were throwing mud at the American Institute of Certified Public Accountants's (AICPA) call for broad disclosure of both financial and nonfinancial performance data (see Newswatch, "Disclosure War: Day 1,095," page 15).

The AICPA's position on nonfinancial data, found in the group's just-released manifesto on U.S. financial reporting practices, sounds reasonable enough: Investors need information relevant to the task of making capital allocation decisions, and in an era of fast-paced global competition, that means proof of management acumen and operating know-how that simply can't be found in backward-looking accounting yardsticks. Few people would argue with the concept, but many financial executives were horrified by the AICPA's suggestion that the Securities and Exchange Commission require corporations to disclose what the study calls "high-level operating data and performance measurements." They contend that throwing open the books would saddle corporations with costly and complex reporting chores and impose enormous competitive and legal risks.

Whirlpool first disclosed its nonfinancial performance targets in 1991, and has been revealing results selectively at analyst meetings ever since. "Yes, your report card is out there and everybody gets to look at it each year. But with [important] constituencies, we think we're gaining something," observes Callahan (see "Whirlpool's Report Card," page 422). As for potential competitive costs, "You don't really have to lose a lot from competitor knowledge of how you're going about your business," he maintains. More germane, he says, is that by putting nonfinancial performance data on a pedestal, "you keep a little heat on yourself. That makes everybody more committed."

Investor Heat

There's another good reason to think hard about the costs versus the benefits of fuller disclosure: institutional investors are starting to demand better signposts of long-term operating savvy.

An early hint of such pressures came in an April 1993 speech by Edward V. "Ned" Regan, who was then winding up his 14 1/2-year stint as comptroller for New York state, a job that put him in charge of more than $50 billion in state pension assets. In the speech to chief financial officers, Regan issued this warning: "Someday, a public pension fund is going to file a resolution with a major company and ask it to disclose its standards of employee satisfaction, its measurements of quality of goods or services. And when this occurs with performance measurement, I hope every CFO in this room is prepared."

Since leaving his state post, Regan has served as chairman of a blue-chip committee of the Competitiveness Policy Council, created and funded by Congress in 1991 to develop recommendations for national strategies and policies to enhance the productivity and international competitive position of U.S. industry. In 1993, Regan's group completed a report exhorting company boards of directors to press for the release of nonfinancial measures to the investing public. "This is the hallmark of a good CEO and a good CFO," Regan says today from his new position as Distinguished Fellow of The Jerome Levy Economics Institute, in New York. "Unfortunately," he says, "many companies track these factors, but they don't discuss them with their boards, and they don't discuss them with shareholders."

It's particularly vexing, he says, to public pension funds, "which don't have the depth in terms of high-priced portfolio management talent to do deep fundamental analysis. The lonely civil servant needs better standards for judging the potential performance of companies in the portfolio."

Then again, when an investment strategy aims to reflect the performance of stock market indices, which is the case with many public pension funds, Regan continues, "you have a fiduciary responsibility to stay informed about the long-term prospects of the companies you invest in. What better way to do this than to look at nonfinancial as well as financial statements?" A political realist at heart, however, Regan concedes that "there are a lot of reasons why people want this boat to move slowly. When you talk about quality of goods, employee satisfaction, and so forth, the benchmarks by which you can put corporate performance in a relevant framework are missing at the moment."

Indeed, few major companies are disclosing anything that resembles meaningful operating data. Standing next to Whirlpool on the edge of innovation is Skandia Assurance & Financial Services, the large Swedish insurance company that made headlines last summer when it released its first annual report on intellectual capital. Skandia obviously wants shareholders to appreciate its genius for identifying and leveraging discrete pockets of marketplace knowledge. But others who are now pushing nonfinancial performance internally are gun-shy when it comes to disclosure. For several years, American Express Co., to name just one, has been measuring both employee and customer satisfaction, and recently began linking its performance in these areas to executive pay, in addition to financial goals. Still, the travel and financial services giant has no plans to release such data to investors, says Susan Miller, vice president of corporate communications.

But change will come eventually, say the experts, because so much latent support for nonfinancial measures is ready to spring to life. "The impetus for all this is the group that's scrambling for more active participation in corporate governance," says Krishna Palepu, a professor at Harvard Business

WHIRLPOOL'S REPORT CARD

Whirlpool executives grade their performance with both financial and non-financial metrics. Below are examples of their report-card categories:

FINANCIAL:
Economic value added
Return on equity

CUSTOMER SATISFACTION:
Market share
Customer satisfaction (*by survey)
Brand loyalty
Brand preference
Satisfaction with service
Trade-partner satisfaction
Product availability

TOTAL QUALITY:
Worldwide excellence (quality) score
Defect levels
Cycle time
Service incident rates

PEOPLE COMMITMENT:
Employee commitment survey

GROWTH AND INNOVATION:
Percent new product sales

School who has been researching best practices in investor relations.

Consider a recent move by the board of the California Public Employees' Retirement System (Calpers), the influential public pension fund that wields $78 billion in assets. Calpers is beginning to add workplace practices, such as self-managed teams and job rotation, to its list of attributes that define good corporate governance. Soon, companies in Calpers's so-called Failing 50 list, the 50 worst performers in its portfolio, will have the fund breathing down their necks for progress reports concerning workplace activities.

Of course, the idea of using state pension fund assets to press for better treatment of working folks (read: voters) has a convenient political ring to it. Calpers, in any case, made its move after a study by the Gordon Group Inc., a consulting firm in Newton, Massachusetts, unearthed a correlation between negative financial results and poor workplace practices. Calpers had commissioned the study after board members heard Labor Secretary Robert Reich urge pension funds to add workplace practices to their investment criteria. Fiduciary duty, says Richard Koppes, Calpers general counsel, required the board to investigate the link, and when a link was found, to act on it.

The labor unions and their pension fund managers are also climbing on the bandwagon. "We're searching for indicators that in the labor relations area would provide evidence that the company is conducting business in a way that would maximize its ability to produce value," says Ed Durkin, co-chair of the Council of Institutional Investors, who, as director of special programs at the United Brotherhood of Carpenters, counsels the trustees of 180 funds managing $14.5 billion of union pension money. "Investors can't get involved on the level of micromanagement," he concedes, but "there needs to be some kind of scorecard, so investors can see how they're doing against national averages, industry averages. At the moment, there is a complete lack of information to allow investors to make a judgment of nonfinancial performance."

Not surprisingly, another voice calling for disclosure of workplace practices is that of William Patterson, corporate affairs director for the International Brotherhood of Teamsters, who advises the union on corporate governance concerns and pension fund trustees on their handling of $46 billion in assets. "We represent patient capital, and we think that, ultimately, investing in employees and corporate citizenship will add to the bottom line," he says.

Vision versus Results

Companies that now do a good job of collecting and analyzing operating data most likely were pushed in that direction by a company chief bent on seeing that a new strategy was properly executed. "The measurement is the tail that wags the dog," says David Norton, president of Renaissance Strat-

THE PARAGON AND THE PARADOX

Ask the pros of the performance measurement trade which company they would crown the paragon of virtue, and more often than not they'll nominate Analog Devices Inc., the $700 million maker of integrated circuits based in Norwood, Massachusetts. Analog, guided by chairman, CEO, and co-founder Ray Stata, has graded itself since 1986 with a scorecard of 25 percent financial and 75 percent nonfinancial measures. Among the metrics joining sales and income on Analog's top sheet are on-time delivery, time-to-market for new products, and product quality.

So what has this pioneer learned? "The company needs a process by which the balanced scorecard is set, deployed, monitored, and diagnosed," says Robert Stasey, director of quality improvement and the guru who dispenses wisdom to other companies benchmarking Analog's system. That is to say, Analog considers the way it manages its measures just as important as the results themselves. Twice yearly, Analog executives "diagnose," or evaluate, the system for weaknesses.

Such an approach will help Analog address what Prof. Marshall Meyer, of the University of Pennsylvania's Wharton School of Management, calls the "performance paradox." In time, Meyer's research shows, all measures "run down." Largely because either performance improves or people "game" the system—they

boost, say, earnings per share by increasing leverage rather than core profitability—and variability of the measures declines. Without variability, executives can't easily distinguish good from bad, and they can't set new targets that drive improvement.

Meyer says that at a handful of large companies, quality and customer satisfaction measures have already become so widely used, and thus exhibit so little variability, that the executives are casting about for new yardsticks of performance, such as customer behavior. His prediction for companies in the future: "A world in which we'll cycle through measures with ever greater rapidity. No performance measurement is immutable, especially nonfinancial measures. They're always changing." The conundrum for managers: "Reconciling people's need for consistency with the firm's need for inconsistency."

That Analog has adopted a system to manage its measures makes the company a rare bird, and perhaps a smart one, too, in skirting the performance paradox. Stasey says the firm's balanced scorecard changes little each year, but over several years' time it changes dramatically, owing to rising customer expectations and standards of performance. The latest addition to the scorecard? An annual index of employee satisfaction.

---

egy Group, in Lincoln, Massachusetts. "Strategy is taking on a different focus than it has in the past," he explains. Norton, along with Prof. Robert Kaplan of Harvard Business School, developed the concept of a "balanced scorecard" of financial and nonfinancial measures. Strategy in most companies no longer remains stable, he argues. CEOs are creating visions that move every few years. And the only way to get the organization to turn vision into reality is with the right nonfinancial measures. "You really have to get at the drivers, the lead indicators," he says, and those are nonfinancial.

"You can't begin to change anything unless you can measure," adds Vito Fabiano, vice president of finance, information technology, and administration for Pitney Bowes Inc.'s $2 billion (in sales) mailing systems division. Fabiano is now working hard to refine how the Stamford, Connecticut, company uses its year-old performance measurement system, which monitors customer loyalty, employee satisfaction, value versus the competition, financial progress, and value to other carriers and the U.S. Postal Service to which Pitney Bowes provides products and solutions. The objective of the measurement system is straightforward enough—communicate to the troops which goals are important and ensure that people align their efforts to solve the company's most pressing problems.

How well do the nonfinancial measures link to the financial ones? On a grand scale, the connection is only intuitive, says Fabiano. Loyal customers lead to repeat sales, and repeat sales yield income. More directly, though, Fabiano has found that by increasing the number of "very satisfied" customers, the days sales outstanding figure dropped by several days, freeing up $15 million in accounts receivable.

Keeping Tabs

Three years ago, Whirlpool's David Whitwam announced four "value-creating objectives" that committed the company to its current path. He then publicly set yearly targets: 6 percent revenue growth, 18 percent return on equity, 10 times quality improvement, 5 percent cuts in total costs, and 90 percent of customers saying they are "extremely satisfied." Says Whitwam: "Cost, quality, productivity, and customer satisfaction are what, collectively, drive shareholder value, and many of the related measures are nonfinancial. That simple fact becomes a powerful tool when you acknowledge it, then operate and assess your business accordingly."

The building of Whirlpool's measurement system dates to the company's acquisition of the home appliance business of Philips Electronics in 1989. To bring the company's growing global business together, Whitwam called on 15 "one-company challenge teams," led by senior executives, to unify the way the company worked. Ralph Hake, executive vice president of the North American Appliance Group, who at the time was corporate controller, led his team around the world—to Europe, Asia, and Latin America—to benchmark such companies as Nestlé, Fiat, Hitachi, and Mitsubishi, and to recommend measurements to obtain world-class performance. "Unless you put visible measures in place that you can quantify," says Hake, "it's very hard for people to manage them."

Inventory management is one area that has already benefited. The company now keeps daily tabs on availability—measuring whether specific SKUs (shop-keeping units) are in the right warehouse in the right region at the time when customers order

one of Whirlpool's ranges, dishwashers, refrigerators, and so on. "We have a whole family of measures around availability," says Hake.

Whirlpool formerly had very strict inventory control, but plants made stock to inventory, not to order, so despite full warehouses, availability was often poor. Using nonfinancial measures, Whirlpool has significantly improved performance, says Hake. Better still, "we financed essentially one half of the [Philips] acquisition in Europe by working capital reduction," he says. The acquisition, made in two parts, cost Whirlpool about $961 million.

Every month now, Hake gets a top sheet of all financial and nonfinancial measures. A lot of that data then goes to the board at bimonthly meetings, which begin, like analyst meetings, with a review of the nonfinancials. Says board member Bob Burnett, "I think they're doing a better job [of disclosing nonfinancials] than anyone else in the industry." Burnett, retired chairman and CEO of Meredith Corp., is a member of eight corporate boards. "They have really assigned accountability at every level in such a way that there's no doubt where or how the control or authority is exercised or where the responsibility lies," he says.

A version of the top sheet, including more than two dozen measures with specific targets, also determines Hake's pay. "I'm expected to deliver the financial numbers," he says, "but my incentive is also based on customer satisfaction, quality, productivity, trade-partner satisfaction, and the growth numbers."

Still, releasing all this material to the public is a dicey game of knowing what to hold close to the chest and what to lay on the table so that competitors won't profit from the information. That's why, although Whirlpool discloses measures and targets, it reveals results selectively. "I don't want my good friends next door to really understand how I'm driving loyalty or making progress in it," says Callahan. At analyst meetings, he adds, "we'd throw a chart up on the screen, and there would be a whole batch of numbers on it. It's not a handout. But we'd pick two or three numbers and highlight them, and the next slide would come up before they could get their pencils out." Overall, Callahan never worried all that much about operating statistics slipping out. There's a large gulf between knowing a company's performance statistics and executing programs to deliver value, he says. Then again, "if you don't disclose much beyond bottom line data, people will find out sooner or later anyway. A supplier talks or an OEM talks. That stuff isn't very private."

Analysts, for their part, are happy with what Whirlpool has been giving them. "That type of [nonfinancial] information is helpful in terms of setting benchmarks and seeing improvement," says Larry Horan, vice president and appliance analyst at Prudential Securities Inc., in New York. He particularly likes data on new product development, service performance, and the satisfaction of Whirlpool trade partners such as Sears, Roebuck & Co.

The Link to Performance

The missing link in performance measurement—an airtight correlation between financial results and progress in operating activities—won't be dug out of the ground. It will come from research that shows once and for all that better quality, faster cycle times, and so on drop more value to the bottom line than they cost. But until that evidence begins to pour in, many people will find it hard to justify efforts to supplement dollar measures with indicators of operating strength and knowledge.

Nonfinancial data, albeit numerical, tend to strike many people as simply too soft. In many cases, researchers can't determine whether good financials are the cause or effect of good nonfinancials. For example, the September 1994 draft of a new report to the Department of Labor by Sarah Mavrinac and Neil Jones, two doctoral candidates at Harvard Business School, concludes that while measures of workplace practices and customer satisfaction can serve as reliable leading indicators of future financial performance, one can't ignore the impact of variable forces such as the competitive arena, customer power, or quantum leaps gained from new technologies.

At this point, nobody's holding his or her breath waiting for Corporate America to mount the slippery slope of full, legal disclosure of indicators of

---

FINDING THEIR SMILES

An annual report to warm the heart. That's what you get if you're a stockholder of the AES Corp., the $500 million (in revenues) Arlington, Virginia, independent power producer. Among the highlights in the most recent report: operating earnings soared 51 percent, and return on equity reached 23 percent. Just as compelling, opposite the graph of earnings on the first page of the 1993 report, is a graph of values, of integrity, fairness, social responsibility, and—yikes—fun! Employees, who hand out value grades ranging from 1 to 10, gave AES an average grade in fun of 8 last year.

Other nonfinancial measures revealed in the annual report, although more routine, show a company eager to tell stockholders its performance story: accident rates are only 58 percent of the industry average; sulfur dioxide and nitrogen oxide emissions together averaged 58 percent below permitted levels. Power plant uptime averaged 92 percent, while sales backlog has dropped slightly, from $29 billion to $27 billion.

But does the company believe the touchy-feely stuff is useful to users of the report? "A lot of what we're trying to sell is our reliability," says CFO Barry Sharp, "so we're trying to show we're reliable, safe, and clean." Customers want to know AES is financially strong, of course, but they care first about how well the company will deliver on its promises, he says. The report, he feels, helps give shareholders, analysts, and customers that comfort.

As AES senior management learned, however, when you've wrapped a company in high-minded values and mistakes happen, as they invariably do, faces get red very quickly. Two years ago, a lapse of integrity temporarily hammered the stock price; workers at the Shady Point, Oklahoma, site had doctored water-treatment reports that go to the Environmental Protection Agency. The incident plunged top managers into a dark period of introspection. But they emerged as convinced as ever that their corporate value system was worthwhile, and they reaffirmed their decision to give frontline teams plenty of decision-making authority.

377

nonfinancial performance. Tighter correlations, not to mention safe harbor rules, are needed before corporations will budge en masse.

And the pioneers? They're busy testing and refining these management tools, and they don't seem to be sweating over the small stuff. Just ask Michael Callahan. "Do we understand all the connections between the value drivers and the financials? No. Are we trying to map them? Yes. The point is to believe in the connections."

Bill Birchard, a freelance business writer from Amherst, New Hampshire, is a regular contributor to CFO.

PART II

Materials to Facilitate Performance Measurement, Management, and Appraisal System Design and Implementation

SECTION I

QUESTIONNAIRES

- Performance Management Practices Questionnaire
- Profile of Your Actual/Ideal Performance Management Program
- Performance Management Workshop Evaluation—Short Form

Performance Management Practices Questionnaire

Instructions: First, for each of the following statements, please indicate how often an excellent manager *should* do each of the statements. Please place a check (✓) to indicate this level of frequency in the appropriate column.

Second, please think of your own *behavior* as a supervisor/manager. Then, indicate how frequently you *do* each of the following by placing an "x" in the appropriate column. Please be certain that you have assessed your observations of your own behavior and *not* what you intended to do.

	Never	Seldom	Occasionally	Frequently	Always
A. Strategic Performance Planning Linkage					
1. Insure that goals of your strategic work unit (SWU) are consistent with strategic company goals.					
2. Insure that your employees are aware of operating company goals.					
3. Insure that employees are aware of corporate goals.					
4. Establish clear, specific work unit goals and standards linked with operating company goals.					
5. Help staff members understand how their jobs contribute to company goals and corporate goals.					
B. Gaining Employee Commitment					
6. Communicate high personal standards informally—in conversation, personal example, etc.					
7. Demonstrate strong personal commitment to, and persistence in, achieving your unit's goals.					
8. Ask staff members to participate in setting deadlines for the achievement of their goals.					
9. Build warm, friendly relationships with the people in your work group, rather than remaining cool and impersonal.					
10. Conduct work unit meetings to increase trust and mutual respect among members.					
11. Attempt to get a "feel" for work unit morale.					
12. Emphasize cooperation as opposed to competitiveness among members of your work group.					
13. When conflicts arise, make an effort to work them out with the individuals involved.					
C. Setting Work Unit Goals					
14. Establish clear-cut goals for every direct report.					
15. Develop measures to evaluate programs toward work unit goals.					
16. Develop an awareness of the methods of measurement for your work unit goals.					

Page 1 of 3

	Never	Seldom	Occasionally	Frequently	Always

17. Make certain there is a frank and open exchange of ideas in work-group meetings.

18. Hold meetings that are well-organized and well thought out.

19. Insure staff members have a clear understanding of what was decided at the end of work-group meetings you conduct.

20. Ask if staff members have a clear understanding of their duties and responsibilities.

21. Provide staff members with clear-cut decisions when needed.

D. Negotiating Individual Performance Goals and Standards

22. Give staff members a chance to influence the performance goals and standards that are set for their jobs.

23. Ask staff members to participate in deciding on which goals are most important.

24. Make the best use of staff members' skills and abilities when making assignments.

25. Explain to staff members the factors used in evaluating their performance.

26. Set clear-cut, individual assignment measures.

27. Set clear-cut work standards (measures of behaviors and outcomes).

E. Observing Employee Performance

28. Pay close attention to what staff members are saying when they talk to you.

29. Communicate your views honestly and directly during discussions of staff members' performance.

F. Documenting Employee Performance

30. Consider all relevant information when appraising staff members' performance.

31. Make every effort to gather information to enable you to accurately evaluate an employee's performance.

G. Giving Feedback and Coaching Employees

32. Provide training with specific behavioral feedback to enable employees to improve their performance.

33. Provide a climate whereby staff members can be completely open in telling you about their mistakes.

Page 2 of 3

384

	Never	Seldom	Occasionally	Frequently	Always
34. Prepare employees to fill in for each other when key people are absent or unavailable.					
35. Help employees develop specific plans to improve their performance.					
36. Work with employees to determine their realistic short-term career objectives.					
37. Give employees verbal feedback on how well they are doing on their jobs.					
38. Give staff members written feedback on how well they are doing on their jobs.					
39. Recognize and praise excellent performance.					
40. Recognize staff members for good performance more often than criticizing for performance problems.					
41. Notice and show appreciation when staff members have put in extra time and effort.					
42. Go to bat for your employees with your superiors when your employees are "right."					
H. Conducting Formal Performance Reviews					
43. Work with employees to reach mutual agreement on performance appraisals.					
44. Give employees written performance appraisals consistent with the feedback you have given them informally during the performance period.					
45. Sit down frequently with employees to review their overall performance.					
46. Provide employees with the information they need regarding pay and other compensation policies.					
I. Rewarding Performance with Pay					
47. Make every effort to be fair with staff members regarding their pay.					
48. Relate rewards (salary increases, recognition, promotions) to excellence in job performance rather than to other factors such as personal relationships.					

Profile of Your Actual/Ideal Performance Management Program

Think about the history of Performance Management in your organization. Mark with an "A" on the scales (1–7) below where you ACTUALLY are, and mark with an "I" where IDEALLY you would like the organization to be within three years (1 not at all—7 a great deal).

I. MY ORGANIZATION…

A. 1 _____ 2 _____ 3 _____ 4 _____ 5 _____ 6 _____ 7
Encourages managers to involve employees in key organizational decisions.

B. 1 _____ 2 _____ 3 _____ 4 _____ 5 _____ 6 _____ 7
Regularly communicates senior management's "vision" and objectives throughout the organization.

C. 1 _____ 2 _____ 3 _____ 4 _____ 5 _____ 6 _____ 7
Expects every employee/manager to contribute in achieving the organization's most important objectives.

D. 1 _____ 2 _____ 3 _____ 4 _____ 5 _____ 6 _____ 7
Is an outstanding place to work.

II. IN MY ORGANIZATION, THE PERFORMANCE MANAGEMENT SYSTEM…

A. 1 _____ 2 _____ 3 _____ 4 _____ 5 _____ 6 _____ 7
Is an ongoing management process, with meaningful communication which is linked to the critical plans and objectives of the organization.

B. 1 _____ 2 _____ 3 _____ 4 _____ 5 _____ 6 _____ 7
Was developed with input from employees/managers throughout the organization.

C. 1 _____ 2 _____ 3 _____ 4 _____ 5 _____ 6 _____ 7
Is "owned" by every manager/employee and seen as one of their most critical responsibilities.

D. 1 _____ 2 _____ 3 _____ 4 _____ 5 _____ 6 _____ 7
Includes *extensive* orientation and training for everyone impacted.

E. 1 _____ 2 _____ 3 _____ 4 _____ 5 _____ 6 _____ 7
Is viewed as a *valuable* tool for managing how work gets done and how well each individual is performing.

F. 1 _____ 2 _____ 3 _____ 4 _____ 5 _____ 6 _____ 7
Is legally defensible.

III. IN MY ORGANIZATION…

A. 1 _____ 2 _____ 3 _____ 4 _____ 5 _____ 6 _____ 7
Senior management is *INVOLVED/COMMITTED* to the successful implementation of our performance management system.

B. 1 _____ 2 _____ 3 _____ 4 _____ 5 _____ 6 _____ 7
Middle management is *INVOLVED/COMMITTED* to the successful implementation of our performance management system.

C. 1 _____ 2 _____ 3 _____ 4 _____ 5 _____ 6 _____ 7
Supervisors are *INVOLVED/COMMITTED* to the successful implementation of our performance management system.

D. 1 _____ 2 _____ 3 _____ 4 _____ 5 _____ 6 _____ 7
Employees are *INVOLVED/COMMITTED* to the successful implementation of our performance management system.

E. 1 _____ 2 _____ 3 _____ 4 _____ 5 _____ 6 _____ 7
There is a direct link between "strategic/business planning" and the performance management system.

F. 1 _____ 2 _____ 3 _____ 4 _____ 5 _____ 6 _____ 7
The performance management system is used to integrate other key systems (i.e., quality improvement, productivity improvement, succession planning, etc.).

G. 1 _____ 2 _____ 3 _____ 4 _____ 5 _____ 6 _____ 7
Appraisal results are used for promotion decisions.

H. 1 _____ 2 _____ 3 _____ 4 _____ 5 _____ 6 _____ 7
Appraisal results are used for compensation decisions.

I. 1 _____ 2 _____ 3 _____ 4 _____ 5 _____ 6 _____ 7
Appraisal results are used to determine training needs.

IV. THE TRAINING PROVIDED IN SUPPORT OF OUR PERFORMANCE MANAGEMENT SYSTEM...

A. 1 _____ 2 _____ 3 _____ 4 _____ 5 _____ 6 _____ 7
Teaches how to define a job so that it accurately reflects the work to be done.

B. 1 _____ 2 _____ 3 _____ 4 _____ 5 _____ 6 _____ 7
Teaches how to develop qualitative and quantitative definitions of successful performance (standards).

C. 1 _____ 2 _____ 3 _____ 4 _____ 5 _____ 6 _____ 7
Teaches how to keep track of one's performance relative to the standards which are in place.

D. 1 _____ 2 _____ 3 _____ 4 _____ 5 _____ 6 _____ 7
Teaches how to provide positive feedback for a job well done.

E. 1 _____ 2 _____ 3 _____ 4 _____ 5 _____ 6 _____ 7
Teaches how to provide corrective feedback for those areas needing improvement.

F. 1 _____ 2 _____ 3 _____ 4 _____ 5 _____ 6 _____ 7
Teaches how to use appraisal forms and follow appraisal procedures.

G. 1 _____ 2 _____ 3 _____ 4 _____ 5 _____ 6 _____ 7
Teaches managers how to solve performance problems.

H. 1 _____ 2 _____ 3 _____ 4 _____ 5 _____ 6 _____ 7
Teaches how to use this system as an employee development tool.

I. 1 _____ 2 _____ 3 _____ 4 _____ 5 _____ 6 _____ 7
Gives ample opportunity for managers/supervisors to practice their skills before returning to the job.

J. 1 _____ 2 _____ 3 _____ 4 _____ 5 _____ 6 _____ 7
Includes ways to measure how effectively skills are being used back on the job.

Performance Management Workshop Evaluation: Short Form

1. The workshop *content* was appropriate and useful.

5	4	3	2	1
Extremely Appropriate				Not at all appropriate

2. The workshop teaching and training *methods* were appropriate and effective.

5	4	3	2	1
Extremely Appropriate				Not at all appropriate

3. The workshop *materials* provided for me were appropriate and useful.

5	4	3	2	1
Extremely Appropriate				Not at all appropriate

4. The workshop *instructor(s)* was (were) effective.

5	4	3	2	1
Extremely Appropriate				Not at all appropriate

5. The workshop provided *useful and practical* ideas and suggestions I can apply in my organization.

5	4	3	2	1
Extremely Appropriate				Not at all appropriate

6. I *know and understand more* about performance management than I did before the workshop.

5	4	3	2	1
Extremely Appropriate				Not at all appropriate

7. *Overall,* the workshop was a beneficial and useful experience.

5	4	3	2	1
Extremely Appropriate				Not at all appropriate

8. What did you find *most effective,* useful, appropriate? _____
_____
_____

9. What did you find *least effective,* useful, appropriate? _____
_____
_____

10. Would you *recommend* this workshop to others interested in the design, implementation, and evaluation of performance management systems? _____ Yes _____ No

    Why or why not? _____
_____
_____
_____

SECTION II

CASES

- Kathy Berndt

- USA Car Rental

- Midwest Hospital

- Performance Management, Organization Culture, and Organization Strategy in an Insurance Company

- A Case of Alleged Sex Discrimination in Performance Appraisal

- Performance Measurement and Management at IBM

Kathy Berndt

No one seemed to know the real Kathy Berndt. She came to the organization three years ago with considerable experience in another state. She immediately began to work very hard and while she did not socialize with her colleagues, certainly was not disliked. Her first supervisor was very lax in monitoring and managing Kathy. His perspective was, "Professionals can manage themselves, that's why we pay them!" There were a few complaints from clients, but no one took that to be a problem. Kathy seemed to work quietly and efficiently. When her original supervisor retired, she was assigned to Marsha McCoy. Marsha was relatively new to the organization and had recently received a promotion to supervisor. After about three months, Marsha received a complaint about Kathy from a client. (Actually Marsha's boss, the Division Chief, told Marsha about it.) Marsha felt that one complaint was not a problem, it could easily be a personality clash or an unreasonable client; they usually were. After a few more months Kathy's reports began coming in incomplete or late. She flatly refused to take on a few of a colleague's cases when the colleague went on vacation. Kathy said she was too busy. Whenever Marsha inquired how things were going, Kathy always said "fine." When Marsha decided to ask about a specific case she hadn't received a report on, Kathy blew up. She resented her professional expertise being questioned. Marsha tried to explain her reasons for checking, but Kathy stormed out of the office. The following week the two met and Kathy politely agreed to discuss any or all of her cases with Marsha. She also agreed to get her paperwork in on time. After a month, Kathy's paperwork hadn't improved. She seemed to have an emergency meeting or appointment whenever Marsha wanted to discuss cases. Marsha knew the Division Chief would soon ask her how Kathy was doing.

USA Car Rental

USA Car Rental is in the top four in the car rental business. It has maintained market share for the last several years despite erosion of market share for #1 and #2 Hertz and Avis. It has a history of financial soundness and earning a substantial return on investment. Its sales force is extremely competitive and successful in selling major corporations on granting "exclusives" to USA Car Rental for substantial discounts for their corporations. Although competitive in this area USA Car Rental still will not "buy business" by entering into agreements which are below cost. Thus, it has lost some major clients, such as IBM, because of their unwillingness to write "bad" business.

USA Car Rental has begun to recognize they may be the next to lose market share if they do not carefully manage their business. There are many new competitors on the horizon such as Budget, Thrifty, American International, MPG, and others who are beginning to grow in market share. Through a recent survey USA discovered that only 15% of the public have ever rented a car, whereas nearly 90% have flown in an airplane. This led USA to discover a new market, the leisure renter, the "first time or few time" renter as a critical customer for future success. They already have a history of renting to younger customers (i.e., 21 years of age) than others in the car rental business. Therefore, they may have an opportunity to build brand loyalty if they can capture the leisure car rental market. They also have cost estimates from which they have discovered that family vacations might even be cheaper and permit spending more time at the desired destination by flying on a discount airline (such as People Express and Continental) and renting a car upon arrival. Thus, USA decided to market to the first time or few time car renter.

With their philosophy of not giving away business, they have decided they are going to market by providing the best customer service possible by differentiating business customers from leisure customers and spending far more time with leisure customers in explaining the details of the rental agreement, providing directions as to hotels or resort areas, providing special give-aways to children traveling with their parents, etc. For this effort the central person is the car rental agent, the representative of USA Car Rental who has the specific responsibility of making a friend of the leisure renter and selling them various car rental packages such as upgrades, collision coverages, and vehicle upgrades. The Corporate Director of Training, Jane Younger, has become central in the corporate strategy for its new marketing efforts, with the responsibility of training customer service representatives to provide the best customer service possible *and* to exceed the competition by at least 10% on *all* customer service standards.

Instructions: You are Jane Younger, Corporate Director of Training and Development at USA Car Rental. You have been given a specific responsibility of directing the corporation's new marketing thrust with the strategic objective of accomplishing a long-term increase in market share via improved marketing skills of customer service representatives. You are to design a performance appraisal system, initiated by a specific performance appraisal measure and followed by a strategy for recruitment, selection, training and development, and motivation. What would you do?

Midwest Hospital

Midwest Hospital is a 700 bed facility which is clearly a leader in a locale known for health care. The organization has recently undergone a strategic planning exercise and is led by a strong CEO with strong backups in each of the vice presidential positions, especially in the personnel/human resource function. The organization has a tradition of using management by objectives (MBO) and has done so for a number of years. Its managers are skilled at the MBO approach. The organization has determined from its strategic planning that it has five "key success factors" which establish performance targets for each managerial work unit. These include growth in market share, quality of patient care, financial management (and cost reduction), program planning and implementation, and human resource management.

The human resource function is not only strong in its leadership, it is strong in several areas, with backups in each such as training and development, compensation, data base management, and its employee relations function. The employee population generally is young with some turnover, but also has some long-term employees who have been there more than twenty years. The organization retains many employees who are successful, however, it is also proud of the number of individuals who have left and have gone to jobs in other organizations.

The human resource manager and the CEO have generally decided that some attention to the performance appraisal system is now needed. Clearly, they wish to leave the MBO system intact, but have a strong need for a focus on specific job content for each employee in the organization. Better customer relations and human resource management are strongly desired by the CEO and are seen as a way of improving market share as well as rendering higher quality patient care.

The CEO has also become concerned recently that the top level management system needs a succession planning component to ensure the replacement of higher level managers who leave for assignments outside the organization. He is particularly proud of having his organization perceived as a training ground and wants to find a system whereby the organization can retain the very best for its own operations. He also has become concerned with the issue of corporate culture and wants an assessment of the organization's current corporate culture. He believes it is strong and well functioning and focuses on performance, and that the organization "supportively confronts" employees to help each individual do their best.

The CEO's other major concern is a performance appraisal system for non-exempt employees. Basically the organization has attempted to use a MBO system for these employees, but it has not been perceived as successful, and it is not widely or systematically used throughout the organization. He is concerned that everyone in the organization perform as well as possible and believes firmly that good performance appraisal systems require performance planning, management of performance, and effective performance review and reward systems. He has asked for a detailed examination of this system and for specific recommendations.

Instructions: You are Sam Majors, the vice president of human resources for this facility which employs over 3000 individuals. You've been given an hour to make a presentation to the vice presidents and the board, proposing a performance appraisal system specifically designed to enhance the performance of non-exempt employees as well as a methodology for succession planning for managerial jobs. You were specifically asked to diagnose the existing situation, develop the methodologies, and provide a detailed implementation methodology for your strategy. What do you recommend?

Performance Management, Organization Culture, and Organization Strategy*

Organization Background:

Large insurance company.

Paternalistic; good job security; many long-term employees; conservative; technical competence, seniority, and loyalty rewarded.

Considerable variance in degree to which policies are implemented; considerable autonomy across divisions.

Organization has been financially successful throughout its history.

Environment changing drastically in 1980s, with deregulation and increased competition.

Current strategic thrust: Move to a diversified financial services organization.

Current emphasis: cost-cutting, staff reductions, job restructuring, early retirements, efficiency, and productivity.

Younger employees and managers being brought in at high, market-driven salaries.

Top management now verbally supports excellence in human resource management.

Numerous programs and systems to improve performance have been tried, few have had staying power.

Recent reorganization into Profit (line units) and Value (staff units) Centers—autonomous units, with performance measures yet to be determined.

Performance Appraisal System:

Revised several times, most recently two years ago by a high-level task force of line and staff managers.

Leniency perceived, hence forced distribution installed, with distribution published each year.

Merit pay amounts driven directly by rating level attained.

Current appraisal forms require Overall Rating on five-point scale, with vast majority in level three, described as "Fully Successful," but perceived as merely "Average."

"Performance Objectives" and "Management Factors" (e.g., control, communications) now evaluated, but performance standards typically not set.

Enormous variability in compliance with system procedures across work units.

Numerous specific forms comprise the system, including ratee's self-assessment form, performance development form, action planning, overall rating (with comments) form, etc.

Three-hour training in performance appraisal offered, but voluntary.

Considerable dissatisfaction (based on surveys) with rating accuracy, with forced distribution, with equity; a "paperwork exercise required by Personnel."

Related Human Resource Management Programs:

Succession planning system in place at executive level, but criteria not generally known and not tied to appraisal forms or results.

Promotion process not formalized, with appraisal results used casually, if at all.

One-week management development program offered to middle management; little formal training at executive level; neither directly aimed at performance appraisal/management skills or responsibilities.

Several reward and recognition programs in place (e.g., bonus, incentive rewards for excellence, recognition programs), but not well integrated or publicized.

Job evaluation system often used as mechanism to give promotions. Internal "consultant" group working on quality, on cost reduction, on work redesign, but are not linked to appraisal efforts.

Strategic planning process quite sophisticated and beginning to filter through organization, indicating specific strategic direction, with emphasis on performance measurement, on quality, on respect and dignity for people and customers.

The Mandate:

The top level executive group (CEO, Chairman, etc.) asked corporate human resource staff to "fix" the performance appraisal system within six months.

Executive V.P., Administration delegated task to a subordinate (Vice President, Human Resources), who delegated it to a three-person group of human Resource Managers of Compensation, Organization Development, and Employee Relations; the group hired a consultant.

What should the consultant recommend?

*Prepared by Craig Eric Schneier, Craig Eric Schneier Associates, Princeton, NJ.

A Case of Alleged Sex Discrimination in Performance Appraisal*

Jane Burroughs and John Watson are both employed as technicians in the pathology lab of Central Methodist Hospital, a major medical center in the core of a major city. They both hold specialist degrees and are licensed pathologist's assistants. Both have been employed in their jobs for five years.

Last month, Dr. Clarence Cutter, the chief pathologist and supervisor of the lab, decided to reorganize his operation. He decided that supervising the work of both assistants was taking up too much of his time. He reasoned that if he were to promote one of them to a mid-level supervisory position, he could reduce the time he spent in direct supervision. Dr. Cutter presented his argument to Fred Wunderlich, the hospital's director of personnel. Wunderlich agreed and added that Dr. Cutter could probably use even more help in the lab. He suggested that either Burroughs or Watson be promoted to a new job titled Administrative Assistant to the Pathologist and that a new person be hired to fill the vacated lab technician position. Thus, a new structure was developed for the department in which two lab technicians reported to an administrative assistant, who in turn reported to the chief pathologist.

The next task for Dr. Cutter was to decide which of his lab technicians to promote to the new position. In order to make the decision, he pulled the latest six-month performance evaluations he had made on Burroughs and Watson. Exhibit 1-1 reproduces their performance review results. On the basis of the performance reviews, he promoted John Watson to the administrative assistant position.

Exhibit 1-1. Six-Month Performance Reviews for Burroughs and Watson

Employee: _____ Jane Burroughs _____   Supervisor: _____ Dr. Cutter _____
Department: _____ Pathology _____   Date: _____ 11-28-76 _____

Work Quantity		Work Quality		Cooperation	
Far below average	_____	Far below average	_____	Far below average	_____
Below Average	X	Below Average	_____	Below Average	X
Average	_____	Average	X	Average	_____
Above average	_____	Above average	_____	Above average	_____
Far above average	_____	Far above average	_____	Far above average	_____

Employee: _____ John Watson _____   Supervisor: _____ Dr. Cutter _____
Department: _____ Pathology _____   Date: _____ 12-24-76 _____

Work Quantity		Work Quality		Cooperation	
Far below average	_____	Far below average	_____	Far below average	_____
Below Average	_____	Below Average	_____	Below Average	_____
Average	X	Average	_____	Average	_____
Above average	_____	Above average	X	Above average	_____
Far above average	_____	Far above average	_____	Far above average	X

Upon learning of Watson's promotion, Burroughs went to Dr. Cutter and demanded that he justify why he promoted Watson instead of her. He told her that he was not obligated to present a justification to her; that he was perfectly within his rights as chief pathologist to make such a decision and that she should rest assured that his decision was made on grounds that were fair and equitable to her and Watson.

*Prepared by Judy D. Olian, College of Business and Management, University of Maryland, College Park, MD.

This explanation did not satisfy Burroughs, and she filed a formal complaint alleging sex discrimination in a promotion decision both with Mr. Wunderlich, the personnel manager, and Robyn Payson, the Hospital's Equal Employment Opportunity officer.

A hearing was scheduled by Wunderlich to resolve the issues. Wunderlich and Payson constituted the review board at the hearing, and Cutter and Burroughs were invited to present their cases. In the hearing, Burroughs opened the case by presenting her formal complaint: Both she and Watson have identical credentials for their jobs and have equal tenure on the job (five years). In addition, it is her belief that she and Watson have performed equivalently during this period of time. Therefore, according to her charge, the only reason Dr. Cutter could possibly have had for promoting Watson over her would be her sex. She noted that a decision of that nature is in clear violation of the Sex Discrimination Act of 1984 which reads in part:

It is unlawful for an employer to discriminate against an employee on the grounds of the employee's sex, marital status or pregnancy—

(a) in the terms or conditions of employment that the employer affords the employee;

(b) by denying the employee access, or limiting the employee's access, to opportunities for promotion, transfer, or training, or to any other benefits associated with employment;

(c) by dismissing the employee; or

(d) by subjecting the employee to any other detriment.

(Part II, Div. 1, Par. 14(2) of the Sex Discrimination Act 1984.)

Dr. Cutter countered by justifying his decision on the basis of actual performance review data. He argued that sex had nothing whatsoever to do with his decision. Rather, he presented to the board the latest six-month performance evaluations, which showed Watson to be performing better than Burroughs on three performance dimensions: (1) work quantity; (2) work quality; and (3) cooperation (see exhibit 1-1).

The performance results served to anger Burroughs further. She requested that the hearing be adjourned and reconvened after she had a chance to review the results and prepare her case further. Wunderlich and Payson agreed and rescheduled a second hearing two weeks later.

At the second hearing, Burroughs presented the following list of grievances with regard to the promotion decision and the information upon which it was based:

1. The decision is still in violation of the Sex Discrimination Act because the way the performance evaluation was carried out served to discriminate against her on the basis of sex. Her reasoning on this point included the following charges:

(a) Dr. Cutter is biased against females, and this factor caused him to rate males in general above females in general.

(b) Dr. Cutter and Mr. Watson are in an all-male poker group that meets on Friday nights, and she has systematically been excluded. Thus, ties of friendship have developed along sex lines, which created a conflict of interest for Dr. Cutter.

(c) Dr. Cutter has said to her and to others on several occasions that he doubts females can carry out managerial tasks because they must constantly be concerned with duties at home and they get pregnant.

2. The measuring device itself failed to include a number of activities she carries out that are critical to the functioning of the lab. For example, while Dr. Cutter and Watson are talking over coffee, she frequently is cleaning up the lab. She says that, although Mr. Watson's work is good, he tends to concentrate on all visible work outcomes, and leaves much of the "invisible work," like cleaning up, to her.

3. The timing of the performance review was bad. She charged that it was unfair to her to base the decision on only one six-month evaluation. Dr. Cutter has a total of ten performance reviews for each of them. Why didn't he base his decision on all ten, rather than on just the latest review?

4. Also with respect to timing, Ms. Burroughs pointed out that her review had been made a month earlier than Mr. Watson's. She charged that December 24 was Christmas Eve and the day of the lab's office party. She charged that the spirits of the occasion (liquid and other) tended to shade Dr. Cutter's judgment in favor of Watson.

Issues for Discussion:

Put yourself in the position of Mr. Wunderlich and Ms. Payson. Decide whether there is any justification to Ms. Burroughs' charges, or if Dr. Cutter is justified in his decision. In making your decision, address yourself to the following questions:

1. Is the measuring instrument itself at issue in this case?

2. If your answer above is yes, what kinds of recommendations would you make for changing the instrument?

3. Are problems of administration an issue in this case?

4. If your answer is yes, what changes in administration would you recommend?

5. Do you think the problem would have arisen if Dr. Cutter adopted and followed a policy of open feedback on performance review results?

CASE STUDY:
PERFORMANCE MEASUREMENT AND MANAGEMENT AT IBM

Prepared by:
Craig Eric Schneier, Ph.D.
Craig Eric Schneier Associates
5 Chadwell Court
Pennington, NJ 08534
(609) 737-6867

397

IBM: COMPANY SNAPSHOT*

ILLUSTRIOUS HISTORY

1. Values-driven company
2. World-class marketing, service
3. "Hire the best" philosophy
4. Keep (almost) everyone; job security, no layoff philosophy
5. Perennially profitable
6. Model for management, leadership

HARSH CURRENT REALITIES

1. Performance problems
   - EPS down 33%
   - Market share down 38%
2. Many key products (e.g., PC's) judged to be mediocre
3. Downsizings (via early retirement, redeployment, attrition, etc.)
4. Rare public "dirty laundry"
   - CEO dissatisfaction, "threats"
   - Forced distribution rating system**
   - Top-level executive exodus
5. Senior officer defections, staff changes
6. Reorganizations; spin-offs
7. New products

* Highly selective.

** Recent *WSJ* and *NYT* articles attached.

398

BUSINESS STRATEGY AND PLANS:
"THE NEW IBM"*

STRUCTURE	CULTURE	GOALS
Autonomous business units	Faster decision making	Mesh products/services more closely with marketplace
Joint ventures with others in the industry	Less job security	Continue research leadership
Elimination of thousands of jobs	Higher performance expectations	Get products to market faster
	More candor in communications	Boost mainframe demand
	Guidance versus dictates from corporate staff	
	More autonomy, discretion down the hierarchy	
	More risk-taking	

*See e.g., *Business Week*, December 16, 1991.

399

IBM Is Said to Plan Tougher Reviews of Performance of Employees in U.S.

By Paul B. Carroll
Staff Reporter of *The Wall Street Journal*

International Business Machines Corp. plans to stiffen its evaluations of U.S. employees' performance, in a move that should continue to reduce its work force, industry executives said.

In Armonk, N.Y., an IBM spokesman declined to comment. But the industry executives said they expect the tougher performance guidelines to be announced internally this week.

The executives added that they expect IBM to cut at least a few thousand more jobs next year through the program. IBM has already said its world-wide work force will decline by at least 17,000 this year, to 367,000, but earnings have been weak all year, and IBM is widely expected to continue shrinking itself.

Under the new guidelines, IBM will more strictly enforce a system under which it ranks employees on a numerical scale. Few employees now carry a rank below three, but the guidelines will force managers to rank people as fours. Anyone with a rank that low will face pressure to resign, and quickly.

In the past, when a weak employee was given a checklist for improving his performance and was given a certain deadline, he was said to be on "a measured mile." But these days, the employee will get just 30 or 60 days to improve or be fired, instead of perhaps six months. So, one manager says, the new guidelines mean employees may find themselves on "a measured 100 yards."

Although the industry executives said it's not clear how many people will quit or be fired because of the new guidelines, they said they expect perhaps 10% of IBM's U.S. work force to be ranked as fours. That translates to about 20,000 people, of whom at least a few thousand can be expected to leave the company.

Even though the new guidelines won't take effect until next year, many employees will probably leave this year. That's because of a program that provides two weeks of severance pay per year of employment to people who volunteer to leave this year. That package shrinks to one week a year in 1992, so people who are under any sort of pressure may decide to leave quickly.

"I think this is a long-overdue revamping," said Sam Albert, a former IBM executive who is now a consultant in Scarsdale, N.Y. "They're cleaning out the dead wood."

As part of the new guidelines, IBM is also expected to promise more rewards to those who perform best. That is in keeping with statements from IBM executives that they don't view firing as a major way of cutting employment. Rather, they say they view firing as just one of several ways to "raise the bar" for IBM employees and improve the quality of the IBM work force.

IBM's standards for itself "have to be escalated to be more competitive, so the people have to be more competitive," Walt Burdick, a senior vice president, said in an interview this summer. He added that "we want to be a high-demand, high-reward company."

IBM's stock rose $1.375 to $103.625 in composite trading on the New York Stock Exchange yesterday and can be expected to rise further if investors become convinced that IBM is really serious about cutting costs.

The Wall Street Journal, October 1, 1991.

Using Psychological Pressure at I.B.M.*

By Webster Brown

It was a pleasant summer day in 1964 when I took a seat alongside about 250 others, in an auditorium in Poughkeepsie as a new employee of the International Business Machines Corporation. Fresh from engineering school, I was brimming with enthusiasm over what I expected would be a long and successful career at one of America's most exciting companies. I.B.M. had just announced System 360, whose tremendous power first carved out a market for the mainframe.

But I no longer feel much loyalty to I.B.M. My pride dissipated in recent years as I watched I.B.M. betray one of its basic values—respect for the individual. In its relentless pursuit of excellence, I.B.M., like many other American enterprises under competitive siege in recent years, has turned from a challenging and caring employer to one ruled by fear and intimidation. Benevolence has become malevolence. People once praised for their excellence now fear for their jobs.

That is how, after 28 years of loyal service, I joined some 65,000 others who from 1986 through 1991 cut their careers at I.B.M. short, by leaving or taking early retirement. Almost two years ago, on a bright spring day in East Fishkill, N.Y., where I.B.M. has its chip and packaging manufacturing plant, I signed a covenant not to sue I.B.M. for age discrimination, handed in my badge and, after standing in line, received my incentive pay for taking early retirement.

I retained a modicum of dignity by retiring prematurely, at age 54. If I had stayed, I would probably have been weeded out under an appraisal system, which gets tougher each year, that seems designed to sweep the company clean of employees who, however loyal and competent, no longer fit in at I.B.M.

While publicly maintaining that it has not abandoned its no-layoff policy, I.B.M. has initiated a psychological reign of terror over employees under the guise of quality improvement. While purported to raise productivity, I.B.M.'s new performance appraisal system actually determines which employees are most expendable by rating them, along a curve, according to their usefulness to the business and how well they do their job. The 5 to 10 percent with the lowest rating every year are put on 30 days' notice. Improve or be dismissed.

For many, this presents a Catch 22. I.B.M.'s full employment policy means some departments are underutilized, leaving many employees without meaningful work that would allow them to earn a high ranking. Meanwhile, other workers are doomed by overwork. As people have taken early retirement, employees working in departments operating closer to capacity have taken on heavier workloads—and are condemned if they are unable to do their jobs well.

After Christmas of 1989, I found myself ranked at the bottom. I had been transferred from the design to the product assurance department. Management changes and reorganizations had disintegrated my modest network of colleagues until I was isolated, without contacts. As an older, higher-positioned and higher-paid worker, I was easy prey. I.B.M. considered people like me the least productive, least flexible and least desirable.

As a semiconductor design engineer, I was too specialized to qualify for many jobs outside of I.B.M. and too long in the corporate cloister to be seen as a desirable recruit. But retirement was a more attractive option than remaining in what I viewed as an increasingly abusive and dysfunctional company. Caught between the demands of a changing I.B.M. and their sensitivity toward their employees, many of the most talented managers had quickly dropped back to staff positions. Their replacements were a grimmer type. Younger and self-serving, their personal ambitions took precedence over those of I.B.M. or their employees. They arrogated technical responsibility from the engineers, helping transform I.B.M. into a "top down" organization.

The authoritarian management, the lost empowerment of employees and the fear that manifests itself in low morale would take years to correct. The walk out of the woods would be as long as the walk in. The company that reached the clearing would be I.B.M. in name only.

Webster Brown, formerly an engineer at the International Business Machines Corporation, is part-time office manager of the National Council of Alcoholism of Putnam County.

* *New York Times,* March 22, 1992. Reprinted with permission.

IBM PMM "CASE"
Questions for Group Discussion

1. What problems do you detect with IBM's PMM system? _____

_____

2. What additional data would you want in order to assess IBM's PMM system? _____

_____

3. What are the "diseases" (underlying causes) of IBM's PMM problems? _____

_____

4. What specifically should IBM do to address its problems? _____

_____

402

SECTION III

ROLE PLAYS

- The Performance Review
- April Company
- The Best Laboratory Technician
- Central City Recreation Department

The Performance Review

Role for Supervisor (George/Georgette)

You supervise several clerical and administrative employees, including Claire. She has good secretarial skills but her job is really an administrative assistant. She must gather and compile data for reports, prepare the budget, keep track of expenditures, and complete personnel records for the group. She seems only to want to do secretarial work, however. You have given her "Satisfactory" ratings but do not feel she deserves a promotion. She did forget to complete an important report a few months ago.

Role for Subordinate (Claire)

You are an excellent secretary who works for George/Georgette. Your boss always seems to want you to do things beside clerical work, but you like that type of work best. You feel you deserve a promotion as your ratings are fine and you have heard no complaints about your work. Everyone says you are the best worker in the group. You have been with the organization several years longer than your boss. You can't understand how you got a few "Satisfactory" ratings last time but know that won't happen this year. You really need the extra salary that will come with your promotion.

April Company*

Role for Miss Mary Alice Tame, Manager, Women's Wear

You have worked for the April Company for twelve years, starting as a clerk and making slow but steady progress. You hope eventually to become head buyer for the entire chain. You have been in your present job (manager of the women's wear department of the largest April store in the area) for two years. Forty-three people work for you, in three areas. The "college shop," with excessively high turnover, has always been a problem. The assistant manager of this area, Linda Wakefield, has been in that job for one year, and her performance review is due. Linda came to the April Company with two years of experience with a major competitor. You hired her for this position because she seemed bright, energetic, and fashion conscious and had a college degree and relevant experience. During the past year she has been as efficient and effective as you had hoped, but she also seems bossy and conceited and often fails to follow proper procedures. You have often seen her socializing with male managerial personnel during working hours, and several of her subordinates have commented that she is "very friendly indeed" with some of these men. Still her record is good—a 13 percent increase in volume over the past year, and turnover in her group is down by 50 percent. She is an excellent merchandiser, and you would like to keep her. You are afraid that she will take criticism badly, yet her behavior has become a problem.

Role for Miss Linda Wakefield, Assistant Manager

A year ago you were hired by Miss Tame to manage the April Company college shop. The responsibilities were significantly greater than the job you then held, with a major competitor, so you jumped at it. You are twenty-five and look even a little younger. You are proud of your figure, and you dress to show it off. After all, you believe that people in the fashion business should appear to be in that profession. You plan to be a success in fashion retailing. You have spent many hours of your own time keeping abreast of the latest trends. Even so, you have managed to find some worthwhile male company at the store. The fact that you have substantially increased business and reduced turnover in your group should demonstrate your competence. Unfortunately, you doubt that "old-maid" Tame sees things that way. If she would order some of the things you have suggested, your increase would probably double. This is one of the items you plan to mention during your upcoming performance-evaluation meeting.

Place yourself in the interviewee's position. How would you react to this interview? How would you feel afterward?

Comment on the effectiveness of the interview. Did it accomplish the objective of informing the employee of his/her current performance standing? Did anyone win or lose?

What suggestions would you give to the interviewer?

*From M. Sashkin, *Assessing Performance Appraisal,* University Associates, 1981.

The Best Laboratory Technician*

Consider the following scenario:

You are the manager of a group of research scientists and laboratory technicians in a chemical research and development firm.

Recently, you have become aware that one of your best laboratory technicians, Rosena Marie Marley, has been showing some performance inconsistency after receiving consistently high performance evaluations since joining your group five years ago. You're not sure whether there is a real decline in performance, though you've noticed that Rosena has become more introverted and is not as active a participant in the group research sessions (which are usually very lively). While she used to spend a lot of time informally and enthusiastically discussing any ideas that occurred to her with other project members, she seems to be doing less of that now. You've also noticed that Rosena's been coming in to work a little later (though she still finishes what she needs to do) and has been spending more time than usual on the phone. You don't know whether her home life is running smoothly or why she seems to be showing these subtle changes in behavior.

While there are no *obvious* signs of poor performance today, you're worried that performance might deteriorate in the future. After all, you have plans to promote Rosena to a project manager at a future point. In fact, you anticipate an opening in a project management position in about six to eight months. You don't know whether her performance will return to its usual pattern by then, but you're also worried that she might lose out in the competition if her behavior pattern is fluctuating. There are also project deadlines coming up in the near future.

Role for Supervisor

You have called Rosena in for a chat. Your objective is to determine what the problem is, whether it is long term or temporary, and what to do about it.

Role for Rosena Marie Marley

All facts in the case regarding your performance and your history are essentially true. There are no personal problems. You are unsure what is happening to your performance and why. Maybe the job is no longer interesting.

Your supervisor is about to discuss the situation with you.

*Prepared by Judy D. Olian, College of Business and Management, University of Maryland, College Park, MD.

Central City Recreation Department*

Role for Terry Roberts, Director of Recreation

You are director of the Central City Recreation Department. You are in your early forties and have been involved in physical education, recreation, and industrial education most of your life. Your staff consists of eight full-time recreation workers, a large number of volunteers, and an assistant director. You have worked hard in this job and, over the past seven years, feel that you have had considerable success in building up the city's recreation programs. You are particularly pleased with the good working relationships you have been able to develop with local high schools and business firms.

You are about to hold an annual performance review session with your assistant director, Lynn Morrison. Lynn, who has a B.A. in physical education, started working with the department one year ago, immediately after graduating from college. You gave Lynn primary responsibility for dealing with local business and industry, and it is this area that especially bothers you. You have received several phone calls from reliable community members, both industrial managers and retailers, over the past two months, complaining that Lynn has been pressuring them to donate equipment for the city recreation programs. You are worried that Lynn might have destroyed all the good will that it took you years to develop. Other than this problem, Lynn has been a committed hard worker, really caring for the children involved in the community programs. You wonder how well Lynn relates to adult participants, in light of this problem with business leaders. Although you do not think any severe action, such as firing Lynn, is at present justified, you do feel that the problems you have identified must be resolved.

Role for Lynn Morrison, Assistant Director of Recreation

You graduated last year from State University with a bachelor's degree in physical education and were lucky enough to find the sort of job you had hoped for. One of your ideals in going into recreational activities was to help children develop their physical and social skills, and this job gives you a chance to make just such an impact.

You like your boss, Terry Roberts, and believe your work is appreciated. The major responsibility Terry gave you this past year was dealing with the business community, whose support is crucial for effective program implementation. By sponsoring teams or even whole programs, local businesses improve their public relations and the department receives much-needed equipment. Because the city council is unwilling to provide the support the department needs, Terry has developed good relations with local firms and gained their support. Even so, the children desperately need new equipment. You have had to use equipment that should have been thrown away long ago. You have tried to convey this situation to a number of business managers and have even suggested to some of them that they might receive more business from the children (and their parents) if they loosened their purse strings a little. After all, it is only natural for the recreation-program participants to support the merchants and industries that support them.

Speaking of support, you realize that is one thing you could use more of from Terry. In fact, you have placed that item on your agenda for the annual performance review session, which will commence shortly.

Place yourself in the interviewee's position. How would you react to this interview? How would you feel afterward?

Comment on the productivity of the interview. Did it accomplish the objective of informing the employee of his or her current status in the organization? Did anyone win or lose?

What suggestions would you give to the interviewer?

*From M. Sashkin, *Assessing Performance Appraisal*, University Associates, 1981.

SECTION IV

Practical Suggestions for Each Part of the Performance Measurement, Management, and Appraisal Cycle

- Performance Measurement, Management, and Appraisal: A Strategy Execution Tool
- Planning for Performance Management and Appraisal
- Managing Performance
- Reviewing and Appraising Performance
- Developing Performance
- Rewarding Performance
- Designing, Implementing, Administering, and Evaluating Performance Measurement, Management, and Appraisal Systems
- Prototype Format/Worksheet
- Sample Performance Tasks, Behaviors, Competencies, Objectives

Performance Measurement, Management, and Appraisal: A Strategy Execution Tool

Performance Appraisal (PA) System Problems, Symptoms, and Potential Cures

THE CRITERION PROBLEM:
Deciding What to Evaluate

SYMPTOMS:
- Ambiguity in roles and responsibilities of each job
- Job performance is difficult to quantify
- No clear statement of overall objectives of units or organization

POTENTIAL CURES:
- Job analysis and credible position description
- Outcomes for each job identified
- Overall goals of units and of organization set

THE JUDGMENT PROBLEM:
Appraising Performance

SYMPTOMS:
- Disagreement on ratings
- Reviewing official changes ratings
- Appeals, grievances, accusations of bias, discrimination

POTENTIAL CURES:
- Observable, behaviorally-based criteria
- Performance documented over time
- Rater training and practice
- Effective communication of performance expectations

THE POLICY PROBLEM:
Using the Results of the Appraisal

SYMPTOMS:
- Top management fails to reward managers who are excellent in staff assessment and development
- Marginal performers receive promotions or incentives

POTENTIAL CURES:
- Top management actually uses PA itself
- Policies governing use of PA consistently applied
- Performance-contingent reward system in operation

THE REALITY PROBLEM:
Recognizing Managerial Work and Organizational Culture

SYMPTOMS:
- Appraisal forms not completed
- Managers complain about time requirements
- System perceived to belong to designers, not users
- Personnel specialists take "enforcer" role, not "advisor" role
- System revised frequently

POTENTIAL CURES:
- Implement PA using The Performance Management (PM) Model

Why Do Performance Appraisal Systems Fail?

Managers   Not accountable for Performance Improvement
                                Management
                        Not trained in Performance Management

EEO   Lack of job-relatedness

Psychologists   Inaccurate/error/attributions

Employees   Annual performance appraisal vs. ongoing performance
                        management

**Human
Resources**   HR Department, not managerial responsibility

Executives   Not linked to the strategic plan

Performance Measurement, Management, and Appraisal: Description and Scope

The Performance Management Process (PMP) is a key managerial process. Together with a company's compensation, reward and recognition process, and promotion and succession process, the PMP is a primary vehicle for performance measurement, development, and improvement at the organizational, unit, team, and individual levels.

The PMP includes the following activities:

1. Collaborative determination of performance *criteria or measures* (i.e., "what to measure?") for individuals, teams, units, and by inference, the entire organization.

2. Collaborative determination of performance *standards or targets* (i.e., "what level of performance is expected?") for each performance measure.

3. Collaborative determination of *how* the criteria will be *measured*; that is, what data will be used to assess whether the standard or target has been met (i.e., "how will we know how well we have performed?").

4. *Communication* of the criteria and standards or targets to all those affected by them.

5. *Monitoring* performance throughout the year in order to identify and solve problems, or potential problems.

6. *Evaluation* of performance against pre-determined standards or targets.

7. *Feedback* of appraisal, candidly, thoroughly, and specifically.

8. *Development* and *improvement* of performance via identification of strengths to build on and developmental needs to address.

9. Attaching *consequences*—positive and negative, financial or nonfinancial—to performance.

Linking Strategy to Performance Measurement: Company Examples

COMPANY	STRATEGIC PERFORMANCE FACTOR	PERFORMANCE MEASURE
Alcoa	Safety	Improved safety record
Au Bon Pain	Quality Customer Service	"Mystery Shopper" survey covering: — Food quality — Physical environment — Display — Service
Chemical Bank	Customer Service	Customer satisfaction ratings (survey)
Federal Express	Quality	Index: missed pick-ups, lost/damaged packages, late packages, reopened complaints
Xerox	Customer Service	Customer satisfaction ratings (survey)

Tying Performance to Strategy

STRATEGY EXECUTION

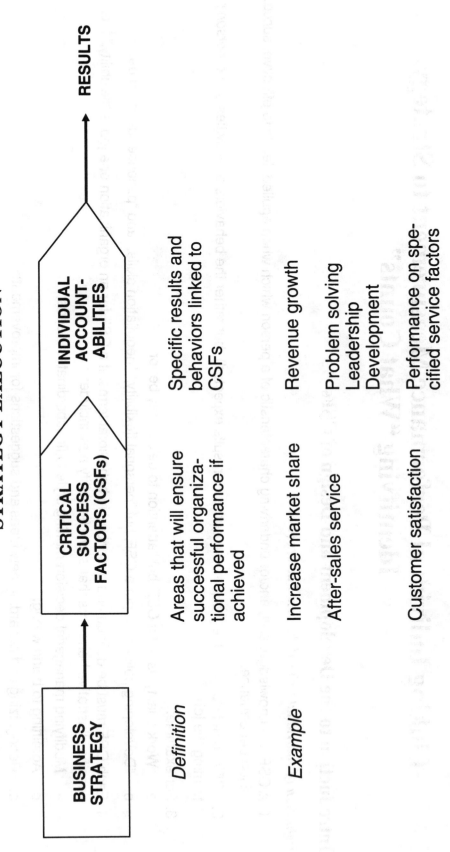

	BUSINESS STRATEGY →	CRITICAL SUCCESS FACTORS (CSFs)	INDIVIDUAL ACCOUNT-ABILITIES → RESULTS
Definition		Areas that will ensure successful organizational performance if achieved	Specific results and behaviors linked to CSFs
Example		Increase market share	Revenue growth
		After-sales service	Problem solving Leadership Development
		Customer satisfaction	Performance on specified service factors

417

Linking Individual Performance Measurement to Strategy: Identifying "What Counts"

Introduction to the Development and Design of CSFs

Definition of Individual Critical Success Factors (CSFs)

1. A CSF is a knowledge, skill, and/or underlying characteristic of a person which when applied, leads to effective, successful job performance.

2. CSFs do not describe the *job* (i.e., the duties or results expected), but rather the behaviors or activities of the *person* performing the job.

3. For example:
   a. "Work quality" is not a CSF, but "attention to detail" may be; or
   b. "Developing policies" is not a CSF, but "personal flexibility," "negotiation skills," and "patience" all could be.

4. Each CSF must be defined and described in behavioral terms. If a CSF for an organization or a job is "flexibility," then specific, illustrative behaviors that *show* flexibility may include:
   a. Modifying managerial decision-making style to fit subordinates' needs;
   b. Admitting to being wrong;
   c. Recognizing and rewarding new ideas and suggestions for improvement;
   d. Providing opportunities to disagree; and
   e. Revising plans and goals as new information is obtained.

Objectives of Developing CSFs

1. Create and communicate a set of shared values and a common vision.

2. Form common, relevant, clear standards that define success for use in human resource systems.

418

Guiding Principles for Developing CSFs

1. CSFs will be linked to corporate strategy and business goals.

2. Line management will be actively engaged in developing the CSFs.

3. CSFs will be developed to assist supervisors in judging performance and potential using a consistent, unbiased tool.

4. CSF data will be appropriate for use as inputs into major human resources systems:

   a. Performance Management
   b. Management Training
   c. Career Development
   d. Succession Planning
   e. Promotions
   f. Selection

419

The Performance Management Cycle

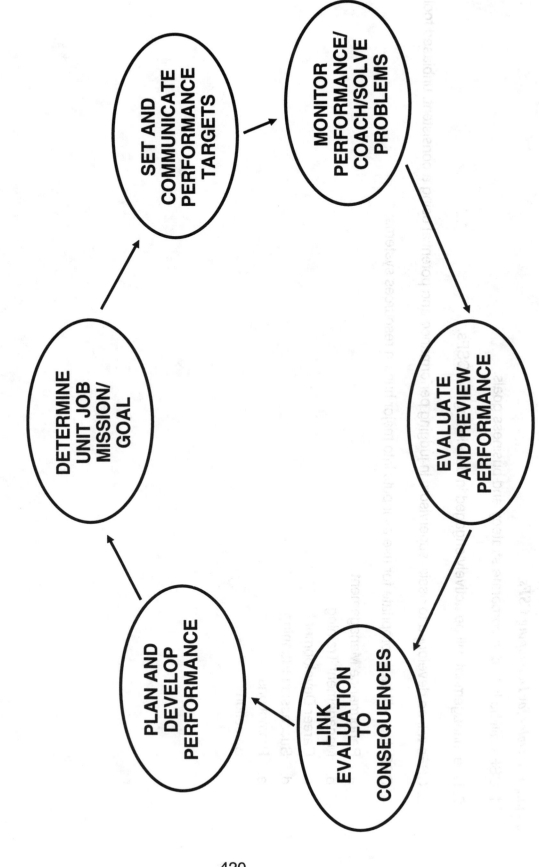

Performance Management:
A Step-By-Step Action Plan for Managers

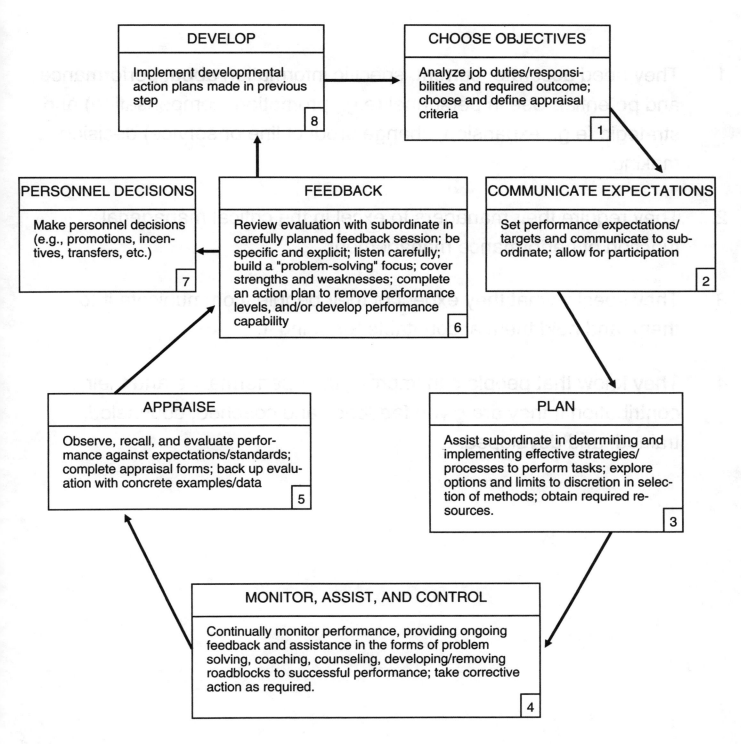

DEVELOP

Implement developmental action plans made in previous step

8

CHOOSE OBJECTIVES

Analyze job duties/responsibilities and required outcome; choose and define appraisal criteria

1

PERSONNEL DECISIONS

Make personnel decisions (e.g., promotions, incentives, transfers, etc.)

7

FEEDBACK

Review evaluation with subordinate in carefully planned feedback session; be specific and explicit; listen carefully; build a "problem-solving" focus; cover strengths and weaknesses; complete an action plan to remove performance levels, and/or develop performance capability

6

COMMUNICATE EXPECTATIONS

Set performance expectations/targets and communicate to subordinate; allow for participation

2

APPRAISE

Observe, recall, and evaluate performance against expectations/standards; complete appraisal forms; back up evaluation with concrete examples/data

5

PLAN

Assist subordinate in determining and implementing effective strategies/processes to perform tasks; explore options and limits to discretion in selection of methods; obtain required resources.

3

MONITOR, ASSIST, AND CONTROL

Continually monitor performance, providing ongoing feedback and assistance in the forms of problem solving, coaching, counseling, developing/removing roadblocks to successful performance; take corrective action as required.

4

Why Do the Best Run Organizations Have Performance Management Systems?

1. They need accurate, current, specific information about performance and potential: Use in personnel (e.g., promotion, compensation) and strategic (e.g., expansion, change product line or service) decision making.

2. They require their managers to excel in the critical managerial function of performance management.

3. They specify what they expect of their people, communicate it to them, and hold them accountable for doing it.

4. They know that people can improve their performance and their contribution if they are given feedback and coached, counseled, trained, and developed.

Performance Management:
Your System's Objectives/Uses

A.   What is your system **really** used for now?

1. _____
2. _____
3. _____
4. _____
5. _____
6. _____
7. _____
8. _____

B.   What **should** your system be used for?

1. _____
2. _____
3. _____
4. _____
5. _____
6. _____
7. _____
8. _____

Planning for Performance Management and Appraisal

Terminology in Performance Measurement

WHAT?

1. WORK OUTCOMES (Quantitative Standards)

    - What is produced by a work unit or an individual?
    - Results
    - Objectives
    - Goals
    - Work Product
    RESULTS DESIRED

HOW?

2. WORK BEHAVIORS (Qualitative/Behavioral Standards)

    - How is the work outcome produced?
    - Activities
    - Tasks
    - Duties
    - Work Process
    ACTIONS REQUIRED

What is Appraised as Performance in Organizations?

RESULTS: Observable, measurable output or contributions by an individual or work unit	**EXAMPLE:** Cash drawer balance at end of day (within a $1.00, 99% of the time). Project completed within 5% of budget. No product returns during the warranty period.
BEHAVIOR: What a person does at work. Often observable physical movements or activities	**EXAMPLE:** Smiling and making eye contact for a doctor's receptionist. Applying a brush coat for a housepainter. Organizing work and setting priorities for a manager.

Measuring Performance: The Options

- **Task-based; job specific**

- **Behavior-based**

- **Competency-based**

- **Results-based**

The Basic Performance Planning Format

Name _____   Performance Period from _____ to _____

Date _____   Performance Review Date _____

Outcomes   Expectations (Numerical Measures)
(What is to be accomplished?)   (Usually quantity, quality, or cost improvements)

  1.
  2.
  3.
  4.
  5.   **What?**   **How Measured?**
  6.
  7.
  8.
  9.
10.

Tasks (How are the outcomes   Expectations (Behavior Standards)
to be achieved?)   (Usually behavior criteria)

  1.
  2.
  3.
  4.
  5.   **How?**   **How Well?**
  6.
  7.
  8.
  9.
10.

Defining Behavioral Performance Levels

Example 1

BEHAVIOR

PERFORMANCE LEVEL

RESULTS ORIENTATION

Desire for Improvement, Sense of Urgency, Flexibility

☐ Waits for guidance and direction before taking action. Fails to respond to others in a timely manner. Often unwilling to change in response to conditions.

☐ Generates some ideas geared toward improvements. Generally can work within time constraints. Has some difficulty responding to change.

☐ Cites improvements that can be made and takes action to make them a reality. Always meets deadlines. Readily responds to changes and adopts new approaches.

☐ Identifies opportunities for improvement before others. Eagerly accepts challenges and responsibilities. Accomplishes work in advance of deadline. Is effective at persuading others to adopt most practical approaches.

431

Example 2

FACTORS

INITIATIVE

Develops original approaches and encourages the creativity of others. Seeks increased responsibility, is self-starting, and able to proceed with minimal direction.

EXAMPLES FOR UNIT HEADS

- Develops originality in decision making by being less cautious and conservative and taking prudent risks.
- Avoids premature censoring of ideas and is not concerned about whether or not ideas are flowing in a logical sequence.
- Encourages peers and subordinates to seek and establish new programs/practices that better serve the organization and its clients.

432

Suggestions for Negotiating Goals

1. Objective is a practical outcome both supervisor and employee can live with

2. Participants are problem solvers, not adversaries

3. Avoid early "bottom line"

4. Focus on interests (what each wants/needs), not on positions

5. State expectations, interests clearly and concisely, without emotion or bias

6. Discuss issues, not people

7. Make offers

8. Listen to the other party

9. Ask for clarification, elaboration

10. Test for understanding

Examples

ACTION	MEASURE	END RESULTS	TIME FRAME
Reduce	Overhead expenses	By 15 percent	By March 1992
Establish	Alternative distribution channel	By signing 1 local dealer in 10 target markets	By January 1992
Install	Computerized billing system	To achieve 95 percent customer billing accuracy	By September 31, 1991
Reduce	Documentation processing time	By 10 percent	For fiscal year 1991/92
Create	Document retrieval system	To access any traffic document within 15 minutes	By October 15, 1991

What Is Wrong with These Goal Statements?

GOAL STATEMENT	MISSING ELEMENT	GOAL STATEMENT
1. Reduce processing time for traffic documentation in 1991	End result	Reduce processing time for traffic documentation by 10 percent in 1991
2. Customers should receive delivery notification ASAP	Action	Develop customer delivery notification procedure for staff by April 30
3. Improve documentation accuracy by 10 percent by March 31	Measure	Reduce number of reported document errors by 10 percent by March 31
4. Hire one traffic coordinator	Time Frame	Increase staff by one traffic coordinator in third quarter 1991

Competency Development Worksheet*

Step I: List a few of the "best" (most successful) managers in your organization.

_____   _____

_____   _____

Step II: Describe a few specific incidents when one or two of these successful managers were particularly effective. What did they **do** that led to their success?

Step III: Review the incidents described above. What "competencies"— i.e., knowledge, skills, abilities, motives, personal characteristics—enabled these individuals to take effective action?

*Data from numerous people and jobs must be compared at each step.

Essential Steps for Developing Competencies

1. Form panel of job "experts" to determine and agree upon measures of success for the job group.

2. Identify successful members.

3. Identify underlying competencies contributing to success.

4. Interview sample of successful job holders to gather examples of "critical incidents."

5. Derive specific competencies from incidents.

6. Compare competencies derived from "critical incidents" to those specified in step 3, and to competency profiles of less successful job holders.

Managing Performance

Performance Problem Solving:
Problem Sources and Solutions

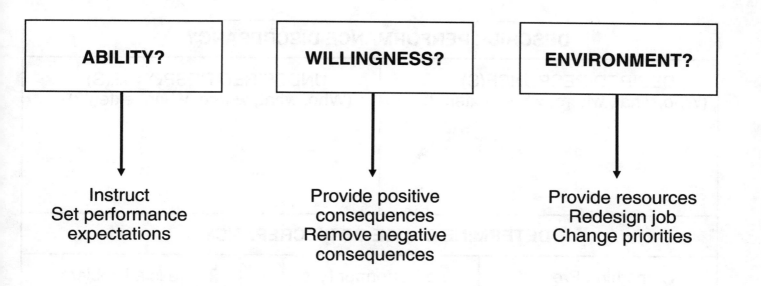

Performance Management Action Plan: Monitor, Assess, and Control Performance

DESCRIBE PERFORMANCE DISCREPANCY		
DESIRED RESPONSE(S) (Who, what, where, when, extent?)		**UNDESIRED RESPONSE(S)** (Who, what, where, when, extent?)
DETERMINE CAUSE OF DISCREPANCY		
Something Prevents the Work from Being Done	The Performer Has a Knowledge or Skill Deficiency	There is a Problem with the Work Itself
Competing Priorities?	Has Never Done It Well?	Standards? Feedback?
Job Procedures?	Practice?	Incentives?
Workflow?	Training?	Consequences?
Adequate Resources?	Job Aids/Guidelines?	Other?
Other?	Other?	Other?
Other?	Other?	Other?

Coaching Guidelines

Poor performance on the part of employees can usually be traced to one of the following reasons:

1. The employee does not know what is expected.
2. The employee does not know how he/she is doing.
3. The employee cannot do the job because he/she does not know how.
4. The employee lacks organizational support and help from the manager.
5. The organization and the manager have developed a poor working relationship.

Coaching is an attempt to overcome performance weaknesses and build on performance strengths. Coaching is actually a set of relationships between a manager and employee, rather than a series of skills to be taught. It can take many forms, including analyzing performance problems, identifying performance that can be improved, correcting improper or dangerous practices, discussing work with an employee to get his/her point of view, and providing assistance and encouragement to the employee.

Some general characteristics of coaching are:

1. Involves face-to-face guidance and instruction.
2. Meant to improve job effectiveness and efficiency.
3. Based on manager's job knowledge or developmental opportunities he/she can provide.
4. Requires a large amount of patience and energy.
5. Insures close attention to individual employee needs.
6. Happens daily rather than on infrequent occasions.

Remember, a good coach:

1. Has a sincere interest in helping employee to improve.
2. Has a thorough knowledge of position requirements and objectives.
3. Arranges for positive and progressive work to be approved and rewarded by superiors.
4. Operates from the sidelines (i.e., does not try to "play" and "coach" at the same time).
5. Recognizes individual differences.

Listening Techniques*

Reflecting Content (or paraphrasing)

Employee: I just don't know. I've been trying very hard to keep my mind on the job, but I don't seem to be doing any better.

Manager: You've been concentrating but not seeing much improvement.

Reflecting Feelings

Manager: Hi, Amy, how are things today?

Amy: Not very well really.

Manager: Oh? You're feeling a little low today?

Amy: Yeah—things just aren't fair.

Manager: You're sounding a little defeated.

Reflecting Meanings (You feel...because)

Employee: My boss is driving me crazy. I never know what's expected of me, and then I'm told I'm not meeting his expectations.

Manager: You feel frustrated because he's inconsistent.

Reflecting Implications

"If what you're saying is true, then we'd be able to..."

"That would cause us to change our plans on..."

"Have you thought about the effect of that..."

Summary Reflections

"Let's see if I can restate some of your major points so far."

"You seem to be coming back to two major points, which are..."

"Your bottom-line position seems to be..."

*Source: Adapted from Zima, *Interviewing*.

Performance Management Action Plan: Interim Review

INTERIM (MIDYEAR) PERFORMANCE REVIEW	
Briefly summarize overall performance (positive and negative) to date:	
What specific performance expectations/objectives/sub-objectives are not being met?	
Detail plans (e.g., changes in job scope, supervision, or job assignment; coaching, counseling, training) to improve performance:	
Action Required	Target Date of Completion
Supervisor _____ Date _____	Employee _____ Date _____

445

Setting "Stretch" Goals

If.... **Then the goal...**

GOALS are

Too High — Demotivates employee and/or is ignored

Realistic and Challenging — Inspires achievement and encourages improvement.

Too Low — Lowers the standards of the organization and inflates reward expectations.

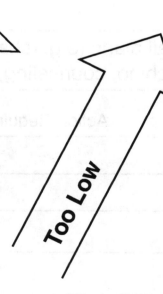

Reviewing and Appraising Performance

An Example of a Performance Diary

Employee's Name: _____

For the period from_____ to_____

Instructions:

Below you are to record your observations of the performance of your employees. Only behaviors, not conclusions or judgments about behaviors, not assumptions about knowledge, not numbers, and not frequencies. Examples of behaviors should be in the form of action verbs such as points, speaks, inserts, describes, types, presents, lectures, demonstrates, helps, etc. It would be especially useful if each of these words were accompanied by further examples of what your employee did in performing this activity. The more specific you can make the examples, the better. Please remember that the quality of your observations, and the documentation thereof, are absolutely critical for accurate performance ratings.

1. Task: _____ Date: _____

_____

2. Task: _____ Date: _____

_____

3. Task: _____ Date: _____

_____

4. Task: _____ Date: _____

_____

5. Task: _____ Date: _____

_____

6. Task: _____ Date: _____

_____

7. Task: _____ Date: _____

_____

8. Task: _____ Date: _____

_____

9. Task: _____ Date: _____

_____

ABCs of Documentation

HINT

A manager's notes about a subordinate's progress and performance provide critical information for completing the performance assessment. Your documentation should be:

1. **Accurate:** Record objective facts concerning actual performance rather than stating evaluative opinion.

OPINION	FACT
Tom is a good manager.	Tom challenges his people to make major improvements, but is also very supportive and cooperative with their Directors.
Sam's work is excellent.	Sam completes his work on time, and anticipates his managers' and grantees' questions.
Joe is responsible.	Joe meets his obligations and admits when he makes a mistake.

2. **Behavioral:** Describe specific behavior rather than making vague statements.

VAGUE	SPECIFIC
Undependable.	Is never on time for meetings and always misses deadlines.
Develops good working relationships with peers.	Actively listens, asks questions when meaning is unclear; gives positive feedback, but isn't afraid of giving constructive criticism.

3. **Consistent:** Record both positive and negative behaviors. Keep the same basic format and level of detail for each person. Maintain documentation on all persons in a given work group. Periodically, review the collective documentation to be sure that desired quantity, quality, and consistency are maintained.

450

Questions to Obtain Peer Input on Performance Evaluation and Development*

1. States own position forcefully and logically but supports group position, even if not his/her own, once decision is made?

2. Is an effective manager of people (for managers only):

   a. Sets clear expectations?

   b. Coaches to improve performance?

   c. Evaluates fairly?

   d. Provides useful feedback?

   e. Develops staff?

3. Is an effective leader of individuals and teams:

   a. Understands and communicates Ratings Group and Department strategy, goals, key business issues?

   b. Sets and communicates overall direction consistent with Ratings Group strategy/goals?

   c. Elicits input from all relevant parties on key issues/decisions?

   d. Instills confidence and respect in others?

   e. Motivates/challenges people by setting clear, challenging, relevant goals?

   f. Has presence, makes an impact, has energy?

   g. Is trusted?

   h. Leads the ratings process and committees efficiently/effectively?

   I. Is sought after as a "mentor"?

---

* Not all questions may be relevant to any given incumbent.

451

4. Has adequate (or better) technical knowledge, analytical skills, given position and experience?

5. Operates team, unit, department in efficient manner, assigning/utilizing scarce resources effectively?

6. Prioritizes work, tasks so effort, energy is focused on important issues?

7. Cooperates with others across and within unit/department; is truly a "team player"?

    a. Openly and candidly shares information?

    b. Assists others?

    c. Encourages cross-unit moves to develop people?

8. Communicates well:

    a. Verbally, both one-on-one and in front of groups?

    b. With those (e.g., issuers; press) outside the Ratings Group?

    c. In writing?

    d. Listens, is approachable?

9. Is sensitive to and creative in uncovering business development opportunities; follows up to assure action is taken?

10. Is innovative in developing new business, given position and experience?

452

Sample Performance Descriptions and Definitions

RECOMMENDED PERFORMANCE CATEGORY TITLES	ALTERNATIVE PERFORMANCE CATEGORY TITLES	DEFINITIONS
Exceeds Expectations	Exceptional Mastery Outstanding	The employee's performance clearly surpasses the fully competent level for this period. The person who reaches this level of excellence does so through truly unique and exceptional application of knowledge, skill, and/or ability that may be difficult to sustain over time.
Meets Expectations	Fully Competent Excellent	The employee's performance is what would be expected of a person who is fully experienced and qualified. The person who reaches this level of performance can be depended upon to consistently attain the expected results.
Developing	Needs Improvement Satisfactory	The employee's performance is in need of development to reach a level that would be expected from a fully competent employee. The person at this level of performance may be learning and developing skills or competencies, or may be new to the job, and is displaying those behaviors expected of someone moving in a positive direction toward full competence.
Below Expectations	Marginal Unacceptable	The employee's performance does not meet what is required. Performance is unsatisfactory and no recent, significant development progress or improvement has been evidenced. Improvement is essential; corrective action may be required.

The Normal Distribution Fallacy

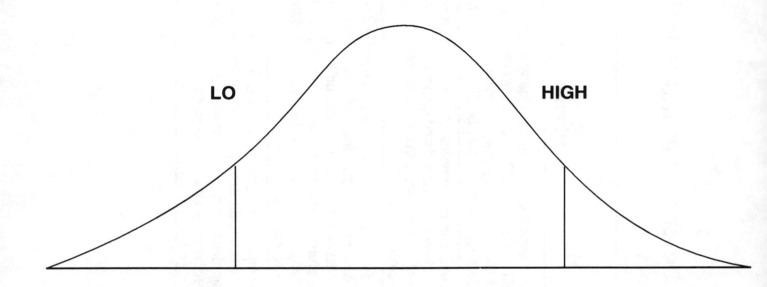

Does a performance distribution follow a normal curve? (particularly for small numbers of rates?)

Probably not:
How many subordinates do you have?
Did you select them at random?
Is it possible that they are all "above average"?

If one subordinate is "very outstanding," another who is clearly not as good may still be outstanding.

Compare to absolute standards—not relative standards.

Restriction of Range

Over some period of time, raters probably should have some out-standing, some average, some unsatisfactory employees.

Leniency: Jack the Ripper gets a 10 out of 10 on the "humanity" scale. (Otherwise he might have his feelings hurt.)

Central Tendency: Everybody is about average. (I can't really say Joe is better than John or I'll have morale problems.)

Strictness: Make 'em reach! Keep 'em on their toes! Nobody is perfect! (Bo Derrick and Robert Redford are maybe a 6, on a good day.)

Avoiding Judgment Errors

HINT

Accurately evaluating or rating others is one of the more difficult, yet vital, responsibilities of managers. They are continually confronted with situations in which they must make judgments and consequently direct, coach, evaluate, and reward people based on their judgment. Below are some of the common judgment errors to look out for:

	ERROR	TIP
Contrast	An individual is considered to be exceptional because he or she is surrounded by mediocrity or considered to be a poor performer because of surrounding stellar performance.	Evaluate each individual against goals and standards negotiated at the beginning of the performance cycle. Do not evaluate them against one another.
Recency	Individuals are evaluated based upon the most recent things they have done, positive or negative, with little thought to their performance over the entire appraisal period.	Evaluate individuals based on their performance over the *entire* performance period.
Primary	An individual's evaluation is based on first impressions—the individual performed very well, or very poorly, initially and this is what remains in the forefront of the manager's mind, regardless of subsequent performance.	Evaluate individuals based on their performance over the entire performance period.
Halo	A general impression, favorable or unfavorable, based on one aspect of performance is used as the basis for judging all aspects of performance. For example, an individual who works long hours may be considered to be productive.	Write goals and standards with each individual that balance all the key job responsibilities and evaluate against them.
Familiarity	A manager is comfortable with someone possessing characteristics similar to his or her own and evaluates them more favorably.	Stay focused on an individual's performance.

456

ERROR		TIP
Negativity	Negative behavior or poor performance is weighed more heavily than positive performance because of problems it causes.	Keep a written record of performance over time for accurate, balanced recall of positive accomplishments and problem areas.
Attributions	A specific cause, reason, or motive is attributed to an individual's behavior. This attribution may or may not be the actual cause of the behavior, but it determines a manager's evaluation. For example, an individual is not producing; a manager assumes that this is because he or she is lazy and the manager rates him or her poorly because of laziness.	Evaluate based on concrete data about an individual's performance. Don't make assumptions that you have not tested with the individual.
Leniency	A manager evaluates all individuals as exceptional.	Recognize that for individuals to develop and grow, for their own and the organization's benefit, they must receive accurate, honest feedback about performance. Evaluating everyone as exceptional jeopardizes your credibility as a manager and robs them of a valuable opportunity to improve.
Strictness	A manager evaluates eveyone strictly because he or she is a "tough grader."	Remember that a fair evaluation for good work is vital to maintain morale and ensure good work.

457

Solutions to Bias in Rating:

- Develop performance standards

- Be aware of bias threats

- Develop outcome and behavior data base (i.e., documentation)

Giving Constructive Feedback

Criticize:

- Behavior
- From actual observation
- By sharing ideas
- What is happening now
- A few points

Don't Criticize:

- The individual
- From what you *assume* an action means
- By giving advice
- What happened a long time ago
- By overloading the person with everything that's wrong

459

OPINIONS

1. Mary's work is excellent.

2. Sam has a poor attitude.

3. Sue's turnaround time is too slow.

4. Frank doesn't know MAC's traffic procedures.

FACT

Mary works well with customers, returns phone calls quickly, tracks slow shipments, and determines alternatives to speed delivery to meet customer schedule while incorporating MAC's costs. Accurately processes all necessary documentation.

Sam is late at least one day a week, does not deliver telex to others when they come in, and responds to questions with only a yes or no, excluding important details.

Sue's monthly reports are one week late (or later) at least half of the time and she often does not return customers' calls within 24 hours (the standard).

Frank rarely completes the necessary documentation and does not contact the appropriate people within the department.

Performance Feedback:
Behaviors Versus Inferences*

Inferential

Tells about how other person feels; makes "you" statements

Cannot be observed or verified

Agreement is difficult

Uses the verbs "to be," "to know"

Uses absolutes

General/abstract

Value judgment

Attributes causes or motives

Behavioral

Tells about the event

Can be observed and verified

Makes agreement easier

Uses action verbs

Differentiates clearly

Concrete/specific; doesn't use adverbs

Free of values

Not locked into attributing causes or motives

Examples

You don't care...

You don't know...

You don't take into consideration...

You need to be more conscientious.

You should know these things.

Good work.

You are never here when I need you.

You always come late when we have meetings.

Examples

The report contained a very concise, useful conclusion.

Your language with the client was vague.

Six absences in two months is not acceptable.

The contract omitted a vital section.

The data analysis was inaccurate according to my figures.

I observed you interrupting that subordinate.

* Adapted from Sandra O'Connell, *Manager as Communicator,* Harper & Row.

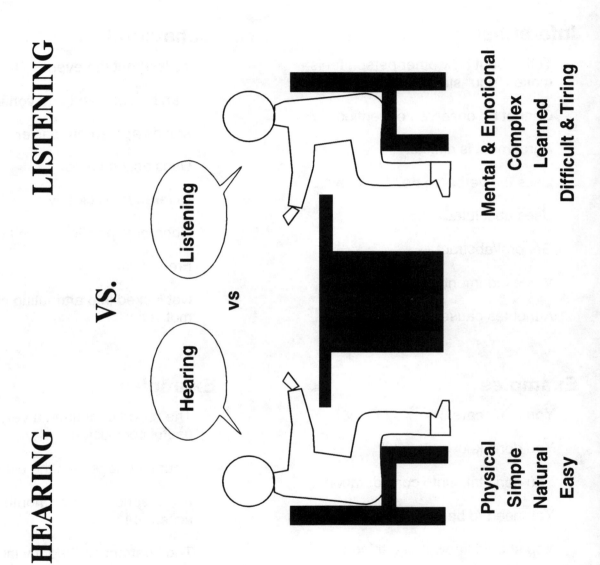

A Listening Test

1. When someone talks about something remote, boring, or uninteresting, do you tune out?

   _____ Points

2. Do you smile, nod, or say "uh huh" to fake attention?

   _____ Points

3. Do you let people's physical appearance, facial expression, or accent interfere with your listening?

   _____ Points

4. Do you conclude before you are through listening?

   _____ Points

5. Do you interrupt to take over the conversation?

   _____ Points

6. Do you let personal prejudices, biases, or subjective prejudgments block your listening?

   _____ Points

7. Do you prepare your responses while the other person talks?

   _____ Points

8. Do you let commonplace distractions interfere?

   _____ Points

9. Do you make excuses instead of dealing directly with the issues?

   _____ Points

10. Do you daydream, doodle, or fiddle with things while the other person talks?

    _____ Points

SCORING	POINTS
Always guilty	0
Almost always	2
Usually	4
Infrequently	6
Almost never	8
Never	10

TRAINER'S INFORMATION SCORING KEY

80 to 100	Excellent
70 to 79	Average
69 and Below	Clean Your Ears Out

463

Clear Standards = Clear Expectations

HINT

The following problems in miscommunication can be avoided by heading them off early.

"BUT WHAT I TOLD YOU WAS..." If you clarify and openly express your expectations, there will be fewer surprises and more focus on objectives of mutual interest. Problems often arise when you believe that you made your expectations clear, but actually you did not.

YOUR WAY VERSUS THEIR WAY. One difficulty in disclosing your expectations is that you must be able to separate your personal standards from the ones that are really necessary to effectively perform the job. How you would do a job is not the issue. You may come in 20 minutes early each day to establish priorities for your day, but that is not something you can reasonably expect from a subordinate. This is the common snafu of expectation exchanges.

AVOID MISUNDERSTANDINGS. This type of misunderstanding is completely avoidable. Let people know what you expect of them and let them know what they can expect of you in return. If you do not tell someone what you need and expect, you are inviting problems. Doing an effective job requires coordinated teamwork. When one member of a team is confused or misdirected, the work quality of the entire team suffers. In any team or group effort there is always a "gestalt effect." That is, the output of the whole team can be more or less than the sum total of each individual's contribution.

When dealing with others, there is always variation in expectations. Before you begin your meeting to set expectations, consider the kinds of things you might expect from your manager and the kind of things you expect of your subordinates. List all the "shoulds" you have in mind for the person, for example, what should he or she:

1. Do more of?

2. Do less of?

3. Continue to do?

4. Know about?

Once you've made a list, ask yourself if the subordinate knows all of the things on the list. If your hunch is that he/she knows only 10 percent, your job is to make your expectations clear.

464

Receiving Feedback

HINT

Equally important as providing feedback, is receiving feedback. Remember that coaching and counseling is a two-way street. Managers and subordinates should be prepared to receive, as well as give, feedback.

T - A - C - T stands for things you must do when receiving feedback:

THINK BEFORE YOU ACT

It is vital that you come to the performance assessment session prepared. That means you have worked through and thought about what you want to say and accomplish.

Maintain a positive attitude. A negative attitude won't do you any good. The assessment discussion can be a real opportunity for you to set goals and advance your career. Your manager can be a resource to help you do this. Work with your manager as a member of a team. The objective is to improve performance.

ACCEPT CRITICISM GRACEFULLY

Try not to be overly sensitive, or delicate. Most people learn more from their mistakes than from their successes.

No one is perfect. Sometimes you may feel that you are being unfairly criticized for things that are not your fault. Using tact, tell your manager what you feel is unfair about the criticism. But recognize that within every criticism, there is always at least a grain of truth.

No single criticism should crumble you. It's not life or death. You can always change your habits without changing your identity, or who you are. Try not to be overly defensive.

Listen for the meanings behind the words. Try not to interrupt when you hear about your past performance. You may want to take notes as you listen, but you need to maintain eye contact also.

465

CONVERSE DIRECTLY

When you share your views, maintain direct eye contact with your manager. There is nothing worse than trying to talk to people when their eyes are wandering. It breaks down communication.

Be aware of your body language. Your body talks in hundreds of nonverbal ways. Try to keep your message consistent with your body language. For example, if you sit slouched, you're sending a message that the discussion isn't important. Be aware that even when you are not speaking, your gestures, facial expressions, movements, and posture communicate what you are feeling and thinking.

Avoid aggressive, manipulative, or negative behavior. How do you respond to criticism without being aggressive? When you need to respond to an unfavorable comment, use the pronoun "I" rather than "you." "You" sounds accusatory. It is confrontative and aggressive. Saying things like "You didn't tell me" or "Well, you always do it that way" or "You are not a good listener" can make your manager defensive. "I" is tactful, but assertive.

TELL YOUR MANAGER YOUR POINT OF VIEW

Don't leave the discussion without sharing what is on your mind. Try not to ramble on; make your comments factual, concise, and to the point.

Don't hesitate to write out an agenda or checklist of what you want to say. An agenda helps ensure you'll leave the discussion with no unfinished business.

466

Basic Communication Rules to Use in Difficult Performance Review Sessions

1. Before responding in conflict or stressful situations, *paraphrase* what you have learned in terms of what was said with respect to both content and affect.

2. *Be an active listener*—respond physically to the speaker by facing the employee and by establishing eye contact. Don't glance around the room or stare off into space. Keep your eyes on the speaker and show that you are genuinely interested in him/her.

3. *Don't interrupt.* Your employees are fully aware that your experience is broader and bigger, your operation more involved, and your scar more pronounced. But control the urge to offer this valued information. Instead, listen carefully—you might learn something.

4. Listen without *evaluating,* don't try to judge the "goodness" or "badness" of what the other person is saying—just try to see the world as they see it.

5. Don't project *motives* on to other people; in other words, don't attempt to determine why they are telling you what they tell you—just try to understand what they have said.

6. Use *"I" statements* when you speak, but don't just say "I." Try to think from the "I" position by recognizing that what I say is only my opinion or thoughts and that I cannot speak for other people. Don't beat upon employees by using the corporate "we" as your army.

7. Use an *affective verb* such as "I feel," or "I sense," etc. Try to get in touch with your own emotions.

8. Be careful with *questions.* Don't use them to probe for motives, etc.—only use them to clarify what has been said. Check yourself to see what your motivation is for asking a question. Further, in asking questions, stay on the subject, and help the speaker clarify himself, through the use of questions. It's also a way for the manager to guide and control the situation.

Developing Performance

Development Approaches*

A number of development approaches are used by companies, each with varying degrees of frequency and success.

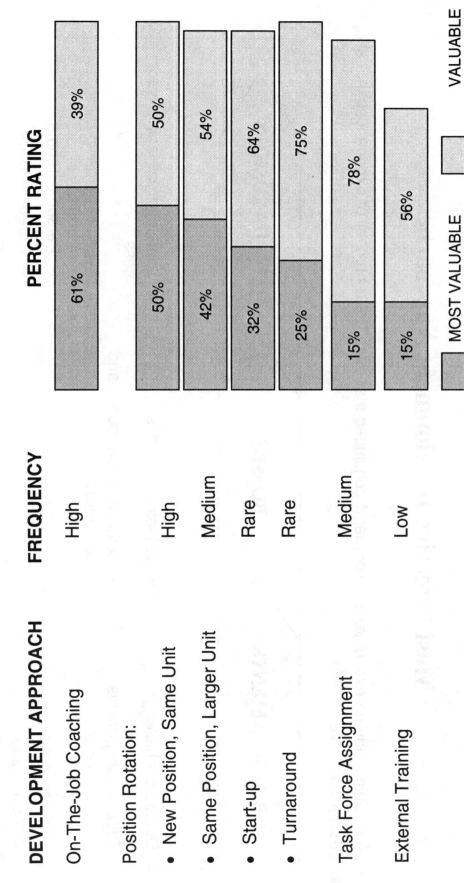

DEVELOPMENT APPROACH	FREQUENCY
On-The-Job Coaching	High
Position Rotation:	
• New Position, Same Unit	High
• Same Position, Larger Unit	Medium
• Start-up	Rare
• Turnaround	Rare
Task Force Assignment	Medium
External Training	Low

PERCENT RATING

MOST VALUABLE   VALUABLE

On-The-Job Coaching: 61% / 39%
New Position, Same Unit: 50% / 50%
Same Position, Larger Unit: 42% / 54%
Start-up: 32% / 64%
Turnaround: 25% / 75%
Task Force Assignment: 15% / 78%
External Training: 15% / 56%

*Source: Sibson & Company, Inc., Princeton, NJ, survey.

Most Effective Development Approaches

One notable study on executive development* concluded that there are a number of experiences that shape successful executives.

```
┌─────────────┐┌─────────────┐┌─────────────────┐
│ JOB         ││             ││                 │
│ ASSIGNMENTS ││   BOSSES    ││   HARDSHIPS     │
│             ││             ││                 │
└─────────────┘└─────────────┘└─────────────────┘
```

- Degree of challenge
- Type of assignments
  - Start-up
  - Turnaround
  - Task Force
  - Rotation

- Values and politics
- Lessons from good and bad bosses

- Learning from lack of success
- Types of hardship
  - Personal trauma
  - Career setback
  - Changing jobs
  - Business mistakes
  - Subordinate performance problems

472

*See "Developing Executives Through Work Experience"; Center for Creative Leadership.

Three Phases of the Development Discussion*

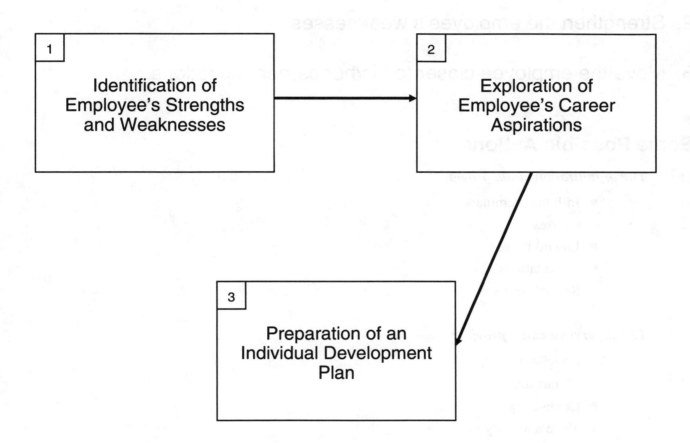

*Dave Daniel, American Chemical Society, Washington, D.C.

Development Discussion: Individual Development Plan

1. Capitalize on the employee's strengths.

2. Strengthen the employee's weaknesses.

3. Move the employee closer to his/her career aspirations.

Some Possible Actions

The organization could provide:

- In-house seminars
- Classes
- Lateral moves
- Job rotations
- Special projects

The supervisor could provide:

- Coaching
- Mentoring
- Counseling
- More authority

The employee could pursue:

- External courses
- College and university programs
- Outside reading
- Extra duties
- Special projects

Development Plan Example

Instructions: Using the completed evaluation, indicate both performance strengths and development needs. The development needs are areas that will improve or enhance performance in the current position. Also indicate the actions required to meet the needs, who is responsible, and the date to complete the actions. This should be completed during the one-on-one discussion with the employee when planning for the next performance cycle.

Strengths: Identify any abilities or capabilities that merit special recognition, other than Performance Factors.

Consistently exhibits an ability to effectively train the department's new employees.

_____

_____

Developmental Needs: Describe specific areas that need improvement or will enhance the development in the current position. Include any goals or performance factors that received a "Meets Some Expectations" or "Below Expectations" rating. Also, specify recommended developmental actions (e.g., training, seminars, closer supervision) to address developmental needs. Indicate who is responsible and the date action will take place.

NEEDS	ACTION	WHO'S RESPONSIBLE	DATE
Improve timeliness	Develop work plan and schedule due dates	Sue (*employee*)	5/15
Develop supervisory skills	Designate as project team leader	Tom (*manager*)	6/1
Broaden experience	Rotate department job duties	Tom, Sue, Bill (*manager and employees*)	10/1

A performance discussion took place which included the employee's development plan for the next performance cycle.

_____   _____

Manager   Date

475

Action Planning to Develop Performance

OPTIONS IF PERFORMANCE EXCEEDS EXPECTATIONS				
Promotion	Increase Responsibilities, Duties in Present Position	Provide Developmental Job Assignment	Send to Training to Increase Knowledge, Skills, Abilities	Provide Awards, Incentives, Increase Compensation
Advantages				
Disadvantages				

OPTIONS IF PERFORMANCE MEETS EXPECTATIONS			
Increase Performance Expectations or Standards	Provide Periodic Training to Maintain Knowledge, Skills, Abilities	Provide Developmental Job Assignment	Provide Incentives to Increase Performance
Advantages			
Disadvantages			

OPTIONS IF PERFORMANCE DOES NOT MEET EXPECTATIONS				
Terminate	Transfer to Another Position	Provide Immediate Remedial Training to Increase Knowledge, Skills, Abilities	Lower Performance Expectations or Standards	Revise Job Duties, Remove Responsibilities, Increase Supervision, Provide Job Aids, Revise Methods
Advantages				
Disadvantages				

Discussing Developmental Issues

Open the Discussion by Focusing on Goals, Expectations, and Personal Job Objectives

Explain the discussion as an opportunity for the manager to discuss his or her progress and goals in the department. Pose the following questions:

1. How do you feel about the progress you are making in the department?
2. What kinds of things are you doing to help in that progress?
3. What kinds of things are you doing that may be hindering that progress?

The idea of progress should be kept in the forefront of the discussion so that any comments or behaviors can be related to whether they work for or against the manager's progress. People should not be put on the defensive by the interview becoming a formal opportunity to spell out weaknesses. If a subordinate is convinced that the interview is motivated by a sincere interest in helping him or her achieve goals, talking about correctable weaknesses will be much less threatening.

Establish if there is a Conflict Between the Subordinate's Goals and the Facts

After the matter of goals and objectives has been thoroughly explored, the manager should draw upon the subordinate's own observations, if possible, in establishing the existence of a conflict between actual performance and/or behavior and the facts. When the person has a blind spot, or does not own up to the facts, the manager may have to challenge or confront fallacies or distortions of reality.

Confrontation calls attention to discrepancies in the position, including those between:

1. What people say and what they do.
2. What people feel and what they say.
3. Their words and their body language.
4. Their self-image and the way they are seen by others.

Confrontation can use a format such as, "On the one hand, you say you are well organized, yet in the last assignment several deadlines were missed. How do you account for that?"

Confrontations are, of course, most effective when there is mutual trust. They must be handled skillfully and sensitively and always with the focus on barriers to job progress or improvement.

477

After giving the person a chance to present his or her case, the manager must identify whatever facts have been distorted or ignored. They must then be presented for mutual examination in an objective, positive way. Moral judgment should be avoided. The ultimate aim should be to get the person to see that he or she is working against the very objectives he or she wants to achieve. Whenever possible, the person's own remarks about the facts should be used. This reduces the possibility of defensiveness and also results in greater ownership of the facts.

Allow the Subordinate to Determine the Consequences

Rather than explaining the consequences that will result if certain weaknesses are not corrected, the emphasis should be on questions that force the person to confront the ultimate consequences if the facts are ignored or the behaviors go uncorrected. For example, "What do you think will happen to your goal of a promotion if the reports on interpersonal problems with your colleagues continue?"

Develop an Action Plan to Improve Behavior

Once the behaviors have been identified and accepted, the person should be encouraged to suggest ways to overcome a particular weakness or problem. Sometimes recognition and acceptance of the problem is enough incentive to solve the problem. Provision should also be made to indicate what the manager will do to help overcome the weakness or solve the problem. In closing the interview, the manager should seek a commitment as to when the problem will be solved or when significant improvement can be expected. The person should also be involved in determining how the improvement will be measured or in deciding when the correctable weakness has in fact been corrected.

Follow Up

Another meeting should be scheduled to discuss progress. When there is an improvement in behavior, the person should be complimented at the earliest opportunity. If there is little change in behavior or the change proves temporary, developmental counseling must be tried again. If the problem continues to go unresolved after several attempts, depending of course on the seriousness of the problem, further action may be required.

478

Providing Developmental Feedback to Managers: Subordinate Input on Manager's Skills at Performance Appraisal and Development*

FOR MY MANAGER, THIS ITEM CURRENTLY IS...

PERFORMANCE MANAGEMENT	A Strength	A Proficiency	A Developmental Need
1. Sets clear, fair, relevant performance expectations	☐	☐	☐
2. Communicates performance expectations effectively	☐	☐	☐
3. Monitors my performance to assess my progress	☐	☐	☐
4. Provides ongoing candid feedback on my performance	☐	☐	☐
5. Encourages me to participate in expectation setting, feedback, and performance evaluation discussions	☐	☐	☐
6. Listens to my points of view	☐	☐	☐
7. Is an effective coach and problem solver, enabling me to improve my performance	☐	☐	☐
8. Evaluates me fairly and accurately	☐	☐	☐
9. Gathers input on my performance from appropriate, relevant parties to augment his/her data base	☐	☐	☐
10. Identifies developmental needs and effectively designs opportunities for me to attain my career objectives	☐	☐	☐

* To be distributed to and completed anonymously by a manager's subordinates; full data to be shared with manager and his/her superior and discussed.

479

FOR MY MANAGER, THIS ITEM CURRENTLY IS...

LEADERSHIP	A Strength	A Proficiency	A Developmental Need
11. Sets a vision and direction for our department/unit/team consistent with Ratings Group strategy	☐	☐	☐
12. Communicates Ratings Group strategy and how our department/unit/team and my position fit into it	☐	☐	☐
13. Is an advocate for the position of our department/unit/team, yet is consistent with goals and needs of entire Ratings Group	☐	☐	☐
14. Leads our department/unit/team effectively, due to communi-cation skills, analytical skills, business acumen, "political" skills	☐	☐	☐
15. Facilitates everyone on our team/in our unit having a voice in decision making and contributes in a meaningful way	☐	☐	☐

480

Rewarding Performance

Performance Management: Managerial Consequences?

- What happens to managers for doing a good job in performance management?

- What happens to managers for doing a poor job in performance management?

- Managers (raters) evaluated on competence in managing performance?

   — Influences their bonus?
   — Influences their promotions?
   — Influences this job assignment?

Rewarding Performance

Often Overworked	Often Overlooked (or underused)
Company-wide competitive base salaries	Expanding the number of managers eligible for bonuses related to achievement of strategic milestones
Stock options	Performance units; phantom stock
Annual merit increases	Lump-sum merit plans
Large, special-purpose cash awards, privately awarded	Regularly scheduled public recognition events
Annual performance reviews	Performance reviews on a variable schedule adapted to the anticipated achievement of strategic milestones
Large bonuses granted at year-end	Smaller cash awards given rapidly after achievement of strategic success

Conditions Necessary to Link Pay to Performance:

- Performance dimensions must be readily measured

- All critical performance dimensions must be captured by the system and standards set for each

- Performance must be important to the employee and employer/manager

- Performance must be under employee's direct control

- Monetary incentives must be compatible with other outcomes important to the employee

- Monetary level and merit differences must be meaningful to employee

- System must be affordable

- Relationship between manager and employee must be one of mutual respect, trust, openness, effective communication

Designing, Implementing, Administering, and Evaluating Performance Measurement, Management, and Appraisal Systems

Basic Considerations in the Choice of a Performance Management System

- Organization Strategy

- Organization Financial Conditions

- Economic Environment

- Organizational Culture

- Organizational Technology

- Purposes of Performance Measurement

- Managerial Skills in Performance Management

- Managerial Accountability for Performance Management

- Top Management Support

- Relation to Other Human Resource Systems

- User Input in Design and Implementation

- Number and Type of Position Covered

- Orientation/Training

- Schedule for Implementation

Linking Performance to Consequences

PERFORMANCE CONSEQUENCES*

PERFORMANCE DATA	Base Salary	Bonus	Promotion	Demotion	Termination	Job Assignment	Developmental Action
1. Past performance	● Primary	● Primary	● Primary	◐ Secondary	● Primary	● Primary	● Primary
2. Sustained performance/ performance trend	◐ Secondary	○ Minor	● Primary	● Primary	● Primary	◐ Secondary	◐ Secondary
3. Potential	○ Minor	○ Minor	● Primary	○ Minor	○ Minor	● Primary	● Primary

Legend:
- ● Primary determinant
- ◐ Secondary determinant
- ○ Minor/negligible determinant

*Does not include verbal praise, public recognition, special awards, etc.

Performance Management (PM): Three Implementation Approaches

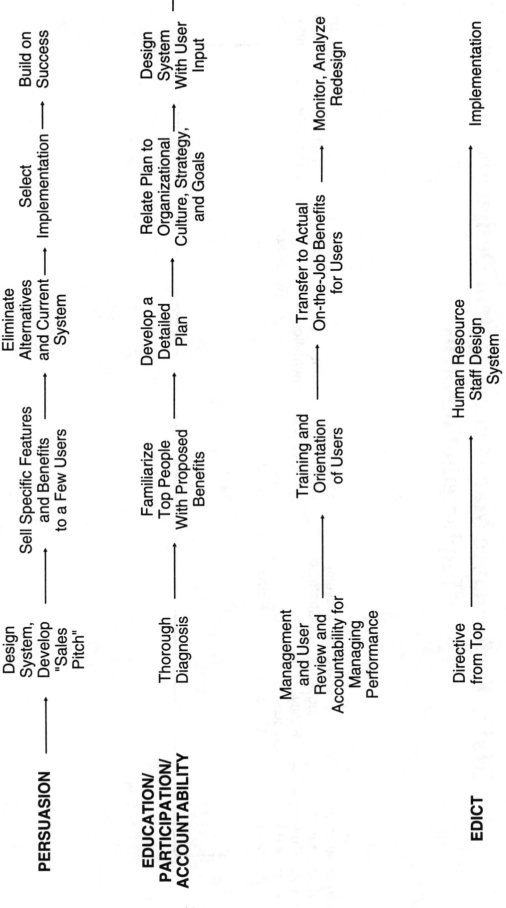

PERSUASION

Design System, Develop "Sales Pitch" → Sell Specific Features and Benefits to a Few Users → Eliminate Alternatives and Current System → Select Implementation → Build on Success

EDUCATION/ PARTICIPATION/ ACCOUNTABILITY

Thorough Diagnosis → Familiarize Top People With Proposed Benefits → Develop a Detailed Plan → Relate Plan to Organizational Culture, Strategy, and Goals → Design System With User Input

Management and User Review and Accountability for Managing Performance → Training and Orientation of Users → Transfer to Actual On-the-Job Benefits for Users → Monitor, Analyze Redesign

EDICT

Directive from Top → Human Resource Staff Design System → Implementation

491

Major Performance Management System Design and Implementation Steps

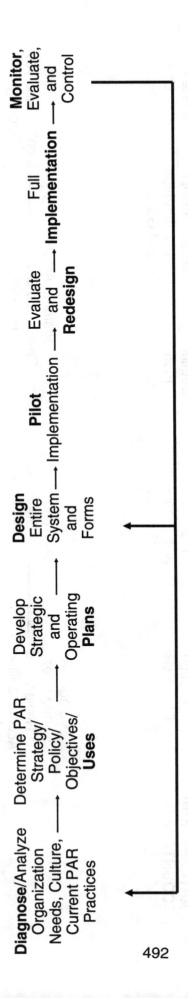

Diagnose/Analyze Organization Needs, Culture, Current PAR Practices → Determine PAR Strategy/ Policy/ Objectives/ **Uses** → Develop Strategic and Operating **Plans** → **Design** Entire System and Forms → **Pilot** Implementation → Evaluate and **Redesign** → Full **Implementation** → **Monitor**, Evaluate, and Control

492

Implementing Performance Measurement, Management, and Appraisal Systems: Guiding Principles and Their Key Implications

1. **Managers are accountable for managing subordinates' performance and for operating the process effectively:**

   a. Each manager's performance evaluation will be based, in part, on how well he/she is judged to have managed subordinates' performance.

   b. The relative weight of the measure of performance management will always be substantial but will vary by manager according to total number of people directly or indirectly managed and number and level of direct reports, as well as the manager's other performance expectations in any given evaluation period.

   c. Managers are responsible and accountable for their subordinates' effective use of the process (e.g., failure to utilize, inconsistent evaluations, unfair evaluations, inappropriate expectations/standards, failure to develop subordinates, lack of candor, etc.).

   d. To help assure that consistent expectations are set for people across departments within a position, unit executives will meet at the beginning of an evaluation cycle (i.e., annually) to discuss the performance expectations they will communicate and reach consensus on the level of performance expected. (These consistent expectations will then "cascade" down throughout the hierarchy within departments.)

   In addition, unit executives will meet at the end of an evaluation cycle (i.e., annually) prior to communication of final assessments. They will review anticipated evaluations and achieve consensus as to the evaluation that should be given for like performance across departments. (These consistent assessments of performance will then "cascade" down throughout the hierarchy within departments.)

2. **Both results obtained and the manner by which results are obtained (i.e., the behaviors exhibited) are determinants of success in any position:**

   a. Both results and behaviors will be measured and evaluated for each position, but relative weights may vary depending on position accountabilities in any given evaluation period.

   b. Behavioral performance expectations and targets for results will be identified and communicated to each ratee by the manager at the outset of each evaluation period; end-of-period evaluations will be made against these (or an updated version of) expectations.

3. **All relevant parties will participate candidly in all phases of the process:**

   a. Input from ratees themselves, their peers, their subordinates, their "customers" (internal and external), and their superiors will be obtained and utilized.

   b. Performance measures, targets, objectives, and standards, as well as developmental needs and actions required to address these needs, will be collaboratively determined by managers and their subordinates.

   c. Discussions about performance will be candid.

4. **Teamwork and collaboration are essential to success of the company:**

   a. In addition to team members' and team leaders' performance, team performance itself, where appropriate, will be evaluated.

   b. Teamwork is a performance criterion for all levels and position.

5. **Performance will be linked to consequences:**

   a. The primary determinant of compensation is (documented) past performance.

   b. Fair, but not equal, treatment across people is expected regarding reward allocation, unless performance is equal; differentiation, in the allocation of consequences, is encouraged and expected.

6. **Managers are accountable for their units' performance; team leaders for their teams' performance:**

   a. Appropriate performance measures for team, unit, and organization performance will be determined and utilized.

   b. Individual performance is most heavily weighted for individual contributors, but the team's or the unit's performance is most heavily weighted for managers.

494

Improving the Performance Measurement and Management Process: Illustrative Questions for a Project Team

1. What are the *objectives* of the performance measurement, management, and reward processes?

2. Are these objectives being *met?* If so, why? If not, why?

3. What are the underlying *causes* of any problems and what is the data base which confirms these causes?

4. Have *prior attempts* to solve these problems failed? If so, why?

5. Who must *"own"* these processes? Do they? If not, how can they become *process owners?*

6. What are the *"critical success factors"* (i.e., what it takes to succeed, as individuals, teams, units, the organization)? How do these vary across components?

7. What *principles* will govern design and operation of the performance measurement, management, and rewards processes? (E.g., how will results, versus personal characteristics, be weighted?)

8. What are the *implications* of these principles? (E.g., subordinates will assess their managers.)

9. *Who will approve* these principles and implications? How will their approval be obtained?

10. What *skills* are required to implement the new process? How will these be built?

11. What *reward* and *recognition* mechanisms are currently, and should be, utilized? How effectively are they utilized? Why?

12. How will performance be tied to *consequences,* both positive and negative?

13. What are the mechanisms to hold *managers accountable* for measuring, managing, improving, and rewarding performance?

14. *Who is performing* these activities well now? Why are they successful?

15. What other uses for the *"critical success factors"* (i.e., what it takes to succeed, as individuals, teams, units, the organization) are there? (E.g., succession, selection.) How will these uses best be served?

495

16. What is the *"right" design?*

17. How will the *current process* be redesigned?

18. What changes in *systems* (e.g., compensation), *structure* (e.g., design of managers' jobs), *skills* (e.g., setting goals), and *style* (e.g., accepting performance feedback from subordinates) are necessary to see real, lasting improvement in these processes?

Knowledge and Skills Needed to Help System Users

KNOWLEDGE/SKILLS*	ROLES					
	Needs Assessor	Program Designer	Program Purchaser	Trainer	Program Evaluator	Coach
1. Problem solving		•				•
2. Data analysis	•		•		•	
3. Listening	•			•		•
4. Communication						
a. Written		•				
b. Oral				•		•
5. Measurement					•	
6. Evaluation	•				•	
7. Interviewing	•				•	
8. Adult learning		•	•	•	•	•
9. Cost/benefit analysis			•		•	
10. Project planning	•	•			•	
11. Project management	•	•			•	
12. Budgeting			•			
13. Survey design	•				•	

* Does not include technical aspects of system design; not an exhaustive list; dots in cells indicate special emphasis on the indicated skill for the indicated role.

Assessment of Skill-Building Options

CRITERIA

DELIVERY OPTION	Relevance:		Required Time:		Required Skills of Trainers/ Managers	Out-of-Pocket Cost
	Content	Method	Trainers/ Managers	Trainees		
1. Classroom						
a. Internal	●	◐	○	◐	○	◐
b. External	◐	◐	●	○	●	◐
2. Self-study	●	◐	●	○	○	◐
3. Coaching	◐	◐	○	◐	◐	●
4. OJT	●	◐	○	○	◐	●

Typically a:	
●	Strength
◐	Can be a strength or weakness
○	Weakness

PM Tasks and Suggested Training Program Content*

PM Tasks	Training Program Content
Observation of work behavior	Knowing what to observe and how often to observe Recognizing the behaviors to be observed when they are evidenced by ratees Processing knowledge of the ratee's job Making representative observations free from perceptual biases Making observations within the perspective of some standard or criteria
Storage of observations	Storing information for later use
Recall of observations	Retrieving the majority of the observed information when required
Judgment	Evaluating the appropriateness of the observed behaviors in light of some standard or criteria Using the judgments to complete a performance appraisal form Ability to make accurate judgments relatively free from bias and prejudice and without fear of dealing with negative consequences of harsh (but accurate) ratings
Feedback	Providing complete, accurate feedback to the ratee on his/her performance in a "problem-solving" performance appraisal review session, as well as throughout the entire appraisal period Providing complete, accurate information on performance levels, potential, developmental needs, etc., for use by the organization in human resource decision making
Coaching	Providing information to ratees on relative importance of various aspects of job Communicating specific expectations in all areas of job performance Pointing out deficiencies (and strengths) in performance Instructing ratees in correct ways to perform Providing opportunities to practice correct performance
Counseling	Identifying organizational and individual obstacles to improved performance and effective strategies/plans to overcome them Setting realistic, challenging goals for future performance Providing various rewards (e.g., verbal praise) for desired performance Establishing a climate of trust and supportiveness

*From V. McCaleb, S.J. Carroll, and C.E. Schneir, *Performance Appraisal and Review Systems*, Scott Foresman, 1982.

How Performance Management (PM) Supports Total Quality Improvement (TQI)

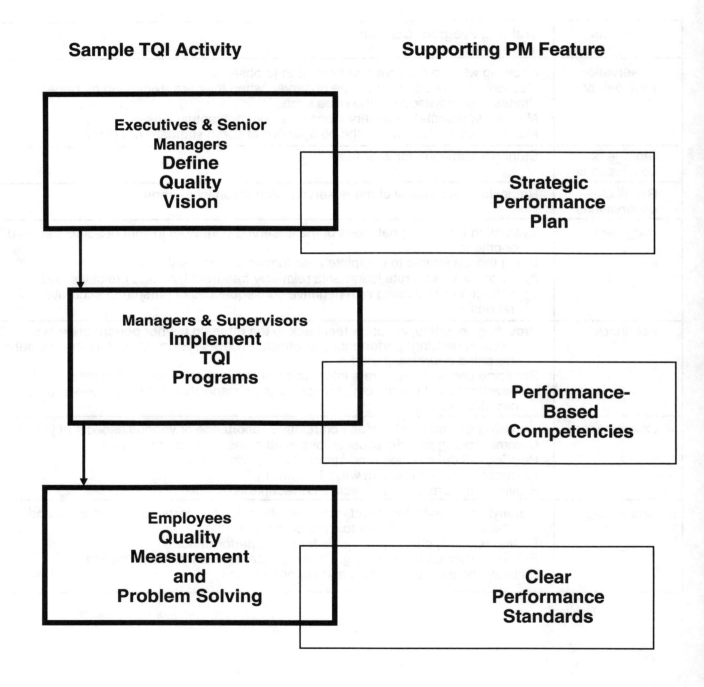

Sample TQI Activity

Supporting PM Feature

Executives & Senior Managers **Define Quality Vision**

Strategic Performance Plan

Managers & Supervisors **Implement TQI Programs**

Performance- Based Competencies

Employees **Quality Measurement and Problem Solving**

Clear Performance Standards

Conditions Conducive to Resistance to Change:*

- If the nature of the change is not made clear to the people who are going to be affected by it

- When different people see different implications in the job proposed changes (e.g., that they are doing a poor job, or would lose power, or that leaders intend to force them into a new and strange situation)

- When those influenced by the change feel a real conflict between the strong forces pushing them to make the change and strong forces deterring them from the change

- When the persons influenced by the change feel strong outside pressure put upon them to make the change

- If the change is made on personal grounds rather than upon impersonal requirements such as objectives, unmet needs, or other aspects of the present situation

- If the proposed change process does not take into account the established customs and institutions of the group

*Prepared by Judy Brown, Aspen Institute, Wye, Maryland.

Measurement and Management of Performance: Necessary Conditions

1. Compelling business need

2. Links from strategy to critical success factors to performance measures

3. Line-driven design and implementation

4. Managers' accountability defined and built into assessment of their performance

5. Top executives use system

6. Link to consequences (pay) direct, quick

7. Managers' skill needs addressed via on-the-job assistance

502

Prototype Format/Worksheet

Performance Management Worksheets

A. Name _____   Position _____   Department _____

Manager _____

B. PERFORMANCE OBJECTIVES

Completed at Beginning of Year:

Completed at End of Year:

Key Result Areas:

	Objective	Measure(s)	Target(s)	Result	EVALUATION*			Comments
					Does Not Meet Expectations	Meets Expectations	Exceeds Expectations	
1.								
2.								
3.								
4.								
5.								
6.								
7.								
8.								
9.								
10.								
11.								
12.								

Date completed: _____   Date completed: _____

*Can be used without a rating scale or evaluation categories; narrative assessment only.

C. CRITICAL SKILLS

	Completed at Beginning of Year:	Completed at End of Year:			
	ILLUSTRATIVE BEHAVIORAL AND OUTCOME STANDARDS	EVALUATION			COMMENTS
		Does Not Meet Expectations	Meets Expectations	Exceeds Expectations	
Analysis	• • • • •				
Management	• • •				
Communication	• • •				
Leadership	• • •				
Business Development	• • •				

D. OVERALL EVALUATION

(Best represents evaluations on each Objective and Critical Skill)

Comments:

Does Not Meet Expectations	Meets Expectations	Exceeds Expectations
☐	☐	☐

_____
_____
_____

E. DEVELOPMENTAL PLANNING

Key Strengths

_____
_____

Key Developmental Needs

_____
_____
_____

Action to be Taken to Address Developmental Needs

_____
_____
_____
_____

Comments about Potential...

To Perform in Current Position More Effectively...

_____
_____
_____

To Assume Additional Responsibility...

_____
_____

F.

_____   _____
Employee Signature   Date

_____   _____
Manager Signature   Date

_____   _____
Reviewer Signature   Date

Mid-Year Review Worksheet

A. PERFORMANCE OBJECTIVES

Key Result Area:

Objective	Measure(s)	Target(s)	Mid-Year Progress/ Assessment
1.			
2.			
3.			
4.			
5.			
6.			
7.			
8.			
9.			
10.			
11.			
12.			

B. CRITICAL SKILLS

Illustrative Behavioral and Outcome Standards

Mid-Year Assessment

Analysis

• • • • • • •

Management

• • • •

Communication

• • • •

Leadership

• • • •

Business Development

• • • • •

Employee Signature _____ Date _____ Manager Signature _____ Date _____

End-of-Year Self-Assessment Worksheets

A. Name _____ Position _____ Department _____

Manager _____

B. PERFORMANCE OBJECTIVES

Key Result Areas:

	Completed at Beginning of Year:			Completed at End of Year:	
	Objective	Measure(s)	Target(s)	Result	Comments
1.					
2.					
3.					
4.					
5.					
6.					
7.					
8.					
9.					
10.					
11.					
12.					

Date completed: _____   Date completed: _____

C. CRITICAL SKILLS

	ILLUSTRATIVE BEHAVIORAL AND OUTCOME STANDARDS	COMMENTS
Completed at Beginning of Year:		**Completed at End of Year:**

- Analysis
-
-
-
- Management
-
-
- Communication
-
-
-
- Leadership
-
-
-
- Business Development
-

511

D. DEVELOPMENTAL PLANNING

Key Strengths	Key Developmental Needs	Action to be Taken to Address Developmental Needs
_____	_____	_____
_____	_____	_____
_____	_____	_____
_____	_____	_____

Comments about Potential...

To Perform in Current Position More Effectively...

_____
_____
_____
_____

To Assume Additional Responsibility...

_____
_____
_____
_____

Sample Performance Tasks, Behaviors, Competencies, Objectives

Examples of Job Tasks
Secretary

1.   Process, type, and distribute written materials.

2.   Manage office operations.

3.   Communicate by writing, speaking, and listening.

4.   Input information into data and/or word processing equipment.

5.   Keep written and electronic records; update records.

6.   Make arrangements and process details for employees and department.

7.   Maintain and update physical and/or electronic files; retrieve information from files as needed.

8.   Operate equipment; perform preventive maintenance on equipment.

9.   Answer phone—screen and route callers, take messages.

10. Order and store supplies.

11. Act as liaison between own department and other departments.

12. Tabulate and/or compile information.

13. Duplicate (film or copy) records, communications, information.

14. Receive requisitions, invoices, or requests and process.

15. Compose or draft written materials.

Examples of Job Tasks
Computer Programmer

1. Input information into data and/or word processing equipment.

2. Maintain and update physical and/or electronic files; retrieve information from files as needed.

3. Implement solutions to problems.

4. Develop and enhance existing systems including preliminary design, detail design, programming, system testing, conversion to system, documentation procedures and operating techniques; maintain system.

5. Develop, test, implement, and document programs.

6. Plan, lead, or participate in problem-solving meetings.

7. Compose or draft written materials.

8. Define problems and generate solution alternatives.

9. Document programs and systems developed.

10. Process, type, and distribute written materials.

11. Evaluate effectiveness of solutions implemented.

Examples of Job Tasks
Manager

1. Direct the production of departmental products.

2. Communicate by writing, speaking, or listening.

3. Assess overall resource utilization of work unit and determine assignment schedules of work and resource allocation.

4. Control projects in area of responsibility by establishing standards, measuring work in progress, interpreting results, and taking corrective action.

5. Review and approve work of others.

6. Assign/set performance expectations.

7. Interact with others through speaking, writing, listening.

8. Communicate with employees and/or superiors.

9. Analyze situations by collecting relevant input, setting measurable objectives, determining resources needed to meet objectives.

10. Participate in long-term and strategic planning process.

11. Develop staffing plans; recruit personnel for company openings according to staffing plans; interview and hire personnel.

Customer Service Representative (CSR) Appraisal

Dealing with Others

Task: Customer Service

(Building customer relations by the concern extended to customers which recognizes them as individuals and makes their lives more pleasant by resolving their problems, and by making them more comfortable and at ease. It is the behavior CSRs demonstrate that influences how positive customers feel about National. It is also how we present ourselves and convey our excitement about our work, our confidence in ourselves, and co-workers in delivering the best car rental service possible.)

CSR NAME:_____ TASK WEIGHT: _____%

In the space provided below, please describe your observations of the CSR you are evaluating. Be certain that what you write are descriptions of what you have observed the employee doing during the performance period. Use words such as enters, smiles, inserts, orders, puts, etc. to describe CSR actions. Once you have documented your observations, compare your documentation to the five rating levels below and check the rating that best indicates the employee's level of performance. Documentations:

_____

_____

_____

_____

5. **WELL ABOVE STANDARD:** Greets customers with a smile while making eye contact; anticipates customer's problems and provides whatever is necessary to make customers become more comfortable and co-workers more effective; asks customers what they need and tells them that we are there to serve them; checks with customers to determine if the car was satisfactory and makes notes of problems with the car to give to service; makes best presentation of self—uniform is neat, clean, and tidy; explains in detail to customers rental processing procedures; quickly communicates positive feedback to co-workers and discusses concerns in private; keeps composure even when customers are irate with the CSR and the Company; tells customers about the organization and what makes it a good place to work.

4. **ABOVE STANDARD:** Acknowledges customers by using a greeting when they are standing in line behind the customer being serviced; makes eye contact with greeting; recognizes changes and/or contributions of co-workers and follows up with specific compliments; checks to be certain that customers have been heard accurately by saying, "Did I understand you to say that...?"; makes positive comments about the organization and its employees to customers; tells people over the phone what they are going to do for them before putting them on "hold"; makes certain customers understand what is expected before an activity/procedure is to begin by asking the customers if they fully understand before proceeding; makes suggestions or initiates methods to improve organizational performance; encourages the work of co-workers by letting them know when they have done a good job; works to ensure cooperative, not competitive, efforts with co-workers; makes time to help train new CSRs in rental processing.

3. STANDARD: Listens to customer's needs, apologizes for car problems, and lets them know that she/he will do their best to respond to their needs; greets customers over the phone by telling them whom they are talking to and asking how they may be of help; says please and thank you when interacting with customers; grooming is well maintained, wears clean clothing, is careful with personal hygiene, meets dress code standards; gives directions by showing on the map how to get to where the customer wishes to go; explains to customer specifically what is in the rental agreement in ways the customer can understand; uses name when addressing them such as Mr., Mrs., or Ms.; demonstrates respect for property and equipment by ensuring that proper care is given to equipment and appearance of public areas are clean and tidy; greets customers before customer greets them; asks customer what problems they may have had with the car; makes suggestions about ways to improve customer and service performance; tells co-workers when they have done a good job.

2. BELOW STANDARD: Does not greet others and attempt to make them feel good about our organization; does not ask how they may be of help or service to the organization; does not use customer's name when addressing them; hair is not clean nor well groomed; does not tell others when they have done exceptional work; is not specific with customers in explaining the cost of coverages or what effect waivers have on their coverages; does not use a greeting when answering the phone; puts customers on hold without telling them that they will be on hold or why they are on hold.

1. WELL BELOW STANDARD: Does not listen to others—interrupts customers, closes their station with customers waiting, does not greet others with a smile, or make eye contact; hair and dress are not clean, uniform is soiled or does not meet the dress code; makes unfavorable comments about the organization to customers or co-workers; does not support the efforts of co-workers; does not monitor work area to ensure counter is clean and equipment is well maintained; does not explain rental procedures to customers or call them by name; discusses customers problems in public; puts people on "hold" on the phone without telling them what is happening or hangs up on customers; complains about the organization to customers and does not make suggestions or work to improve the situation; make-up is overdone; does not make positive comments when possible; discusses co-workers' problems with customers; takes credit for others' work; uses abusive language with customers; criticizes co-workers for providing excellent customer service.

RATING

□	□	□	□	□
Well Below	Below	Standard	Above	Well Above

Behaviors for the Managerial Dimension of Leadership

Principle/practice: Leadership _____ %

Effective managerial leadership consists of fully accepting the responsibility for performance, establishing high and reasonable performance standards, working as a team, achieving goals, providing employees with feedback, inspiring others, providing technical as well as professional guidance, fostering honesty, delegating tasks that match employees interests and skills, delegating challenging work, and acting on employee improvement and professional growth.

Below, please write specific behaviors that you believe are descriptive and typical of this manager's performance in leadership during this performance period:

_____

_____

_____

Please rate the behaviors you have described by reviewing the levels of performance shown below and circle the number below that is most indicative of the manager's performance in leadership.

Lowest   1   2   3   4   5   6   7   Highest

Check one: Signature: _____

( )   Supervisor's evaluation

( )   Self evaluation   Date: _____

( )   Other (e.g., peer, subordinate, second-level supervisor)

---

7 EXCELLENT   In initiating projects, meetings are held to explain objectives and rationale; meetings are followed by specific written documentation detailing objectives, tasks, and roles; all possible efforts are devoted to insure results are achieved by due dates and within resource limitations; holds subordinate managers accountable for achieving negotiated goals and fully accepts the responsibility for his/her goals; does not make excuses or blame others if goals are not achieved; performance expectations are discussed, negotiated, and distributed to all who may be impacted; problem solving is a team effort, in problem identification, solution generation, criteria for selecting among alternatives, decision making, and planning to implement and evaluate projects; employees are given recognition (in public and in private) of their contributions and tasks are delegated in order to achieve employee growth/developmental needs as well as organizational objectives.

6 VERY GOOD   Negotiates objectives with subordinates and contacts them to insure that feedback on good performance is given specifically and immediately; performance standards are high, attainable, and behaviorally specific; what is to be done and how it is to be approached is specified through discussion/negotiation; success is communicated to and shared with subordinates; assigns tasks to employees that are developmental and based on employer strengths; informs the organization of circumstances even if not always favorable to this manager; accepts full responsibility for failure as well as success; resolves conflicts by integrating the interests of work units; rewards effective performance.

Page 1 of 2

Keeps informed on technical developments in areas of responsibility by attending personnel meetings, listening to more technically competent subordinates, and reading relevant publications; uses group problem solving to aid in decision making and building commitment; encourages group effort in problem definition and the generation of alternatives; in delegating tasks insures that employees know specifically what decisions are to be made by the manager and for which decisions they need to inform the manager and which ones they can make without informing the manager; career counseling meetings are held which integrate assignments with organizational objectives and employee strength/interests; employees know where they stand and the magnitude of their contributions; constant monitoring of progress toward objectives by holding progress meetings and requiring progress reports.

Seeks responsibility for success or failure of work unit; employees' goals are negotiated and stated in specifically numerical and/or behavioral terms; subordinate performance expectations and the manager's are identical; feedback is continually given on performance in specific terms; performance deviations are addressed candidly and immediately; group problem-solving meetings within work unit and across organizational lines are frequently held where the manager listens and uses the information offered in these sessions; in assigning tasks employees are informed of performance expectations, methods of measurement, decision-making latitude, and resource limitations; moderate risks by employees are encouraged; motivation is primarily based on the use of rewards for effective performance.

Does not blame others for lack of success in his/her work unit; assigns tasks that are based on employee competence, interests, and developmental needs; may tell an employee that they offered a "ridiculous" solution in a group problem-solving meeting; does not follow up and provide specific feedback to insure that goals are accomplished; employees don't know "Where they stand with the boss"; plans to evaluate group problem-solving efforts are not developed; employees generally know what contribution they make, but feedback on specific actions taken and the rationale for those actions is not given; communication is primarily "top down."

Devotes time and energy to employee development by letting employees know of seminars, availability, etc.; evaluations on performance come as a surprise to subordinates; tasks delegated are simple and routine and do not enhance promotion possibilities; performance standards are unclear and feedback given is not timely nor specific; work unit does not share a common perception of goals and methods to accomplish goals; does not listen in group problem-solving meetings and use suggestions in developing creative and effective solutions; continually reminds subordinates of their unsuccessful efforts without acknowledging successful efforts; fails to resolve employee conflicts.

Interrupts others to deny responsibility for lack of success in work unit; not only withholds unfavorable information, but also "colors" information to make it appear only in the best possible way for the manager; performs familiar, routine tasks and delegates tasks that exceed employee's skills and information; when compiling lists of employee performance expectations the manager and the employee have two different lists; tells an employee that they did a "good job" two weeks ago; employees are often surprised to discover that they have made decisions that the manager did not want them to make; does not attend professional meetings or review relevant journals; becomes defensive, interrupts, or changes the subject when discussing technical matters with competent subordinates; attempts to motivate by punishment.

Sample Managerial Competencies: Fortune 500 Company

Understanding of People

Understanding of Groups and Interpersonal Relations

Expressive Communication Skill

Planning Skill

Organizing Skill

Results/Rewards Focus

Institutional Perspective

Competencies

Competency	Description/Examples	Rater Comments (Optional)	Employee Comments (Optional)	End-of-Period Rating
Sense of Priorities	<ul><li>recognizes relative importance of various activities to organization, particularly those of other departments</li><li>is able to see beyond departmental lines in planning and conducting own work</li><li>has sensitivity to work and problems of other units</li><li>demonstrates flexibility and ability to compromise</li><li>is not controlled or manipulated by situational or short-lived pressures</li><li>keeps a balanced perspective of the organization's priorities even under pressure</li><li>•</li><li>•</li></ul>			
Personal and Interpersonal Skills	<ul><li>initiative, i.e., engages in self-starting behaviors</li><li>realistically assesses own strengths/weaknesses</li><li>emotional resilience—responds effectively to emotional reactions by others</li><li>flexibility; is open to new ideas; is willing to experiment with new approaches or methods; is interested in stretching his or her abilities through self-initiated learning</li><li>is able to respond to power situations without blame, recrimination, or oppressive behavior</li><li>•</li><li>•</li></ul>			

Sample Managerial Competencies: Fortune 500 Company

Financial Knowledge

Market/Customer/Client Knowledge

Organization Knowledge

Strategic Thinking and Decision Making

Observation Skill

Creative Thinking Skill

Entrepreneurial Skill

Illustrative Individual Critical Success Factors/Competencies

1. **LEADERSHIP SKILLS**

   a. *Creates Shared Vision:* Defines, communicates, and reinforces a common sense of purpose and set of values that are adopted by subordinate employees.

   b. *Motivates and Empowers Others:* Influences, convinces, directs, and persuades others to accomplish specific objectives; provides sufficient latitude to allow subordinates to achieve specific objectives.

   c. *Credibility:* Engenders the respect and confidence of others based on personal influence and reliability or organizational authority.

   d. *Integrity:* Demonstrates consistency in beliefs, words, and behaviors.

   e. *Sensitivity:* Alert to the motivations, attitudes, and feelings of subordinates and using this knowledge positively to direct behavior and achieve desired results.

   f. *Develops People:* Identifies and addresses principal development needs of subordinates; provides frequent, effective feedback about accomplishments, strengths, and development needs.

   g. *Group Skills:* Plans, conducts, and participates in meetings in which the collective resources of the group are used efficiently.

2. **CONCEPTUAL SKILLS**

   a. *Strategic Thinking:* Identifies, interprets, and addresses key influences on the effectiveness and efficiency of the unit and company.

   b. *Conceptualizing:* Understands and formulates ideas and possesses the ability to communicate and implement these ideas to improve plant performance.

   c. *Creativity:* Identifies imaginative approaches and solutions to problems or potential problems.

525

3. **RESOURCEFULNESS**

   a. *Utilizes Resources:* Recognizes when and where to go to get assistance inside and outside the plant.

   b. *Organization Sensitivity:* Recognizes the need to involve specific people and functions to achieve the unit's and company's objectives; deals effectively with organizational authorities and realities.

   c. *Organization Know-How:* Builds and uses an informal network to achieve desired objectives.

4. **ANALYTICAL SKILLS**

   a. *Problem-Solving:* Identifies the root cause of a problem (not the symptoms), develops and analyzes alternative solutions, and recommends or implements the best course of action.

   b. *Analysis:* Knows how to conduct the most effective quantitative and qualitative analyses to be used for problem solving.

   c. *Financial Analysis:* Understands and applies basis business analysis in evaluating alternative situations.

5. **MANAGEMENT SKILLS**

   a. *Planning:* Develops a course of action to achieve defined objectives.

   b. *Organizing and Delegating:* Structures and assigns responsibilities based on demands and abilities; provides sufficient latitude and authority to achieve objectives; establishes follow-up processes to allow for timely corrective action.

   c. *Decision Making:* Selects and supports an effective course for achieving desired results in a timely manner.

   d. *Negotiation:* Identifies appropriate situations, perceives parties' core demands, and persuades parties to relinquish secondary demands, while maintaining positive relationships; enters negotiations with desired outcomes and fair alternative negotiations in mind.

   e. *Fortitude:* Posseses strength to withstand pressure from numerous internal and external sources that threaten to impede progress/effectiveness.

526

Example of a Work Unit Outcome

JOB TITLE: **Director of Human Resources**

Result/Outcome
Desired: Recruitment of Qualified Staff
- Recruitment time per hire (days)
  Present _____ Target _____ Actual _____
- Recruitment cost per hire (average $)
  Present _____ Target _____ Actual _____
- Performance during probationary period
  (average rating)
  Present _____ Target _____ Actual _____

Result/Outcome
Desired: Absenteeism Reduction
  Measured in days lost and cost.
  Present _____ Target _____ Actual _____

Result/Outcome
Desired: Salary (Compensation) Control
  Previous Year $ _____
  Current Year
        (Budgeted) $ _____
  Actual $ _____

Measures Used in Management-by-Objectives Measurement

Type A units sold
Transfers due to unsatisfactory performance
Training programs
Minority persons hired
Warranty claims
Items entered in a ledger
Days off the job
Mileage per replacement vehicle
Turnover
Sales
Tools replaced
Reduction in expenses from previous period
Extent of contribution and amount of innovation in the project (i.e., highly creative ideas)
Rejects
Pedestrian-vehicle accidents
Visits to the first-aid room
Cost of material used in training
Reports completed by X date
Community complaints received
Maintenance budget plus or minus
Grievances received
Profit by product line
Mileage per replacement tier
Potential contribution to total sales and profits
Returned goods
Research projects completed on time and within budget
Traffic accidents
The rate at which individuals advance
Transfers at employee's request
Employees ready for assignment
Units constructed
Days tardy
Earnings on commissions
Length of service
EEOC complaints received
Units produced
Claims received and processed
Containers filled to capacity
Discharges
Plus or minus budget
Dollar savings realized from projects
Burglaries
Errors in filing

Housing units occupied
Cost of each research project against budget
Damaged units shipped
Value of new cost-reducing procedure
Days sick
Percentage of profits to sales
Garbage cans emptied
Contributions and suggestions made via the suggestion program
Ratio of maintenance cost to product cost
Calls per day
Penetration of the market
Number of repairs on warranty
Time to reach expected results
Injury accidents
Letters typed
Minority persons trained
Cost of maintenance per machine
Number of promotable persons
Number of new versus old units sold
Successful completion of a course
Number of crimes against persons
Number of disgruntled customers
Results of a morale or attitude survey
Cost of spoiled work
Calls answered
Return of invested capital
Gallons used per vehicle
Amount of downtime
New customers per month
Customers maintained for one year
Customers paid by end of month
Delinquency charges
Percentage of deliveries on schedule
Number of customer complaints as a percentage of monthly purchase orders
Percentage of rejects in total monthly volume
Ratio of factory repair time to total production hours per month
Number of units service-free during warranty period
Cost per unit of output per month
Equipment utilization time as a percentage of monthly available hours

Rock Art at Leirfall

02.2018–06.2018
Stjørdal,
Norway

Vingene
Constantin Frommelt

→ 81

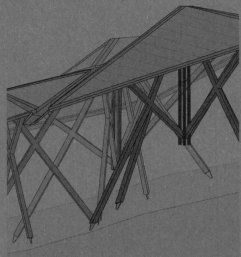

Felsenshelter
Julia Mair

→ 84

Rock Art Shelter
Lucie Thamas

→ 87

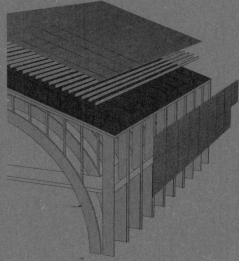

Petroglyph
Michelle Schmidt

→ 90

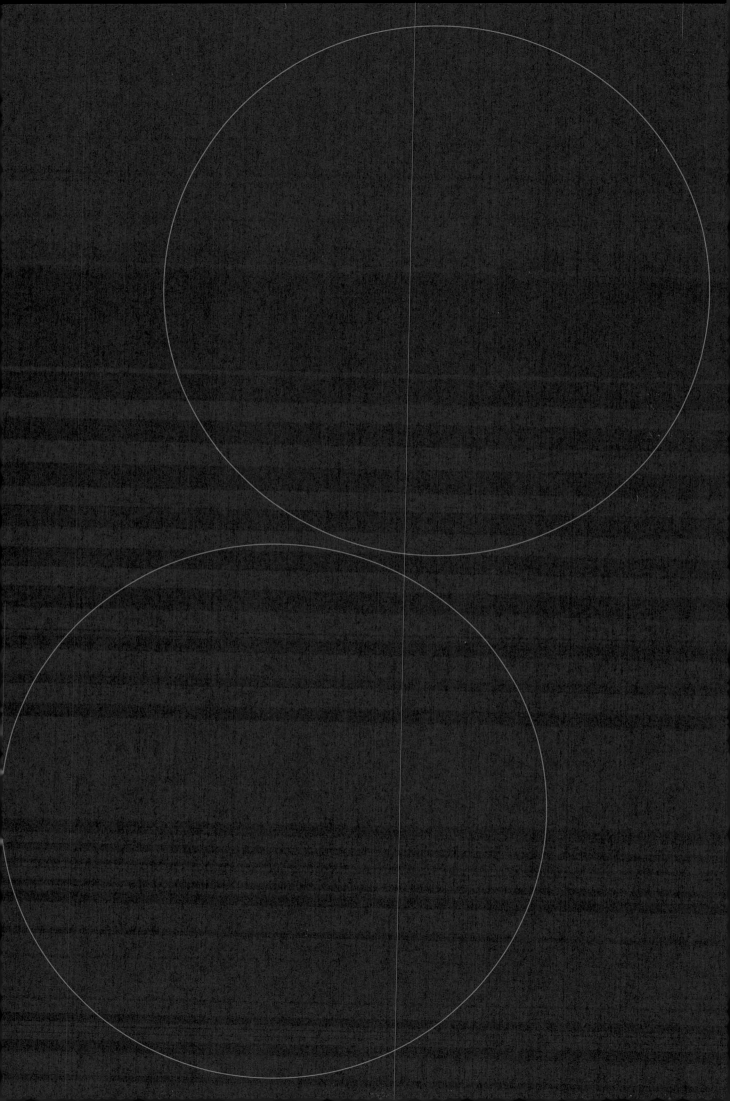

Studio

University of the
Crafts
02.2020–08.2020
Landgraaf,
The Netherlands

Workshop

Pavilion at
Slot Schaesberg
19–21.08.2020
Amsterdam,
The Netherlands

Studio

Alpine Towers
02.2019–06.2019
Schaan,
Liechtenstein

Workshop

Alpine Towers
14–24.03.2019
Vaduz,
Liechtenstein

→ 26, 92, 142

CRAFTING
WOOD

STRUCTURE & EXPRESSION

Urs Meister,
Carmen Rist-Stadelmann,
Machiel Spaan (eds.)

 PARK BOOKS

Erasmus+ is the European Union's most successful education programme. 'Strategic Partnerships' are projects in which at least three organizations from three different programme countries work together. In addition, non-university organizations can also participate in a Strategic Partnership if, by doing so, they generate added value towards the implementation of the project objectives.

The European Community promotes Strategic Partnerships in order to improve the quality and efficiency of European education systems.

Academic freedom is the freedom to learn as much as one desires. (Rudolf Virchow)

Dr Stefan Sohler,
Director of the National
Agency for International
Educational Affairs

Mag. phil. Clarissa Frommelt,
Head of Erasmus+ Higher
Education

In this spirit, the project 'Wood: Structure and Expression' has put into effect an interdisciplinary cooperation between universities and building praxis so as to establish innovative and creative partnerships between these two realms over the long term. The project partnership consists of three university partners, the Amsterdam Academy of Architecture, the Norwegian University of Science and Technology (NTNU) in Trondheim and the University of Liechtenstein, as well as two creative timber construction companies from Liechtenstein and the Netherlands.

The specific expertise of the three partner universities in the fields of design and architectural theory, combined with the partnered timber construction companies' practical know-how of building construction and assembly, enriches the project and offers an important breadth of knowledge and experience. This transfer of knowledge, achieved through the interconnection between praxis and universities and the resulting holistic approach, which combines architectural, constructional, cultural, economic and ecological issues with aspects of the encounter between differing cultural spaces, adds another important facet of innovation to the Erasmus+ project 'Wood: Structure and Expression' for the higher education sector.

The project was implemented to a very high standard, and we at the national agency responsible for Erasmus+ education in Liechtenstein honour the strengthening of ties between education, research and innovation that was brought about by the project 'Wood: Structure and Expression' at the University of Liechtenstein.

Introduction

Carmen Rist-Stadelman,
Urs Meister

Roughly, by a complex system I mean one made up of a large number of parts that interact in a nonsimple way. In such systems, the whole is more than the sum of the parts, not in an ultimate, metaphysical sense, but in the important pragmatic sense that, given the properties of the parts and the laws of their interaction, it is not a trivial matter to infer the properties of the whole.[1]

Wood is considered to be one of the most original materials with which man began to build dwellings. In depictions of primitive huts, we first encounter trees interwoven with branches that are still rooted and used as supports. In later representations, trees are felled and trunks, branches and twigs are used to construct primitive skeletons and eventually to build roofs and walls, and joints were knotted with fibres and cords. Even if we know that these archetypes of building correspond to a retrospective view and the didactic pretensions of the architectural theory of the Renaissance, we can still argue that timber construction and later carpentry developed from this basic taxonomy of joining building components, which used a limited number of tools to furbish beams and boards out of a tree trunk in order to erect structures and enclose space. The principles are still the same today: stick, connection and structure are the central elements of a game, in which stability, economy of means and the pursuit of congruence and beauty must be kept in balance. The laws of interaction of the parts must not only be observed, but constantly redefined in order to obtain a whole that is more than the sum of its parts. Persistent work is required to give the building inner tension, complexity and ultimately radiance. The design process follows less the architect's will to form than his ability to deal with the logic of the material and its properties.

This has become a leitmotiv and recurring theme in the methodology of the design studios of the three schools of architecture throughout the whole process. In this three-year Erasmus+ programme, students and lecturers from Amsterdam Academy of Architecture, the Norwegian Technical University in Trondheim, and the University of Liechtenstein focused on designing structures in wood. In the focus of the partnership, the three design studios were run in parallel and were complemented by joint workshops. The implementation of a special session at the International Congress for Structure and Architecture 2019 in Lisbon and a symposium held in Amsterdam in 2020 made our experiences and results accessible outside the project partnerships and positioned the programme in the European discourse. Today, wood is one of the most up-to-date building materials and offers an incredible wealth of possibilities. Modern timber construction with the currently available means bridges the gap between solid carpentry and complex digital manufacturing processes. Hence the future of timber construction is open to complex developments, which we should aim for in our schools of architecture. We would like to express our sincere thanks to all those involved for their great commitment and the diverse support we have received over three years.

1   Herbert A. Simon, *The Architecture of Complexity*, Pittsburgh 1962

1 CRAFTING THE MODEL

Tectonics in Education

Carmen Rist-Stadelmann

Materials influence the design and appearance of our built architecture. It is therefore important to consider materials as a whole, as a unity of form and construction, and to make them understandable for students as a driving force, as the origin of form and construction in the design process. But how do we offer our students a way to understand the meaning of these aspects? We can achieve this through a tectonic discourse that promotes a sensitivity to materials and generates a sense of joy in and curiosity about the interaction between materials, design and construction. In other words, the symbiosis between art and technology in design and realization. The practice of working at full scale at the University of Liechtenstein over the past ten years has contributed to the tectonic discourse about various materials in the teaching of architecture in Europe.

The culture of joining

Tectonics is therefore the study of joining individual parts together to make up a whole, to create an object of architecture, if you will: it is the study of the inner structure of an artwork. Tectonics, as the aesthetic expression of laws of construction, demands a structural design that cannot be easily separated from the work of the architect who designs it, nor can it be considered separately from the artistic mastery of building. (Kollhoff, 1993)

In order to fulfil today's requirements of technology and building physics, we must layer the various construction materials. Or to use Gottfried Semper's terminology, we must use them for cladding. Layered materials lead to a packaged architecture involving many participants and professionals. As a result, our understanding of the material-specific joint has been lost, and this can be seen in the often questionable use of materials in contemporary architecture where they are no longer used because of their properties, but primarily because of their appearance. The art of joining the materials logically, proceeding from the individual piece to create a new whole, has been lost over the course of history, starting with industrialization and continuing with computerization today. We miss this art now. Due to this loss, we no longer see an interplay between design and construction based on the properties of the materials. That is why it is important to revive the culture of joining and the interaction between art and technology, bringing it back into the discussion and raising awareness of it.

Tectonics, with its implied hierarchy in construction, from coarse to fine, is directly suitable for achieving this. For Gottfried Semper, the joining of rigid, rod-like parts to create an immovable system is indisputably the most important and, at the same time, most difficult task, as he explains in *Style in the Technical and Tectonic Arts* (Semper, 1879a). Here he divides the purposes of tectonics into four tasks. These include the frame with corresponding filling, the lattice as a complicated framework that is made by joining rod-like structural elements

to form a system that creates a surface, the supports and the structure, which is formed by an integration of the supports with the frame (Semper, 1879b).

In Gottfried Semper's understanding of tectonics, based on these four tasks, construction is by nature multi-layered. For him, it is important for tectonic joining that architecture always supports structure plus cladding, whereby the use of materials depends on the construction, thus making design and construction come together as one entity. Thus the appearance corresponds with the technology used. Adolf Loos wrote the following on this subject: "The principle of cladding, which was first articulated by Semper, extends to nature as well. Man is covered with skin, the tree with bark." (Loos, 1898a) This analogy between tectonics and human anatomy shows that the skin as cladding is always joined constructively to a person's insides; it is part of our body. That is why it is important for Loos that the cladding may not be confused with cladding materials. "The law goes like this: we must work in such a way that a confusion of the material clad with its cladding is impossible." (Loos, 1898b)

Semper's definition of tectonics or Loos's analogy with the human body, however, do not tell us how this tectonic interaction can be resolved. They refer to the secretive relationship between constructional joinability and appearance and involve the connection between the built object and our perception. The 'how' remains unexplained between art and technology. However, it is precisely this lack of clarity that enables a creative space for construction and design that should be taught more strongly, rediscovered and placed at the focus of the design and construction process when training architects. In order to join very different materials in this complex design process as understood in tectonics, we require basic knowledge about the materials to be used.

Material consciousness

Every material possesses its own language of forms, and none may lay claim for itself to the forms of another material. For forms have been constituted out of the applicability and the methods of production of materials. (Loos, 1898c)

All of the efforts by an architect to do high-quality work ultimately depend on his or her curiosity about the material to be used. This requires material consciousness and, more than anything else, knowledge of their properties and the possible ways they can be implemented. Because, as Loos accurately said, not all materials are alike.

We can achieve this necessary material consciousness by promoting a sensibility to materials when teaching architecture and, besides imparting theoretical knowledge, by holding the material in our hands, and by working and designing with it. In his book *The Craftsman*, Richard Sennett divides material consciousness into three phases. He describes the first phase as metamorphosis—when the material changes. For him, metamorphosis takes place by developing the material further into a type form, establishing a judgement about its use in a combination of forms and reflecting about its area of application (Sennett, 2008a).

He identifies the second phase of material consciousness as presence. This comes about for Sennett through in the processing of materials by leaving behind trademarks or by marking the material or by making production processes visible. That is, how the material is processed and how we ultimately join materials to one another (Sennett, 2008b).

The anthromorphosis, the third area of material consciousness, is described by Sennett as what happens when an unprocessed material is ascribed human qualities. When we speak of real material or beautiful material, that is, when built objects are assigned human traits and properties (Sennett, 2008c).

Material consciousness according to Sennett—when it finds its way into teaching architecture—means that students become familiar with different materials and their different physical states during their

Figure 1–5
Construction process of the model workshop, Liechtenstein, 2017

architectural studies. They must know how different materials can be processed, how they can be developed further and joined tectonically from the small to the large. In brief, students should learn how materials should be used in building in accordance with their properties and how this interplay ultimately influences the appearance. In this process, the marks of production, influenced by the choice of tool for each material and visible in the way the material is joined to the building, also play a significant role. However, these marks are not restricted merely to the traces left by tools but can also include structural marks. This means that marks are also created by a multitude of steps carried out as part of the different requirements and that these are connected to one another while building. The production process includes a specific combination made up of empirical experience and intellectual reflection, and these can hardly be separated from one another. Here, the hand carrying out the work is important, as it processes the material with the respective tool or machine. The tool is therefore an extension of the hand, which brings us to an important point: the interaction between hand and mind.

Interaction between hand and mind

For the sportsman, craftsman, magician and artist alike, the seamless and unconscious collaboration of the eye, hand and mind is crucial. As the performance is gradually perfected, perception, action of the hand and the thought lose their independence and turn into a singular and subliminally coordinated system of reaction and response. (Pallasmaa, 2009)

When this collaboration between hand and mind comes to bear with material consciousness in combination with tools in architecture, the result is highly interesting in terms of materials and construction technique. In the study of architecture, theory and praxis come together through hand and mind. This happens when everything that is taught as theory and is stored in the mind as knowledge, beginning with material consciousness right up to construction requirements, is put into practice using the hand and the tool.

The hand touches small objects with the thumb, cradles them in the palm and grasps them with the entire hand. The fingers touch, the hands grasp and feel, and the collaboration between hand-wrist-lower arm acts as a whole. The exchange of information between eye and hand is strengthened by repetitions. The hand first of all has to be sensitized by the tips of the fingers. After that, it can turn to the problem of coordination, then comes the integration of the hand into wrist and lower arm. Once the interplay of knowledge, which is made up of theory and praxis, has been learned, when eye and hand are familiar with one another, what results is an invaluable aspect in the teaching. Thanks to this dialogue, long-term design habits develop, and these habits lead to a switching back and forth between solving and finding problems, which supports the symbiosis between construction and outward appearance, or to put it in other terms, the unity of art and technology.

And when this interaction is transferred to the design process, what is achieved is an interplay among sketch, models, building at full scale and drawing. This fruitful inclusion was part of the three-year Erasmus+ project 'Wood: Structure and Expression'. In this project by the University of Lichtenstein, headed by Dr Carmen Rist-Stadelmann and Professor Urs Meister in cooperation with the architecture department at the Amsterdam Academy of Architecture and NTNU Trondheim, research was carried out into joints made of rod-like timber elements, and these were tested in a real design. The starting point was the long tradition of joinery, which has taken on different forms in different cultures, but always has the task of dealing with the transfer of forces in timber structures. Here, we concentrated on purely timber joints without considerable steel reinforcements in order to enrich the structures influenced by our culture with experiences and discoveries from other cultures.

With the basic knowledge acquired in this way, and by developing our own connecting nodes at a scale of 1:1, the students first created a spatial load-bearing structure that could form a roof to protect the prehistoric rock drawings made by Vikings near Trondheim in Norway from further erosion and which—together with several infrastructural buildings—can welcome visitors from all over the world to an open-air museum. Joining and thinking tectonically was therefore provided for in the task itself. As the design process involves using the material itself, the result is a material consciousness in the three phases outlined by Sennett. The hand executes what the mind thinks. Theory and praxis are brought together, and the students learn through the experience they have gained.

Learning through experience

But the result is the student's own experience and possession, because it has been learned rather than taught. Learning is better than teaching because it is more intensive: the more we teach, the less students can learn. (Albers, 1982)

Students can learn and gain a good understanding from their own experience when they build at a scale of 1:1. In other words, when they work hands-on. Working in this way offers students plenty of opportunities to gain experience, something that became apparent when we built the model workshop for our university. Many years of experimenting with building at a scale of 1:1 at our university have shown that just having contact with the material is enough to gain a new understanding of it.

While building the model workshop, we noticed that wood was the material that was driving the design and the subsequent manual labour. The design process began with a five-day workshop as part of the Erasmus+ programme, in which eight load-bearing structures were developed and then built on site at a scale of 1:1. The parameters for the load-bearing structures were set in advance, as the tunnel-shaped form best complied with the existing building regulations on the designated site.

Of the eight supporting structures, the two design studios of Dr Carmen Rist-Stadelmann and Professor Urs Meister analysed four structures as the next step. These were then further developed with the students and built as prototypes. From these, a small jury of lecturers and students selected the structure that was ultimately to be realized. The selection criteria that were decisive were that the supporting structure formed both wall and ceiling constructively, that the structure was developed from the material, and that the tectonic approach was fulfilled. The structure also had to be built and realized by the students themselves, without specialists and without much computer work, and that the expectations of craftsmanship and artisanal aspects were also satisfied.

For the fabrication process, the students built moulds into which the long and narrow timber boards could be inserted and then fixed together into segmental arches. With a tectonic understanding, these prefabricated segmental arches were joined on site to create a new whole. The segmental arches are hinged at the crown, rest on a timber sole plate and are interwoven with one another. The timber sleeper is, in turn, held by the floor beams, which are designed to withstand tension. The finished floor on the floor beams provides information about the floor construction through its laid timber formwork. It thus visibly unites construction and appearance.

The model workshop was an ongoing process in which the students resolved different structural parts in different teams. The project was developed further in joint presentations while construction proceeded simultaneously. In a 1:10 scale model that one student group built during the construction process, it was possible to assess all decisions and then to build them on site at a scale of 1:1 and vice-versa, thus resulting in an interesting interplay between theory and praxis using both the model and reality.

The construction process was carried out as teamwork involving 62 students and 3 lecturers. After 15 weeks of intensive building, detailing and designing, the model workshop was ready at the end of the semester, meaning it could be opened ceremonially. In addition to relocating and connecting the machines, participants carried out the last work during the summer holidays, so that the workshop could go into operation for the 2017–18 winter semester. The model workshop has proved its worth so far and enjoys a high level of acceptance among students.

The fascinating thing about this way of learning through experience gained by working on a real object was seeing how strongly the students identified with the construction task and how this increased as the process went on. It was also exciting to see how they gained experience and confidence in working with wood as a material as construction progressed. And how they naturally switched back and forth between the different scales to check construction details and aspects in real life. Their learning was learned and not just taught.

The tectonic ambition

Technology, when spoken poetically, leads to architecture.
(Auguste Perret)

The use and application of materials influence the design and appearance of our built architecture. So it is of great importance to gain more in-depth knowledge of how to handle a material in its form and construction, beginning during one's architectural studies. It is all about really living the tectonic discourse, promoting a sensitivity to the material, in short, about generating a sense of joy in and curiosity about the interaction between material, its design and construction, that is, the symbiosis between art and technology in the design and realization process.

In addition, it is important to perceive of material as a whole, as a unity of form and construction, and to make it understandable for students as a driving force, as the origin of form and construction in the design process, and it is increasingly important that this be cultivated in teaching architecture. Tectonic joining plays an important role in this process. To achieve this, we must be able to join parts together to form a whole and in this way gain an understanding of the materials used to make them. Put briefly, we must be able to master the interplay between art and technology. This can be achieved if our expectations of tectonics are already experienced while we study architecture, and appearance and construction can merge again to become a whole, to achieve unity.

References

Albers, Josef. 1982. Josef Albers. In *Rainer Wick, Bauhauspädagogik*: 159. Cologne: DuMont.
Kollhoff, Hans. 1993. Über *Tektonik in der Baukunst*: 7. Braunschweig; Wiesbaden: Vieweg.
Loos, Adolf. 1898a. Das Princip der Bekleidung. In *Adolf Loos, Gesammelte Schriften*: 140. Vienna: lesethek.
Loos, Adolf. 1898b. Das Princip der Bekleidung. In *Adolf Loos, Gesammelte Schriften*: 141. Vienna: lesethek.
Loos, Adolf. 1898c. Das Princip der Bekleidung. In *Adolf Loos, Gesammelte Schriften*: 139. Vienna: lesethek.
Pallasmaa, Juhani. 2009. *The Thinking Hand*: 82. Chichester: John Wiley and Sons.
Semper, Gottfried. 1879a. *Der Stil in den technischen und tektonischen Künsten*: Vol. II: 199. Munich: Friedr. Bruckmann Verlag.
Semper, Gottfried. 1879b. *Der Stil in den technischen und tektonischen Künsten*: Vol. II: 201. Munich: Friedr. Bruckmann Verlag.
Sennett, Richard. 2008a. *Handwerk*: 162–176. Berlin: Berlin Verlag.
Sennett, Richard. 2008b. *Handwerk*: 177–184. Berlin: Berlin Verlag.
Sennett, Richard. 2008c. *Handwerk*: 184–196. Berlin: Berlin Verlag.

A Universe of Wood Joinery

Machiel Spaan

All down the centuries, collections of details, material properties and building techniques have inspired architects and designers to improve their craft and innovate their products. It was with this goal in mind that the German architect Gottfried Semper documented the four most important building materials in his book *The Four Elements of Architecture (1851)*: stone and masonry work, wood and joinery, textile and weaving, ceramics and moulding. Semper classified the four materials according to construction technique and architectural appearance. His classification offers insight into the mutual relationship between materials and their deployment, thereby offering a platform for renewal.

In *De wetten van de bouwkunst* (2009), architecture historian Petra Brouwer discusses the 19th-century knowledge revolution in relation to architecture books from the period. According to Brouwer, we should not view these textbooks as a reflection on the architecture of the period, but rather as vehicles for renewal. The books gather together material properties, building techniques and construction principles and reveal the relationships among them. The collected knowledge improves our understanding of the craft. The catalogue of classified examples reveals not only the qualities and rules but also the limitations, thereby increasing insight and encouraging improvement. Current conditions and requirements, as well as the desire to do things better, led to unprecedented solutions that expanded the catalogue. The book *Wood and Wood Joints* by Klaus Zwerger is a collection of imaginative wood structures from all over the world. "Only when one can observe and study a building as part of a larger group of comparable buildings, one's findings will be informed by the bigger picture and thus more meaningful."

Compiling references is a form of collecting and an aid in grasping the structural and architectural principles of wood construction techniques and accompanying joints. Classifying references allows us to reveal the origins and logic of the joints so that we can analyse the architectural principles of each of them. The expertise of the craftsman is encapsulated in every joint and detail. The sharpness of the saw-cut, the ingenuity of the dowel, the clever assembly, and especially the efficient transfer of forces. That said, every joint is also rooted in contextual conditions such as topography, culture and civilization.

Is this act of collecting a valuable aspect of architectural education? And do collecting and cataloguing enhance our understanding of the craft? *A Universe of Wood Joinery* explores these questions by discussing two *Crafting Wood* educational projects in which we analysed and designed wood structures and accompanying details. First during an analysis and design exercise where we drew wood joints in a uniform manner, and second during a hands-on workshop where we made wood trusses.

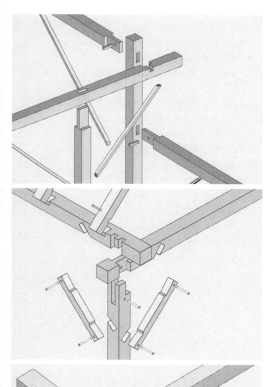

Figure 1–3
Wood joints drawn by students

Part of the *Crafting Wood* project involved analysing traditions of wood construction. In the spring of 2018 a group of students studied wood joints from the Netherlands, Norway, Japan, Switzerland and North America. We drew the joints of selected structures in a uniform style, namely an isometric at a 30–60 angle. We then drew the structures designed by students in the same way. The act of drawing helped us to study the details and explore the world of wood joints. We drew, made and analysed joints. We searched for the identity and essence of the joint, the language of the craftsman. We zoomed in and out and compared traditions. That process taught us about the balance between authenticity and universal values. A uniform drawing technique allowed us to compare construction, building technology and atmosphere.

The result of the drawing exercise was an elucidating 'matrix' of wood joints. The classified joints told us about context, form and assembly. We learned about the differences and similarities. It was no exhaustive and scientifically underpinned catalogue but an associative compilation that inspired further study and design. The catalogue was a personal and subjective representation, a starting point for further reflection on new solutions and possibilities. "Every new experience is measured against past experiences and assessed in relation to it. That results in standards that are subjective and that—as discussions with colleagues from academia and craftsmanship alike reveal—are continually changing or are being substantiated," writes Klaus Zwerger in his book *Wood and Wood Joints.*

The completed drawings revealed differences between the hierarchically composed American, Norwegian and Dutch constructions, the stacked structures from Switzerland, and the ingenious Japanese 'puzzle constructions'. But there were also similarities between the restrained Japanese, Norwegian and Swiss joints.

A series of student designs was based on structures with flexible joints that move in response to horizontal forces such as the wind, which can be very strong and unpredictable in Norway and the Netherlands. The joints in roofs are composed in such a way that the whole construction can sway with the wind. History teaches us that this technique goes back to the construction of Viking ships, which boasted flexible and moveable joints that could withstand the force of the waves. Many Norwegian carpenters also came to the Netherlands during the Golden Age to craft roof trusses and ships' hulls.

A number of student designs consisted of stacked joints. Beams and/or planks were alternately stacked and connected to one another with the help of overlapping notches. Sturdy walls on the inside and outside supported the roof beams. In the Alps, the vertical loads of thick layers of snow are carried to the ground by these stacked structures. Communities in mountainous areas were often small in number, so wood structures had to be simple and easy to construct by a limited number of people. In the Netherlands and Germany you can see a tradition of solid wood constructions that originated in the Alps.

The Japanese tradition of wood construction is timeless. Joints are made in such a way that they are completely hidden from view. All that is visible are the beams that are held together. Every single connecting piece, wedge and notch is concealed. The joints of the Stave Church in Norway look similar to these Japanese joints. Students designed joints of ingenious and precisely made forms inspired by Japanese traditions. These inventive joints, which can support forces acting in a number of directions, have their origins in a tectonic phenomenon. Earthquakes in Japan inspired the development of wooden structures with a high degree of elasticity to withstand vibrations and ensure stability. Japanese joints do both. They move with the vibrations without falling apart.

A number of wood joints are also based on techniques of prefabrication, a form of construction that is widespread in America. These 'loose' construction principles stimulated the students. Prefabricated trusses and components are assembled on site.

A remarkable example of prefabrication is the Thorncrown Chapel by architect E Fay Jones. This open and layered structure is set in a pinewood forest. The construction consists entirely of components

Figure 4
Workshop Trondheim, 2018

that can be handled by two people. The limited dimensions and the quality of the wood determined the construction: a series of pine columns, beams and diagonals. Larger components were assembled on site and then hoisted into position.

Classifying wood construction from all over the world helped students to explicitly adopt a position of their own in relation to design. Compiling and comparing examples gave each wood joint a fixed position within the collection. In any setting, a wood construction results from a combination of individual preferences and contextual and cultural background. Topography, climate and civilization influence the nature of wood joints. "Only by looking at the elements under a wide lens can we recognize the cultural preferences, forgotten symbolism, technological advances, mutations triggered by intensifying global exchange, climatic adaptions, political calculations, regulatory requirements, new digital regimes, and, somewhere in the mix—the ideas of the architect that constitute the practice of architecture today," writes architect Rem Koolhaas in *Elements of Architecture,* an inexhaustible compendium of relevant architectural elements from the history of architecture.

The classified drawings offer insight into contextual differences and similarities. In addition, the exploded isometric drawings show all components of the construction and the way they are combined in a joint. Both the shape and form of assembly are illuminated in an intuitive manner.

6 roof frames

A second relevant project in this regard was a workshop held in Trondheim in the summer of 2018. The starting point for this *Crafting Wood* workshop was the wooden roof structure of the *Haltdalen Stavkirke* from the 11th century. Thirty-two students from three schools constructed six wood trusses that together formed the spatial structure of the chapel. We worked in two specialist workshops, each with its own space, tools and skilled craftsmen. A variety of joints were made and tested at full scale in both workshops. The joints of three trusses were made with saws and chisels according to traditional techniques; the details of the other three trusses were made using modern saws, drills and milling machines.

Students worked in groups to design and make the wood joints that appealed to them. The joints were then gathered in a central space so that students could touch and test them for strength and manipulability. The students could reflect on the nature of joints within a universe larger than the individual detail or product. In plenary working sessions, students compared and shared their understanding of the details on the table: on how they were made, the tools used and the efficiency of the transfer of forces. All the details became part of a shared collection and classified according to the insights of the students. This exchange 'on the table' was repeated a number of times, and the collective exchange of views made it more efficient, precise and easier to design the wood joints. The details were refined from sketch model to well-considered mock-ups and then incorporated into the collection.

Work then moved to the construction site, where the details became part of a truss 4.5 metres wide and 4 metres tall.

As stated, we worked in two workshops, each with its own tools, equipment and drafting techniques. The way of working in the manual workshop differed from that in the machine workshop, and each had its own learning curves and results.

The manual workshop was also the actual construction site, where components were sawn to size and assembled. The relationship between joint and structure was explored repeatedly on the spot, initially through sketches, and then by laying out the whole truss on supports and positioning the elements to be connected on top of and beside each other. In this way, we could see the joint in relationship to the whole structure. The slow character of the manual workshop—it simply takes a long time to make a detail—ensured that the focus was put on the material. It became a matter of crafting the wooden beam

as best as possible with the available tools. The craftsmen present shared with the students their knowledge of working with the saw and chisel—handling the material, holding the chisel, moving the saw, supporting the beam. When sawing with a handsaw, the hand and arm directly encounter the changing grain and knots. Bit by bit, the tool becomes an extension of the hand. A narrative and intuitive handbook with the dos and don'ts that apply in the craftsman's workshop: the realization that the forces acting parallel to the wood fibre of the pine-wood beam can be far greater than those acting perpendicular to it. That a dowel cannot withstand large forces but can only keep components in place. And that the dovetail joint can absorb forces acting in various directions.

In the machine workshop the students worked with electrical equipment, such as circular saws and drilling and milling machines. Machines make it possible to test an idea in reality quickly and without too much difficulty. This allowed the students to think in terms of variations and part solutions. They could compile their own collection of mock-ups and choose from them. The machine workshop was located some distance from the construction site. Prefabricated components were prepared in the workshop and then transported to the site for assembly. The wood we worked with in the machine workshop was Gluelam. The grain in the composite beams was multi-directional because of the criss-cross way they were glued. As a result, the uncontrollable nature of the knots in the trunk was eliminated. The wooden beams were exact in their dimensions and the direction of forces could be easily predicted. Computer drawings are mostly used in the modern-day workshop. From the drawing of the whole truss, students could zoom in on the individual joint.

In the machine workshop, attention shifted from materials to tools. Machine tools create a distance between the hand and the material. Technology moves fast, and safety instructions, gloves and googles increase the distance further. Caution is therefore advisable. The machine comes between the hand and the material. As a result, mastering the material 'just like that' is not so easy.

After the construction site had been tidied, what remained was a wood construction consisting of six trusses featuring more than 30 classified details of joints in wooden beams. Together they constituted a narrative about tradition and modernity, craft and the machine, slowness and speed, strength and beauty. The collection offered insight into the intentions of the designers.

The trusses made in the traditional workshop were exuberant in their use of materials and expressively artisanal joints. Half-lap and dovetail joints were embraced and formed the starting point of the construction. Ornaments were added to each truss: a carved dragon, a decorated tip of a beam, a candleholder. Traces of the saw and chisel revealed the process of making and lent the trusses an artisanal quality.

The three trusses made in the machine workshop were based more on concepts, such as minimizing the use of materials or creating an asymmetrical, abstract or balancing construction. What mattered most was the form of construction, reflecting a desire to innovate and push back boundaries, as expressed by the joints. Flying in the face of tradition, the dowel was deployed to connect elements in a number of places. The cuts of the circular saw and the rounded corners of the milling head indicated the materials used.

The six trusses encouraged innovation, the first three fed by respect for tradition and the way traditional solutions can inform future solutions. The machine-made trusses were informed by an urge to deploy tools optimally and thus arrive at new smart solutions.

Collecting and classifying

The drawing exercise speaks to both the design approach and research approach of the student. Analysing existing wood joints and allotting them their rightful place in the collection is a valuable lesson. Every discovered wood joint becomes part of the collection, inspiring the designer and providing pointers for design.

igure 5
even Trusses, Trondheim, 2018

17

Figure 6
Wood joints, 1:1, Trondheim, 2018

The making exercise goes a step further. Here the student steps into the shoes of the craftsman. In addition to a knowledge of form and assembly, the student is also challenged to master the material and its characteristics such as weight, grain and so on. Actually working with the material makes it clear that the tools at hand help determine the design and finished product.

Through the act of drawing, students collected and classified wood joints. These constituted a coloured representation of reality, offering insight into a wealth of ways to use wood. They broadened the horizon and provided opportunities to explore new perspectives. Moreover, the drawings provided a good form of representation because they facilitated every idea. The pencil allowed us to explore the collection and each individual joint, without having to take gravity into account. Imagination was given free rein.

The reverse was the case in the making exercise. The act of making confronted us directly with the resistance of the material. We explored the properties and possibilities with our own hands. We engaged directly with the wood. Imagination made way for physical contact. The intrinsic knowledge of the craftsman helped us to refine our understanding of the material and tools. Here the collection was not committed to paper but shaped by hand through the material.

The 'living' collection of wood joints made during the process helped everybody to adopt a position and refine their own design. In the end, the six trusses constituted a collection that enabled us to reflect on the role of the workshops, tools and materials in design.

In designing, an architect balances technique and beauty, crafts and arts. In *De wetten van de Bouwkunst*, Brouwer describes how the handbooks of Vitruvius address both the theoretical and practical knowledge of architecture together. "Manual craftsmanship is the continual and repeated training in an activity that involves shaping by hand the sort of material that is required, until it complies with the intended design. Intellectual reasoning can illuminate and explain the objects crafted." The process of collecting and classifying the drawn wood joints stimulated this intellectual reasoning. And the collection of wood joints made with one's own hands forms a 'manual' for mastering hands-on craftsmanship. Seen in that way, collecting and classifying are welcome tools in learning to understand the use of materials and craft and their significance in design.

Connected Knowledge

Bjorn Otto Braaten,
Ian Siem,
Arnstein Gilberg

The development of computer numerical controlled (CNC) milling machines has renewed interest in traditional carpentry joints. The use of machines to make complicated timber joints paves the way for large-scale production of timber structures in a modern industrial context. An interesting question is how these digitally produced timber joints, untouched by the human hand, relate to the understanding of the properties of wood, structural concepts, cultural identity, aesthetic aspects and individual experience of traditional craftsmanship. What characterizes the difference between them? What is gained and what is lost in this development?

Some aspects in this discussion concern measurable and objective facts. Others can only be studied as part of a continuously changing, subjective and intersubjective cultural context. Very often, this kind of discussion tends to be polarized between a seemingly non-value-based, rational and 'objective' position, and a value-based ethical or aesthetical 'subjective' position. In this paper, we will present and discuss a method called the Four-Quadrant Model, which helps us investigate these matters in a more balanced way through different perspectives and ways of understanding that include both objective and subjective positions.

Four-Quadrant Model (FQM)

Through a series of books, the American philosopher Ken Wilber has developed and presented a map for human knowledge called the 'Integral Approach'. It attempts to be comprehensive, balanced and inclusive, and embraces science, art and morals. Its vision is to establish a comprehensive, all-inclusive or integral map that includes the best elements of knowledge, experience, wisdom and reflection from all major human civilizations: pre-modern, modern and post-modern.

The Integral Approach consists of five main elements: 'Levels', 'Lines', 'States', 'Types' and 'The Four Quadrants'. 'Levels' refer to the developmental stages of the phenomena. 'Lines' refer to the different areas of development, and 'States' refer to different states of temporary character (like states of consciousness: deep sleep, dream sleep, awake, altered, etc.). 'Types' refer to different aspects such as gender, personality types, etc. 'The Four Quadrants' refer to a way to investigate a phenomenon by differentiating four perspectives and then recombining the information (Wilber, 2001).

Though all these elements work together as a whole, we will, in this context, focus on the Four-Quadrant Model (FQM).

The FQM (figure 1) may be seen as an upgraded version of the tripartite classical model of Ethics, Aesthetics and Science, or 'the Good, the Beautiful and the Truth' (Wilber, 2000).

To understand the architecture of the FQM, we can divide it into its different building blocks. On the right side, the two quadrants (Upper Right and Lower Right) deal with everything that can be measured or positioned in time and space. These are the objective aspects of facts. However, these facts are not fixed 'truths' that don't change. History

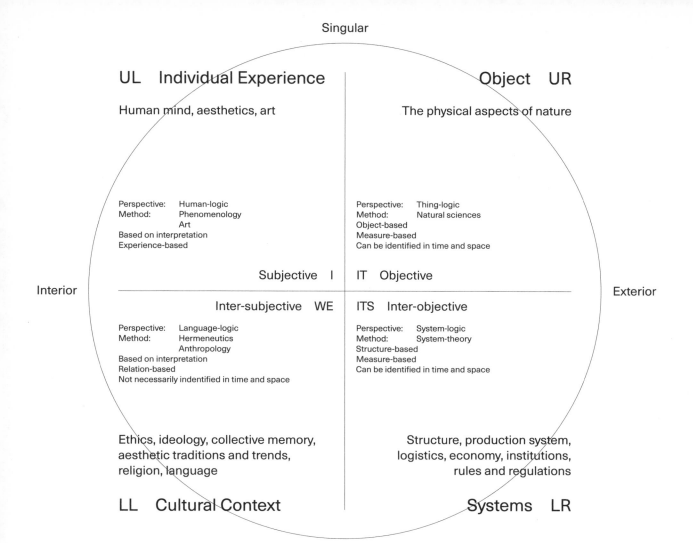

Singular

UL   Individual Experience

Human mind, aesthetics, art

Perspective:	Human-logic
Method:	Phenomenology
	Art
Based on interpretation	
Experience-based	

Subjective   I

Object   UR

The physical aspects of nature

Perspective:	Thing-logic
Method:	Natural sciences
Object-based	
Measure-based	
Can be identified in time and space	

IT   Objective

Interior

Inter-subjective   WE

Perspective:	Language-logic
Method:	Hermeneutics
	Anthropology
Based on interpretation	
Relation-based	
Not necessarily indentified in time and space	

ITS   Inter-objective

Perspective:	System-logic
Method:	System-theory
Structure-based	
Measure-based	
Can be identified in time and space	

Exterior

Ethics, ideology, collective memory, aesthetic traditions and trends, religion, language

Structure, production system, logistics, economy, institutions, rules and regulations

LL   Cultural Context

Systems   LR

Plural

Figure 1
The Four-Quadrant Model (FQM). This version of the FQM is adapted by the authors for this specific context (see 'Adapting the Model to Our Cause')

shows that development of better equipment for measuring or studying the phenomena at hand may fundamentally change the way we understand or see the object. (This, however, is an example of the aspect uncovered by the 'Levels' category in the Integral Approach). Upper Right (UR) is the behavioural aspect of the phenomena, or its nature as an object that can be observed. This is the field of the natural sciences. Lower Right (LR) is the objective plural aspect of the phenomena, the system aspect. Here, structures and links that the phenomenon at hand is part of may be discovered if they are not easily visible in the upper right quadrant, where they are studied as a singular entity. This is the field of system theory.

On the left side of the model, the perspectives are fundamentally different. The Upper Left and Lower Left represent the subjective aspects of the phenomenon. They cannot be measured, observed or defined in time and space like those on the right side. These perspectives are defined either by subjective individual experience (Upper Left) or by shared intersubjective experience based on interaction and dialogue (Lower Left). Hermeneutics, the science of interpretation (Gadamer, 1975), is an example of a method of the lower left quadrant, while phenomenology (Husserl, 2013; Heidegger, 2010) and the arts are methods and ways of investigating the Upper Left quadrant.

On basis of this, the Upper Left can be seen as an 'I' perspective (internal, singular, subjective); the Lower Left a 'We' perspective (internal, plural, intersubjective); the Lower Right as an 'Its' perspective (exterior, plural, inter-objective); and Upper Right an 'I' perspective (exterior, singular, objective).

As noted in the introduction, the FQM offers a set of methods that includes both objective and subjective perspectives. Now it is easy to see how the different quadrants are part of the whole, how they represent different perspectives, and how they are interconnected. A phenomenon observed in one of the quadrants will automatically inform

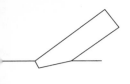

Figure 2
The single-step joint

and influence the three others. Something observed as a 'fact' in the Upper Right will, for instance, always be seen within a cultural context, through epistemological, ontological and language-based concepts in the Lower Left. When these change, the fact may be translated and understood in a different way.

In terms of using the model, it is important to be aware of three different steps that need to be taken. The first step is to separate the phenomenon we want to investigate into the four quadrants. The next step is to isolate the investigation in each of the quadrants, so that the potential of each perspective is fulfilled. To stop here, however, will quickly lead to some kind of reductionism, subjective or objective. The last step, recombining the information and seeing how the different perspectives inform each other in a new complete picture, is therefore crucial.

Adapting the model to our cause

The Integral Approach and the Four-Quadrant Model is used to discuss and analyse a multitude of phenomena in different contexts like medicine, education, economy, politics, etc. (Wilber, 2001). In discussing structural wood joints in this context, we have chosen to make some small adjustments of words headlining each quadrant. In the Wilber model, the headline for the Upper Right (objective exterior / it) quadrant is 'Behavioural'. In our model we have chosen to use the headline 'Object' to make it clearer that this is how the phenomenon appears when externally observed as an object. The headline for the Lower Right (interobjective exterior / its), 'Social', is here called 'System' to emphasize the system-logic perspective. Lower Left (intersubjective internal / we) is changed from 'Cultural' to 'Cultural Context', and Upper Left (subjective internal / I) is changed from 'Intentional' to 'Individual Experience' to make it easier in this context to understand the profile of the quadrant. However, the concepts, perspectives and content of the four quadrants remain unaltered from the Wilber model.

We will now show how the Four-Quadrant Model can be helpful in discussing the qualities of a timber joint. As an example, we will use a joint that is common in traditional Norwegian structures and traditional Japanese buildings, and is now also available for industrial production by 3D milling machines: the single-step joint (figure 2).Following the previously mentioned procedure, we start by separating the different aspects of the joint: the object perspective (UR), the system perspective (LR), the cultural context (LL) and the individual experience (UL).

1   The object perspective (UR)
In this perspective, all the things that can be measured, weighed and observed will be taken into account. In addition, how it works as a singular structural element is important information. 'The single-step joint: a traditional carpentry joint with new possibilities' is an in-depth paper on the way this joint works (Siem, 2017). It describes failure modes and how forces are distributed, the importance of the fibre direction in the wood, and the consequences of variable angles between the horizontal element and the inclined compression element, etc. Other important aspects of the joint are what kind of wood is used and what part of the tree is used and its percentage of humidity. The precision between the two connected structural elements can be measured and, if put into a laboratory, the capacity to take forces can be documented. All this is information that belongs in the Upper Right quadrant.

2   The system perspective (LR)
If we look at the single-step joint from a system perspective, the focus shifts from looking at the joint as a singular, isolated element to seeing how it works as part of a system. This could be many different systems. First, it is the structural system that can tell what specific function the joint performs in a building. Then there is the system of production that tells if it is made in a small, local workshop or part of large-scale industrial production. How does the joint relate to an economic system? How much does it cost to produce? What are its characteristics within a sustainable system? Is it transported over long distances or is it 'short travelled'?

The system perspective helps us to better see the function of the joint in a bigger context. Things that would remain hidden if it is only studied as a singular object become clearer, and sometimes surprisingly so. For instance, can the extreme refinement of traditional Japanese carpentry be understood better by seeing its function in the simple structural systems of the traditional house, where the joint represents a negotiation between structural stiffness and flexibility? Instead of rigid diagonals that would cause serious damage in the event of earthquakes, the joints fitted together with wedges may be shaken but easily mended by tightening the wedges.

3   The cultural context (LL)

What is good and what is bad, what is important and what is not, what generates knowledge (epistemology) and how we understand our world (ontology), all belong in the Lower Left quadrant. Because this deals with human values and culturally defined worldviews, it cannot be measured, weighed or even identified in time and space, as with UR and LR. For an orthodox natural scientist, this is the muddy and unpredictable field of meaning, belief and interpretation. Still, it is quite obvious that even a natural scientist does not observe objects outside a given cultural context which will influence what is seen and the way the facts are interpreted.

Because this quadrant deals with the cultural value aspect, this is also where different points of view concerning what is 'good' and what is 'bad' about the joint belong. It is, in short, where the ethics of the joint are highlighted. Some may be surprized that it is possible to discuss the ethics of a joint, but we will see that the value-perspective between traditional carpentry and industrial production of joints can be quite different. This is of course a complex matter, so in this brief presentation of the simplest way of using the FQM, we will just bring out a couple of examples.

Within the context of producing timber joints, whether traditional or industrial, there is a shared attitude that 'wood is good'. However, even if the human-made and machine-made step-joint is equally strong and functions in the same way, there are some important differences concerning the production. Sustainability is an important ethic factor in our time, and even if wood is regarded as a sustainable material, large-scale industrial production may not be seen as sustainable owing, for instance, to long-distance transport.

Industrial production will provide the product, but not the human act of making, since it is made by milling machines. In a society and cultural context where global industrial products are plentiful, some will say locally handmade products in general, and traditional craftsmanship in particular, have a value in themselves. The act of making, is, by some within the field, actually seen as important as the product, because the knowledge is in the hand; it is an embodied experience, not just a question of cognitive knowledge (Godal, 2018; Greve and Nesset, 1997). If this 'silent' knowledge developed by the act of doing disappears, a way of thinking that is not based purely on reductive production logic and instrumental thinking may disappear. On the other hand, the potential for new understanding and new ways of making very intricate timber joints through new production methods may also be the 'lifesaver' of the timber joint in modern house production.

4   The individual experience (UL)

The Upper Left quadrant is based on how each individual experiences the phenomenon in question and is, by definition, subjective. This does not necessarily mean that this experience is limited to the individual, because many people will experience the same thing in a similar way. On the other hand, we will never exactly know what each one of us experiences, because we all have a different background, different sensibility and so on. To acknowledge, in this context, the individual experience of the specific single-step joint is therefore crucial. All objective aspects, system aspects and cultural context aspects are ultimately filtered through a person, with his or her level of understanding, sensibility, prejudice, preferences and knowledge.

The aesthetic experience of a specific single-step joint has not only an intersubjective aspect related to norms and preferences within

the cultural context, but also an individual, subjective aspect in the way each individual experiences these aesthetic properties. If the joint is made by a 3D drilling machine, how for instance do the rounded corners fit with the rest of the formal qualities of the structure? If it is made by hand, is the precision of the craftsman's work using traditional tools satisfactory? If there are rough edges, do they give a sloppy impression or are they expressions of functional understanding?

The individual experience of the single-step joint may be based on both physical aspects, emotional aspects, cognitive or knowledge-based aspects, and intuitive aspects.

5   Recombining the four quadrants (UR/LR/LL/UL)

By differentiating how the single-step joint works in four different perspectives, we get a wider picture. Each of the quadrants may contain true or truthful information about the single-step joint, but only partly, reductive truths. By recombining them, we can acknowledge the contribution of each perspective and achieve a more balanced discussion.

In this case, the discussion about aesthetics may be informed by how the single-step joint was produced (by whom, with what tools, where, production cost, etc.), if the aesthetic expression is focused on a slick surface or a more unpolished consequence of the forces working within, and finally, what values it represents as a cultural artefact.

It is now possible to see how the analysis of the forces working within the joint and the production process (whether industrial or traditional) are connected to explicit intersubjective paradigms and individual preferences.

Using the model

When recombining the four perspectives of the Four-Quadrant Model, we come to understand that there are potentially many different aspects and factors that could be included as part of the investigation. For those used to discussing or investigating phenomena mainly from one or two perspectives, this model may seem quite complex. On the other hand, to use the FQM without taking into account the four main elements (levels, lines, states and types) of the Integral Approach may be seen as a drastic simplification.

This is a classical dilemma in dealing with matters of complexity and depth. How can complex matters be discussed in a manageable way without missing their complex nature? Using the Four-Quadrant Model can be seen as a first step in solving this dilemma. The next step would be to take into consideration and identify the different levels of each of the four quadrants, from gross to subtle and causal. After that, the discussion or investigation could develop into states, lines and types.

However, to be able to use the FQM as an operative tool, we need some training. During the spring of 2018 the FQM was presented and used in the master level theory course Timberstructures B (7.5 ECTS) at the Faculty of Architecture and Design at NTNU in Norway. (This course was closely linked to a 15 ECTS architectural design course called Timberstructures A.) During the five weeks of the course, the 14 students would submit an essay where they used the model as tool for discussing a specific joint system. The students would use a freely chosen building or built structure as a case to discuss the context of their specific joint system. In addition to a text of at least six pages (maximum 50% pictures or diagrams), the students were encouraged to fill in key-words of their analyses into a graphic representation of the FQM. The essays are available as an internal NTNU booklet entitled 'Joint Systems: A Collection of Student Essays' (Siem, Braaten and Gilberg, 2018).

Information about the model was provided through articles to read and a lecture. In addition to presenting the Integral Approach, the lecture focused on how the FQM could be relevant to discussing architecture and architectural elements like joint systems.

As a typical transdisciplinary topic, the architect's way of working is a very good example of an integral way of thinking in practice. Designing a building is a complex negotiation of technical, economic, ethical and aesthetic elements, and the architect needs to be trained

in considering all these elements and their interrelationships simultaneously. The students in this master-level course were, through their previous years of studying and designing architecture, well prepared for the multi-perspective thinking represented by the FQM.

By studying the 14 essays, we became aware of some aspects of using the FQM by beginners that seem to be typical.

The overall impression was that almost everybody managed to use the model in a relevant way. This means that they discussed their joint system based on the FQM in the text. All 14 essays show an ability to differentiate between the objective (UR/LR) and subjective (UL/LL) perspectives in the model. Two essays did not strictly follow the form by putting the discussion into the quadrant headlines. One of them, probably because of discomfort with the rather formalistic structure, and the other interestingly integrated the FQM into a more 'essayistic' text. This last one in particular was a highly competent text where the author fully understood and expressed the intention of the FQM through a more literary form.

As with all models, the quality of its use depends on the skills of its user. A couple of texts showed just a rudimentary understanding of the model and its intentions. This may have been because they felt the form to be restrictive and were unable to break out of the form or to develop enough skills and understanding to use it in a more elaborate way. It must be pointed out that the time to develop this skill and understanding was limited to five weeks. However, at least four or five of the essays show exemplary use of the model, where the separate perspectives were understood and the relationship between them was discussed in a concluding section.

A very good example in using the model is an essay where the student first briefly introduces the built structure by explaining its history, building process and use. The structural joint system is steel dowels, and the author describes different stages of development in using dowels and steel plates in bigger timber structures and how the forces are distributed through the joint (UR). Through the system perspective (LR), the author describes in depth the nature of the building's structural system and how torsional and bending forces are working, based on the dowel joints. In discussing the cultural context (LL) of the structure and joint-system, the author explains the specific interest in the area for using timber in new and inventive ways that point to the future and back to regional traditions. A very relevant and interesting story of the relationship between cultural identity and development of wood as structural material in large buildings is told. The author also clearly explains his close relationship with the building (UL) from early age, and how he enjoyed the appearance of the visible steel dowels which made him understand, in a simple way, how the structure actually worked. Finally, in the recombined part the author discusses how the structural system and the use of dowels are rooted in a tradition where timber structures and regional identity are closely linked. He points out how the joint system (UR) combines influences from the other three quadrants and is not a purely technical detail with a strictly functional meaning.

What seems to be the most challenging quadrant for many students is that of cultural context (LL). Even if many of the descriptions of how the forces work in the joint-system (UR/LR) are somewhat superficial, this is probably not because the students don't understand it, but because detailed information or laboratory tests have been hard to provide in such a short time.

However, discovering and understanding the relationship between the objective facts of the technology perspectives (UR/LR), and assessing these within a cultural context, seems to be an even bigger challenge. It is crucial for an architect to understand how the language we use (LL) and the way we conceptualize objective facts (UR/LR) consciously and unconsciously implies valuation, moral positions and ideology. This is very evident in the discussion between 'traditionalist' and 'technologist' concerning the different qualities of a handmade and robot-made wood joint. What is 'good' and why it is 'good' is just partly a question of objective, measurable facts. It is also a matter of intersubjective valuation of what is important, of aesthetics, and of the construction of identity. This is exactly where the FQM is very helpful, because it clarifies the nature of this interrelatedness.

Another aspect that shows it takes some time and effort to integrate the way of thinking that the FQM represents is the quality of the graphical abstracts the students were asked to make. All of the graphical abstracts showed general topics and categories related to the four quadrants, rather than visualizing specific and detailed information about the joint system. The potential of the graphical abstract was thus not fulfilled. This, however, is important information for the team of teachers. Since it was the first time this specific task was tried out, the students had no template to use as reference. Next time around, this will be provided, and hopefully the result will be improved. It also informed the team of teachers that even if the students could reflect surprisingly well in written texts about the joint system using the FQM, it perhaps requires a higher level of understanding to extract the most relevant information in a graphical abstract. This makes the graphical abstract even more interesting as a tool for developing understanding of how the FQM works and skills in using it.

Since the architect's role in the design process is clearly not only to take care of the aesthetic aspects, but also to be the one who recombines all the different elements of the building process into an architectural whole, it is important to have tools to deal with such matters of complexity. The FQM provides one such tool, and the students in the course specifically expressed that they saw the benefits of having such a structured way of conducting analyses and discussions. Through the course, they not only improved their technical knowledge of the properties of wood, but they were also able to discuss these matters in a way that is relevant for them as practicing architects.

Connected knowledge

All building processes in a modern society are based on interdisciplinary work. At its best, it is a fluent flow of information, knowledge, creativity and decision-making among competent representatives of the different disciplines. Too often, however, interdisciplinary groups are bothered by misunderstandings and bad communication due to different disciplinary traditions, ways of thinking and interests.

Among the small group of teachers (consisting of one engineer, one architect and one architect/craftsman) that for some years have been developing the master course 'Timberstructures' at NTNU, there is one specific aspect of interdisciplinary work that is crucial for good cooperation. This is the willingness and openness among participants, not only to acknowledge each other's competence, but also to learn and develop some basic knowledge in the different fields. This willingness to dig into and integrate the perspective of another discipline is probably one of the most important elements in transdisciplinary work. If this does not happen, the situation will often be that each member of the group remains in the somewhat simplistic position of thinking that things would be better if only their specific discipline's view was dominant.

This is where the FQM becomes a helpful tool, because its concept is to structure a discussion about a phenomenon around four basic perspectives and that, as isolated perspectives, they all carry potential truths, but only part truths. It is the combination and cross-connection of the quadrants that provides the bigger picture. To learn to use the FQM is to develop competence and a willingness to see things from different points of view. People who have developed this skill to a certain level, in combination with a high level of competence within their field and some basic training in group-work dynamics and self-knowledge, are carriers of what is here meant as 'Connected Knowledge'. These individuals would be very attractive partners in interdisciplinary and transdisciplinary work.

In the discussion about revitalizing the wood joint as part of a new area of timber structures, there is a huge potential for combining knowledge and skills among several professionals, among them architects, engineers, craftsmen and building historians. By using the FQM as a structuring and helping tool in the research, we can ensure that the best of each professional field could together pave the way for new inventions and higher quality production in the field of modern timber-based architecture.

References

Gadamer, H-G, 1975. *Truth and Method*, translated by G. Barden and J. Cummings. London: Sheed and Ward.
Godal, J.B. 2018. Om det å lafte. Fagbokforlaget.
Greve, A. and Nesset, S. (ed.), 1997. *Filosofi i et nordlig landskap*. Universitetsbiblioteket i Tromsøs skriftserie Ravnetrykk nr. 12.
Heidegger, M. 2010. *Being and time: a revised edition of the Stambough translation*, State University of New York, Albany.
Husserl, E. 2013. *Ideas: General Introduction to Pure Phenomenology*. Routledge.
Wilber, K. 2000. *A Brief History of Everything*. Shambala, Boston.
Wilber, K. 2001. *A Theory of Everything*. Shambala, Boston.
Siem, J. 2017. 'The Single-step joint—A traditional carpentry joint with new possibilities'. *International Wood Products Journal*, 8: sup 1, 45–49. Taylor and Francis Group, UK.
Siem, J, Braaten, B.O. and Gilberg, A (ed.), 2018. *Joint Systems: A Collection of Student Essays*. NTNU.

Models 1:100
1:10
1:1

During three workshops in Trondheim, Amsterdam and Vaduz, students of the participating studios made models of structures and details of selected buildings and their own designs. The analytic model stands for different building traditions: the Norwegian wood tradition that goes back to the Vikings, the Dutch wood tradition and its relation with shipbuilding and the urban vernacular of the traditional wooden buildings of the Rhine valley near Liechtenstein. Large scale models were finally used in the design studios in order to transport the knowledge of the previous research phase into the project work of each student and to cultivate the power of hand drawing as a design tool.

The models were essential in helping students to gain insight into the qualities of the façades and the used materials and joints. We came to understand that working at a large scale echoed the difficulties of working with wood as a building material. In the process, we discovered the value of modelmaking as a crafted object unmediated by the computer. The selection underlines the role of drawings and models as instruments of knowledge that fuse the conception and construction of buildings and offers a fundamental insight into the crafting of wooden façades and making a handmade model.

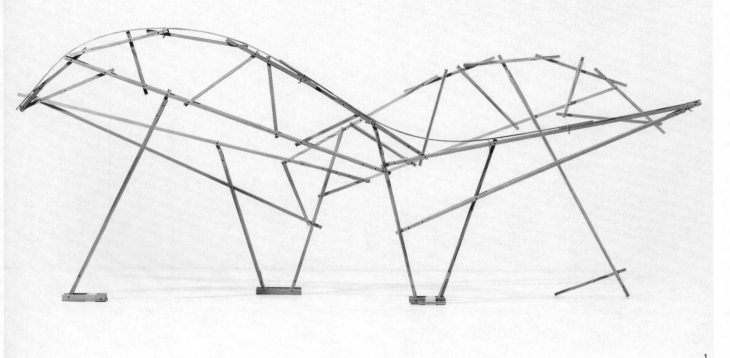

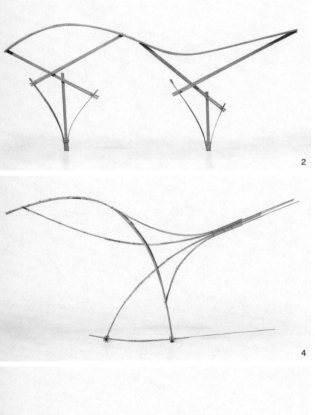

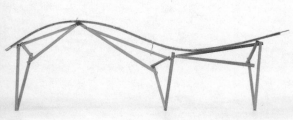

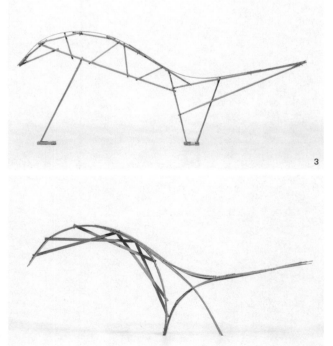

Bell shaped roofs

1	Tom Vermeer, Richard Doensen
2	Daria Dobrodeeva, Charlotte Mulder
3	Tom Vermeer, Richard Doensen
4	Evie Lentjes, Anouk van Deuzen
5	Sung-Ching Lo, German Gomez
6	Laurien Zwaans, Anne-Roos Demilt

Towers

7   Shefket Shala, Anna Prüller, Bertille Bourgarel
8   Danny Kok, Sandra Oeler, Arthur Rundstadler
9   Evie Lentjes, Rikke Jensen, Arno Wust
10 Anne-Roos Demilt, Bunjamin Sulejmani, Alex Escursell

Roof frames

11	David Kerle
12	Jakob Fliri
13	Andreas Negele

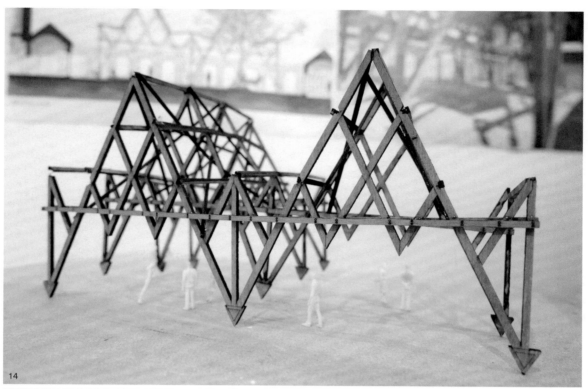

14

15

Roof frames

16

17

18

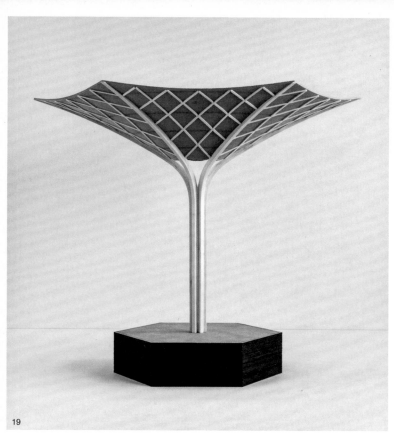

19

20

21

32

22

Towers

23

24

Towers

25

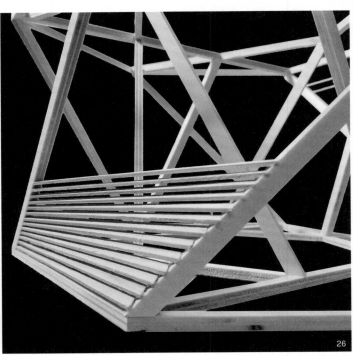

26

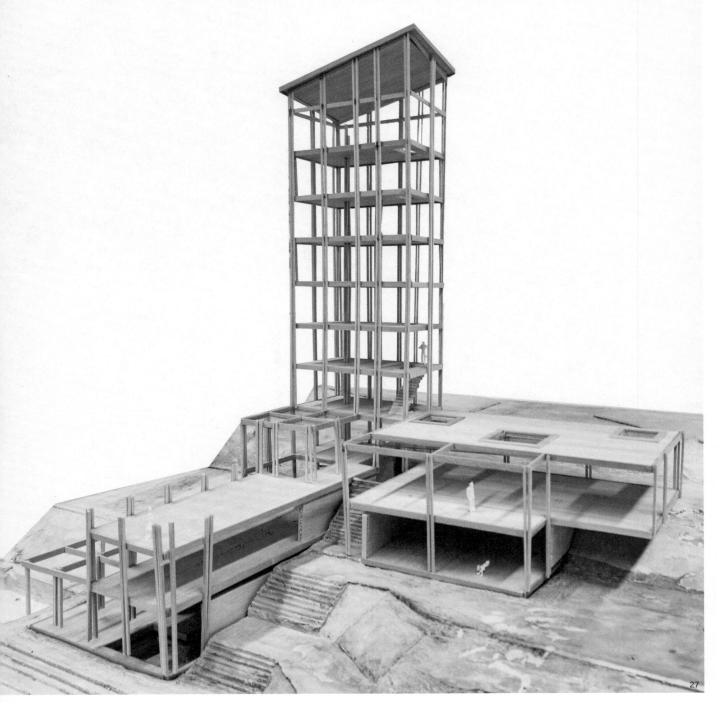

27

28

29

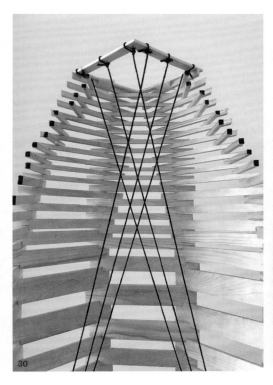

30

31

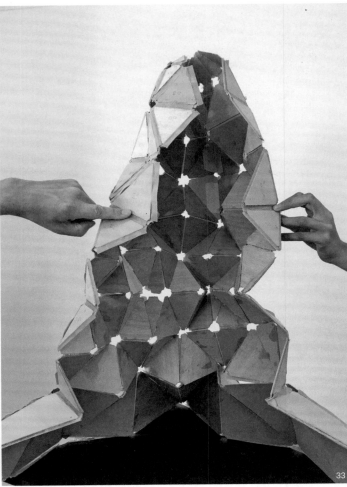

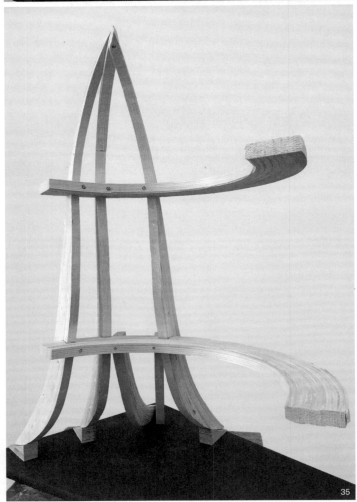

Bell shaped roofs

28–29 Danny Kok, Ayla Azizova
30–31 Anne-Roos Demilt, Charlotte Mulder
32–33 Evie Lentjes, German Gomez
34–35 Noury Salmo, Anna Torres

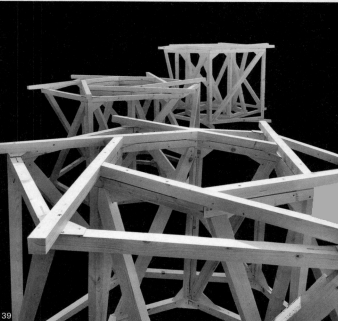

Nodes

36   Gebhard Natter
37   Alex Carrasco Escursell, Gilles Gasser, Luis Martín Cea,
        Iñigo Villanueva Gutiérrez
38–39   Gebhard Natter
40   Final result, Workshop Trondheim, 2018
41–44   1:1 mock-ups of details, Workshop Trondheim, 2018

40

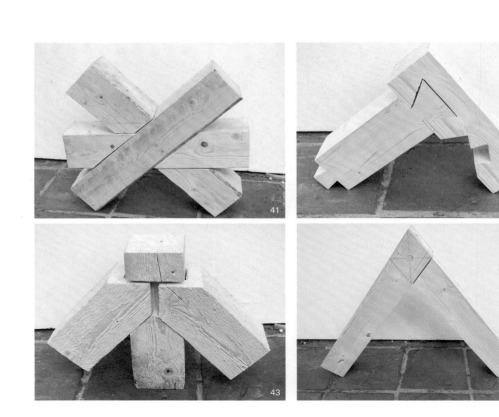

41

42

39

43

44

45

Pedestals

50

51

42

Towers

50   (background) Danny Kok, Sandra Oeler, Arthur Jean-Pierre, Henri Rundstadler, Anne Roos Demilt, Bunjamin Sulejmani, Alex Carrasco Escursell (foreground) Edwin Frei, Bejan Misaghi, Silvia Daniela Doherty Riubrugent, Shefket Shala, Anna Prüller, Bertille Beatrice Agnes Marie Bourgarel
51   German Gomes Rueda, Christian Meier, Ben Quinn, Attila Truffer, Agathe Philippine Cheynet, Iñigo Villanueva Gutiérrez
52   Noury Salmi, Aline Rabea Koger, Esteban Vincent, Roger Borteele, Ayla Azizova, Gebhard Natter, Berenice Lea Marie Aubriot

52

Towers

53–54   Anna Tores, Luis Martín Cea, Mar Gonzalez Campos, Evie Lentjes, Rikke
          Jensen, Arno Léon Oreste, Alfred Wust
55   (foreground) Anna Tores, Luis Martín Cea, Mar Gonzalez Campos, Evie Lentjes,
          Rikke Jensen, Arno Léon Oreste, Alfred Wust
          (background left) Adan Carnak, Júlia Ros Bofarull, Gilles Benjamin Theo Gasser,
          Charlotte Mulder, Maik Goop, Anna Garcia Molina, Pia Weber
          (background right) German Gomes Rueda, Christian Meier, Ben Quinn, Attila
          Truffer, Agathe Philippine Cheynet, Iñigo Villanueva Gutiérrez

56

Towers

56   (foreground) Noury Salmi, Aline Rabea Koger, Esteban Vincent, Roger Borteele,
Ayla Azizova, Gebhard Natter, Berenice Lea Marie Aubriot
(background) Danny Kok, Sandra Oeler, Arthur Jean-Pierre, Henri Rundstadler,
Anne Roos Demilt, Bunjamin Sulejmani, Alex Carrasco Escursell

46

2 TECTONIC REFLECTION

The Age of Timber

Machiel Spaan

During the Wood Symposium held at the Academy of Architecture in Amsterdam, several speakers argued for the use of more timber in construction.

> *Only when one can observe and study a building as part of a larger group of comparable buildings, will one's findings be informed by the bigger picture and thus be more meaningful.*
> (Klaus Zwerger in *Wood and Wood Joints*)

In a distant past we built our houses from wood sawn from the trees of nearby forests, or from trees the rivers carried to us from German and Swiss forests. Architects and carpenters were one with the grain and hardness of all kinds of wood. Woodworking skills were passed on from master to apprentice. In our post-war efforts to rationalize construction, we ended up in a world of concrete. Building traditions, skills and knowledge of wood gradually disappeared; woodworking techniques were no longer developed.

Now that the climate debate is catching up with us, it seems time for a change. Dutch architects advocate the use of much more timber in construction. Timber is made available to us by nature, it stores CO_2, and it provides a healthy indoor climate. In addition, timber structures are easy to assemble and can be dismantled and reused. How practicable is this idea of building with timber to the concrete-loving building sector of the Netherlands? And what is involved in this seemingly simple shift from concrete-oriented to timber-oriented thinking? We will have to renew timber applications and constructions to make them suitable for today's circumstances and regulations. And how can traditional knowledge contribute to this new step towards an 'Age of Timber'? These were the questions that arose during the Wood Symposium held at the Amsterdam Academy of Architecture on Friday 22 November 2019. The four speakers presented four perspectives that gave attendees plenty of food for thought.

During an impressive argument, Klaus Zwerger of the University of Vienna showed that in timber construction, innovation is of all times. It is a consecutive and continuous process that involves adapting to circumstances, improving techniques and availing oneself of new possibilities. Development processes in the Dutch timber construction tradition came to a standstill some 70 years ago. Timber construction and knowledge of structures and connections were no longer passed on to the next generation. Artisans with knowledge of wood properties and joinery are now scarce. Dutch engineers lack the expertise to calculate the efficient complex constructions necessary to create dimensioned and sustainable timber constructions. How can we remaster the necessary knowledge, skills and traditional methods? Is it possible to reintroduce the master-apprentice structure?

In an ecological structure, we use timber in a material-specific way: tensile forces in the direction of the grain, pressure forces perpendicular to the grain. Because of its properties, timber lends itself well to assemblage. Swiss structural engineer Mario Rinke presented

smart and efficient timber constructions that can be assembled as well as disassembled: ingeniously curved trusses composed from slender, tension-loaded slats and a dome construction made of pressure-loaded beams. Bespoke steel joints ensure that the structures are easy to disassemble. Rinke compared them with laminated joists, glued constructions that cannot be disassembled and reused. Wouldn't using the latter mean: creating a new kind of 'timbery' concrete? We can remaster the knowledge of timber assembly and apply it in today's construction technology.

Where do we get our building materials? What is locally available and what can we grow and harvest on the spot? The Zestien Eikenschuur by Hilberink Bosch Architecten in Berlicum is an inspiring example.

It shows that trees can provide many building materials: not only beams and planks in different shapes and sizes, but also residual wood, shingles and bark can be used as building materials. One-third of Dutch forests comprise pine trees for paper production. Two-thirds comprise oak, Douglas fir and larch; the latter two are widely used for construction. If we better manage and diversify Dutch forests we will be able to extract even more and higher-quality local timber. If we earmark wood varieties for the purpose for which they are most suitable, we can handle our stock efficiently and ecologically. This way, dozens of dwellings will grow in the Dutch forests every day. What is the best way to organize this learning process? Who has the space and time to experiment? If we want to innovate, we have to facilitate experimentation. And things may go wrong. Who will take responsibility?

Architect and lecturer August Schmidt presented construction workshops with students from all over Europe in Trondheim. Students learned how to build and design with the material and playfully discovered new ways to stack, connect and span—and learned from each other's traditions. The design and construction of Schmidt's own house are experimental as well. Connections and constructions are tried and tested on the spot. His own house is a laboratory to develop timber detailing and assembly techniques. The coming of the Age of Timber may be a matter of time, but starting it is easier said than done. Innovation requires the remastering of knowledge and skills of the material and its applications. This intrinsic knowledge belongs to the designer and the builder. We have to attune legislation and regulation to its use. Experience shows that it takes more than a decade for rigorous innovations to penetrate the capillaries of the building sector.

Designers, builders, the industry, government and education can join forces to develop a new vocabulary together. Being open to new ideas helps. In Europe, there is a lot of useful knowledge about timber constructions, and this can inspire and accelerate our timber construction transition. In this process, experimentation will play a crucial part. It is at the joinery works, the building site, the architect's self-built house and the experimentation site that we can pass on the craft by hand and discover the future. Not at the drawing board!

Three Projects

51

Sixteen Oak Barn

Berlicum,
The Netherlands
Hilberink Bosch
Architects

Plugged and Stacked

Andelfingen,
Switzerland
Rossetti + Wyss
Architekten

Sponhuset

Trondheim,
Norway
Arkitekt August
Schmidt AS

Sixteen Oak Barn

In 2017, seven century-old oak trees on a farm appeared to be in poor condition. To breathe new life into an old tradition, the architects used the wood from the oaks and traditional timber construction techniques to construct a new shed on the site, where a motley collection of run-down structures needed replacement. Along with nine additional trees, a total of sixteen trees were sawn with a mobile sawmill into beams for the bearing structure and planks for the exterior walls. Beams containing pieces of phloem were processed into slats, while bark and soft sapwood were added to the poured concrete. Short lengths of oak were cut into tiles for the roof.

Chance is an important aspect of the building's aesthetics. It lends the contemporary shed a vibrant appearance in which old and new work wonderfully well together.

Annemariken Hilberink

Berlicum, The Netherlands

Project contributors:
Architect: Hilberink Bosch Architects, Berlicum
Structural engineer: Raadgevend Ingenieursburo van Nunen, Rosmalen
Timber construction: Zandenbouw b.v., Aarle-Rixtel
Photographer: René de Wit, Breda

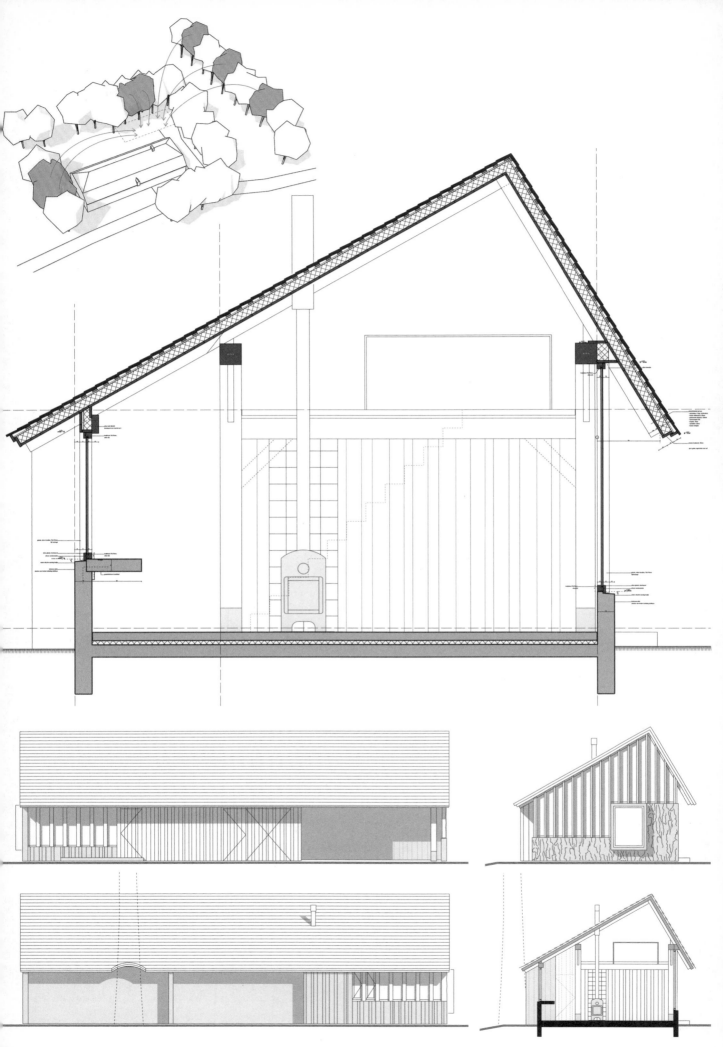

53

Sixteen Oak Barn

Plugged and Stacked:
The Maintenance Depot in Andelfingen as Modern Industrial
Log Construction

Mario Rinke

In 2015 a new maintenance depot for utility vehicles was built in Andelfingen (Canton Zurich, Switzerland). The building is 16.50 metres wide, 30 metres long and 8 metres tall, and was to be constructed in timber. Inspired by the simplicity of a kit of parts, planar components were developed for the roof and walls to integrate both the loadbearing structure and the building envelope, and to facilitate fast and simple assembly. This was possible because of modern industrial fabrication techniques that allow traditional log construction to be transferred to a large-scale industrial building type. The process of stacking and plugging two-metre-high laminated timber components along the length of the entire building, and then slotting the roof beams into the walls and the multilayer boards on top, made it possible to erect the building with just a few additional iron fasteners in just four days. The Glulam wall components are completely straight and can even be used for another building later, embodying the concept of a material bank for future construction cycles. Only through close cooperation between architects, engineers and contractors could such a strong relationship between the materials, construction principles, structure and architectural expression be achieved.

Andelfingen, Switzerland

Project contributors
Architect: Rossetti + Wyss Architekten AG, Zollikon
Structural engineer: Dr. Lüchinger und Meyer Bauingenieure AG, Zurich
Timber construction: Erne AG Holzbau, Stein
Excavation and concrete construction: Landolt + Co. AG, Kleinandelfingen
Glulam components: Hüsser Holzleimbau AG, Bremgarten
Photographer: Jürg Zimmermann, Zürich

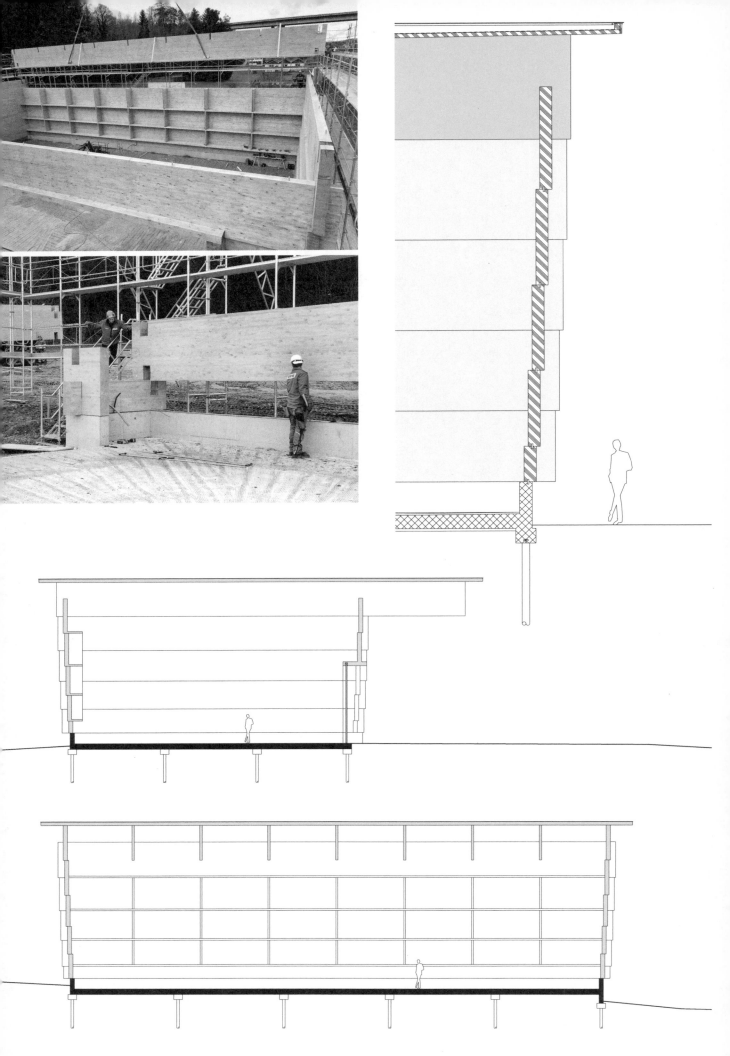

Maintenance Depot

Sponhuset

Dikehaugen 12 is a small one-family house situated among trees on the outskirts of the city of Trondheim, Norway. The complex comprises three saddle-roof volumes (dwelling, sauna and annex), all constructed in timber and clad in pine shingles.

Energy efficient and environmentally sustainable, the house is compact but its flexible floor plan creates plenty of living space. Natural materials allow the sturdy construction to breathe. The low-maintenance building includes unpainted exterior surfaces that can age with the weather and untreated indoor surfaces that do not require surface treatment. The distinctive design and layout of the volumes allows the complex to blend into the natural surroundings.

Made of timber, plant-based and recyclable materials, the house features simple and sound solutions, and its clear architecture is designed to ensure a long lifespan. Heated floor space is limited, and there is more unheated multi-purpose space to provide plenty of flexibility and facilitate activities during snowy winters and wet summers. The building binds CO_2 in its construction. At the end of its lifespan, the building will produce a minimum of non-recyclable waste.

August Schmidt

Trondheim, Norway

Project contributors:
Architect: Arkitekt August Schmidt AS, Trondheim
Structural engineer: Dipl. Ing. August Schmidt
Timber construction: Artic Nord Bygg AS
Photographer: Pasi Alto

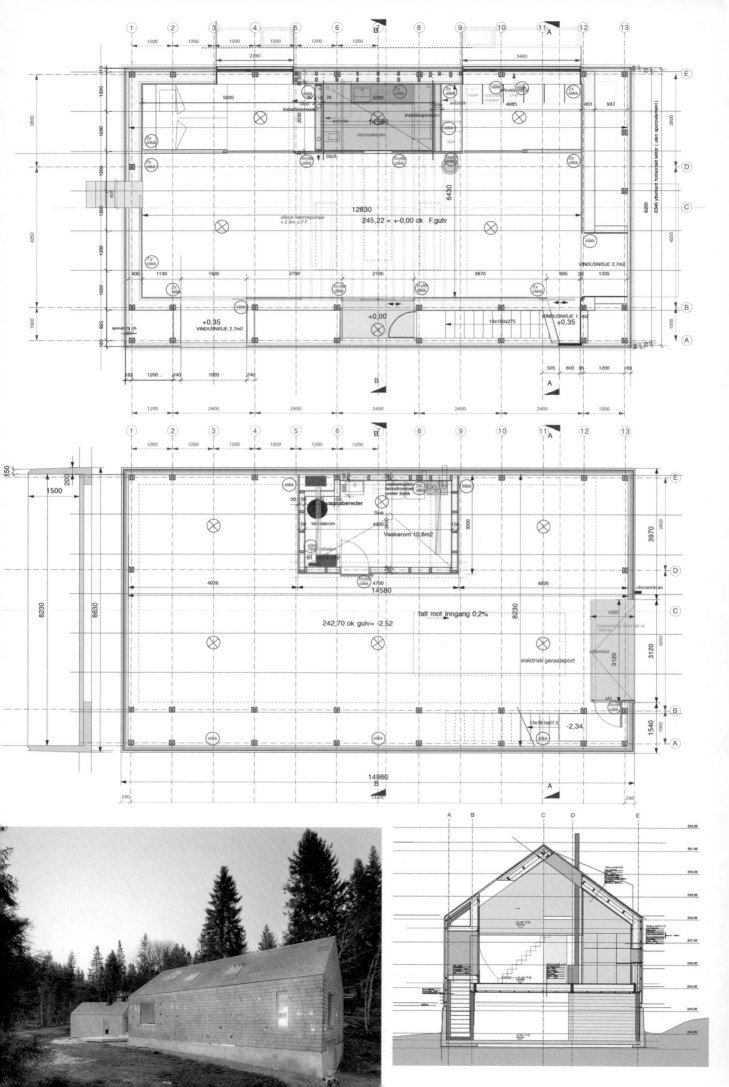

Sponhuset

Evolution of the Wood Joint: 'How Did Tradition Stimulate Innovation in Historic Wood Architecture?'

Klaus Zwerger

Summary of lecture by
Klaus Zwerger at the Amsterdam
Academy of Architecture
on 22 November 2019,
by Machiel Spaan

'Can tradition stimulate innovation?' Klaus Zwerger answered this question with a resounding yes. To him it isn't even a question; it's a given. He immediately posed a follow-up question: 'How did tradition stimulate innovation in historic wood architecture?' A professor at the Faculty of Architecture and Design at the University of Technology in Vienna, Zwerger is an expert on the development of historical wood architecture. He has documented in words and images countless examples of timber structures encountered on his travels and categorized them according to theme and development. A selection of his discoveries can be found in his publication *Wood and Wood Joints*.

Making something without any basis in knowledge that has been passed down is simply leaving things to chance, said Zwerger. There is little chance it will result in successful innovation. Developing tradition further on the basis of trial and error leads to progress much more often. Zwerger cited in this context the American sociologist Edward Shils: 'The tradition of empirical knowledge embraced both the knowledge of how to adapt an inherited model of a tool or a machine so that it would be appropriate to the better performance of recurrently given tasks and the knowledge of how to use the tool efficiently.'[1]

Zwerger continued his introduction more quotes from Shils: 'Mastery of traditional empirical knowledge is [...] capable [...] of becoming detached from the tradition through efforts to see how work could be done more efficiently.'[2] And importantly: 'It is the tradition which permits the discernment of the opening to invention.' According to the English architects and researchers Robert Brown and Daniel Maudlin, we can discuss the development of historical wood architecture from the angle of the value of tradition 'as a creative, adaptive and reflective process within modernity.'[3]

The palisade wall

The first image that Klaus Zwerger showed was a drawing of a palisade like that built by Roman soldiers to defend their strongholds. Such walls were strong but temporary, because they derived their strength from the resistance of the piles driven into the ground, which rotted away over time. It took some time before a better solution was devised, because traditional ways of working and construction methods did not change without a reason. It wasn't easy to convince a builder or craftsman to adapt their way of working. Often, a tradition was only revised if external conditions forced a reassessment. For example, if changing climate conditions or material scarcity forced people to reconsider the use of materials. Or if the social development from an agrarian society to a society of employees changed the requirements for living and working conditions. Farmers used their houses in a very different way to people who leave home in the morning and return in the afternoon to eat, watch television and go to sleep. Even today, when we spend a lot of time in front of the computer, new conditions are imposing themselves: interior spaces are better insulated and sealed off from

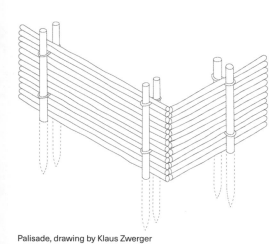

Palisade, drawing by Klaus Zwerger

1   Shils, Edward. 1981. 'Tradition.' The University of Chicago Press.
2   Ibid.
3   Brown, Robert and Maudlin, Daniel. 2012. 'Concepts of Vernacular Architecture.' In *The Sage Handbook of Architectural Theory*, edited by Greig Crysler, et al., 340–354. Los Angeles, et al.: Sage Publications.

the world outside. This leads to new timber construction techniques and details.

Innovating is not a recent phenomenon. Ever since the palisade, timber construction has undergone extraordinary development. Conditions have continually led to modifications and improvements to construction methods and details. During his lecture Zwerger presented ten examples to demonstrate that innovation is anything but a contemporary phenomenon. Quite the contrary, it has a long tradition.

1   Corner joints

A sturdy corner makes a house so secure that it can be raised off the ground, supported by stone foundations. Over time and in response to local conditions, woodworkers developed methods to prevent beams from sliding out of position and to protect their ends from the weather. Various dovetail joints (through, half-blind, secret and overlapped dovetails) demonstrate the inventiveness of the maker, each in its own way.

iu, Romania

Molzegg, Austria

2   Pagan support pincer and sword

The triangular facade plane beneath the pitched roof above the log structure does not stay upright all by itself. Craftsmen developed details to keep the beams in position. Several pincer constructions are clearly visible. A sort of sword driven vertically through all beams forms part of the triangular facade plane, thus ensuring stability almost invisibly.

henbach, Switzerland

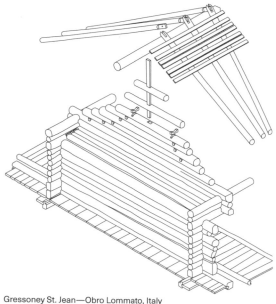

Gressoney St. Jean—Obro Lommato, Italy

3   Round shapes

When it comes to log construction we usually think of rectilinear shapes. But curved walls and roofs on timber sheds and chapels can also be functional and lend such buildings additional structural stability. Turning each successive beam slightly inwards results in a curved roof shape that makes a structure much stronger and more stable.

Nadasa, Romania

Ulucz, Poland

4   Columns of stacked wood

The walls of log buildings are limited in length owing to the maximum length and stability of available wood. Stability was achieved by placing cross-walls perpendicular to the outer wall, but these sometimes stood in the way. So smart woodworkers came up with hollow columns made of stacked wooden beams. These columns ensure stability, strengthen the walls close to the roof edge and strengthen and protect the logs joined lengthways. In churches they served as significant supports to dissipate the roof load.

Pihjalavesi, Finland

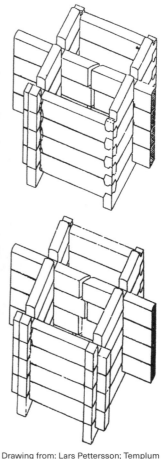

Drawing from: Lars Pettersson; Templum Saloense; Helsinke 1987: fig. 261–3, 4.

66

5 Forked columns

Placing the house on columns lifts it clear of the ground, protects it against water and vermin, and allows the floor structure to dry fully. But such 'pillars' also make a structure vulnerable; if one of them fails or collapses, the house will also collapse. Woodworkers devised forked columns to prevent them from sliding and, at the same time, strengthen the base layers of the structure.

jiazui, China

Stübing, Austria

6 Anchor beams

The growth of urban populations also increased the need for taller buildings. Longer beams allowed for the construction of houses with multiple floors after carpenters had introduced anchor beams. Long beams facilitated their construction, specifically their reinforcement. But irregular bracing determined the position of wall openings and impaired the appearance of facades.

uedlinburg, Germany

Marburg, Germany

7 Frame construction

As wood for construction becomes scarcer, declines in quality or decreases in dimensions, traditional methods of construction no longer suffice. The one-storey frame structure designed in response to these limitations offers a number of advantages. A different window arrangement can be made on each floor, and floors can be stacked in a staggered manner to create cantilevered volumes.

Rothenburg, Germany

Markgröningen, Germany

8 Hammer beam roof

A scarcity of materials also leads to innovative roof structures. An example is the 'hammer beam' roof, consisting of a number of short beams. By constructing the roof structure out of a series of rigid triangles, builders could achieve a relatively large span without depending on tie beams that require long and straight material. For the proper execution, skilled woodworkers were needed. Decoratively executed details visibly expressed an appreciation of churches and other representative buildings.

Woolpit, England

Tarrant Crawford, England

9 Hanging pillar

The need for large column-free spaces increased with large buildings for large numbers of people. To avoid the use of columns in spaces, all sorts of smart structures were devised to divert the forces acting on the central part of the truss to the walls rather than vertically downwards. The search ultimately led to a beam structure that distributes the forces to the eaves' walls directly or via the inclined roof-shaping structural members. This 'hanging pillar' ingeniously disburdens the previously heavily burdened horizontal beams.

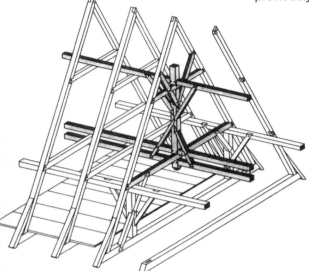

Image from: Albrecht und Konrad Bedal; Dachstühle im Hofer Land vor 1650; in: Beiträge zur Hausforschung I, 1975: 126–173.

Égreville, France

10 Natural protection

Protecting the timber structure of buildings from the weathering effects of the sun, rain and snow extends their lifespan. That can be achieved with cladding, conventionally using boards and shingles, or using greenery. The leaves of espaliers planted in front of the facade offer protection from both the rain and sun. Green facades also produce oxygen and create microclimatic cooling.

Eidsborg, Norway

Lupitsch, Austria

Timberdutch! Considering Dutch 'Conceptional Wood'

Tibor Joanelly

Mind the gaps! Not so long ago, the Franco-Swiss architects Bakker & Blanc refurbished a huge old barn in the picturesque valley of the River Saane in Fribourg, lying at the foot of the medieval town. Since the 16th century the barn has been called Le Werkhof, a designation that carries meanings of necessity, bustle and skill in its name. The barn was erected for the production of boats, and after a devastating fire some years ago, the architects launched a concept for its reconstruction, mainly based on references to ships and shipyards.

The story behind that story is simple: Fribourg, in the 16th century, was well known for the production of wood for construction, mainly from oaks and beech trees, some of which was even shipped to the Netherlands. There the wood was processed for the housing and shipping 'industry' of the time. The geographic gap between the hilly heart of Switzerland and the plains of Holland was closed with the simple force of water and difference in altitude.

Talking today about the past and future of timber construction and the hopes that it implies—hopes that are guided towards a sustainable use of resources—seems to unravel a whole bunch of gaps. There are gaps between places of cultivation, processing, manufacturing and the use of wood or timber products for the building industry. There even are gaps to be acknowledged between industry and craftsmanship in general and between engineering calculation methods and traditionally transmitted knowledge in particular, which give rise, among other issues, to problems around the provision of warranties. More than that, there are gaps to be found between different modes of thinking, between tacit knowledge and conceptual thinking—and also between academia and practice. If they were not enough, there are, besides an apparent gap between past and present, gaps to be discerned between good examples and the large mass, between rural areas, and between small buildings and large estate development. And on and on.

It may be worth staying a bit longer with history. Amsterdam, the brick city par excellence was, at least until the 15th century, constructed in timber. Some brick facades within the inner ring today are, in fact, only facades covering a timber structure. Brick was introduced after large fires 1421 and 1452, but some buildings were only masked—a detail that can be verified by finding facades where upper stories project, because that is only made possible with an underlying traditional timber structure.

These remnants seem to tell us a lot about the proverbial Dutch pragmatism. They also tell us a lot about the conceptual possibilities of composite constructions that are able to serve different masters. And they explain how timber constructions could convincingly find their way back into dense cities, at least in terms of architectural expression.

Of course, this would need some further gaps to be bridged. In doing so, one has to start with a new assessment of fire regulations, as was successfully undertaken in Switzerland in 2015. The new regulations propelled innovation in the timber construction industry. Another area of assessment is the development of reliable calculation

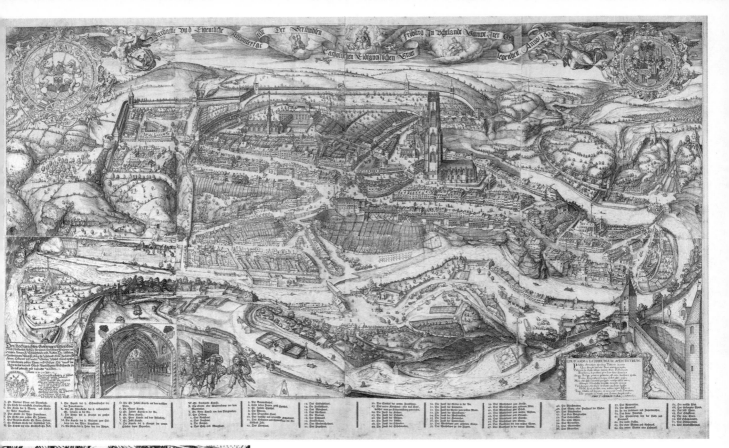

Figure 1
Le Werkhof in Fribourg/Switzerland, a barn from 1555 where boats
were built to transport timber downstream.
a   *Martiniplan*, Martin Martini, 1606
b   Detail
Picture credits: Courtesy of Musée d'art et d'histoire Fribourg

models that allow for more efficient structures, since the financial aspect implicated here is crucial for a broader proliferation of timber construction systems. It seems that the notion of efficiency is something that is promising for both stimulating new technologies and fulfilling the thrifty and therefore sustainable use of such systems.

Efficiency is not something that has been only requested for the benefit of investors. Another look at history—or tradition if you want to call it that—makes this obvious. But the historic perspective also has its pitfalls. The Grubenmann family in Switzerland had acquired a knowledge of wide-span timber structures that allowed them to use similar structures to bridge valleys as well as large spaces for churches. Their implicit knowledge led in the 18th century to spans of more than 60 metres or 36 × 21 metres respectively—without the type of calculations that would be required today!

Unfortunately, the Grubenmanns were unable to offer proof in terms of scientific knowledge, and so they were no longer allowed to build. For today, it would be interesting if it were possible to develop state-of-the-art calculation models for timber structures that are easy to apply and bolster intuition—and could also provide structural proof.

Viewed conceptually, composite structures like those we find in some old Amsterdam houses have the potential to bridge another gap that has already been mentioned: the gap between city and countryside. Building in a dense environment calls for different construction systems, not only due to fire regulations or height, but also due to standards, regulations, costs, comfort and the like.

Even under the paradigm of sustainability, building in the countryside implies detached houses, or at least settlements with only a few storeys to provide forms of privacy or spaces that accommodate different needs from those in the city. And it also implies a different metabolism of construction materials. Besides the fact that most people still live outside cities, for instance in Norway, building in the countryside engenders different construction systems as well as different solutions regarding the adaptability or reuse of structures. Timber, in any case, can provide fruitful solutions—or to put it differently: there is no ideal and generalizable construction technique.

Of course, bridging the gap between good will and reality is no easy task. And it doesn't happen by itself. Let us return to Fribourg. Not long ago the canton and state of Fribourg launched an architectural competition for a police administration building. One of the constraints that the architects had to respect was the use of the state's own wood.

Figure 2
'Tara-Space' at Le Werkhof in Fribourg/Switzerland, representing the shipping and trade connection to the Netherlands. Some remains of the old oak structure are still visible. Photo: Bakker Blanc architects, Marco Bakker

Figure 3
The material of the wooden structure for the administration building of the cantonal police in Fribourg by Deillon Dellay Architects was obtained from the communal forests. Photo: Mélanie Rouiller

(It should to be noted that many communities in Switzerland still hold their own wood resources.) The winning and now realized project is an interesting concept with a completely timber internal structure and an aluminium shell that is reminiscent of car bodywork, perhaps because the plot is situated between highways and car infrastructure.

Stimulating the use of wood requires subsidies and even state pressure. One good example is Norway, where wood technology was pushed by the government in the lead-up to the 1994 Winter Olympics.

And in the Netherlands? In December 2019 the Dutch Supreme Court upheld the decision by a lower court that forced the government to reduce CO_2 by 2020 at a rate of 25% compared to 1990. Such efforts may not happen without courageous changes in the building industry and without legal compulsion.

Without going too much into sociological or philosophical details, change is only possible if structures are bound not too tightly. Or to put it differently, there has to be, in every relationship, be it human or among things or even between notions, a certain degree of freedom to allow for the unexpected to occur, to allow for surprise. And here, of course, the gap plays a crucial role. A gap exactly marks that field of underdetermination and uncertainty where new things can occur and change is possible. Gaps should therefore not be bridged too firmly. In relation to the above discussion, it becomes clear that solutions may well be situated between construed oppositions, such as tradition and modernity, academia and practice, or city and countryside. Mediators can develop enormous efficiency.

Historically, 'Superdutch' was such a mediator. The now widely discredited architectural 'style'—or better, the attitude towards architecture implied by the term—can be seen as an attempt to bridge architecture's aim for autonomous expression and the realities of neoliberal policies and markets in the 1990s. The 'closing of the gap' was made possible by raising conceptual thought to the realm of architecture, striving for a strong assertiveness of architectural ideas.

But we all know about the affirmative outcomes of this experiment—and about the aesthetic, economic and political consequences such as arbitrariness, massification and populism that paralleled architecture as it framed unbridled growth. So, maybe 'Superdutch' really has lost credibility. But what about reconnecting to the spirit of the 1990s? What about combining Dutch conceptual thinking with what has been set up by craftsmen in remote Swiss valleys and Norwegian fjords? I would like to propose here a new 'thing-in-between-the-gaps': Why not talk about 'Timberdutch'?

The Ecology of Timber Construction

Cathrine Johansen Haanes
and Haakon Haanes,
Nøysom arkitekter

The renewed relevance of timber

Building with timber is increasingly becoming the new standard for sustainable architecture, and not without merit. As a building material, timber has lots of qualities that mark it out from its competitors.

Timber is a renewable material, when harvested sustainably. In Norway, for example, productive forests are growing faster than they are being cut down. In 2017, numbers from the Norwegian Institute of Bioeconomy Research (NIBIO) showed that the volume of Norwegian forests has tripled since the 1920s, and the forests are growing twice as fast.[1] There are several reasons for this, such as the regrowth of traditional cultural landscapes, longer growing seasons due to climate change, and more intensive forestry.

Timber is a climate-friendly material when used locally. As trees grow, they capture CO_2, which is then stored in building materials made from wood. When timber is compared to other building materials, this stored CO_2 is often counted. In addition, wood is soft and malleable, and normally does not need much energy to process into building materials.

Timber has benefits for indoor climate. The internal structure of wood allows for moisture to pass through its body, which evens out temperature and relative humidity levels. Its complex structure creates a good acoustic environment, and the visual, tactile and olfactory qualities of wood provide a subjective feeling of comfort and warmth.

Finally, wood has properties that make it easier to recycle or reuse than many other materials. It can be downcycled as bioenergy or components for fibre boards or other composite products, or preferably, it can be reused directly.

All these qualities make wood from local forests that are managed and harvested properly the obvious champion of sustainable building materials by today's standards.

However, from an ecological perspective, most of the qualities noted above have less to do with the actual sustainability of timber as a material than with its role in minimizing a building's negative environmental impact. Being a renewable material with less negative impact on global warming, and with fewer human health and ecological disruptions than its competitors, does not make wood a sustainable building material in itself.

To go deeper into the sustainability of timber as an architectural building material, we have to go into the ecology of timber construction.

The ecological benefits of building with wood

From an ecological perspective, sustainable development can be defined as 'the goal of fostering adaptive capacity and creating opportunities'[2]. The study of interrelationships in nature teaches us that the capacity to adapt to changing circumstances and create opportunities is crucial to healthy ecosystems, and a rich and diverse nature. Human beings are part of nature, and have adapted to nearly every climate on

1 Dalen, Lars Sandved (2017, 28. Aug) Nye rekordtall for skogen i Norge. From https://www.nibio.no/nyheter/nye-rekordtall-for-skogen-i-norge)
2 Holling, C.S. (2001) Understanding the Complexity of Economic, Ecological and Social Systems. From https://link.springer.com/article/10.1007/s10021-001-0101-5

earth, but we seldom think about how we are reorganizing our contemporary environments to increase or decrease our ability to continue to adapt and create opportunities.

Looking at the tradition of timber construction, we can see that wood as a material has been a central building block of human adaptation to a diverse range of circumstances. This is due to qualities of wood that are seldom mentioned in a sustainability context; the simplicity, versatility and understandability of timber as a building material.

Wood is simple in that it follows the logic of all carbon-based life forms. The wood we use is dead, but it still needs to breathe and move, or it will rot, twist, turn and disintegrate. You can cut through it using simple tools, but so can insects and rodents. Many species have evolved a capability to digest wood, and if the living conditions are right it will be home to life forms like fungi and bacteria. It will burn if you set fire to it. It will change colour if exposed in the sun. All these qualities are often seen as a problem with wood, but they have been predictable and understandable for humans through the ages. As a life form adapted to its different environments over millions of years, trees and wood are an integral part of many ecosystems, and for better and worse, they always have a role to play.

The versatility of wood is also due to many of the properties listed above. Modern humans have marvelled at how enormous structures of stone and marble have been erected without the technology we have today, but few have done the same with wooden structures. A tree can be processed into building materials using only manual labour and simple tools. It can be transported easily, as it floats on water and glides on the snow. Wood as a building material is strong, but weighs little. It can be combined in a variety of ways, from carefully constructed joints to crude nails hammered into it. Untreated wood is not particularly (though wood dust can be carcinogenic) harmful to work with, neither for you nor for other living organisms. Different species of trees, and the different parts that make up trees, provide a variety of benefits to constructions and buildings, and traditional knowledge of timber construction has found uses for most varieties.

The result of the simplicity and versatility of timber is its inherent understandability as a building material. One of the oldest building materials we have, timber has been shaped into a variety of forms for various purposes. Logs have been stacked on top of each other, sticks have been lashed together, and columns, beams, joints and other components have been shaped, formed and combined into a multitude of structures that can be used and reused in a variety of ways, inspiring creativity and embracing the unexpected. The traditional and intuitive understanding of timber as a building material has made it the material of choice where trees grow, sparking artistic, inventive, useful and robust architecture. When it comes to sustainability in an ecological perspective, this is the greatest merit of timber as a building material.

The complexity of modern building materials

The evolution of timber structures based on material availability, tradition and creativity, is long and rich, but at some point it changed its course, leading to the way we often build with timber today. The question is whether many of the qualities that made traditional timber structures sustainable have been lost in the process.

There has always been a conflict between the natural qualities of timber and our need for a controlled environment, but in recent decades our ability to change the properties of timber has increased greatly. When constructed correctly and with high-quality timber, structures can be left untreated without adverse effects. This was the norm in countries like Norway up until the 19th century.[3] Timber can also be treated in ways that preserve its inherent qualities, such as the ability to transport humidity. But for the sake of ease and economy, a wide variety of synthetic treatments have been invented to alter the natural qualities of timber, transforming it into something else. Timber treatments to avoid susceptibility to fire, rot, insects, bacteria and fungi and discolouration have environmental impacts that go beyond altering its properties. Naturally, most substances that prevent timber from

transporting water through its cells, being eaten by bacteria or fungi, or catching fire, are harmful to nature and people.

Timber as a building material also has natural limitations when it comes to structural strength and durability, and the quality of wood differs within a single tree, between individual trees, and between species. As wood increasingly became a commodity, the ability to grow fast, providing steady and reliable income, became the favoured property of trees. With the decline in our understanding of which trees, and parts of trees, were best suited for different purposes, the evolution of timber construction became a matter of finding ways to use trees that grew fast in large plantations, like spruce. As a result, a range of complex composite materials have been invented, partly by physical reorganizing the material and partly by adding products like glues, bitumen, cement, metals and plastic films to the mix. Many of these materials are harmful to the environment and/or energy intensive in their production.[4]

One of the main challenges in contemporary architecture is that neither users nor specialists, like architects, really understand what new buildings are made of. A timber building, for example, is not always what it seems. A study by the VTT Technical Research Centre in Finland, referred to in Lars-Erik Mattila's article 'Reclaiming expertise' in *The Finnish Architectural Review*[5], claims that the timber content in new timber structures in Finland is only 16–32 per cent. The jungle of composite materials is not made easier to navigate by the fact that product names have replaced the names of materials, and that the architectural design process, more often than not, revolves around choosing products from a catalogue or computer database, and importing them directly into a building information model. The model contains all the specifications of the materials, making the architect's job easy, but that makes it difficult to understand the ecological impact of the building they have designed. The sticker 'wood' attached to a variety of composite materials becomes a trap for both professionals and laymen, alienating us from our built environment.

From building blocks of innovation to specialized elements

Another major development in modern timber construction is the rise of prefabricated components. Until recently, the versatility of timber structures had been preserved with modern innovations, at least in Norway and other parts of the world where timber frameworks have been, and still are, the most common way to build small buildings. Modern stud-frame construction can be seen as the pinnacle of this development, with the sawn planks available at every building store providing versatile building blocks for an ingenious, simple and economic construction system that stimulates creativity and problem solving for architects, carpenters and self-builders.

The versatility of the stud frame makes it ideal for self-building, which has been a common way to build homes in Scandinavia as a result of municipal schemes and individual efforts. It wasn't until after the Second World War that self-building stopped being a tool for providing affordable housing. Concrete and steel became the materials of choice for mass housing in cities, and industrial construction methods and eventually prefabrication gradually became the norm for efficient building. For many people, this efficiency and ability to stack hundreds of people on top of one another in itself is synonymous with sustainability.

When the timber industry discovered that it could produce cross-laminated glued components that could combat reinforced concrete, it was perhaps rightly seen as a revolution in timber construction. A revolution that is still gathering steam, under the pragmatic call to descrease the environmental impact of the building industry. However, in the process the versatility of timber as a building material seems to have been abandoned. Huge prefabricated elements constructed in a factory can carry heavy loads, providing the opportunity to build towers of timber, but the timber used is highly specialized in its function, and almost impossible to reuse. In its current form, it can compete with concrete, but only by becoming like it.

3 Berge, Bjørn (2001): *The Ecology of Building Materials* (English Edition) Architectural Press, p. 434
4 See for example Berge, Bjørn (2001): *The Ecology of Building Materials* (English Edition) Architectural Press
5 Mattila, Lars-Erik (2019): Reclaiming Expertise. *Arkkitehti / Finnish Archietctural Review 5–2019*

A call for an ecological approach to timber construction

The evolution of timber construction is not over. We need to reinvent contemporary timber construction to make it simple, versatile and understandable again. In an ecological perspective, without these qualities, timber materials will not continue to be the sustainable building blocks for innovation they once were. In a world that is increasingly turning to smart technology to solve our adaptation, too often we forget that we are also smart and adaptable. Timber is traditionally a material that takes our intelligence seriously and facilitates the creative adaptation of our environment through simple structures. Whether through the rediscovery and renewed appreciation of the genius of existing methods of timber construction, or through new ways of adapting traditional techniques of timber construction to new challenges and new settings, the future will show whether we can reinvent contemporary timber construction in a way that conserves the ecological qualities of building with timber.

3 TWELVE WOOD STRUCTURES

Studios

Rock Art at Leirfall

02.2018–06.2018
Stjørdal,
Norway

Alpine Towers

02.2019–06.2019
Schaan,
Liechtenstein

University of the Crafts

02.2020–08.2020
Landgraaf,
The Netherlands

All participating students worked on the same topic in our design studios. Each of the three project partners was responsible for the content and organization of one design task, which was then carried out jointly. By choosing wood as the main material, we clearly focused on regional traditions of timber construction in the three countries. Each country developed its own traditions, crafts and sources that shaped local building methods and specific details. In addition, the sites and topics relate to specific tasks in the three countries. The integrated workshop with a hands-on component enriched the studio projects. The collaboration with lecturers from the three participating universities in the fields of design, construction and structural engineering deepened the studios and offered a wide range of knowledge and experience throughout the whole project.

Leirfall in Stjørdal is one of the biggest rock art sites in Norway. There are several groups of carvings on the site, and the largest group is on a rock surface about 22 by 20 metres in area. The carvings mainly date from the late Bronze Age (1800–400 BC in Norway) and consist of geometrical patterns and the representation of footprints and boats. Most well-known, however, is the procession of thirteen human figures arranged in a line. At the head of the procession, a much larger male figure with a pointy face seems to hold a sword. Two of the figures in the procession are carrying something between them. This procession is unique in rock carving sites in Norway, and probably depicts some kind of ritual. The site is a steep slope at the northern edge of a cultivated field, where you arrive from the flat river valley. It is open to the public and guides can be arranged on a daily basis during the summer months. From October to May the rock surface is covered with thick carpets to protect the carvings.

The rock carvings were discovered in the early 19th century and are already showing signs of erosion and damage. If they are not physically protected, they will disappear within a relatively short time. The assignment was to design a timber structure that provides shelter for the rock art at Leirfald III.

02.2018–06.2018
Stjørdal, Norway

Vingene

Rock Art at Leirfall   Constantin Frommelt

Vingene

Rock Art at Leirfall   Constantin Frommelt

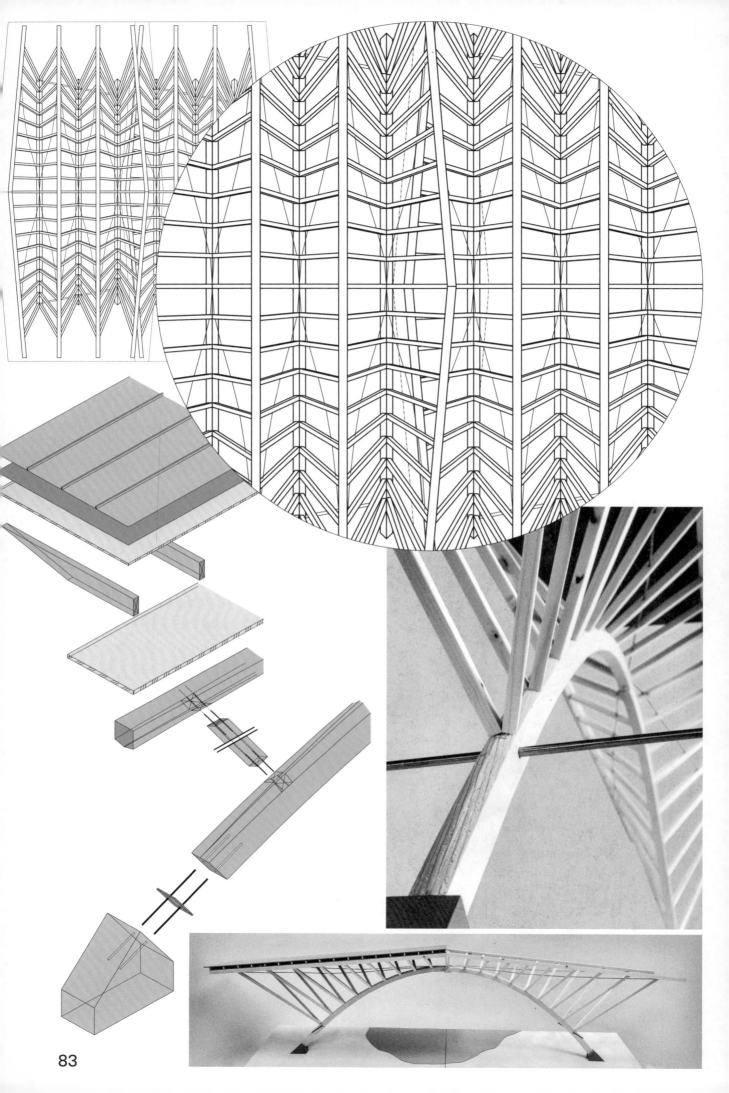

83

Felsenshelter

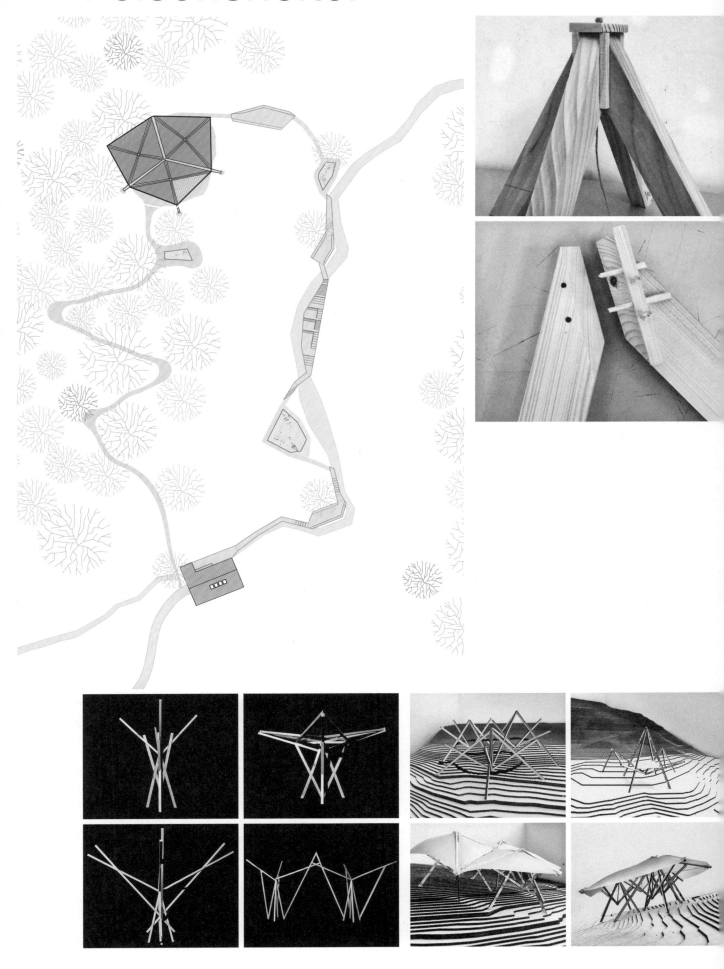

Rock Art at Leirfall   Julia Mair

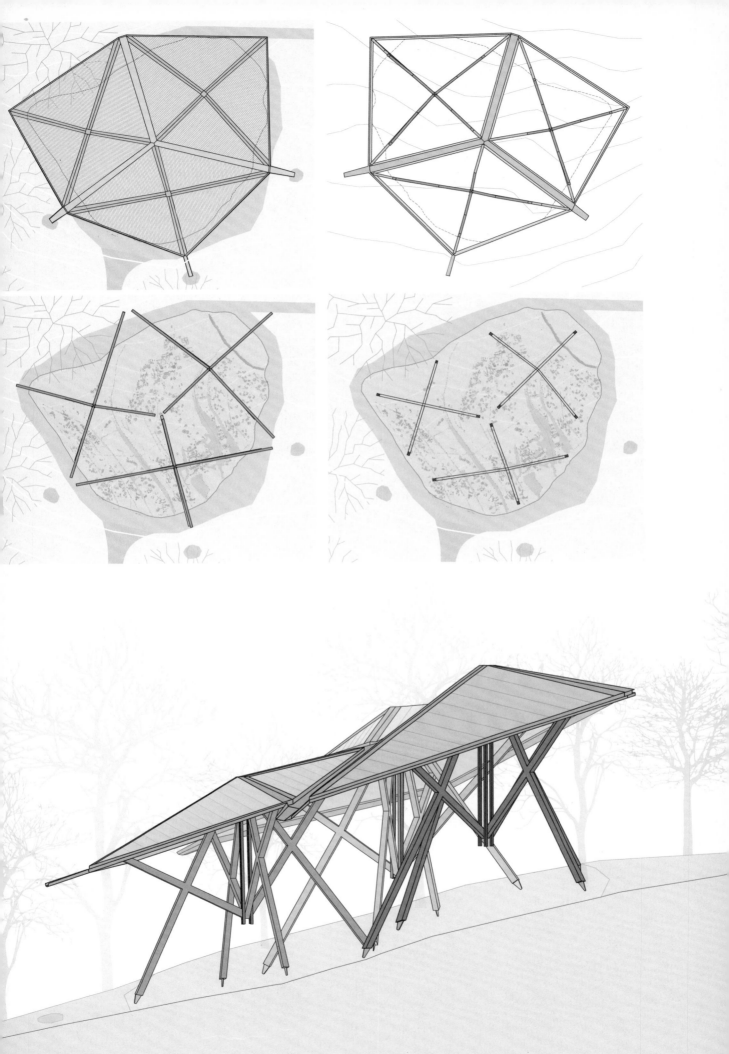

Felsenshelter

Rock Art Shelter

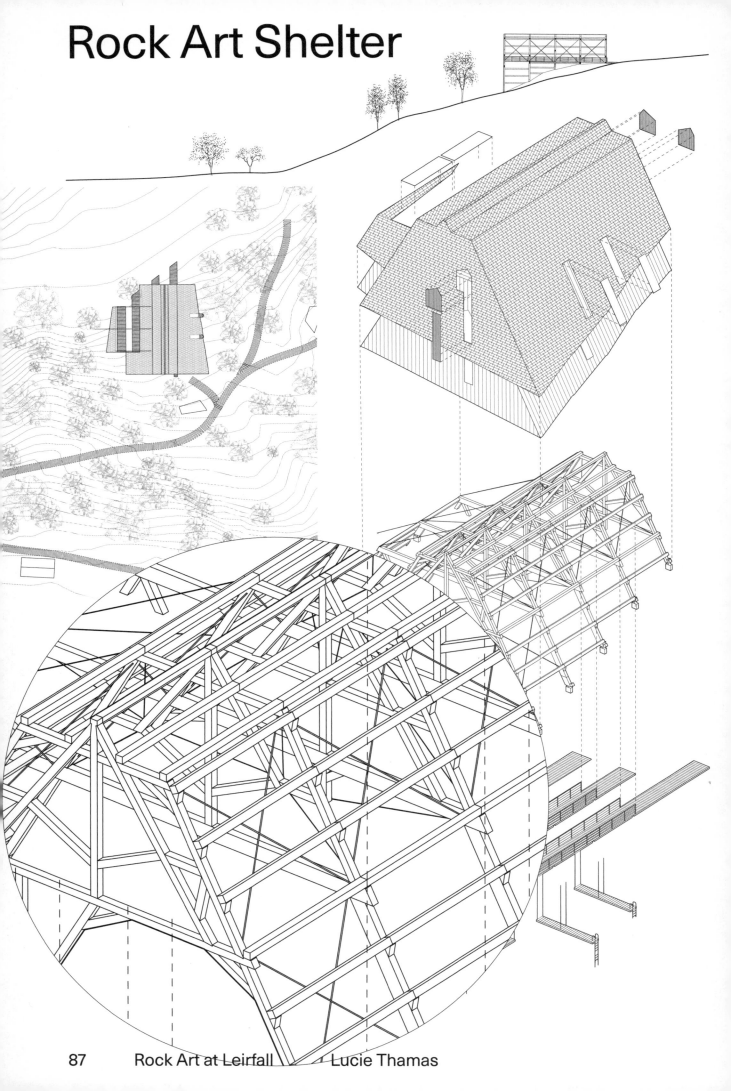

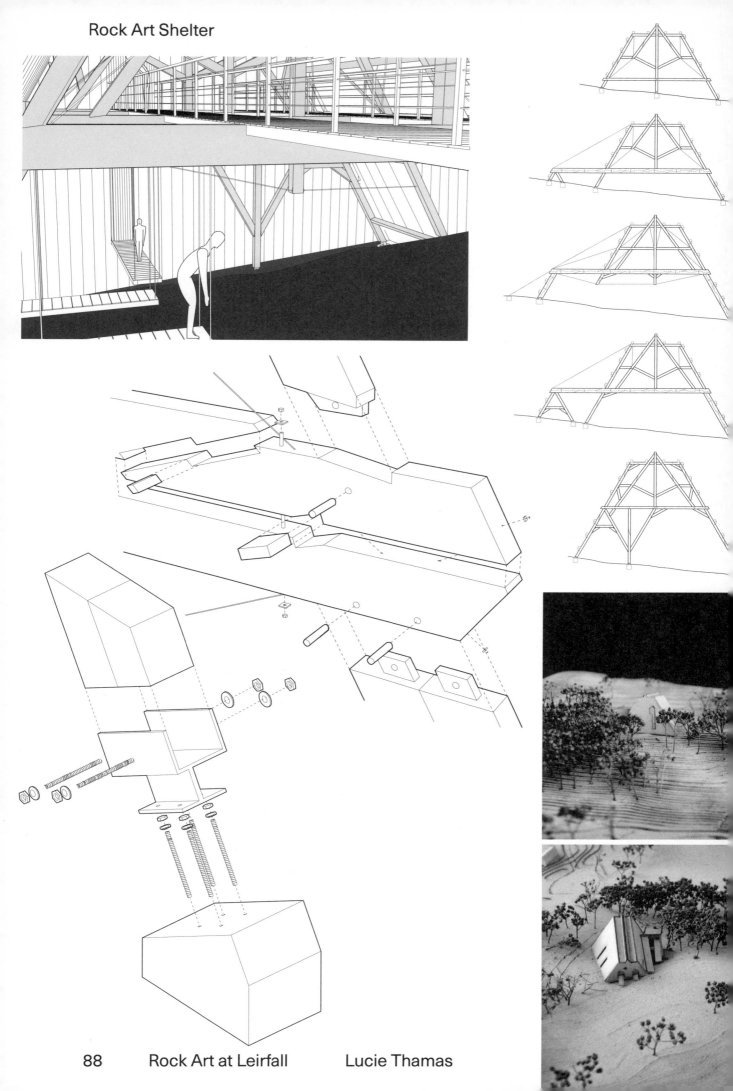

Rock Art Shelter

Rock Art at Leirfall   Lucie Thamas

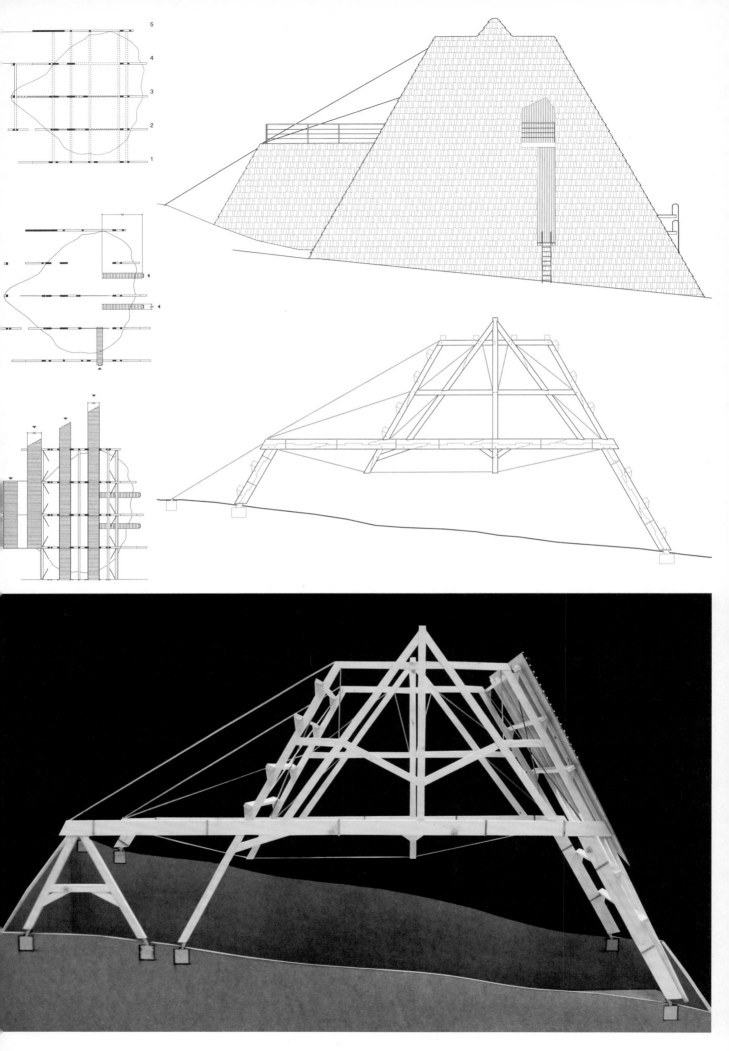

89

Petroglyph

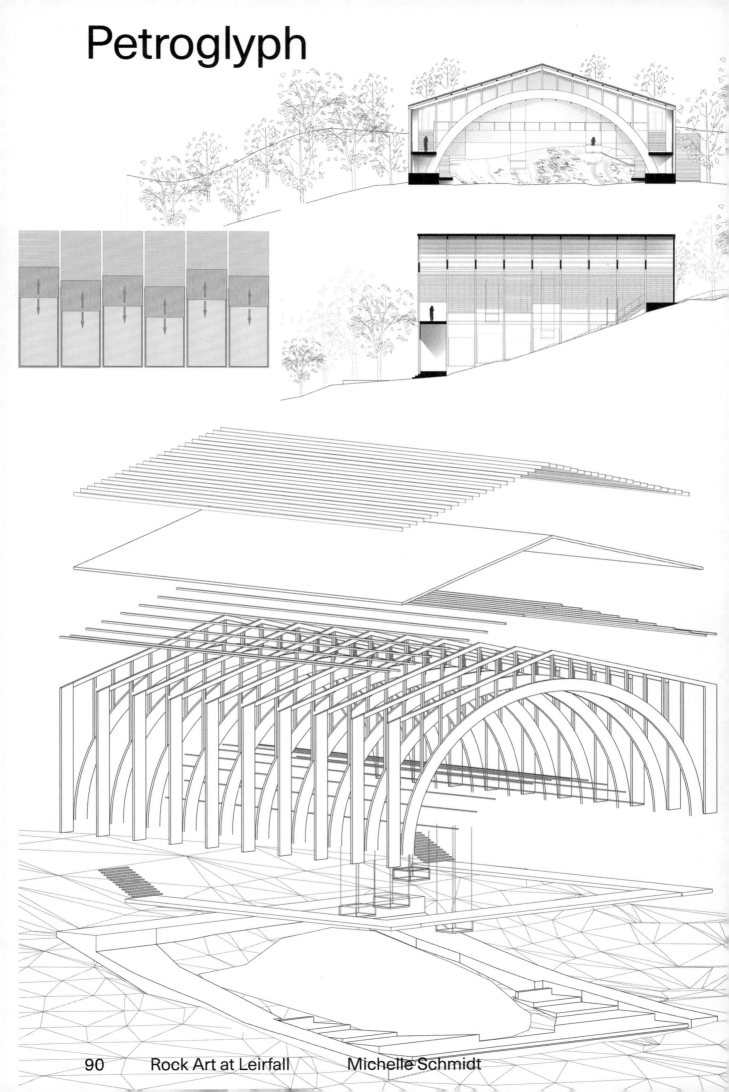

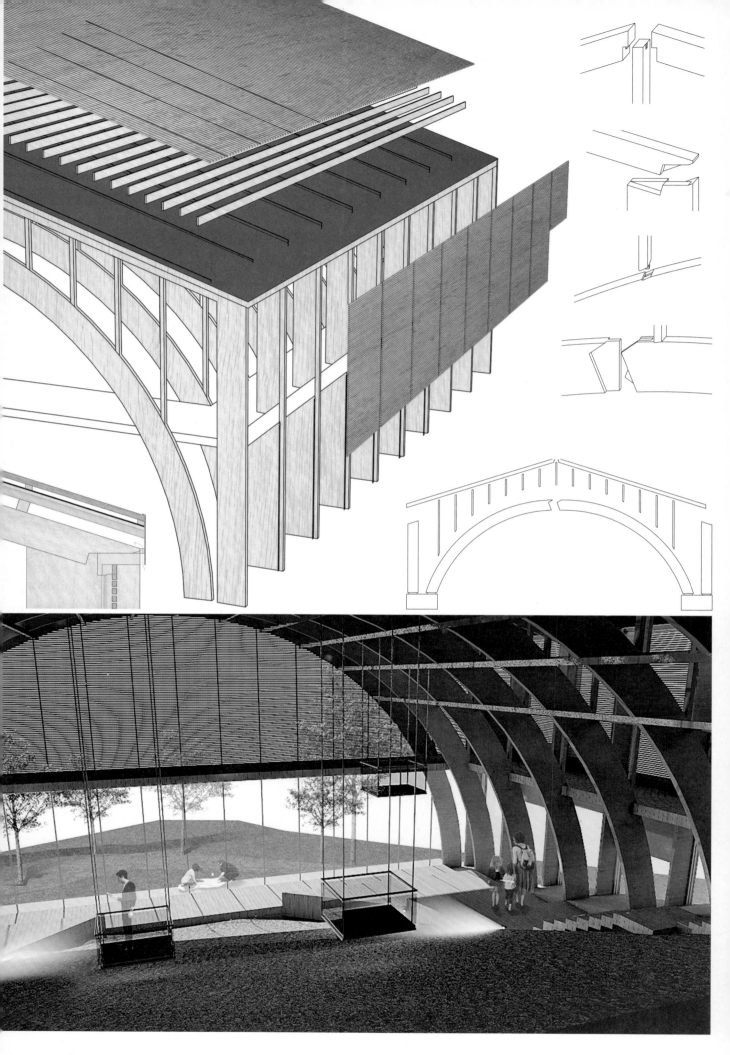

Two wooden observation towers are planned in the forest above Schaan. Wood is the obvious material for rural buildings, especially for a tower in the forest. The construction will reach a height of about 35 metres, allowing visitors to enjoy a view over the treetops. The careful connection to the existing paths and surrounding area is also part of the project. Wood occupies a central position in the alpine building culture of recent centuries, particularly in the region of the Rhine Valley. Students analysed this culture. The tradition of timber bridges by the Grubenmann carpentry dynasty from Appenzell in the 18th century and the later translation of the typology of the covered timber bridge into the efficient framework system of Howe in the Vaduz-Sevelen Bridge across the Rhine are just as much part of the investigation as the construction of the Norwegian stave churches and the suspended column structures of Eastern European bell towers.

Against the backdrop of the discussion about sufficiency and creation of regional value, we are interested in the tectonic properties of the solid material and its intrinsic suitability for tectonic elements. The joining of individual parts regains enormous significance. Modern mechanical processes can create timber connections that were previously made by hand. The use of locally grown hardwood also adds new themes. In the interplay between traditional knowledge and modern technology, a new 'hybrid timber construction' is postulated, lending new meaning to the classic theme of carrying loads. The conception of a handcrafted timber structure, developed for modern production techniques, should offer an alternative to standardized, industrially produced timber structures. Thus, 'archaic' and 'advanced' techniques are both used to reinterpret the richness of traditional timber with today's manufacturing techniques.

02.2019–06.2019
Schaan, Liechtenstein

Spiralis

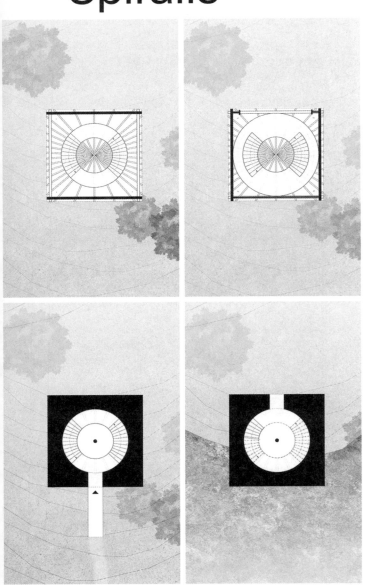

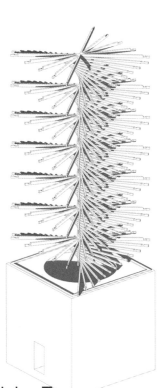

Agathe Cheynet, Alina Koger,
Bejan Misaghi, Tobias Oswald

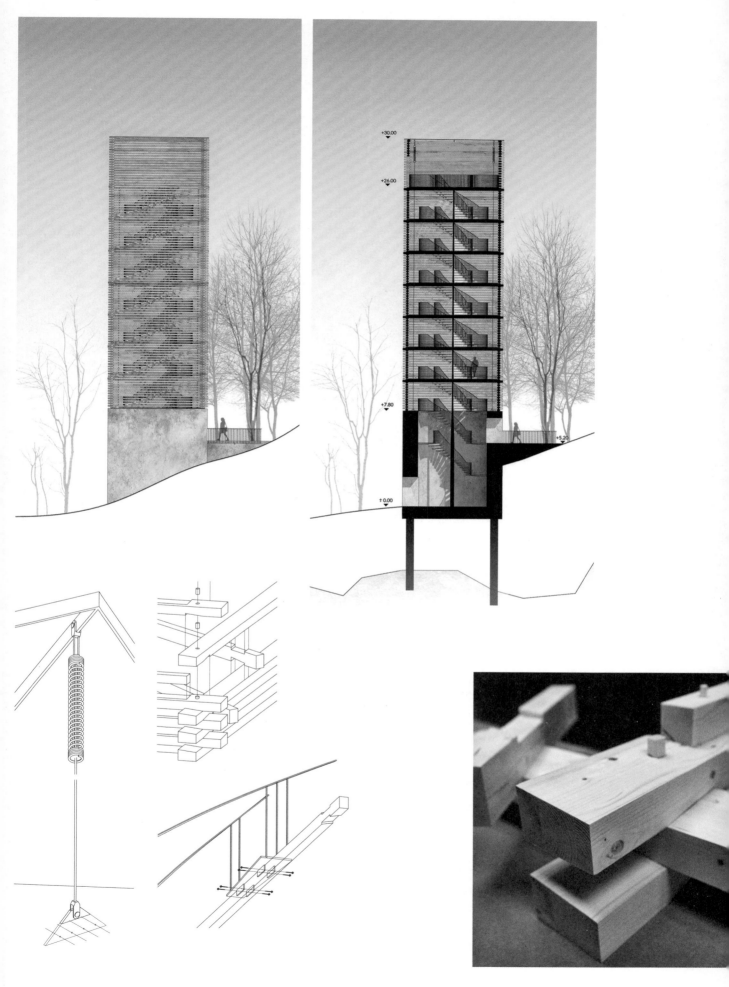

Agathe Cheynet, Alina Koger,
Bejan Misaghi, Tobias Oswald

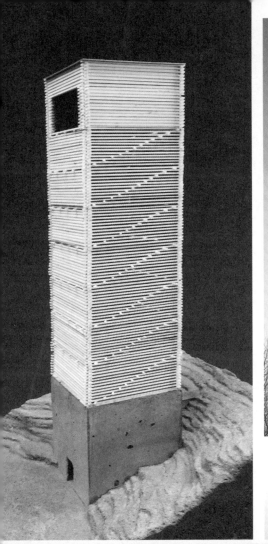

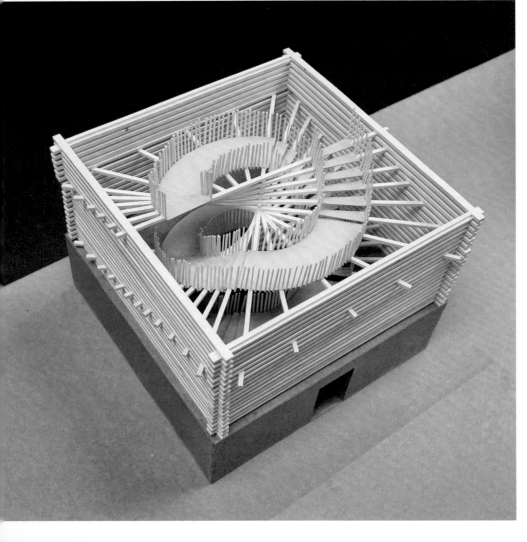

AXXXV

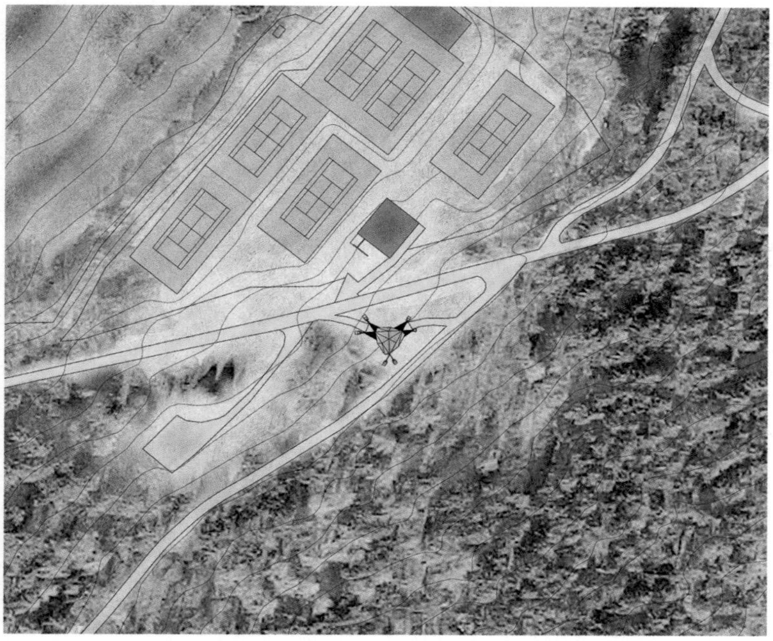

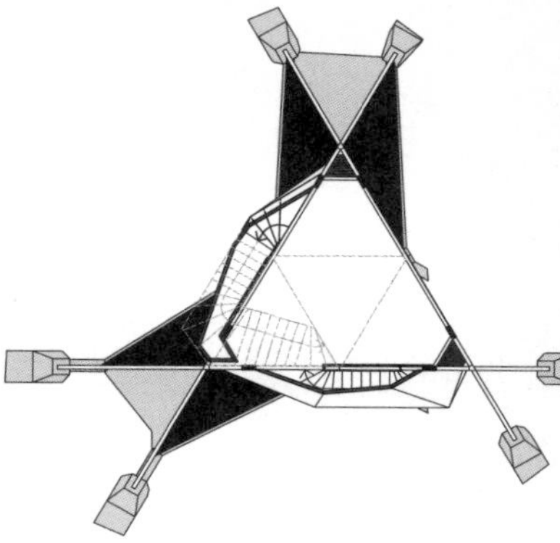

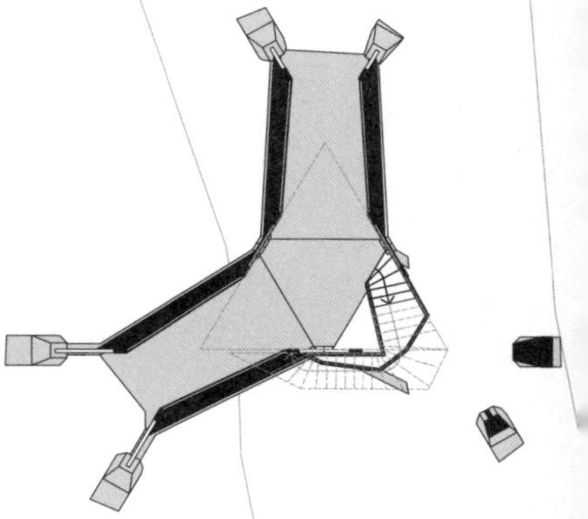

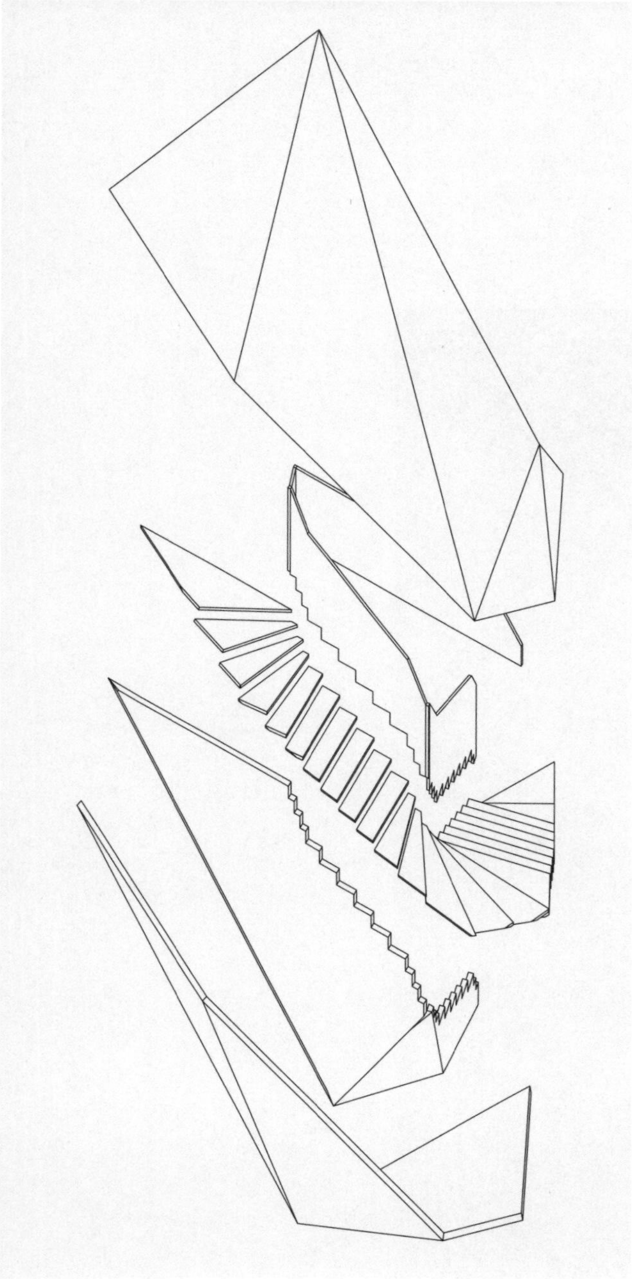

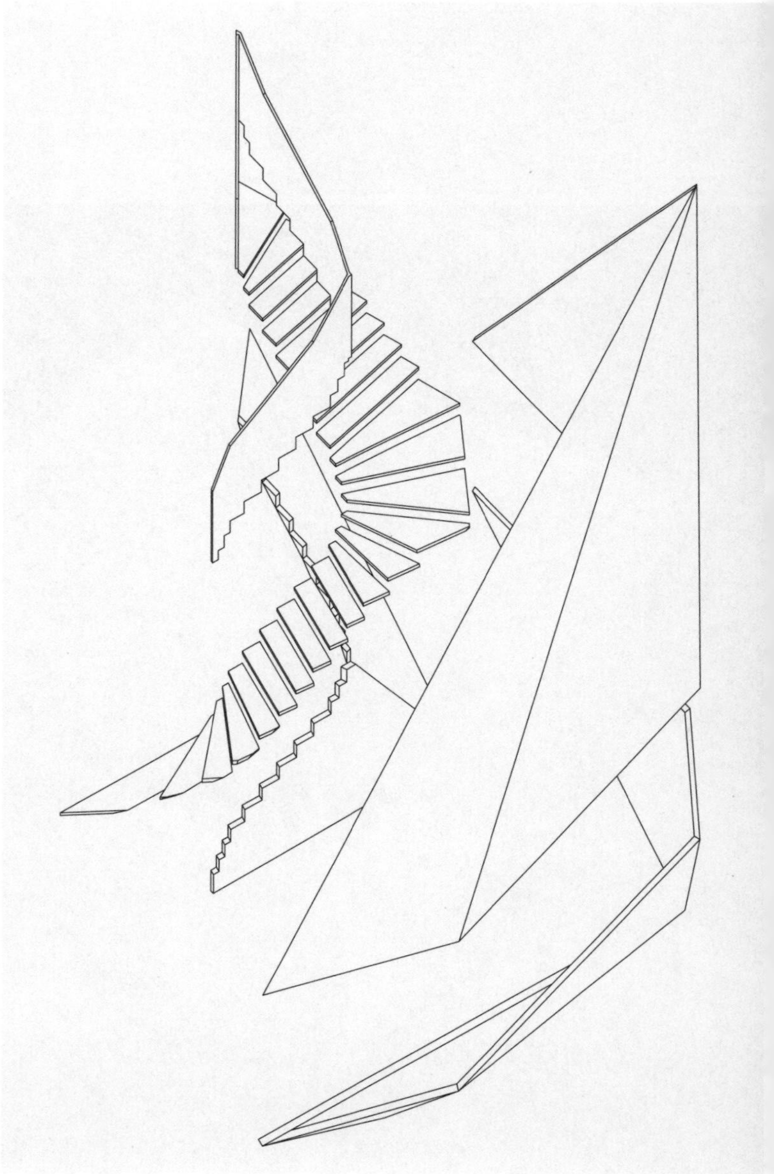

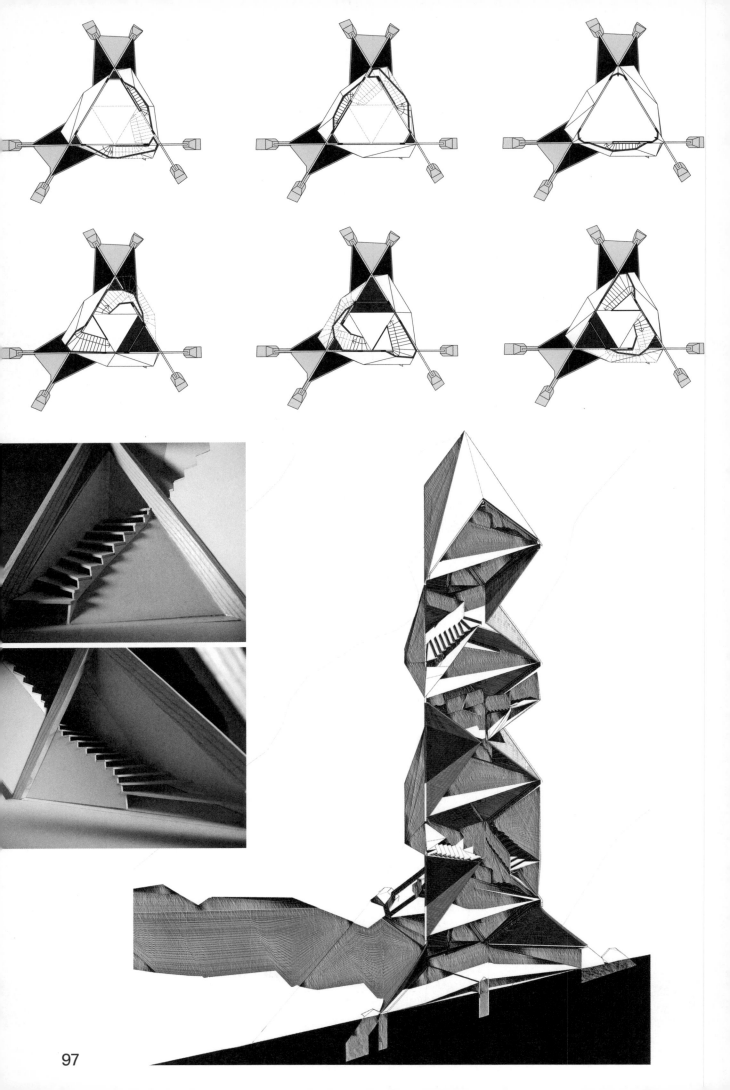

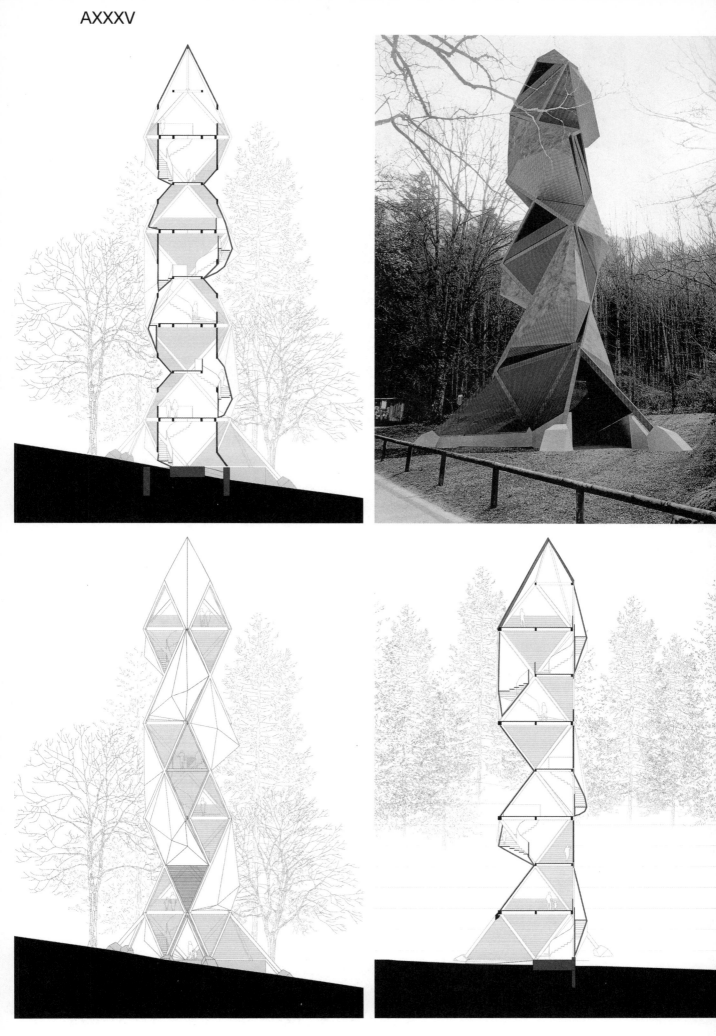

Intertwined

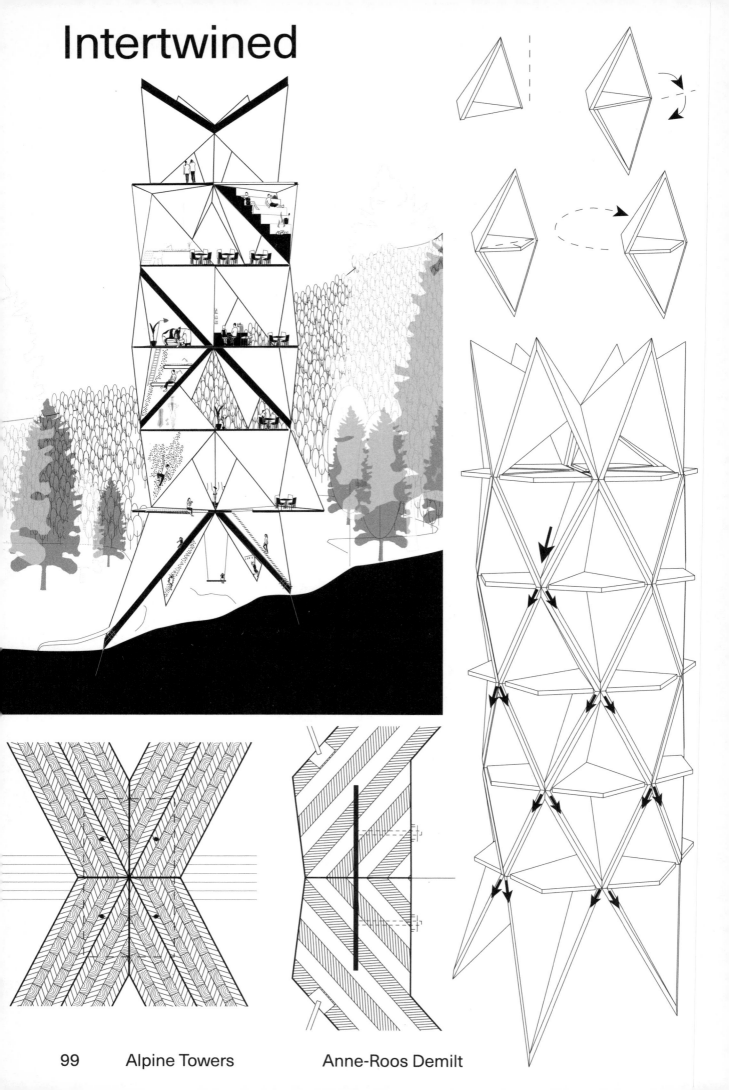

Intertwined

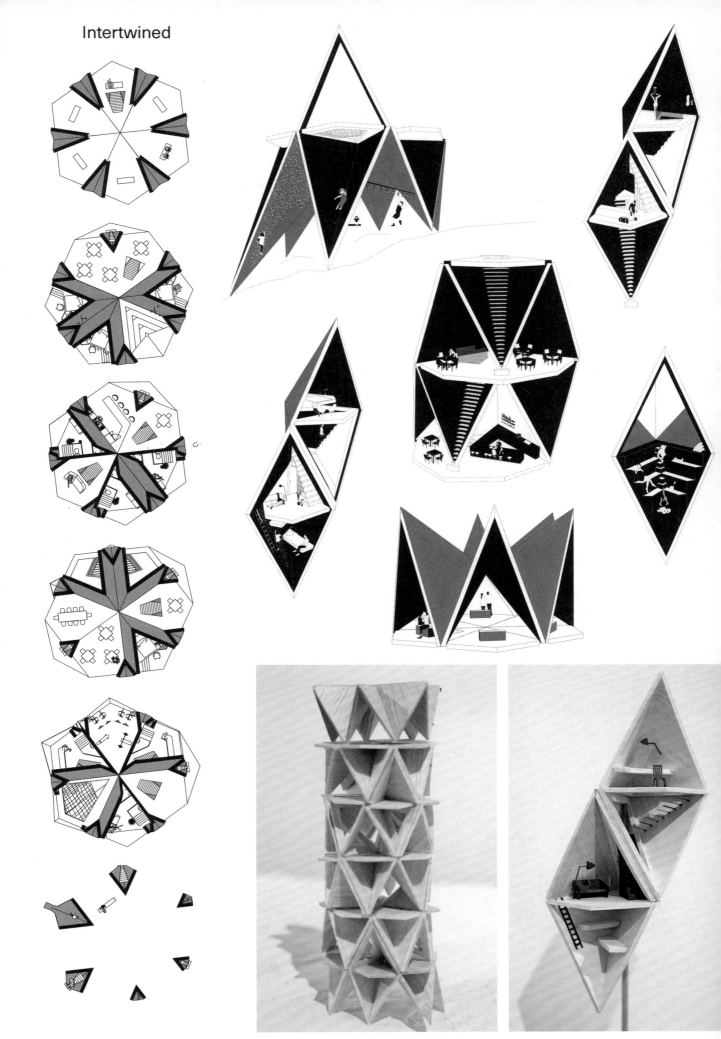

Alpine Towers   Anne-Roos Demilt

Rotation Entgegengesetzt

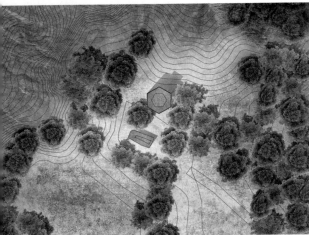

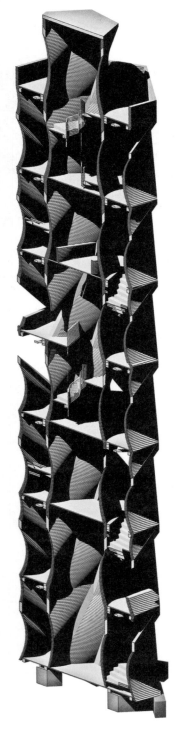

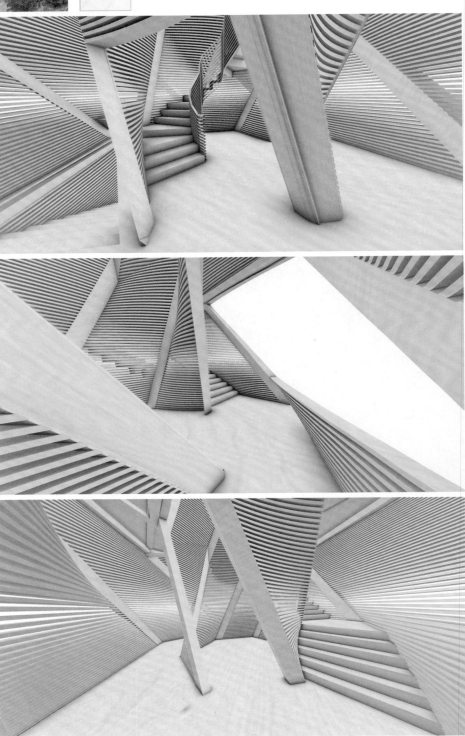

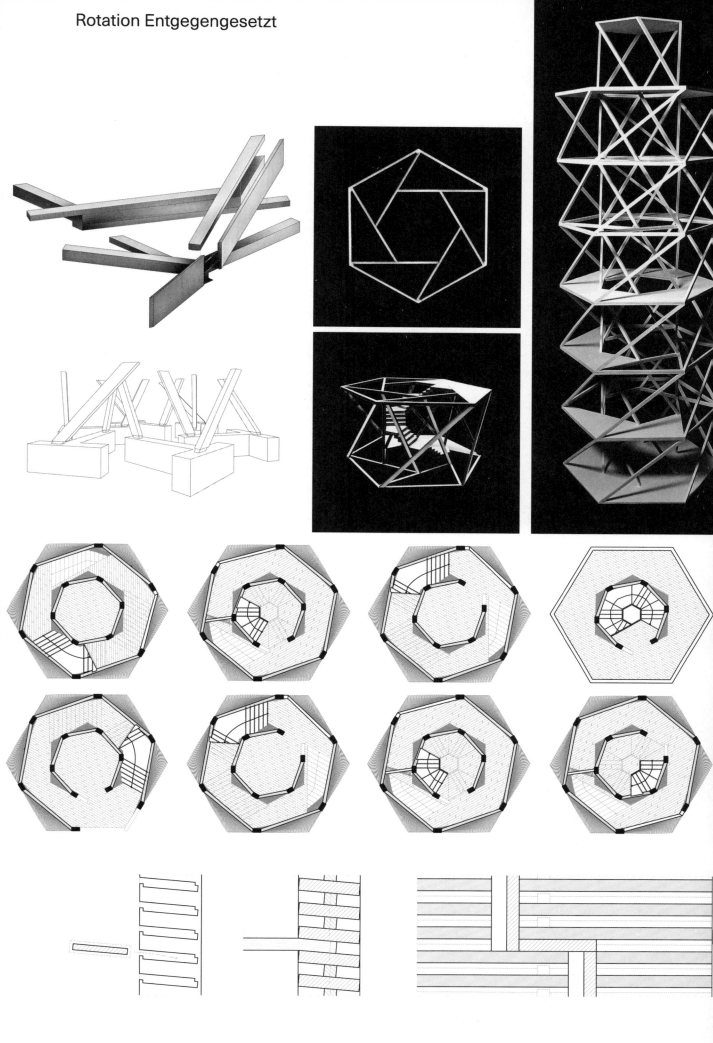

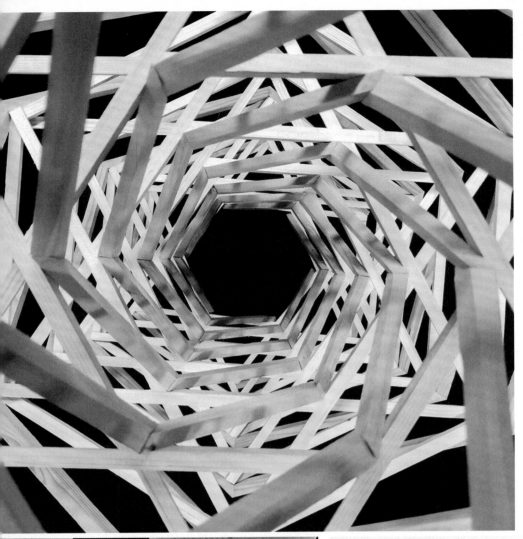

The assignment was to design a University of the Crafts on the historic site of Schaesberg Castle in Landgraaf. The *Landgoed Slot Schaesberg* Foundation wants to rebuild Schaesberg Castle and the associated *Slothoeve* in a historically and scientifically responsible manner and to redesign the surrounding area. The castle is both a cultural-historical attraction and a location for education and training to promote craftsmanship. The University of the Crafts consists of workshops for the development of traditional building-related crafts, labs for innovative techniques, and a research centre with documentation, library, exhibition and other facilities. The new building will be part of the historic ensemble of the castle site and should relate to the existing artefacts of the castle.

Design themes included the tectonics of the materials used, the merging of old and new crafts, historic and modern architecture, restoration and transformation. Local wood was an important building material for the construction, cladding and interior. From the first to the final week, students utilized spatial design and communicated with scale models, ready-mades and mock-ups. In *The Craftsman*, the sociologist Richard Sennett argues that old and new crafts are a crucial part of our daily lives. Archaeologist Langland writes in *Creaft* that our surrender to machines actually leads to decline. At a time when we are becoming increasingly cut off from the world around us, that is not only tragic but downright dangerous. A craft is a profession in which something is made by hand. We should become a *homo faber* again, the kind of person who makes things. That could be our salvation

02.2020–08.2020
Landgraaf, The Netherlands

Craft Forum

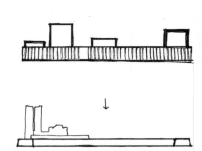

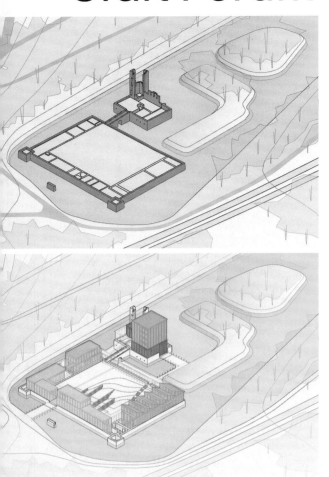

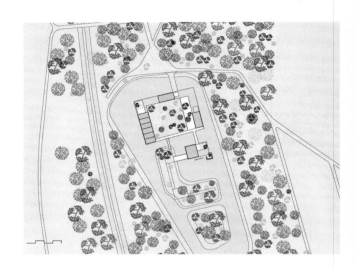

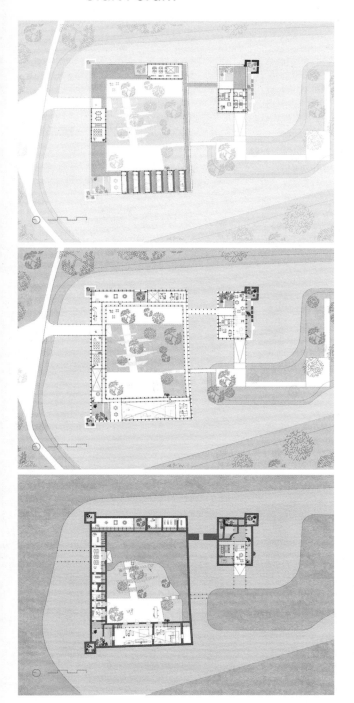

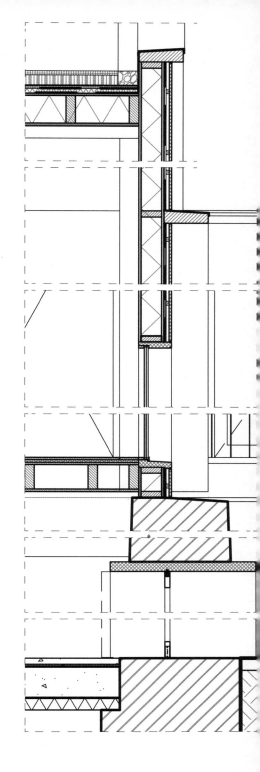

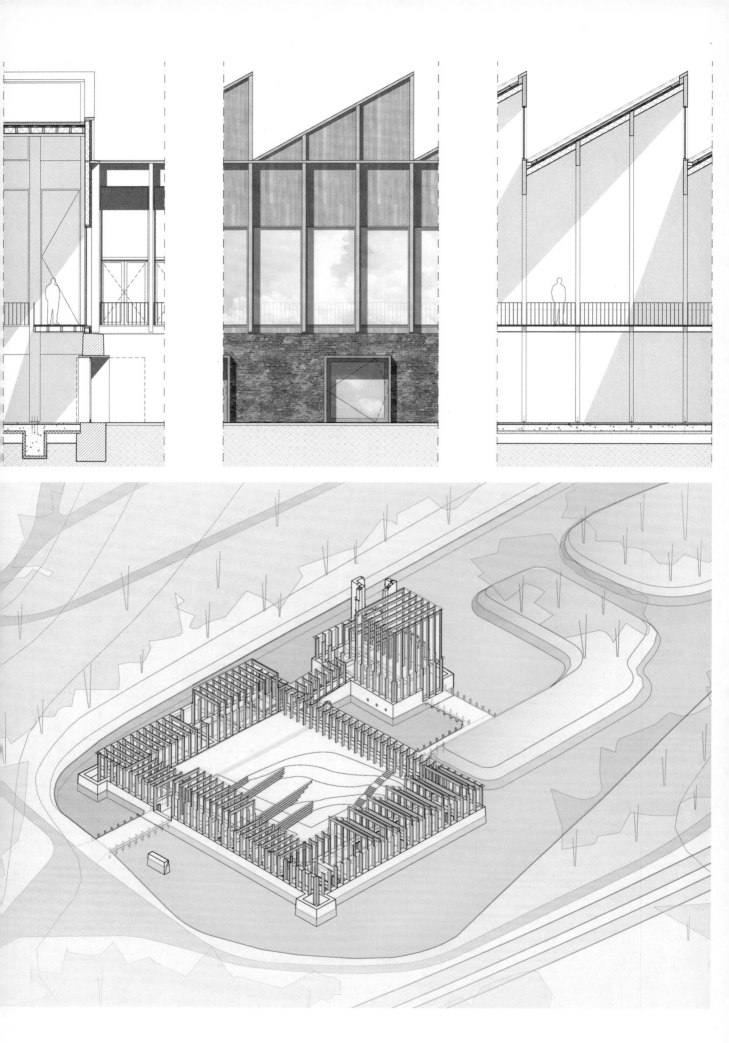

107

Horizontal Promenade

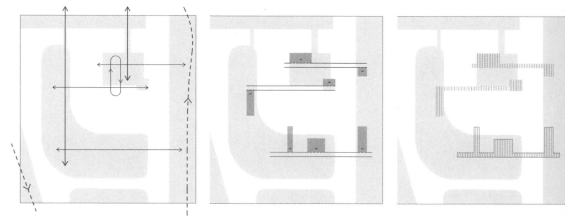

Clément Molinier, Laura Villaverde Díaz,
Xavier Granados Esteve

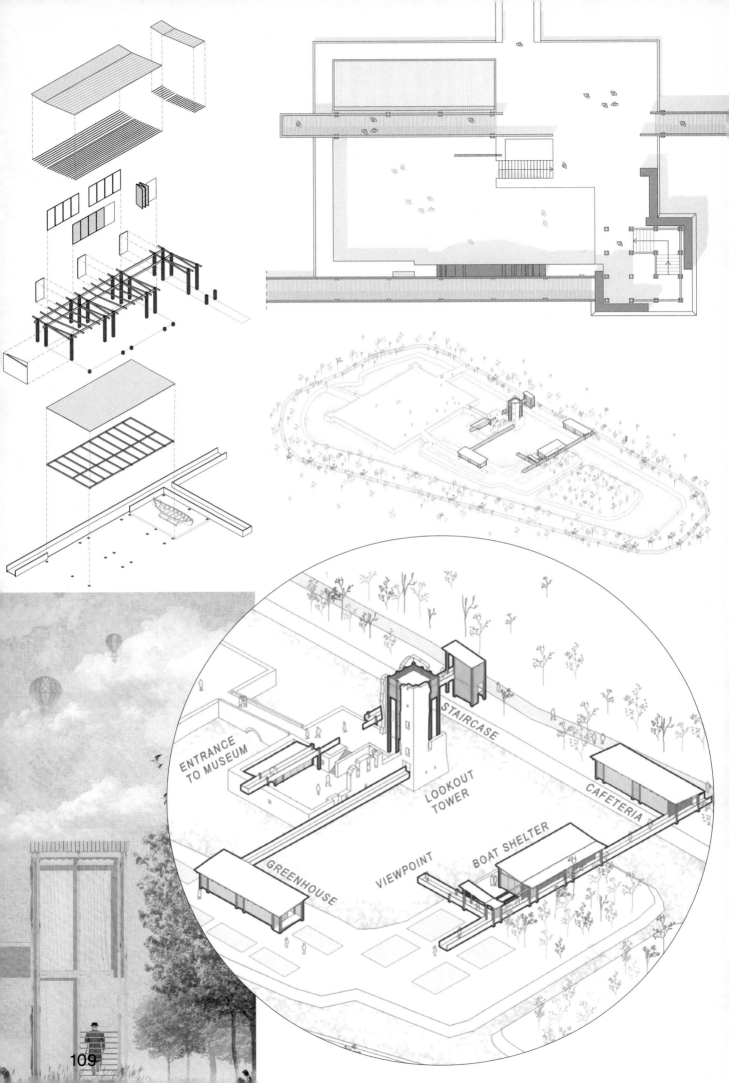

ENTRANCE
TO MUSEUM

STAIRCASE

LOOKOUT
TOWER

CAFETERIA

GREENHOUSE

VIEWPOINT

BOAT SHELTER

109

Horizontal Promenade

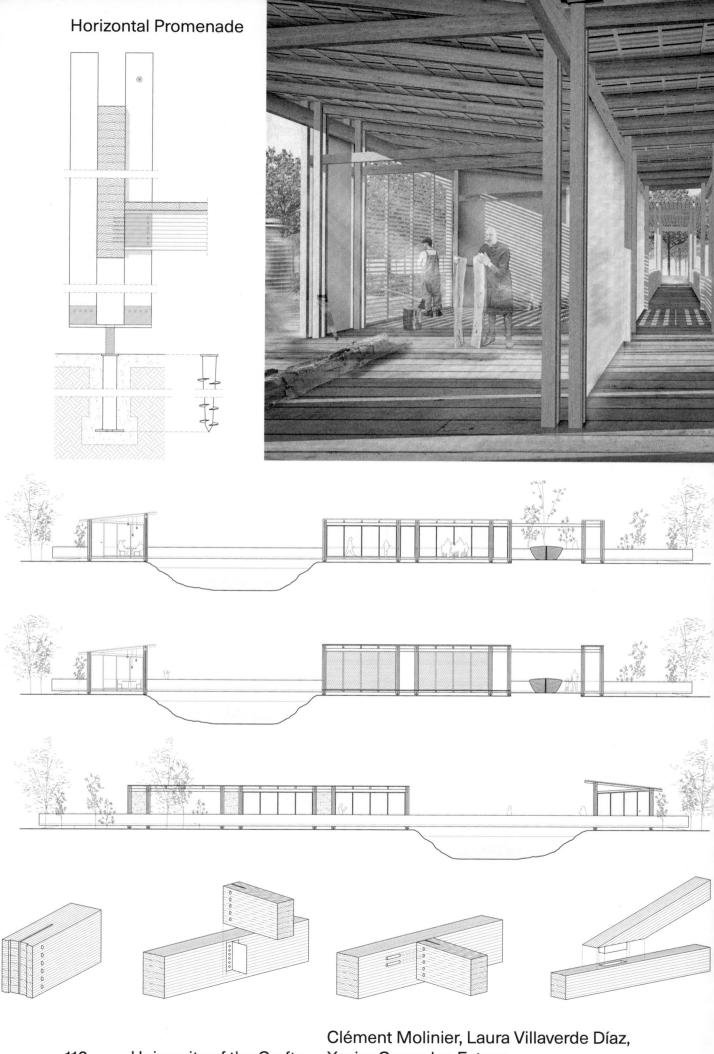

Clément Molinier, Laura Villaverde Díaz,
Xavier Granados Esteve

Momentum–Reaction

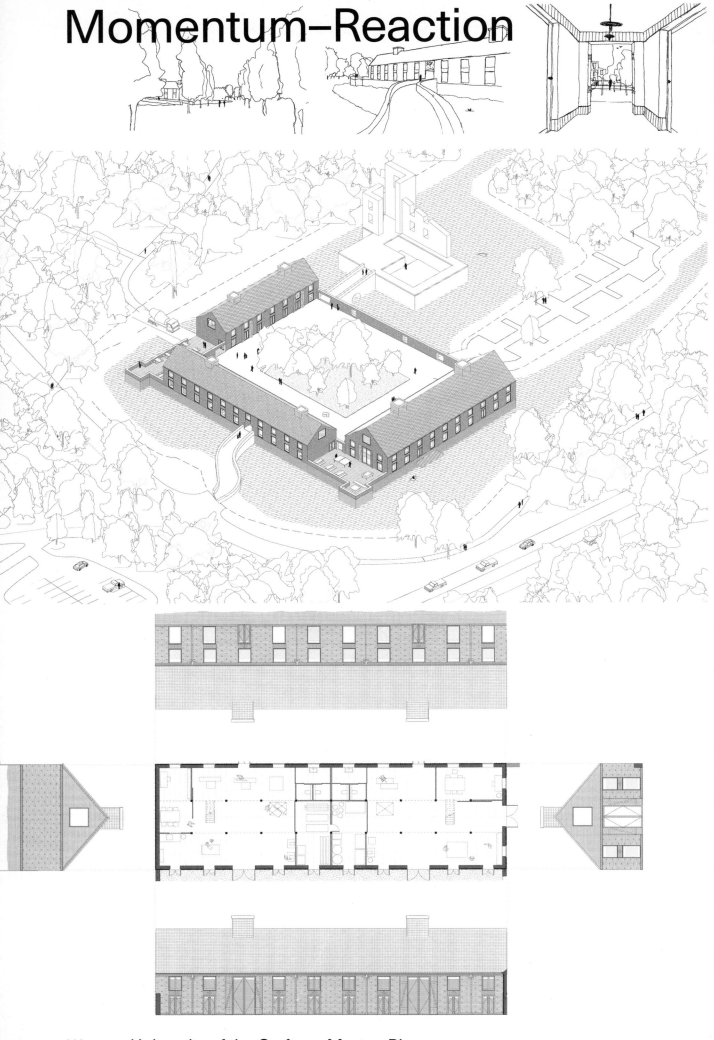

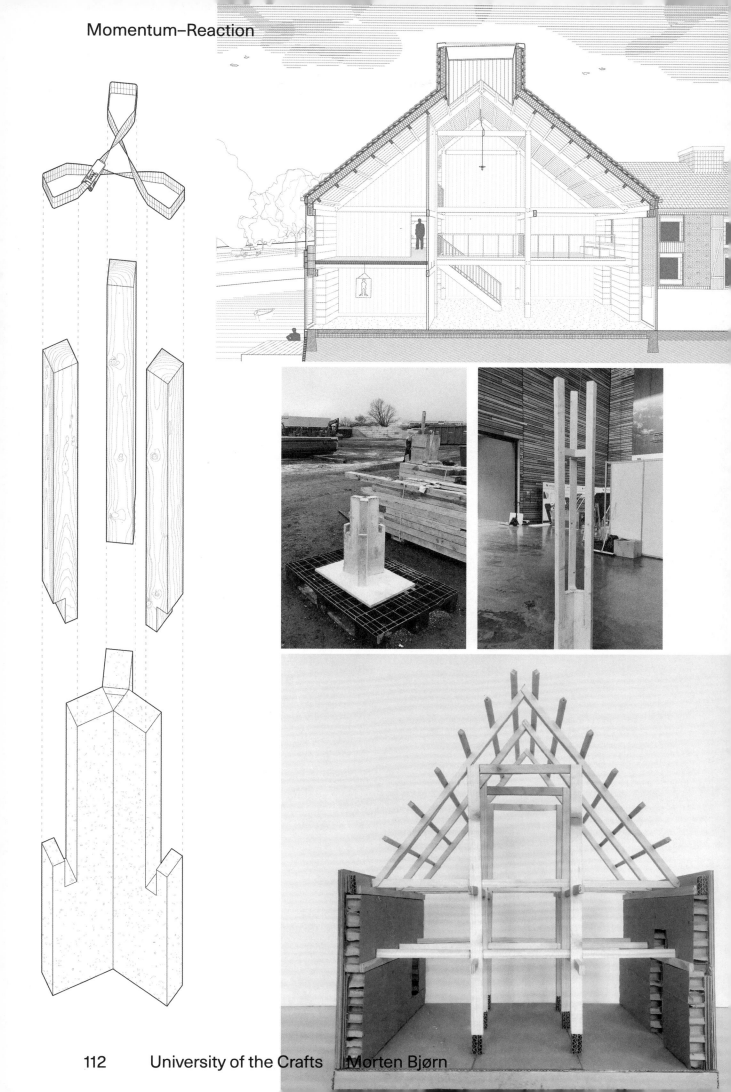

LEER KANTOOR

113

Craft Village

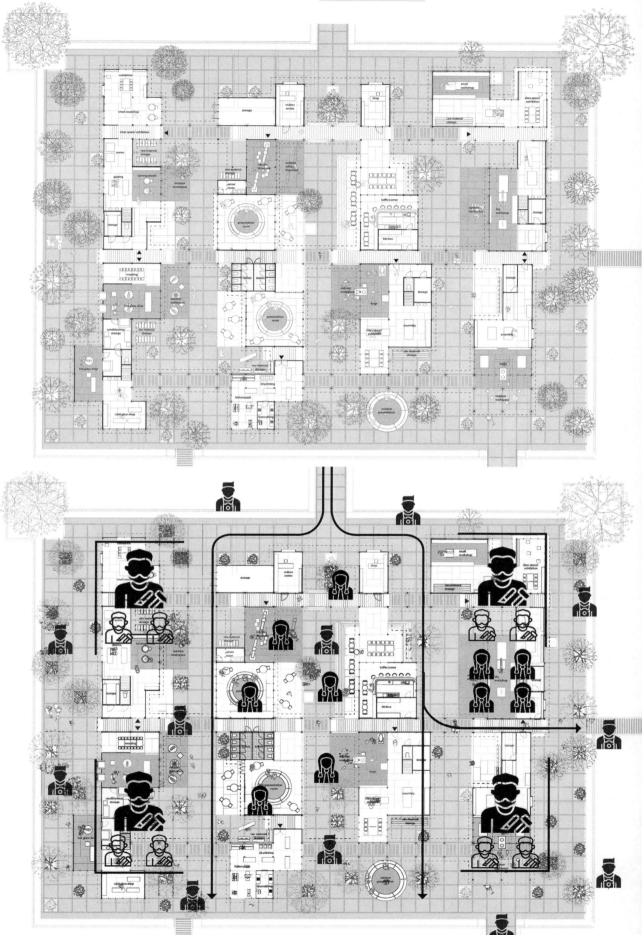

115

Craft Village

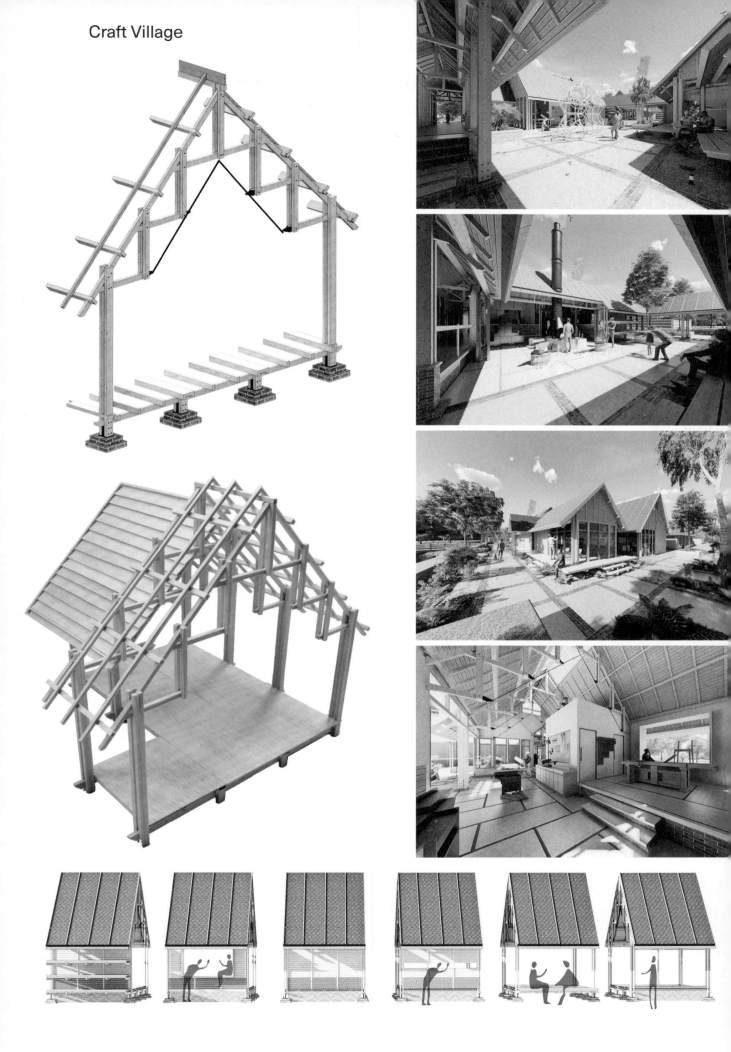

4 CRAFTING WOOD HANDS-ON

Full-Scale Timber Architecture as an Educational Tool

an Siem,
Bjorn Otto Braaten,
Arnstein Gilberg

Figure 1
a   Inside, front screen to the right
b   Upper platform
c   Front screen

The Faculty of Architecture and Design at NTNU in Norway has used full-scale building as an educational tool for several years. In one of the series of courses, designing and building a permanent project for a client has been the driving force for developing knowledge and skills in timber architecture and timber structures. In this paper we present three of the projects, sum up our earlier dissemination about pedagogic methods we have presented at ICSA conferences, and show how the Four-Quadrant Model (FQM) can be used.

At ICSA 2013 we presented a birdwatching tower (figure 1) and discussed the pedagogic methods we used to help students to gain increased insight into the development of architectural concepts, and the inherent properties of materials, structures, workmanship, fabrication, erection of structures, collaboration and communication (Siem et al, 2013).

At ICSA 2016 we presented a Star Cube (figure 2) and discussed the pedagogic methods we used to inspire and guide students in developing individual projects, working in groups on chosen projects for further development, and working as an architectural studio to develop one project in detail (Siem et al, 2016). A multi-perspective model based on the 'Integral Approach' developed by Ken Wilber was introduced. This model, called the Four-Quadrant Model (FQM), is adapted for discussions and research within the field of architecture and architectural structures (Braaten et al, 2019) and used to discuss a specific joint in the structure later in this paper.

The third project, called 'The Change Observatory' (figure 3), focuses on the changes in the area the installation is built. When arriving at the site, you are guided by a bridge into the building. Inside, you can choose to go up the stairs to enjoy a wide view of the area, or you can continue walking to an opening into the dark core of the structure, where you can observe the water underneath the building. Inside the core is a stairs down into the water. When you look at the building you can see four steel legs entering the water. These are welded to steel piles in the ground.

The project is built at the mouth of the River Orkla. On the site, the variation in water level depends on amount of flow in the river and the tidal water in the sea. Underneath the structure, it can be dry land or almost two-metre-deep water.

In this paper, we want to use the FQM (Braaten et al, 2019) to discuss one of the details in the presented full-scale project where the structure and structural detailing is an important part of the architecture. By using the model, we will discuss the detail from a technical, cultural and aesthetic perspective.

The chosen detail is shown in figure 6 and based on the same joint system as shown in figure 2.

When using the FQM, you must be aware of three different steps that need to be taken. The first step is to separate, or differentiate, the

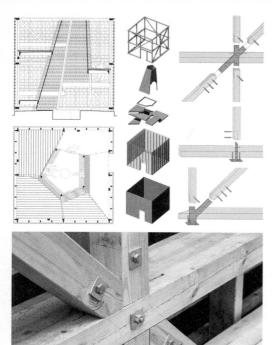

Figure 2
Star cube

Figure 3–4
The Change Observatory

phenomenon we want to investigate into four categories of perspectives (the four quadrants). The next step is to isolate the investigation in each of the quadrants, so that the potential of each perspective is fulfilled. The last step is to recombine the information and see how the different perspectives inform one another in a new, complete picture. This last step is important, because without it the separation and isolation steps may lead to subjectivist or objectivist reductionism.

Separation into four quadrants

When discussing a topic, people often think they are discussing the same thing, but they are unaware that they are actually discussing different aspects of a phenomenon. To help make the discussion clearer, the separation into the four quadrants shown in figure 5 is a good start.

The quadrants contain an objective natural scientific perspective of the detail (UR), an inter-objective system perspective (LR), an inter-subjective cultural context perspective (LL), and a subjective individual experience perspective (UL). The details of this will be discussed in the next chapters.

Isolating the four perspectives

1   The physical aspect of the detail (UR)

The detail chosen for discussion is a joint where five structural elements in a truss meet, as shown in figure 6. Technically, a slot is cut into the timber elements as shown in the centre image, and a steel plate is inserted into the slot. On this picture, just three timber elements are shown. On the picture to the right, we see all the elements in the K and the bolts with steel washers. The drawing on the left shows numbers positioning the steel plate and the bolts in the joint.

To design a joint like this, it is important to understand the design criterion based on the inherent orthotropic material properties and the possibilities of the production process. Through international joint research, design rules are developed and formulated in Eurocode 5 (CEN, 2004). When axial loads are transferred from one structural element into the joint, the forces pass from the timber element through the bolt into the slotted steel plate and then in the opposite direction into the other timber element. Many parameters influence the chosen design. The force value affects the diameter and number of bolts needed. The number of bolts in a row, the distance between them, the distance to the end or the edge of the timber element, and the thickness of the timber are all important elements that determine the capacity of each bolt. There are many possible design solutions when considering timber geometry and limitations in production methods.

2   System perspectives (LR)

The system perspective helps to see the aspects of the joint in a bigger context. By shifting the viewpoint from the joint as a single point to part of a structural system, production system, economic system, etc. we may see hidden characteristics. Let us take a closer look at the structural system, production system and logistics.

Figure 7a shows the core structure in timber. The darker parts indicate the steel plates in the joint. The figure shows how the joints and the timber elements create a stiff core with an opening into the centre which can carry the horizontal wind loads, and transfer the vertical loads down to the four supporting columns. The strong and stiff joints make it possible to choose a system with cantilevered platforms (figure 7b).

The production system and economic system make it rational to use the joint system in the trusses in the core, but not in the platforms. In the core, with its large loads, it is necessary to use the strong and more expensive system.

Our workshop contains modern equipment for producing timber details, components and structures. The workshop makes it possible timber prefabricate complicated full-size structures with the discussed detail at nearly furniture quality. Hand tools are used on site, so it is

Singular

UL   Individual Experience

Human mind, aesthetics, art

By exposing the steel dowels and the washers, it is possible to understand and to read how the detail is working in the structure.

Object   UR

The physical aspects of nature

Joint — timber/steel plate/steel dowel/steel washers. The force value affects the diameter and number of bolts needed. The number of bolts in a row, the distance between them, the distance to the end or the edge of the wood element and the thickness of the wood are all important elements concerning the capacity of each bolt.

Subjective   I | IT   Objective

Interior

Exterior

Inter-subjective   WE | ITS   Inter-objective

The process resulted in choosing timber as the main material, since it for so long time has been the dominating material in the region. It also resulted in using modern production methods in production steel parts based on the newer oil-related industrial development.

The joint and the timber elements make a stiff core with an opening into the center which can carry the horizontal wind loads, and transfer the vertical loads down to the support of the four columns. The strong and stiff joints makes it possible to choose a system with cantilevered platforms.

Ethics, ideology, collective memory, aesthetic traditions and trends, religion, language

Structure, production system, logistics, economy, institutions, rules and regulations

LL   Cultural Context

Systems   LR

Plural

Figure 5
The Four-Quadrant Model (FQM) for the detail in the Change Observatory

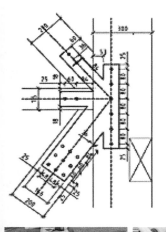

Figure 6a–c
Joint in the Change Observatory

not possible to produce the discussed detail. These possible production systems affect both the prefabrication system and the transportation system. It is necessary to produce volumes that can be transported by road and assembled on site.

The digital drawing system makes it possible to study 3D digital models of the structure, and to transfer geometry to the engineering calculation programmes and to the laser-cutter system for producing the steel plates with holes as shown in figure 6.

3   The cultural context (LL)

The building project was a collaboration between NTNU and the municipality of Orkdal, an industrial community close to Trondheim. Orkdal has an impressive industrial history, strongly connected to the local industrial inventor and architect Christian Thams, who started producing prefabricated timber houses for exportation worldwide in the early 20th century. He later initiated large industrial companies and thus created the basis for a solid industrial culture in the area. Today Orkdal is the largest industrial municipality along the Trondheim fjord, now focusing on oil-related business.

The municipality wanted us to cooperate with local industry and develop a built object appropriate to the cultural context of the area. We arranged meetings with local producers so that the students became aware of the local possibilities. The process resulted in choosing timber as the main material, since it has been the dominant material in the region for a long time. It also resulted in using modern production methods to manufacture steel parts based on the newer oil-related industrial development.

When Norway was preparing the Winter Olympics of 1994, Glulam was used as a structural material for the largest arenas. This led to a process whereby a new production technique was developed to produce

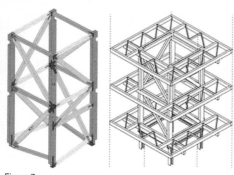

Figure 7
a   Core structure
b   Core and platform structure

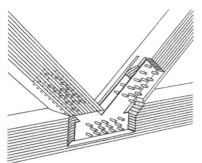

Figure 8
Dowel joint

stiff and strong joints for transferring loads. Figure 8 shows a typical K-joint and a section of the arena with the highest loaded joint. To produce joints, slots are cut in the timber and holes are drilled, steel plates with holes are inserted into the slots and dowels are pushed into the holes. The principle was well known, but was not previously used in large structures in Norway. Since then, the joint principle has been used in large-span sports arenas, the largest timber bridge span in the world, and largest timber building in the world. The joint can now be characterized as an important part of Norwegian culture in building large-span timber structures.

4   The individual experience (UL)
       Individual experience is by nature subjective, so the description of a detail through this perspective will vary from person to person. For this reason, some tend to dismiss this perspective. Two things about this perspective are therefore important to remember. The first is that even if we talk about individual experiences, we often share these experiences in an intersubjective way, meaning for example that aesthetic experiences are based on shared cultural references and context. The second is that, at the end of the day, the perspectives from the three other quadrants are interpreted through the senses, emotions and minds of individuals. To not acknowledge this perspective is therefore to supress or hide important information. This may soon result in conflict in discussing the interpretation of the objective facts in the UR/ LR quadrants.
       Typical aspects of the joint in this quadrant would be how an individual responds to the aesthetics of the joint. Is the steel plate slotted into the wood in a precise way? If the steel washers have a quadratic shape, are they positioned precisely in parallel order? As we can see in figure 6, the washers on the vertical timber element are not parallel. Some will see this as a lack of aesthetical quality; others will not pay any notice to it at all. By exposing the steel dowels and washers, we can understand and read how the detail works in the structure. For some, this is a quality. Others would maybe prefer to hide this so it looks more like a traditional timber joint without steel.
       Aside from the aesthetics, there is an aspect of individual emotional response to the production process. Some may take pride in the local industrial history and identity and therefore appreciate the combination of timber as a traditional material and the high-tech steel plate system. Others who interpret local tradition and identity more in relation to traditional timber craftsmanship may see the joint as a hybrid and an expression of pragmatic modern industrial technology.

       Recombining the perspectives

All these four perspectives represent important aspects of the joint. Individually, however, each of them represents reduced information about a complex matter. This is maybe hard to see, because it is almost impossible not to unconsciously make connections between the quadrants. For example, we may automatically assume that because of the strength of the steel dowel joint, it is 'better' than a traditional timber joint without steel. The objective fact is that it is stronger (UR), not better (LL). Depending on the context, a weaker traditional timber joint may sometimes be a 'better' solution than a stronger steel dowel joint.
       Recombining the reductive perspectives of the four quadrants in a conscious way is therefore important in getting the big picture. Only in this way will the FQM work as a helpful tool for a balanced discussion of the various phenomena.
       Looking at what the different aspects of the quadrants provided in terms of information, we observe that some combinations work harmoniously. The physical properties of the joint and the way it contributes to a large-scale Glulam timber structure in an industrial production system align well with local identity and intersubjective values focused on industrial history and contemporary high-tech. If individuals experience the mix of tradition and the high-tech solution of the joint as beautiful and maybe even identify with the industrial tradition on a personal level, the joint in this context can be seen as strong (UR),

effectively organized (LR), good (LL), beautiful and meaningful (UL). However, a different view of local identity or a preference for pure timber structures, may give a more conflicted picture.

Conclusions

We have now tested how the Four-Quadrant Model contains an objective natural scientific perspective (UR), an inter-objective system perspective (LR), an intersubjective cultural context perspective (LL) and a subjective individual experience perspective (UL).

So what is achieved by using the FQM? By recombining some vital aspect of each quadrant, we can see more clearly the interplay between the wider context, the aesthetics and the technical specifics of the joint. This balances out any tendency for one specific perspective, objective or subjective, to dominate the discussion.

Dealing with complex matters like architecture without making drastic reductions into technological, cultural or aesthetic reductionism calls for a way of thinking that considers the bigger picture without losing the complexity of the combined aspects. The FQM provides a tool for balanced communication and discussion between the various participants within the building industry and the field of architecture in general.

Within architectural education and structural engineering education, the FQM represents a map to train students in complexity thinking and in understanding the importance of connected knowledge. For the teachers, too, the FQM structures the components of knowledge in a way that one-perspective thinking is avoided. At a time where the building industry really needs to change practice and promote production and solutions that are drastically more sustainable, this is crucial.

By our brief and preliminary testing of the FQM on a specific structural joint, it is also necessary to ask what is not achieved?

As noted in an earlier paper on the subject, 'Connected Knowledge' (Braaten et al, 2019), the FQM represents one of five main elements in the Integral Approach. For those not familiar with this approach, our experience is that using the FQM is a manageable first step. The Integral Approach, however, covers a much more comprehensive and complex field. The simplifications (though complex enough for beginners) achieved here by focusing on the FQM without 'levels', 'line', 'states' and 'types' (the other main elements of Integral Approach), have been made purely for pedagogical reasons. The next step could be to include 'levels' in the FQM, which would provide differentiations between developmental stages in each quadrant.

A model and a method are never better than the way they are executed. Also, the FQM may be used in a way that doesn't align with the full potential or the basic intentions of the Integral Approach. Training, discussions and knowledge seeking are the best medicine in developing the use of the model in a constructive, intelligent and comprehensive way. When this is achieved, the FQM may have an important impact, not only within education, but also within research and sustainable industrial development.

To develop the use of the FQM within our own pedagogical context, the next step would be to test the model on more groups of students, so that we can better see the thresholds in the learning trajectory and support the students properly through the rapids of multi-perspective thinking. An interesting test would also be to use this model to support a real 1:1 social context with various participants in the next full-scale construction project.

References

Siem J., Braaten B. O., Alto P., Manum B. and Gilberg A. (2013) *The advantage of full-size construction as an educational tool in architecture education*, ICSA 2013.
Siem J., Braaten B. O., and Gilberg A. (2016) *Full scale in four months—Objectives, methods and results*, ICSA 2016.
Braaten B. O., Siem J. and Gilberg A. (2019) *Connected Knowledge*, ICSA 2019.
CEN (2004) *Design of timer structures—part 1-1: general common rules and rules for buildings*, Standard no EN 1995-1-1, Brussels: CEN.

The Aspect of Craftmanship: Innovation and Expression

Urs Meister

Today, the wooden house is produced by machines in factories, not by the craftsman in his shop. A traditional, highly developed craft has evolved into a modern machine technology.
(Wachsmann, 1930)

Konrad Wachsmann's introduction to his 1930 book *Building the Wooden House: Technique and Design* reads amazingly up to date against the background of the rapid technical development in contemporary timber construction. While Wachsmann purposefully focused on the systematization of elements in house construction only to subsequently suffer failure with General Panel Corporation, which he founded in the USA together with Walter Gropius, his research remains a milestone in 20th-century industrial construction. "Each technically pure construction has its own characteristic forms. Hence, the new method of working wood does change the external face of the building. A new form has to emerge." (Wachsmann, 1930) Wachsmann illustrated this in his book with cubic, modern wooden structures in the style of the *Neues Bauen* ('New Building') à la Giedion, which had little in common with traditional wooden houses. The "face of the building" ought to evolve in a modern sense from the construction, and a new working method would ideally lead to a new architectural expression.

Today, modern timber construction is no longer characterized by the will to mass produce, but lies rather in the contrast between classic craftsmanship and digital production. In recent years, this has led to a multifaceted discussion in architecture, which is again experiencing a strong orientation towards exploring craftsmanship and the artisanal. In addition to the utility of innovative technical solutions, this is reflected in the effort to offer more importance in varying degrees to the legibility of production and thus of craft. Today it is also interesting to see how a 'craftsmanly expression' can be realized and deployed as an instrument of design. In the spirit of Gottfried Semper, construction that results purely from the material and its statics requires an exaggeration for an expressive power to emerge and the building to become architecture. This exaggeration requires a creative will to make use of the varied options offered by traditional craft, to do so freely and to use new technologies to make an innovative contribution to the expression of craftsmanship.

Self-evident knowledge

A look at books written for carpenters gives us untold new clues as to how structure and materiality can advance production methods for timber construction. The manifestation of traditional timber structures draws its energy from the immediacy and impact with which the constructional elements interact. Each component is legible, be it in solid, post-and-beam or framework construction. Even with the interior wall panelling of rooms or the facades of timber buildings, the beams and boards are largely recognizable and give the architecture a profoundly human scale and grain, regardless of the building's size.

124

As the carpenter was one with the architect until the Baroque period, at least for timber buildings, "conception, design, sizing and execution all lay in his hands" (Zwerger, 1997). The tasks of the architect were wide-ranging, extending to the practical work of the handcraft itself. It is not for nothing that the German word for carpenter (*Zimmermann*) implies the creation of space in that it contains the word for 'room' (*Zimmer*), and conversely, that the *tektōn*—Greek for an artisan, especially a carpenter—is hidden in the word architect. In Japanese, lastly, the word for carpenter is *daiku*, literally 'great artisan' or 'master builder', and actually even takes on the role of cabinetmaker. "As the age of the Baroque dawned, a development took place which was to change the whole nature of building. Designing and planning, the creative act, hitherto the result of practical experience, was to be theorized by and for more and more specialists." (Gerner, 1986). The divergence of craftsmanship and conception in timber construction has advanced inexorably since industrialization. Bringing these loose ends back together is our duty, and the place where this can happen is within architectural education.

It is revealing that carpentry originally scarcely defined itself through drawings. The regionally cultivated tradition of timber construction helped to ensure that a skilled carpenter could rely on his experience for the conception of buildings. "In Russia drawings only started to appear at the end of the 17th century. When working drawings eventually started to be used, these were frequently the work of artists whose familiarity with engineering sometimes left much to be desired." (Zwerger, 1997). Zwerger describes this knowledge as self-evident, as being *taken for granted*. The rules for making timber joints were learned in an apprenticeship, enlarged upon in the journeyman years and finally mastered in one's own work, and thus handed down via oral but above all manual dissemination.

This *self-evident knowledge* is described by Josef Killer in his book about the Grubenmann family of master builders, in the description of the famous roof truss of the church in Baar from the year 1645: "Particularly worthy of mention is also the craftsmanship of these roof trusses. All the connections are not only lapped or mortised, but also secured with wooden nails of oak or beech. Age-old construction principles, which had always been passed down and improved, formed the basis of every wooden structure. Since at that time there was not yet any means to make a structural calculation of the roof structures, all the dimensions were established on the basis of experience, in many cases even based purely on intuition. After all, certain rules governing the normal execution of the work emerged over time, and these could be continually improved by observations of the built structures." (Killer, 1942)

The loss of this traditional chain of knowledge has taken place over a short time: "In hardly 100 years the knowledge accumulated over some 1,300 years, constantly extended, refined and adapted to new tasks, has been allowed to seep away," notes carpenter Nishioka in regret about this development in Japan (Zwerger, 1997). The traditional cultural heritage can only be maintained in niches today, as the economic pressure of industrial production has become too strong. In order to counteract this crisis, it is necessary in architectural education to emphasize an understanding of the culture of construction and the importance of craftsmanship.

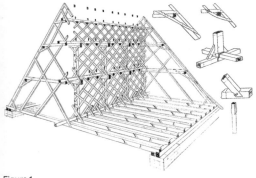

Figure 1
Roof structure of the church in Baar, 1645

Structure and expression

We seek to anchor the cultivation of an experimental and nevertheless practical interpretation of artisanal approaches to timber construction with interdisciplinary architectural projects. As part of the Erasmus+ project 'Wood: Structure and Expression', three architecture schools from Norway, the Netherlands and Liechtenstein are working together with local craftsmen to achieve this goal. In so doing, the contemporary European discussion on designing with wood is supported and new paths with regard to structure and expression are presented. Within this framework, a timber observation tower in the forest above Schaan, Liechtenstein, will be designed and constructed in 2019. The structure

will reach a height of about 35 metres and allow views out over the treetops. In an international workshop on site and in the carpentry workshop, the potential of the raw material will be explored in models and prototypes up to a scale of 1:1. In the individual universities, different projects will be developed from these approaches. Ultimately, a tower project will be selected from the students' designs and then, over the summer, it will be developed further and detailed. The construction of the forest tower is planned for autumn 2019 and will be realized with the help of students from the University of Liechtenstein.

Timber is the obvious choice for a building material for rural utilitarian structures, especially for a tower in the forest. But timber also occupies a central position in the Alpine building culture of the past centuries, particularly in the region of the Rhine Valley, Liechtenstein, Eastern Switzerland and Vorarlberg. This will be researched by the students in analytical work. The tradition of the 18th-century timber bridges by the Grubenmann family of master builders from Teufen and the later interpretation of the typology of covered timber bridges in the efficient Howe Truss system (Birrer, 2011) in the Rhine bridge between Vaduz and Sevelen are part of the investigation, as are the construction methods of the Norwegian stave churches and the king-post structures of Eastern European bell towers.

Natural acumen

Covered timber bridges were common in Switzerland since the Middle Ages and provided protected routes for transporting goods and people between north and south. The roofs provided protection for the structure and formed a shaded space in the open landscape above the river that can still be experienced today in the surviving examples. However, the quantity of supports required in the riverbed made the structures highly vulnerable to floodwaters. Starting in the 15th century, larger spans were sought and hanging trusses up to 30 metres were built. The master-builder family Grubenmann from Teufen initiated a veritable boost of innovation in bridge construction in the 18th century. Jakob Grubenmann's family first ran a carpentry business, whose initial work was to cover the roofs of church steeples but soon moved on to building entire roof structures. These were often designed as hanging trusses or strutted frames. With this knowledge, the field of work soon extended into bridge construction and timber structures with increasingly long spans were built. An apex was reached by Hans Ulrich Grubenmann with the construction of the Schaffhausen Bridge in 1758, which soon achieved international fame: "As a monument to the ingenuity of an Appenzellian carpenter, Hans Ulrich Grubenmann of Teufen, who has through his own efforts managed to achieve a new level of architecture, the timber bridge over the Rhine at Schaffhausen is a worthy object of universal admiration." (Storr, 1784) And still further: "Considering the magnitude of the plan and the daring of the structure, it is astonishing that the master builder is a common carpenter without any scholarship, without the slightest knowledge of mechanics and utterly inexperienced in the theory of mechanics. This extraordinary man is named Ulrich Grubenmann, a common rural man of Teufen, a small village in the canton of Appenzell, who was very devoted to the drink. He has a tremendous amount of natural acumen and an astounding affinity for the practical part of mechanics, and he has by himself made such extraordinary progress in his art that he is rightly counted among the most inventive master builders of the century." (Coxe, 1792)

Emphasis is given to the background of the unstudied carpenter, who developed his means of construction entirely on his own. Grubenmann later took the knowledge he gained from building bridge structures and transferred it to long-span roof trusses for church buildings. His impetus to apply his knowledge of design and materials to create wooden structures with ever-greater spans is due to an investigative spirit that is not academic but rather craftsmanly. Grubenmann also participated in the international competition for a bridge over the River Derry in Ireland and sent a model of his design. The client had to be convinced with both drawing and model; the models were made to a scale of 1:40 and constructed in precision work. Even the interlocking

Figure 2
Model of the Grubenmann bridge in Schaffhausen

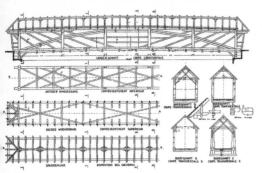

of the timbers in the arches and the bolted connections of individual
slats were built. Even today, the impressive drawings and models have
hardly lost any impact as communication tools.

Construction languages

In 1871, a good one hundred years after Grubenmann's Schaffhausen
Bridge was erected, a toll bridge over the Rhine was built between
Vaduz and Sevelen with a span of 136m, and it still survives today as
the last of what was once seventeen covered wooden bridges in the
Alpine Rhine Valley. Although it is reminiscent of the hitherto familiar
covered wooden bridges, its means of construction has little to do with
the hanging truss bridges of Grubenmann. The Liechtenstein state
technician Peter Rheinberger used the efficient Howe Truss system,
a radically simplified timber structural system that was combined with
steel elements. The construction system was originated by the American design engineer William Howe, who in 1840 developed a trussed
framework of timber beams with pretensioned vertical iron rods. This
in turn was based on the lattice truss bridges of the American engineers Stephen H. Long and Ithiel Town. Their trussed systems, which
were still built purely of wood and spanned up to 60 metres, subsequently served as models for the iron lattice bridges in Europe.

The sides of the bridge each consist of two paired Howe Trusses
that function as vertical longitudinal girders with vertical tie rods and
a series of diagonal timber compression struts. The bridge still capti-
vates onlookers today with the elegance of its length and its imposing,
enclosed interior where the tight rhythm of the diagonal struts creates
an expression of strength. The timber structure is exceedingly adaptable and has already survived diverse modifications and repairs, with
measures to the load-bearing structure only needed in isolated locations. The shingled roof and the board facades were conceived as
wearing surfaces that are also replaced on a regular basis. The construction of the wide-span bridge can be attributed to the development
of steel construction and the idea of rationalization. Despite all its discernible craftsmanship, the bridge's simplification to an elementary
and repetitive structure of latticed trusses gives it a distinctly industrial
character. The bridge as a system could be stretched considerably
further, with its extent limited only by the number of supporting piers
anchored in the riverbed. Hence, as a system conceived for mass production, it is exceedingly American, can be executed with a minimum
variety of wood joints and stands out clearly from the delicate carpenter
construction of Grubenmann.

The developmental advances in the construction of timber bridges
that were decisively driven by Grubenmann and Howe were mainly
due to the pursuit of longer spans with greater material economy and
the premise of utilizing available timbers. The elaboration of their systems can be characterized as a *construction language*: "Just as languages emerge and develop into entirely different forms as a function
of varied boundary conditions, construction languages also emerge
and develop in dependence on different factors (...). The history of construction technology can be written as the rise and fall of ever-new
construction languages that find their expression in the continual production of ever-new 'texts' in these different languages." (Lorenz, 2005)
Language is something that is in flux and must continually evolve. A
driver of change is the will to innovate. Yesterday and today alike, the
basic driving forces in constructing with wood, aside from fulfilling a
clearly defined task, are specifically the search for expression from
the design.

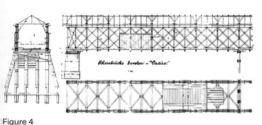

The soul of things

How can simple means be used to obtain maximal expression from
the construction? A roof structure that is unique in this regard is the
barrel roof structure of the Zollinger roof developed in the 1920s. Nearly
forgotten today, this lamella construction constitutes a reticular shell
structure consisting of relatively short boards, which are held together

Figure 5
Gut Garkau, Hugo Häring, Scharbeutz, 1926

Figure 6
Construction of the model workshop at the University of Liechtenstein, 2017

at the junctures with steel screws and can be installed together with the wooden cladding with skilled manual labour. With this small-scaled timber construction system, it is possible to produce impressive structures of industrial dimensions. Hugo Häring built the famous barn at Gut Garkau in 1926 using the Zollinger construction method. Not only does the expressive form of its cross-section embrace its organic formal vocabulary, but in the purity of the repetitive and diamond-shaped wooden slats that set the rhythm of the structure, Häring doubtless also recognized what he called the "essence of the object": "He (like the great American architect Louis Kahn later) ascribed to things a 'design will', which the architect helps to assert as an act of empathetic aid. Thanks to his assistance, the soul of things builds its enclosure by itself, so to speak, and differentiates it according to the specifications placed upon it." (Pehnt, 1982). Without planks or rafters, the principle developed by Friedrich Zollinger in 1921 offered not just savings of timber but also the advantage of prefabrication in a sawmill, and it was used for a wide variety of functions—from market halls to hangars to church spaces. The industrial type was also well suited for centrally managed sales and distribution by proprietary companies.

A place of production

The Zollinger roof served as a reference for another project, in which three schools of architecture worked together as part of the Erasmus+ project 'Crafting the Façade' (Meister, Rist, Spaan, 2018). The three-year programme explored the potential of stone, brick and wood as building materials based on their regional significance. In a one-week workshop on the topic of wood, students from the Glasgow School of Architecture, the Amsterdam Academy of Architecture and the University of Liechtenstein worked in teams to develop models and prototypes for the construction of a model workshop. These designs embodied the starting point for further development in an experimental process in which the students, working in close collaboration with a carpentry business, took up the structural concepts and developed them all the way to the realization of the entire building. The load-bearing structure of the model workshop consists of curved boards that have underspanned in an undulating pattern. Despite the delicacy of the boards, this counter-tension ensures sufficient static height and leads to an innovative system with few references. The assembled, additively arranged structure is extremely delicate and elegantly demonstrates the internal stresses intrinsic to the wood. In the design and production of the model workshop, the concept of craftsmanship did not only apply just to the actual work done by hand, but was understood much more as the experimental engagement with the logic of joining the board lamellae into a characteristic expression. The continual change between the level of detail and its tangible reality, on the one hand, and the entirety of the building on the other, in a kind of reverberant design process, seems to us to be crucial for the achievement of innovative architecture. The constant sharpening and honing in a process with changing perspectives and varied distances to that which is being designed increases not only the constructive precision, but also the quality of the design as a whole.

Vertebrae and spinal discs

When studying multi-storey wooden structures, you cannot ignore the Asian pagoda towers. The 67-metre-tall octagonal tower of the Fogong Pagoda (Wooden Pagoda of Yingxian) is regarded as the oldest existing specimen in China and is also the tallest historical post-and-beam structure in the world. Built over four decades and completed in 1095, the building consists of two interlocking octagonal wooden pillars. Sacred figures are centrally positioned on multiple storeys. The passage between the inner and outer octagons is accessible, as are the outer verandas, which offer views of the city and landscape. Radial beams, brackets and supporting pillars interconnect to form a stable trussed framework per storey. The cylindrical void in the middle of the

Figure 7
Cross-section of the wooden Fogong Pagoda in Yingxian, 1095

References

Birrer, P. 2011. Geschichte. In: *Die alte Rheinbrücke Vaduz–Sevelen. Entstehung und Umgang mit einem Kulturdenkmal.* Vaduz: Gemeinde Vaduz.

Coxe, W. 1792. *Briefe über den natürlichen Zustand der Schweiz, Vol. II, pp. 1, 2.* Zürich: Orell, Gessner, Füsslin and Comp.

Gerner, M. 1986. Das Zimmerhandwerk, in Schadwinkel, H., Heine, G.; *Das Werkzeug des Zimmermanns.* Hannover: Th. Schäfer.

Killer, J. 1942. *Die Werke der Baumeister Grubenmann*: 69. Zurich: ETH Zürich.

Kocher, L. 2016. Holz auf Holz. In: *Werk, Bauen 11–2016.* Zurich: Verlag Werk AG.

Ledderose, L. 2009. Ten Thousand Things: Module and Mass Production in Chinese Art. In: Nerdinger, W. (ed.) *The Art of Timber Construction: Chinese Architectural Models*: 40. Berlin: Jovis.

Lorenz, W. 2005. Archäologie des Konstruierens—Eremitage, Walhalla, Neues Museum Berlin. In: Jahrbuch Ingenieurbaukunst in Deutschland: 172. Hamburg.

Meister, U. Rist-Stadelmann, C. Spaan, M. 2018. *Crafting the Façade: Stone, Brick, Wood.* Zurich: Park Books.

Pehnt, W. 1982. Ruhm durch einen Stall: Dem Protagonisten des ,Neuen Bauens' zum 100. Geburtstag. *Die Zeit*, no. 21. Hamburg.

Storr, G. K C. Alpenreise, Leipzig, 1784, quoted in: Killer, 1942.

Wachsmann, K. 1930. *Building the Wooden House: Technique and Design.* Transl. by Peter Reuss. Basel, 1995. Originally published as Holzhausbau—Technik und Gestaltung. Basel: Birkhäuser.

Zwerger, K. 1997. *Wood and Wood Joints: Building Traditions of Europe, Japan and China*: 57. Basel: Birkhauser.

pagoda results from the stacking of the constructional rings and replaces the central mast of earlier pagodas. "The stacked, alternating rings function like the vertebrae and discs of a spinal column. Nature combines sturdiness with flexibility in this structure, while also minimizing material and weight." (Ledderose, 2009). This also makes the building more resilient, which provides greater resistance to earthquakes and storms. The curved roof forms set atop one another are a reflection and expression of a complex timber construction.

The master builders opted for smaller components in most cases. The characteristic projecting canopies are supported by complex bracketed systems and the total number of timber parts adds up to about 30,000. It is not surprising that a high degree of standardization was sought, and thus the ratio of height to width of the individual elements remains constant at 3:2. This high level of pre-industrial standardization is reflected in the Yingzao Fashi, a collection of Chinese building standards compiled by construction official Li Jie that was published in 1103. The manual primarily aimed to rationalize public buildings and established not only dimensions, but also labour hours for the individual elements as a basis for calculating the total time needed for construction. The system could easily be disseminated, making its application economical, and thus the manual reinforced the specific strengths of a modular system. The Yingzao Fashi not only created the basis for the standardization of building parts, but also represents a milestone in the history of mass production in China (Ledderose, 2009). In the European context, such approaches were as unthinkable at that time as the quantity of timber structures that could reach heights over 100 metres. Today we can only marvel at such buildings and at their longevity. Together with their beauty and strength, they radiate a will to innovate that should inspire us.

Production as driving force

If the physical skills of craftspeople had central importance in tradition as a driving force in the choreography of production, and this has meanwhile become obsolete for industrial timber construction, then a new way must be found in contemporary, hybrid fabrication processes to derive creative potential from production. It must also be possible today to process the material by hand to varying degrees and to ultimately leave a visible imprint of the manual work done on it. Craftsmanship does not solely refer to the activity done 'by hand' with hand tools, but extends to include a vastly more diverse selection of production methods that are used in the artisanal sense. These days, the range of tools that serve in handcrafted production as an extension of the human body is enormous, and this allows for the emergence of entirely new expressive profiles.

Against the backdrop of the discussion on sufficiency and regional value creation in the construction sector, we have a reawakened interest in the particularities of solid timber and its inherent suitability for clear-cut, tectonic elements. The joining of the individual parts thereby regains significance, as today's mechanical processes make it feasible to make timber joints that were previously made by hand. The use of locally grown hardwood adds additional new themes. In the interplay of traditional knowledge with modern technology, a new *hybrid timber construction* is postulated that will give new meaning to the classic theme of bearing loads. It is the idea of handcrafted timber construction that has been developed for modern production techniques and which will form an alternative to standardized, industrially produced timber construction. Thus, both 'archaic' and 'advanced' techniques should be used equally to reinterpret the wealth of traditional timber joints with today's production techniques (Lorenz, 2016) Thus, the relative importance of industrial fabrication and craftsmanship must be renegotiated in the search for a timber architecture whose production processes intertwine in a future-oriented way.

Experiments with Glueless Laminated Wood

Niels Groeneveld,
Werkstatt

Modern timber construction consists of a broad range of techniques, many of which originated in old crafts and traditions. Carpenters used to explore forests in search of trees with the right curve or trunk shape so that they could create structural elements that optimized the direction of the grain. Special timber joints were designed to take up specific forces (pull, push, torque, etc.). Carpenters could 'read' the quality of wood by examining it closely. Even today, a solid knowledge of past techniques remains essential in bringing timber construction forward and truly innovating. In these modern, competitive times when labour is expensive, it is increasingly hard to work with traditional techniques. To maintain and nurture a 'timber building culture', old techniques must be adapted and further developed, while radically new techniques must also be found. Within the framework of the 'Crafting Wood' research project, the goal is to bridge the gap between old and new craft, strengthening continuity of knowledge about timber architecture. Three projects centred on this theme, each of them relating to a specific case: the curved timber roof structure of the gate tower at Schaesberg Castle. All three projects searched for an alternative, contemporary reconstruction of this timber structure.

Schaesberg Castle gate tower

The architecture office Werkstatt and Machiel Spaan initiated three research projects together with students from the Amsterdam Academy of Architecture to achieve this goal. They focused on an analysis of an alternative reconstruction of the former central tower of Schaesberg Castle in the province of Limburg in the south of the Netherlands. This ancient stone tower had an eye-catching, slate-clad, 'bell-shaped' roof, supported by a timber structure. The original tower structure remains something of a mystery, because the original plans were lost. An analysis has been made based on the few sketches, measurements, photographs and comparable structures that still exist.

The remarkable bell shape is clearly visible in photographs of the exterior. Only one interior image reveals some information about the tower's octagonal loadbearing structure. It does, however, reveal something interesting about the structure: a 22.5 degree vertical rotation of the tower's central cross-shaped main structure relative to its square stone base. This is the result of the octagonal horizontal section, which makes up the facetted bell shape, consisting of eight single-curved surfaces. Heavy solid oak members were used for the main structure. The structure's overall height of approximately 9 metres is at the limit of what is possible with single members. The structure was likely composed of multiple members to reach the total height.

ower of Slot Scheasberg, Landgraafa

The goal of the O4 research studio was to understand the differences and similarities between traditional and high-tech methods, and to apply this knowledge to a design assignment: the complex roof structure of Schaesberg Castle's central tower. The O4 studio explored two traditional and two contemporary techniques of joinery and construction. Seventeenth-century shipbuilding methods provided interesting insights into creating curved geometries, by harvesting and applying pre-curved timber beams from curved trees. The use of naturally grown 'Y joints' from tree branches also provided insight into benefiting from nature's most efficient joinery skills. In contrast, digital methods such as CNC milling and laminating show the current state of the timber industry. CNC-milled cross-laminated timber structures have succeeded in combining 'skin' and 'structure', creating possibilities to 'open up' spaces that were formerly occupied by loadbearing structures. And of course the technique of laminating makes it possible to create precise and efficiently curved structures by using fast-grown softwood available locally. The aim was to apply a combination of these techniques to create 'contemporary' fragments of the curved roof structure, thereby generating valuable insight into the future role of wood in organic architecture.

'Krommers' to build the hull of a ship, 16–17th century

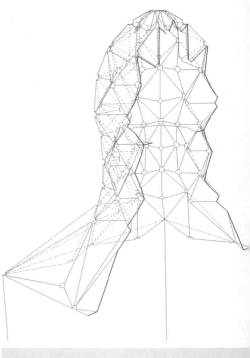

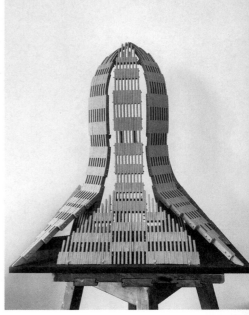

Erasmus Wood workshop—Amsterdam Academy of Architecture, with the Universities of Trondheim and Vaduz

Designing with wood requires specific knowledge about the material because of its natural, anisotropic properties. The only way to truly understand this is to work with the material at scale 1:1. The curved shape of the Schaesberg tower structure provided a valuable starting point. The structure's complex geometrical facets posed multiple challenges for this physical exercise. The aim of the workshop was to create a 'pavilion' or roof structure, consisting of curved timber trusses, derived from the shape of the tower's cross-section. The top side of the trusses had to follow the exact curve, while the bottom side and supports could be designed freely. Giving students certain restrictions in terms of shape, dimensions and quantity of material yielded an interesting collection of ideas. The result was a diverse collection of timber trusses, together embodying the wealth of solutions offered by timber construction.

Slotlab—Research by Werkstatt

The O4 studio and Erasmus workshop ran parallel to the Slotlab research project initiated by Machiel Spaan and Material Sense Lab for the IBA 2020 (Internationale Bauausstellung) in Parkstad. Slotlab invites young designers to reconstruct parts of Schaesberg Castle using modern, innovative methods. Architecture office Werkstatt was asked to reconstruct the traditional bell-shaped roof structure of the castle's central gate tower using innovative timber construction techniques.

The original structure that supported the remarkable roof consisted of solid beams sawn from big oaks that are now scarce in the region. These big structural beams made the space beneath the roof impenetrable. Werkstatt wanted to free up this space so that visitors could experience the roof structure up close. In addition, there was a desire to make use of wood harvested locally. This mostly comes from smaller trees that call for different construction methods. To this end, Werkstatt investigated the ideas of the very first timber engineers who in the early 19th century built innovative timber structures out of composite timber, also called 'laminated timber structures'. Numerous thin layers of timber are pressed to form a strong, thick beam. Structures of this kind are increasingly common today, but a lot of glue is involved. In the past, they featured smart connections of steel or timber. That makes it possible, in theory, to dismantle the structure and reuse the timber. This aligns more with the current tendency to consider the sustainable use of materials and circularity. Unfortunately, midway through

the 19th century, this pioneering work by a handful of timber engineers was overshadowed by the arrival of wrought iron. Today, the use of timber in construction is on the rise, because it has a positive CO_2 footprint, in contrast to steel and concrete. In the new design for the top of the tower, Werkstatt sought to achieve a high level of material efficiency by resisting the wind load and gravity with a combination of curved and straight timber components. In this way, structural material can be added where the forces are greatest, and material can be minimized in other places, resulting in an elegantly slender structure. Space is kept open in the centre of this structure for a spiral stairs and a round platform to allow visitors to experience the tower to the full. In addition to a fully digital model, one rafter was built at a scale of 1:3. Freshly sawn Douglas fir from the locality was laminated and fastened without the use of any glue, with just mechanical connections of steel and timber. In this way, assumptions and expectations could be physically tested and confirmed: the structure turned out to be very strong and stable, retaining its exact shape after the removal of the mould.

Werkstatt picked up where the 19th-century engineers had left off, combining their ideas with the most modern timber construction techniques. And thus the new tower roof was a homage to more than two centuries of innovation in timber construction, bridging new and old.

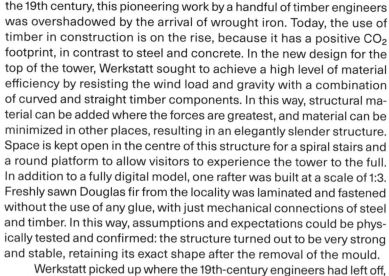

Workshops

Seven Trusses

25.08–2.09.2018
Trondheim,
Norway

Alpine Towers

14–24.03.2019
Vaduz,
Liechtenstein

Pavilion at
Slot Schaesberg

19–21.08.2020
Amsterdam,
The Netherlands

During the whole programme, three workshops for all participants ran in the three countries. The goal of each workshop, which was an essential part of the project studio, was to become familiar with wood, with its properties and with the culture of wood construction of the region. In the workshops, participants first surveyed historical and recent wood constructions, and then worked in teams to build models by hand at scale 1:20 or 1:10. In the second part, students studied and experimented with structural elements at scale 1:1. During the final days of the workshop they built a structure at full scale.

For centuries, carpenters have crafted wooden joints and the production methods have been bound by traditions. Many cultures developed their own joinery traditions, and in cultures such as the Chinese or Japanese, these traditions have been especially strong. In Europe, the traditions for structural joinery are closely related but with regional differences. Today, the development of digitally controlled milling machines has provided renewed interest in structural wood joints. It is now possible to produce them effectively and economically with high precision. Therefore, the design needs to be informed both by industrial parameters and by traditional carpentry knowledge.

The task of this workshop was to develop and build a timber roof structure. The discussions included architecture, space, structure, joints and timber as a material. An important focus in the discussions was on the detail, and the differences found between structural wood joints made manually by hand and electrical hand tools, machines and robots. By making structural details with different sets of tools, the participants learned about the properties of wood and how wood can be used in inventive ways. By bringing the detail back to the centre of the architectural design, we can enable architecture to regain the important synthesis of structure and expression.

25.08–2.09.2018
Trondheim

During the workshop in Liechtenstein, the students started with building towers of wooden slats at scale 1:20. Structures that defy gravity and absorb horizontal forces were sketched. The models never lie: by pushing and pulling the slats, we understood the distribution of forces and were able to increase the stability. In this way, twelve structural principles for a 35-metre-high tower at the base of the mountain in Liechtenstein were created over time.

In groups of students from the different schools, we elaborated six chosen structures. The scale was then increased to 1:5, which resulted in models of seven metres tall. The glued or adhesive joint of the 1:20 model had to be replaced by 'real' structural joints. The weight of the material and the precision of the saw cuts were important factors in the execution. Twelve hands worked resolutely on one tower, designing while making. Connections arose via the experiment and were refined over the course of the days.

After four days, the six seven-metre-high wooden structures were transported to the village square in Schaan and hoisted, assembled or stacked on top of each other. The structures formed an inspiring ensemble of six towers, each with a character of its own. Six different structures, each with its own story, delete laws and connections. They demonstrate the creativity of the designer and the workmanship of the craftsman. Thinking and doing formed a stimulating field of tension which was assimilated in unique creations, showing that a fascinating voyage of discovery full of setbacks and successes lies hidden between concept and reality. These prototypes underline the experimental approach of the whole project and mark the starting point for the building of a tower in Liechtenstein, which will be built in collaboration with the students.

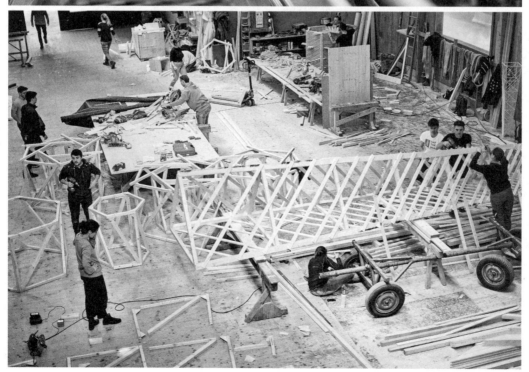

The goal of the workshop was to get in touch with wooden structures and to strengthen a tectonic approach towards both tradition and innovation of wooden structures. In combining traditional crafts manship and industrial production, the workshop aimed to research solutions that develop new ways to use wood. During the workshop students experimented with structural elements at scale 1:10. With wooden laths, constructions that are capable of forming members of the structure of an expo pavilion were developed.

The location for the pavilion is the square in front of Slot Schaes berg for the Slotlab exposition for IBA Parkstad. The pavilion is an experiment in making a temporary and removable wooden roof struc ture, whose elements should be easy to dismantle and to transport on a small truck. The pavilion is a temporary structure assembled with wooden joints, constructied with as little steel as possible and no glue added.

During the workshop we investigated different structures and systems. First at scale 1:10, thereafter with mock-ups and finally at full scale. The starting point was the shape of the pitched roof of the castle tower. The final designs, unique in shape, structure and joints, express an ambitious attitude towards the innovation of the craft.

19–21.08.2020
Amsterdam

 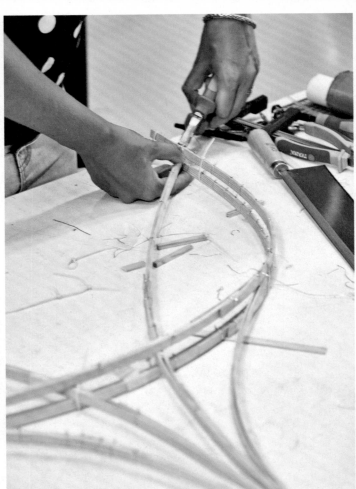

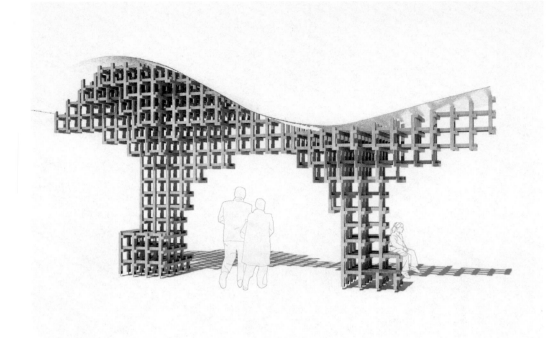

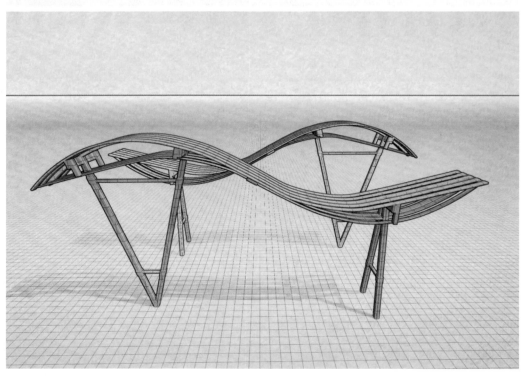

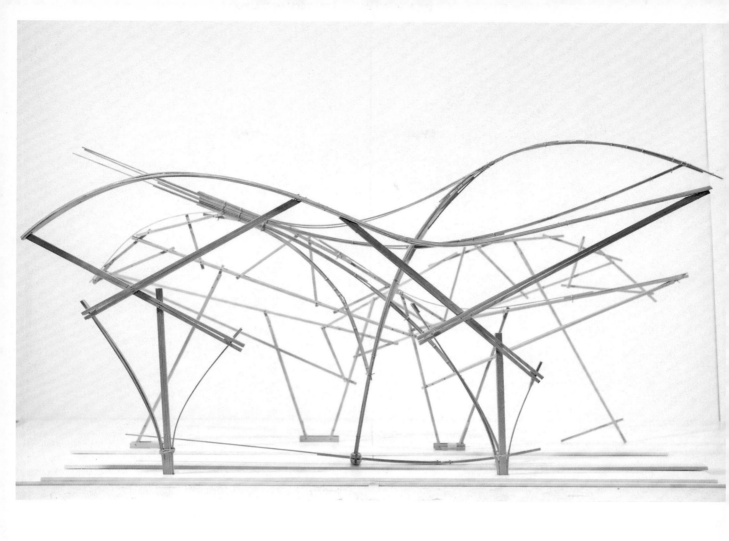

Trondheim 25.08–02.09.2018	Vaduz 14–24.03.2019	Amsterdam 19–21.08.2020
NTNU Trondheim	NTNU Trondheim	NTNU Trondheim

Trondheim — NTNU Trondheim

Ragnhild Skoglund
Marte Midtlyng
Lars Gustav Rogne
Juni Palmstrom
Johan Dolmseth
Michael Hongyu Peng
Haakon Bergsholm
Eline Eide Bye
Arild Megard
André Berlin
Martin Vilhemson
Johanne Thoresen Mofoss
Ingrid Sondov
Teachers:
Siem Jan
Gilberg Arnstein
Bjørn Otto Braaten

University of Liechtenstein

Natalie Marinelli
Denise Pfleger
Nick Ulrich
Zoran Miletic
Pascal Büchel
Andreas Negele
Daniela Huber
Teachers:
Carmen Rist-Stadelmann
Urs Meister

Amsterdam Academy
of Architecture

Art Kallen
Jesse Stortelder
Anouk van Deuzen
Sander Gijsen
Milo Greuter
Maro Lange
Loretta So
Susanne Vruwink
Noury Salmi
Susanna Scholten
Charlotte Mulder
Matilde Bazzolo
Teachers:
Machiel Spaan
Jochem Heijmans
Niels Groeneveld
Jan Loerakker
Serge Schoenmakers
Yukiko Nezu

Vaduz — NTNU Trondheim

Júlia Ros Bofarull
Gilles Gasser
Luis Martín Cea
Mar Campos
Alina Koger
Esteban Borteele
Alex Escursell
Anna Molina
Arthur Rundstadler
Pia Weber
Ben Quinn
Arno Léon Oreste
Alfred Wust
Berenice Aubriot
Bejan Misaghi
Silvia Riubrugent
Anna Prüller
Bertille Bourgarel
Agathe Cheynet
Iñigo Gutiérrez
Teachers:
Arnstein Gilberg
Bjørn Otto Braaten

University of Liechtenstein

Sandra Oeler
Shefket Shala
Maik Goop
Gebhard Natter
Bunjamin Sulejmani
Rikke Jensen
Christian Meier
Attila Truffer
Edwin Frei
Teachers:
Carmen Rist-Stadelmann
Urs Meister
Christoph Frommelt

Amsterdam Academy
of Architecture

Danny Kok
Anne Roos Demilt
Charlotte Mulder
Ayla Azizova
Anna Tores
Evie Lentjes
German Gomes Rueda
Noury Salmi
Adan Carnak
Teachers:
Machiel Spaan
Nina Knaack
Marcel van der Lubbe

Amsterdam — NTNU Trondheim

Andreas Nielsen
Christina Schieferle
Clément Molinier
Gianmarco Pistoia
Giovanni Dello Loio
Johanna Kieft
Jostein Wigenstad
Julia Kapinos
Julie Bovier
Kotryna Navickaite
Laura Bergelt
Laura Villaverde
Melanie Vercauteren
Sjaak Velthoven
Sofie Gustafsson
Sofie Luise Fetting
Xavier Granados Esteve
Teacher:
Arnstein Gilberg

University of Liechtenstein

Chun Yin Kelvin Au
Shona Beatje
Morten Bjørn Jørgensen
Finn Buchanan
Carlos Vazquez
Roberto Villaseñor
Gregorio Candelieri
Elias Said
Libat Eden
Marie Mikulová
Herolind Elezi
Zaal Siprashvili
Lars Gassner
Nick Conrad Ulrich
Gabriela Ponechalová
Lucia Schachtner
Tata Zakaraia
Giorgi Evsia
Teachers:
Carmen Rist-Stadelmann
Urs Meister
Christoph Frommelt

Amsterdam Academy
of Architecture

Laurien Zwaans
Tom Vermeer
Anne-Roos Demilt
Daria Dobrodeeva
Richard Doensen
German Alfonso
Charlotte Mulder
Evie Lentjes
Sung-Ching Lo
Anouk van Deuzen
Teachers:
Machiel Spaan
Niels Groeneveld
Marcel van der Lubbe
Gerald Lindner

Arnstein Gilberg
is an architect and Associate Professor at Faculty of Architecture and Fine art, NTNU Trondheim, Norway. He teaches tectonics and working with full-scale constructions. Course manager for master course 'Timber structure' and a part of the Erasmus+ project 'Wood: Structure and Expression'.

Haakon Haanes
is co-founded Nøysom arkitekter just after graduating from NTNU in Trondheim in2015. Before studying architecture, Haakon studied philosophy and psychology for two years in Oslo, which sparked an interest for working with the broader questions concerning our built environment, such as sustainability and ecology. Together with Cathrine, Haakon has written several articles about architecture, ecology and alternative housing strategies. He has also held lectures, talks and arranged workshops with the other partners in Nøysom arkitekter. Haakon has also worked for several years with city planning and placemaking at The City Planning Office in Trondheim and The Agency of Planning and Building Services in Oslo. In addition to being partner in Nøysom arkitekter, Haakon is currently employed as an urban planner in Asplan Viak in Oslo.

Annemariken Hilberink
studied Architecture at the Technical University Eindhoven from 1983–1990. Received the 2nd price in the Archiprix 1990, the best Dutch graduation projects, with a design for a mountain station in Austria. Worked at several smaller architectural firms. Received a starter stipend of the Fonds BKVB on which she started her own architectural firm. In 1996, together with Geert Bosch, she formed the office Hilberinkbosch architecten. She has been involved in teaching at several Academies of Architecture, most recent as a member of examiners in Arnhem. Also worked as a member of Architectural advisory services in Etten-Leur and Venlo.

Tibor Joanelly
is an architect, publicist and teacher. He received his degree in architecture at the Federal Institute of Technology in Zurich (ETHZ) and worked in numerous well-known Swiss architectural offices. Next to his practice, he led atelier discourses with Swiss architects such as Christian Kerez, Valerio Olgiati and Livio Vacchini. He published essays and articles in architectural magazines. Tibor Joanelly was teaching at the Budapest University of Technology, at the ETHZ and at the University Liechtenstein. He currently lectures on Architectural Critique at the University for Applied Sciences in Winterthur and he is an editor of the Swiss architectural magazine werk, bauen+wohnen. He is engaged in several book projects as well as in architectural practice.

Cathrine Johansen Haanes
was born in the arctic city of Tromsø in Northern Norway. She studied architecture at The Norwegian University of Science and Technology (NTNU) and graduated in 2014 with a diploma project called 'The Way to Satori', a space for contemplation of nature on the mountain of Fløya in Tromsø. In 2015 she co-founded Nøysom arkitekter with Trygve Ohren and Haakon Haanes. The trio is most known for their urban ecological pilot project, 'Experimental Housing at Svartlamon', a self-build scheme were five families have been able to build their own low cost row-houses made largely from reused materials. The project has sparked a broad national and international interest in the young office, which was nominated to The European Union Prize for Contemporary Architecture—Mies van der Rohe Award 2019 and introduced as emerging architects in Architectural Review in May 2019. In addition to working as an architect, Cathrine writes and lectures, together with Haakon, about architecture, ecology and alternative housing strategies.

Urs Meister
is graduated in architecture from the ETH Zurich. He is a professor of design and construction at the Institute of Architecture and Planning at the University of Liechtenstein and partner of the architecture office Käferstein & Meister Architekten AG in Zurich. Coordinating Erasmus Intensive and Erasmus+ programmes since 2003, he was responsible together with Carmen Rist-Stadelmann for the programme 'Wood: Structure and Expression'.

Mario Rinke
is Professor at the Faculty of Design Sciences at the University of Antwerp. Trained as a structural engineer and working in the field of architecture for some years, he is teaching and researching construction in the realm of architecture. Genuinely interested in transformation processes between areas of knowledge, materials and institutions as well as structural thinking, he is specialised in hybrid material concepts, early reinforced concrete and early industrial timber (glulam). After working as a design engineer for major offices in London and Zurich, he ran his own practice in Zurich for several years. Mario Rinke holds a Diploma degree in civil engineering from the Bauhaus University Weimar and a PhD from ETH Zurich. He was senior researcher and lecturer at the architecture department at ETH Zurich and the senior lecturer at the Lucerne University of Applied Sciences and Arts. Currently, he serves as a member of scientific committees, as a reviewer for journals and is a founding member of the International Association of Structures and Architecture (IASA) and currently secretary the management board.

Carmen Rist-Stadelmann
graduated in Architecture from the Technical University Vienna, Austria and received her doctoral degree the same university. She has practiced professionally in Austria and Malaysia and is currently Master academic director at the Institute of Architecture and Planning

at the University of Liechtenstein. She runs design studios at undergraduate and graduate level and her current research project 'Hands-on: An added value for teaching in architecture' focuses on building on a scale of 1:1 with students and professionals as part of their architectural education. She is the coordinator of 'Wood: Structure and Expression', funded by the European Commission, which focuses on the tectonic method for connecting wooden joints to a structure on a scale 1:1.

August Schmidt
established his private practice, Studio Sjellsand, in Trondheim in 2005. After finishing engineering studies in Austria, he pursued architecture studies in Graz, Stuttgart and Trondheim. He has worked in various architect firms in Austria, Germany, Canada and Norway, where he graduated and settled down in 1996. His early training in masonry and carpentry is evident in the craftsmanship and detailing in his projects. The link between form, construction and materials is the basis of his teaching at NTNU, and in his internationally published projects. August specializes in small self-built housing which strives towards quality in every inch.

Machiel Spaan
is an architect, co-founder of the Amsterdam firm M3H Architecten and has taught at various architecture programmes in the Netherlands and beyond for over twenty years. Recently he published *The Wandering Maker*. Spurred by his own observations, *The Wandering Maker* discovers the value of street, building, house and detail. He unravels constructions, cleans up, repairs and transforms; searches for a conscious way of dealing with the available material as a sustainable alternative for the fast conceptual and object-oriented approach. Machiel Spaan is involved in the Erasmus program since 2008.

Harm Tilman
is editor-in-chief of the Architect, an independent and opinion-forming professional journal and platform in the field of architecture, urban design and interior design. Website, magazine and events inform and inspire spatial designers and place their work in a broader social and cultural context. Before he has been coordinator at the Rotterdam Academy of Architecture. Tilman graduated from Delft University of Technology in 1984, after his studies worked as an urban designer and researcher, gave lectures and supervised projects at various educational institutions in the Netherlands and abroad. He is also the author of numerous publications in the field of modern architecture and spatial planning.

Werkstatt
is an Eindhoven based architecture practice founded by Raoul Vleugels (1985) and Niels Groeneveld (1985). They focus on sustainable building in wood, for which they have drawn considerable attention. In 2021 they were rewarded the Jonge Maaskantprijs for their contribution to a sustainably built environment. Their projects have developed from a radical ecological approach to a distinctive architecture in which sustainability is clearly expressed.

Klaus Zwerger
studied at the University of Applied Arts in Vienna. Alongside and afterwards he worked as carpenter, joiner and artist. In 1991 he became assistant at the University of Technology in Vienna. Since then he extensively travelled in most European countries, in East and Southeast Asia in order to study and investigate historic wood architecture. In 2012 he habilitated at the Vienna University of Technology. In 2015 he held a guest professorship in Tokyo. He gave numerous presentations and lecture series predominantly in China. He widely published in German, English, Chinese and Japanese language. Recently he expanded his research focus to Northern Laos and Vietnam.

Credits

Editors: Carmen Rist-Stadelmann, Machiel Spaan, Urs Meister
Contributions by Carmen Rist-Stadelmann, Urs Meister, Machiel Spaan, Niels Groeneveld (Werkstatt), Bjorn Otto Braaten, Jan Siem, Arnstein Gilberg, Annemariken Hilberink (HilberinkBosch Architects), Mario Rinke, August Schmidt, Klaus Zwerger, Tibor Joanelly, Cathrine Johansen Haanes, Haakon Haanes (Nøysom arkitekter).
Translation: Billy Nolan, David Koralek
Final editing: Billy Nolan
Design: SJG / Joost Grootens, Dimitri Jeannottat
Lithography: Marc Gijzen
Printing: Wilco Art Books

ISBN 978-3-03860-235-4

Park Books
Niederdorfstrasse 54
8001 Zurich
Switzerland
www.park-books.com

© 2021 The authors and Park Books AG, Zurich

Printed in the Netherlands

Picture credits:
Bruno Klomfar (p. 11), Jonathan Drew (p. 27, 151–152, 154), Thomas Lenden (p. 30–33), Niels Groeneveld (p. 38–39), Miro Kuzmanovic (p. 42–46), Rene de Wit (p. 54–55), Jürg Zimmermann (p. 57–59), Pasi Alto (p. 61–63), Klaus Zwerger (p. 65–69), Musée d'art et d'histoire Fribourg (p. 71), Marco Bakker (p. 72, figure 2), Mélanie Rouiller (p. 72, figure 3), Museum zu Allerheiligen, Schaffhausen (p. 126, figure 2), Carpenter Wiedenkeller, A. Wiedenkeller, St. Gallen (p. 127, figure 3), Liechtensteinisches Landesarchiv, Vaduz (p. 127, figure 4), Seiher+Seiher (p. 128, figure 5), Darko Todorovic (p. 128, figure 6), Zhongguo gujianshu, in: Lothar Ledderose, *Module und Massenproduktion im chinesischen Holzbau* (p. 129, figure 7), Darko Todorovic (p. 143–148), Miro Kuzmanovic (p. 149). All other pictures by students and teachers.

Special thanks to:
Clarissa Frommelt and Stefan Sohler, Agentur für Internationale Bildungsangelegenheiten, Vaduz
Frommelt Zimmerei Ing. Holzbau AG, Vaduz
Bouwbedrijf van Engen, Kockengen
Slot Schaesberg en Slotlab, Landgraaf
IBA Parkstad, Heerlen
Gemeinde Schaan, Liechtenstein

Park Books is being supported by the Federal Office of Culture with a general subsidy for the years 2021–2024.

This project has been funded with support from the European Commission. This publication reflects the views only of the author, and the Commission cannot be held responsible for any use which may be made of the information contained therein.